THE CATHOLIC SCHOOL

THE CATHOLIC SCHOOL

ITS ROOTS, IDENTITY, AND FUTURE

Harold A. Buetow

CROSSROAD · NEW YORK

1988
The Crossroad Publishing Company
370 Lexington Avenue, New York, N.Y. 10017

Second Printing, 1988
Library of Congress Cataloging-in-Publication Data

Buetow, Harold A.
The Catholic school : its roots, identity, and future / Harold A.
Buetow.
    p.   cm.
  Bibliography: p.
  Includes index.
  ISBN 0-8245-0857-2
  1. Catholic Church—Education—United States.   I. Title.
LC501.B628 1988   87-25387
377'.82—dc19   CIP

CONTENTS

ACKNOWLEDGEMENTS

To thank adequately everyone who helped in the writing of this book would be impossible. Good people beyond number, at the cost of selfsacrifice in time and effort, have contributed by reading and commenting upon the entire manuscript or offering suggestions about their area of expertise, providing valuable insights from long experience, detailing problems, sharing their vision, giving hospitality and cooperation, and imparting some of their commitment and enthusiasm. The following deserve special mention.

For dedication far beyond the call of duty in his meticulous readings of the manuscript and valuable suggestions, I am indebted to the Reverend Thomas G. Gallagher, Secretary for Education, United States Catholic Conference, Washington, D.C., and, for their painstaking work on details, to Sr. Margaret Patrice Gurley, O.S.F., and her associates at Neumann College, Aston, Pennsylvania.

Among my colleagues at The Catholic University of America are especially Avery Dulles, S.J., Department of Theology; Sr. Catherine Dooley, O.P., and Raymond J. Studzinski, O.S.B., Department of Religion and Religious Education; and Sarah M. Pickert, Department of Education. And I cannot forget many students over the years, especially Maria Ciriello, O.P., Alyson M. Muff, Daniel C. Napolitano, the Reverend William P. Saunders, and Thomas W. Small.

In other places are, alphabetically, John J. Augenstein, Warren, Ohio; Michael Bakalis, Dean of the School of Education, Loyola University, Chicago; Michel Bureau, S.J., Paris; the Reverend Mark Campbell, San Diego; Denis Collins, S.J., University of San Francisco; Paddy Crowe, S.J., Dublin; Richard Cunningham, Secretary, Catholic Education Council for England and Wales, London; Michael Daly, Principal, St. Joseph's School, Ronkonkoma, New York; Patricia C. Deeley, school board member, Merrick, New York; Philomena Dineen-Reardon, Surrey, England; Sr. Elizabeth Anne Di Pippo, Sister of St. Ursule de Tours, Paris; Eileen Doyle, S.C., Dublin; Vincent Duminuco, S.J., Secretary for Jesuit Education, Rome; Geoffrey Duncan, of the National Society, Church of England, Westminster.

Sr. Clare Fitzgerald, Boston College; Sr. Mary Fitzpatrick, Faithful Companions of Jesus, Paris; Peter Hackett, S.J., Campion Hall, Oxford University; the Reverend Charles Kohli, Pastor, St. Joseph's Church, Ronkonkoma, New York; Ernest E. Larkin, O. Carm., Chicago; Thomas Martin, Dean of the School of Education, Marquette University; Alfred McBride, O. Praem., National Catholic Evangelization Association, Washington, D.C.; Edward McDermott, S.J., University of San Francisco; Sr. Anne Murray, S.S.L., St. Louis High School, Rathmines, Dublin; the Reverend Msgr. Kevin Nichols, Barnard Castle, England; Sr. Renee Oliver, O.S.U., Citizens for Educational Freedom, Washington, D.C.; Sr. Kathleen O'Sullivan, S.S.L., Newmarket, England; the Reverend Msgr. John Portman, Coronado, California; Ken Sarubbi, Dean of the School of Education, De Paul University, Chicago.

Jerry Starrett, S.J., Fordham University; Sr. Lourdes Sheehan, R.S.M., National Catholic Educational Association; Mary Thatcher, Cambridge, England; David Thomas, Regis College, Denver, Colorado; Sr. Mary Peter Traviss, O.P., University of San Francisco; Sr. Maureen Vellon, R.S.H.M., and her community at Marymount School, Paris; Michael M. Winter and the Fellows and Staff of St. Edmund's House, Cambridge University, England; the Reverend Msgr. John F. Meyers and the many other members of the staff of the National Catholic Educational Association who recommended the small grant from the Knights of Columbus' Fr. Michael J. McGivney Memorial Fund for New Initiatives in Catholic Education; and the staff of the libraries at Cambridge and Oxford Universities, Neumann College Library, the Mullen Library and the Law Library at The Catholic University of America, and the Library of Congress, for living up to the librarians' habit of generous service.

Chapter 1

INTRODUCTION

Some years ago, there appeared a book which synthesized people's questions about whether Catholic schools were the best answer to the formation of Catholic youth. In print, it sent shock waves through the Catholic-school community. The objections to the Catholic school were essentially seven. The book maintained that general schooling can and should be separated from religious formation, that Catholic-school religious formation is too formal to be effective in real life, that Catholic schools are relics of a siege mentality, mediocre as a result of their stringent fiscal condition, divisive in a pluralistic society, contradictory to the spirit of ecumenism, and consuming time, effort, and money that might be better spent in other ways.[1]

These objections will not go away. Added to that fact and intertwined with it has been a perhaps too easy attitude toward identifying the Catholic school. But now "the party's over": fiscal problems have become more pressing, and there is a new urgency about the effectiveness of models other than the Catholic school for religious formation, such as Sunday school, released time instruction, adult education, catechetical centers, and the Confraternity of Christian Doctrine. The time has come for us to decide whether Catholic schools, at least as we have known them, should endure.

We cannot make that decision unless we know the identity of the Catholic school. To explore that identity is the purpose of this book.[2] But before we can embark on the exploration, we have to know what we are going to be talking about. That means definitions[3] of some basic items which we shall be discussing, like philosophy, education, schooling, and specifically *Catholic* education and schooling.

1

PHILOSOPHY

Ironically, "philosophy" is one of those words whose definition depends on one's philosophy. Hence, we can attempt here only a descriptive definition. The word comes from two Greek words: *philia*, meaning love, and *sophia*, meaning wisdom. Philosophy is, at the very least, a love of wisdom.

Love

The Greeks had three major words for love. That is not even to mention minor ones, and it does not include *romantic* love, a more modern invention exemplified by Romeo and Juliet and St. Valentine's Day. The lowest form of love was *eros* — love in the sense of desire, a getting, an *elan vital*, an *esprit* — a thing of life, as opposed to *thanatos*, death.[4] (The "erotic" does not, as some people have it, deal only with the sexual: it can even have to do with the desire for learning!) The highest form of love eventually became *agape*. This was a spiritual love, having to do mostly with man-God and God-man relationships, which frequently involved ecstasy ("standing outside oneself").

For the love of wisdom which constitutes philosophy, that leaves us with *philia*, a love of "friendship." A distillate of the writings on friendship shows friendships based on passion, on pity, on pleasure, on companionship, on professional advantage, on camaraderie-in-arms, on intellectual agreement, on mutual admiration, on spiritual conviction, on personal advancement, on hero worship, on protection, on fear, on need, on loyalty, and on many other things.

Most friendships incorporate several of these elements at once. Whatever lofty purpose friendship may serve, it is always voluntary and a reciprocal thing, a giving as well as a getting, and is something generous and expansive. The love relationship that must exist between us and the second half of the word "philosophy," wisdom, is analogous to friendship — analogous because complete friendship can exist properly only between persons, each of whom subordinates him/herself to the other.[5]

Wisdom

Wisdom has as its base the Old English *witan*, meaning to know. At its base must be common-sense experience, with elements of insight, judgment, sensibleness, foresight, discretion, perspicacity, astuteness, and sagacity. But it is different from and above all of these. Wisdom has ultimates in view. It commonly suggests the habit of profound reflection upon people and events and an ability to reach conclusions of universal as well as immediate value. Wisdom indicates discernment based not only on factual knowledge but on judgment and insight: thus people can be wise even though their fund of knowledge be small. A Japanese proverb says, "Knowledge without wisdom is a load of books on the back of an ass."

Secular wisdom is, at its highest level (which is speculative), an integration of all the sciences, skills, and disciplines, through the mediation of philosophy, theology, technology, and art. At the next level down, this integration discovers the absolutes of life that are to be implemented with concrete decisions. At the level of the situation itself, the entire chain can enter and can modify events for better living. Wisdom is a product of the searching intellect, of the outer reaches of people's thoughts, and of concerned answers to the eternal problems of life and death, God and man, time and eternity.

Christian wisdom is more than simply secular wisdom at its highest level suffused with the Christian faith-life. At the heart of Christian wisdom is Christian theology, which must be in constant touch with all the specialized knowledge and skills and arts involved in wisdom. Christian wisdom as the core of Christ's Gospel message must promote the self-sacrificing love of God and of others, and guide it into building a better community and hence a better civilization.

Christian wisdom provides "heart." It generates greater sensitivity to persons, warmer loyalty to friends, and stronger trust in the community. Christian wisdom is at home with pluralism of doctrine and of value systems, because it is convinced that all doctrines and value systems, insofar as they are true, will eventually converge into the Risen Christ, Wisdom itself. Christian wisdom also fosters a disciplined liberty that in turn encourages cooperation. This is because disciplined liberty is a self-sacrificing attitude which, if genuine, is characterized by both joy and self-effacement.

Christian wisdom manifested in the New Testament points powerfully to Christ's desire to give every human being a fair chance. Furthermore, the love that is at the heart of Christianity brings the decisions of Christian wisdom beyond justice to the richness of mercy and generosity. It stimulates the growth of the sense of stewardship, the dynamic force for good in the civic community, new insights into the disciplines of learning, and new syntheses. In this process, contemplation suffuses action and action enriches contemplation.[6]

Although the concept, if not the practice, of wisdom is unfamiliar to many people today because of its omission from current schooling, it has a long and noble tradition in the history of humankind, in the East as well as the West. In the West, its honorable position goes back to the very roots of our civilization. The Jewish Scriptures are full of attempts to arrive at wisdom. The wisdom of Solomon became legendary, and an entire segment of the Old Testament is called "wisdom literature."[7] In the New Testament, Luke says that Jesus as he grew "increased in wisdom and stature, and in favor with God and man." Jesus advised his followers to pursue wisdom, as did St. Paul and others.[8]

Likewise, the ancient Greeks;[9] Socrates, Plato, and Aristotle were so concerned with the pursuit of wisdom that their works are suffused with it. Rome followed Greece. Concern about wisdom has been a constant tradition of humankind from that time to the recent past. When Charles W. Eliot (1834–1926) was president of Harvard, he had the inscription on the 1890 gate to Harvard Yard read: "Enter to grow in wisdom. Depart better to serve thy country and mankind." And T. S. Eliot (1888–1965) wrote these pregnant lines:

> Where is the Life we have lost in living?
> Where is the wisdom we have lost in knowledge?
> Where is the knowledge we have lost in information?[10]

When we named our own species, we called ourselves *Homo sapiens* — "wise humankind." Whether that attribute proves to be deserved will depend on the way humankind looks toward wisdom. The survival of *Homo sapiens* is going to depend on whether humankind has achieved a measure of wisdom. Dr. Jonas Salk said: "Metabiological evolution involves the survival of the wisest. Wisdom is becoming the new criterion of fitness."[11] Catholic utterances affirm that position: "Indeed the future of the world is in danger unless provision is made for men of greater wisdom."[12]

Benefits of Philosophy

Bob Dylan said, "He who isn't busy being born is busy dying." A healthy, well-developed philosophy of life is the framework of human growth and happiness. Among the areas well served by a solid personal philosophy are the development of critical thinking, the formation of the educated person, and the pursuit of greater comprehension of oneself and others.[13]

Christianity Needs Philosophy

Christianity needs philosophy. Christianity began with many mysteries — for example, the divinity of Christ — which were inexplicable in ordinary language. When St. Peter said to Christ, "You are the Christ, the Son of the Living God" (Matt. 16:16), how was one to understand that? Did it mean that Christ was an extraordinary *creature*? Did it mean literally God? An answer with some precision would have to await later councils of the Church and their philosophical definitions of nature and of person: two natures, divine and human, subsisting in one person who is divine. This controversy, which illustrates the need for philosophical thinking, also gave rise to a nuanced concept of the high dignity of *personhood*, a philosophical concept which in the West has given preeminence to the dignity of all other persons as well as Jesus.

Christian revelation is not a philosophy. But early Christianity used the classical philosophy of the times, in practically every application providing new insights. An outstanding example is the first words of St. John's Gospel: "In the beginning was the word." The philosophers of the time meant by "word" a mind behind the world, ordering everything, a nebulous idea not always understood in the same sense. Christianity said: this means the Word of God, the Thought of God Himself who has actually become a Man.

So "Christian" philosophy was Christian in two ways: in its *origin* (the apostolic need to communicate) and in its *purpose* (to explain Christian revelation with sufficient precision so as to avoid errors). But it is not specifically Christian in its *content*, because it overlaps with the human or natural philosophy which was already there. The adjective "Christian" is extrinsic to it, as when we speak of American philosophy. Philosophy as such has no qualifications, any more than mathematics or chemistry does.[14] But to develop a complete worldview, one must use both philosophy and faith. Using the insights of both faith and reason—revelation and philosophy—and the openness of both, it has been possible to develop Christian positions on many areas—including schooling and education.

Relationship of Philosophy to Theology

For some, the matter of a Catholic philosophy is problematic, an oxymoron in which the noun "philosophy" means an untrammeled pursuit of truth that is contradicted by the adjective "Catholic," which arrives with the baggage of established doctrines. But a Catholic philosophy *is* possible if we agree that revelation has a merely extrinsic influence on philosophy, that is, by letting a philosophy know if it has come to a conclusion contrary to faith, in which case the matter must be reexamined from the viewpoints of both philosophy and faith.

Philosophy thereby remains autonomous, while at the same time discovering at its heart its own insufficiency in the pursuit of a wisdom applicable to all of life. Anyone who says that philosophy can be completely sufficient of itself means that the order of grace has no place in the human spirit and that the supernatural enters nature like a germ, parasite, or other foreign body into a living organism.

While philosophy can benefit from theology, theology can also benefit from philosophy. Philosophy can help theology to express more precisely and more systematically the mysteries of salvation: more precisely against heresies or false interpretations, and more systematically in organizing the mysteries of salvation in the light of wisdom. Theology can help solve humanity's great philosophical problems and can use philosophy as a discipline that can help to understand, define, or defend the content of faith.

Philosophy cannot substitute for theology: theology is the study of God and, despite common elements, philosophy has a different object. But philosophy can partially assimilate a supernatural message in its system of ideas without diminishing its own autonomy. Revelation has an influence on philosophy. No system of philosophy in the Western world today can ignore the existence of Christianity. Attempts to do so are in fact trying to render Christianity useless as a worldview or to relegate it to another level of life than the intellectual. It is, therefore, not only possible, but advantageous and necessary, to speak of philosophies of Catholic schooling and education. And those philosophies cannot exclude revelation and theology.

Theological concepts can be applied *within* the community of faith (for example, the attempt to bring mature religious consciousness toward wholeness), or *beyond* it (for example, the relevance of theology to the teaching of mathematics). Although some of the concerns of the theology of education are within the community of faith (the theology of the Church, for example, with which we shall deal briefly in chapter 6), it is perhaps with matters beyond the community of faith that theology of education is more concerned.

Theology of Education

In attempting to establish the identity of Catholic schools, it is necessary to delve into theology as well as philosophy. Education, being like work or social justice or marriage an important area of human life, must be involved in some way with theology. We have theologies *of* many things — culture, history, play, sport — because there is an application of theology to these matters as legitimate as to the sacraments.[15] And no "theology of education" is a completed work — it is ongoing.[16]

Theology of education can be, furthermore, a respected academic discipline:

> Unlike mathematics, physical science, or aesthetics, education does not constitute a distinct and unique domain of knowledge. Its main contributory disciplines are psychology, sociology, history, and philosophy. In this it is like medicine, whose main contributo-

ry disciplines are anatomy, physiology, chemistry, pharmacology. Less fundamental in education are other disciplines that are involved, such as social administration and statistics. . . . Theology of education has similarities with the former group; it is certainly not at all like the latter group (statistics).[17]

Furthermore, there can be Islamic and Jewish theologies of education, and denominational ones like those of Lutheranism, Anglicanism, and Catholicism. All can provide a legitimate and possible (but not necessary) source of understanding education. The claim of some educationists to secularity for their discipline does not exclude the influences of other forms of life, like religion or art.[18]

All who are engaged in education, if they are to preserve their integrity, must seek to make sense of their work in terms of the rest of their outlook on life: if a humanist a humanist understanding, if a communist a communist understanding, and if a Catholic a Catholic understanding. Further, Catholics working in Catholic schools must be engaged in not only the *study* of the relations between theology and education, but also in the *doing* or *practicing* of theology. Catholics will be helped in their critical educational tasks by reflecting on their professional work in the light of their faith.[19]

EDUCATION

"Education" comes from the cognate Latin words *educere* and *educare*, which mean "to lead out." Classical Latin literature uses these words in various contexts: nautically, to launch; biologically, to give birth. In education, they mean leading out all the potential that is in a person: a process of becoming. Education is not merely a descriptive science, or even merely a social science. It is, in part, an experimental science, because one of its purposes is to secure an exact knowledge of facts. It is also in part a speculative science, because another of its purposes is to explain ultimate realities, establish ideals, and settle transcendent goals. Even more, it is in great measure a normative science — a moral science. But, in the strict meaning of the term "science," which deals with observation and the classification of data, education is not a science at all. It is, at least equally, an art.

Education is not the same as learning, training, rearing, discipline, schooling, or indoctrination. The German language has two words for education — *Erziehung*, which means "instruction," and *(Aus)bildung*, which means "formation" — and the latter is closer to the essential definition. Genuine education involves information, formation, and transformation. It contains both monologue and dialogue. The ancient Greek Pythagoras spoke of education as that which enables a person to become what he or she is.

Although an essential definition of education is difficult, efforts to define it give insights into its various facets. John Dewey insightfully defined education as "the participation of the individual in the social consciousness of the race."[20] Lawrence Cremin gave a cogent definition of education as "the deliberate, systematic, and sustained effort to transmit, evoke, or acquire knowledge, attitudes, values, skills, or sensibilities, as well as any outcomes of that effort."[21]

Education implies something of *value*, just as it involves *knowing* and *understanding* in depth and in breadth. It implies reference to a rather long period of time, and an opening to the future. It sees the necessity of interpersonal interactions: many kinds of understanding can be attained only through close relationships with other human beings. It implies *wholeness*: it involves the entire person and affects all of that person's relationships — with self, with others, with things, and with ideas.

For Catholics, Pope Pius XI summed up a working definition of education when he wrote in 1929 that education "consists essentially in preparing man for what he must do here below in order to attain the sublime end for which he was created."[22] John D. Redden and Francis A. Ryan elaborated:

> Education is the deliberate and systematic influence exerted by the mature person upon the immature through instruction, discipline, and the harmonious development of all the powers of the human being, physical, social, intellectual, aesthetic, and spiritual, according to their essential hierarchy, by and for their individual and social uses, and directed toward the union of the educand with his Creator as the final end.[23]

While some aspects of these last definitions could be applied to secular education, the inclusion of spiritual development and the ultimate goal as union with the Creator are distinctive features of Catholic schools.

The real, or essential, meaning of education will depend on one's underlying philosophy. Idealists' definitions most closely approximate the etymological origins of the word. For them, education means a familiarizing of students with the transcendent. It brings out of students a whole world of ideas that are in some way already there. Classical Realists, on the other hand, look upon education as an introduction of the student to the objective order of reality, a mediation between the person of the student and the world of reality. The predicament here is that the knower, unlike a camera that tries to capture reality, is inextricably involved in the process so that one's perception of reality, even for the Realist, is to some extent subjective.[24]

For Pragmatists, education means setting up circumstances that enable the student to solve problems—problems that cause a disturbance, or disequilibrium, within the student. Through resolving these problems, the student grows. Though the ultimate end is the student's growth, there is no predetermined direction: the relevant thing is the *process*. Positivism, of which Pragmatism is a branch, sees the person as coming into the world as a *tabula rasa*, an empty blackboard, which has as its function to become as fully written upon as possible. The only thing that can write on that blackboard is experience; the person with the most fully written-up blackboard is the most experienced and the most fully educated. Existentialists look upon education as providing choices for the student: by making choices the student finds his authentic self.

— Catholic educators can cull from the various philosophies and their definitions of education only within limits. The wide cores that are unique to each thought pattern are completely different from one another, and some are hostile to everything Catholicism stands for. Catholics cannot, for example, retain their Catholicism and at the same time adhere to Positivism's God-excluding scientism, Pragmatism's view of the person, or atheistic Existentialism's libidinousness and chaos. To be eclectic has its dangers. When it goes beyond mere beginnings, to pick a little of this and a little of that can be a sign of an immature or weak person. Attempting eclecticism means, for one thing, not seeing that one's life of thought must ultimately be an organized, consistent whole. Eclectics in thought are in some ways like "washline" researchers, who copy the positions of various scholars on filing cards and then, when it comes time to write, hang all these positions out on the washline of their text without having involved themselves very much in the thinking process.

SCHOOLING

Education is not necessarily the same as schooling. One can receive an education outside school and one can miss an education in school, all the way to the level of the Ph.D. All fifty states in the United States require parents to "educate" their children, but only thirty-eight states make attendance at "school" compulsory. The school is irreplaceable, "for it is society's most important institutional response to date to insure the right of each individual to an education and, therefore, to full personal development."[25]

But what is a school? One dictionary provides thirteen definitions of the word used as a noun. Fish swim in schools. Horses are schooled. An organized body of scholars and faculty constituted a "school" in the medieval university. A group (as of artists) showing a common influence and similarity is referred to as a school, as is a source of instruction like "the school of experience." The original Greek *scholē* meant leisure; proper schooling still requires a certain amount of leisure.

Those who think of a school as a place are reminded that Socrates had his educational dialogues in the *agora* (marketplace) and Aristotle used a colonnaded cloisterlike arrangement for walking. And yet schools in basements, schools in abandoned buildings, and schools that don't look like schools have had to defend their being schools to government officials. A "school" in one state may not be a "school" in another. The definition is more than semantic: there is a marked increase in litigation over where children may receive their education to satisfy legal requirements. Where there is mandatory schooling, children found during school hours in places that do not fit legally acceptable definitions of "school" face truancy charges, and their parents criminal charges.

The common legal usage of the word "school" at the beginning of the twentieth century was that the school was "a place where instruction is imparted to the young."[26] That 1904 definition permitted courts to find that a home instruction program taught by a former government-school teacher was a valid schooling experience. In 1934, the Illinois Supreme Court described the school as a "place where systematic instruction in useful branches is given by methods common to schools and institutions of learning."[27] In 1956 a California court held that the word "school" could mean the building in which instruction took place, or the body of people within the building engaged in giving and receiving instruction.[28]

Parents teaching their children at home have argued that the home is a school.[29] Statutes requiring compulsory attendance at a "school" and authorizing criminal sanctions for nonattendance elevate the importance of defining "school." Perhaps policy makers should rather consider what is an "education," and compel children of specific ages to receive an education rather than to attend school. This would allow parents to satisfy the requirement without sending a child to a school building. If policy makers prefer the term "school," they should be sure to include the required elements in their definition.

But, as with "education," real or essential definitions of "school" differ, and depend upon one's philosophy. Different philosophies have defined the school variously as a place where a miniature kind of life takes place, or a place where instruction takes place, or an agent of the community, or a place for teachers to perform, or a place for individual opportunity. To ask what constitutes a *good* school makes matters even more complicated. In major areas often thought to affect school achievement, research shows little agreement: class numbers, heterogeneous classes, per-pupil expenses, school size except for egregious extremes, or wealthy school facilities.[30]

CATHOLIC EDUCATION AND SCHOOLING

Because of the lingering objections to Catholic schools, a definition of the Catholic school is even more necessary than a definition of other schools. The building of government schools on the prominent hills of the hamlets, towns, and cities of America suggests that they are intended as the modern counterpart of temples and cathedrals. Agnes E. Meyer, at the time the influential wife of the owner of *The Washington Post*, reflected that concept well when in 1948 she wrote, "When we realize . . . that the public school is the chief vehicle for mutual love, forgiveness and tolerance between all races, classes and creeds, it becomes an act of vandalism to attack it and an act of piety to work toward its improvement."[31]

Catholic schooling has been categorized as "private," in contrast with "public" schooling. This differentiation has pejorative connotations. The "private" is at times equated with the "personal"; it signifies a separation from common purposes, from meaningful participation in the common weal, and from interest in helping society for the better. The word "public," on the other hand, has a variety of senses, all with more acceptable overtones than "private." The *Oxford English Dictionary* shows the complexity of the word "public" in saying that the "exact shade [of meaning] often depends upon the substantive qualified," and gives as examples "the public ministry of Jesus," "public affairs," and a "public hall."[32]

There is no such thing as a "private" school.[33] By its nature, every school takes its students from the public and returns them there, for good or for ill; uses texts and other materials from publishers who are public; forms its curricula partly in accord with its vision of public needs; abides by at least minimal public standards set by the State; accepts teachers who were trained in publicly approved institutions according to publicly certified criteria; and so on. The only ways in which Catholic schools differ from their "public" counterparts are in their goals, their methods of funding, and their administration by Church authorities.

Catholic-school goals will be discussed at length in chapter 4. Suffice it to say here that the goal of forming good Christians is consonant with the best interests of the nation: Daniel Webster said that "whatever makes men good Christians makes them good citizens." Catholic-school funding is from a variety of sources—bingo, bake sales, tuition, free-will donations—frequently at great sacrifice. Catholic-school administration (to be discussed later, chiefly in chapters 8 and 9), like its counterparts elsewhere, is sometimes efficient and sometimes not, but almost always much less expensive.

It is more accurate and more appropriate to designate Catholic schools as "denominational," "church affiliated," or "nongovernment" schools, and government-funded ones as "government" schools. This is the terminology we shall use. If, because of the setup in the United States, unique in the Western world in its deliberate attempt to omit formal religion from government schools, this terminology seems to point to a startling parallel to totalitarian regimes, let that be a matter for further thought.

With the same purpose of clarifying terms, we note also that some scholars and politicians label the Catholic school as a conservative phenomenon. Catholic schools are, in truth, both liberal and conservative: liberal in the sense of the long-accepted definition of liberalism as that which wants to free, conservative in the sense of the older generation saving for the younger generation that which it considers best. We must, however, be careful of both terms. Catholic schools are not "liberal" in the sense of being radical, prodigal, or not bound by orthodoxy. And they are not "conservative" in the sense of the nostalgic rather than the authentically traditional. Some Catholics who call themselves "conservative" have a very selective memory of the past and no knowledge of the modern Church.

In approaching closer to what Catholic schools *are*, let us begin by saying that the definition of "Catholic" is difficult. "Good Catholics" used to be rather universally considered to be those who believed in the truths of the faith, lived up to the Church's moral requirements to the best of their ability, and practiced their religion by attending Mass regularly and frequenting the sacraments, especially penance and the eucharist. Today, for some, the concept of a "good Catholic" is broader. For such thinkers, Roman Catholics are all who accept the formal Church, acknowledging the authentic authority of the pope in cooperation with the bishops of the Church. Catholics who have problems with specific doctrines, which they say do not pertain to the heart of the matter or which have to do with disciplinary regulations, cite tensions in the Church involving concerned people all the way back to the New Testament confrontation of St. Peter by St. Paul. But Pope John Paul II, on his visit to the United States in September 1987, asserted that dissent from the *magisterium* (teaching authority of the Church) is incompatible with being a "good Catholic."

The Catholic must be initiated into the faith through baptism; and the good Catholic professes belief in at least the basic truths of the faith and the basic practices required by the Church. The truths of faith are presented in various formulas like the Nicene Creed. They were beautifully summarized in recent times by Pope Paul VI.[34] The Vatican's "General Catechetical Directory" groups them under four basic headings:

> the mystery of God, Father, Son and Holy Spirit, creator of all things; the mystery of Christ, Word incarnate, who was born of the Virgin Mary, suffered, died and rose again for our salvation; the mystery of the Holy Spirit, present in the Church and sanctifying and guiding it until the coming of Christ, our Saviour and Judge, in glory; the mystery of the Church, the mystical Body of Christ, in which the Virgin Mary has the highest place.[35]

In our text, the terms "Catholic," "Catholics," and "Catholicism" will be used to indicate the actual practice of the Roman Catholic community in the field of education, the de facto policy of the Church. This tradition is consonant with Catholic philosophy and theology, but is not necessarily the *only* possible actualization of Catholic faith. The "tradition" is therefore tradition with a small *t* and cannot be construed to be necessarily the official position of the Roman Catholic Church.

Some say it is impossible to define a specifically Catholic education or school. In the sense of Catholic Christian education being an open, critical study of the meaning of life which seeks to advance the personal development of pupils, some claim that there can no more be a characteristically or distinctively Christian form of education than there can be a distinctively Christian form of mathematics. They claim that education, like mathematics, engineering, and farming, is governed by its own intrinsic principles and not by reference to extrinsic theological factors: they observe that a bridge will hold up and a crop will mature for Christians and atheists alike.[36] But do the parallels hold? Are these other forms of knowledge like education, which is by its nature value-laden? Education is in great measure applied philosophical anthropology. Catholic Christianity can therefore have great applicability.

There is yet another objection to the possibility of Christian education:

> [A]n education based on a concern for objectivity and reason, far from allying itself with any specific religious claims, must involve teaching the radically controversial character of all such claims. An understanding of religious claims it can perfectly well aim at, but commitment to any one set in the interests of objectivity, it can either assume or pursue.[37]

Some theological systems do have this difficulty, but the Catholic system is not one of them. In Catholicism, critical inquiry and controversial examination flow directly and necessarily from the values to which the theology is committed.

By and large the Church sees the Catholic school as a privileged place which is potentially a temple because of the sacredness of its pursuits, and a beacon, lighting the way to a life of moral courage and providing leadership for the necessary Catholic responses to current change. In perceiving its schools in this way, the Church reveals a classicist orientation, emphasizing objective moral values and unchanging truth.

From a legal point of view, Canon Law makes the definition of the Catholic school seem simple. Canon 803 reads:

> 1. That school is considered to be Catholic which ecclesiastical authority or a public ecclesiastical juridic person supervises or which ecclesiastical authority recognizes as such by means of a written document.
> 2. It is necessary that the formation and education given in a Catholic school be based upon the principles of Catholic doctrine; teachers are to be outstanding for their correct doctrine and integrity of life.
> 3. Even if it really be Catholic, no school may bear the title *Catholic school* without the consent of the competent ecclesiastical authority.[38]

But there is more to it than those legal aspects. The Catholic school is, in fact, an ecclesial base community. The word "ecclesial" is important. The school is the starting point for full participation in the life of the Church. The child is in school for a good period of time. The school has access, as well, to the children's parents. So the parish has the opportunity to form this nucleus. The school can be a local church's opportunity to confront non-community with an existing community.

We have other leads to a definition of Catholic schooling and education. One lead is from the Catholic school's functions, another from its characteristics. The Second Vatican Council's *Declaration on Christian Education* speaks to the Catholic school's functions:

[The Catholic school] develops a capacity for sound judgment and introduces the pupils to the cultural heritage bequeathed to them by former generations. It fosters a sense of values and prepares them for professional life. By providing for friendly contacts between pupils of different characters and backgrounds it encourages mutual understanding. Furthermore it constitutes a center in whose activity and growth not only the families and teachers but also the various associations for the promotion of cultural, civil and religious life, civic society, and the entire community should take part.[39]

The U.S. bishops summarized the functions of the Catholic school into three: the delivery of Jesus' *message*, the formation of Christian *community*, and the performance of *service* in Jesus' name.[40] Bishop David Konstant provides some characteristics:

Catholic education should be characterized essentially by its communication of a perspective of human life centered in Jesus Christ; by its respect for the individuality and integrity of all; by its consequent concern with education for freedom, proceeding by way of illumination rather than indoctrination; and by its promotion of a sense of justice and of mission. A first concern of the Church's educational mission must be for the poor and disadvantaged. In a word its task is redemptive.[41]

A definition of the Catholic school, whatever else it indicates, must contain the teaching of faith. This means a place where evangelization should take place—an introduction to the gospel for children who may come from homes that have never heard the good news. The difficulty in trying to apply Catholic faith to culture, as Catholic schools must do, is that Catholic schools must do it without allowing faith to be submerged by culture, and at the same time not allowing culture to become subservient to faith. Enculturation is permissible, acculturation is not. Enculturation, not unlike socialization, is the process by which an individual learns the traditional content of a culture and assimilates its practices and values, whether ancient Greek or modern European. Acculturation, on the other hand, is a process of borrowing that results in new and blended patterns.

Faith is not culture. But there is a sense in which faith needs culture to incarnate itself. Culture can be, say, Irish or Polish; but faith, though needing culture, is not dependent on any one culture. Faith can enter a highly imperfect society and transform it. Faith can make a Catholic home or parish better, *always* converting, *always* Christianizing. When Catholic schools do this, the Catholic community regards them as a contribution made to the country as a whole. In fact, it is important to realize that the "Catholic school does not see itself as an alternative to the State school, but as a complementary institution at the service of the citizen."[42] Most essential throughout is the constant *reflection* by the Catholic community about meaning, about motivation, about curriculum, about community, and about all else.[43]

The Catholic-school graduate has to live up to all the complex dimensions of Christianity. To be a Catholic means not only to say "Lord, Lord," but to do the will of the Father. The pupils must be convinced that they have to *do* something about their faith, even if they do not know what, and have to look for ways to act. The Catholic-school graduate must present something of substance to society. That may mean something different in American society from British, French, or German society. Involvement means engagement in the social, economic, and racial problems of the society.[44]

Also, there is a duty to ensure that the distinctive Catholic character of the school is always maintained, not only in theory, but also in practice.[45] This distinctiveness means not only Catholic orthodoxy, but also adherence to the founding and maintaining religious community in the school's situation in time and place. But Catholic schools, while having many elements of sameness, are also different from one another: "the diverse situations and legal systems in which the Catholic school has to function in Christian and non-Christian countries demand that local problems be faced and solved by each Church within its own social-cultural context."[46] And the sameness of Catholic schools does not do away with their diversity:

> The elements [that are] characteristic of all Catholic schools . . . can be expressed in a variety of ways; often enough, the concrete expression will correspond to the specific charism of the religious institute that founded the school and continues to direct it. Whatever be its origin—diocesan, religious, or lay—each Catholic school can preserve its own specific character, spelled out in an educational philosophy, rationale, or in its own pedagogy.[47]

Always, in putting a definition of Catholic schools into practice, one must be mindful of the possible need for change. If, in one's conception of the nature of the Catholic school, one does not take the possibility of change into consideration, one may find oneself teaching a kind of religion "which [pupils] will be likely to reject as being among other childish things to be abandoned on leaving school."[48]

Last but not least, the entire citizenry must realize that the Catholic school is important.[49] In accordance with its mission, "while policies and opportunities differ from place to place, the Catholic school has its place in any national school system."[50] And no matter how they are defined, Catholic schools are to be models of unity, coordination, service, and commitment, with effective relationships with other schools: government, proprietary, and other church-affiliated, as well as Catholic. In fact, the relationship with government schools should be based upon the realization that "it is there that much of the future of our society lies, [and] [n]ationally the vast majority of Catholic youngsters are enrolled in public schools."[51]

CONCLUSION

Can a Catholic school remain Catholic without attention to its identity and the development of a Christian philosophy and theology? Not for long. The Catholic school without a Christian philosophy does not become neutral: it comes under the influence of the current community ideology, or nationalism, or secularism, or faddism. Its mind and its heart then become those of a different corporate community. Today more than ever before, unless a particular Catholic school is considering the principles that give it its Catholic identity and is trying to live by them, it does not deserve to stay in existence.

Catholic schools should continue not only because they are in existence and can't be wished away. They should continue because they stand for specific, positive ideas. They are needed "to develop intellectual faculties in a systematic way, to strengthen the ability to judge, to promote the sense of values, to establish a point of reference"; the Catholic school is, furthermore,

> a contribution to the development of the mission of the People of God, to dialogue between the Church and the community of mankind, to the safeguarding of the freedom of conscience, to the cultural progress of the world, and sometimes to the solution of problems created by public deficiency. . . . The Catholic school points *per se* to the purpose of leading man to his human and Christian perfection . . . [and] is also an educational community where the meeting of collaboration between all the workers of the area takes place.[52]

The Catholic school makes its "own positive contribution to the cause of the total formation of man. The absence of the Catholic school would be a great loss for civilization and for the natural and supernatural destiny of man."[53]

On the other hand, Catholic schools which adhere to their identity cannot be perceived as being the sole answer to the furtherance of Catholicism and its ideals. In Holland, West Germany, and France, Catholic schools have for over two generations been financially sup-

ported by the State,[54] and yet Catholicism in those countries is confused, lethargic, or barely recognizable.

Yet one of the ways that Catholic schools could be made truly
Catholic and more effective, their worth discovered, and their future
made more secure, is to obtain renewed insights from a reconsidera-
tion of their identity. The material of this book is intended to aid this
task, and will help do so if it is reflected upon, discussed, and lived.

ORGANIZATION AND USE OF THIS BOOK

To give an overview of where the various positions on Catholic-
school identity come from, we present, next, material on the *opponents'
mind-set* and on the *proponents' mind-set*. Then we use all-embracing
categories based ultimately upon Aristotle to encompass the areas of
schooling and education which we shall treat. This begins with a
discussion of *goals*. Goals are from some points of view the most
important aspect of a school: one cannot measure the degree of success or failure of a school (or anything else) unless one can compare its
achievements against its goals. Aristotle said that no wind is helpful to
a ship without a destination.

Goals guide our next consideration: *curriculum*. Curriculum is very
important, containing as it does all that the school offers in the way of
education. Next we consider those *partners* who are responsible for
getting it done, the secondary agents: the family, the Church, and the
State. We treat fourthly the *atmosphere*, conditions, or climate, of
schooling and education: the external, which is that emanating from
society, such as whether society encourages and cooperates with
schooling; and the internal, such as the nature of the physical building
and the spiritual atmosphere.

Fifth are those who get Catholic schools where they want to go:
teachers, whose professionalism, faith, and personal dedication make
them the instruments and immediate representatives of the entire
enterprise to students, parents, and community. Last in our treatment are *students*, who are first in the sense that it is for them that the
entire school adventure exists. In fact, the primary agents of education are God and the student. God sustains the entire effort in existence. But without the student's selfactivity, there is no education, no
matter how good the other resources. The *questions for discussion*, at the
end of each chapter, are to help readers to discover whether they
understand the meanings, implications, and inferences of the text,
and to apply the material further.

The notes of each chapter expand the text and provide further
reading. Books and materials are not usually listed in both notes and
suggested bibliographies, but only in one or the other. Even though

some books are relevant to more than one chapter, bibliographies do not usually repeat materials from one chapter to another.

QUESTIONS FOR DISCUSSION

Do the reasons why parents send their children to Catholic schools suggest a definition of the Catholic school — even a descriptive definition?

Can one easily deduce with certainty a definition of Catholic education by asking questions about what Catholic education *ought* to be, what education *has been*, or what it *might be*?

Is it true, as some scholars contend, that there can be no science of education because human conduct can never be objectively predicted and controlled?

What is your vision of the good person, the good life, the good society, which education tries to promote?

What are the pros and cons of metaphorically describing the Catholic school as a factory (turning out as many pupils as possible), a theater (to capture the imagination and interests of youth), and a temple (where a reverence for learning is instilled)?

What are the implications of defining the function of the school as a rear-view mirror, presenting the best of what has gone on in the past; a weathervane, pointing to the way society's winds are currently blowing; a beacon, a light for change in a world that is perhaps heading for the rocks of destruction?

May the Catholic school be defined in any legitimate way by the presence of religious, sisters especially, on the faculty?

Socrates said that the unexamined life is not worth living. Erasmus believed that, for the masses, the examined life is no better. As applied to Catholic schools, with whom of the two do you agree, and why?

Instead of wasting time and effort in discussing philosophies of education, why not simply try things out, and if they work, just use them without being troubled about underlying philosophies?

SUGGESTED BIBLIOGRAPHY

Abbott, Walter M., and Joseph Gallagher. *The Documents of Vatican II*. New York: Guild Press, 1966.

All sixteen official texts promulgated by the ecumenical council, with good translations from the Latin and notes and comments by Catholic, Protestant, and Orthodox authorities.

Adler, Mortimer J. *The Paideia Program: An Educational Syllabus*. New York: Macmillan, 1984.

A modern-day Aristotelian makes proposals on education and curriculum, taking into account his previous books on the *paideia* (1982, 1983).

_____. *Ten Philosophical Mistakes. Basic Errors in Modern Thought — How They Came About, Their Consequences, and How to Avoid Them.* New York: Collier Books, 1987.

An Aristotelian critique of characteristic positions of modern philosophers.

Benedictine Monks of Solesmes, eds. *Papal Teachings: Education.* Boston: Daughters of St. Paul, 1979.

A collection of papal encyclicals on education.

Bogolovsky, B. B. *The Ideal School.* New York: Macmillan, 1936.

The author advances the selfhood of the pupil and its importance in Idealism. He reviews those elements (e.g., learning environment) that represent the ideal educational experience.

Brann, Eva T. *Paradoxes of Education in a Republic.* University of Chicago Press, 1979.

A classicist approach to liberal education.

Broudy, Harry S. *Building an Educational Philosophy.* New York: Prentice-Hall, 1954.

The Realist author discusses the realist perspective on the structures and dynamics of personality.

Copleston, Frederick. *A History of Philosophy.* 8 vols. Garden City, N.Y.: Doubleday, 1962.

An extensive introduction to the history of philosophy, from ancient Greece to today, examining the major trends.

Denton, David, ed. *Existentialism and Phenomenology in Education: Collected Essays.* New York: Teachers College Press, 1974.

Presents current investigations in education by leading existentialists and phenomenologists.

Dewey, John. *Democracy and Education.* New York: Macmillan, 1916.

An exposition of Dewey's type of Pragmatism (Instrumentalism). (This is perhaps Dewey's most significant work.)

Donohue, John W. *Catholicism and Education.* New York: Harper and Row, 1973.

Explores the impact of Vatican II upon Catholic education. Examines educational theory and the individual goals of education, and concludes with a discussion of the social goals of Catholic schools.

Ferm, Vergilius, ed. *History of Philosophical Systems.* Paterson, N.J.; Littlefield, Adams, 1961; New York: Books for Libraries Press, 1970.

A collection of essays discussing philosophies of different historical periods and cultures. Though brevity prevents in-depth analysis, the book will serve the beginning student well in providing overviews.

Fitzpatrick, Edward A. *Exploring a Theology of Education.* Milwaukee: Bruce Publishing, 1950.

To arrive at a theology of education, examines major Church doctrines, the liturgy, spiritual writings, and the teacher. Examines also the nature of knowledge, will, and love.

Flannery, Austin, ed. *Vatican Council II: The Conciliar and Post Conciliar Documents.* 2 vols. Northport, N. Y.: Costello Publishing, 1975.

The primary source documents, with notes and footnotes.

Gutek, Gerald L. *Philosophical Alternatives in Education.* Columbus, Ohio: Charles E. Merrill, 1974.

Reviews the primary philosophies of life and presents them as educational philosophies. Discusses the elements of schooling (e.g., curriculum) in terms of each of the educational philosophies.

Hocking, William E. *Types of Philosophy.* 3rd ed. New York: Scribner's, 1959.

Presents in a thorough manner the various life philosophies. Focuses on truth and values and how each of the life philosophies addresses and resolves the issues in these areas.

Mann, Jesse A., and Gerald F. Kreyche, eds. *Reflections on Man, Perspectives on Reality, Approaches to Morality.* The Harbrace Series in Philosophy. 3 vols. San Diego: Harcourt Brace, 1966.

Anthologies that offer a pluralistic approach to the basic issues in philosophy, giving the beginning student a substantial introduction to different perspectives on the contemporary American scene. Each volume presents materials from various viewpoints: classical and scholastic, dialectical, naturalist and pragmatist, analytic and positivist, and existentialist and phenomenological.

McDermott, Edwin J. *Distinctive Qualities of the Catholic School.* Washington, D.C.: National Catholic Educational Association, 1985.

This is the first essay in the NCEA Keynote Series of fourteen booklets for the pre-service and in-service education of Catholic school teachers. Others in the series are *A History of Catholic Schooling in the United States; Development and Public Relations for the Catholic School; Governance and Administration in the Catholic School; Catholic School Finance and Church-State Relations; Student Moral Development in the Catholic School; The Parent, the Parish, and the Catholic School; The Teacher in the Catholic School; Curriculum in the Catholic School; Catechetics in the Catholic School; Methods of Teaching in the Catholic School; Total Development of the Student in the Catholic School; Research and the Catholic School;* and *Code of Ethics for the Catholic School Teacher.*

Pope Pius XI. *The Christian Education of Youth.* New York: America Press, 1936.

This 1929 encyclical was the most important document on Catholic education until Vatican Council II, and still offers valuable insights.

Yzermans, Vincent A., ed. *Pope Pius XII and Catholic Education.* St. Meinrad, Ind.: Grail Publications, 1957.

Examines the addresses of Pope Pius XII concerning education in areas like the modern environment; the religious, moral, and intellectual training of youth; the Christian conscience; and solid religious training.

Chapter 2

WHY SOME PEOPLE ARE AGAINST CATHOLIC SCHOOLS: OPPONENTS' MIND-SET

Black-hatted "bad guys" and white-hatted "good guys" are as American as apple pie and ice cream. They are the stuff of American art forms: drama, film, short stories, novels, television. Their story is full of action, law and order, mythic figures, practicality, "good guys" winning and "bad guys" losing. Very often, the identity of the black-hatted and white-hatted figures depends on the viewer. Catholic-school proponents, for example, see "bad guys in the black hats" in some aspects of United States history, many modern philosophies, and various psychological theories of personal formation. The opponents' mind-set sees in black hats those Catholics who want their separate schools to be on a par with government schools. Today, though, the appearance of the good guys and the bad guys is altered. Both now wear Brooks Brothers suits and no hat, and the suit color of both sides is gray, the design usually pin-striped. Both sides are generally more subtle, usually not malicious, and likely to be sincere. And their demeanor is more "O. K. Chorale" than "O. K. Corral."

UNITED STATES HISTORICAL OVERVIEW[1]

Catholics in the thirteen original colonies were an insignificant and powerless minority: In 1790 they numbered no more than thirty-five thousand in a population of over four million. Catholic colonists wanted the education of their children to be Catholic. Those who could, sacrificed by sending their children abroad to colleges and to convent schools in Europe. There was, at the same time, a wide, sweeping intellectual revolution: the rationalistic and faith-excluding so-called "Enlightenment." The principles of this "Age of Reason" also provided a philosophical base for the unfolding work of the Founding

Fathers. Though the developing "new nation" never lost the Puritan's sense of America's special destiny as a chosen nation, the theme of rationalism also perdured.[2]

One of the most serious complaints about the United States situation in the early national period voiced by the church's Councils of Baltimore (which began in 1829) pertained to the laws by which some of the states denied the Church the right to possess property. This resulted in the well-known difficulty called trusteeism, and sometimes hindered the progress of schools.

During the decades before the Civil War, the popular Puritan hope for the Kingdom of God on earth led to desires for reform. One of the areas of reform was schooling. The most effective educational crusader at the time was Horace Mann (1796–1859). Dedicated to eliminating sectarian religion from government schools, he was equally convinced that the schools must instill the historic Protestant virtues. William H. McGuffey (1800–1873), through his millions of reading books, helped shape the national mind in forging an even closer bond between schooling and Protestant virtues. The same could be said of the enormously popular works of instruction written by two New England ministers, Samuel G. Goodrich (1793–1860), known as Peter Parley, and the prolific Jacob Abbott. Most of these works contained anti-Catholic prejudices.

During the westward movement, two factors affecting the expansion of the Catholic Church were immigration and conversions to Roman Catholicism. Resentment of both resulted in their being a not unmixed blessing. The country was at the time experiencing the most violent religious discord in its history. This embraced especially the phenomena of American nativism and anti-Catholicism.[3] They were the results of a militant religious tradition and the Protestant majority view of the United States' destiny as a Protestant nation. Anti-Catholicism also offered to many a motive for Protestant solidarity.

Political fears exacerbated the situation. Every immigrant ship at a wharf struck fear into the hearts of insecure politicians. To them it seemed that the ideologically united Irish were dooming decency, order, justice, and sound social principles (translation: "a conservatively structured society"). Immigration also spawned economic fears in those who worried about losing their jobs with the influx of cheap labor.

The "Protestant crusade" also gave birth to inflammatory anti-Catholic publications. Wild tales of nuns like "Maria Monk" were especially popular. And the agitation went further than words. Near Boston, after years of mounting tensions, on August 11, 1834, a well-organized group burned the Ursuline convent in Charlestown. Between 1840 and 1842 in New York, the political rift widened further with the school crisis, answered forcefully by the blunt and perhaps pugnacious Catholic bishop John Hughes, "Dagger John," who served from 1842 to 1864. Up to his time, public funds throughout the country were being given to church-affiliated schools.

When the powerful Public School Society in New York withheld funds from parish schools, Hughes argued that in justice the parish schools should be given a share of the school fund (which fund was raised by the taxation of Catholics as well as Protestants) or, in the alternative, that Catholics be exempt from the taxes they were paying into the common school fund. He objected to Catholics paying taxes "for the purpose of destroying our religion in the minds of our children." The Public School Society rejected his argument. The final result of the bitter fray was that no school teaching religious sectarian doctrines was thereafter to receive money from the common school fund. The government-school/church-school dichotomy deepened.

In contrast was the contemporaneous peace-loving bishop of Philadelphia, Francis Patrick Kenrick. When the nativists threatened violence, Kenrick issued a conciliatory statement. His quiet and dignified conduct did not prevent the eruption, in May 1844, of wild and bloody rioting. Two Roman Catholic churches and dozens of Irish homes were burned, militia fired point blank among advancing crowds, a canon was turned against St. Philip Neri Church, and for three days mob rule prevailed in the city and its suburbs. Thirteen people were killed. Ever since, in the face of confrontations the preferability of the Hughes or Kenrick procedures has been argued.

As industrialization and other influences wrought changes in the nation, the influence of the Enlightenment, with its dichotomy between education and manual labor, its opposition to the principle of schooling for the masses, and its consequent disinclination for the lower classes to attend school, began to subside. When in addition it became increasingly obvious that for the first time in history a government-school pattern was to be attempted without religion, it became equally clear that the Church was going to have to step up its schooling efforts.

Toward the end of the nineteenth century, the fact that some of the anti-Catholic bigotry continued even in high places was, to the average Catholic, awesome. It showed even in President Ulysses S. Grant's speeches of 1875,[4] and in the many proposals for an amendment to the Constitution by Senator James G. Blaine that absolutely forbade government funds for church-affiliated (especially Roman Catholic) efforts. Variants of the "Blaine Amendment" succeeded in appearing in many state constitutions.

The turn of the century, roughly from 1885 to 1917, was critical for organized religion. Materialism and its cult of success, pragmatism, naturalism, and hostile extensions of Darwinism permeated the country. The shifting patterns of immigration put the Protestant establishment, already hurt by the Civil War, in a worsened position and led to a revival of the movement to restrict immigration and to new outbreaks of nativism, like the short-lived American Protective Association.

Just as the Supreme Court reflected the mood of the time in its 1896 Plessy decision supporting "separate but equal" treatment for blacks, so too the Court reflected popular prejudices concerning Catholics. Most of the cases of church-state relationships pertained to schooling. They were tried in state and federal courts, and the opinions did not evidence much consistency.

In the early twentieth century there were developments concerning students, in both theory and practice. With regard to theory, government schools had been welcoming the introduction from abroad of the ideas of Johann Pestalozzi (1746–1827), Johann Herbart (1776–1841), and Friedrich Froebel (1782–1852), which contributed to the growth of progressive education. The government schools were also interested in the tests and measurements movement of Edward L. Thorndike (1874–1949), who held the principle that everything that exists, exists in quantity and can be measured. Catholic educators could not completely accept the naturalism of Pestalozzi, the determinism of Herbart, the pantheism of Froebel, the empiricism of Thorndike, nor progressive education because of what they considered undue permissiveness for the child and a forgetfulness of original sin.

In the area of practice, Catholic-school students comprised several minority groups of immigrants, who were blamed for many of society's ills. Catholic educators tried to meet this prejudice by making their students not only Catholic, but also American. For Catholic immigrant parents, the parish was the familiar unit from their places of origin; an integral part of this, especially among the Germans, was the parish school. The parish school could not help but separate immigrant children to a certain extent from their foreign-sounding and foreign-looking parents; but it made the transition slower than the government schools did and therefore, in the light of subsequent research, psychologically more sound.

In the 1960s, the terms "post-Puritan" and "post-Protestant" began to be applied to the United States. The age of the White Anglo-Saxon Protestant (WASP) and the age of the melting pot, if there ever was one, began to come to a close. Many terms began to describe the culture of this time, such as "secular," "permissive," "the death of God," and "the great moral revolution." The country was experiencing a basic change in moral and religious attitudes. All traditional structures, such as the parish church and school, were questioned. Equally seriously, laymen were finding that they had been forced to divorce their faith from the modes of thought by which they dealt with their life and work in the world. Declining growth rates and widespread budgetary problems lessened the institutional vitality of the churches, as well as every other institution.

For many reasons, youth showed an estrangement from traditional forms of religious nourishment. Sydney E. Ahlstrom summarized these characteristics into three—the first metaphysical, the second moral, and the third social:

> 1) A growing commitment to a naturalism or "secularism" and corresponding doubts about the supernatural and the sacral; 2) A creeping (or galloping) awareness of vast contradictions in American life between profession and performance, the ideal and the actual; 3) Increasing doubt as to the capacity of present day ecclesiastical, political, social, and educational institutions to rectify the country's deep-seated woes.[5]

To thinking Catholics, all of this showed at least as much as any previous history the need for church-affiliated schools. But Catholics committed to the sacral aim of "saving souls" had grave problems with the identity of some Catholic schools, which they perceived as producing an atmosphere in which the traditional faith did not seem to flourish sufficiently.[6]

THE PHILOSOPHICAL BACKGROUND

Catholics as well as their opponents claim to be "humanistic." By that both sides mean they are prohumankind. But "humanistic" has at least two meanings.[7] One had its roots in Greco-Roman rationalist culture, and the other in medieval Christianity. These two strands continue to form our cultural heritage. The Protestant Reformation, striking a note of faith and man's dependence on God, emphasized one side of this polarity. The Enlightenment stressed the other: reason and science, and the potential of man. Both strands—faith and reason—went into the formation of the American Republic, whose history is full of the tension between these poles.

The optimistic humanistic values of the Enlightenment countered the repressive and pessimistic elements of Calvinism. Cotton Mather and Jonathan Edwards did not believe in the basic good nature of man, nor did the writers of the U.S. Constitution; hence the Constitution's ingenious system of checks and balances against the selfish instincts of people. The Founding Fathers were classicists as well as Protestant Christians and, as good British subjects, had been as familiar with the Scottish Enlightenment thinkers as they were with Calvin's *Institutes*. It was a unique synthesis of these two traditions that brought about the American civic religion that sustains the U.S. polity.

Today, with the demise of mainstream Protestant cultural hegemony, the Enlightenment side of the polarity—the "reason" side—has gained the ascendancy in our culture, including in our government schools. The result has been a reaction in the form of a twentieth-century "Great Awakening" of Protestant Christianity, which includes fundamentalist Christian churches and schools. Contributing to the tensions are the philosophies of Pragmatism, Empiricism, Positivism, Secularism, Naturalism, Materialism, and some theories of personal development.

Pragmatism

The time of the "bad guy in the black hat" was the time of the development of the philosophy that has come to dominate the United States and to some extent the contemporary world: Pragmatism. Charles Sanders Peirce (1839–1914), an engineer and logician; William James (1842–1910), a psychologist and philosopher; and—most important of all for education—John Dewey (1859–1952), philosopher and lawyer, were founders of one form or another of that philosophy at Harvard. James's charm and lively style helped get it off the ground. Later historical circumstances made Dewey better known and more influential.

In popular parlance, "pragmatism," the "pragmatic," and the "practical" are words dear to the American heart. To be pragmatic means to be active in affairs; it stresses the disposition to be busy. To be practical means to be disposed to here-and-now decisions and action rather than to speculation or abstraction. They all mean the avoidance of being an unrealistic visionary, an "absent-minded professor," or a dreamer—all of whom Americans abhor.

But being practical or pragmatic is not the same as being philosophically pragmatistic. As a philosophy, Pragmatism sought to imitate the laboratory techniques of positive science, at that time undergoing tremendous growth, especially in the United States. It received stimulation from the promulgation of the Darwinian theory of natural selection, then also acquiring prominence. It was the nineteenth-century world of laissez-faire economics, in which industrialists reigned supreme and young children had to work in mines and mills. As evolution taught the "survival of the fittest," Pragmatism taught that the true idea is the one that survives the clash with experience. (So Oliver Wendell Holmes could say, "Truth is the majority vote of that nation which can lick all others.")

Then there was the United States frontier experience of the time: cities were growing larger in a shift from the farms, the railroads were moving westward, and technology was dominant. Pragmatism emphasized action and the changing character of knowledge and truth. It fit right in with the U.S. deemphasis on intellectualism, prompting one humorist of the time to propose the slogan "Ready! Fire! Aim!" and an opponent to change another popular saying to "Don't just *do* something — *stand* there!"

Peirce, the founder of Pragmatism, held that as a person proceeds in his pursuit of truth, he is faced with obstacles. In such cases the person undertakes inquiry, which is Peirce's definition of thought. Inquiry ceases when the obstacles and doubts are removed. Then new obstacles arise, and the process is repeated. Peirce gave instructions for making ideas clear through his famous "pragmatic maxim," which states: "Consider what effects, that might conceivably have practical bearings, we conceive the object of our conception to have. Then, our conception of these effects is the whole of our conception of the object."[8]

James saw the importance of Pragmatism, claiming that its success, if it came about, would be of the same degree of importance as that of the Protestant Reformation. He emphasized the duty of each individual to make his own experience a decisive factor in his thought and action. With the influence of Darwin in the background, and James's training in medicine and psychology in the foreground, James considered that the main function of thought is to help establish "satisfactory relations with our surroundings." James also asserted that we may have a right to hold a religious or metaphysical belief, but only when the belief in question would supply a psychological benefit to the believer, when evidence for and against the belief is equal, and when the decision to believe is weighty.[9]

James's formulation of Peirce's pragmatic maxim was: "The pragmatic method . . . is to try to interpret each notion by tracing its respective practical consequences." In James's words, the pragmatic method means "the attitude of looking away from . . . principles, 'categories,' supposed necessities; and of looking towards . . . fruits, consequences, facts."[10] John Locke had been the archetypical British philosopher, and James performed in the same capacity for the United States: he emphasized populism, moralism, hard-won optimism, homely examples, rhetorical vigor, and the energies of the will rather than the subtleties of the intellect.

Dewey, far and away the most famous and influential of the pragmatists, espoused Pragmatism especially in the field of education. He taught in universities just at the time when accreditation was taking hold. Teachers from all over flocked to the University of Chicago and Columbia University, where he taught, and they brought his ideas back home. In Dewey's theory of inquiry, a "felt need" impels the inquiring person to reintegrate the situation which has presented a problem. Intelligent reflection enables the inquirer to settle the problematic situation by offering solutions to be tried. So thought becomes an instrument in helping a person to adjust himself to the new in experience. (Thus Dewey's version of Pragmatism is called Instrumentalism.) Dewey was very much concerned with the public character of a true statement or, as he called it, a "warranted assertion." The warranted assertion became, in fact, Dewey's version of "truth."

Major Positions

Pragmatism holds to the following fundamental theses, with not every pragmatist subscribing to all and with varying interpretations from one to another. Pragmatists emphasize the pliable nature of reality, the practical function of knowledge, concern with action, constant change, and the priority of actual experience over a priori reasoning (that is, knowledge not requiring experience). In addition, the meaning of an idea or proposition resides in the practical consequences that result from its use or application.

Truth is, to put it crudely, "what works." Peirce put it less crudely when he defined truth as the "limit towards which endless investigation would tend to bring scientific belief." Pragmatists understand ideas as instruments and plans of action. They thus emphasize the functional aspect of ideas. Lastly, in methodology pragmatists believe that people's interpretations of reality are motivated solely by considerations of utility for themselves, and that this is justified.

Evaluation and Current Status

On the positive side, Pragmatism enjoys the immense prestige, and value, of practical knowledge. Also, it has replaced the dubious ideal of philosophy as being exclusively a system of eternal truths with a valid emphasis upon the authentic character of human reason. Pragmatism has thus become vitally involved in current intellectual life. It has succeeded in its critical reaction against some high-blown nineteenth-century thought.

Perhaps the greatest shortcoming of Pragmatism is its excessive concern with what is here and now *relevant*. It thus confines itself to limited horizons, and can exclude areas of *importance*, such as humankind's spiritual nature, human freedom, and the person's ultimate destiny. Although it is true that the thinker should concern himself with what is relevant, one should speculate about *all* aspects of being. That which is important has an inner weight of its own, even when not perceived as relevant. What many people have perceived as being relevant here and now has often in the long run turned out to be unimportant.

Lack of Consonance with Catholicism

Catholicism can accept Dewey's historical contribution to enlivening classrooms that were lifeless, boring, dull, and ineffective. It also easily accepts Dewey's insistence upon the use of intelligence. And it can accept his use of the method of problem solving (which, however, Dewey did not discover, but only emphasized). As for the rest of Pragmatism, however, it and Catholicism have nothing in common.

William James defined Pragmatism as "the attitude of looking away from first things, principles, 'categories,' supposed necessities; and of looking towards last things, fruits, consequences, facts."[11] This sits uneasily with Catholic philosophies of life and education. Pragmatism's verification principle as being solely empirical data cannot permit of the existence of the transcendent and immanent God of Catholicism. Truth for the pragmatist is sociologically certified agreement. This admits of the equation of prevalency with normalcy—hardly an acceptable criterion for Catholic morality. Catholicism, though admitting the importance of experience, sees Pragmatism as overemphasizing it. For one thing, this overemphasis makes dubious the possibility of religion for the person who has not had an immediate experience of God. Many Catholic educators also find it hard to take the pragmatist's definition of the teacher as only a facilitator. The philosophies congenial to Catholicism see the teacher as having something to say—insights to share, traditions to hand on, knowledge to impart.

Pragmatists are exceedingly distrustful, if not downright disdainful, of what Catholics have traditionally found necessary for philosophical integrity: abstractions, ultimates, absolutes, moral values in a world other than the empirical. Pragmatists see the origins of religion in the desires of humankind and rule out divine revelation—again unacceptable to Catholics. Pragmatists see the worth of religion (as of everything else) solely in its consequences and in whether it works for an individual; Catholics see religion as having objective worth whether or not it pleases a specific individual at a given time.

Pragmatism sees the child as the center of the educational enterprise: curriculum must be child-centered, experiences must center around the student, and there must be little regimen or structure imposed on the child. Catholicism sees God as the center of the enterprise: God who sustains all in existence, whose will constitutes the only right and good, and belief in whom necessitates a certain amount of structure. Pragmatism does not believe in anything a priori; Catholicism has much of it. Pragmatism stresses scientific inquiry as the basis of all learning; this methodology stops short of addressing the spiritual nature of the person.

Pragmatism's Roots: Empiricism and Positivism
EMPIRICISM

Pragmatism, of which the American James was an originator, is close to Empiricism, of which the British Locke was an originator. In the pursuit of knowledge, Empiricism emphasizes experience, especially of the senses, and reliance upon observation, experimentation, or induction rather than upon such other rational means as intuition, speculation, deduction, or dialectic. The empiricist, in contrast to the empirical researcher, looks upon his methodology as the *sole* road to truth.

Locke, learning from such scientists as Isaac Newton, the famous physicist, affirmed that in the beginning the human mind is a "white paper, devoid of characters." It has no innate *ideas*, but only innate *powers*. It is a "clean slate" (*tabula rasa*), to be written upon through sensation of the external world. The influence of this concept has been a major factor in schools' demands for a multiplicity of sensory materials.

The Scottish David Hume drew his mentor Locke's system to its logical conclusions. Hume claimed that man's knowledge is confined to the phenomena he can experience: "nothing is ever present to the mind but perceptions." For Hume, not only the external world but even the knowing subject vanished. Before that time, most scholars who wrote about the person called their work *De anima* ("On the Soul"), basing their writing on what they considered the most important aspect of the person; for the followers of Locke and Hume that would be impossible.

The essence of sensationalist thought was expressed by the eighteenth-century Etienne Bonnot de Condillac. Condillac is famous for imagining a lifeless statue. If one gives the statue a sense of smell, the statue will come to the point of desiring. If the sensation of touch is added, the statue will acquire a consciousness of an external world, and so on with the addition of all the senses. In other words, given the senses the entirety of human experience will follow. Empiricism limits knowledge to the order of experience, and treats the human intellect as simply a more powerful sense faculty of the brain. The intellect does not get beyond the material order.

Critics, however, charge that, though sense experience may be required to begin the process, there is more to knowledge than what the senses provide. People do form universals, or concepts. And the person can, in the realm of knowing, be self-reflective: although the eye, for example, cannot see itself seeing, the intellect can be aware of its own act as it places it. While Catholics do not reject the process of empirical research, they do reject Empiricism for many reasons, most importantly for its undue emphasis on sensation and experience at the expense of insights.

POSITIVISM

Auguste Comte (1798–1857) was the founder of Positivism. From about 1830 onward, Comte claimed that the development of science and of the Industrial Revolution was giving birth to a new culture—a culture deriving all of its important principles from science. The new methods and principles were to be applied to a new science, which Comte named sociology.

Comte summarized it all into his "law of three stages." He held that in the earliest stage of the human race, intellectually its lowest, humankind looked to theology for an explanation of phenomena and for meaning. The next higher stage came when people looked to metaphysics for explanations. Humankind's highest stage, however, arrived when people looked for explanations only to facts, observable phenomena, the "positive" data of experience, and beyond all that to pure logic and pure mathematics. This meant abandoning all inquiry into causes or ultimate origins, because these areas belong to the theological or metaphysical stages of thought, now held to be superseded. And the individual repeats in his personal growth and development that of the human race. (This is the theory of "recapitulation," which says that ontogeny is the recapitulation of phylogeny.)

Comte believed also that satisfactory social organization could be achieved only after the reorganization of all knowledge along "positive" lines. This would base social science on physical science, treating social phenomena in purely physical, nonanthropomorphic language. Consistent with the orientation of nineteenth-century continental social thought, best known today in the works of Karl Marx and Friedrich Engels, Comte conceived of humanity at large as a "social being," a kind of superperson. Humanity alone is real and the individual is only an abstraction. Like one of his early mentors, Claude-Henri Saint-Simon (1760–1825), Comte founded a "religion" of veneration for and cult of "the Great Being: Humanity."

In the English-speaking world, Herbert Spencer (1820–1903), though critical of the French Comte, attempted a similar task. In sociology, the French Emile Durkheim (1858–1917) was Comte's principal important disciple. In the same family, Logical Positivism is a movement which aims to establish an all-embracing Empiricism based solely on the logical analysis of language. Linguistic Analysis and Analytic Philosophy make language and its analysis central.

In education, Positivism emphasizes the empirical sciences in the curriculum. The "verification principle" of Positivism is that nothing has meaning unless it can be verified by scientific methodology. All areas, even ethics, are empirical sciences. Ethical propositions can be meaningful without being factually true or false, for they are not used to describe some special kind of entity, like goodness, but are used rather to express an "emotive attitude." Ethics is not concerned with favoring one moral way of life over another, but is the examination of the logic of ethical propositions.

Religious propositions, too, are neither true nor false, but may be meaningful only in declaring a particular attitude toward life and the world. In fact, religion is disposed of along with metaphysics. Humankind cannot attain a superior kind of knowledge of transcendental entities, such as God, the Absolute, mind, soul, or substance, because those are inaccessible to natural science. The Behavioristic Psychology of such as the U. S. Burrhus F. Skinner (b. 1904), a derivative of Positivism, construes mental dispositions as being similar to physical properties (for example, malleability, brittleness, electrical conductivity).

There are some valuable truths in the positivist movement. It has, for instance, cautioned against the dangers of too much a priori speculation and smug absolutisms. It has insisted upon clarity of thought and precision in the use of language. It has called upon common sense in philosophizing. On the other hand, some positivists have themselves observed that it is "nonsense" to say that metaphysics is nonsense, and some from outside Positivism have claimed that Positivism, despite its antipathy to metaphysics, has its own metaphysics, with its own rival theory of first principles. Some outsiders observe that Positivism's verification principle, by its own standards, is self-refuting because, not being itself empirically verifiable, it has to be meaningless.

Many feel that Linguistic Analysis suggests that philosophy is nothing more than wordplay which can never be concerned with problems of real existence. Any philosophy which assumes, for example, that the statements of mathematics and the natural sciences constitute the total domain of the true, the meaningful, or the knowable, is certain to stir objections in the areas of aesthetics, ethics, and religion. Lastly, Positivism's attempt to discard as useless or meaningless whatever has no place in an intellectual system based on mechanics seems an unwarranted limitation on the extent of human experience. Catholics disagree with Positivism for its rejection of traditional religion in favor of the worship of "the Great Being Humanity," its nonacceptance of metaphysics, its limitation of law to man-made statutes, its restriction of the school curriculum emphasis to science, and its reduction of even ethics to empirical sciences.

Secularism: Voltaire

Another strain of the modern mind is secularism. Here the main influence is Voltaire (Francois Marie Arouet, 1694–1778), who is perhaps most famous for the statement attributed to him, "I disagree with what you say, but I will defend to the death your right to say it." His influence in education is not in the area of methodology, as with Positivism, but in the areas of content and purpose.[12]

Doctrinal Synthesis

Voltaire's major work was in the philosophy of history, which was completely different from anything that had gone before. To build indirectly a case against Christianity, he began his history with China; he spoke of its antiquity, its strength, and its laws. Depicting the religion of China as a philosophical, nonrevealed religion, Voltaire praised it highly. Then he gave a short treatment of India, from which he went to Persia, Arabia, and Mohammed. He omitted the Old Testament completely, and gave not more than a couple of lines to Jesus Christ.

Among his basic points were, first, the omission of any divine providence over humankind. The development of humankind was completely secular and had nothing to do with religion. Second, he denied any plan of redemption: in addition to his omission of any treatment of the ancient Jews, he also omitted mention of the supernatural mission of the Christian church, which for him is a purely human institution. There is no Christ, and no divine plan of salvation. Third, he attacked the ages of faith. He obscured all of the beneficent purposes and accomplishments of the Church. The welfare of man comes from freedom *from* religion. Fourth, the principle of Voltaire's social doctrine and program is that progress is made without religion: there is in society a "law of becoming" which works as a natural law.

Evaluation and Influence

Among Voltaire's followers was Edward Gibbon (1737–1794), well-educated, British, and a personal friend of Voltaire. Gibbon's most famous work, *The Decline and Fall of the Roman Empire*,[13] shows a definite Voltairean influence. It contrasts pagan civilization with Christian barbarism and attributes the fall of Rome to the triumph of Christianity. Another close follower was Condorcet, Voltaire's editor. Condorcet's major work is *Sketch for a Historical Picture of the Progress of the Human Mind*.[14] It was he who enunciated the rigid "law of progress" (humankind is progressing ever upward), still invoked in many circles. Voltaire also influenced Hegel, whose doctrine in turn lives on in Marxism, as well as in Comte and other influential thinkers.

From the viewpoint of historical science, it is impossible to write without some principles of inclusion and omission — principles of selection, arrangement, and emphasis — which are based upon one's philosophy. Voltaire's principles of selection started the rise and spread of historical atheism. He and his successors attempt to explain history as though there were no God, or as though the influence of religion in history were nil, or both.

Voltaire's doctrine of Secularism had, and continues to have, an influence on the field of education in chiefly two areas. The first is in the authorized secondary agencies of education. These normally consist in a delicate, and preferably harmonious, balance between family, Church, and State. Negatively, secularism banishes the Church from that balance. Positively, secularism gives the State the exclusive right to educate. Second, Secularism continues to have an overwhelming influence over the content of the curriculum. Negatively, it banishes in varying degrees the content of religion from the material taught. Positively, it means a Voltairean understanding of human history, especially in the area of social studies.

Studies of current textbooks demonstrate that this philosophy is still very much with us. A 1984 study of twenty of the best American history textbooks available, by Robert Bryan, claims that the "role of religion . . . is 'neglected and distorted'."[15] There is consensus in the textbooks that after 1700, Christianity has no historical presence in America. Not only are the textbooks incomplete in their mention of the role of religion, but they include errors of fact, are superficial in their treatment of religion in history, and treat historical problems with "anachronism, discontinuity, and oversimplification."[16]

Anachronism is visible in the description of attitudes and beliefs of the past, making them appear irrelevant and unimportant. An example of discontinuity is present in the references to "the Puritans," without any attempt at explanation of who the Puritans were. Both the anachronism and the discontinuity foster a snide attitude of superiority over the past that is unbecoming and damaging to true understanding and appreciation of the past. The student using these books, says the study, will leave not with a heightened understanding of his heritage, but with a contempt for it.

The oversimplification consists in vague generalities that make it impossible to get at specifics. The texts treat events in which religion played a significant role as if there were no religious influence involved. Bryan provides as examples the omission of any mention of the Quaker and Protestant leaders who headed the abolitionist movement out of religious conviction, and the agitation of the Know-Nothing party which strongly influenced the successful movement for a "monopolistic public-school system."

One of the most systematic efforts to study values in textbooks of the nation's government schools, begun in 1982 and concluded in 1985 under the auspices of the National Institute of Education, made similar conclusions about history and social-science textbooks. This study of popular government-school textbooks stated that most of the texts ignore religion in American history and society, attributed in part to the authors' deep-seated fear of any form of active, contemporary Christianity.

The texts teach, at least implicitly, that religion has no relevance to contemporary life, but is something old-fashioned, or at best a quaint and colorful aspect of certain, especially foreign, cultures; that Protestantism in particular is without importance except as a minor aspect of black American culture; that religion, especially Judaism and Christianity, has been merely incidental to the main course of world history; and that religion was of some importance in colonial times because English settlers wanted to get away from persecution and Spanish settlers wanted to convert the Indians, but by 1800 religion had ceased to have much influence in American life.[17]

Lack of Consonance with Catholicism

What makes secular humanism different from any church-related humanism is that secular humanism excludes traditional theism. Secular humanists reject anything that could be described as supernatural or otherworldly, such as life after death. They emphasize instead human experience and scientific knowledge. Although its adherents claim that secular humanism has no religious pretensions, and a definition is difficult, it meets the criteria set by many for being a religion in itself.[18] Secularists do not want Catholic schools, or anything such schools represent, to exist. Catholics for their part find that Secularism by definition completely separates the sacred from the secular and makes the sacred meaningless. This is diametrically opposed to Catholic belief that "the sky hangs low," that the sacred is here and now interwoven with the secular.

Yet we must be careful about terms here. The secularism opposed by Catholics acknowledges only this world in the way that empiricism holds only quantitative avenues to truth. But secularization can be Christian.[19] It can mean fitting Christian philosophy and theology to the world. Secularization for the Catholic can mean the persistent use of all knowledge, skills, and arts to explore the ultimate mystery of the human and the divine. And secularity can mean an altogether proper love of the world: the dedication, out of loyalty to Christ, of the Christian community's life to God, the world, and humankind because of the intrinsic value of each.

Naturalism: Rousseau

Another vast philosophical influence over the modern mind is Naturalism. The greatest figure in founding this area of thought is Jean-Jacques Rousseau (1712–1778).[20] In 1762, at the height of his powers, he published two basic books: *The Social Contract* and *Emile*.[21] The latter was subtitled "on education," and is one of the most influential books in the field.

Doctrinal Synthesis

Whether Rousseau was a philosopher or not is controverted. His novels were indeed instruments for propagating philosophical thought, as the novels of others, like Jean-Paul Sartre, have been. *Emile* consisted of a program of education for happiness and for a natural way of life that was uninhibited. *Emile's* philosophy shows education as being derived from three sources: nature, humankind, and experience. Nature is independent of humankind, and the other two — humankind and experience — must be directed in nature's way.

Emile denies human limitation of any kind, including the religious doctrine of original sin. It is predicated on the assumption that humankind has no evil inclinations; all one needs to do to bring about a good human being is to bring out humankind's natural good nature. The book represents the first time that anyone ever suggested a system of education omitting religion. Education is an unfolding from within, like a flower from a bud. The teacher is harmful rather than helpful, because society, represented by the teacher, corrupts. The cultivation of the arts and sciences is what has made humankind artificial rather than real. Whereas theretofore education was considered a process — the word graduation being from *gradus*, meaning a "step" — Emile was liberated from formal education, for education to Rousseau is an uninhibited natural growth. What results from this is permissiveness of the same type Rousseau had tried to achieve in his own development.

Evaluation, Influence, and Lack of Consonance with Catholicism

Rousseau redefines the means and methods of education. He destroys the traditional structure of education and replaces it with an unfolding from within. He relegates the arts, sciences, and disciplines to a secondary place, or denies them altogether. He changes the role of the teacher from that of causal agent to that of guide. He makes the normative aspects of education nothing external, but rather the self and its natural tendencies. He promises that humankind will be restored to a natural blissful state. He does not consider any ultimate goal. He claims that humankind can retain the disciplines, arts, and sciences of Western culture through a "natural" system of education (which others point out would undermine secular cultures as well as religion). He does not conceive the formation of the individual in terms of the intellect, but stands at the fountainhead of anti-intellectualism. And he overturns a heritage which goes back to the Greek *paideia*. Rousseauian philosophy calls into question any possibility of qualitative excellence in education.

Rousseau's influence is almost entirely in the area of method, not in the area of content, as with Voltaire. The three educationists most influenced by *Emile* were Johann Basedow (1723–1790), and the previously-mentioned Pestalozzi and Froebel. These three, part of the "psychological school" of educators, are the fathers of modern education, making Rousseau its grandfather. In the United States, the two most influential followers of Rousseau were James and Dewey. Dewey's Naturalism resulted in his complete rejection of the supernatural and made him extremely critical of traditional religion. His book *A Common Faith* is essentially a plea for a divine reality that is only a symbol which is representative of all humankind's ideals.[22] The function of religious faith for him is that of unifying people in the pursuit of their highest ideals.

Naturalism has had many other important adherents, some of them very influential in education. For George Santayana (1863–1952), religious beliefs belong to the sphere of poetry and therefore are not to be taken literally. For Alfred North Whitehead (1861–1947), an "Idealistic Naturalist," God is neither infinite nor omnipotent, but is a great companion, the fellow sufferer who understands. Charles

Hartshorne (1897–1979) claimed in addition that God must be found within the world process, a participant in cosmic evolution. Catholics see in Naturalism a denial of the limitations of humankind and consequently of any need for redemption.

Materialism

In general, Materialism, which has many forms, means an emphasis on the material at the expense of the spiritual. In the forms applicable here, a deistic Materialism would allow that there may be a spiritual creator of the universe, but he does not interfere with the created universe, the latter being explainable only in terms of mechanical and physical laws. Materialism describes the human brain as being no more than a mechanism that behaves in a deterministic way. In terms of ethical attitude, Materialism prescribes that people be interested mainly in sensuous pleasures and bodily comforts and hence in the material possessions that bring these about.

Ludwig A. Feuerbach (1804–1872), a very influential example, argued in his book *The Essence of Christianity*[23] that religion is an illusion, a dream of the human mind. God is no more than the attributes which people find in themselves, a mere outward projection of humankind's inward nature. Humankind creates its own gods. Hence the proper worship of man is man. Feuerbach was endorsed by many extremists in the struggle between Church and State in Germany and by those who, like Karl Marx, led the revolt of labor against capitalism. Marx had called religion "the opiate of the people."

The adherents of a religion whose exemplar taught detachment and "had nowhere to lay his head" cannot accept Materialism. And it is inherently contradictory for a materialist to favor the essence of Catholic schools' contributions to education.

Atheistic Existentialism

A relatively recent phenomenon is Existentialism. Existentialism objected to the degradation of the individual from a person into a thing that accompanied an age of mechanization and the technological interchangeability of parts which had begun to extend to people as well as machines. The more recent existentialist thinkers, such as Martin Heidegger (1889–1976), Jean-Paul Sartre (1905–1983), Gabriel Marcel (1889–1973), and Karl Jaspers (1883–1969), sought to understand individuals as they exist in what the existentialists consider a meaningless world.

One must make allowances in this highly individualistic theory for great differences from one thinker to another. In general, however,

Existentialism is a theory that man's individual existence precedes his essence. Jean-Paul Sartre explains the significance of this key concept:

> What is meant here by saying that existence precedes essence? It means that, first of all, man exists, turns up, appears on the scene, and only afterwards defines himself. If man, as the existentialist sees him, is undefinable, it is because at first he is nothing. Only afterwards will he be something and he himself will have made what he will be. . . . Not only is man what he conceives himself to be, but he is also what he wills himself to be after this thrust toward existence. Man is nothing other than what he makes himself.[24]

Existentialism stresses such intensely subjective phenomena as anxiety, suffering, feelings of guilt, angst, anomie, alienation, and general disgust with human life in order to show the need for making decisive choices through a utilization of freedom in an uncertain, contingent, and apparently purposeless world. Under its umbrella, aside from the fact that existentialists are all individualists, are only two broad groups: the nontheistic, or secular humanist, group and the theists.

Major Positions

As its name implies, Existentialism has a special concern with the problem of human existence. The person comes into the world devoid of "whatness," or essence, committed only to his existence. He forms his own "whatness" (that is, his personhood) by what he appropriates to himself: his choices, to which he commits himself, reveal what he is becoming.

One of the first principles of Existentialism is that existence is always particular and individual. It is always *my* existence or *your* existence, and not a given manifestation of the same universal substance. One important reason for the existentialists' interest in the individual is that most existentialists see the abstract and the universal as an indignity toward people because, they say, these categories reduce the individual person to an object. By insisting on the individuality and nonrepeatability of human existence, Existentialism is sometimes drawn to regard one's inevitable coexistence with other people as a condemnation or alienation of people.

It is also true, however, that some existentialists see a coexistence that is not anonymous (such as a mob's would be), but is founded on personal communication which assists man's authentic existence. Thus there are two kinds of intersubjectivity: one is the I-thou, a personal relationship between two individuals, with the "thou" being another person or God; the second is an impersonal relationship with the anonymous mass deprived of any authentic communication.

Existentialism's premises allow for taking often opposing directions. One direction is to hold that humankind creates itself by itself, thus assuming to itself the function of God. Those who go in this direction are atheists. People in this group, like Sartre, Camus (1913–1960), Franz Kafka (1883–1924), and the dramatists of the theater of the absurd, have been more influential than the theistic group. For them, humankind is the new transcendent and the ultimate reason. These existentialists concentrate more on the gloom, anxiety, and absurdity of life than do their theist counterparts. The absence of God makes death an absolute. In frustration, some regard death as an absurd stupidity and others as a ludicrous monstrosity. Death is not the only negation, however: emptiness, frustration, annoyance, and sorrows are recurring themes in the short stories of Kafka, the novels of Sartre, and the plays of Camus.

Existentialists have a consuming interest in the nonrational, by which they mean whatever escapes man's comprehension. They often term this the absurd. For Sartre, the absurd is the absolute gratuity or contingency of things: since for him there is no God, there is no reason for either the existence or the essence of the things of the world; they just are, and because they are what they are without reason, they are absurd. Other aspects of existence upon which existentialists have focused are dread of the failure of one's choices, "shipwreck" upon insurmountable "limit situations," guilt inherent in the responsibilities that derive from making choices, boredom from the repetition of situations, and the absurdity of one's dangling between the infinity of one's aspirations and the finitude of one's possibilites. A person achieves what Heidegger calls "authentic existence" when he understands the impossibility of all of the possibilities of existence.

Evaluation, Influence, and Lack of Consonance with Catholicism
Though Existentialism has affected modern thought in many areas, it is in the field of art that its influence has penetrated most deeply, and through art it has penetrated still other areas of life, like education. The art form in which Existentialism has made its particular mark is literature. Existentialism's interest in individuals and its rejection of the abstract in human affairs explains why much existentialist writing has taken the form of the novel, the short story, the autobiographical essay, and the play. Through their literature existentialists show their basic concern about the question of what it means to be a

human being. Their typical themes are freedom, responsibility, bad faith, and absurdity.[25]

Many regard the existentialist view of existence as unbalanced. Initially a legitimate protest about legitimate concerns, Existentialism became, according to critics, too extreme. Pertaining to truth, existentialists have developed over and against their original legitimate warning about the rigid rationalism at the time of the philosophy's origins, the development of a denial of the relevance of any general or abstract truth concerning persons, their nature, and their activity. Having protested correctly against the artificiality and hypocrisy of much in bourgeois morality, Existentialism became for some a repudiation of every standard of objective morality.

Catholics reject atheistic Existentialism as being unbalanced, without the Christian virtue of hope, a repudiation of objective standards of morality, and an excessive exaltation of subjectivity and relativism. Catholics see all of this as leading to anarchy and chaos. Atheistic Existentialism's themes of the absurd, the denial of the speculative and of all absolutes, the alienation of man, the acceptance of man as the ultimate reason, death as final, despair, and the like, make it essentially incompatible with the *raison d'etre* of Catholic schools.

SOME THEORIES OF PERSONAL FORMATION

Some current theories of personal formation disagree with claims that Catholic schools, when conjoined with a proper home environment, can bring about an excellent formative influence on child growth and development.

Sigmund Freud

Sigmund Freud (1856–1939) brought to the world a hitherto overlooked dimension of the human person, especially in the areas of formation and responsibility. He presented his own idea of the origins of religion.[26] He called religious ideas illusions — fulfillments of "the oldest, strongest, and most urgent wishes of mankind."[27] He wrote:

> [T]he terrifying impression of helplessness in childhood aroused the need for protection — for protection through love — which was provided by the father; and the recognition that this helplessness lasts throughout life made it necessary to cling to the existence of a father, but this time a more powerful one. Thus the benevolent rule of a divine Providence allays our fear of the dangers of life; the establishment of a moral world order ensures the fulfillment of the demands of justice which have so often remained unfulfilled in human civilization; and the prolongation of earthly existence in a

future life provides the local and temporal framework in which these wish fulfillments shall take place.[28]

All religious doctrines are illusions and can neither be proved nor disproved, according to Freud. Inasmuch as science is the only road which can lead a person to a knowledge of reality, one must reject religious illusions as being neurotic relics worthy only of children. Freud claimed that "the two main points in the program for the education of children today are the retardation of sexual development, and premature religious influence."[29] The rational operation of the child's intellect must replace both. Freud decided: "Men cannot remain children forever; they must in the end go out into 'hostile life.' We may call this 'education to reality.'"[30]

Much of contemporary psychonalytic thinking has moved beyond Freud, and there have been many objections to Freud's views. One objection, from ethnocentrism, points out that Freud's view of the primeval creation of God the Father is congruent with the religion and familial relations of the Viennese Jewish society in which Freud lived. The psychiatrist Karl Stern accused Freud of reductionism. He said that for Freud, "God is *nothing but* the father, in fact anything in the spiritual order is 'nothing but.'"[31] Gregory Zilboorg agreed, saying, "Such a reduction, if applied to science, would make science come off as an art of making mechanical toys or cutting out paper dolls, or as a diabolic vision of gigantic derricks and bulldozers."[32]

Despite Freud's misunderstanding of or hostility to religion, some Freudian insights are contributory toward and consonant with Christian insights.[33] Freud was, for example, one of the few psychoanalytic theorists to perceive that there is something drastically wrong with human nature—an equivalent to the Judeo-Christian notion of "original sin." Freud recognized the unconscious element in human personality and indicated that individuals go through stages of psychic development which, if fixated, can cause psychic difficulty. The person has biological and psychic functions that are equivalent to what Freud terms the *id* and the *ego*, which need training in order to be subjugated to the requirements of society. As for what Freud calls the *superego*, it may be similar in some respects to what the Christian calls conscience.[34]

Others

By and large, psychology says we should accept ourselves as we are: We're all "okay," and we need only to learn "to be ourselves." Catholics feel that psychology overemphasizes the notion of self-esteem and "feeling good about yourself," and argue that this can be used to justify undesirable behavior. Christianity says we need constant transformation. And if humankind is not in need of a savior, Christianity loses its point. Far better than concentration on the self, says the New Testament, is for a person to be forgetful of self. Whereas the basic therapeutic criterion might be to ask, "Will it meet my needs?" or "Will it make me feel good?" the Catholic criterion is, "Is it objectively true? Objectively good?"

Four other issues distance psychology and Catholicism: freedom versus determinism, the appropriateness of a reductionist view, the need for moral perspectives, and the basic view of humankind. The doctrine of total psychic determinism poses a threat to the Catholic notion of people's freedom and responsibility. Catholicism sees a person's behavior as being purposive action, over and against mechanistic causal forces which drive one's behavior willy-nilly in one direction or another. The reductionist view of psychoanalysis, especially in its beginnings, reduced all human behavior to explanations in terms of instinctual derivatives. Catholic thinkers have, to the contrary, been anti-reductionistic, often to a fault. They have explained human behavior only on the highest levels of psychic organization—as matters of intellectual perception and willpower.

Morality is one of the most telling areas of difference between psychoanalytic theories and Catholic perspectives. The Catholic perspective tends to see human behavior in moral terms, and therefore tends toward hyper-responsibility. The tendency in psychoanalysis has been diametrically opposed, appealing to unconscious determinants and instinctual drives, seen as biologically or socially based forces, or both. Psychology does not have much use for the idea of sin. Still another divergence between the Catholic view and the psychological is the fact that the Catholic view of humankind is supernatural: humankind is related to the divine Creator and specifically ordained by the Creator to a higher existence. This has no relevance for any natural science, psychology included.[35]

Some specific theories of personal formation have a very mechanistic or animalistic concept of human beings, like that begun by Ivan Pavlov, who demonstrated the conditioned response. Perhaps the most famous of these theories is that which is called the "stimulus-response bond," or more simply the "s-r" theory, wherein all human activity is limited simply to responses to stimuli. For this theory, even the higher mental processes are mechanical, and development and learning take place within a social context which provides the conditions of learning. Animalistic theories of human personality do not admit any high spiritual principle in humans. A summary of their position could be to say that the best-integrated and most perfect personality would be a well-oiled machine with all parts functioning properly for the good of the whole.

Other theories, while not essentially or directly hostile to Catholicism in the process of personal formation that is education, may be considered indifferent to the transpsychological dimensions of religion. Among these is the analytic theory of Carl Jung, which defined personality in terms of the ideal state of integration toward which the individual is tending. The ultimate goal of personality development for him may be summed up in the term "individuation." The self is the center of personality, holding together all the other systems which revolve around it, and providing equilibrium and stability. The self is the goal of life, constantly motivating one's behavior and bringing one to a search for wholeness.

Jung believed that individuation is sought especially through religion; religious experiences bring a person as close to selfhood as is possible. But Jung's critics assert that, as a matter of fact, such figures as Christ and Buddha are as different expressions of the archetype of self as one will find. And Jung's ideas of the nature of religion would not meet the approval of all. He says, for example:

> Religion appears to me to be a peculiar attitude of the human mind, which could be formulated in accordance with the original use of the term "religio," that is, a careful consideration and observation of certain dynamic factors, understood to be "powers," spirits, demons, gods, laws, ideas, ideals or whatever name man has given to such factors as he has found in his world powerful, dangerous or helpful enough to be taken into careful consideration, or grand, beautiful and meaningful enough to be devoutly adored and loved.[36]

He further indicates his subjective and pragmatistic approach to religion when he says:

> [T]he one who has it [religious experience] possesses the great treasure of a thing that has provided him with a source of life, meaning and beauty and that has given a new splendor to the world and to mankind. . . . And if such experience helps to make your life healthier, more beautiful, more complete and more satisfactory to yourself and to those you love, you may safely say: "This was the grace of God."[37]

CONCLUSION

The minds of many who are opposed to Catholic schools have been formed by some of the less inspiring aspects of United States history, by opposing philosophical backgrounds, and by some theories of personal formation. Because these influences are in the intellectual air we breathe, despite their inherent incompatibility with Catholicism many Catholics, including those involved in schooling and education, have absorbed them. Though this process has been without blame, it is all the more tragic because such Catholic "leaders" in turn pass such ideas on to their charges. The next chapter will explain the mind-set of those who favor Catholic schools.

QUESTIONS FOR DISCUSSION

What are the full and complete consequences to schooling of pragmatism, empiricism, positivism, secularism, naturalism, materialism, atheistic existentialism, and Darwinian evolutionism?

Why does Rousseau's naturalism make impossible any qualitative excellence in education?

Many of the people whose thought patterns are described here are sincere and good people. Is there no way that Catholics can establish rapport with them?

What are the good points from the mind-set of Catholic-school opponents which Catholic schools might beneficially incorporate? The bad points which Catholic schools must avoid if they are to remain Catholic?

If more persons were to consider people as the highest good, and thus as the object of kindness and other virtues, would not the human race make more progress more quickly than it has?

Is the influence of religion in history something of which to be proud or ashamed?

Is there evidence of secularism in schools today? If no evidence, what would be the potential consequences of secularism's inclusion? If there is evidence, what are the actual consequences of that inclusion?

How does secular humanism differ from church-related humanism?

Is humanism a religion? Is there any evidence that it is being taught in government schools?

Would there be anything wrong with Catholic schools teaching the psychological emphasis on self-esteem and the need for one to feel good about oneself?

What are the differences in ways in which Catholic schools perceive morality and personal formation over and against the way many psychologists do?

SUGGESTED BIBLIOGRAPHY

Ausmus, Harry J. *The Polite Escape: On the Myth of Secularization.* Athens, Ohio: Ohio University Press, 1982.

Traces varying interpretations of secularization in history, sociology, and theology, and concludes that secularization has brought humankind to a state of nihilism.

Barnes, Wesley. *The Philosophy and Literature of Existentialism.* Woodbury, N.Y.: Barron's Educational Series, 1968

On the introductory level, this book examines Existentialism as a modern philosophical, sociological, psychological, and literary phenomenon, and also provides brief descriptions of existentialists.

Barrett, William. *Irrational Man.* Westport, Conn.: Greenwood Press, 1977.

A comprehensive introduction to existentialist thought, recounting its historical emergence and the perceptions of individual thinkers.

Bloom, Allan. *The Closing of the American Mind.* New York: Doubleday, 1987.

The United States is sinking into moral illiteracy, the result of decades devoted to moral relativism. America's colleges, which are supposed to educate the best and brightest to learning and service, train to hedonism, promiscuity, and the refusal to distinguish between forms of behavior. The roots of the disease go deep: into the deformation of the family and the loss of the elite's religious impulse. A key step on the way back to national moral health is the teaching of classical philosophy.

Camus, Albert. *The Myth of Sisyphus and Other Essays.* Trans. Justin O'Brien. New York: Vintage, 1955.

A collection of essays addressing the meaning of life, built around the theme of suicide.

———. *The Plague.* Trans. Stuart Gilbert. New York: Knopf, 1969.

A novel written in reaction to World War II. Camus portrays man's condition as nonsensical and futile, but focuses on man's attempts to make sense of the world through bravery.

Cassirer, Ernst. *The Philosophy of the Enlightenment.* Princeton, N.J.: Princeton University Press, 1979.

The Enlightenment of the eighteenth century continues to influence thought, especially its concept of the dominance of reason. Cassirer attempts to analyze and synthesize the ideas of the age.

Dawson, Christopher. *The Crisis of Western Education.* New York: Sheed and Ward, 1961.

Dawson asserts that the crisis of the West has its origins in the secularization of Western culture and the revolt of the rest of the world against the West's dominance. Education, he says, is called upon to play a saving role yet cannot, because it is at once the product and reservoir of the forces which have produced the crisis. He suggests that it is the study of Christian culture (not to be confused with the Christian faith) which alone can enable Western education to solve its own problems and hence to safeguard Western culture.

de Lubac, Henri. *The Drama of Atheist Humanism.* New York: New American Library, 1963.

Today's atheism, claims the author, is different from the atheism of the past in that it maintains humanistic qualities. In the final analysis, though, atheistic humanism will not promote man's survival.

Gay, Peter. *The Enlightenment.* Rev. ed. Greenville, N.C.: Touchstone Books, 1985.

A good exposition of the intellectual strains of the Enlightenment by a proponent.

Grene, Marjorie. *Introduction to Existentialism.* University of Chicago Press, 1970.

A brief but solid description of Existentialism, focusing on its treatment of values and human individuality though the thoughts of Kierkegaard, Sartre, Heidegger, Jaspers, and Marcel.

Flower, Elizabeth, and Murray B. Murphy. *A History of Philosophy in America.* 2 vols. New York: Putnam, 1977.

A comprehensive discussion of the philosophies from Puritanism to Pragmatism that have contributed to the American mind.

Ford, Marcus Peter. *William James's Philosophy: A New Perspective.* Amherst: University of Massachusetts Press, 1982.

Argues interestingly that James's conception of truth adheres to that of Realism. Also gives attention to James's views on religion, science, and metaphysics.

James, William. *Pragmatism* and *The Meaning of Truth.* Cambridge, Mass.: Harvard University Press, 1978.

In the first, James examines Pragmatism as a method and theory of truth; in the second, he defends his theory of truth. Valuable introduction by A. J. Ayer.

————. *The Will to Believe* and *Human Immortality.* New York: Dover Publications, 1956.

In the first, James discusses the interrelationship of belief, will, and intellect; in the second the question of survival after death, rebutting philosophically the theory that thought and personality die with the brain.

Lamont, Corliss. *The Philosophy of Humanism.* 6th ed. New York: Ungar, 1982.

A thorough outline of humanistic beliefs. These eliminate the classical approaches as meaningless because of their failure to withstand the verification process. Advocates humanism as an optimistic approach to man's condition.

McCarthy, Patrick. *Camus: A Critical Study of his Life and Work.* London: Hamish Hamilton, 1982.

An historical examination of Camus' life, with emphasis on the controversial aspects of his writings.

Masaryk, Thomas Garrigue. *Humanistic Ideals.* Trans. W. Preston Warren. Lewisburg, Pa.: Bucknell University Press, 1971.

Together with a realization that man's ideals are always changing and in need of constant evaluation, man's scrutiny of his ideals for living can help humanity achieve its potential.

Rousseau, Jean-Jacques. *Emile.* Trans. Alan Bloom. New York: Basic Books, 1979.

A novel; one of the most influential books in the world in education, in behalf of naturalism.

Sartre, Jean-Paul. *Being and Nothingness.* Trans. and intro. Hazel E. Barnes. New York: Pocket Books, 1966.

A description of being and its relationship to consciousness, the latter of which Sartre concludes is nothingness.

————. *Essays in Existentialism.* Ed. and Intro. Wade Baskin. Secaucus, N.J.: Citadel Press, 1965.

A collection of Sartre's works on faith, freedom, aesthetics, and metaphysics.

————. *Search for a Method.* Trans. and Intro. Hazel E. Barnes. New York: Vintage, 1968.

An attempt to reconcile Marxism with existentialist thought. Examines man's relation to history, the nature of reason, and man's existence. Barnes's introduction clarifies some of Sartre.

Schilpp, Paul A., ed. *The Philosophy of John Dewey.* Evanston, Ill.: Northwestern University Press, 1939.

Thorough but uneven essays on Dewey's views on education, epistemology, logic, science, and metaphysics.

Spencer, Herbert. *Education: Intellectual, Moral, and Physical*. Paterson, N. J.: Littlefield, Adams, 1963.

Another extremely influential work, this one in behalf of positivism in education.

Taylor, Richard, ed. *The Empiricists: Locke, Berkeley, Hume*. Garden City, N.Y.: Dolphin Books, 1961.

Essays on and excerpts from the three philosophers in an advanced style.

Chapter 3

THE THINKING BEHIND THOSE WHO FAVOR CATHOLIC SCHOOLS: PROPONENTS' MIND-SET

Catholicism, like Christianity in general, doesn't entangle itself inextricably with any one culture, ideology, or philosophy. Catholicism tries to be acceptable to all people of all times. Nevertheless, it must have a language, a way to appeal, a method of being heard. It was in this way that the New Testament, showing itself favorable to the dominant culture of the time, adapted current philosophies and terminology, much of it Hellenistic.[1] What had been in the Greek *paideia* the formation or *morphosis* of the human personality became for Christians *metamorphosis*, as in Paul's advice that Christians "be transformed in the newness of your mind."[2]

An early Christian principle with regard to non-Christian learning and literature was to "take the best and leave the rest." So it is today. Catholic Christianity marches to a different drummer than our times' Pragmatism, Empiricism, Positivism, Secularism, Naturalism, Materialism, and some kinds of Existentialism, and the relativism, subjectivism, and historical prejudice and theories of personal formation which they spawn. That leaves some forms of Realism, Idealism, and Existentialism for Catholicism to accept, use, or adapt.

Both Realism and Idealism have a rationalistic orientation—that is, they emphasize aspects of reason. Begun by Plato (427?–347B.C.) and Aristotle (384–322B.C.), enduring through the later Greeks and adopted by the Romans, they had distinct elements in medieval Scholasticism and have modern counterparts. Because they do not change substantially, they are sometimes grouped under the term Perennialism. Because (in contrast with Existentialism) they assign priority to essence over existence, they are also grouped under the term Essentialism.

These philosophies hold that certain basic ideas and disciplines essential to our culture are formulable and should be taught at all

50

times to everyone. In education as well as in other areas, these classical philosophies enjoyed a favored position at least up to the Second Vatican Council (1962–1965). Classical Realism especially was very much reflected in Pope Pius XI's 1929 encyclical, *The Christian Education of Youth*, whereas Vatican II's *Declaration on Christian Education* is also open to other approaches.

REALISM
Meanings
In popular parlance, being "realistic" to the average person means facing reality squarely, in a way that is not impractical or visionary. That is not, however, what we mean by Realism in a philosophical sense. There, the philosophies on the Realist spectrum are called Moderate Realism, Classical Realism, Naive Realism, Commonsense Realism, Thomism, Neo-Thomism, Neorealism, Critical Realism, Representative Realism, and so on. When we use no other designation here, we shall be referring to Classical or Moderate Realism. This kind of Realism means the viewpoint that accords to the objects of humankind's knowledge an existence which is independent of whether a person is perceiving or thinking about them. It asserts that the ultimate principle of being is not the mind of a person, but rather what exists beyond or outside one's mind. The word "outside" in this context does not necessarily imply a spatial sense, as though the mind were located within the human brain and reality outside it.

History
Aristotle
Realist terms go back to ancient Greece and to a dispute about universals: What, for example, is the status of "man" as predicated of John and Mary? Aristotle developed Moderate Realism from the mixture of Absolute Realism and Idealism in Plato.[3] Aristotle insisted that human knowledge is basically abstractive, and that abstraction depends upon a series of experiences with reality by way of the senses. The chief difficulty in Aristotle's Realism is to explain how the self-same object can exist in two orders of reality: in the extramental as actuality, and simultaneously in the mind as universality. How is it possible for "humankind" to "be" (exist) in the mind, if being is, as Aristotle's Realism claimed, identical with an objective order?

Thomas Aquinas and His Successors
Probably the most ambitious attempt to preserve the doctrine of Moderate Realism was that of Thomas Aquinas (1225–1274).[4] Although not the first to use Aristotle, and much indebted to Augustine,

Pseudo-Dionysius, and other Neoplatonists, he reversed a system with which most Catholic thought had been identified for a thousand years: Platonism, as continued in, for example, the Neoplatonism of St. Augustine. Thomas wrought a synthesis of faith and reason as stimulated by the knowledge explosion of his day, as Maimonides attempted to do for Jews and Avicenna for Muslims.

Thomas's system was the apex of the Scholastic philosophies. Among his topics having a bearing on education were God, truth, man's intellectual powers, free will, true understanding, man and the state, man's last end, habits, choice, love, pleasure, fear, virtue, sin, law, grace, faith, prudence, justice, courage, Christ, and many more. Thomas came to be for the next seven hundred years the major thinker upon whom Catholic expression depended.

Promoted vigorously by the Church[5] and widely influential in catechetical instruction, Neoscholastic philosophy and theology (a modern outgrowth of Thomism) was for a long time the chief vehicle and common language in which the Catholic faith was articulated. Yet, unlike its medieval predecessors, it became closed to the world in which it lived, marked by defensiveness and hostility, and more disposed to reject alternative views than to engage in constructive dialogue with them. Armed with a fixed catalogue of answers narrowly oriented, it tended to classify both biblical thought and patristic theology as mere precursors of its own synthesis, which it considered final.

As a result, it became unproductive and relatively sterile. Respected theologians began to diverge from Neoscholasticism in decisive respects. One was Karl Rahner, a German Jesuit (1904–1984). He saw the most characteristic element of modern thought as its focus on human existence, a perspective he called its "anthropocentric turn." He judged that anthropocentrism is not, at its core, hostile to Christianity. In fact, he argued that systematic theology today, if it is to make a real contribution, has to be theological anthropology. In 1912, W. P. Montague of Columbia University, Ralph Barton Perry of Harvard, and four others got together a volume called *The New Realism*.[6] Though they differed among themselves, their New Realism (or Neorealism) agreed on three major points: (1) things do not depend for their existence upon their being known; (2) the relations between things are as objective and independent of man's consciousness as are the things themselves; and (3) things are grasped directly by the mind rather than indirectly through mental copies as supposed by John Locke.

Other realists as well as critics of Realism noted that Neorealism failed to extricate itself from the egocentric predicament and proposed no satisfactory explanation of the mind's proneness to error. The egocentric predicament referred to the question of whether one's mind can, for example, be compared to a camera, which records the reality before it with utter objectivity, inasmuch as an individual is always and necessarily involved personally in the interpretation of the data that comes in.

Major Positions

Realists begin with everybody's major concern: to distinguish between what people term reality and what they suspect to be merely products of their own cognition. Therefore the role of the universal in reasoning and in reality is a major concern. Take, for example, "personness" or "chairness," that which makes a being a person or a chair. Do they truly exist? If so, where? In the mind? Outside the mind? If the latter, then where? Somewhere in outer space? Sufficiently nearby to be within the experience of people? Realism allows to the nature of a universal a distinct existence in reality outside the mind.

Another issue important to realists is whether the existence of external things enters human cognition in direct confrontation. Against those viewpoints which regard objects as comprising mere private instances of disconnected sense fragments, Realism professes objects to be real enduring substances: though the knower transcends the object, the object does not depend for its existence upon the knower. The physical properties (of, for example, the moon) perceived or perceivable (for example, grayness or hardness) are in some degree actual properties of the object.

A final issue is the mathematical and scientific constructs which have been so beneficial in the human struggle for mastery over nature. Unlike philosophies that regard scientific laws and theories as freely chosen constructs devised by scientists to describe reality, Realism holds that laws and theories have determined and real counterparts in things.

Evaluation and Current Status

Realism, rather than being a doctrine of the existence of things, is primarily a doctrine of cognition. It regards cognition as the object most present to oneself: a person knows his own thought processes more intimately than he knows anything else. In the field of science, Realism's opposition to retaining a merely instrumental status for laws and theories remains vigorous. The Association for Realistic Philosophy has as its declared purpose the critical clarification and defense of its basic theses, especially of Moderate Realism: for example, the thesis of the contemporary relevance of the classical tradition of Platonic and Aristotelian philosophy and the practical value of Realism in providing immutable and trustworthy principles for individual and social action.

Consonance with Catholicism

Realism posits the existence of an external world. The objects of our senses, real in their own right, exist independently of their being known to, perceived by, or related to the mind. Yet the realist perceives problems within people of arriving at a knowledge of the external world, because of difficulties in the intellect and other aspects of knowing; the Catholic adds to these a belief in the effects of original sin.[7]

In their perception of the good life, realists may by virtue of their philosophy alone stop with the present world. The Catholic goes beyond to a life of grace and a supernatural destiny. Truth for the realist consists in fidelity to objective reality; Catholics agree, but also affirm transcendental reality that comes from the free communication of the Divine Being. The goal of life and of education for the realist may be found in this world; for the Catholic it consists in the life and teachings of Christ. Some forms of Realism, like the Thomistic synthesis, would embrace the teachings of Catholicism as well as the basic tenets of realist philosophy.

IDEALISM
Meanings

One of the most technically correct dictionary definitions of "Idealism" says that it is "a theory that mind or the spiritual is of central importance in reality." It goes on to provide an example:

> a theory that regards reality as essentially spiritual or the embodiment of mind or reason esp. by asserting either that the ideal element in reality is dominant (Platonism) or that the intrinsic nature and essence of reality is consciousness or reason (as in Hegelianism).[8]

Unlike Realism, which may be said to hold that all things measure the person's mind, Idealism tends to regard the mind of the person as the measure of all things. It stresses the central role of the idea or the spiritual in the person's search for meaning. The ultimate principle of philosophy is mind. Reality for idealists issues from intelligence or from spirit, and is ultimately nothing more than a dimension of that spirit. ("Idealism" should really be called "Idea-ism"; in English, however, it is easier and more euphonic to say "Idealism.")

But idealists' views, like those under other philosophical umbrellas, may vary: some idealists emphasize that reality exists essentially as spirit or consciousness, others that universals are more fundamental than sensory things, others that (as the idealist minimum) whatever exists is known to people in dimensions which are chiefly ideas.

One of the earliest and simplest forms of Idealism is Plato's. He saw two worlds existing: the world of appearances and the world of forms. The world of appearances consists of all kinds of changing phenomena, instability, and what we perceive with our senses. The world of forms consists of the world of ideas, and is unchangeable. One aspect of Plato's concept—that we are born with powers of perception that quickly atrophy in mundane existence—is reflected in Wordsworth's ode, "Intimations of Immortality."

Plato argued to the existence of the world of ideas in two ways. One is mathematical. Take, for example, the number five: no one has ever sensed it in the world of appearances; written on a schoolboard, it is only a symbol, and only chalk. The same is true for the triangle, square, circle, and so on. So these must all exist in the world of ideas.

Plato's second argument was from the existence of the world of abstractions. We say that one rose is better than another, or one friend better than another. We can do this, Plato said, because in the world of ideas or forms we have a knowledge of the perfect rose and the perfect friend. In that world, there is one Form or Idea which is supreme. Plato described this in his famous "Allegory of the Sun." In a modern heliocentric version, that allegory would go like this: In the beginning was only the sun, but it was so full of energy that it couldn't contain itself. It spewed forth gases, which coalesced into planets, and then an evolution of life forms took place, climaxing in people, who could see the sun by its light. All the world of appearances came from the sun.

The Form of the Good is like that. All else came from it, in a "cascade of creation." In a waterfall from the Form of the Good (the sun) came manifestations which are three in number but really all one: goodness, which is the supreme form of the moral domain but contains also the elements of truth and beauty; truth, the supreme form in the ontological domain, but also containing goodness and beauty; and beauty, the supreme form in the aesthetic domain, also containing truth and goodness. Each of these three in turn produce other forms. To take goodness as an example, it produces such forms as wisdom, courage, and temperance, which in turn produce other forms, cascading all the way down to the world of appearances.

How people come to a knowledge of the world of ideas Plato explained in his most important allegory, that of the cave.[9] We are chained in a cave, our backs to the entrance, facing the rear wall of the cave. Outside the entrance, the sun (the Form of the Good) shines. Between the sun and the mouth of the cave is the world of forms or ideas; these forms and ideas are reflected on the cave's rear wall. It is only the reflections on the rear wall — the world of appearances — that ordinary people can see. The object of life is to free ourselves from our chains, escape outside into the sun, and turn around (con-version) to face the world of ideas.

If one does convert toward the sun, one's eyes will have to get used to its blinding light. Should one return to the cave, one's eyes must get used to the darkness again. Also, one finds it difficult to explain one's vision to the people in the cave, because of the principle of ineffability (the impossibility of putting such tremendous insights into words) and because most others simply can't listen: not all can endure the pain of breaking the chains of ignorance.

There are many others forms of Idealism. Whereas idealists generally agree that the ultimate reality is spiritual, they do not agree on whether there is only one Absolute, a few, or many. In Hegel's Absolute Idealism, the rational and the real are capable of being equated. Monistic Idealism emphasizes the primacy of the One (as the Absolute or Nature) rather than of the many. Pluralistic Idealism, in contrast, emphasizes the multiplicity of selves and their individual experiences. There is also Personal or Personalistic Idealism, also called Personalism, emphasizing the significance, uniqueness, and inviolability of personhood.[10]

History

In addition to Plato's cave and other metaphors was his notion[11] that the soul is the eldest of all things and that the physical is the product of the spiritual. Though no medieval thinker can be regarded as idealist in the modern sense, there were precursors of modern Idealism. In more recent thought were George Berkeley (1685–1753), Gottfried W. Leibniz (1646–1716), and Immanuel Kant (1724–1804). Kant, the foremost thinker of the Enlightenment and one of the greatest philosophers of all time, was a Subjective Idealist. (His system is also called Critical Idealism and Transcendent Idealism.) In his first major work, Critique of Pure Reason,[12] he saw that a radical empiricism would entail skepticism, and a radical rationalism would ultimately lead to sterility. He therefore maintained that the objective world must be constituted by the organizing forms and categories of mind.

Kant claimed that, just as Nicolaus Copernicus had explained the apparent movement of the stars by ascribing them partly to the movement of the observers, he, Kant, had shown that in knowing, it is not the mind that conforms to things but things that conform to the mind. The objective realm of experience is only phenomenal (that is, consisting of things observable through the senses), not of the mind (what he called "noumenal"). His second major work, *Critique of Practical Reason*,[13] is the standard source for his ethical doctrines. Morality for him is in the form of a law that demands to be obeyed for its own sake — a law, however, not issued by some foreign authority but representing the voice of reason. Hence his "categorical imperative": "Act only on that maxim through which you can at the same time will that it should become a universal law."

Transcendent Idealism emphasizes that what is fundamental in reality is that which transcends sense experience, namely, the primacy of the spiritual and the intuitive over the material and the empirical. Under this aspect, nineteenth-century Transcendentalism was a movement in New England which stressed the presence of the divine within man as a source of truth and a guide to action. In Europe, Idealism continued as a movement into the early twentieth century.[14]

In the United States, most idealists came to fall into two groups: personal and absolute. Personal idealists conceive reality as a self or as belonging to a self, and are usually theistic. Absolute idealists hold that reality is included within one complete system, present to an all-comprehensive Mind called the Absolute; they tend to be pantheistic. The history of Idealism in the United States is mostly a record of protest by religiously oriented thinkers against various forms of Materialism, Naturalism, and Positivism. Most came to their position out of a search for a rational basis for morality and religion.[15]

Major Positions

As opposed to Materialism, which holds that the basic substance of the world is matter and that the world is known primarily through material forms and processes, Idealism denies that mind originates from or is reducible to matter. All together, Idealism is frequently opposed to Skepticism, which doubts everything, and often to Atheism, because the idealist frequently extrapolates the concept of mind to take into account an infinite Mind. Idealism's basic direction may be gleaned from such of its typical aphorisms as that "reality reveals its ultimate nature more faithfully in its highest qualities (mental) than in its lowest (material)."

One of Idealism's basic doctrines is the *concrete* universal: the universal that is also a concrete reality. Rather than the fixed, formal, or abstract universal, this concrete universal is essentially dynamic, organic, and developing. A second principle concerns the contrast between contemporaneity and eternity. Whereas other philosophers deal with matters of contemporary interest, idealists take in epochs in the broad sweep of history, viewing the contemporary scene "under the aspect of eternity."

Third is the idealists' doctrine of internal relations and the coherence theory of truth. Non-idealists tend to say that two things simply being related to each other does not bring about any change in the things themselves: any such relationship is merely external. Idealists look upon reality as more subtle than this: for example, it is part of the essence of a brick that it is related to a wall. Just so, ultimate reality consists of a whole system of interrelated propositions. As for truth, it consists in the coherence of propositions with one another to form a harmonious whole. A spy can be judged a hero or a villain only in relation to a total system of international relations and a particular philosophy of history.

Fourth is the dialectical method. Idealists delight in arguments (dialectics), which in this sense means systematic Socratic techniques of exposing false beliefs and eliciting truth by means of rational discussion. They do this for several reasons. They want to penetrate into the entire coherent system of truth, to arrive at new discoveries to be integrated with earlier knowledge, to remove the contradictions present in human knowledge, and to have a new incorporation into a higher truth of whatever truth is presented in lower judgments. A fifth idealist principle is the centrality of mind. To idealists, matter can be explained by mind but not vice versa. Sixth and last is the transmutation of evil into good. Josiah Royce, for example, held that the larger whole is the Absolute Mind, which keeps all evils under control.

Idealists also posit several questions which they consider to be of utmost importance. The first is, "What is the ultimate reality?" History has provided two answers. On one extreme is the eighteenth-century empiricist David Hume, who held that the ultimate reality is the moment-by-moment flow of events in the consciousness of each person (which for him is also what defines the person). This compresses all of reality into a solipsistic present, the momentary sense experience of one perceiver. The other extreme answer is represented by seventeenth-century idealist Baruch Spinoza (1632–1677), who defined ultimate reality as that which can exist and can be conceived only by itself. His pantheistic Idealism posited the ultimate reality to be God, or Nature, or Substance. Hegel called Spinoza's dogmatic absolutism a lion's den into which all tracks enter and from which none returns. Most forms of Idealism are somewhere between the empiricist Hume and the idealist Spinoza.

Another question important for idealists is, "What is given?"—that is, what are we starting with? Idealists assert that collective human intellectual inquiry has come to provide us at the outset with innumerable order systems, and this creative intelligence through a long period of time called history has produced our various sciences and disciplines. Logically, therefore, "the given" is the complete transformation of the earth by its inhabitants; history shows this of the past, and today's flights to outer space portend the transformation of the entire universe in the future.

A third question of utmost importance to idealists is, "What position should one take toward temporal change and becoming, and toward the presence of ends and values?" Idealists answer that reason discovers a basic order in *nature*, which is coherent. This in turn creates such *cultural* institutions as the State, and these together constitute the cultural order of a civilized society. Last is the *private* order, or family. The cultural order has priority, and the enhancement of the values of all three orders is a civilized people's basic moral objective.

Evaluation and Current Status

There are many criticisms of Idealism. Moderate Realism, as we have seen, insists that things exist independently of the human mind. The Cambridge philosopher G. E. Moore (1873–1958) prepared a famous "Refutation of Idealism," and the Scientific Realist Bertrand Russell (1872–1970) prepared a similar argument.[16] They recalled the distinction between a subject's act of perceiving and the perceptual object of this act, and claimed that the *esse est percipi* ("to be is to be perceived") argument failed to take this distinction into account.

Logical Positivism sees as a basic weakness Idealism's rejection of the notion of empirical verifiability, according to which every proposition claiming to be true must be verified by investigating the sense experience in which its terms originated. Linguistic Analysis analyzes Idealism's technical terms and attempts to prove that they are replete with ambiguities and double meanings. Finally, and most interestingly, Karl Marx (1818–1883) and his followers adapted the dialectical argument of the Idealist Hegel and then used it effectively to develop Dialectical Materialism, an enemy of Idealism. Marxism thus provides a significant alternative to Idealism's spiritual emphases.

Between 1875 and 1900 almost every professor of philosophy in the United States was an adherent of Idealism. Idealists remained in the majority for another decade or so, bequeathing many religious teachers and ministers. Idealism did not retain this position, however, for a couple of reasons. One was the internal disputes within Idealism. Spiritual monism and spiritual pluralism, for example, are opposite types of Idealism. Personalism rejects Absolute Idealism, and atheistic spiritual pluralism sharply conflicts with the theistic. Another reason was that in an increasingly "scientific" and technological age Idealism came to be regarded as unscientific or at least insufficiently imbued with the scientific spirit. The trend of U.S. thought went from Idealism to Naturalism, which was the way John Dewey developed.

Idealism does, however, provide evidence of itself being a possible reflection of some permanent aspects of the human spirit, and in this sense at least shows itself to be potentially a perennial philosophy. Although at present on the wane in the West, Idealism has survived many other periods of crisis and been reborn to remain with us.

Consonance with Catholicism

A purpose of Catholic education is to provide educative experiences for the student that contribute toward the formation of Christian values and life. Catholic education utilizes the life and teachings of Christ as the model to stimulate directional development. Catholicism as well as parts of Idealism are both concerned with the realization of the self in the context of a relationship with the Ultimate Being. In this respect, Classical Idealism (such as the Christian Platonism of the Church Fathers) and Christian Personalism (especially of people like Emmanuel Mounier and Maurice Nedoncelle) are eminently acceptable to Catholics.[17]

CHRISTIAN EXISTENTIALISM
Meaning and History

Catholic existentialists see the major issues of Existentialism as being inextricably intertwined with humankind's history. The problem of what one is in oneself, for example, was present in Socrates' imperative, "know thyself." The stance of a person's withdrawal into one's spiritual interior as held by such existentialists as Gabriel Marcel (1889–1973) was already present in St. Augustine.

The one who gave inspiration to modern Christian Existentialism was the Danish Lutheran pastor, Søren A. Kierkegaard (1811–1855). As he saw it, many of his countrymen regarded Christianity too much as a doctrine to be grasped only intellectually. For him, if one wanted to call Christianity a doctrine, one should see it as a doctrine that must be realized in existence; one must exist in the doctrine, not just speculate on it. For Kierkegaard, the absurd (which is, as we said in chapter 2, whatever escapes humankind's comprehension) is Christ: the fact that God became a person out of love for humankind is incomprehensible to human reason.

Christian existentialists see man's existence as being constantly faced with many other possibilities, too. (Christian Existentialism gives primacy to the concept of possibility for humankind: temporally, it gives priority to existence's stretch to the future over the past or the present.) From among the possibilities, one must make a selection and then commit oneself. So consciousness (or awareness) and freedom are constant Christian existentialist themes. Persons become fully existent only when their consciousness makes them vividly aware of all the problems, conditions, and decisions of human living.

People should achieve consciousness by being reflective beings whose lives are interpenetrated with thought. People are to be fully alive to the richness of each experience, vibrantly alert to all the anguish and care of existence. Among life's risks, the most serious is the possibility of a person descending into inauthenticity or alienation. Against this degradation the theistic forms of Existentialism— such as those of Marcel or of Karl Barth (1886–1968)—held out the guarantee of transcendent help from God, which in turn is guaranteed by faith.

Too many people are mere followers whose judgments only echo others. The person of existence is the thinking person, the person of decision, the free person. One becomes free by taking a personal interest, by making decisions, and by consciously following one's choices. Far from the disinterestedness demanded by science, the existential self must be personally involved and must make decisions with passionate concern. Being fully committed to life, such a person is aware that with freedom goes the heavy burden of responsibility.

Because these possibilities are constituted by man's relationships with other people and with things, existence is always a being-in-the-world, in a concrete situation that conditions choice. Existentialism is therefore opposed to solipsism ("I alone exist") and to epistemological Idealism (that the objects of knowledge are mental).

Marcel's "theater of sincerity" shares many of the concerns of the existentialists, but not their ultimate viewpoint. The drama in his writings consists in discovery by which successive layers of disguise are stripped away and the self is revealed. Marcel is distinguished from other existentialists in that he holds open the possibility of genuine love, and views freedom as the drama opening upon communion and ultimately upon transcendence.[18]

Influence

In theology, Barth started a "Kierkegaard revival," which he expressed as "the relation of this God with this man; the relation of this man with this God." Barth saw this as the only theme of the Bible and of philosophy. Karl Jaspers (1883–1969) emphasized more and more the religious nature of faith. In transcendence, faith is the way to withdraw from the world and to resume contact with the Being beyond the world. Faith is life itself, because it returns to the encompassing Whole and allows itself to be guided and fulfilled by it. For Rudolf Bultmann (1884–1976), the theologian of the demythologization of Christianity, inauthentic existence is tied to the past, to fact, and to the world, while authentic existence is open to the future, to the nonfact, and to the nonworld — to the end of the world and to God.

The influence of Existentialism has penetrated education also, though it has not been widely written about. The existentialist Carl Rogers (1902–87) deplored modern schooling's "education from the neck up."[19] The existentialist sees education pretty much in terms of human becoming, an allowing process whereby the individual becomes who he is. Existentialist themes of the concrete and specific rather than the universal or general apply to education, as would such other themes as the value of the individual person and freedom of choice. Existentialists for the most part see education as bringing forth from the child something latent and then cultivating it. They see the treasure that is hidden in each child as something strictly personal.

The Jewish Martin Buber's (1878–1965) theories on the "I-Thou" relationship have influenced Christian Existentialism.[20] Unfortunately, however, although important existentialists like Nicholas Berdaiev (1874–1948), Buber, Marcel, and Jaspers are theists, atheistic Existentialism has probably been more influential.

Evaluation

Affirmatively, Existentialism is to be congratulated for its awareness of the inhumanity that a misguided technology can bring about by its tendency to regard people as mere numbers. Negatively, in addition to adapting some of the relevant evaluations of atheistic Existentialism from chapter 2, we can say even of some Christian Existentialism that it has so exalted the inwardness, subjectivity, and absolute freedom of the individual that social life becomes in their system philosophically difficult, if not impossible, to defend. And, say some, if the principles of Existentialism were carried to their ultimate conclusion in such fields as education and politics, the result would be chaos and anarchy.

Consonance with Catholicism

Theistic Existentialism can be consonant with Catholicism. That human beings revolt, as Existentialism did, against dehumanizing modern industrial and technological applications is most acceptable to the Catholic notion of the person. That human beings abhor totalitarian movements that submerge or rob them of their individuality, Catholicism — following Sacred Scripture — applauds.

Existentialists emphasize an aspect of the person that Catholics treasure: freedom. This is both one's crown and, because it brings with it responsibility, also one's cross. For both Existentialism and Catholicism, this responsibility is the foundation for commitment. Both responsibility and commitment are essential elements for one to become a productive contributor to the narrow community of school and the broad community of people. Both Existentialism and Catholicism want to introduce the student to not only skill development in school, but also to the fine arts and humanities.

For both Existentialism and Catholicism, the humanities are an essential vehicle to present the problems, dilemmas, and growth of humankind. Such subject areas help in the definition of the self. Although in this process many existentialists work only in cooperation with the self, there is nothing in their philosophy that says they cannot proceed, as do Catholics, in cooperation with divine grace. The attempt to open Catholic pedagogy to the values contained in existentialist philosophy, though perilous, seems justifiable.

Indeed, the educational documents of the Church, once firmly classicist, suggest that they now tilt toward Existentialism. Pius XI's stern encyclical of December 31, 1929, on *The Christian Education of Youth*, for example, written when Italian Fascists were requiring boys to spend Sundays in military drill, devoted much attention to the rights of the family and the Church in schooling and education. The Pope applied elements of Thomism to emphasize universalism and supernaturalism as distinctive features of Christian pedagogy. Vatican II's *Declaration on Christian Education*, in contrast, sees human nature as neither static nor fixed, but undergoing continual metamorphoses which must be acknowledged and understood:

> Whereas Pius XI in his Encyclical primarily related education to the vocation of three institutions: the family, the Church and the State, the *Declaration* formulates its opinions by starting from the dignity of the "person," which gives every man the right to a human education (n. 1), and from the dignity of the "children of God," which gives all the baptized the right to a Christian education (n. 2). Hence the viewpoint of Pius XI may be qualified as institutional, in contrast to the existential orientation of the *Declaration*.[21]

This movement in education away from Aristotelian categories and toward personalist, phenomenological, and existentialist types of thought is concordant with new knowledge of cultural differences. The *Annuario Pontificio*, a Church directory published annually, lists roughly twenty-five hundred Catholic jurisdictions around the world. They range from Aachen, West Germany, to Zomba, Malawi.

The jurisdictions that are not in totalitarian countries contain Catholic schools.[22] These schools differ considerably from one culture to another, because they have been shaped by diverse histories and are vehicles for transmitting quite different local cultures. (We hope that, although this book on Catholic-school identity is written with a United States bias, it will have some relevance to other cultures as well.)

Theology is increasingly concerned with the idea of conversion. Bernard Lonergan makes clear that conversion is not just an acquisition of new concepts, but is also a reorientation of the subject, an about-face on various levels of functioning. Conversion is existential and intensely personal, and can be experienced, according to Lonergan, in terms of the intellectual, moral, and religious modes of human consciousness.[23] Intellectual conversion is the central concern of Lonergan's book *Insight*. Moral conversion, described in both *Insight* and *Method in Theology*, takes place when the criteria of one's decisions change from satisfactions to values.[24]

Theistic Existentialism does not differ from the atheistic branch in its subjectivism, the dramatic quality of the human condition, and the need for freedom and authenticity. Whereas, however, atheistic Existentialism is pessimistic in its underlying conception of the human person in his or her nothingness, theistic Existentialism prefers to stress the person's greatness. Existentialists give attention not only to the person of the student, but also to the educational process. To both the person and the process of education, they apply three existentialist categories: encounter, dialogue, and authentic involvement.

Encounter is "a situation in which man is placed in contact with a reality that affects him in his inmost being and exercises a decisive influence on his life."[25] Encounter with God is an essential dimension of that experience. In the problem of bringing about an encounter that depends on God's grace and man's freedom, the educator's role is limited to mediation: educators must remove the obstacles and create favorable dispositions in their pupils.

As for dialogue, M. Navratil defines it as

> a process whereby two subjects make use of speech in order to arrive at a mutual understanding of what each is thinking and living by, and as a result of which they can, to some extent, manage to reconcile their respective viewpoints and ways of being.[26]

Inasmuch as the adult educator dominates the still undeveloped person of the child, is it possible for the educator-student relationship to be one of true dialogue? The fact is that educators must not regard themselves as perfect persons. They, too, need the help of other persons, even children. "Our pupil forms us," writes Martin Buber.[27] It is in this sense that the Second Vatican Council declares that children contribute in their own way to making their parents holy.[28]

Existentialist involvement results from free choice, and means both participation and the unreserved giving of self to a project or a person. This involves authenticity, which consists in being true to one's inmost "self." Existentialists hope that involvement as a pedagogical category will result in an understanding of and approach to the authentic existence of the student throughout the educational process, and in fostering the development of the pupil's committed existence.

Encounter, dialogue, and involvement are all consonant with the advocacy of social awareness in Catholic theology. That theology no longer advocates flight from the world, but commitment to the world's transformation:

> Thus, the relationship between the world and the final stage of the reign of God is not one of total discontinuity. When a person works for the betterment of the world and human society, he or she is promoting the reign of God.[29]

CONCLUSION

Although Catholicism does not entangle itself inextricably with any one culture, ideology, or philosophy, but offers itself to all people of all times, it must nevertheless have a language in which to be heard. Just as the New Testament adopted acceptable philosophies of its time, moderns do the same. Today, moderate Realism, classical Idealism, and theistic Existentialism provide easy roots for Catholic philosophies of education and schooling.

Classical Realism harkens back to Aristotle, received new vigor with St. Thomas Aquinas (whose synthesis of faith and reason dominated the seven hundred years after his death), and was explained for later times by such as Etienne Gilson, Jacques Maritain, Robert M. Hutchins, and Mortimer Adler. Realism accords to the objects of a person's knowledge an existence which is independent of the person thinking about them. The ultimate principle of being is not the mind of the person, but rather what exists beyond, objectively. Truth, too, is objective, being the correspondence of what is in the mind to reality.

Because Realism became closed to the world, was marked by defensiveness, and refrained from dialogue, its popularity waned, and theologians like Karl Rahner have gone along with the "anthropocentric turn" of modern thought. While the 1929 encyclical *The Christian*

Education of Youth reflected Realism, Vatican II's 1965 *Declaration on Christian Education* and subsequent documents have been more open to other philosophies.

Idealism is a theory that mind or the spiritual is of central importance. It is more accurately called "idea-ism," which word represents its emphasis, but "Idealism" is more euphonious. One of its typical aphorisms is that "reality reveals its ultimate nature more faithfully in its highest qualities (mental) than in its lowest (material)." Among Idealism's major positions are a view of the contemporary scene "under the aspect of eternity," a theory of truth in which propositions must cohere with one another to form a harmonious whole, delight in dialectics, the centrality of mind, and the ultimate triumph of good over evil. Like Moderate Realism, Classical Idealism is consonant with Catholicism. A purpose of Catholic schooling is an education that provides Christian principles and values. Both Catholic schools and Idealism are concerned with the realization of the self in the context of a relationship with the Ultimate Being.

Christian Existentialism is another worldview possible for Catholics. Existentialists derive their name from the fact that they give existence priority over essence. People form their own selves, becoming fully existent only when vividly aware of all the problems, conditions, and decisions of human living. People should therefore be wholly alive to all the anguish and care of existence. Against the degradation of inauthenticity or alienation, theistic Existentialism holds out the guarantee of transcendent help from God, which in turn is guaranteed by faith.

The person of existence is the thinking person, the person of decision, the free person. Far from the disinterestedness demanded by science, the existential self must be personally involved, have passionate concern, and be fully committed to life. With all this goes the heavy burden of responsibility. Existence is always a being-in-the-world: that is, one's existence takes place in a concrete situation which conditions choice.

Theistic Existentialism, despite criticisms, is consonant with Catholicism in such areas as revolt against dehumanizing technological applications to the person, abhorrence of movements against individuality, and opposition to the concept of the school as a factory. Catholicism shares with theistic Existentialism a desire for individual freedom, personal authenticity, commitment, responsibility, the use of the humanities as a vehicle to present the problems of humankind, emphasis on personal conversion, the dramatic quality of the human condition, the greatness as well as the uniqueness of the person, and, in the process of education, the three existentialist categories of encounter, dialogue, and authentic involvement.

The following chapters will apply these philosophical foundations to the goals of the Catholic school, the partners in the process, the curriculum, the Catholic-school atmosphere, teachers, students, and leadership.

QUESTIONS FOR DISCUSSION

Should we have a separate Catholic school system? Why or why not?

Catholics claim a reverence for, and a desire to teach, truth. As Pilate asked, what is truth?

Which philosophy today do you think is overall the most suitable to be the basis of a Catholic philosophy of education?

How do Catholic-school proponents differ from their opponents on basic questions of life, like the nature of ultimate reality, the definition of the person, and the optimal relationship that should exist between the person and reality?

SUGGESTED BIBLIOGRAPHY
Realism

Adler, Mortimer. *Aristotle for Everybody: Difficult Thought Made Easy*. New York: Macmillan, 1978.

Adler sets forth the truths he has learned from Aristotle, explaining them in a way that is intended to make them easily understood by everyone.

_____. *Six Great Ideas*. New York: Macmillan, 1981.

Discusses truth, goodness, beauty, liberty, equality, and justice. In a very simple style, guides the reader to some basic tenets of Realism.

Allard, Jean-Louis. *Education for Freedom: The Philosophy of Jacques Maritain*. Notre Dame, Ind.: University of Notre Dame Press, 1982.

The thought of Maritain applied to education in a thought-provoking work.

Aquinas, Thomas. *Summa Theologica*. Vol. I. *The Existence of God*. Part 1, questions 1–13. General ed. Thomas Gilby. Garden City, N. Y.: Doubleday, 1969; Westminster, Md.: Christian Classics, 1981.

Thorough, clear, orderly, classic approach to such questions as the existence of God, God's nature, human existence, reality, and so on.

_____. *Thomas Aquinas: The Teacher—The Mind*. Trans. James V. McGlynn; intro. James Collins. Chicago: Henry Regnery, 1959.

A translation of Aquinas's *De Magistro* with commentary.

Gilson, Etienne. *God and Philosophy*. New Haven, Conn.: Yale University Press, 1979.

The metaphysical problem of God in an historical perspective, this work emphasizes a discounting of the positivist denial of the existence of God. Valuable for the novice to philosophy.

Maritain, Jacques. *An Introduction to Philosophy*. New York: Sheed and Ward, 1962.

For students, an introductory treatise to the principles of Thomism by a modern French Thomist philosopher.

Mascall, E. L. *He Who Is: A Study in Traditional Theism* (New York: Longmans, Green,

1943); *Existence and Analogy: A Sequel to "He Who Is"* (idem, 1949); *Words and Images: A Study in Theological Discourse* (idem, 1957); *The Openness of Being: Natural Theology Today* (Philadelphia: Westminster, 1971).

Four essays in natural theology or philosophical theism, by an Anglo-Catholic priest writing in the tradition of Gilson and Maritain. Contain useful critical comparisons with rival philosophical doctrines common in the English-speaking world.

Pegis, Anton C., ed. *Introduction to St. Thomas Aquinas.* New York: Modern Library, 1948.

A selection of Aquinas's works, including brief discussions of God, epistemology, and the nature of man.

Pieper, Josef. *Introduction to Thomas Aquinas* (New York: Pantheon, 1962).

An attractive introduction by a German Thomistic philosopher whose writings are characterized by clarity, simplicity, and profundity.

Spangler, Mary M. *Principles of Education: A Study of Aristotelian Thomism Contrasted with Other Philosophies.* Lanham, Md.: University of America Press, 1983.

For beginners, discusses the essential factors in the education process from the viewpoint of Aristotle and Aquinas, and contrasts them with Renaissance thought, Naturalism, and Experimentalism.

Wild, John. *Introduction to Realistic Philosophy.* New York: Harper and Brothers, 1948.

A comprehensive but readable study of Realism, with contemporary examples. Includes discussions of Plato, Aristotle, Augustine, and Aquinas.

Idealism

Bouillard, Henri. *The Knowledge of God.* London: Burns and Oates, 1969.

In the tradition of French idealistic personalism.

Collingwood, R. G. *An Autobiography.* Oxford: Oxford U. Press, 1939.

The last testament of one of the last great British idealist philosophers. An attractively written story of Collingwood's rejection of the version of Realism represented by John Cook Wilson, Ernst Mach, G. E. Moore, and Bertrand Russell, which came to displace Idealism in the British universities. Collingwood stresses the inadequacy of this Realism to educate for moral and political values.

Louth, Andrew. *The Origins of the Christian Mystical Tradition from Plato to Denys.* New York: Oxford, 1981.

A rich survey of patristic spirituality, particularly Origen, Gregory of Nyssa, Dionysius the Areopagite, and Augustine. Introducing the Christian writers are three chapters on the philosophy of Plato, Philo, and Plotinus. The conclusion examines the extent to which Platonism was transformed by the patristic authors. (Note: Because of the increased scope which Platonists give to intellectual intuition, for them there seems to be an overlap between the realms of philosophy and theology, which an Aristotelian would regard as illegitimate.)

Mounier, Emmanuel. *Personalism.* Notre Dame, Ind.: University of Notre Dame Press, 1970.

In this advanced text, the author differentiates personalism from individualism. He contends that the problem of personalism lies in man's struggle to achieve consciousness for himself and for society as a whole, and concludes with a discussion of how personalism can be applied to the present.

Mouroux, Jean. *The Meaning of Man.* New York: Doubleday, 1961.

A Christian personalism, with special emphasis on the religious dimension.

Pontifex, Mark, and Illtyd Trethowan. *The Meaning of Existence.* London: Longmans, 1953.

Pontifex and Trethowan are Benedictine monks who have been open to the contributions of the French personalists, owing to the Platonism of monastic theology.

Richards, M. C. *Toward Wholeness: Rudolf Steiner Education in America.* Middletown, Conn.: Wesleyan University Press, 1980.

A critical and appreciative description of the philosophy, organization, curriculum, and methodology of the Waldorf School movement in America. Steiner, an Austrian philosopher whose genetic psychology serves as the foundation for this pedagogy, developed his unique approach from the idealistic *Naturphilosophie* of the poet Goethe. For an example of how some of Steiner's insights can be appropriated by Catholic spirituality, see Noel Dermot O'Donoghue, *The Holy Mountain: Approaches to the Mystery of Prayer* (Wilmington, Del.: Michael Glazier, 1983).

Slesinski, Robert. *Pavel Florensky: A Metaphysics of Love.* Crestwood, N.Y.: St. Vladimir's Seminary Press, 1984.

A study of the Russian Orthodox priest-theologian Florensky (1882–1943?), analyzing his experiential methodology, his antinomic theory of truth, and his sophiological conception. Florensky conceives his "concrete idealism" in radical opposition to Kant's subjectivistic idealism.

Smith, Robert Houston. *Patches of Godlight: The Pattern of Thought of C. S. Lewis.* Athens: University of Georgia Press, 1981.

In the principles of Lewis's "Christian objectivism" Smith finds a Platonistic Christianity such as that of Clement of Alexandria or Origen, during the second and third centuries.

Trethowan, Illtyd. *An Essay in Christian Philosophy.* London: Longmans, 1954; *Absolute Value: A Study in Christian Theism.* London: Allen and Unwin, 1970.

See Pontifex above.

Von Hildebrand, Dietrich. *What Is Philosophy.* Chicago: Franciscan Herald Press, 1973; *An Analysis of Human and Divine Affectivity,* idem, 1977.

Von Hildebrand represents a school of phenomenological realism, known as the Munich school. (According to many interpreters, the later work of the founder of phenomenology, Edmund Husserl, veered off in the direction of absolute idealism.) Historically, Von Hildebrand presents himself in continuity with the Franciscan school in the scholastic tradition.

Wincklemans, de Clety. *The World of Persons.* London: Burns and Oates, 1967.

Attempts to show that at the heart of experience there is a central activity called life-act. The task of education, as of ethics, is to realize reflectively this life-act in its full possibilities. The implanting of knowledge by the teacher is formative.

Christian Existentialism

Cain, Seymour. *Gabriel Marcel.* South Bend, Ind.: Regnery/Gateway, 1979.

A simply written introduction to the thought of Marcel. Deliberately portrays him not in relation to his peers, but as an individual whose thought was based on personal revolt against idealism.

Collins, James. *The Existentialists: A Critical Study.* Chicago: Henry Regnery, 1951.

A study of Sartre, Jaspers, Marcel, and Heidegger by a Catholic philosopher, with a summary of five existentialist themes.

Cooper, David E. *Authenticity and Learning: Nietzsche's Educational Philosophy.* Boston: Routledge and Kegan Paul, 1983.

Examines the educational theories of the German philosopher.

Earle, William, James M. Edie, and John Wild. *Christianity and Existentialism.* Evanston, Ill.: Northwestern University, 1971.

This concisely written introductory collection of essays provides both theistic and nontheistic viewpoints to explain the impact of existentialist thought on religion, notably Christianity.

Friedman, Maurice. *Martin Buber: The Life of Dialogue.* 3d rev. ed. University of Chicago Press, 1976.

Provides a clear and comprehensive synopsis of Buber's philosophical leanings, especially on the nature of evil, the problem of God, and man's being. Although Jewish and not Christian, suggests possible applications to education, religion, psychology, and anthropology.

Kierkegaard, Søren. *The Concept of Anxiety.* Trans. Walter Lowrie. Princeton, N.J.: Princeton University Press, 1980.

An advanced description of man's various interpretations of original sin.

_____. *Either/Or.* Trans. David F. Swenson and Lillian Marvin Swenson. Princeton, N.J.: Princeton University Press, 1971.

Volume I of this two-volume work is the "either," volume II the "or." Kierkegaard summons the reader to decide between alternative philosophies of life.

_____. *Fear and Trembling* and *The Sickness Unto Death.* Trans., intro., notes by Walter Lowrie. Princeton, N.J.: Princeton University Press, 1974.

A challenging discussion of faith in which the author maintains that man does not reach self-actualization until he has surpassed mere ethics and arrived at a religious state. The road requires a person to overcome a sense of fear and trembling.

Kohansky, Alexander S. *Martin Buber's Philosophy of Interhuman Relations.* Rutherford, N.J.: Fairleigh Dickinson University Press, 1982.

An analysis of Buber's thought, structured around the theme of communication. The author presents the thesis that the human race's paramount crisis is that humankind's existence is built around the conflict that results from difficulty in communicating with the world.

Krapiec, Mieczylaw A. *I-Man: An Outline of Philosophical Anthropology.* New Britain, Conn.: Mariel Publications, 1983.

A representative textbook of Lublin Thomism, prepared for a course on the philosophy of man. An abridged version, prepared by Francis J. Lescoe and Roger B. Duncan, was published in 1985.

Lescoe, Francis J. *Existentialism With or Without God.* New York: Alba House, 1974.

A clear exposition of the thought of Kierkegaard, Marcel, Buber, Heidegger, Sartre, and Camus, with special stress on the question of God.

Luijper, William A. *Existentialist Phenomenology.* Pittsburgh: Duquesne University Press, 1960.

An original synthesis of existentialist themes such as knowledge, intersubjectivity, and freedom, using the writings of Marcel, Heidegger, Merleau-Ponty, and Sartre. Luijper is the author of several other books in the same vein.

Macquarrie, John. *Existentialism.* Harmondsworth, England: Pelican Books, 1972.

A careful interpretation of Existentialism as compatible with Christian thought.

Malantschuk, Gregor. *Kierkegaard's Thought.* Ed. and trans. Howard V. Hong and Edna H. Hong. Princeton, N. J.: Princeton University Press, 1971.

A comprehensive analysis of Kierkegaard's thought pattern as applied to specific topics. A good companion to Kierkegaard.

Marcel, Gabriel. *Tragic Wisdom and Beyond.* Evanston, Ill.: Northwestern University Press, 1973.

A not-too-simple study of the nature of man and his existence, the role of philosophy in today's world, and other philosophical questions.

_____. *Creative Fidelity.* New York: Crossroad, 1982.

In this discussion of man's existence, the author attempts to differentiate between his philosophy and Idealism; Christian undertones.

Wallraff, Charles F. *Karl Jaspers, An Introduction to His Philosophy.* Princeton, N.J.: Princeton University Press, 1970.

This introduction to Jaspers emphasizes the German interpretation of existentialist thought.

Woznicki, Andrew N. *A Christian Humanism: Karol Wojtyla's Existentialist Personalism.* New Britain, Conn.: Mariel Publications, 1980.

Examines the philosophical works of Karol Wojtyla, later Pope John Paul II, as an exemplar of the school of Lublin Thomism:

> Commencing with Maritain's and Gilson's existentialist interpretation of Thomas Aquinas' metaphysics, the Lublin philosophers have adapted and incorporated within their realist metaphysics, not only the insights of such contemporary existentialists as Heidegger, Jaspers, and Marcel, but also the methodology of phenomenologists such as Max Scheler and Roman Ingarden. (p. v.)

The Christian Tradition

Buetow, Harold A. *Of Singular Benefit: The Story of U.S. Catholic Education.* New York: Macmillan, 1970.

A history of Catholic schooling in the United States from its beginnings through the 1960s. Updated by *A History of United States Catholic Schooling* (Washington, D.C.: National Catholic Educational Association, 1985).

Dolan, Jay P. *The American Catholic Experience.* Garden City, N. Y.: Doubleday, Inc., 1985.

A good history of the Catholic ethos from colonial times to the present.

Ellis, John Tracy. *American Catholicism.* 2nd rev. ed. University of Chicago Press, 1969.

Deals with developments in Catholic education, the changing relationships of the Church to its own members and to society in general, and especially with arguments for and against the ecumenical movement brought about by the Second Vatican Council.

Rausch, Thomas P. *The Roots of the Catholic Tradition.* Wilmington, Del.: Michael Glazier, 1986.

An intelligent and well-organized introductory explanation of what it means to participate in the Roman Catholic faith tradition.

Chapter 4

WHAT CATHOLIC SCHOOLS
AIM AT: GOALS

WHAT GOALS ARE: DEFINITION

What, from your schooling, would be of value, if you found yourself in the Robinson Crusoe situation: cast up alone on a gadgetless island, having to face months or years of living alone? Boy Scout or military survival skills would be handy, but once you had built your lean-to and your fire and found food, what then? What of the world's rich lore would your memory resort to for solace, good living, or entertainment? Your answer will depend in great measure on what the goals of your education had been, and the extent to which they had been accomplished.

To refer to the end points toward which schooling strives, people speak interchangeably about aims, goals, and objectives. We think the term "goals" more appropriate for a variety of reasons. One is that goals seem more long-ranged and comprehensive than other terms. Most of all, though, we like its connotations in athletics. Goals in athletics are specific and definite: you run into the end zone or you do not, put the ball into the basket or do not, hit a two-bagger or do not. The goals in athletics are taken seriously, worked at, sacrificed for, and sweated over. In this analysis, goals differ from aims, which are more nebulous, and from objectives, which are often matters of hopes, dreams, and velleity. A new Catholic-school modality avoids quibbling over terms: some Catholic schools are developing mission statements, declarations of basic assumptions or presuppositions, from which flow statements of goals and objectives.

Goals are a travesty if they are only motherhood statements or catalogue front matter for appearance's sake, that are seldom implemented by school personnel. Rather, effective goals answer ultimate questions like "why?" and look for the essential "shoulds." To be meaningful, goals need frequent and careful scrutiny that prioritizes and assesses consequences, for goals shape the direction of activities. The degree to which goals are intelligently derived and expressed in real and specific terms directly affects the clarity of the process, the content of the curriculum, and the nature of the enterprise.

From the viewpoint of their essence, goals should not be remote and high sounding, but close, detailed, specific, and meaningful. From a temporal viewpoint, they can be ultimate (looking to the future) or proximate (concerns of here and now). Whereas ultimate goals might be relatively constant, proximate goals need to be flexible and ever changing to meet the challenges of the day. We must all face change, which frequently necessitates the abandonment of nostalgia. Nostalgia, which is one of the most inaccurate forms of memory, differs vastly from solid historicity.

WHY GOALS?

Everyone who knows thoroughly the "how" of a calling will probably always have a job; but everyone who knows thoroughly the "why" of a job will more likely be the boss. The only way to judge the success or failure of any enterprise is to determine how well it has met its goals. Degree of success equals performance over and against goals. As to the ultimate success or failure of education, however, "all external tests of success, while useful, should be treated with caution."[1] Perhaps because the formulation of meaningful goals is difficult, schools have by and large neglected them. John Goodlad assessed the documents pertaining to United States schooling over the past two hundred years, including the current guidelines of all fifty states. He concluded that the area is "a conceptual swamp," and that "the schools suffer from lack of a clearly articulated mandate and so are peculiarly susceptible to fads and fashions."[2]

The lack of goals is at times due not to laziness or neglect, but to deliberate philosophical positions. Some existentialists, for example, prefer that each individual set his or her own personal goals. Pragmatists pay little or no attention to goals because, at bottom, they deny metaphysics. For them, *the* goal is "growth," but they make no decision on growth *whither*. With Catholic schools, sometimes lack of attention to goals is mere mindlessness.[3] Yet the children who will graduate from secondary schools in A.D. 2001 are already alive. And the question of what sort of community we want in A.D. 2001 is not being addressed in sufficient depth by either Catholic or government schools.

WHENCE CATHOLIC SCHOOLS' GOALS?

The Judeo-Christian vision has usually given careful attention to the formulation of real and specific goals, and "Catholic education is an expression of the mission of Christianity."[4] Schools that are truly Catholic therefore set up end points deliberately conceived and set out for achievement at specific points along the way. For this reason, Catholics are sometimes accused of being "absolute" and "unbending"; the truth is that for Catholics education, like life, is teleological: it has a purpose and an end. In considering the sources of goals, Catholics have much about which to be proud, imaginative, and creative. By and large, the sources of Catholic goals are twofold: the New Testament, and the liberal arts and humanist traditions.

New Testament

For the ancient Greek culture that was prevalent in New Testament times, the word *paideia*, essentially untranslatable, meant literally that which an older generation considered worthwhile to hand on to the younger generation (*pais*, "child"). Thus, *paideia* can mean culture, civilization, education. Werner Jaeger says it had several essential characteristics, among them belief in the value of the individual and intellectual freedom, and a focus on the relationship of education and character building.[5]

In the New Testament, what in Greek *paideia* had been the formation or *morphosis* of the human personality became *metamorphosis*, a more profound formation than the Greeks expected. St. Paul spoke of this when he wrote to the Romans asking them to undergo a renewal of their spirit: to "be transformed in the newness of your mind."[6] The purpose of human existence in accord with New Testament concepts is to change one's heart—*metanoia*. It is through transmitting the transcendent values of the Gospel that Catholic schools contribute toward the Church's salvific mission: "It is precisely in the Gospel of Christ, taking root in the minds and lives of the faithful, that the Catholic school finds its definition as it comes to terms with the cultural conditions of the times."[7]

Liberal Arts and Humanist Traditions

The concept of the goal of education making better human beings goes back to the ancient *paideia* of the Greeks, the *humanitas* of the Romans, and the classical liberal arts that had as their goal to free the person "to become what he is": to free one from the shackles of dependence that bind all human beings from the moment of their conception onward. This concept remained essentially the same in the Western world for about two thousand years.

Catholic schools must take into consideration these goals of liberal education so as to form graduates into persons of curiosity, adventure, and human understanding, who have learned to live with ambiguities, uncertainties, and stubbornly held opinions, and can distinguish between what is important and what is not. The true humanist, the Judeo-Christian witness to God, can be a countervailing intellectual force to a technological society that needs the humanist's conscience.

WHO DECIDES GOALS?

All who are interested in Catholic schools should take part in the formulation of the schools' goals. All the partners should be involved: parents because their position gives them the primary rights and duties, the Church because of its concern for the spiritual, and the State because of its legitimate concern for the public welfare. Since the dominant vision more accurately and comprehensively defines the school than anything else does, it must arise out of the school community itself. Its formulation must include faculty, students, staff, family, and all other constituents of the school. Then it will be lived, and will unite the school community.

With particular reference to the Church and its attendant institutions, from early Christian times to the present there has been an emphasis on the offices of pope and bishop. But Vatican II inspired a shift to an emphasis on the Church as "the people of God"—*all* the people—and involved the concept that governance involve the governed: that there be shared responsibility and participatory decision making. In Catholic schools in the United States, the National Conference of Catholic Bishops (NCCB) in its national catechetical directory, *Sharing the Light of Faith*, noted that a "representative board, responsible for the total educational program, should be involved in catechetical planning in every parish."[8]

HOW TO DETERMINE GOALS

Aside from existentialists, who would leave the matter to individuals, the two major positions with respect to the determination of goals are the experimental approach (an inductive, a posteriori method), and the philosophical approach (a deductive, a priori method). In view of many of the questions inherent in goal making, the feasibility of the experimental approach is difficult to conceive. Catholics for the most part choose a philosophical approach, looking to authoritative sources for guidance.

A model of how to determine goals for schools—*any* schools—is that of John Goodlad. Indicating that schools cannot adequately meet all of society's expectations, he begins with philosophical principles, then includes data derived from facts learned about the community and its students. He suggests that there is a major gap between what society *envisions* schools accomplishing (goals) and what schools *actually do* (function). Until one recognizes the gap and clearly defines the educational needs, it is impossible to develop a model of what schools *should* do.

The most widely used model on which to develop educational goals is the rational model of Ralph W. Tyler, written in 1947.[9] He posits four stages that are interrelated and not rigidly sequential. Tyler's initial stage begins with an analysis of three data sources: society, students, and subject-matter specialists. His second stage is to formulate these data into general goal statements. Then he filters the general goal statements through two theoretical screens, one based on one's particular philosophy of education and the other on a psychological conception of learning. This serves to clarify the goals further, assuring that the derived goals are congruent with the values, functions, and aims of the specific educational institution, consistent with one another, comprehensive and not too narrow in scope, economically and practically feasible, and attainable by the intended learner. The last stage is to state the goals in specific, measurable terms that define the *behavior* anticipated and the *content area* in which this behavior should operate.

The rational design of Tyler's model accounts for its popularity, but at the same time for criticism on the basis that goals and curricula are not in practice developed that way. Critics of this stage-approach claim also that this analysis necessitates inferences and value judgments, which are based on one's own philosophical perspective: existentialists weigh heavily the learner's needs; pragmatists favor contemporary society; traditionalists value subject-matter specialists' data; and so on. Another criticism is that Tyler's model is generally used literally instead of evaluated critically. Others assert that the model does not provide a basis for resolving conflicting value judgments. Still other critics object to this model as being "top down," seeing it as diminishing teachers' and students' direct participation in the selection of goals.

Catholic schools use a mixture of the "top down" and "bottom up" models, depending on local situations. Their proposed solution to criticisms of the top-down model is the formation of committees of teachers and sometimes parents as well as students to work together to present, discuss, and clarify goal proposals. This might benefit teachers by providing them with a more direct leadership role in the school, parents by providing a vehicle for having ideas heard and taking responsibility for the school's emphases, and students by providing them with a valuable learning experience, familiarizing them with the importance and nature of goal selection, and fostering leadership skills. It might benefit the entire enterprise by establishing a sense of community. Values conflicts, left unresolved in Tyler's rationale, do not as often present a problem to Catholic schools, which have a more clearly defined homogeneous system of values than pluralistic government schools.

WHICH GOALS?
In General

History has provided many individual goals for Catholic and other schooling, among them conveying information, usefulness, saving one's soul, physical and moral discipline, vocational education, formation of a "lady" or "gentleman," training of patriotic citizens, promotion of national ideals and culture, students' psychological development, creative expression, conformity with the findings of science, adaptation of the individual to the constants in society, social efficiency, and preparation for the reconstruction of the social order. While history provides insights, goal clusters must constantly be examineed to assess anew for an optimal educational opportunity the balances and integration between, for example, intellectual development and character formation, cognitive skills and affective needs, and happiness and perfection.[10]

The first important attempt at developing a healthy balance in educational goals was the work of B. S. Bloom and his colleagues, who produced a taxonomy which divided learning into three domains: the cognitive, the affective, and the psychomotor.[11] The attempt omits moral goals, however, and shows no awareness of any necessary relationships between the various kinds of objectives within the different domains.[12]

What the area of goals and curriculum planning needs more than a categorization is a logical map, with a perception of mutual relations and relative positions of importance.[13] Instead of a logical map, Goodlad comments, "one finds long lists of goals and objectives for the separate subject fields, . . . lists of proficiencies students are to acquire for high school graduation or grade-to-grade promotion."[14] His analysis of education-related documents over the past two hundred years reveals that four broad areas of goals have consistently emerged: academic, vocational, social/civic/cultural, and personal.[15]

Obviously, the formulation of goals is a complex philosophical task, a task that involves detailed work in epistemology, philosophy of mind, psychology, and other areas. Yet the intense work of discussing goals can provide Catholic schools with the opportunity to sort out

life's true gold from fool's gold, the passing fad from solid development.

Catholic-School Goal Clusters

Catholic education distinguishes between ultimate goals and proximate ones. The ultimate goals remain constant and unchanging: they
center around the person's union with God. Catholic schools' ultimate goals are absolutes that hold for all students regardless of
race, culture, or religious affiliation. The proximate goals are more
flexible: they reflect the changing needs and demands of society.
All Catholic-school goals are consonant with the foundational principles of the United States. The historian Henry Steele Commager said
that "after 1880 it might indeed be maintained that the Catholic
Church was one of the most effective of all agencies for democracy and
Americanization."[16] Whatever the priorities of individual Catholic
schools, Catholics in general see the sense of the Jesuit motto formulated in the sixteenth century: *Ad maiorem Dei gloriam,* "To the greater
glory of God". More specifically, today's goals pertain to God, to
others, and to self, and contain a category that pertains overall to all
three.

Overall

Catholics do not forget their humanist heritage. H. I. Marrou lists
eight characteristics of that humanism: the goal is the adult, not the
child; emphasis upon the development of the entire person; primacy
to moral considerations; emphasis upon the development of the person as a person, wholly and not just in any special part; development
of the person rather than the technician; emphasis on a literary as
opposed to a scientific culture; emphasis upon the value of tradition;
and emphasis upon development of "polyvalence": someone with insight and good judgment, someone having ability in the theoretical
sphere as well as the practical.[17] Altogether, the goals of classical humanism, allowing for variations through more than a thousand years,
meant an education based upon a literary culture, rigorous intellectual training, the development of leadership qualities, the fulfillment of
the whole person physically and morally, an education based upon
established truth, the perception of established values, and the realization of universal philosophies.

Yet the humanist heritage has not always remained the same. With
the Renaissance, the meaning of the terms "humanism" and "liberal
education" began to change. In the eighteenth century, a liberal education was a matter of acquiring good taste, reasonably defined intelligence, and a social poise which would enable one to move easily and

without embarrassment in the world of public affairs; the concerns were the virtually synonymous liberality, elegance, civility, and style. In the early nineteenth century, education came to be equated with hard work, and the formation of character emerged as one of its most important objectives. But there was no clear consensus about the type of character which would be best suited to a world characterized by accelerating social and economic mobility and the combined impact of the Romantic rebellion and the Industrial Revolution.

In the midnineteenth century, some educators argued that a liberal education should approximate as closely as possible the intellectual vigor of earlier times. Others were convinced that the summit of endeavor must be to examine the methods by which the reasoning human mind achieves its degrees of conquest over the world of sense. Still others, for example T. H. Huxley, defined a liberal education as one which would equip its recipients to be "ready, like a steam engine, to be turned to any kind of work and spin the gossamers, as well as forge the anchors, of the mind."

As the nineteenth century moved toward its later years, the West lay wide open to the impact of the knowledge explosion. The integration of the many fields of knowledge was fragmented, and career preparation superseded earlier ideals as the true purpose of education. In the advance of science and technology, the predominantly moral dimension of education withdrew. That direction has continued from that time to this. Certain themes emerge as characteristic of modern notions of "humanism" in education: an existentialist emphasis on personal authenticity, a pragmatistic primacy to humankind rather than to God, a romantic approach to truth, and a focus upon process rather than content.

Some of these notions contrast with the classical humanism from which Catholic schools derive their sense of goals. Classical humanism is based upon intellectual discipline, while modern humanism moves toward a romantic approach to the individual's inner truth, and openness in personal relationships. Classical humanism is concerned with the development of the whole person in universal and established terms, modern humanism with the development of the person in individual and unique terms. Classical humanism has to do with the development of leadership qualities, modern with the development of the ability to lead a full and intense life. Classical humanism is authoritative, truth and knowledge being established; modern humanism leaves one free to express one's inner feelings. Classical humanism is based on established values, modern on personal values. Classical humanism embraces the development of universal philosophies, modern the development of individual and unique ones.

Humanism in the Western tradition, as understood by Catholics, begins with a study of the supernatural. It is essential that one have an appreciation of divine revelation and the physical presence of God in the world, God's revelation of Himself to humankind being the most critical event that has ever happened in history.

The relativistic position of our culture notwithstanding, Catholic schools recognize the importance of clarifying one's own value system and gaining a knowledge and understanding of opposing systems. They try to convey the clear sense of mission and purpose which permeates all aspects of their program in academic excellence: union with God, discipleship, faith development, and community service, all based on a shared religious value system. Catholic-school goals are amplifications of the U.S. bishops' summary (noted often in these pages) of message, community, and service.

While realizing the limits of what schools can be expected to do, the Church has at the same time declared the specific mission of the Catholic school to be "a critical, systematic transmission of culture in the light of faith and the bringing forth of the power of Christian virtue by the integration of culture with faith and of faith with living."[18] The individual culture is, however, to be subordinated "to the integral development of person, to the good of the community and of the whole of mankind,"[19] not the other way around.

After years of discussion, a group of Catholic chaplains in England came up with the primary goal of Catholic education as "the establishment of a relationship of trust with the institutional Church, in the context of which the individual will reaffirm, or make for the first time, a personal commitment to Christ."[20] Among the advantages to this goal definition, they saw the following. Faith is not merely a grasp of doctrinal statements, but a personal commitment to Christ. While that decision is in the making, their goal, if accomplished, has the individual in a relationship with the community. The goal is concerned with personal relationships. And it is flexible, because it can apply to all aspects, levels, and settings of educational programs. But goals are numerous and

> can vary, as place and needs vary, in degree and measure. . . . It is also useful to compare the pastoral goals set up in one region with those set up by episcopal conferences closest to it geographically or culturally.[21]

Overall goals usually need to be applied to the various levels of schooling in different ways, depending upon the readiness and ability of the students. The elementary school is awesomely important to the pliable years. Even the school building should incorporate this awareness. And even the elementary school can demonstrate the proper attitude toward minority groups, the handicapped, and the *anawim* — society's poor, powerless, and disadvantaged. Lastly, it is possible even on the lowest levels of elementary schooling to use the latest technological techniques to help in the presentation of the content of doctrine, notions of community, and opportunities for service.

On the secondary level, the school should give special attention to the problems of adolescence: a careful balance between acne-plagued, awkward, insecure, self-conscious adolescents and their openness, enthusiasm (especially for the downtrodden), and high sense of morality and ideals (especially in the area of justice). The high school should present the demands of the personal and social teachings of the Church. High school opportunities for service as part of the educational experience should go deeper and broader than at the elementary level. On all levels, commensurate with the student's stage of growth and development, the school's task is to provide

> a synthesis of culture and faith, and a synthesis of faith and life: the first is reached by integrating all the different aspects of human knowledge through the subjects taught, in light of the Gospel; the second in the growth of virtues characteristic of the Christian.[22]

In sum, Catholic schools' overall goals have to do with education for total wellness. Total wellness, far from being merely passive, is an active process through which an individual becomes aware of and makes choices toward a balanced existence: stimulating the mind through curiosity and creative thinking; reaching out and developing meaningful relationships with others; setting aside quiet time for reflection and relaxation; developing skills that will allow one to understand, express, and manage one's full range of emotions; pursuing a life that has motivation, purpose, and meaning; and exercising and eating for maximum performance.

At the same time, each school's goals are and must remain *unique*. Among the sources of uniqueness are generous and energetic constituencies, enriching specialization, a vision that facilitates good decisions, and adaptation to needs. A good example of such uniqueness is St. Anselm's Abbey School, Washington, D.C., which adapted its goal statement to its religious founder:

> Through our specific form of educational apostolate, we hope to extend to our students and through them to the broader public something of the spirit of St. Benedict, as expressed in his Rule: a

sense of peace and fraternity, a respect for the value of work, an appreciation for the mystery of God's creation, personal self-discipline, and the development of personal talents for the service of others.[23]

The Loreto Sisters of Dublin put nicely their schools' overall goals for their students as being

> growth in the ability to love. This involves an awareness of God's love, an acceptance of oneself, and a respect for others. It grows through experience and knowledge: the experience of human relationships and prayer, and knowledge gained through reflection on life situations and the study of theology, scripture, and liturgy. These good relationships with God, self, and others will mature where there is a healthy discipline. This discipline in turn is not mere external order, but is built upon qualities such as unselfishness, self-control, and respect for persons, all of which lead to the development of a fully integrated person.[24]

With overall goal formation, as always, Jesus is the model for what gives the Catholic school its specific character:

> The Catholic school is committed thus to the development of the whole man, since in Christ, the perfect man, all human values find their fulfilment and unity. Herein lies the specifically Catholic character of the school. Its duty to cultivate human values in their own legitimate right in accordance with its particular mission to serve all men has its origin in the figure of Christ. He is the one who enobles man, gives meaning to human life, and is the model which the Catholic school offers to its pupils.[25]

Toward God

Education to faith in and encounter with God is an important part of the purpose of a Catholic school. Both faith and education "aim at encouraging people really to be people."[26] Once they have been educated in the faith, Christians have the obligation to bring the Gospel to others "by the example of their lives and the witness of the word, . . . so that others, seeing their good works, might glorify the Father and more perfectly perceive the true meaning of human life and the universal solidarity of mankind."[27]

Catholic-school pedagogy aiming at encounter with God distinguishes between the truths of Catholicism and "those that can be equally accepted and realized by nonbelievers: for example, human

dignity and freedom, or universal brotherhood."[28] The vertical encounter with God to which Catholics aspire is effected through faith
and prayer.[29] For Catholics, the notable sacrament of this encounter
with God is Christ, the "image of the invisible God," whose incarnation "is for us people and for our salvation."[30]

Toward Others

The *social* dimension of Catholic-school goals encourages fulfilling
social obligations for the welfare of the community.[31] This participation with the Church in being a leaven to the world differs from "do-
goodism." It must be all-encompassing: "The work of Christ's redemption . . . takes in . . . the renewal of the whole temporal order. The
mission of the Church, consequently, is . . . to permeate and improve
the whole range of the temporal."[32] And the "social nature of man
shows that there is an interdependence between personal betterment
and the improvement of society."[33]

The Catholic school's sensitivity toward others should involve a
sense of community that extends "toward others in the educational
community, in the other communities that they may belong to, and
with the entire human community."[34] This community is different
from all others, going as it does beyond the laws of mere fraternal
dialogue: the Christian idea takes into account God's having endowed
man with a spiritual and moral nature, and "calls for mutual respect
for the full spiritual dignity of men as persons."[35]

What the Church today calls community, New Testament times
called *koinonia*, meaning a unique fellowship in the life of the Holy
Spirit. The U.S. bishops, referring to this "unique fellowship," said:
"Community is at the heart of Christian education not simply as a
concept to be taught but as a reality to be lived."[36] To paraphrase the
U.S. bishops, the community aspect is intended to offer clarity and
vigor to faith, to foster living in the spirit of Christ, to encourage
participation in the liturgy, to motivate involvement in the apostolate,
and to eliminate any alienation that may be caused by youth's disen-
chantment with some institutional and organizational forms and
functions.

It means a growth in Christian fellowship through personal relationships of friendship, trust, and love, especially by way of the Eucharist, which is a sign of community and *the* cause of its growth.
Integral personal growth is impossible without an integral social life,
and it is the crucial task of education to foster an understanding of
this. Creating readiness for growth in community through worship
and through the events of everyday life is a wholesome part of the task

of Catholic education. Community is to be lived in the Catholic school.

Community includes education to the imperatives of justice. Catholic schools face a risk in presenting justice as a goal. If they accept a role as a carrier of messages for justice, an agent for change in society, this risks offending the rich and powerful, some of whom support Catholic institutions. But the risk must be taken, because the result of justice and love will be the peace on earth which all people seek.[37]

The Church's schools, then, are to provide education not primarily for power, or "as a means of material prosperity and success, but as a call to serve and to be responsible for others."[38] The call to service is the New Testament *diakonia*. This service should be to the Church and to the world. As the U.S. bishops wrote: "Christ did not intend it [the Christian community] to live walled off from the world any more than He intended each person to work out his destiny in isolation from others."[39]

This interest in and collaboration with others for the right ordering of social and economic affairs should be such that whatever work students choose—law, clerking, cleaning, business, medicine—their choices reflect a concern for others and a bias toward the poor (*anawim*), an essential feature of the Judeo-Christian tradition. The "preferential option for the poor" should especially include developing countries. On the theory that it is much better to teach the poor how to fish than to give them a fish, service to the poor should be most especially in the area of education, "raising human dignity and promoting more human conditions."[40]

The desire to build a better world should involve a positive attitude to work, pupils seeing in it a means of developing themselves, of serving others, of building up the world, and of promoting justice and peace. This in turn involves making demands on leadership to assume responsibility for changing harmful structures as well as finding opportunities for channeling efforts into relieving those in need.[41]

In this tradition, Catholic schools should bring about a rapport between Catholic students and the work they will enter, make them courageous in facing the responsibilities of their profession, and make them take part in answering the questions that arise specifically in their professions: how their caring shows in their handling of the employment of people, how they make financial decisions, and the like.

Since Jesus is "the alpha and the omega, the first and the last, the beginning and the end,"[42] he is the Model in our quest for peace and in our search for community. Jesus is, in fact, the center of our solidarity with the entire human race.[43]

To Self: the Personal

How one puts into order the personal goals of educational formation will depend upon such underlying philosophical questions as one's definition of personhood and how perfectible one believes the person to be. In general, Catholic schools' personal goal is to communicate to pupils what it means to be fully human in the light of Christ. This implies a sense of worth as a person created by God for God. It involves the development of the capacity to be a thinking, reflecting, and discerning Christian.[44]

From every social background, "we are to produce the kind of men and women so desperately needed by our age — men and women not only of high culture but of great personality as well."[45] The attractive personality which Catholic schools should be forming preclude the smug, respectable, unkind, cold, aloof, others-can-go-to-hell-I'm-saved kind of person we sometimes see. The attractive Catholic personality begins with the capacities which the student has naturally: "one must aim at encouraging the human spirit to develop its faculties of wonder, of understanding, of contemplation, of forming personal judgments and cultivating a religious, moral and social sense."[46]

The formational aspect of the Catholic school should gradually open people to see life as it is and to create an attitude for life as it should be.[47] The Catholic school's formation should be integral and harmonious:

> Due weight being given to the advances in the psychological, pedagogical and intellectual sciences, children and young people should be helped to develop harmoniously their physical, moral and intellectual qualities. . . . Moreover, they should be so prepared to take their part in the life of society that, having been duly trained in the necessary and useful skills, they may be able to participate actively in the life of society in its various aspects. They should be open to dialogue with others and should willingly devote themselves to the promotion of the common good.[48]

The school's general goal is to be "a place of integral formation by means of a systematic and critical assimilation of culture. A school is, therefore, a privileged place in which, through a living encounter with a cultural inheritance, integral formation occurs."[49]

It deserves repeating that the Catholic school should synthesize culture and faith, and faith and life. Rather than being culture-bound, however, the Catholic faith transcends all cultures. The Church emphasizes often the Catholic school's complete Christian formation of the human person as a totality.[50] Church law synopsizes the matter:

> Since a true education must strive for the integral formation of the human person, a formation which looks toward the person's final end, and at the same time toward the common good of societies, children and young people are to be so reared that they can develop harmoniously their physical, moral and intellectual talents, that they acquire a more perfect sense of responsibility and a correct use of freedom, and that they be educated for active participation in social life.[51]

This totality comes from new life in Christ. It will therefore embrace Jesus as the model for the person.

INTELLECTUAL, AFFECTIVE, MORAL, AND PHYSICAL

Although Catholic philosophers of education might debate the relative position of the *intellect* as a goal of Catholic schooling, none subscribes to an anti-intellectualsim of the type sometimes seen in United States history[52] and in some movements in education. Most Catholics are sufficiently philosophically attuned to realize that linguistic and abstract forms of thought are in some measure for all people, and Catholic schools can be proud that research indicates solid intellectual achievement.[53] The greatest intellectual virtue is wisdom. Everyone needs at least enough wisdom to unify life's experiences. But for the Christian, that is not enough.[54] Christian wisdom, indeed, goes beyond visible realities to those which cannot be seen: "The Catholic school should teach its pupils to discern in the sound of the universe the creator whom it reveals and, in the achievements of science, to know God and man better."[55]

The *affective* (or emotional) dimension of Catholic education to total wellness means, essentially, cultivating a good heart. It consists in the acquisition or strengthening of specific attitudes and values related to Christian truth and revelation. It involves students' learning to quiet themselves, resulting in discovering their personal meaning. This will, hopefully, result in their finding an understanding that leads to a sense of peace. This peace, or inner harmony, is an important place to begin if we are to be whole and healthy individuals. Knowing who they are and having the courage to be that unique self helps students to keep their life in balance. An unhealthy lifestyle, compounded with anxiety, distracts from the ability to function fully as people.

Education, dealing with such areas as the formation of the "good person," the "good life," and the "good society," is essentially a *moral* enterprise. It deals with the best of what it means to be human. It includes, of course, the spiritual. Every good school should provide bases for ethics and values,

> to draw out the ethical dimension for the precise purpose of arous-
> ing the individual's inner spiritual dynamism and to aid his
> achieving that moral freedom which complements the psychologi-
> cal. Behind this moral freedom, however, stand those absolute
> values which alone give meaning and value to human life.[56]

Catholic-school emphases might differ from one philosophical position to another — idealists emphasize character formation and the vision of God, for example; existentialists, authenticity and trueness to
self — but Catholic schools are more likely than their government-
school counterparts to be more normative and prescriptive, using
more "oughts" and "shoulds."

While all persons must live according to their own conscience,
educated Catholics do this as members of a community of moral
wisdom: the Church. The process is facilitated by clear instruction in
Christian moral values, based on the Gospel and Church teaching.
Although the religious dimension of morality does not alter the psychological pattern of moral development, instruction in Christian morality is distinctive: It includes the alienating force of sin, the healing
power of grace, Christian hope, and the judgment of God's truth.
Moral education is, of course, to be adapted to the age and understanding of the pupil.

One of the areas in which some Catholics are easily influenced by
Platonic and neo-Platonic ideas (at least in popular conceptions) pertains to the *physical*: the body. Plato saw the body as the prison of the
soul. Platonists think of the goal of life as being to free the soul from
this body-prison. In this viewpoint, the functions of mortification and
penance are to do just that: free the soul from its bonds and enable it
to soar heavenward.

The Christian view is based upon different philosophical principles.
The body, instead of being the prison of the soul, is in substantial
union with it. To have a live human being means having both body
and soul together in that kind of unity — otherwise you have merely a
corpse, or a disembodied soul. Theology adds that God created the
body and therefore the body is good. God reinforces this by His Son's
coming into the world by way of the Incarnation: that is, Jesus took
upon himself a human body.

Therefore, added to high academic standards, a complete education must develop physical skills as well. The physical dimension

encourages activities which contribute to high-level wellness; this includes appropriate use of exercise and of the health-care system, and avoidance of negative influences like tobacco, alcohol, and other harmful substances. It prepares students to make informed decisions about their health care and lifestyles.

JESUS AS PERSONAL MODEL

For every aspect of personal formation at its fullest, Jesus Christ is the model and the center: "Since Christ Jesus, Word of God Incarnate, is the ultimate reason why God intervened in the world and showed himself to people, he is the centre of the Gospel message in salvation history."[57] At Epiphany, which is the feast that celebrates God's showing His Son to the world, we say a prayer that fits this notion: that God "draw us beyond the limits which this world imposes, to the life where your Spirit makes all life complete." All in Catholic schools try to conform to the image of God's revelation of His Son as a person.[58]

The Educated Person as Goal

The goal that wraps up all others is contained in the notion of "the educated person." Views of what an educated person is have varied. For Aristotle, the educated person was a man who led a life of contemplation. For Plato, it was the philosopher-king. Socrates was a stonecutter, but also a soldier, a teacher, and a citizen par excellence. In the Renaissance, the educated person was "the universal man." In current society, the term "educated person" frequently embraces a view which favors relativism and pluralism, with no reference to anything transcendent. In a free and democratic marketplace of ideas, all ideas— true and false ones, good ones and bad—are equal; what is worthwhile is to be discovered by individuals for themselves.[59]

With that as the current *Weltanschauung*, can a person who remains faithful to the Catholic religion be an "educated person"? Critics say no, giving among their reasons the following. Educational positions are relativistic, and Catholic education has absolutes. Education is based on inquiry, Catholicism on authority. Education tries to deal, for the most part, with pure reason; Catholicism contains "givens" from revelation, to which the Catholic has an attitude of acceptance. For the critics education is an on-going process and Catholicism aims at a "finished product." And critics say that educated persons think for themselves, while Catholics think what they are told to think and believe what they are told to believe.

John M. Hull counters these arguments by stating that the Christian *can* be an educated person:

In the New Testament, especially the Epistles, [the Christian] finds numerous exhortations to achieve an alert, watchful, vigilant, inquiring, and discriminating spirit. The Christian view of man is that, like the educational view, he is unfinished; the Christian context of that process is that the image of God is being daily renewed in us. Christian anthropology, therefore, goes hand in hand with a developmental view of human personhood. As for authority vs. freedom, we must distinguish between two concepts of authority: the authoritarian and the authoritative. The authoritarian person contains no criteria and offers no reasons: He is right because he says so. The authoritative person, on the other hand, has his authority because of specific reasons, gives specific criteria based on research or the quality of arguments. Catholics believe that God's authority is authoritative. He and His Church do not, like frustrated parents, shout, "Do as you're told!" . . .

Lastly, the highest realms to which we are called in Christian spirituality do not call for the mere passive obedience of easily-led sheep, dependent children who are to take up our cross and not our syllogism. Christ calls us to be disciples, learners, . . . constantly challenged by Christ's question to the apostles, "What do you think?" We are to have a spirit of critical openness — not the proud spirit of complacency that sometimes characterizes the academic, but the humble attitude of one who knows that he has much to learn.[60]

In fine, educated Catholics would ideally look something like this. They are personally educated to the maximal point of their intelligence. They are morally formed to do God's will in their unique circumstances. They are free of encumbrances that might keep them from developing to their full potential. They are emotionally warm but controlled. They are sensitive to others and to the world around them. They reflect upon values, meanings, and problems. They strive for wisdom. In action, they achieve being responsible. They are firmly rooted in their family and also have durable bonds with people outside their family. They have developed the ability to love properly. They have achieved self-identity, freedom, and self-fulfillment.

Liberation as Goal

In Catholic-school circles, the goal terms that would have to be taken into consideration at least as much as "educated person" would be "liberation" and "salvation." As for the first — liberation, or freedom — critics accuse Catholic schools of intending a predominantly domesticating effect, espousing as their goals such concepts as good behavior and conformity. Opponents say that, contrary to Emile

Durkheim's concept of the disciplined person as one who is autonomous, rational, and altruistic, Catholic schools jeopardize and diminish authentic human life and allow real humanity to wither. Antago-
nists accuse Catholic schools of suppressing their students by means of
a morality of fear and legalism rather than by a delight in goodness.
These same accusers continue that it is not unusual for youth to cast
off what they consider to be the alien, smothering net of the forms of
life which Catholic schools impose in the names of "freedom" and
"liberation."[61]

The truth is that the goal of Catholic schools is "the development of
man from within, freeing him from that conditioning which would
prevent him from becoming a fully-integrated human being."[62] The
concept is as old as God's deliverance of the Jews in the Exodus, as old
as Jesus' declaration of his aim "to set free the oppressed." Jesus'
Gospel dissolves the dualistic image of this life versus afterlife, body
versus soul. The resurrection is the epitome of this unified concept.
When in the Lord's Prayer we pray, "Give us this day our daily bread,"
the well-fed think of the Host in the Mass; poor people who have had a
hard time finding food for their children think of the unity between
the struggle for daily bread and Jesus' call to create the Kingdom of
God "on earth as it is in heaven."

Liberal education, after the ancient Greek ideal (another of our
intellectual inheritances), frees the mind for its proper functions: emphasis upon pure over applied knowledge, the thoughtful and realistic
selfpossession which is necessary for the good life, reflective commitment to values, rejection of knowledge as power, and eliminating the
unexamined life which, according to Socrates, is not worth living.
That kind of liberal education also frees its recipients from an unre-
flective acceptance of the world as it is, and liberates its subjects to see,
as Jean Piaget wrote, the possibility of running the world in a different
way. This means, as Marxists and others (including the Church) have
discovered, that liberal education is a risky business: it can subvert the
established order.[63]

Because of confusions, and because the "liberation theology" of
people like Paolo Freire and Gustavo Gutièrrez[64] was widely publi-
cized, the Congregation for the Doctrine of the Faith on March 22,
1986, issued an instruction on the subject. Part of the problem, said the
document, is that many people no longer know the true meaning of
freedom. The spontaneous definition of many people would be that "a
person is free when he is able to do whatever he wishes without being
hindered by an exterior constraint and thus enjoys complete independence."[65] The Congregation took the position that true liberation

requires the criterion of truth and a right relationship to the will of others. Truth and justice are therefore the measure of true freedom. By discarding this foundation and taking himself for God, man . . . instead of realizing himself . . . destroys himself. . . .

Freedom is not the liberty to do anything whatsoever. It is the freedom to do good, and in this alone happiness is to be found.[66]

Pope John Paul II has since written a letter to the Brazilian bishops in which he favors liberation theology, provided it is integrated into the mainstream tradition of the Church.

The effort to free thought and will from their limits has led some to consider that morality as such is an unreasonable limitation, not to be tolerated. Humankind, in order to become its own master, is to go beyond morality. In this view, God is the other obstacle to humankind's freedom.[67] Catholics counter that humankind's going beyond the moral law and becoming independent of God, far from giving true freedom, destroy it. The essence of humankind's ongoing temptation is contained in the serpent's words in the first temptation: "You will be like God."[68] Succumbing to this temptation alienates the person not only from God, but from oneself.

The fact that the Church, as an indirect part of her mission, "is firmly determined to respond to the anxiety of contemporary man as he endures oppression and yearns for freedom,"[69] makes the Church the object of accusations of being an obstacle on the path to liberation: her *magisterium* (teaching authority) is said to be opposed to freedom of thought, and her constitution, which is hierarchal, to be opposed to equality. The truth is that, although the Church has made mistakes, the "diversity of charisms in the people of God, which are charisms of service, is not opposed to the equal dignity of persons."[70] And by "opening itself to divine truth, created reason experiences a blossoming and a perfection which are an eminent form of freedom."[71]

Morality is essential to true liberation: "to the salvific dimension of liberation is linked its ethical dimension."[72] True liberation essentially entails not only truth, but also love. Before one can achieve the economic and social changes that will help humankind, one must first "appeal to the spiritual and moral capacities of the individual and to the permanent need for inner conversion."[73]

This conversion is of the *mind* from error, illusion, and rationalization, toward truth; of *moral* concepts from the pragmatistic and the utilitarian toward commitment to values and responsible action; of *religious* attitudes toward the power of love. In Bernard Lonergan's concept, this total conversion is a *metanoia* which turns to God, and goes intellectually from group bias toward attentiveness, reason, and judgment; morally from egotism towards rational responsibility; and religiously from partial insights to the primary intelligible, known through the knowledge that arises from love.[74] Liberation as a Catholic goal of education will adopt the established forms of knowledge, and then add a deep faith in human creativity, a hope without much limit, and a "profound love of the world and of men."[75] Education should not end in stagnant inaction, but the action in which it results should be prudent and meaningful.

It is therefore necessary to work simultaneously for both inner personal conversion and the improvement of structures. Both must take into account the historical situation of a nation and the cultural identity of its people. And when the time comes for action, the rights of true freedom, without which there can be no real liberation, are to be respected; systematic violence is to be avoided as opening the way to new forms of servitude; and a morality of means, which questions the path of revolution, is to be kept in mind. Throughout, the "primary task, which is a condition for the success of all the others, is an educational one."[76]

Salvation as a Goal

The other Catholic term mentioned above as a goal of Catholic schooling is "salvation," which in this context means holiness. Holiness, by connotation perhaps a standoffish term, really means wholeness or total wellness. "Salvation"—*sotēria* in Greek, *salus* in Latin, *Heil* in German—means "health."[77] The Old High German *Heil* was one of the origins of the English "whole," thus showing the affinity between "holiness," "wholeness," and "salvation."[78]

The holy life, the saved life, consists in the fullness of Christian practice and the perfection of love.[79] For Catholics, whatever their vocation, this life in faith "is their greatest responsibility."[80] Although the forms which holiness takes are many,[81] it is one in being "cultivated by all who act under God's Spirit and, obeying the Father's voice and adoring God the Father in spirit and in truth, follow Christ, poor, humble and cross-bearing, that they may deserve to be partakers of his glory."[82]

What is to be saved and made holy is not just a person's soul, but (in the Hebrew view of the human person as one entity) the person as soul, the person as body, the person corporate as well as individual; the person physical, mental, and spiritual; the person in individual life, in social, political, and economic life; the person in relation to other people as well as to God; the person under pressure from inward drives, from the past, from history, and from race; the person in sexual, intellectual, and emotional life. It is for the salvation of people that Jesus died, rose, and ascended. God's salvation goes on and on and out and out; its only frontiers are the edges of the universe.

Salvation in the biblical sense includes education; the relation of education to salvation is that of the part to the whole. Salvation and education are not ancillaries to religion and the Gospel, nor mere implications or applications of the Gospel; they are essential parts of the Gospel. It is God's purpose that each member of humankind become wholly mature vis-a-vis God, oneself, and other people. Education has a vital role in the fulfillment of that purpose.

CONCLUSION

We speak of goals rather than of targets, aims, and objectives, mostly because of the connotations of goals in athletics: specific, taken seriously, prepared for, worked at, sacrificed for. Goals answer ultimate questions like "why?" and look for "shoulds." Goals are necessary to give direction and to judge the enterprise's degree of success. Catholic schools, an expression of the mission of Christianity, receive their goals from such sources as the New Testament (for example, *metamorphosis* and *metanoia*) and the tradition of humanism.

All who are interested in Catholic schools should have input into their goals: society at large, the State, the Church community, parents, and (particularly) the school community of faculty, students, and staff. In this shared responsibility and participatory decision making of committees of teachers, parents, students, and others working together to formulate meaningful, specific, close, and detailed goals, the process as well as the result can have many beneficial results. Not least among them is to establish a sense of community and to provide a vision that will be lived and will unite.

Catholic-school goal clusters are consonant with the best of the humanist heritage and of the historical foundations of the United States. They establish a relationship of trust with the institutional Church, can vary from time to time and place to place and school level to school level, uniquely define and represent the individual schools, and aim at total student wellness. Goal clusters center around the person's union with God, include a social dimension, and embrace the intellectual, affective, moral, and physical reaches of the self. Throughout, Catholic-school goals have Jesus as their model. The commonly enunciated goals of "educated person," "liberation," and "salvation" have for Catholic schools specific meanings which are in many ways unique.

Catholic-school goals should be reflected in and implemented by the curriculum. This will be the subject of our next chapter.

QUESTIONS FOR DISCUSSION

Can an existentialist ever fail in goals or fail an examination?

Who is best prepared to set up schools' goals: teachers, sociologists, philosophers, psychologists, political theorists, parents, or others? Why?

In what way(s) is the Catholic school an expression of the mission of Christianity?

What should be the personal qualifications of those who participate in the formulation of Catholic-school goals?

Do schools — church-affiliated as well as government — exist primarily to promote the interests of the individual, or of society, or both?

In deciding which goals to enunciate, what considerations should obtain?

In the presentation of goals, is there any balance that should be kept between the practical and the theoretical?

If you were the chairperson of a Catholic-school Goals Committee, how would you go about establishing your school's goals?

Is it possible to include in Catholic schools, under any aspects of their goals, the teaching of subjects like racism, poverty, world development, war and peace, secularization, and economics?

What is your idea of the educated person?

In your opinion, what priority of goals should the Catholic school seek to achieve?

How can we determine whether a school's goals are being achieved?

SUGGESTED BIBLIOGRAPHY

Ferm, Deane William. *Third World Liberation Theologies*. Maryknoll, N.Y.: Orbis Books, 1986.

A systematic survey of the principal liberation theologies from Asia, Africa, and Latin America.

———. *Third World Liberation Theologies: A Reader*. Maryknoll, N.Y.: Orbis Books, 1986.

Judiciously edited selections from the diversity of liberation theologies.

Goodlad, John. *A Place Called School: Prospects for the Future*. New York: McGraw-Hill, 1984.

A critical analysis of United States schools, suggesting that serious gaps exist between what society expects and what actually happens; contains suggestions for improvement.

Kaplan, Martin, ed. *What Is an Educated Person? The Decades Ahead*. New York: Praeger, 1980.

Presents papers developed at two conferences sponsored by the Aspen Institute for Humanistic Studies, attended by European and American scholars. Among the questions addressed is "What is an educated person?"

Maritain, Jacques. *Education at the Crossroads*. New Haven, Conn.: Yale University Press, 1961.

From the viewpoint of Classical Realism, shows the problems of a school system that is more concerned with techniques than goals.

_____. *The Education of Man*. South Bend, Ind.: University of Notre Dame Press, 1963.

Intended as the complement to *Education at the Crossroads*, this work includes Maritain's principal texts on education.

National Catholic Educational Association. *The Catholic High School: A National Portrait*. Washington, D.C.: National Catholic Educational Association, 1985.

Assesses the current state of Catholic high schools in terms of administration, teachers, students, goals, and curriculum, and suggests agenda for improvement.

Tyler, Ralph W. *Basic Principles of Curriculum and Instruction*. University of Chicago Press, 1949.

A classic model for determining how to organize a curriculum; also includes an area on goals.

Vaile, Scott J. *Catholic Education*. Dayton, Ohio: National Catholic Educational Association, 1968.

Discusses a Catholic philosophy and goals of education.

Chapter 5

HOW CATHOLIC SCHOOLS PROPOSE TO GET THERE: RELIGION AND VALUES IN THE CURRICULUM

DEFINITION

There is no unanimous agreement on a definition of curriculum. The etymological meaning of "curriculum" is "little race course"—here, the track one has to run in order to catch up with oneself. Technically, it is "the label for a programme or course of activities which is explicitly organized as the means whereby pupils may attain the desired objectives, whatever these may be."[1] Curriculum embraces all those academic, moral, social, and physical experiences the school fosters for the growth of its students.

Curriculum differs from "course of study," curriculum being the more comprehensive of the two terms. On the speculative level, curriculum is that which contains those activities, content, processes, values, and institutional arrangements as intended, as emphasized, and as experienced in the school ambience in connection with the school's educational purposes. In practice, it is the interaction of student and school personnel in an educational environment directed toward a predetermined goal. These matters may or may not be included in the course of study. The course of study, organized mostly for classroom use, usually refers to the printed school document which gives a formal statement of the required content and often the sequence of the various subjects taught.

CURRICULUM THEORY

Curriculum theory is a large and complicated area. Many contributions come to it from sciences like history, philosophy, anthropology, psychology, and sociology. Catholic schools study these contributions with care. The problem of Catholic schools is somewhat analogous to what William Jennings Bryan is reported to have said during the Scopes "monkey trial" of 1925: "It is better to trust in the Rock of Ages than to know the age of the rocks; it is better for one to know that he is close to the heavenly Father than to know how far the stars in the heavens are apart." The problem is to seek out the relative domains and emphases for both religious and secular knowledge.[2]

Philosophical Principles

Realist principles put the student in contact with as much of reality as possible. The subject matter has to be logical, orderly, and based on the universal laws of reality which ultimately aid the faculty of reason. Knowledge is valuable for its own sake, not just for use. The curriculum is to be based on universal truths, thus making it less flexible than pragmatists or existentialists might wish. And unity or integration is inherent in the logical unity of knowledge.

Most realists would say that religion, being also an important part of reality, it should be an important part of the curriculum. Subjects like sex education, which are intrinsic to human nature, belong to schools as an extension of church and family, with students not only raising questions, but being taught objective right and wrong. Because realists see the educated person as being both practical and speculative, they prefer a liberal education followed by an apprenticeship over vocational education. They also prefer intellectually oriented content over the skill-oriented, and objective standards over subjective experiences. They permit electives only after a liberal-arts foundation.

Idealist curricular principles emphasize giving the student ideas by stressing the accumulated wisdom of society and whatever will open the mind to all the mind's possibilities. Idealists favor basic courses like history, philosophy, literature; strive for the integration of new knowledge with the entire range of what has already been learned; and aim for modern adaptations and updating of the richness of the "seven liberal arts," which served the Western world well for over fifteen hundred years. They consider religion essential to the curriculum because the person's spiritual being is foremost in importance. Like realists, they advocate courses such as sex education as suitable at the appropriate time and manner, and only in the framework of moral values. Idealists would not permit vocational training if it meant eliminitating or substituting for any basic courses. And the acquisition of credits is only incidental to the goal of personal formation.

Positivist principles, which include those of pragmatists and empiricists, place major emphasis on science and technology over the humanities, favor practical values over speculative knowledge (the unexamined life is worth living), espouse usefulness, emphasize practical problem solving, encourage the experiential, stress the teaching of *skills*, and prefer the relevant to the important. The positivists' verification principle—the way in which they verify the truth of any potential part of the curriculum—is purely scientific: what is not quantifiably measurable is of little or no value. Obviously, most of the basic principles of the positivist family run counter to the values of Catholicism.

Existentialist principles concern what will provide personal identity and authenticity; freedom from outside coercion; preparation for life choices, action upon them, and responsibility for them; provision for guided choices for the student; subjects that allow self-expression; opportunities for self-unfolding, self-in-becoming; the humanities over science; subjects that provide opportunities for self-appropriation of truth (for example, comparative religion, values, sex education); a minimum of required courses; the adjustment of the curriculum to the pupil's individual needs in order to prevent lack of student self-esteem through failure; and electives at all ages, to introduce every child to the joy of learning. Catholic agreement with some of these principles is mostly a matter of degree.

Curriculum Organization

In organizing their curricula, Catholic educators need to be cognizant of curriculum planning versus syllabus tinkering; the nature and implication of knowledge and experience; the relationships between means and ends; the differences between relevancy and importance, education and schooling, and rigidity and flexibility; and the meaning, value, and place of truth.

Syllabus tinkerers have no vision of the school as a whole, no sense of creating a community in the school who care and provide for the person. Thoughtful curriculum designers and planners, on the other hand, take cognizance of the impermanence of all things and of the need for ongoing conversion and growth of persons and ideas.[3] These curriculum theorists distinguish areas of knowledge and experience which an intelligently organized curriculum will satisfy.[4] They see general education as concerned with more than intellectual development. Meaning "is the essence of the life of man, not the processes of logical thinking only but the life of feeling, conscience, inspiration and other processes not retained in the strict sense."[5]

One possibility of curriculum organization is the means-end model. This develops a set of desired goals and plans the organization of the best means to achieve them.[6] In general the most widely used model for curriculum design is still that of Ralph Tyler, written in 1947 and mentioned in our discussion of goals in chapter 4. John Dewey presents *relevancy* as a prime principle for curriculum design. He wrote:

> A curriculum which acknowledges the social responsibilities of education must present situations where problems are relevant to the problems of living together, and where observation and information are calculated to develop social insight and interest.[7]

Catholics, without denying the place of relevancy, add the weightier consideration of *importance*. Whereas the adjective "relevant" raises the question, "relevant to what?," the "important" stands on its own. The "relevant" is open to fads, the "important" more to what has lasting value. The "relevant," referring to things like life skills, making money, or pleasure, is a light-weight in comparison with the "important," which has a great inner weight of its own that carries it. One who makes decisions based on an opinion of what is here and now relevant may later see matters differently.

Since Catholics believe that their curricular concerns must be for *education*, and not just for *schooling*, they oppose purely pragmatistic principles of curriculum design. For example, they do not agree with the emphasis upon experience as the sole determinant of the validity of knowledge. Thus Catholics see the notion that curricula are to be practical to the exclusion of the theoretical as a false dichotomy. The curriculum should be both practical and theoretical, realizing that overly practical people may end up efficiently going at supersonic speed with their lives, but in the wrong direction, and the overly theoretical person may end up as an absent-minded professor. Whereas some say that knowledge is power, Catholics emphasize the concept that ideas move the world and see wisdom as being higher than knowledge: "The intellectual nature of man finds at last its perfection, as it should, in wisdom."[8]

Catholic schools should have the ability to discern what is valuable in current curricular theories and incorporate it into their schools. In New Testament times, the Christian curriculum reflected the best of the Hebrews, Greeks, and Romans. St. Augustine later encouraged the Christian curriculum to take the best from non-Christian sources and leave the rest. And today's Catholic-school curriculum should seek to use the best of current curricular discoveries in order to imbue Catholic youth with the spirit of Christ.

Important to a Catholic curriculum is belief about *truth*. Truth is achievable, so the curriculum should present more than mere matters of opinion. Finding truth may at times be difficult, and therefore the curriculum should teach its preciousness. Truth is one; therefore the curriculum should not be fragmented, nor a mere scramble for credit, nor a matter of complete student election. Truth is important, so the curriculum should encourage and present the cogent rather than the merely persuasive. Truth, when obtained, is sure, and therefore words like "absolute" and "dogma," forbidden in the curriculum of some philosophies, are acceptable to Catholics. Truth is perceivable in stages, and therefore there is no conflict between a child-centered and a subject-centered curriculum.

Truth is vast, and therefore requires arranging the curriculum into areas of manageable proportions or logically distinct forms or disciplines: school "subjects." Because truth is one, these units are not discrete, but rather overlap and interpenetrate. There must therefore be a certain degree of integration.

Curriculum Integration

Coming from the Latin *integer*, which means "whole," *integration* implies that the combined elements — parts, factors, details — are so intimately connected with one another that a perfect whole results. We speak of the integration of races in the United States into a single people, or of the automobile as an integration of a multitude of machine parts, or of an integrated economic and political system.

In curricula, integration means combining elements that are otherwise taught in separate courses or departments into one. Integration, in this context, means the organization of teaching matter to interrelate or unify subjects usually taught separately. It is possible, for example, through integration to teach health, science, and safety together. One theory holds that the subject of "religion" could integrate the entire curriculum. Integration makes vast demands on the knowledge and ability of the teachers involved, however, and in less competent hands can "degenerate into pursuits which, however interesting, have little or no educational value."[9]

Among the areas of special importance to Catholic schools are religion and values. Catholic schools usually favor their being in the context of a foundation in the liberal arts, or — in elementary and secondary schools — in remote or proximate preparation for the liberal arts.

LIBERAL ARTS

The beautiful word "liberal" can mean many different things. It has been used for the Enlightenment of the eighteenth century, as a banner under which some politicians muster support, as a shibboleth for occasional student revolts, as the rationale for many government programs, as an equivalent of permissiveness, and many more. Its root, however, is from the Latin *liber*, which means "a free person" over and against a *servus*, or "slave." The "liberal arts," with which Catholic education strives to prepare people for life, have as one important function to free one from prejudice, ignorance, and narrow-mindedness, to become truly oneself.

Education in the liberal arts has its origin among the ancient Greeks. It was based not only on the free man, but on the distinctive purpose of the mind to pursue knowledge, and on the fact that knowledge can reach reality. Humankind need not live with only deceptive appearances, doubtful opinions, and unsupported beliefs. A liberal education can free the mind to function according to its true nature — freeing reason from error and people's conduct from wrongdoing.

These views did not define education in terms of knowledge or skills that may be useful, or look for a justification in "the predilection of pupils, the demands of society, or the whims of politicians."[10] Rather, these views embraced knowing as a distinctive human virtue, and education as a fulfillment of the mind. And "because of the significance of knowledge in the determination of the good life as a whole, liberal education is essential to man's understanding of how he ought to live, both individually and socially."[11] The views were those of classical realism; they have been embraced by such Catholic theoreticians as John Henry Newman and Jacques Maritain as well as by such others as Matthew Arnold, Robert M. Hutchins, and Mortimer Adler.

Although liberal education is intended to be comprehensive, it does not aim at the acquisition of encyclopedic information. Nor does it seek the specialist knowledge of the person fully trained in the details of a particular branch of knowledge, or the technician's knowledge of practical applications. It aspires to sufficient immersion in the concepts, logic, and criteria of disciplines for a student to be able to pursue knowledge further, and sufficient generalizations for a widely structured experience.[12]

Essentially what Catholic education wants from a liberal education is a person who is free and thus able to attain to God. It is in the area of the liberal arts that one can best "recognize that over and above what is visible, the reality of which we discern through the sciences, God has given us an intellect which can attain to *that which is*, not merely the subjective content of 'structures' and developments of human consciousness."[13] The liberal arts have other advantages, like "bringing the human race to a higher understanding of truth, goodness, and beauty, to points of view having universal value."[14] Education in the liberal arts counteracts a propensity toward exclusive concentration upon scientific and technical progress, which has dangers:

> [It] can lead to a certain phenomenism or agnosticism; this happens when scientific methods of investigation, which of themselves are incapable of penetrating to the deepest nature of things, are unjustifiably taken as the supreme norm for arriving at truth. There is a further danger that in his excessive confidence in modern inventions man may think he is sufficient unto himself and give up the search for higher values.[15]

This is not to say, however, that science is without positive values, among them

> exact fidelity to truth in scientific investigation, the necessity of teamwork in technology, the sense of international solidarity, a growing awareness of the expert's responsibility to help and defend his fellow men, and an eagerness to improve the standard of living of all men, especially of those who are deprived of responsibility or suffer from cultural destitution.[16]

Pope John Paul II, in fact, stated that teachers should show young people that "science and faith have different yet complementary views of the universe and of history."[17]

RELIGION

Catholic schools embrace the formal teaching of religion. But even in a Catholic school religion remains a delicate subject and entails problems. Some schools are of the opinion that religion should permeate the entire curriculum. Others view their parish schools as part of the entire faith community, into which religious curricula should be integrated. Still others prefer to view the integrity of each subject, including religion, on its own merits, with its own academic criteria. This last view does not, however, treat religion as a mere add-on to what government schools are doing.

Definitions

Religion has traditionally meant the tie that binds a human being to the immanent and transcendent God. Contemporary culture, however, sees religion's tie as to whatever is central in one's life, the ground of being, that which gives a person direction for the basic questions in life — for example, spouse, dividends, children, whiskey. Religion is the answer to the implacable question that the thinking person cannot avoid: "What gods do I choose to serve?" In the context of humankind's age-old search for meaning and purpose, the Catholic Church sees religion as dealing with the profundities:

> Men look to their different religions for an answer to the un-
> solved riddles of human existence. The problems that weigh heavi-
> ly on the hearts of men are the same today as in the ages past.
> What is man? What is the meaning and purpose of life? What is
> upright behavior, and what is sinful? Where does suffering origi-
> nate, and what end does it serve? How can genuine happiness be
> found? What happens at death? What is judgment? What reward
> follows death? And finally, what is the ultimate mystery, beyond
> human explanation, which embraces our entire existence, from
> which we take our origin and towards which we tend?[18]

The Catholic Church sees religion as providing a balance between other-worldly and this-worldly concerns:

> It is a mistake to think that, because we have here no lasting city,
> but seek the city which is to come, we are entitled to shirk our
> earthly responsibilities. . . . But it is no less mistaken to think that
> we may immerse ourselves in earthly activities as if these latter
> were utterly foreign to religion, and religion were nothing more
> than the fulfilment of acts of worship and the observance of a few
> moral obligations.[19]

There are other terms whose definitions are important with respect to religion in the curriculum. Among them are evangelization, cate-chesis, religious education, and theology. They are not rigorously separate. *Evangelization* means preaching the Gospel of Christ with a view to converting the hearer to Christ. Christ gave his Church the work of "preaching the gospel to all nations." Although we think of evangelization as primarily preaching to those who have never heard the Gospel, the new conversion of minds and hearts to God — Christians' as well as others' — is something that must go on daily.

Catechesis is an action which seeks to evoke a living, conscious, and active faith in one who already believes. It intends to evoke a deeper "yes" to the meaning of Christ and the Church. Among the compo-nents of catechesis are instruction, dialogue, content mastery, ques-tions, answers, and religious experience (as found in Church commu-nity, prayer, liturgical celebration, and acts of love, mercy, and justice). Catechesis includes values and moral education, inasmuch as commitment to Christ and the Church involves values and moral consequences. Catechesis is not the same as instruction, which is explaining the doctrines and practices of the faith. Instruction is part of catechesis, but catechesis goes further. Not content with an increase of knowledge, it goes toward improving the quality of faith, making it more informed, more mature, and better understood.

Religious education is based on the idea that human life involves a number of important fields of knowledge that contain religious/moral meaning: for example, the worlds of science and of the arts. A person who has an education is one who has an adequate grasp of each of these. Education also has an important connection with the development of reason. When applied to religion, these aspects of education, though not without criticism, aim to give youth an understanding of the world of religion from the inside, with sympathetic insight. Religious education differs from *theology*, the latter leading one to participate in, reflect upon, and analyze *religious* experience of all kinds.

Lessons from History

Religion in the Catholic-school curriculum must contain applications to current affairs, an acknowledgement of the problems students face, and a recognition of their worldview. So it has been since New Testament times. Early Christians did not spurn the curriculum of their time. They saw such studies as good *in themselves*, because they contained truth. Christians, like the rest of humankind, were in search of truth, and though the truth contained in poet and philosopher might not always be religious truth, there was often an evident agreement between poet, philosopher, and Holy Scripture. Secular learning was full of erudition and wisdom. Christians saw Greek philosophy as having reached the heights of wisdom that the human intellect could achieve without the help of divine revelation.

Further, the Church Fathers saw the robust teaching handed down from the leading Greeks as a *means* — to the Christian personal formation they wanted to encourage. In fact, when they faced the uneducated pagan nations of the north, they found the Greek learning of their time a better foundation for Christian education than the fanatical asceticism of some of their own uneducated Christians.[20] Most Church Fathers looked upon secular learning as an indispensable supplement to the Bible. Lastly, they saw the Greek *paideia* as a practical *necessity*. The educated portion of the Western world of the time had been schooled in it and, if the Christians wanted to address its leaders, they would have to do it in terms of the only education those leaders knew.[21]

Catholic curriculum designers must continue to use the best of secular education. They must also be sensitive to accuracy in the transmission of their Christian cultural heritage: papal statements (encyclicals, briefs, bulls, addresses, letters, allocutions, and so on), teachings of councils, statements of the local magisterium. A brief look at historical documents[22] reveals the care which the Church has taken to keep the true faith.

Why Continue?

The presence of religion in education accords with part, at least, of the Catholic Church's position: "Complete education necessarily includes a religious dimension. Religion is an effective contribution to the development of other aspects of a personality in the measure in which it is integrated into general education."[23] And the best of the United States tradition is in accord with that Roman Catholic teaching, as the provisions for religion in the Northwest Ordinance of 1787, for example, and similar legislation testify. There continues to be, in some quarters, the recognition that religious education is essential to democracy, and that inadequate attention to religious education and the threatened collapse of modern civilization are related as cause to effect.

Religion is of the utmost importance in the Catholic-school curriculum. Pope John Paul II stated that it is the teaching of religion that identifies the Catholic school:

> [The Catholic school] would no longer deserve this title if, no matter how much it shone for its high level of teaching in non-religious matters, there were justification for reproaching it for negligence or deviation in strictly religious education. . . . The special character of the Catholic school, the underlying reason for it, the reason why Catholic parents should prefer it, is precisely the quality of the religious instruction integrated into the education of the pupils.[24]

John Paul gave further details of this position later when he said: "I insist on the upholding of Christian catechesis in Catholic schools, of its carefully adapted presentation, its doctrinal correctness, and its great respect for the mystery of God."[25]

The presentation of the Roman Catholic religion in the Church's schools is consonant with the best ideas of the Republic and fulfills Daniel Webster's dictum that whatever makes men good Christians makes them good citizens. The hierarchy of truths in the Roman Catholic message

> can be grouped under four basic headings: the mystery of God, Father, Son and Holy Spirit, creator of all things; the mystery of

Christ, Word incarnate, who was born of the Virgin Mary, suffered, died and rose again for our salvation; the mystery of the Holy Spirit, present in the Church and sanctifying and guiding it until the coming of Christ, our Saviour and Judge, in glory; the mystery of the Church, the mystical Body of Christ, in which the Virgin Mary has the highest place.[26]

This creed is not meaningless jargon irrelevant to the way life is lived.[27] The Catholic religion has a bearing "not only with what has to be believed, but with what has to be done," and entails "the obligation to live and grow, under the guidance of the Holy Spirit, in the new life communicated by Jesus Christ."[28]

In practice, it is neither the devout priest, zealous religious educator, informed curriculum expert, or philosopher of education who legitimates this kind of education; it is society. Education cannot be divorced from its cultural context. Another difficulty is that Catholic-school religious educators have at times given in to what lawyers disdainfully call "form over substance"—more concern with style, method, or process than content. There is no doubt that some attention to methods is important: to create interest, for example, to engender motivation, and to encourage involvement. Religious educators must take into account age, ability, and social background. But education in religion is more than methods.

Form and substance are really inseparable: one does not wrap a Christmas gift in litter bags, nor garbage in pink ribbons. Catholic schools, while being aware of the importance of style and process, must place their emphasis on substantive content. This is more difficult today than before; the difficulties explain, but do not excuse, the galloping religious illiteracy among youth and the tendency of many current religion programs to be thin on content.[29] For one thing, there is today more theological speculation than in the past, making it harder to draw as heavily on settled Church teachings. For another, this is a time of child-centered rather than content-centered education. And some Church teachings today are being explained more often in the language of Scripture and experience than in exact formulas—in many ways a good development. Other methodological difficulties include the questions of how to evaluate and grade religion, and how to set standards.

A difficulty outside methodology is as old as the Prophets: the teaching of how religion is to be practiced. The Prophets had to struggle against a belief in the possibility of reconciliation with God through ritual rather than through genuine repentance. Jesus had to struggle with some contemporaries for whom, as for their predecessors, religious practice had replaced genuine inner life. And Jesus was condemned to death by very pious people, in the name of God and for the sake of religion.

The last of the difficulties we shall mention in the presentation of religion today[30] is that of formulating a catechetical instrument to match current Catholic self-understanding—for example, to do for the newly emerging Church what the Baltimore catechism did for the late nineteenth century. Though thought is at times given to the formulation of such an instrument, many are not sure it can be done, given today's highly accentuated cultural and other differences. There must be further dialogue between the Church's magisterium and theologians to indicate the truly essential elements of the mystery of Christ that must be taught to youth.

In the face of all these difficulties and more, why continue to try to teach religion in the Catholic school? For one reason, religion has a dynamic power to change people, institutions, and cultures for the better. For another thing, religion has a sustaining influence on a democracy like the United States. The prestigious Brookings Institution, a liberal think tank, after three years of analysis arrived at this conclusion:

> In a highly mobile and heterogeneous society like the United States, the values based on religion are even more essential to democracy than they may be in more traditional societies, where respect for freedom, order, and justice may be maintained for some time through social inertia or custom. . . . Banishment of religion does not represent neutrality between religion and secularism; conduct of public institutions without any regard to religion is secularism.[31]

Again, religion is important to help students, schools, and society arrive at a much deeper appreciation of life. Essential is constant *reflection*: reflection about motivation, about curriculum, about community, about "vocation" rather than "careers." The religion lesson needs to be in part an examination of conscience on the school's behavior.[32] Another reason for facing the difficulties to continue to teach religion is the teaching of commitment—*religious* commitment, which is deeper, longer lasting, and with different objects than other kinds of commitment. (We shall go into more detail on this in chapter 8, on teachers.) In 1974 the German National Synod made the realistic judgement that religious instruction in the schools will have been worthwhile from the point of view of the Church if pupils, when they leave school, feel that a religious commitment is not pointless or stupid. It should enable them to see how commitment can be an enrichment of their personality. . . . [33]

Through faith, people have a new vision — a new vision of God, a new vision of the world, and a new vision of themselves. Doctrine is the basis for a way of life. Catholic schools, as well as the rest of the Church, must teach this doctrine accurately, faithfully, and fully. The doctrine's probing of the religious dimensions of life must not be narrow, and it must encourage other disciplines to examine their own fields of study.

How to Present Religion in the Catholic School

All agree that the presentation of religion in the Catholic school will help form leaders for the Church, encourage students to become active participants in their local congregation, and help students to perpetuate their religious heritage. Though the presentation of religion may not be pastoral, it would provide the sources and resources necessary for students to reaffirm adherence to certain fundamental doctrines which are the heritage of the Church, to develop a meaningful outlook on life, and to become better members of their Church. The overall purpose of this kind of inclusion of religion in the curriculum would be the ancient *fides quaerens intellectum*, "faith seeking an understanding of itself."

There are, however, fine points. One of them is to decide *how* the religious goal of Catholic schools can be accomplished. Most Catholic educators agree that religion should be taught not indirectly but explicitly, systematically, with the purpose of imparting commitment as well as mere knowledge,[34] and in an up-to-date fashion.[35] A key question, however, is whether religion should be presented by way of integration, permeation, or separation. The answer to this is important for one's definition of a Catholic school.

In the specific context of religion in Catholic schools, integration means presenting a learning and a living which are fully integrated in the light of faith. In this sense, instruction in religious truths is not just one more subject, but is perceived and functions as *the underlying reality* in which a student's experiences of learning and living receive their coherence and their deepest meaning. It is brought about by teachers who manifest an integrated approach to learning and living in their lives. It is further reinforced by interaction among students within their own youth community, which is to be a community of faith: a community the building of which is the prime explicit goal of the school, and a faith that is living, conscious, and active. Religion is thus at the center, not only of the subject matter of the curriculum, but also of the very personhood of the student.

This concept of integration can be of crucial importance, in view of modern pressures to compartmentalize life and learning and to isolate the religious dimension from all other aspects of life. Proponents of integration note that it is impossible to separate the "secular" from the "religious" in *any* important endeavor, including education. And a program of integration only reinforces the idea that no single item makes a school Catholic: not the subjects offered, or the methods used, or the teachers. That uniqueness is in the living union that integrates the entire educational experience.

A second way in which religion can be accomplished in church-affiliated schools is by way of *permeation*. "Permeate" is from the Latin *permeare*, "to pass through." In its general meaning, the word implies diffusion through all the pores of some entity, like rain through sand. In terms of the Catholic school, permeation implies a diffusion of religion into all other content areas.

Many assert that permeation of religion is *the* necessary mode for the teaching of religion. The Second Vatican Council (1962–1965), for example, further revealed this kind of thinking. It put Catholic religion and theology in dialogue not only with other religious traditions and with atheism, but also with such academic disciplines as sociology, psychology, philosophy, the natural sciences, anthropology, the history of religions, and the like. Further, the Council emphasized a strongly practical side of religion in attempting to confront massive social issues like hunger, racism, war, poverty, the women's movement, and the sexual revolution. Since Vatican II, many continue to see a deepened sense of permeation as a great need.[36] At the same time, Catholic educators must not consider curricular subjects as mere adjuncts to faith and must preserve the integrity of each subject.[37]

The third way of including religion in the curriculum of the denominational school may be termed either *segregation* or *separation*. It divorces religion from the rest of the curriculum and contains it in separate courses taught at certain hours on certain days, the same as other subjects. Separation establishes criteria for evaluating religion as a science. It makes religion an equal partner with the rest of the humanities and has religion participate in interdisciplinary and interdepartmental studies. This concept maintains that such inclusion of religion in the curriculum suffices to preserve the identity of an institution as Christian. It helps students formulate a set of values consonant with the Christian tradition and implements the goals of the institution for values education.

Liturgy

Learning the truths of faith should also

> be at the service of active, conscious and genuine participation in the Church's liturgy, not only by explaining the meaning of the rites, but also by training the faithful for prayer, for thanksgiving, for penance, for confident prayer of petition, for a sense of community, giving them a proper understanding of the symbols—all of which are necessary for a proper liturgical life.[38]

Liturgy does not stand entirely on its own: it celebrates deep and affective times in life, and rites of passage like birth, First Communion, Confirmation, marriage, and death. The liturgy is not only words; it is color and light, gesture and movement, texture and color, music and chant, sign and symbol. While liturgies must be about meaningful things, they must celebrate the common things people live with. Thus liturgies recognizing new faculty members in the school are for students often more passionate than those liturgies about "the poor as other." Liturgy is not primarily a tool for religious education, however; it is first and foremost the worship of God and the reactualization of the Lord's redeeming work toward us.

Proper liturgy is a mystery which attracts, yet causes awe. It contains something of that awed spirit which impelled Moses to take off his shoes before the burning bush because he stood on holy ground. Current liturgical practice—with its use of the vernacular, its domesticity, its familiarity—may at times occasion a reduction of this feeling of awe before the sacred. "Living through" salvation history by way of the liturgical year has formational value for a person by recalling the meaning of life as a whole and its various segments. At the center of the yearly cycle is the paschal mystery: the death and resurrection of Jesus. All else leads up to this climax or follows as effects.

Liturgical celebration is a religious event ministering to the total human being: mind, heart, soul, senses, sentiment, intuition, poetic instincts, faith purpose. Some feelings are particularly noteworthy: feelings of awe and reverence which lead to worship, feelings of gratitude which lead to thanksgiving, feelings of guilt which lead to repentance. Especially where children's liturgies are concerned, there must be room for adaptation and spontaneity.[39]

Central to the liturgy is the Eucharist, which "is the summit of both the action by which God sanctifies the world in Christ, and the worship which men offer to Christ and which through him they offer to the Father in the Spirit."[40] Educators should see to it that children come from the Eucharist with the Christian human values of "acting together as a community, exchanging greetings, the capacity to listen, to forgive and to ask for forgiveness, the expression of gratitude, the experience of symbolic actions, conviviality, and festive celebration."[41]

For effectiveness, the Church makes suggestions. The liturgy requires, for example, that people be properly disposed, fully aware, actively engaged, and have the requisite pedagogy, taking into account their age, condition, way of life, and standard of religious culture.[42] In addition to praying with others in the liturgy, pupils must also be trained for solitary personal forms of prayer in their proper place.[43]

Life Experience

To share in the liturgy may lead to vivid learning of many things about God and other religious areas. But other human experiences, too, have an implicit connection with truths of faith. Faith, if it is to survive, must be of a piece with one's experience of life. Looking at the stars can impart some religious truth, and those who can't do it because of city lights lose an opportunity. One must be careful, however, not to exaggerate the ability of experience to lead to religion.

Life experience will inevitably expose a person to considerations of morality. Some challenge the idea that moral values rest on religious beliefs.[44] They point to the moral understandings of philosophers like Socrates and Aristotle, which were based on the use of unaided reason and observation. They point to scriptural texts, like St. Paul saying, "Gentiles who do not have the law keep it as by instinct. . . . They show that the demands of the law are written in their hearts. Their conscience bears witness. . . . "[45] People *do*, of course, derive motivation for their values from many sources besides religion. And people are expected to use their heads in forming their moral code and values priorities. But in forming a right conscience it helps to take into consideration the conclusions of the community of wisdom, the Church.

Even within Christianity there are two schools of thought on the relationship of morality and religion. One school holds that we must emphasize the huge body of Church teaching about what is right, starting with the moral teaching of the Gospels right up to current questions. As with doctrine, so with morals: There is development. This is not to be understood as being relativistic, but in the sense that no Catholic teaching in any area is exhaustive. Although subjective factors like intent, feeling, stress, circumstance, and passion may lessen the degree of responsibility, knowledge of objective principles is important. The Catholic belongs to a community of moral wisdom and lives meaningfully as a member of it.

The other viewpoint emphasizes that we must teach students to make up their own minds: thoughtful personal decision is the essence of morality. This leads to the moral autonomy that is consonant with the dignity of personal maturity. Catholic teaching holds this view as acceptable so long as it is understood that we are not to have free-wheeling morality working without a definite content. A certain amount of knowledge is required for moral decisions. We need the ability to predict the probable outcome of specific actions, insight into our position, awareness of others, and understanding—none of which are innate. In sum, Catholic teaching holds to a synthesis of both reason and Church teachings having a bearing on morality. If either goes its own way without the other, the result is confusion.

VALUES
Background

Every reflective person has to have asked during his or her lifetime, "How should I live, and how can I find out how to live?" It is important to know the difference between what is noble and what is base, to know what is to be defended and what to be loved, the difference between toughness and callousness, and what true courage and self-discipline are. These are all values. They constitute an important part of the Catholic-school curriculum. Most essays on moral education are ultimately variations either on Plato's claim that virtue can be taught by fostering insight into moral truth or on Aristotle's contrary insistence that good dispositions are acquired only by practice. This classic standoff has never been resolved, but wise parents and teachers have always encouraged both insight and practice.

On the one hand, Plato's emphasis upon insight has been bolstered during the past decade by Lawrence Kohlberg's theory of the stages of moral development. Kohlberg himself asserted that his research shows that "youths who understand justice act more justly."[46] Of course, the reflective moralist is not necessarily a moral person. Talleyrand could probably have solved cases of conscience as accurately as the Curé of Ars. On the other hand, for years churches have sponsored programs of community service for young people which reflect the Aristotelian emphasis upon building character through concrete experience.

Opponents of Catholicism say that the goal of building values, or a system of morality, on the basis of universal and fundamental ethical truths is misguided. For them, the best way to live must be established as the result of a process, personal and social, which cannot formulate any answers in advance. For Catholicism's opponents, one's own ethical judgments may not apply to other persons or distant cultures, and relativism is in the air. Catholics can concede that circumstances alter cases, and that sometimes we cannot know enough to judge. That is not relativism, however, but prudent discretion, concern, and realization of the nature of the individual. Relativist principles mean that we cannot prescribe how people ought to live. Many classroom-methodology texts on values[47] deliberately match Secular Humanism's documents. The Catholic Church's approach to values is different at its very base:

> It must, of course, be recognized that in the course of history civilization has taken many forms, that the requirements for human living have changed considerably and that many changes are still to come. But limits must be set to the evolution of mores and life-styles, limits set by the unchangeable principles based on the elements that go to make up the human person and on his essential relationships. Such things transcend historical circumstances. . . .
>
> Consequently, it is wrong to assert as many do today that neither human nature nor revealed law provide any absolute and unchangeable norms as a guide for individual actions, that all they offer is the general law of charity and respect for the human person. . . .
>
> Since revelation and, in its own sphere, philosophy have to do with the deepest needs of mankind, they inevitably at the same time reveal the unchangeable laws inscribed in man's nature and which are identical in all rational beings.[48]

Definition

Distinct from morals, ethics, and virtues, values are hard to define. Clyde Kluckhohn defined a value as "a conception, explicit or implicit, distinctive of an individual or a group, of the *desirable*, which influences the selection from available modes, means and ends of action."[49] Most literature on values says that a true value is one that is prized and cherished, publicly affirmed when appropriate, freely chosen from among alternatives, and acted upon with consistency and repetition. But values can be in the realm of velleity and not practiced: a thief can hold the value of honesty, a drinker the value of sobriety.

Importance

Values are important in education because education is essentially a moral enterprise. Education by its nature deals with normative concepts (what *should* be) with regard to such basics as the "good person," the "good life," and the "good society." Definitions of the "good" mean values and morals. Inasmuch as another term for education is "personal formation," and this most often reaches people when they are young and impressionable and lasts for life, what values are presented is important not only for the individual but for society and the world.

Values in schooling and education are more important today than ever, because this is a time of crisis for their absence. The world has achieved brilliance without wisdom and power without conscience. Of late, educational liberals as well as conservatives have recognized the impossibility of the "values-neutral" approach and of the nonjudgmental ethical relativism that has been advised for government schools for at least the past two decades.[50] Catholic schools by their nature add a high dimension of interest to these facets of education.[51]

The Responsible Agents

Some scholars think that values can be taught directly and openly only in church-affiliated schools. Most, however, agree that nothing is value-free, that—despite protestations to the contrary—values are taught directly and openly in government schools as well, and that the only differences are in strategies and in the particular values taught. As we shall see in subsequent chapters (especially chapters 6 and 7), the family, the Church, the State, and society all have rights and duties in imparting values, but at the same time all have difficulties. What, then, of educators: teachers, administrators, counselors, and other staff? Because the school is where all the formal agents of education meet, it may rightly be expected to carry a considerable measure of responsibility for imparting values.

Their Sources

For convenience, we may speak of the sources of values as being threefold: God, neighbor, and self. In the Western world values, like morals, come from the transcendent and immanent God of the Judeo-Christian tradition. (In other regions, they come from other gods.) This is true even for atheists, because no one now alive knows what it would be like to live in a world without religion. It is even more true for the educator in the Catholic school, who is in a special way committed to God.

The second source of values is our neighbor, considered not narrowly as the person who lives next door, but broadly as all of human society extending through space and time in the past and present. Values are thus taught by sciences like anthropology and history. There are also sociological influences on values formation: for example, one's peer group, socioeconomic status, country of origin, and rural or urban residency. Americans, for instance, are often characterized as being obsessed with facts, from which they tend to reason inductively, and are suspicious of broad generalizations. They are achievers, intent upon visible results, thriving on competition. Physical comfort and material wealth are values which for them constitute progress. But some other societies reason deductively, do not have as much of a temporal orientation, do not emphasize material things, and do not see the value of looking to the future.

Finally, the self has a role as a source of values. Gender, for example, can be a determinant of values: parents and others present male children with bats and balls and guns and female children with dolls and carriages, allow crying from girls but not from boys, and in other ways impart gender-connected values. Race determines values, in that those who are oppressed or in other ways given differentiating treatment will develop different values than the majority.

One's myths are another determinant that shapes varying values. Contrary to the commonplace definition of myth as a tale uncritically fabricated in an arbitrary way, here myth means a traditional story that serves to encapsulate great truths and thus to unfold part of a worldview. And who are one's heroes? There is a great difference between the values of a Jesus Christ over and against those of a modern "celebrity." Physiological considerations also enter in: if Napoleon had been a few inches taller, it could have changed his values and thus the history of Europe; if, in Pascal's famous remark, Cleopatra's nose "had been shorter, the face of the entire earth would have been completely changed"; if Constantine had had insomnia and not dreamed of a Christ-like figure who promised victory if his troops bore the cross on their standards, the shape of the modern world would not be the same. Age is another consideration: older people pose different values from younger ones. Even climate will have a role: Mediterranean values tend to be more easygoing and volatile than the "efficient" values around the North Sea.

For existentialists, the source of values is *all* in the self. Carl Rogers, a counselor with existentialist leanings, said, "I am the architect of myself."[52] The existentialist emphasizes the immediacy of choice in the valuing process. Kierkegaard explains this concern by saying, "the instant of choice is very serious . . . because there is danger that the next instant it may not be equally in my power to choose."[53] If one does not consider the importance of the immediacy of making a subjective choice, "there comes at last an instant when there no longer is any question of an either/or, not because he has chosen but because he has neglected to choose."[54] Catholic educators must always be sensitive to these considerations.

How We Get Values

How They Are Imparted

There is a growing movement in the United States for "character education," "values education," or "ethical education." In government schools it presents questions about whose values are taught and about the possibility of teaching deep and lasting values without religion. In Catholic schools the search for an effective method of imparting values with a religious underpinning goes on. It is important that all educators conduct and keep up with research in all the nuances of imparting values. All too often, pupils who are in every way exemplary at school frequently turn out to be delinquent, criminal, corrupt in politics, dishonest in business, or (of interest to Catholic schools) nonpractitioners of their faith.

One of the traditional ways for imparting values has been *inculcation*, usually through simple teaching methods. Such methods are considered inadequate, however, because intellectual information does not necessarily change beliefs or penetrate deeply. Discussion methods have also been discarded, because they have been thought not to motivate. And peer group methods are frowned upon for the young because of the immaturity and unreliability of youthful participants.

Another method of imparting values has been *integration*, which means bringing values into the curriculum wherever possible. Asking the teacher to function as a role model of integrated values has become problematic. Most educators no longer want that responsibility. In Catholic as well as in government schools, teachers often feel deserted in the front line of the battle against neglectful parents and an indifferent society.

One theory for the imparting of values, a fad a short time ago but now on the wane, is "Values Clarification." This theory was "discovered" and promulgated by such scholars as Louis E. Raths, Merrill Harmin, and Sidney B. Simon. To tell a student that certain values are good would be, according to them, to manipulate and coerce. So their methods are chiefly indirect and address the *process*. Educators encourage students to reveal their values, and then through various strategies try to clarify the values for the students. The methods involve, first, prizing and cherishing: one is encouraged to lose passivity, to realize actively a value position, and to treasure it. The student must then choose one value or values over conflicting ones. Finally, students are encouraged to act upon their choices. To do all this, values clarificators enlist the aid of various strategies.

By way of positive critique, it must be said that the values-clarification process increases awareness of the issues. It also in many ways improves upon traditional moralizing approaches. Nevertheless, some scholars, many of them Catholic, have mobilized against values clarification. They charge that, to the extent that it has a philosophy, values clarification is most in accord with Pragmatism, with some Existentialism mixed in.

And, say the critics, values clarification does not attempt to go any farther than eliciting awareness. In addition to its superficiality (often amounting to banality and triviality), it is based upon an ethical relativity, which in turn is based upon a confusion of pluralism with relativism. Whereas true pluralism favors a proper tolerance for a diversity of ideas, relativism says that there are no right and wrong answers anywhere, especially in ethics and religion.

Further, Catholic philosophers claim, values clarification theories are based on the social sciences' ostracism of ethics in the name of "value-free social science." But there is *nothing* that is value-free, and most values-clarification strategies emphatically indoctrinate in values. In one of its areas of self-contradiction, values clarification on the one hand believes that values are personal, situational, and individually derived, and on the other hand lists values-based behaviors which are inferior and to be eschewed (for example, apathy, uncertainty, inconsistency, and overconformity) and other values which are superior and to be encouraged for all (among them purposefulness, productivity, consideration, and zestfulness). There results a group of "new conformists" who replace "old" values with "new" ones.

Reliance on peer pressure and a tendency toward coercion to the mean in many activities is a criticism leveled at values-clarification *techniques*. Take, for example, the "values continuum" strategy, in which students select positions on issues presented on a continuum from one extreme to its opposite. One of the items presents the question, "How do you feel about premarital sex?" At one end of the continuum is Virginal Virginia, sometimes called Gloves Gladys, who wears white gloves on every date, both physically and metaphorically. At the opposite end is Mattress Millie, who goes out on every date with a mattress strapped to her back, prepared for any and every contingency.[55] Consider the shy, sensitive, fearful adolescent girl, who is tremulously concerned about her standing with her peers and teacher, having to make a choice. Where is she to place herself on the spectrum? Experience indicates it is toward the center—which means, even for the girl of chaste values, no completely negative position.

Furthermore, much of values clarification's content and methods constitute an invasion of the privacy of students and their families. Although it is true that the method permits students to "pass" when the teacher asks them to complete such open-ended sentences as, "My parents are usually . . . ," students will often realize too late that they have divulged more about themselves and their families than they wanted.

Some say also that values clarification, by presupposing very specific views about human nature and society, becomes a kind of "religious" position in its own right. For example, the theory consistently presents the individual self as the final arbiter of the rightness of values and assumes that the good life is one of self-fulfillment. These positions directly contradict the biblical view that God is the ultimate lawgiver and that the good life is to be found only in losing oneself in the service of God and of people.[56]

How They Are Acquired

For the *acquisition* of values, there is a wide spectrum of theories. Catholic philosophers look first to conscience. Conscience is the practical dictate of reason by which one judges what here and now is to be done as being good or to be avoided as being evil. It is a prudent judgment, whose norms derive from the nature of the human person and of his acts. Among other theorists are behavior modificationists and affectivists. Those who dominate the field, however, are the cognitive developmentalists. They are called cognitive because they claim that moral education, like intellectual education, has its basis in stimulating one's intelligence on moral issues. They are called developmentalists because they see the aims of moral education as being a movement through moral stages.

The idea of cognitive moral development goes back at least as far as Plato and Aristotle.[57] Among more recent proponents have been John Dewey, Erik Erikson, and Jean Piaget. Dewey postulated three developmental stages of moral growth in children.[58] Dewey's stages were further refined by Piaget, who brought to bear the tools of social science — principally interviews and direct observation — on Dewey's theoretical definitions.[59] The leading current theorist is Lawrence Kohlberg.

Initially, Kohlberg posited six stages at three levels of development. They begin with the preconventional level, at which the person (usually a child) responds to cultural rules and labels of good and bad, but interprets these labels either in terms of the physical or the hedonistic consequences of action or in terms of the physical power of those who enunciate the rules. The second level is called the "conventional"; it perceives the maintenance of the expectations of the individual's family, group, or nation as valuable in its own right, regardless of consequences. The attitude is not only one of conformity to social order, but one of loyalty; of actively maintaining, supporting, and justifying the order; and of identifying with the group involved in it. Finally, there is the postconventional, autonomous, or principled level, in which there is a clear effort to define moral values as having validity apart from the authority of the groups or persons holding them.[60]

Gradually, Kohlberg became aware that after stage six, the individual often experiences despair. Such a person has developed principles of justice, and yet is faced with the dilemma of an unjust world. Kohlberg therefore announced that he was exploring a seventh stage, which might be described as a "faith" orientation. This stage involves a person's resolution of such questions as, "What is the ultimate meaning of life?"; "Why be moral?"; and "Is there not a religious morality of love, transcendentally grounded, that is finally more important than cognitive development?"

In stage seven the individual advances from an essentially individual to a cosmic point of view. One achieves the moral strength to act on the principles of justice in an unjust world, and the peace of sensing oneself as a part of the infinite whole. This stage examines belief in a fundamental being: God, or Independent Reality. Though religious, it is pantheistic, in that it equates God with the laws and forces of the universe, and no more. Stage seven, says Kohlberg, appears to be achieved most often by those very few persons who have reached stage six in their early twenties. The faith dimension usually comes later in life and is crucial for those who have achieved the postconventional level of moral awareness. This stage is a reflection of a higher kind of "getting it together." Stage seven is not spoken of very much in the literature, however, and not many people have even heard of it.[61]

From a public hungry and thirsty for knowledge about values, for a long time there were not many criticisms of Kohlberg's theories. Indeed, the use of Kohlberg presented many potential advantages in the classroom: effectiveness in peer group discussions, for example, wherein the arguments of students in higher stages can be used to stimulate those in lower stages; the forcing of educators to be open-ended in presenting content, to see benefit in conflict, and to see the need to integrate this with the rest of the curriculum and with students' experiences of life; and increased awareness that morality and religion are not necessarily the same thing.

But criticisms have been growing, mostly from a philosophical point of view.[62] Among them are the following. Kohlberg concluded with observations on what *is*, even across cultural and geographical lines. This may be psychologically and sociologically acceptable. When one goes on to assert, however, as Kohlberg does, that people are in a moral escalator that everyone should board from one stage to another, he steps over from psychology into a philosophical consideration of *what ought to be*. Kohlberg, recognizing this problem, makes the ultimate claim that, while the "ought" of moral judgment cannot be directly derived from the "is" of cognitive development, each has an important bearing on the other.

Again, Kohlberg's theory, being cognitive, is weak on the affective side of morality. It similarly underemphasizes *will* in morality.[63] Then, too, to assert that one stage is higher than another, and that the aim of education is stage growth, demands a philosophic rationale to explain why, which Kohlberg does not provide.[64] Also, some Kohlbergian assumptions, like identifying prevalence with normality, are pragmatistic. But, strangely for one who seems to lean toward Pragmatism, Kohlberg in maintaining that the stages are essentially *developmental* also maintains that they are quasi-innate, in a rather Platonic way. So there is evidence of his theory's not being sufficiently thought out from a philosophical point of view.

Among other philosophical criticisms are that Kohlberg does not take human sinfulness sufficiently seriously, underemphasizes the importance of the influence of the community in moral development, has a gender bias, and does not consider the relationship between the imagination and action lived out in imitation of significant others like parents.

Patterns of Values

Instrumental Value Theorists

Scholars disagree on whether one can present in advance—a priori—a "shopping bag of values," as opponents of the idea sometimes call it. There are basically two points of view. One is that of the *instrumental* (or contributory) value theorists. Their essential position is that values are determined not by anything intrinsic, but only insofar as they help a person—as well as by prevalence, which they equate with normality. Values are only a means to an end, an instrument; they have, therefore, no permanent worth, no absolute character, and no hierarchy. To a starving man a bowl of soup is of more value than an art masterpiece.

Among those embracing the instrumental value theory are those under the umbrella of Positivism. Moral norms in the positivistic view inevitably contain a noncognitive element, and this vitiates them. What look like statements of fact (for example, "Thou shalt not steal") are really expressions of one's feelings toward a certain action. Such value judgments in this theory of emotivism are neither true nor false. Behold the divorce of ethics from science!

For positivists, value judgments are meaningless because they cannot be verified or justified by the empirical sciences. For the pragmatists among them, like Dewey, inquiry, the method applied in the sciences, is a paradigm in moral activity as well. In the same camp are also atheistic existentialists, who eschew all universal norms (except, paradoxically, authenticity). As subjectivists, they insist that a thing is of value only when it is desired, not before. Their critics argue that these relativists are impaled on the horns of a dilemma: anyone who states that "change is *the* determinant," or "there is only one value: never hurting other people," or "there are no absolute values," is thereby stating absolute values, and cannot avoid so doing.

Intrinsic Value Theorists

Catholics cannot accept the instrumental value theory. The basic position of the *intrinsic* value theory, which they espouse, is that values are within persons, intrinsic to their being. To be without them is to be less a person. Such values as truth, goodness, and life are constant, because human nature is basically the same for all people of all time. The person gives a hierarchy to values, in part by determining the merit accorded them in objective reality. It is mostly realists and idealists who are the intrinsic value theorists. Numbered among them are Saints Augustine and Thomas Aquinas, John Henry Newman, Jacques Maritain, Robert Hutchins, and Mortimer Adler.

New Testament Rootedness of Catholic-School Values

To illustrate which values are important from the viewpoint of Catholicism, we could provide many examples. Some are provided by Church documents which point to patterns, among them

> a freedom which includes respect for others; conscientious responsibility; a sincere and constant search for truth; a calm and peaceful critical spirit; a spirit of solidarity with and service toward all other persons; a sensitivity for justice; a special awareness of being called to be positive agents of change in a society that is undergoing continuous transformation.[65]

We shall deal in greater detail with an example that is more familiar: the New Testament.[66] It illustrates the center of Christian values as well as the intrinsic value theory. The Gospel values presented here are to be understood, however, as only an initial statement of Christian values, not an eternal, universal, or complete presentation. We must begin with the observation that Gospel values are admittedly topsy-turvy when compared with those of the world: "The last shall be first and the first shall be last"; "Whoever exalts himself shall be humbled, but whoever humbles himself shall be exalted"; "Anyone among you who aspires to greatness must serve the rest."[67]

Patterns of values to be held and vices to be avoided are discernible throughout the New Testament. Sometimes they are explicitly mentioned together,[68] and elsewhere they are able to be inferred. Certain overall values pertain to *all of one's relationships* — to God, neighbor, and self. Above all and through all is *love* — universal benevolence to all.[69] Another overall New Testament value is *childlikeness*: "I assure you, unless you change and become like little children, you will not enter the kingdom of God"; "The kingdom of God belongs to such as these [little children]."[70]

Still another overall value is generosity, or *wholeheartedness*. When Jesus was asked the first of all the commandments, he answered in part in words that the religious Jew then and now says in his daily prayers, posts on his door frame, and places in an emblem over his heart — the "Shema": "'Hear, O Israel! . . . you shall love the Lord your God with all your heart, with all your soul, with all your mind, and with all your strength.'"[71]

Pertaining specifically to one's *relationship to God* are values that begin with *faith* in a personal God.[72] There is the value of *worship*, the "courtesy paid to worth" — which, considering God's supereminent worth by definition, brings it about that the worship we owe Him is beyond anything we owe to all others. Certain acts of worship, like prayerfulness, are inferrable as other values to characterize worship.[73] *Religion* is a value that acknowledges that all of life is related to God. *Hope* is still another.[74]

A value that pertains to *both God and neighbor* is *reverence*. We live in an age of technology, which sees almost everything as a means to an end and is therefore irreverent. A well-developed Christian personality, to avoid becoming jaded, cynical, and selfish, prizes the value of reverence. Christians need it for God and whatever else supernatural that they believe in, but they also need it for all creatures of earth. This is seen as particularly true of attitudes toward other people, over and against current dehumanization, the indignity of the designation of persons by number instead of by name, and the modern State's emphasis on standardization and efficiency (values not mentioned in the New Testament).

Values with particular reference to *relationships with other people* begin with *neighborliness* — an awareness of the needs of others and a willingness to meet those needs. Charity begins at home, but should not stay there. Followers of Jesus are expected to have the values enunciated by the beautiful words "compassion" (from the Latin meaning "to suffer with") and "sympathy" (from the Greek meaning the same thing). Christians are expected to perform the works of mercy[75] and to live up to their social obligations to vote, pay taxes, join unions, obey legitimate authorities, and so on.

Responsibility is a New Testament value whose root is freedom. As free causes of our own actions or omissions we must be willing to render an account. Under this category are values like *industry*, *frugality*, and *work*. *Peacemaking* is also extremely important: not just passive peaceloving, but active peacemaking. Peace is oneness with God. *Honesty*, a value which means being in harmony with God's justice, is also fitting. Also proper is *integrity*. This is a value that means wholeness: a person with integrity has all the right spiritual parts, and has them in the right place.

Truthfulness is a value that has particular importance, especially in this age of the big lie. Such values as *forgiveness*, *mercy*, *gentleness*, and being *nonjudgmental*[76] can perhaps be summed up in the phrase "the truth of charity and the charity of truth." There must, of course, be *external charity*: against, for example, such vices as calumny and detraction which result from lack of control of the tongue.[77] There must also be *internal charity*, whereby one restrains judgmental attitudes.

The values of the *self*, too, receive New Testament attention. These begin with *humility*, the specifically Christian value and virtue which sees the proper place of God and one's fellowman in relation to oneself. They contain the important value of *joy*, which is too often forgotten in Christianity. Different from pleasure or delight, joy is something deep-rooted and permanent, like a great artist with his masterpiece. Not something pursued in itself, it is more a result—of love. There is *self-control*, which includes *meekness*, *patience* (which John Milton beautifully called a species of courage), *affability*, and *indignation*. With regard to the last, Christianity is not, as some think, a "doormat" way of life, a fact illustrated by Jesus' anger at the hypocrisy of the Pharisees and his actions with the money changers in the Temple.[78]

Self-denial is a personal value which consists of voluntary acts of *repentance*[79] and submission to involuntary *suffering*, physical and mental. *Detachment*[80] is a paradoxical New Testament value which sees material things as a reflection of God, but at the same time sees their place as relative; like a long string of zeroes, material things have a value only when a number, God or service to Him, is placed in front of them. Subvalues here are *contentment* and the *right relationship to money* and other creatures. Finally, the New Testament values *purity*, both internal and external—an interesting value confronting today's age, which meets all sexual problems by encouragement to circumvent consequences in hundreds of ways other than by the word "no."

Some Special Values for Emphasis Today

Service

For Catholic schools, teaching the truths of religion is not enough. Christian *witness* — what the ancients called *martyrion* — is also an essential part of the teaching of religion. What is more, the teaching of religion goes further than theology in incorporating an *active* component: *service to others*, which requires not only a knowledge of theology or of religion, but special skills as well — skills which schools are to train students to exercise in parishes and in civil communities. The bishops of the United States support the notion of service:

> The Christian community should not be concerned only for itself. Christ did not intend it to live walled off from the world any more than He intended each person to work out his destiny in isolation from others. No human toil, no human sorrow is a matter of indifference to the community established by Jesus. In today's world this requires the Christian community to be involved in seeking solutions to a host of complex problems which undermine community within and among nations. Christians render such service by prayer and worship and also by direct participation in the cause of social reform.[81]

Schools, both elementary and secondary, should provide *opportunities* for service. The school is to perceive that service is basic to fulfill the demands of the Gospel in all communities: the family, the church, the neighborhood, the working world, the civic arena, the international scene, and wherever else one sees opportunities to be of help. Each person must serve the other for the good of all: "He who seeks only himself brings himself to ruin, whereas he who brings himself to nought for me discovers who he is."[82]

By making students rub shoulders with poverty and confront important issues (such as defending one's country versus killing other human beings) social service can force students to explore their moral values and the social consequences of their decisions. It might be good for the whole school to discover from time to time a project or projects for service to the parish or civic community. This could help satisfy those teachers and others who have a penchant for social work, could unite the local Church community, make the pupils permanently aware of the needs around them, and — not incidentally — be of assistance in the area of the chosen project.

There are many possibilities for service: tutoring children, working in orphanages, assisting in welfare offices, volunteering in nursing homes, reading and answering mail for the visually impaired, serving as aides in programs for the handicapped. These services may teach students to make sacrifices for other people, particularly those they don't understand or don't like.[83] A respected study indicates that Catholic high schools are succeeding in promoting concern for others as an integral part of the faith.[84]

Justice

Justice is fidelity to right relationships. Because an interest in justice is an essential part of Christian love and because peace is based on justice, education for justice is a very important part of the Catholic-school curriculum. The contemporary world scene convinces everyone of today's great need for teaching justice. One sees concrete situations of injustice in the human family on the political, economic, and socio-cultural levels.[85]

God speaks in many ways, beginning with the Scriptures. In the Old Testament, one's right relationships which constitute justice were with Yahweh, with neighbor, and with the land. Whereas before Sinai religion might be equated with cult and ritual, at Sinai religion expanded to include social responsibility as an inseparably integral part. Since then, to separate justice from worship is considered idolatry. Knowing and praising God in worship are equated with doing justice. Justice is not an application of faith but its substance: a way of living.[86]

A theme unto itself is Mary's Magnificat. In the context of its joy and gratitude, with its roots in the Old Testament, it is one of the most revolutionary documents in all literature. It contains the seeds of a moral/cultural revolution, a political/social revolution, and an economic revolution.[87] Many of Mary's ideas were taken up by her son and expanded in another New Testament theme, the Beatitudes. In this "Charter of Christianity," Jesus challenges the accepted order in society and gives the ground rules for a new economic, political, cultural, and social order.

Another New Testament justice theme is in the criteria for the Last Judgment.[88] These are feeding the hungry, making the stranger welcome, clothing the naked, visiting the sick, and the like. The justice of the first Christian churches constitute another theme: for example, "The faithful all lived together and owned everything in common. They sold their goods and possessions and shared out the proceeds among themselves according to what each one needed," and "[n]one of the members was ever in want."[89]

In the Gospels, Jesus challenges everyone to a new order, whose values are based on the Magnificat values. He challenges the existing order, especially in the Beatitudes:[90] the *economic* order (which addresses resources: "Happy are the poor . . . Do not store up treasures . . . can't be a slave of two masters . . . where your treasure is, there your heart is also"[91]); the *political* order (which addresses power and consists of a basic Christian community: "the gentle inherit the earth . . . pagan great men make their authority felt . . . not you"); the *cultural* order (which addresses meaning and changes the basic understanding of how society should work, with people building the Kingdom rather than becoming rich and powerful: "Happy are those who mourn . . . those who are persecuted; . . . if your virtue goes no deeper than that of the scribes and Pharisees, you will never enter the Kingdom of heaven . . . you know what was said of old . . . but I say to you . . . When you pray, go to your private room"); the *social* order (which addresses relationships: "Why does your master eat with tax collectors and sinners? . . . His disciples were surprised to find him speaking to a woman . . . the poor will inherit . . . if you love only those who love you . . . if you forgive others, your father will forgive you . . . do not judge . . . treat others as you would like them to treat you . . . the greatest must be the servant").

Jesus challenges his friends and other individuals: Peter on Jesus' identity, on forgiveness, in his denial of Jesus;[92] the messengers of John the Baptist; the young man who wished to be perfect; Thomas; the Samaritan woman; Nicodemus; the Canaanite woman; and others.[93] He challenges his disciples: on riches, on the last being first, on who is greatest in the Kingdom, on mission, on leadership.[94] He challenges Judas Iscariot and others concerning priorities.[95] He challenges the crowds: on the Beatitudes, on divorce, on hoarding possessions versus trust in providence, on almsgiving, on choosing guests.[96]

He challenges the people of Nazareth, the people of Jerusalem, and the Jews.[97] He challenges religious and temporal rulers: the Pharisees and Scribes, Zacchaeus, and the rich in the story of Dives and Lazarus.[98] He challenges Simon the Pharisee concerning Mary Magdalene, the Temple authorities concerning the Law, the Temple money dealers, the Sanhedrin and the high priests about his identity, the chief priests concerning their authority, and even Satan.[99] He challenges the colonial rulers: Pilate, Herod, the police, the soldiers, and the centurion.[100]

The Fathers of the Church continued the concept of the importance of justice in the Church.[101] The modern social teaching of the Church has put no less emphasis on the teaching of justice.[102] But, as we said in the beginning of this section, one big obstacle to building a more just society is a lack of deep understanding and true experience of what it means to be materially poor or deprived in some other way.

Many "good" Catholics, for example, are middle-class, either by birth or education, and view life from a rather high point on the social pyramid. We need personal conversion, initial and ongoing, if we are to be prophetic witnesses to Gospel values. To know about the injustices of poverty, powerlessness, exclusion, and marginalization allows an empathy and an understanding which can form the basis for a genuine relationship with the poor. But it is only the living experience of these phenomena that will free us to really grow through knowing them and to take it from there.[103]

Peace

Peace, along with reconciliation, is a fruit of justice. The Catholic Church takes this value seriously. Vatican II enunciated much about peace. It said, for example, that "the Church, whose duty it is to foster and elevate all that is true, all that is good, and all that is beautiful in the human community, consolidates peace among men for the glory of God."[104] It also voiced the wish that those "engaged in the work of education, especially youth education, and the people who mold public opinion, should regard it as their most important task to educate the minds of men to renewed sentiments of peace."[105] Indeed, teaching peace is a good way to develop nonviolent means to fend off aggression and resolve conflicts, and best reflects the call of Jesus both to love and to justice.

Some see peace as a religious activity.[106] Certainly, both justice and peace have a faith dimension, and the Catholic Church's serious concern for both justice and peace is scripturally based.[107] Although in one study Catholic high-school principals ranked understanding of and commitment to peace twelfth on a list of fourteen goals, much is being done about teaching peace and justice in Catholic schools.[108]

Ecumenism

The study of the outlook of our separated brethren is important, and "should be pursued in fidelity to the truth and with a spirit of good will."[109] To begin with, "all men without exception are called to work together; with much greater reason is this true of all who believe in God, but most of all, it is especially true of all Christians, since they bear the seal of Christ's name."[110] Ecumenism also includes Jews. An interesting 1985 research study of Catholic school curricula indicates "a deep appreciation of Jews and Judaism,"[111] especially of Christianity's rootedness in Judaism. This study showed that Catholic high-school as well as college students have the opportunity today not only to be aware of this common rootedness between Christians and Jews, but also to learn of the persecutions, pogroms, expulsions, forced conversions and a whole range of horrible injustices which have all too frequently come from the Christian side and have characterized their "relationship." . . . Courses on the Holocaust have become part of the required courses in high schools, some elementary schools and in almost all the colleges and universities.[112]

The negative image of the Pharisees as an aspect of Judaism requires, and is receiving, correction in Catholic schools. An area of omission is "the lack of emphasis given to guidelines in the proper understanding of the passion of Jesus and the events surrounding it."[113] And more must be done to help Christians to better comprehend the Jewish understanding of *Torah, People,* and *Land.*[114]

As a result of ecumenical programs, from "the treasures of the many traditions, past and present, which are alive in other churches and ecclesial communities,"[115] the spiritual life of Catholics can be nourished. There are many other purposes, among them

> to increase among students a deeper knowledge of the faith, the spirituality and the entire life and doctrine of the Catholic Church, so that they may wisely and fruitfully take part in ecumenical dialogue each according to his capabilities, to direct their attention both to that inward renewal of the Catholic Church itself which will help so much to promote unity among Christians, and to those things in their own lives or in the life of the Church which hinder or slow down progress towards unity; a further purpose is that teachers and students should learn more about other Churches and communities, and so understand better and assess more correctly what unites Christians and what divides them; finally, . . . the aim is that those taking part in them should better realize the obligation of fostering unity between Christians and so be led to apply themselves more effectively to achieving it. They will also be led to do what is in their power to give joint Christian witness to the contemporary world.[116]

An immediately apparent problem is, of course, that these programs, if not properly and carefully done, may lead to students coming away with an attitude of relativism in religion. All involved must be mindful that there "can be no ecumenism worthy of the name without interior conversion. For it is from newness of attitudes of mind, from self-denial and unstinted love, that desires of unity can take their rise and develop in a mature way."[117]

The Future of Values

Many look to such disasters as the nuclear bomb, the Chernobyl accident, or the AIDS epidemic as a hopeful awakening and source of renewed values for humanity. Unfortunately, it usually does not happen that way. The Black Death of 1348, for example, was catastrophic: in some places one out of every two people died. People did not then understand that bacteria caused plagues, nor that rats from seaports in that era of increased navigation could be the carriers. So far as they knew, this cataclysm was a visitation from God in punishment for their sins. One could expect, therefore, a renewal of religious exercises and a concentration upon man's last ends: death, judgment, and eternal sentence. And so there was. But there were also defiant dances of death, and a revival of the ancient epicurean maxim of "eat, drink, and be merry, for tomorrow we die!"

Others look to some kind of wholesome "social mutation" in humankind emerging from a heightened awareness. Unfortunately, there is insufficient evidence to substantiate this. Probably closer to the truth is the fact that decisive turns of values in human history are made not so much by great cataclysms or highly imaginative hypotheses, but by some personage(s) tipping the sensitive scales ever so slightly in one direction or another.

For this to happen, the climate must be right. A sufficient number of people must be prepared. Catholic schools should be helping in that preparation. With very young children, Catholic educators must stimulate them to retain and develop their natural sense of wonder, which schools often kill off. When the young become adolescents, with their sense of wonder preserved, they must be encouraged to develop empathy, a prime value consonant with their maturation process. When they reach adulthood, one of the foremost values they must consciously keep is civility. No matter what our differences, we have a need to keep open the channels of discourse.

In 1982, one hundred and twenty people representing Catholic education from approximately forty countries met at an assembly at Bangkok, Thailand, to take a long-range look at values education. They attempted to arrive at a consensus that respects local situations and prepares for the values of the year 2000. The values they proposed were cultural, admitting that "cultural values equally take shape in a social context." They saw the "Western" world as imbued with the idea of success, not free of a materialistic conception of existence and a competitive spirit.

African cultures, on the other hand, they saw as giving precedence to respect for physical life as the expression of harmony between living persons and their ancestors. In most third world countries, the first values hoped for and eagerly sought are those that are essential to a minimum of human dignity.[118] The assembly chose four major values as decisive for the generation of the year 2000: respect for others as others, creativity, responsible solidarity, and interiority. These are closely interconnected. Like the values of Jesus, they run counter to the value systems of some of our society.

The Catholic school will translate *respect for others* by welcoming the child as he or she is and by avoiding any natural inclination to uniformity. *Creativity* will foster the divergent intelligence, which is the source of inventiveness, as much as if not more than convergent thinking, which is geared to standardized reproduction in the learning process. The Catholic school, if it is to be faithful to its cocreative mission of transforming the world, must foster the creative mission of its teachers and students by including studies of creativity—what it is and how to nourish it. *Responsible solidarity* must replace the spirit of competition and rivalry which too often prevails in schools. *Interiority* stresses the importance of prayer in the school community, and encourages children to formulate value judgments, to give thanks, and to forgive; it leads children to *be* more rather than to *have* more.

Prescinding from that report, all of us, no matter what our philosophy of life, seek the freedom to "be all you can be," the modern slogan equivalent to the ancient Pythagorean goal of education to "become what you are." The personal liberation we seek has its root in self-transcendence. We must in some way get beyond our "selves." This self-transcendence includes an intellectual, a moral, and an affective elevation of ourselves. As intellectual, this conversion and elevation means drawing a definite distinction between the world of immediacy and the world of deeper meaning. As moral, it acknowledges a distinction between satisfactions and values, and wherever values conflict with satisfactions it is committed to values. As affective, this change means commitment to the values of love in the home, loyalty in the community, and faith in the destiny of humankind.

CONTROVERSIAL SUBJECTS

Because of their importance, many controversial areas should be present in the Catholic-school curriculum. Among them are human rights, nuclear energy, the arms race, the unequal distribution of wealth, consumerism, discrimination, and the ecology. Because sex is so omnipresent and so critical as regards values and personal development, it too must be in the curriculum:

sex is the source of the biological, psychological and spiritual characteristics which make a person male or female and which thus considerably influence each individual's progress towards maturity and membership of society.[119]

But the generation-long increase in "openness," "candor," and "information" about sex has not brought any decline in premarital pregnancies, venereal disease, and other sexual problems.

The Catholic Church has maintained that information is only one part of sex education. The other parts have to do with moral and spiritual education.[120] With sex instruction for children, the overtones, for all the reasons given elsewhere in these pages, should be set by the parents. They are irreplaceable.[121] If they do not teach sex in the home, out of embarrassment or for any other reason, they are remiss and, like a dropped stitch, no other party — school, clergyman, or whatever — can make it up.[122]

But silence is not a valid norm of conduct in this matter, above all when one thinks of today's very influential "hidden persuaders." If because of parental neglect or for any other reason the school becomes involved in this delicate matter, sex education must, as with all education, be carried out in agreement with the family.[123] The Church continues to think it important to teach sexual "purity and its radiant splendour," because this "virtue emphasizes man's dignity and opens man to a love which is true, magnanimous, unselfish and respectful of others."[124]

AREAS FOR POSSIBLE IMPROVEMENT

There are some areas where the Catholic-school curriculum might improve. Citizenship education is one. Catholics do not seem to have been trained sufficiently in civic virtue and, if they are to impart their vision of humanity and the world to their communities, there must be greater use of the democratic process by way of more active Catholic participation in civic affairs. Another area for improvement is familiarity with the modern marvel of computers. In Catholic schools computer education must include the ethical and moral questions raised by the impact of this advancing technology.

A really large area for improvement is the fine arts. They are "rightly classed among the noblest activities of man's genius."[125] The Church looks upon art as being not only technique, but beauty — and beauty is truth. The Church has explicitly and repeatedly expressed approval of the arts. Pope Pius XII, for example, wrote: "Art is the most living, most comprehensible expression of human thought and sentiment, the one that most profoundly penetrates the intelligence and sensibility of man."[126] And Vatican II said:

> [L]iterature and art . . . seek to give expression to man's nature, his problems and his experience in an effort to discover and perfect man himself and the world in which he lives; they try to discover his place in history and in the universe, to throw light on his suffering and his joy, his needs and his potentialities, and to outline a happier destiny in store for him. Hence they can elevate human life. . . .[127]

In turn, *sacred* art "should be worthy, becoming, and beautiful, signs and symbols of things supernatural."[128]

It is never too early to encourage artistic taste "so that they [children] can use discrimination in choosing the publications, films and broadcasts that are set before them."[129] In particular, school curricula should provide children with film literacy. Film is the modern popular art form, and film's education involvement is a deep, effective, powerful influence. Film "exerts a strong influence on education, knowledge, culture and leisure."[130] Many films that are considered classics reflect the human condition and "have dealt with specifically religious themes."[131] They can deepen and broaden sensitivity.

Several considerations from a purely practical point of view demand that film literacy be updated and emphasized in the Catholic-school curriculum. By the time students reach eighteen, they will have spent two years before the television screen, longer than time spent on any other activity except sleep. Film is a teacher of morality, so sophistication is necessary. Film is on the ascendancy. New technology is now available which will involve the viewer more and more: for example, buttons installed on seats which the audience can push to determine the course of a film.[132]

The Church's *Decree on the Means of Social Communication* often suggests the inclusion of instruction on the media in school curricula. For one example, it said that if they are to use the media properly,

> [p]rojects designed to effect [instruction and practical experience in each of the media], especially among the young, should be encouraged and multiplied in Catholic schools at all levels . . . and should be directed in accordance with the principles of Christian morality.[133]

Instructions in social communications should be present in religious education.[134] Youth should be encouraged to take up careers in social communications.[135]

And the clergy have "a clear duty to contribute to Christian education in this field . . . with the social teachings of the Church in mind."[136] Catholic leaders ought to be competitive with their message, sponsoring not only dull television programs for the wee hours of Sunday morning when most people are asleep, but emotional, passionate, interesting, comic, sad, suspenseful, dramatic, attractive programs for prime time as well.

CONCLUSION

Catholic-school goals should be reflected in and implemented by the curriculum. The two major qualities that differentiate the Catholic-school curriculum from others are the importance it openly accords to religion and its unique presentation of values. The Catholic school's inclusion of the Roman Catholic religion is unabashedly and without question or doubt a contribution not only to its students, but also to the community and the nation. The ways in which religion should best be present in the curriculum, however, are not as simple as some might think.

In our time of crisis, the values taught in the Catholic school are especially important (again to the community and nation) for their absence. Values originate with God by way of such revelation as the New Testament, with our neighbor broadly considered, and with our selves. Like religion, their inclusion in the curriculum is not as uncomplicated as it may at first seem. Catholic theories differ from others with regard to the imparting and acquiring of values, as well as in the values they prize and cherish.

We shall now see some of the influences on the curriculum placed by such responsible agents as the family, the Church, and the State, the school's external and internal atmosphere, teachers, students, and leadership.

QUESTIONS FOR DISCUSSION

Is knowledge good in and of itself, or only for use (is it an unqualified good or is it to have a market value)?

How is the student's progress in religion to be graded: by the student's knowledge? Faith practice? Good-willed effort? Life commitment?

How does one deal with a Catholic-school student's personal preference for agnosticism or atheism?

Should Catholic schools, especially where a good number of students or teachers are non-Catholic, merely teach *about* religion?

To what extent should there be prayers in the curriculum? Observance of religious holydays?

Can religious instruction for Catholics be satisfactorily provided in government schools?

If one rejects "values clarification" and other modern approaches to the imparting of values on philosophical/theological/religious grounds, how is one to inculcate values successfully?

What is the Catholic schools' unifying principle?

"Morality" comes from *mores*, "the customs of a people." Are persons moral, therefore, if they conform to the customs of their people?

What knowledge is of most worth?

Is it possible to provide a basis for the teaching of morality independent of religion?

Can schooling provide character formation without the teaching of religion?

What are the basic traits and qualities, in the order of importance, which you believe constitute character? Justify your list.

What are the personal character traits which are common to practicing Catholics trained in a good Catholic school and citizens of a democracy?

Should the curriculum be more concerned with intellectual or with moral virtue?

Given present-day realities, many "enlightened" people say that young people are going to do it anyway, so rather than waste time shouting a futile "Don't," maybe we ought only to teach them to do it responsibly. Supply them with the information, the resources, and the devices to eliminate the worst of the consequences of their doing it. Would the same "enlightened" people maintain the same position with drugs as with sex? Why or why not?

If values remain outside the pale of rational discussion and are held as only matters of taste or private intuitions, can they be academically respectable? Are they doomed to be the thinnest parts of the curriculum?

Is today's sex education based on the assumption that good information leads to good behavior? Is this a good assumption?

SUGGESTED BIBLIOGRAPHY

Curriculum Theory

Connelly, F. Michael. *Curriculum Inquiry.* New York: Wiley, 1983.

Provides comprehensive definitions of curriculum and curriculum objectives, and gives case studies.

McNeil, John D. *Curriculum: A Comprehensive Introduction.* Boston: Little, Brown, 1985.

Discusses varied curricular emphases, such as those of humanism, social reconstruction, technology, and academia; gives their characteristics, objectives, and possible future trends.

Walker, Decker F., and Jonas F. Soltis. *Curriculum and Aims*. New York: Teachers College Press, 1986.

Very readable discussion of curriculum theory with an emphasis on prompting thought about the purposes, content, and structure of education. Includes case studies and questions.

Religion in the Curriculum

Felderhoff, M. C., ed. *Religious Education in a Pluralistic Society*. London: Hodder and Stoughton, 1985.

Articles and responses from Westhill College, of the University of Birmingham, on subjects like education and diversity of belief, the educational role of theology, and the legitimacy of religious education in secular institutions.

Giroux, Henry, and David Purpel, eds. *The Hidden Curriculum and Moral Education*. Berkeley, Calif.: McCutchen, 1983.

A collection of essays by authors such as Gilligan, Freire, and Kohlberg, discussing school influences outside the formal curriculum.

Laghi, Pio. "Taking Stock of the Catechetical Renewal," in *Origins*. Washington, D.C.: U.S. Catholic Conference, 1976.

A timely symposium on ways in which catechesis could be renewed in order to give youth important instructions on the Catholic faith.

Lord, Eric, and Charles Bailey, eds. *A Reader in Religious and Moral Education*. London: SCM, 1973.

Articles by scholars on interesting areas of religious education.

National Conference of Catholic Bishops. *To Teach as Jesus Did*. Washington, D.C.: U.S. Catholic Conference, 1973.

In consultation with priests, religious, parents, students, professional educators, and others, the United States bishops deal with many educational problems.

Nichols, Kevin. *Cornerstone*. Middlegreen, Slough, England: St. Paul, 1978.

A forthright presentation of the presence which religion should have in the curriculum.

O'Leary, D. J., and T. Sallnow. *Love and Meaning in Religious Education: An Incarnational Approach to Teaching Christianity*. Oxford: Oxford University Press, 1982.

A theology of revelation, an educational theory, and a curriculum model.

Smart, Ninian, and Donald Horder, eds. *New Movements in Religious Education*. London: Temple Smith, 1975.

Presents the approaches of various experts on new movements in the religious content of the curriculum, many of particular interest to our present work.

Values

Aquinas, Thomas. *Summa Theologica*. 1a 2ae, 7.18–20. Trans. by English Dominican Province. New York: McGraw-Hill, 1964ff.

An excellent primary source for a moral theology based upon Classical Realism.

Aristotle. *Nicomachean Ethics*. Indianapolis, Ind.: Bobbs-Merrill, 1981. (Also in Loeb Classical Library and other editions.)

Aristotle's discussions of "what is the good for man?" in this primary source are still very relevant from a realist perspective. Books I, II, and III especially helpful for the student of values.

Aune, Bruce. *Kant's Theory of Morals.* Princeton, N.J.: Princeton University Press, 1979.

A concise and clear synthesis of Kantian idealist morality from various works of Kant.

Buber, Martin. *I and Thou.* 2nd ed. New York: Scribner's, 1958.

To this Jewish existentialist, encountering "You" is encountering God, and the social sphere is thus given a religious dimension.

Dewey, John. *Moral Principles in Education.* Boston: Houghton Mifflin, 1909.

Dewey discusses the social and psychological factors in moral education from his pragmatistic perspective.

_____. *Theory of the Moral Life.* New York: Holt, Rinehart and Winston, 1960.

A new edition of Part II of John Dewey's *Ethics,* originally published in 1908 and once widely used in ethics courses.

_____. *Theory of Valuation.* University of Chicago Press, 1939.

Valuation as being empirically verifiable.

Dykstra, Craig. *Vision and Character: A Christian Educator's Alternate to Kohlberg.* New York: Paulist, 1981.

Presents adequately the promise of its title.

Gouinlock, James. *John Dewey's Philosophy of Value.* New York: Humanities, 1972.

Collects Dewey's naturalistic and positivistic thoughts serving to clarify and unify his ethical philosophy. Relates Dewey's conception of values to his theory of nature.

Hall, Brian P. *Value Clarification as Learning Process; A Guidebook of Learning Strategies.* New York: Paulist, 1973.

Designed for students and teachers from high school to adult education for growth in clarification of values; contains values clarification exercises.

Hall, Brian P., and Maury Smith. *Value Clarification as Learning Process; A Handbook for Christian Educators.* New York: Paulist, 1973.

Helps for Christian educators to develop their own curriculum for values clarification.

Hall, Brian, Janet Kalven, Larry Rosen, and Bruce Taylor, eds. *Readings in Value Development.* Ramsey, N.J.: Paulist, 1982.

Readings from many sources and many points of view.

Contains a bibliography of positivist authors.

Hersh, Richard H., John P. Milleer, and Glen D. Fielding. *Models of Moral Education: An Appraisal.* New York: Longman, 1980.

Presents six models for moral development: rationale building, consideration, values clarification, values analysis, cognitive development, and social action.

Honig, Bill. *Last Chance for our Children.* Reading, Mass.: Addison-Wesley, 1985.

Criticizes values clarification theory as being "institutionalized public amorality."

James, William. *Essays on Faith and Morals.* New York: New American Library, 1962.

From James's pragmatistic perspective, discusses the nonexistence of a predetermined ethical philosophy.

The Journal of Value Inquiry. An international philosophical quarterly published by Martinus Nijhoff, 9–11 Lange Voorhout, P.O. Box 269, The Hague, Netherlands.

Kay, William. *Moral Education; A Sociological Study of the Influence of Society, Home and School.* London: George Allen and Unwin, 1975.

Traces the social influences of the home, society, and the school on individual moral traits and attitudes.

Kohlberg, Lawrence. *Essays on Moral Development.* Vol. I: *The Philosophy of Moral Development.* New York: Harper and Row, 1981.

Essays Kohlberg wrote after his presentation of his theory.

―――――. "Stages of Moral Development as a Basis for Moral Education," *Moral Education: Interdisciplinary Approaches*, ed. C. M. Beck et al. University of Toronto Press, 1971, pp. 23–92.

Kohlberg here contrasts other approaches to moral education – including the "hidden curriculum" and "bag of virtues" – to his.

Maritain, Jacques. *Education at the Crossroads*. New Haven, Conn.: Yale University Press, 1961.

From Maritain's realist viewpoint, considers moral reeducation a matter of urgency.

Maslow, Abraham H. *Religions, Values, and Peak-Experiences*. New York: Viking, 1964.

Sees "peak experiences" as natural; in a chapter on values, sees values moving from the religious community to that of education.

Meilander, Gilbert G. *The Theory and Practice of Virtue*. Notre Dame, Ind.: University of Notre Dame Press, 1984.

A philosophical account of virtue drawing on Plato, Josef Pieper, and Lawrence Kohlberg.

National Catholic Educational Association. *Vision and Values in the Catholic School: Participant's Guide*. Washington, D.C.: National Catholic Educational Association, 1985.

Resource and planning book for integrating Gospel values within the total curriculum.

Pennant Educational Materials (4680 Alvarado Canyon Rd., San Diego, Calif. 92120). *Values Education Catalogue: Resource Materials for All Ages*.

Phi Delta Kappan, vol. LVI no. 10 (June 1975), "A Special Issue on Moral Education," 659–711.

Various views in articles on the cognitive developmental approach, Kohlberg, values clarification, moral education in several countries, and a reader survey.

Raths, Louis E., Merrill Harmin, and Sidney B. Simon. *Values and Teaching: Working with Values in the Classroom*. Columbus, Ohio: Merrill, 1966.

Considered the first major book on values clarification, it is divided into three sections: theoretical, strategies in the process, and application of the theory.

Rogers, Carl R. *Freedom to Learn*. Indianapolis, Ind.: Bobbs-Merrill, 1969.

Concerned with self-reliant learning and its differences from "conventional" learning. Part IV is concerned with finding and determining values. Good annotated bibliography.

Scharf, Peter, ed. *Readings in Moral Education*. Introduction by Lawrence Kohlberg. Minneapolis, Minn.: Winston, 1978.

Selections focus on the cognitive-developmental approach; excellent foreword describing how the American political situation leads to interest in moral education.

Schulman, Michael, and Eve Mekler. *Bringing Up a Moral Child*. Reading, Mass.: Addison-Wesley, 1985.

A guide for parents by psychological clinicians, challenging the work of Piaget and Kohlberg. Provides examples to show the effectiveness of consistent moral instruction.

Simon, Sidney B., Leland W. Howe, and Howard Kirschenbaum. *Values Clarification; A Handbook of Practical Strategies for Teachers and Students*. New York: Hart, 1972.

Major part of book consists of seventy-nine strategies for values clarification, each with many examples; includes instructions for use.

Simon, Sidney B., Merrill Harmin, and Howard Kirschenbaum. *Clarifying Values Through Subject Matter*. Minneapolis, Minn.: Winston, 1973.

138 · THE CATHOLIC SCHOOL

Discusses three-level teaching for the teacher: facts, concept, and values teaching. Presents short examples of three-level teaching in various subjects, with emphasis on how values can be incorporated.

Simon, Sidney B., and Howard Kirschenbaum, eds. *Readings in Values Clarification.* Minneapolis, Minn.: Winston, 1973.

Selections provide an overview of the values clarification approach. Good annotated bibliography, organized chronologically.

Social Education. Official Journal of the National Council for the Social Studies, 1200 17th Street N.W., #405, Washington, D.C. 20036. Especially vol. 39 no. 1 (January 1975) and vol. 40 no. 4 (April 1976), on moral education.

The January 1975 issue begins with a basic explanation of Kohlberg's theory, then applies it, and includes an article on the teacher's accountability for moral education. The April 1976 issue focuses on the cognitive-developmental approach, and includes an article by Kohlberg and a critique by Jack Fraenkel.

Superka, Douglas. *Values Education Sourcebook: Conceptual Approaches, Materials Analyses, and Annotated Bibliography.* Boulder, Colo.: Social Science Education Consortium, 1976.

Good overview of values education approaches and descriptions of available materials to date of publication.

Taylor, A. E. *The Faith of a Moralist.* London: Macmillan, 1980.

The Gifford lectures of an Anglican idealist metaphysician and student of Plato.

Van Caster, Marcel. *Values Catechetics.* New York: Newman, 1970.

The Christian significance of human values, related to economic and social development, work, freedom, and love and sexuality.

World Religions Curriculum Development Center, 6425 West 33rd Street, Minneapolis, Minn. 55426.

A source for materials incorporating values into curriculums.

Zygon: Journal of Religion and Science. Edited by the Center for Advanced Study of Religion and Science (University of Chicago Press, 5801 Ellis Avenue, Chicago, Ill. 60637).

Periodical committed to seeking to apply science to the advancement of religious and moral ideas. See especially articles by Ralph Wendell Burhoe.

Chapter 6

INITIAL PARTNERS IN
THE PROCESS:
FAMILY AND CHURCH

AGENTS OF SCHOOLING AND EDUCATION

Although it is theoretically possible for education to just *happen*, usually it takes place through partners who work for it: agents. An agent is a person or thing (institution, structure, or other organism) that performs an action through which a result is generated: in short, a vehicle which produces an effect. Agents of education are formal and informal. Informal agents comprise peripheral vehicles like mass media and peer groups. Formal agents are more concrete and direct in their impact. The formal agents of education, those *ultimately* responsible for getting it done, are in turn distinguished as being primary and secondary. These agencies do not work in isolation, but interact. Sometimes, indeed, they conflict.

The *primary* agents of education are God and the student. God sustains the whole educational enterprise in existence, as He does all being. Under God, no matter what excellence one provides in the way of equipment, teaching, and the rest, there has to be student self-activity. If the student is not actively involved, all is in vain. Education is not an individual activity, however, but a social one. In the process, three principal groupings are in partnership: the family, the Church, and the State, and "education which is concerned with man as a whole, individually and socially, in the order of nature and in the order of grace, necessarily belongs to all these three societies."[1] The family, the Church, and the State are the *secondary agents* or partners of education. In this chapter, we shall deal with the family and the Church.

THE FAMILY
Definition of the Family

To evaluate the role, meaning, and importance of the family in the education of children, one must first consider the complex question of what a family is. The *nuclear* family consists of two married adult parents and one or more children (whether generated by the spouses or adopted), all of whom live together. The nuclear family is composed of two generations having different needs, prerogatives, obligations, and functions. It also comprises persons of two sexes which (traditionally) have different though complementary roles and functions. This contrasts with the *extended* family, which includes near relatives and in which collateral lines are kept fairly distinct. We are speaking here of the nuclear family.

In the traditional nuclear family the members of the unit are committed to and responsible for each other. Because, however, in any human institution what is meant to be and what actually is are not always the same, we need to be aware of some of the potential drawbacks of nuclear family life. One must at the same time remember, however, that most drawbacks also contain opportunities for growth — in some cases growth in directions which humankind may need most.

Among the family's challenges, the first concerns sharing, with the other members of the family, time, talents, and possessions. This is not to every individual's liking. There is also the potential loss of privacy, as members of a group tend to impinge on personal space. Third is the alteration of individual freedom, since living in a group situation demands that one consider the impact of one's behavior on others. Still another challenge is rules and regulations: the necessary guidelines often require consideration of others' desires, goals, and values, and at times entail compromise.

A fifth limitation is legal and moral ties. If a child does something wrong, the family as a group is responsible for the wrong and for the disciplinary action to follow. Sixth, the family can easily be the "seed ground" for rivalry, jealousy, and competitiveness, and even serious abuse and neglect. Lastly, a current indictment leveled at the family is that it does not do what it purports to do: the family, which is supposed to be nurturing, caring, and giving, is often just the opposite, a fact which often mars or obscures the constructiveness of the group's activity.[2]

Some authors offer the thesis that the family is dying and perhaps should be abolished.[3] But the dirge for the family is the result of a perceived rather than actual failure. The family itself as an entity need not be judged as the cause of all its shortcomings: the cause may, rather, be the lack of concern and leadership on the part of major societal institutions. Thus, to discuss the family and its various roles and responsibilities we need to be aware of the traditional definition of family and its possible translation into present-day society. For Catholics, as for many religious denominations, the challenges of surviving in a changing pluralistic society have made life increasingly frustrating as the teachings of the Church often conflict with the social messages of the secular culture.

Marriage for the Catholic is companionate, inasmuch as it fosters the growth, development, and friendship of the couple. It is a process: a continuing development rather than merely a static state of life entered into with the public exchange of vows. Because of its sacramental character, marriage is indissoluble: the two people commit to one another not only their persons, but their faith, their relation to God in Christ. One of the primary purposes of marriage—in addition, of course, to the procreation and nurture of children—is the mutual support of the spouses.

Importance

A person's educational formation cannot be understood properly without first considering the critical role which the family plays in the developmental process. Infants require prolonged, constant, and consistent nurturant care. The early stages of the life cycle transpire within the family nest and evolve either favorably or unfavorably, depending in great measure upon how "parental persons" guide the child.

The contribution of the family to the education of youth is so awesomely important that we begin our considerations of agents with this community. Indeed, as Pope John Paul II pointed out, in the new Code of Canon Law the whole treatment of education begins with the word "parents."[4] Marriage is so important that Christ made it one of only seven sacraments. The sacramentality of marriage is something which a couple manifests more perfectly as their relationship grows. In the context of the family and education, the teachings of the Catholic Church are corroborated by information provided by social science research.

The rights of the Christian family are primary not only chronologically, but also in the order of priority. The family forms the earliest and most persistent influence on the child's way of life. All subsequent experiences, behavior, value judgments, and life decisions will mirror the early foundations established by the family.[5] The family, a universal phenomenon, is a critical institution ordained by God[6] to enable children to grow into integrated, self-realizing, and responsible adults.

The reality of the family as a basic unit and bulwark for individual and societal growth is not merely a sociologial or psychological fact: it is also a basic theological fact which is rooted in the heuristic understanding of the Church. The Church has recently begun to use the term "domestic church" to signify the home where parents and children embody, communicate, and concretize the reality of God's saving grace[7] and where "the parents, by word and example, are the first heralds of the faith with regard to their children."[8]

Virtually every society entrusts the family, knowingly or unknowingly, with the task of providing for the child's basic survival needs while simultaneously transmitting societal values, culture, techniques of adaptation, and language. In its "Charter of the Rights of the Family," the Church has summarized many of those rights "that are inherent in that natural and universal society which is the family."[9] Among these rights, "parents have the original, primary and inalienable right to educate . . . their children in conformity with their moral and religious convictions."[10]

Although the constitutions of some democratic states explicitly affirm that the family is the basic unit of society, the word "family" is absent from the founding documents of the U.S. republic. This does not mean that this republic is antifamily, but that our documents simply reflect the age of "Enlightenment" in which they were written: a time that emphasized *individualism* and a desire to protect the freedom of the individual from the overwhelming power of the State.

If the individualist time bomb has not gone off during the two centuries since the Constitution was written, it is because of the accumulated moral capital of the Judeo-Christian heritage of the country. The current legal revolution is both sign and effect of the diluting of that moral capital. But the reality is that the family, not the individual, is the fundamental social reality. The family is prior to the individual, and all persons are born into a family and live their lives as the continuators of that family. And as the mediating structures of the family and the Church are weakened, the age-old confrontations between the naked individual and the omnipotent State increase. Such confrontations ultimately tend toward the absorption of the individual by the State. Paradoxically, the very survival of individualism depends on the survival of the family.

Rights, Responsibilities, and Reasons

Parents have an essential but not exclusive right and duty in education because they are the ones who brought their children into the world, are closest to them, love them the most dearly, know them the best, and have the most intimate and longest-lasting influence over them. The family, a natural society established by God for the procreation and formation of offspring, has a priority of rights over civil society. Christianity teaches that parents, who have conferred life on their children, have a most solemn obligation to educate them. Parents are the first and foremost educators. This does not give them the first competence or the first charism, but the first opportunity. The family is the first school, the basic institution.[11]

One point to be kept in mind when discussing rights and duties in schooling and education is the principle of subsidiarity. Succinctly put, this principle of social philosophy means that the primary responsibility to meet human needs rests first with competent individuals, and only then with the group. Higher levels of community assume this responsibility only when the more basic unit either cannot or will not assume it. Pope Pius XI said that "it is an injustice and at the same time a grave evil and a disturbance of right order to transfer to the larger and higher collectivity functions which can be performed and provided for by lesser and subordinate bodies."[12] As applied to education, the primary right belongs to the family. When civil society provides help as needed, it must do so with due respect and consideration for the wishes of the parent.[13] To every right, however, there is a corresponding duty or responsibility:

> It is . . . the duty of parents to create a family atmosphere inspired by love and devotion to God and their fellow-men which will promote an integrated, personal and social education of their children. . . . It is therefore above all in the Christian family . . . that children should be taught to know and worship God and to love their neighbor. . . . In it, also, they will have their first experience of a well-balanced human society and of the Church. Finally it is through the family that they are gradually initiated into association with their fellow-men in civil life and as members of the people of God.[14]

That serious duty must be maintained, even in the face of the current rapidity of social and cultural change which has altered and sometimes weakened the family's capacities.

The early Christian Fathers appear to have been keenly aware that the deterioration of moral character as well as the general social disorganization during the decline of ancient Rome was related to the deterioration of the family.[15] If that connection is true, our declining family structure is a predictor of what eventually is to become of our own society.

There are negative trends which serve to fragment the Christian family. Especially since the late 1960s psychologists, sociologists, religious associations, and educators' groups have expressed growing concern over the fact that the family has been breaking down into isolated units of mother, father, and children. The *National Catechetical Directory* lists as evidence for the progressive fragmentation of the Christian family the increasing divorce rate, single-parent households, dual-career parents with their accompanying latch-key children, and a rising postponement of marriage due to career pursuits and the pressures of an immature, materialistic society.

This list could easily be expanded to include such current social phenomena as the lack of kinship in the family, confused marital roles, vague and faddish views of child rearing, technological advances which serve to alienate persons more and more (for example, personal television and audio equipment), and the change from the family as the important unit of economic production to the individual as the important unit of economic consumption.

Moreover, the women's liberation movement, which has challenged the traditional roles of males as well as females, has shaken the family structure even further. The position of women has changed for a number of reasons: their increased educational and financial status, a desire (and sometimes need) to work outside the home, a desire for recognition as productive members of the work force, the advent of the pill, abortion legislation which allows choice in mothering and child rearing, and a new confidence on the part of women that they can achieve on their own and gain satisfaction by doing so.

Traditional married life is becoming less and less the rule, and some are searching for an adequate substitute for that intimacy and mutual assistance ordinarily provided by the family. It has been easy for modern society to criticize the conventional family, but underlying the criticisms and fruitless search for family substitutes lie widespread loneliness, isolation, and an alarming increase in suicide rates. As a result of the experimentation in "becoming an individual," there are homeless, deprived children who have little hope of developing into capable, stable, and productive adults. The cult of the individual has, ironically, destroyed many possibilities of self-realization by removing the social and personal supports which encourage it.

Family Roles in Child Development

The first observation we must make about the role of the family and of each member in education is that the teachings of the Catholic Church and the best findings of social science on the subject support one another. For example, Pope John Paul II's *Familiaris consortio* — the most recent major instance of Church teaching on the family — corroborates scientific research and underlines some important aspects of parental education of children. It says that the parental right to educate is essential, original, primary, irreplaceable, and inalienable, and that parental love is the source, animating principle, and norm of such education. Parents, in the eyes of the Church, are called upon to do more than physically beget their children, feed them, and start their moral and intellectual education, only to turn them over to schools to finish the job. The educational role of parents is as basic a responsibility as begetting life in the first place.[16]

The apostolic exhortation, in part an encapsulation of previous Church teachings, makes it the responsiblity of the Catholic parent to form Christian persons who will contribute to the forum of life. It expects Catholic families to teach their children the beliefs of the Church and participation in its practices. But the responsibility of the Catholic parent in educating the child does not end there: it includes forming relationships with and participating in the activities provided by the other educational agents of society. The formation of the kind of mind and heart which is of most interest to the Catholic family is concerned especially with instructing the child in moral and social virtues stemming from unconditional love within the family and parental modeling of virtue.

Parental rights can be neither usurped nor surrendered: according to the papal document, the only instance in which supervision and educational direction can be taken from the parents and delegated elsewhere is in the case of neglect, abuse, a hateful and rejecting familial circumstance, or any combination of these. This often creates difficulties given the current legal stance of some countries. The fundamental right of parents to custody over the education of their children has been recognized by the United States Supreme Court in the Oregon School Case: "The child is not the mere creature of the State; those who nurture him and direct his destiny have the right coupled with the high duty to recognize and prepare him for additional duties."[17] The same right is recognized by the United Nations' Declaration of Human Rights.[18]

The papal teaching insists that the most basic element in the educational duty of parents is love that is both paternal and maternal, which love is the inspiration, soul, and norm of all education. Modern psychology supports this position. Self-esteem, grounded in and stemming from a supportive, loving, and consistent familial structure, is the psychological foundation of the future development of the child's character, value system, and intellectual achievement. Love of God and neighbor, which is the basic Christian law, must begin, both theologically and psychologically, with proper love of self.

Three terms in *Familiaris consortio* deserve attention: person, personalism, and personal. These terms are not to be interpreted as being consonant with the narcissism of the "me" cult, which denies any givens or inherent meanings which one must implement carefully, attend to, or abstain from totally. The Church teaches that the person is not a norm unto himself or herself. Rather, the person, though unique and irreplaceable, is an individual manifestation of and participation in human nature. At a time when Catholic parents and educators, like many other Catholics, are often "selectively obedient" to the Church's teachings, this is important to note.

Familiaris consortio delineates the main truths and principles basic to authentic marriage and human life, supplies a Christian humanism that illustrates God's calling for humanity to enter into and exist in a love for life, and begins to develop a theology of family as a "communion of persons."[19] As an intimate community of love and life, the family has a duty to manifest its inner reality of love. Every demand made of the Catholic family is part of the fundamental mission to love. The four main tasks of the family are to form a loving community of persons, to serve life, to participate in the development of society, and to share in the life and mission of the Church.

Today, the idea that infants might be better cared for by a parent than by alternate care givers is often viewed as a ploy to restrict women to a barefoot-and-pregnant role. Some child-care specialists have blessed the concept that new mothers should be returned to the world of the paycheck as soon as possible, that children are just as well off with a professional care giver as with a mother, and that parents who follow their convenience in these matters should do so without guilt.

Popular opinion often holds that, at the very least, infants can be managed by any competent person, and the infant will suffer no negative result: small children view adults not as resources, but as a sort of controlling gray mass. Some assert that a mother at home is usually too preoccupied—with housework, and with soap operas and the telephone if she's lonely—to have much one-on-one interaction with her preschool children. Some feminists actually go further and suggest that stay-at-home mothers may harm their children with too much attention. Part of the reason for differences in opinion is the definition of child care. Does the only time that counts as true parental child care mean undisturbed down-on-the-floor-with-the-blocks time, while every other real-life activity like having the child go with the mother to the grocery store, doing the laundry, walking the dog, or making dinner doesn't count?

Because the subject is controversial, the United States is the only industrialized nation without a national policy on maternity leave or child-care. In France, 90 percent of three-year-olds attend government-sponsored preschools; in Sweden, parents may choose to work six-hour days until a child is eight years old; in Italy, working women receive two years' credit toward seniority with every childbirth.[20] But for-profit day care in the United States is growing fast, with national chains like Kinder Care and Children's World in the forefront of the growth. For this reason and because of the vast possibilities of errors in philosophical and other approaches with government entry into the field, perhaps the country's lack of national child-care provisions is wise.

Although not all studies produce the same results or conclusions, and no one is suggesting that all children react in the same ways, some observations may be made. It is being discovered that children who spend their early years in day care are growing up different: more hyperactive, less responsive to adults, less curious, less altruistic, less likely to make strong one-on-one relationships. Kindergarteners and first-graders who spend their early years at a child-development center may be more intelligent than their home-reared counterparts, but they may also be more likely to hit, kick, push, threaten, swear, and argue.

One theory is that a child with an insecure mother-attachment may become withdrawn and passive in later years, while a child with a secure attachment tends to be outgoing and have other good qualities. Babies who have been left alone or with a stranger for a while, if they are secure, tend to reunite joyfully with their mother and then return happily to their toys. Anxious-avoidant babies tend to ignore their returning mother. And anxious-ambivalent babies tend to go to their mother but be angry with her, sometimes crying inconsolably for a time. Mothers of this last class of babies generally tend to be less sensitive to their child.

Though few studies have considered fathers, some observations can be made from the studies that exist. Boys at one year of age were found to have a less secure relationship with their fathers if their mother worked full-time. Five-month-olds of working parents interacted less with their father than with their mother—the hypothesis being that the mothers were pushing the fathers out of the way in their rush to spend time with baby at the end of the day. Both parents might speculate on whether, when they're around sixty years old, they will be more likely to remember the first years of their child's life or the satisfaction of their work-place.

Although parents may be individuals first, they usually function as a coalition, depend on one another, and divide the tasks of living and child rearing. Parents are responsible for providing their children with nurture, succor, and stability. They offer themselves as guides, educators, and models so that their children can develop in healthy ways. Jean Piaget showed rather succinctly the importance of parents to children:

> Most values of little children hinge on their image of their father and mother. . . . In essence, they are formed during the long period when the human being is like soft wax: the actions of others, their mental attitudes, the thoughts expressed before the child and for him, leave such a deep mark on his person that (except in the case of a very original personality) he becomes wholly what his elders want him to become, even if he is left free to act as he wishes to.[21]

Pope Paul VI was aware of the same factor when he said that people follow witnesses more readily than teachers.[22] The simple fact is that children need "beacon personalities": those adults who actualize values in their conduct and give the young the desire to emulate them because they seem happy and worthy of respect.

The British Council of Churches put well what is expected of parents:

> [T]he child learns of a love which does not have to be earned and of a forgiveness which is always extended. This is an important basis for his religious growth. . . . Although Christian parents share general nurture with all good parents, they interpret it differently. For them, normal parenthood becomes a priestly calling. . . . The Christian family witnesses to faith by its association with the church.[23]

Among the Council's recommendations is "that local Churches give greater attention to parent education, including especially the Christian understanding of the Bible, modern Christian thought, psychology of children, and the practice of the Christian faith in the home."[24] It also mentions awareness "of the need for suitable literature for the guidance of the parent."[25] Parents must carry out the fundamental functions related to their respective gender roles. The consequences of attempts to obliterate completely the traditional differences between maternal and paternal roles are as yet unknown.[26]

Gender roles differ, however, from gender identity. Security of gender identity is one of the most significant and cardinal factors in the achievement of a stable ego identity. The stability of ego identity relates to the person's self-concept, self-esteem, and maturation. Parents who do not wish to inculcate their children with healthy differentiated sex roles are to be reminded that boys and girls do not obtain sex-linked attributes by some generic gender allocation.

The Catholic Education Council for England and Wales pointed to another recommendation — home-school cooperation:

> The need for close contact between the two main influences on the child, home and school, is great. Parents and teachers can pool their resources in the cases of individual children, the teacher gaining the advantage of the parent's unique knowledge and of information about home circumstances, the parents benefiting from the greater objectivity of the teacher who can draw on experience of a wider range of children and encourage or re-assure parents. . . . in terms of activities there need be no sharp division between what children do at home and at school, between learning and play.[27]

Not too long ago, parents were held strictly responsible for whether their children practiced the religion of their parents. Today, children show many aberrations from the religious and moral practice of their parents, for which, because of the prevalence of so many other influences, not many people hold parents responsible. There seems to be an anomaly here. On the one hand, when the suggestion is made that the State should involve itself with issues of morality (abortion, pornography), the countering argument is invariably that the *family* is the place where morality should be inculcated. But when one gets to the level of the family, those same counter-arguers make the point that parents are not responsible. The end result is that the inculcation of moral values often turns out to be *nobody's* business.

Nevertheless, many continue to argue for the child's right of self-determination in all areas, including religion. Parents' imposition of a particular belief system, this position holds, is tantamount to indoctrination, which consists in the intentional inculcation of beliefs without due regard for rational evidence and argument; for the child this brings about heteronomy rather than autonomy.

In this view the most that can be accorded to parents is the right to provide their children with a religious upbringing in a "weak" sense: no more than revealing to their children that they, the parents, happen to hold a set of religious beliefs and live according to them. Though they may provide their children with an explanation of these beliefs and their related practices, they should stop short of developing the children's own religious commitment in any way; otherwise, they threaten the child's right to self-determination.

Those in the affirmative,[28] on the other hand, argue that parents' handing on to their children their own beliefs is a right — an extension of their right to practice their own religion. Also, religious development is not only consonant with the development of personal and moral autonomy, but is necessary for its true achievement. In addition, when discussing the welfare of children one must distinguish between childish "wants" and real interests. Furthermore, the "conflict" between religious faith and personal autonomy is, when each is properly understood, a false one.

There is a healthy tension between introducing children to parental beliefs and allowing them to express and develop their own points of view. Parents seek their children's rational commitments now, not so that later on the children will firmly adhere to the beliefs of their family, but so that they will have a substantive rational base from which to launch their own personal search for truth. This is especially valuable because society places upon the balance scale the thumb of relentless manipulation in such a way that it is difficult for a child to achieve balanced judgments about religion and many other important values.

In these tensions and risks, good parents should have an active and strong role. The "weak" sense of religious upbringing is not adequate to produce children's real *understanding* of the religious domain sufficient to equip the children with the capacity to make sense of the religious elements of their family backgrounds. "Weak" religious upbringing, in addition, constitutes a threat to the family's organic, holistic character, and increases the attendant dangers of psychic disunity. "Weak" religious education also detracts from the broader family *community* which is sustained by a range of shared practices and beliefs which involve religious elements. And there can be no such thing as "religiously neutral" upbringing (despite contrary arguments from such as John Stuart Mill, who claimed to have been raised in a religiously neutral atmosphere).

Strong religious training, if properly imparted, in no way detracts from a child's open-mindedness. But parents must be aware of the difficulty of harmonizing the desired autonomy of the child with the deeply pervasive nature of religion, and must take certain precautions. T. H. McLaughlin described some of these:

> At an appropriate point, parents should encourage the child to ask questions and be willing to answer honestly and in a way which respects the child's developing cognitive and emotional maturity; make the child aware that religion is a matter of faith rather than universally publicly agreed belief, and that there is much disagree-

ment in this area; encourage attitudes of tolerance and understanding in relation to religious disagreement; indicate that morality is not exclusively dependent upon religion; be alert to even subtle forms of psychological or emotional blackmail; ensure that the affective, emotional and dispositional aspects of their child's religious development take place in appropriate relationship with the cognitive aspect of that development, so that irrational, compulsive or neurotic forms of religious behaviour or response are guarded against; respect the eventual freedom of the child to refuse to participate in religious practices, and so on.[29]

Parents must find ways to educate their children by persuasion rather than compulsion. Their procedures must take into account the long-range possibility that their children will arrive at a position where they may autonomously choose to accept or reject their particular religious faith, and even religion in general. They should understand that, as with the priest and the teacher, the parent can *teach* the faith, but cannot *give* it. At some point, the parent has to "let go, and let God."

The Mother

The mother, during the child's early years, is important for the child's ability to distinguish male and female roles. Though the functions of mother and father may be changing, clear-cut role reversals furnish the children with images of masculinity and femininity which are culturally deviant.[30] The biological makeup of women is related to the nurturing of children and the maintenance of interpersonal relationships, emotional harmony, and expressive-affectional affiliation roles.[31] In most families, the mother is primarily responsible for the nurturant care of the children, particularly when they are small. This includes the emotional as well as the physical care necessary for the child's well-being. This mother-child relationship is influenced by the total family setting and does not transpire in isolation. Furthermore, in order to invest her infant with proper love and care, the mother requires support and the requiting of her own emotional needs. In the most suitable conditions, these come from the husband.

The trust the child develops in parents is a good predictor of the child's future level of development in terms of autonomy, self-esteem, motivation, perseverance, delayed gratification, and self-identity. In the boundaries established between parents and their child lay the child's foundations for trust in the reliability of collaboration, the worth of communication in problem solving, and the general tolerance to work with others in a constructive manner.[32] Erik Erikson contends that the first two or three years of the child's life are among the most important in terms of moral and intellectual development.[33]

During the first six months of life, children begin to develop a sense of trust. As immature as newborn children are, they thrive on attention and need a familiar person or persons to give them things and help them explore. Erikson cautioned against not giving small children the chance to develop attachment. He stressed the need for consistent and constant loving care which ultimately plays a critical role in ego identity and thus in the subsequent tasks of adulthood. During the earliest years of life, it is generally the mother with whom the infant develops the greatest attachment.

Attachment is an enduring tie based on affection focused upon a specific person. The types of attachment depend largely upon the treatment of the child by the mother (or, in cases like legal guardianship or adoption, the mother figure). Healthy attachment depends upon the expectations of the infant toward the mother. If the infant expects the mother to be accessible, responsive, and consequently trustworthy, the child will develop a basic sense of trust. If the mother is slow to respond, less affectionate, and inconsistent, the infant develops an anxious, ambivalent attachment.[34] This insecure attachment leads to a lack of trust and an inability to form substantial bonds with others during the rest of life. Though there has been an abundance of research findings related to mother-child attachment patterns, it is difficult to draw any firm conclusions about how much the mother, in isolation, contributes to the establishment of attachment bonds.

The Father

Researchers have neglected the role of the father during the attachment phase, even though many infants are quite close to their fathers.[35] In the past decade, with an increasing number of mothers joining the work force, it would seem that the father's participation in child care should have increased. In fact, this is not the case. Studies indicate fathers spending very little time with their children, at times an average of only thirty-seven seconds per day.[36] These are obviously statements of fact and not of approval. The best predictor of the time a man spends on child rearing is his work schedule.[37] A study of working parents showed that the female role has still not changed; the mother remains the primary caretaker regardless of her work schedule and occupation.[38]

In general, fathers seem to be less nurturant and more consistent in enforcing rules with their children than mothers are. Interviews with parents found that mothers tend to emphasize keeping their children free from anxiety, whereas fathers talk about moral and personal values. Interviews with children between preschool and highschool years suggest that children detect the difference between parental roles. In general, children describe the mother as affectionate and nurturing and the father as strong, competent, and sometimes frightening.[39]

Fathers do have specific effects on their children which pertain to their role. Boys with high self-esteem, for example, report a closer relationship with their father than boys with low self-esteem. Daughters who are closely bonded to fathers tend to be curious, independent, and highly motivated, whereas girls without close father-daughter bonding tend to be quiet, dependent, and acquiescent.[40]

The Family in Itself

If the family and its educational role are to be saved, it will only be if we understand the essential functions of the family and hold fast to their preservation in a manner which will stand the test of time and social transformation.[41] The family must be appreciated as the basic societal unit that serves the essential needs of offspring and subserves the essential needs of society. There is no other institution which is as well equipped to fulfill all its functions simultaneously. Lying at the center of the Christian family's role and mission is the call: "Family, become what you are".[42] Because of the profound changes which have occurred regarding the function and role of the family, this simple statement has profound implications. The Christian family is at the heart of the Church's mission to exemplify God's love for His children—most especially in the impersonal and neutral life which is currently fostered by an isolationist, individualistic civil society.[43]

"All happy families resemble one another," Leo Tolstoy astutely observed in *Anna Karenina*. Family therapists and psychologists agree. One important ingredient that happy families have in common is the retention of traditions—rituals that families go through together year after year—despite the temptations in these busy times to omit them. These provide needed symbols. Among them are to sing the old songs, say the same prayers, wear certain clothing, eat special food. There is a sense of "correctness" and belonging. In addition to daily domestic living, these rituals apply to rites of passage like birthdays, baptisms, weddings, and funerals; annual customs revolving around civil and religious holidays (Lent, Christmas, Halloween, St. Patrick's Day); and pastimes associated with the seasons.[44] Conversely, families with disturbed children do not try to build traditions. Mealtimes are mundane, bedtimes boring, and leaving the house and returning completely without spirit, all giving children the impression that neither they nor their family are important.[45]

The relationship between the dynamic organization of the family and the integration of the personality of the offspring is important in predicting the future social and learning behavior of the child. Pope John XXIII is alleged to have said, "I go along my way with the simple wisdom I inherited from my home." Initial indications of an extensive current project in longitudinal research are that "a child's social and academic potential is developed in the very early elementary years and that the relationship between the school and the home is a crucial factor in that development."[46]

Family functions must meet two determinants. The first is the biological nature and needs of human beings. The second is the requirements of the particular society of which the family is a social subsystem exemplifying societal *mores*, beliefs, and value systems.[47] Thus, families everywhere, while having disparate ways of dealing with problems, share common functions. There are many complex functions which outline the purpose of the family.

Ideally, the family is designed for two general functions. The first is to be an accepted societal means of perpetuating the human race. The family protects, nurtures, and disciplines the minds and bodies of children during the most critical period of physical, moral, and intellectual growth. The physical functions of caring for a dependent and helpless human being during the nurturing years are obvious. Less obvious is the importance of the family's provision of psychological protection and caring. Without the emotional caring provided by the family, the child would sicken and die at worst, or survive as a psychologically deficient being at best. Secondly, the family is the primary socializing agent during the child's early years. Socialization includes instruction which provides direction in determining identity: who the child sees himself or herself to be in relation to other persons, and to the rules, expectations, values, and roles prescribed by society.[48]

In terms of the socializing process, the family provides role models which will influence the child's future relationships: as heterosexual, friend, spouse, and parent. The family is the teacher of the native language. The family provides social and personal guidelines, all of which help the child to regulate, control, and direct feelings, actions, and general behavior in the world. The family is the incubator for ego and superego formation: for personal self-concept, social self-concept, and style of living. It also provides a center for the formation and advancement of "in-depth" interpersonal relations. In an alienating world, the family is the only unit which consistently furnishes its members with affection, warmth, acceptance, love, understanding, stability, and intimacy. It is the first "group" to which a child belongs and with which he or she interacts, the reference point for later group interaction and identity.[49]

Through intrafamilial experience children also learn about a variety of social institutions like marriage, the family, schooling, and economic exchange. Identification with parents inculcates societal values — examples being ethics and moral development. In belonging to a family, children experience a multiplicity of social phenomena which will permanently influence development, such as the value of belonging to a mutually protective unit, the reward of renouncing one's own wishes for the good of the collective unit, the acceptance of hierarchies of authority, and the relationship between authority and responsibility. The family value systems, role definitions, and patterns of interrelationships enter into the child's development without conscious instruction on the part of the parents.[50]

Socialization concerns teaching the child the basic roles and institutions of society through familial transaction. Another family responsibility in initiating the child into society is enculturation. Enculturation deals with the transmission of symbols from generation to generation. Obviously, there is considerable overlap between enculturation and socialization, and the terms are often used synonymously.

The process of enculturation, which concerns the acquisition of major aspects of one's heritage, is importantly assimilated at the base level via the family unit. Cultural heritage includes tangible matters such as modes of housing or food preferences. Children axiomatically accept less tangible matters — such as value systems, religious beliefs, and status hierarchies — as the proper way of doing things and rarely question them until much later in their development (if then). In a complex scientific and industrial society the family becomes increasingly dependent upon schools to transmit the more complex adaptive techniques due to parents' lack of time and knowledge.

It is becoming more and more apparent that the cultural deprivation of children is almost as harmful as social and economic deprivation. Children who are culturally deprived do not learn readily, have difficulty with symbolic and abstract thought, and have a sparse pool of knowledge and experience upon which to draw during the maturation process. Studies of disorganized families indicate that their children may be both intellectually and emotionally crippled by the time they enter nursery school.[51]

The child develops the fine points of morality gradually. The most clearly delineated theory of moral development is that of Lawrence Kohlberg,[52] which is explained and critically evaluated in our chapter on curriculum. Suffice it to observe here that social-learning researchers claim that family modeling is more responsible for children's moral behavior than Kohlberg's concept of six moral stages. Kohlberg is often unclear about the role of such significant persons as parents in contributing toward the moral development of the child.

By observational learning, children can come to imitate their model's perspective, a process which results in a conceptual understanding of moral issues and a great degree of predictable behavior. The ability to take another's perspective is one of the most important influences on moral action and judgment.[53] Consequently, children's experiences with social situations and varying perspectives affect their moral development. Social intercourse of all kinds offers opportunities for perspective-taking, whether it be participation in the family group or with peers.

Social learning theorists emphasize the use of this perspective-taking ability, stating that a person might have such an ability and never use it. Whether a person does perform a certain behavior depends, in part, upon reinforcement. Social approval, especially by such significant persons as parents, is one of the most powerful reinforcers of behavior. As children learn which actions bring approval or disapproval from their parents, they begin to modify their behavior in view of the expected consequence. Justin Aronfreed thinks that this expectation is what helps lead to the establishment of conscience,[54] and has outlined a range of moral controls ranging from external to internal modes of modification.

Reinforcement and punishment are external controls which are often environmental and help control the child's behavior. Internal controls are influences within the child that guide behavior. For example, a child might resist stealing because of external controls (fear of being caught) or because of the internal control (conscience) which desires to avoid feelings of anxiety and guilt. The internal control is a goal of the socialization process in developing moral behavior. According to Aronfreed, children develop strong internal control when their parents specify exactly what behavior is being rewarded or punished and then *explain* why the behavior is being rewarded or punished. The explanations help the child to become responsible for actions.[55]

Two areas which are important to the moral development of children and involve parents in a major way are the growth of self-esteem and the maintenance of motivation. When children are able to achieve the goals they and others set for them, their concept of self-worth can become a self-fulfilling prophecy. High self-esteem tends to bring success, which in turn further reinforces self-esteem and respect. Self-esteem (or lack of it) thus becomes an important part of the personality.

A study by Coopersmith ascertained three interconnected ways of parent-child relations which indicated the effects of parents on the formation of identity and self-esteem.[56] He found that parents with children of high self-esteem tend to be extremely accepting of their children, set clearly defined limits on their children's actions, and enforce these limits. Realistic limits set on the behavior of children clearly provide a reduction of uncertainty and failure pertaining to parental demands. When standards are ambiguous, children are confused and less able to evaluate the consequences or results of their actions.

Coopersmith also found that parents who had an authoritative (not to be confused with authoritarian) style tend to be competent and independent role models who enforce rules and demand levels of high achievement and are thus associated with high self-esteem in children.[57] These parents also tend to be warm, rational, and receptive to their children's questions, and believe in their competence as parents. Personal characteristics of the parents—such as high self-esteem, competence, consistency, and interdependence—contributed significantly to the level of self-esteem mirrored in their children. Generally, children with low self-esteem tend to have parents who are autocratic, distant, and overly permissive. Children in this type of parental situation feel stupid, powerless, and incompetent; eventually they become passive and compliant.

How much children actually learn also depends to a great extent on their level of *motivation*. One has only to watch the one-year-old child struggle with the process of standing and walking to understand the strong sense of motivation with which all human beings are born. Competence motivation helps explain the child's innate persistence in learning something difficult, such as riding a bike. The motivation to read, which is probably the key to beginning academic competence, is strongly affected by the attitudes and actions of the child's parents. The level of parental interest in the child's academic career, parental hopes for the child's success, and the amount of time parents spend in actively helping the child to learn are good predictors of the child's future success in learning.[58]

In brief, the most important function of the family toward children is to teach them how to love. They can do this by, for one thing, being patient. Children pass through states as they grow, and parents need to remain lovingly tolerant. Also, parents should give their children time. Whether parents consider it "quality time" or not, children need a personal love relationship with their parents, and one of the best ways to foster this is by communicating on many levels—all of which takes time. One of the best ways to do it, next to hugging, is to read aloud to their children. This is important to inspire them, to guide them, to educate them, to bond with them, and to communicate parental feelings, hopes, and fears. This is a long-lasting experience that children savor long after they have grown.

Parents should also be tender with their children: tenderness is a good Christian virtue to develop. This does not exclude a loving discipline, through which the child develops the ability to bear discomfort, control impulses, and steel will. Parents should be affirming, which doesn't mean overlooking faults and mistakes, but does mean nurturing, guiding, and emphasizing what is good in a child. Parents should be forgiving, which is the only way to heal the hard feelings that develop in a family when conflicts grow out of control. Parents should be listening: if they want to get to the big things in the lives of their children, they have to be willing to listen to the little things. And parents must be loyal: in our time of "what's in it for me?" concepts of real love[59] are frequently forgotten. If parents do all these things, perhaps without even thinking about it they will have taught their children about God's love.[60]

THE CHURCH
Definition and Nature of Church

The Church is in many ways important to any consideration of Catholic schooling and education. It is therefore essential that we have some idea of the definition and nature of the Church. In a religiously monolithic society in which there is one dominant religion—Spain with Roman Catholicism, England with Anglicanism, Sweden with Lutheranism, Israel with Judaism—the Church has a relatively clear identity. In a pluralistic society professing religious freedom and deliberate nonestablishment of religion or churches and in which there are many churches, denominations, sects, and cults, as in the United States, the definition of Church—as, for example, in "Church-State relations"—is difficult, if not impossible.

Not having a common ground of definition makes Church-State relations on school issues—about ninety-five percent of Church-State court cases—very difficult. Congress, which exempts churches from some tax and other obligations, has in studied silence left the word undefined.[61] In the area of religion, courts have dealt with sects, cults, denominations, religious societies, lodges, churches, mutual benefit societies, fraternal orders, and a host of other arrangements. The courts search for a "common meaning,"[62] and usually define "church" functionally, often as a building, because they have to settle the location of liquor establishments, gas stations, and so on, which by statute must be located a distance from a church; or to settle property disputes between members; or to decide zoning regulations and variances; or to determine tax regulations.

The courts have also defined church as a voluntary association (usually of Christians), a company of the faithful (again usually Christian), a congregation, a denomination, an organization for religious purposes, a parish, a place for worship, and a religious corporation or society.[63] The courts have admitted that the nature of church can be presbyteral, congregational, episcopal, or hierarchical. Because of the First Amendment, the courts' definitions cannot reflect only established, traditional, conventional churches — whose definitions may be simpler — at the expense of unorthodox ones.[64]

The situation becomes even more complex with an "interdenominational" church which seeks to transcend established denominations and their doctrinal disputes. Although the Internal Revenue Service has admitted its inability to formulate a definition, it has loosely used fourteen criteria which it derived from the forms and practices of recognized churches, and is sensitive to concerns about freedom of religion and discouraging or destroying new churches.[65] In view of this enormously diverse and confusing range of churches in the United States, it is difficult to see any danger of "establishment" of religion in this country.

Even among Catholics there are confusions of definition of the Catholic Church. Aside from the church building ("Let's go to church"), people often use such expressions as "The Church says," "The Church forbids," "According to the mind of the Church," and so on. To be accurate they should rather say, "The Code of Canon Law of 1983 says," "According to Vatican Council II's 'Declaration on Christian Education,'" and "According to the statutes of our diocese." In other words, people sometimes say "Church" when they mean the hierarchy, the proclamations of law, the Church's administration, etc. Some definitions are expressly forbidden:

> The followers of Christ are . . . not permitted to imagine that Christ's Church is nothing more than a collection . . . of Churches and ecclesial communities. Nor are they free to hold that Christ's Church nowhere really exists today and that it is to be considered only as an end which all Churches and ecclesial communities must strive to reach.[66]

In the New Testament, the Church is the mystical body of Christ, the pillar and bulwark of truth, Christ's spotless bride; Christ will be with it to the end of time, and the Holy Spirit will dwell with it.[67] The knowledge that "the Church is us" gives a solid sense of unity. Christ alone is the Lord, and the relationship among all in his Church is fraternal and sororal.

Unfortunately, due to the sixteenth-century attacks on the papacy, Roman Catholic Canon Law circled the wagons and drew the lines of authority tightly. This protection, sometimes evolved into a merely juridical concept of Church. The nineteenth century saw the beginnings of a renewal in the theology of the Church, awareness of which became more widespread with Pius XII's epoch-making 1943 encyclical, *Mystici corporis*. The encyclical returned to the New Testament concept of the Church as "the mystical body of Jesus Christ" and added that "it should not be thought that this organic structure of the body of the Church relates and is limited only to the hierarchy of Church offices."[68]

Vatican II's *Constitution on the Church* takes full cognizance of the revival of the earlier view.[69] All of chapter II of this document speaks of the Church as the People of God. The Church is the helper of the world. The mission of the Church is essentially concerned with *this* life, with the penetration of the dominion of God in this world, as well as with eternal life hereafter. The Church does not want to dominate, but to stand for God's dominion. The Church does not want to interfere with civil society's structures, but to introduce the Kingdom of God into social phenomena as well as into the individual person. The Church inevitably is in a reciprocal relation with the whole of society. The same people who, from a temporal viewpoint, make up society, from a religious viewpoint make up the Church.

In the Church's dialogue with the world, Christians must humbly learn, because the world has much to say that is valuable. In this dialogue, the Church has important things to say to the world, as well as the world to the Church.[70] This dialogue can provide the world with the deepest perspectives on human conduct, and the Christian with a philosophy of life that interprets reality in the light of faith.

Models of the Church

Because of the mysteries involved in definitions of Church, images and symbols have been used from time immemorial to express this profound mystery. We often call them "models." The Old Testament revelation of the kingdom, especially the preparatory books of the prophets, used symbols taken from the life of the shepherd, from the cultivation of the land, from the art of building, and from family life and marriage.

In the New Testament, the Church is a sheepfold, the sole and necessary gateway to which is Christ; a flock, of which God foretold that He would Himself be the shepherd; a cultivated field, the tillage of God; and the building of God. The Lord compared himself to the stone which the builders rejected, which the apostles used as the cornerstone to build the foundation of the Church. The edifice that is the Church has many names to describe it: the house in which God's family dwells, the household of God in the Spirit, the dwelling place of God among men, and, especially, the holy temple. The Church, further, which is called "that Jerusalem which is above" and "our mother," is described as the spotless spouse of the spotless lamb.[71]

Our time also uses models to help give a descriptive definition of the Catholic Church. Each of the models presented by Avery Dulles has strengths and weaknesses, and none is complete of itself. One is the institutional model, the basis of which is the end of St. Matthew's Gospel, when Jesus told the apostles: "Full authority has been given to me both in heaven and on earth; go, therefore, and make disciples of all the nations. Baptize them. . . . Teach them. . . . And know that I am with you always . . . !" The stress here is understood to be on the structures of government.[72] In this model, the Church is the saving institution: "the Church is . . . an institution to which the universal mission of salvation has been entrusted."[73] The Church is not only a fellowship of individuals who are with God and together in Christ; it is also an institution of salvation, a means by which fellowship is generated and sustained by the workings of God:

> The Church, therefore, as people of God, society of the faithful, communion of people in Christ, is the work of God's saving love in Christ. . . . The Church . . . is not only the society of believers, it is also, thanks to its ministerial and saving work, the mother of believers. . . . It is a people on pilgrimage towards the fullness of the mystery of Christ.[74]

Among the advantages of this model is that it makes for order, clarity, and respect. Because its focus is on the preservation of a heritage, the theory has strong endorsement in the official Church documents of the past few centuries. It provides a strong corporate identity for individual members, who know who they are, what they believe, and what their mission is. It instills cohesion, a sense of loyalty, and apostolic zeal.[75]

The model also has at least five liabilities, some of them arising from easily made distortions of the model. First, it has a comparatively meager basis in Scripture and in early Church tradition. Second, it can lead to some unfortunate consequences in Christian life, both personal and corporate. Clericalism, for example, under this model tends to reduce the laity to a condition of passivity. Juridicism tends to exaggerate the role of human authority. There can then be too much concern to fulfill ecclesiastical obligations and insufficient concern to fulfill the law of charity, to have more concern about right relationships with pope and bishops than with the heavenly Father, Christ, and the Holy Spirit.

Third, the institutional model can raise obstacles to a creative and fruitful theology, binding theology too exclusively to the defense of current official positions and diminishing exploratory thinking. Fourth, exaggerated institutionalism can lead to many serious theological problems, like the presentation of the enormous difficulty of admitting the salvation of non-Roman Catholics. And fifth, the monopolistic tendencies of this ecclesiology is out of phase with the demands of ecumenism, dialogue, and interest in world religions.[76]

Another model is the Church as mystical communion — *koinonia*: "As all the members of the human body, though they are many, form one body, so also are the faithful in Christ. . . . The head of this body is Christ."[77] This model points to a visible society, the people of God, and interpersonal communication. It is heavily rooted in Scripture: in the Old Testament, it is reminiscent of Yahweh's covenant with the Israelites that they would be His people and He would be their God. In the New Testament, Christ's Passover established a new covenant whereby a new people of God formed the Church. One of the most powerful New Testament images of this new cohesion is that of the Church as "mystical body"[78] whereby, like organs in a human body, each individual has a role — neither more nor less important than any other — in promoting the mission of Christ, the head of the body.

Among the advantages of this model is its scriptural foundation. Also, it lays the foundation for union in a spirit of love to find the Lord. It points to a warm, interpersonal fellowship within the Church.[79] Among the model's weaknesses are that it could be vague to outsiders, it works best only when the group is small, and it isolates the Church from the rest of humankind because it tends to turn inward.

The most difficult model in the concrete is the sacramental. "Since the Church is not merely the people of God but also, as it were, in Christ 'a sign and instrument . . . of communion with God and of unity among all men' it should be regarded as the primordial sacrament."[80] And all those "who in faith look towards Jesus, the author of salvation and the principle of unity and peace, God has gathered together and established as the Church, that it may be for each and everyone the visible sacrament of this saving unity."[81] Edward Schillebeeckx put it: "for the love of man, Jesus is the human incarnation of the redeeming love of God: an advent of God's love in visible form."[82]

The mystery of Christ's love and activity continues in the Church, the medium through which Christ's work continues. The Church, therefore, is a sacrament, an outward sign through which Christ works and channels his grace and which makes present God's love for man, bridging the gap between heaven and earth.

Among the advantages of the sacramental model are that it presents well the Church as a visible society with the presence of God and preserves the dynamism of the mystery of Christ. Also, in it the Church expresses its divine element in that it sanctifies; it expresses its humanity in that it is always trying to improve and draw closer to God.[83] Among the model's disadvantages is that it is a product of a developed theology which is somewhat esoteric and complex, rather than a product purely of Scripture. It therefore complicates dialogue with religious associations outside the Catholic Church.[84]

Another model is the Church as herald. Like Christ, the Church has the kerygmatic, or witness-giving, duty to preach the Word of God. The Church enables the people of God to share, as they should, in Christ's prophetic office; it also establishes a life of faith and offers to God a sacrifice of praise.[85] Just as the Word became flesh, the proclaimed Word becomes flesh in the visible Church, the Kingdom of God now present.[86] The Church as Herald strives to preserve the integrity of Christ's Gospel.

Among this model's advantages are that it turns outward, it proclaims the Good News, and it emphasizes the missionary role of the Church. Among its weaknesses are that it seems to contain the Gnostic notion that if one hears about Christianity, one will accept it, and if one accepts it one will be saved; and this model misses the element of love.

A more recent emphasis is the servant model of the Church. In entering into solidarity with all humankind and fostering brotherhood, the Church's service, or *diakonia*, is diverse, encompassing both spiritual and temporal assistance.[87] Among the advantages of this model is that it shows the Church in service to the whole world—not only Christians—to develop the world's potential; also, it is outward turning, leads to dialogue, and promotes justice and peace. But it can undercut the mission effort of the Church, and does not fit comfortably into much of the first fifteen hundred years of the Church's existence.

There are other, distorted, images of the Church: an island of salvation in an essentially hostile world, seeing to the works of mercy; a fortress on a hill whose work is defense, entering the world only to provide for and protect itself; a monastery whose only task is prayer, the object of which may be a more humane society; an institution that merely parallels worldly institutions, having the same human services like health care and schools. All of these views are inadequate. The truth is that, although the Church is not of this world and not motivated by earthly desires, it is involved with the world, observing the signs of the times and dialoging with all people to draw humankind closer to God.[88]

Hierarchical Nature

The Church is by nature hierarchical. Chapter III of Vatican II's *Constitution on the Church*, which is devoted to the hierarchical structure of the Church, states at the beginning that Christ established various offices within the Church in order to shepherd the people of God, for the "holders of office, who are invested with a sacred power, are, in fact, dedicated to promoting the interests of their brethren."[89] Today's democratic mentality favors the concept of brotherliness in the Church. There is certainly authority and obedience, but not superiority and subjection for their own sake.

To help to teach the faithful authentically with the authority of Christ, the Church's authority is divided between pope, bishops, priests, and faithful.[90] As the visible head of the Church, the pope is the "pastor of the entire Church, and has full, supreme, and universal power over the whole Church, a power which he can always exercise unhindered."[91] Further, the pope enjoys infallibility "in virtue of his office, when, as supreme pastor and teacher of all the faithful—who confirms his brethren in the faith (cf. Luke 22:32)—he proclaims in an absolute decision a doctrine pertaining to faith or morals."[92]

Proclaiming the Gospel of Christ to people is one of the principal duties of bishops, who are "the principal dispensers of the mysteries of God."[93] The bishops are the visible source and foundation of unity in their local Churches, but insofar as they are members of the episcopal college and legitimate successors of the apostles they are to show such care also for the whole Church.[94] Pope Paul VI declared: "The teaching office of the bishop is for the believer the sign and channel which enable him to receive and recognise the Word of God."[95]

Priests derive their authority from the bishop. Therefore all priests, diocesan and religious, share and exercise with bishops the one priesthood of Christ.[96] Relevant to education, priests share in the responsibility for teaching: "In their role as teachers it is the duty of parish priests to preach the word of God to all the faithful so that they . . . may grow in Christ. . . . They should manifest a special interest in adolescents and young people."[97] They are especially to have zeal in catechesis,[98] and they "have a grave obligation to ensure that the faithful enjoy a Christian education, especially the young."[99] Unfortunately, not every clergyman by virtue of his calling has the qualities required: not all are sufficiently knowledgeable, sensitive, prudent, nonjudgmental, nonauthoritarian, compassionate, open-minded, and flexible.

One must not neglect the share of the laity in the common priesthood which, because through baptism it unites the faithful with their heavenly king, is rightly called a "royal priesthood."[100] The priesthood of the laity, though essentially different from that of ordained priests must be renewed, so that the laity can better participate in evangelization. This work is enhanced through the sacrament of marriage, whereby husband and wife create a Christian home and instill Christian virtues in their children and help others who seek the truth.[101] Unless we remember this, the consequence can be the clericalization of religion. For the most part it is the lay people who have to be the Church present to society. Priests "should carry out their work of teaching, sanctifying and governing in such a way that the faithful and the parish communities may feel that they are truly members both of the diocese and of the universal Church."[102]

The best of the laity emphasize Church as community, as people of God, as celebrating the Good News instead of just listening to it. Clergy who have kept abreast of theology realize that

> [t]hough they differ essentially and not only in degree, the common priesthood of the faithful and the ministerial or hierarchical priesthood are none the less ordered one to another; each in its own proper way shares in the one priesthood of Christ.[103]

They realize that the Church is a communion of people

> gathered together by God and united by close spiritual bonds. . . . there is a common dignity of members deriving from their rebirth in Christ, a common grace as sons, a common vocation to perfection, one salvation, one hope and undivided charity.[104]

Importance

In the particular Catholic school, the local Church — parish, religious community, or whatever — is the sponsoring organization; this is true in many more ways than the financial. The local Church is the reason why the school came into existence, why the school is rooted in Catholic Christianity, and why it has remained a Catholic Christian school. The local Church continuously gives the school the richness of the Christian tradition, subtly exerts its ongoing good influence without interfering with the school's autonomy, is the important speculative model of the Christian community and the practical model of the living faith community, interfaces with the school in a way in which the strengths of each minister to the other's weaknesses, and is a wise, intelligent, and compassionate mediator between the Church at large and the school.[105]

The nature of the local Catholic school is therefore going to be dependent in great measure on the nature of beliefs about the Church. If we are going to expect the school to be a Catholic community — as we must — we have to ask what kind of community we expect the Church to be. In brief, the Church is the model for the faith community that the Catholic school should be. And the Church is the community of moral wisdom from which the school draws.[106]

That is the way it was from the beginning. The primary focus of the early Church was to fulfill Christ's command to "go . . . and make disciples of all the nations. . . . Teach them to carry out everything I have commanded you."[107] It sought to do so through a unity that surpassed conventional boundaries of family and civil structures, a "unity which has the Spirit as its origin and peace as its binding force."[108] St. Luke shows the relationship between the unity of the community and its role in instruction: "They devoted themselves to the apostles' instruction and the communal life, to the breaking of bread and the prayers."[109]

Responsibility to Schooling

The Church has given evidence of her awareness of her responsibility to education "for nearly two thousand years, from the ministry of the early deacons to the present time, and has tenaciously held aloft the torch of charity not only by her teaching but also by her widespread example."[110] And the Church continues to recognize the outstanding importance of the school:

> In nurturing the intellectual faculties which is its special mission, it [the Catholic school] develops a capacity for sound judgment and introduces pupils to the cultural heritage bequeathed to them by former generations. It fosters a sense of values and prepares them for professional life. By providing for friendly contacts between pupils of different characters and backgrounds, it encourages mutual understanding. Furthermore it constitutes a center in whose activity and growth not only the families and teachers but also the various associations for the promotion of cultural, civil and religious life, civic society, and the entire community should take part.[111]

The Church's schools are a visible sign of the Church's concern for all education, constituting one proper fulfillment of its commitment to a theology of incarnation: the existence of church schools signifies the inseparability of the sacred and the secular. In addition, if the Church wishes to make a contribution to education, it is better fitted to do so if it is *engaged* in that enterprise, sharing both its achievements and its frustrations. But Church schools can claim no monopoly of the Catholic effort in education: the witness of Catholics working in government schools, the principles upon which many sensitive and dedicated professionals outside Church schools have built sound practice, and the ethos of many non-Church schools all attest to good education.

Church's Right in Education and Schooling

The Church has a right[112] and a duty in education because people have a spiritual nature as well as a physical one. The Church has rights over a person's spiritual domain. The Church's role is unique, because she has the responsibility for proclaiming the way of salvation (which has a temporal as well as an eternal aspect), of communicating the life of Christ, and of assisting all people to grow into the fullness of that life.

There are at least three other bases that give rise to the Church's rights in education and schooling: social justice, the betterment of human life, and the nature of education as an essentially moral enterprise. Intertwined with these is the Church's perception of herself as a mother who communicates the divine life of grace, and guards and teaches God's revelation.

Social justice provides an eminent right to Church schools. In a modern state, schools are a major carrier of values in society. As a result of that, they are a major shaper of the kind of future society that we are going to erect. As people who are, if you like, "specialists" in the area of values and meaning, the people of God who are the Church have a serious interest in those values and in the shape of the society which those values will form.

To say that the Church should not be involved here gives rise to serious questions about basic rights. The government is putting a particular educational system in place, with a particular set of values, and a particular vision of the future. Proponents of such a system often seem to be saying to Catholics, "You don't have any say in that area; we are going to develop our own type of society." Who should have the say? Only those who are politically powerful? Only the economically powerful? Practitioners of religion focus on meaning, values, and culture: they should have at least an equal say, if not a much more major one, in shaping the society.[113]

A third reason for the right of the Church in education and schooling is the betterment of human life. There is no dichotomy between the supernatural and the natural, the spiritual and human progress, human values and the values of the Gospel. The improvement of the quality of life is directly connected with the Kingdom of God. It provides a groundwork out of which moral and spiritual life can grow.

That is connected with a fourth reason for the Church's right in education and schooling: education is of itself and by its very nature a moral enterprise. The purpose of education and schooling is to dialogue about and to make good people, a good life, a good society. That requires defining what is "good." The Catholic Church has a unique contribution to make here. Because the Church and the world are mutually related, Catholic Church members should be prepared to enter into dialogue and cooperation with others who have completely different ideas from theirs. Catholics individually and the Church communally must be involved, as part of their vocation, in the major problems of the age. In facing these problems, education has a preeminent place: in many ways, it holds the key to the future of the human race.

Intertwined with these reasons for the Church's right in schooling and education is the Church's perception of herself. Arising out of the nature of the Christian religion, she perceives herself as a mother, for one, by virtue of which position she is also

> [t]eacher of nations; so that all who in the course of centuries come to her loving embrace may find salvation as well as the fullness of a more excellent life. To this Church, . . . her most holy Founder has entrusted the double task of begetting sons unto herself, and of educating and governing those whom she begets, guiding with maternal providence the life both of individuals and of peoples.[114]

The Church takes seriously that she "as a mother is under an obligation . . . to provide for [her] children an education by virtue of which their whole lives may be inspired by the spirit of Christ."[115]

The Church sees herself also as communicating the divine life of grace to humankind, "notably in the way it heals and elevates the dignity of the human person, in the way it consolidates society, and endows the daily activity of men with a deeper sense and meaning."[116] The Church's engagement in this educational task stems from an unselfish interest in human formation.[117]

Lastly, the Church sees as part of her vocation the need to be a community which guards and teaches God's revelation. Her teaching authority (*magisterium*) is to be found in the teachings of popes and bishops throughout history and throughout the world on doctrinal and moral matters. It, along with the Holy Scriptures, liturgy, and Christian experience, forms part of the content of catechesis. It includes solemn statements and also the regular day-to-day teachings through which the content of revelation is gradually clarified.[118] The Church's bottom line is: "Every baptized person, precisely by reason of being baptized, has the right to receive from this Church instruction and education enabling him or her to enter into a truly Christian life."[119]

Church's Duty in Education and Schooling

Correlative to every right is a duty. If you have a right to walk on the sidewalk, I have a duty not to push you off. In education and schooling, the Church explains her rights to the public at large, and shows awareness of her duty within herself. The 1918 Code of Canon Law devoted twelve canons (1372 through 1383) to schools. In reiterating the Church's basic right to establish schools, it called for the establishment of schools throughout the Church (canon 1375). It stipulated that Catholic children should not attend non-Catholic schools unless they had permission from the local bishop (canon 1374) and asserted that local bishops should see to the establishment of schools (canon 1379).

Her new (1983) Code of Canon Law succinctly summarizes the Church's cognizance of both the Church's right and duty. Canon 794 §1 states: "The duty and right of educating belongs in a unique way to the Church which has been divinely entrusted with the mission to assist men and women so that they can arrive at the fullness of the Christian life," and §2 of the same canon places on pastors of souls "the duty to arrange all things so that all the faithful may enjoy a Catholic education."[120]

The correlative right and duty are enunciated in a similar way in canon 800. That canon's §1 asserts the right of the Church in general: "The Church has the right to establish and supervise schools of any discipline, type and grade whatsoever"; §2 places the duty of support with the faithful: "The Christian faithful are to foster Catholic schools by supporting their establishment and their maintenance in proportion to their resources."[121] Parents, whose right to freedom of choice the Church often proposes and defends (and which we treat in the next chapter), are reminded also of "their duty to send their children to Catholic schools wherever this is possible, to give Catholic schools all the support in their power, and to cooperate with them in their work for the good of their children."[122]

The local bishop has the greatest share of the responsibility. He has the duty to see to the establishment of "schools imparting an education imbued with the Christian spirit."[123] And schools, once established, are subject to bishops, especially in the area of religious teaching.[124] This duty is shared by all "pastors of souls," who are under a "very grave obligation to do all in their power to ensure that this Christian education [of maturing in Christ] is enjoyed by all the faithful and especially by the young who are the hope of the church."[125] Pope John Paul II expressed his concern: "This problem [the Christian education of youth] is especially close to my heart, because it closely touches the Church, which has not failed to give, in various syntheses, its clear directives in the matter."[126] Duties in education and schooling have also been a prime concern of the Church in the United States.[127]

Advantages of Church Schools

Without getting into crass calculations of financial benefits to the citizenry, the free, equal, and open existence of Catholic schools offers advantages to the State, individuals, society, human activity, and peace. The popes have frequently stated that the prosperity of the State depends upon the proper education of youth.[128] Supreme Court Justice Lewis Powell spelled out further the applicability of that principle to Catholic schools:

> Parochial schools, quite apart from their sectarian purpose, have provided an educational alternative for millions of young Americans; they often afford wholesome competition with our public schools; and in some States they relieve substantially the tax burden incident to the operation of public schools. The State has, moreover, a legitimate interest in facilitating education of the highest quality for all children within its boundaries, whatever school their parents have chosen for them.[129]

On the level of society, the Church's religious mission as expressed through parochial schools "can be the source of commitment, direction, and vigor to establish and consolidate the community of men according to the law of God."[130] The Church develops herself in the service of all people, serves the needs of the common good, and encourages people's conscientious earthly responsibility. With regard to the last, through her members the Church offers to human activity a proper and beneficial mean between otherworldly faith and immersion in earthly endeavors:

> It is a mistake to think that, because we have here no lasting city, but seek the city which is to come, we are entitled to shirk our

earthly responsibilities; . . . But it is no less mistaken to think that . . . religion were nothing more than the fulfilment of acts of worship and the observance of a few moral obligations. One of the gravest errors of our time is the dichotomy between the faith which many profess and the practice of their daily lives.[131]

And through her unhampered teachings in her schools, "the Church, whose duty it is to foster and elevate all that is true, all that is good, and all that is beautiful in the human community, consolidates peace among men for the glory of God."[132]

For individuals, Catholic schools offer meaning to life, teachings that raise the dignity of human nature, proclamations of the rights of man, and a presentation of truths of the moral order. On the meaning of life, lack of which is bringing about varied phenomena (such as an unprecedented number of teenage suicides), "the Church is entrusted with the task of opening up to man the mystery of God, who is the last end of man; in doing so it opens up to him the meaning of his own existence, the innermost truth about himself."[133] The truths of the moral order which the Church teaches in her schools are also elevating: the Church "interprets authentically both revealed positive law and 'the principles of the moral order which spring from human nature itself' and which relate to man's full development and sanctification."[134]

Again, empirical research corroborates Church teachings. James S. Coleman's 1987 research conclusions, for example, argue that, in the three sectors of schooling (public, religious private, and independent private), in those areas in which Catholic schools excel they do so because of "the functional community that exists around a religious body to which the families adhere and of which the school is an outgrowth."[135] This is not, of course, true of government schools, nor of independent private schools. The latter "constitute with few exceptions the extreme of individualism in education"[136] and consist of parents who have individually chosen the school but do not constitute a community outside the school. It is not true of other religious private schools, either, because they constitute only *value* communities rather than *functional* ones as Catholic schools do.[137]

The summation of the advantages of the Catholic Church's schools is in her founder, Jesus Christ:

> The Catholic school without a desire for power and still less for triumphalism, has precisely the ambition to propose simultaneously the acquisition of a knowledge as extensive and profound as possible, the demanding and persevering education of true human

liberty, and the training of the children and the adolescents . . .
toward the most elevated concrete ideal that could be: Jesus Christ
and His evangelical message.[138]

CONCLUSION

The primary agents, coprincipals, or partners of education are God
and the self-activity of the student. The secondary agents are the
family, the Church, and the State. Among the latter, the nuclear
family — married parents and their progeny — comes first not only
chronologically, but also in the order of priority. This God-ordained
institution, this "domestic church," this basic unit of society, this first
school, forms the earliest, deepest, and most persistent influence on a
person's subsequent behavior, value judgments, and life decisions.

The family's role and responsibilities have to do with their begetting
life — not only physical, but also spiritual. Except for cases of neglect,
abuse, a rejecting circumstance, or any combination of these, parental rights can neither be usurped nor surrendered. The basic element
in parents' educational duty is love, which engenders self-esteem and
proper self-love on the part of their children, from which can arise
fulfillment of the basic Christian law of love of God and neighbor. The
family is to form a loving community of persons, serve life, participate
in the development of society, and share in the life and mission of the
Church.

Because people follow witnesses more readily than teachers and
because children need beacon personalities, Christian parenthood is a
serious obligation. Parents should be given training in parenting, in
home-school cooperation and, while preserving child autonomy, in
ways to bring their children up with religion in a secularist society.
The Christian family is at the heart of the Church's mission to exemplify God's love for His children. Because of complications, like
changing male and female expectations, it is difficult to assign precise
roles to fathers and mothers. More research needs to be done in this
area.

The Church is important to any consideration of Catholic schooling
and education. The New Testament refers to this important sacrament of Christ among us in such terms as the mystical body of Christ,
Christ's spotless bride, and the pillar and bulwark of truth. To describe the Church, the New Testament also uses images like sheepfold,
flock, cultivated field, edifice, and mother. Our day also uses "models"
of the Church, none complete of itself: institution, mystical communion, sacrament, herald, servant, saving institution.

The Church is hierarchical, entailing authority and obedience but
not superiority and subjection for their own sake. Proclaiming the

Gospel of Christ is one of the principal duties of bishops. Priests derive their authority from the bishop. Because baptism unites the faithful with their heavenly king, the laity's share in the priesthood is rightly called a "royal priesthood." The laity help constitute the Church as community, as people of God, as celebrating the Good News instead of just listening to it.

In the particular Catholic school, the local Church—parish, religious community, or whatever—is the sponsoring organization in many more ways than financial. The local Church is the reason the school came into existence, why the school is rooted in Catholic Christianity, and why it remains a Catholic Christian school. The local Church continuously gives the Catholic school the richness of the Christian tradition, exerts its ongoing good influence without interfering with its autonomy, is the speculative model of the Christian community and the practical model of the living faith community, interfaces with the school in a way in which the strengths of each minister to the other's weaknesses, and is a wise and compassionate mediator between the school and the Church at large.

The Church has both rights and duties to schooling. The Church has rights in schooling and education because people have a spiritual nature as well as a physical one, because of social justice, because of the need for the complete betterment of human life, and because of education's being essentially a moral enterprise dealing with the "good person," the "good life," and the "good society." Intertwined with it all is the Church's perception of herself as a loving mother. The Church's serious duties to schooling are reflected in Church legislation.

In addition to financial benefits to the citizenry, the equal and open existence of Catholic schools offers advantages to the State, individuals, society, human activity, and peace. These schools offer an educational alternative for youth; provide wholesome competition with government schools; facilitate high-quality education; can be a source of commitment, direction, and vigor to the community of humankind; offer to human activity a proper and beneficial mean between otherworldly faith and immersion in earthly endeavors, and between the faith which many profess and the practice of their daily lives; and foster and elevate all that is true, good, and beautiful in the human community. For individuals, they offer meaning to life, teachings that elevate the dignity of human nature, proclamations of the rights of humankind, and a presentation of truths of the moral order. The Catholic school, under the auspices and complements of the Church, and with no desire for power, wants to educate children toward the most elevated concrete ideal possible: Jesus Christ and his evangelical message.

We shall now turn to that "partner" of schooling and education which many people in our day take for granted as the dominant agent: the State.

QUESTIONS FOR DISCUSSION

How can the family become more effective as an educational agency?

Is it possible for the school to counteract unfavorable influences in children's homes? If so, how?

Is it possible for the home to counteract unfavorable influences on their children in the school? If so, how?

What kind of plan would you formulate for the promotion of effective cooperation between the home and the school for the best education of children?

Is it realistic—even possible—to expect parents to be morally responsible to bring up their children in the parents' religion? Should parents who are concerned that their children be autonomous, rational, emotionally mature, and properly independent provide their children with a religious upbringing? Can parents do this in an open, pluralist, democratic society, which has maximum toleration of diversity and commitment to free critical debate and a minimum toleration of paternalism?

In secularistic and pluralistic societies, why should the Church have any rights in schooling?

SUGGESTED BIBLIOGRAPHY

Family

Adams, Bert N. *The Family: A Sociological Interpretation*. 4th ed. San Diego: Harcourt Brace Jovanovich, 1986.

In clear language emphasizes interpretations of factual material and develops alternative formulations and paradoxes connected with family research.

Anderson, Herbert. *The Family and Pastoral Care*. Philadelphia: Fortress, 1984.

A brief yet thorough presentation representative of a growing body of Protestant works blending theology and pastoral ministry.

Bellah, Robert N., and associates. *Habits of the Heart: Individualism and Commitment in American Life*. Berkeley: University of California Press, 1985.

This scintillating work is destined to be a classic in describing the underlying values and practices which distinguish contemporary life.

Boyer, Ernest, Jr. *A Way in the World: Family Life as Spiritual Discipline*. San Francisco: Harper and Row, 1984.

A sensitive, personal account of Boyer's life as a family person, based on his attempts to bring out the richness of both the Catholic and Anabaptist traditions. His relentless pursuit of genuine Christian community is challenging.

Callahan, Sidney Cornelia. *Parenting: Principles and Policies of Parenthood*. Garden City, N.Y.: Doubleday, 1973.

Touching the nerve center of the problems of U.S. parents in an objective and optimistic manner, presents personal experience, current psychological theories, and sociocultural observations from a wide range of experts.

Collins, Randall. *Sociology of Marriage and the Family: Gender, Love, and Property*. Chicago: Nelson-Hall, 1986.

A college sociology text, incorporates extensive discussion of feminist perspectives. While not overwhelming the reader with data, draws extensively on recent research. Helps the reader see connections between individual biography, family process, history, and social structure.

Curran, Dolores. *In the Beginning There Were Parents*. Minneapolis, Minn.: Winston, 1978.

This brief and easily read book takes the fear out of parenting and gives parents a sense of confidence in rearing and enjoying their children.

————. *Traits of the Healthy Family*. Minneapolis, Minn.: Winston, 1983.

Describing the top fifteen traits of the healthy family chosen by professionals who work with families, presents a practical and comprehensive guide for developing and maintaining successful family life.

D'Antonio, William, and Joan Aldous, eds. *Religion and Families, Conflict and Change in Modern Society*. Beverly Hills, Calif.: Sage, 1983.

An excellent collection of scholarly sociological essays on the relation of church and family.

Family Resource Coalition. *Programs to Strengthen Families*. Family Resource Coalition, 230 N. Michigan Ave., #1625, Chicago, Ill., 60601.

The many resources of the Coalition are of interest.

Friedman, Edwin. *Generation to Generation; Family Process in Church and Synagogue*. New York: Guilford, 1985.

Shows provocative, interesting, and meaningful connections between family dynamics and those of the local church and synagogue.

Goldstein, Joseph, Anna Freud, and Albert J. Solnit, eds. *Before the Best Interests of the Child*. New York: Free Press, 1979; *Beyond the Best Interests of the Child*, idem, 1973, 1979; *In the Best Interests of the Child: Professional Boundaries*, idem, 1986.

A trilogy illuminating the precarious process of child placement, bringing to professionals and the general public the message that child care in settings outside the family is an essential support, but not a substitute, for parents.

John Paul II. *The Role of the Family in the Modern World (Familiaris consortio)*. Boston: St. Paul, 1981.

An apostolic exhortation applying the Roman Catholic tradition to the modern family.

Jorgensen, Stephen R. *Marriage and the Family: Development and Change*. New York: Macmillan, 1986.

Attempts to synthesize the family-development and social-change approaches to the study of marriage and the family. More successful on development than on change.

Kammeyer, Kenneth. *Marriage and Family*. Boston: Allyn and Bacon, 1986.

An introductory sociology text on the family which presents historical and cross-cultural data, and is interested in providing students with information that will help them make important relationship decisions. Fresh and innovative.

Keniston, K., and the Carnegie Council on Children. *All Our Children: The American Family under Pressure*. New York: Harcourt, Brace, Jovanovich, 1977.

A descriptive study of some of the anxieties, worries, and obstacles that a changing society is creating for U.S. parents and children.

Lamanna, Mary Ann, and Agnes Riedmann. *Marriages and Families: Making Choices Throughout the Life Cycle*. 2nd ed. Belmont, Calif.: Wadsworth, 1985.

An easily read introductory sociology text.

Leslie, Gerald, and Sheila K. Korman. *The Family in Social Context*. 6th ed. New York: Oxford University Press, 1985.

A college text; sociologically covers most of the standard topics on the family. Good coverage of studies published in the specialized family literature from the 1950s to the present.

Montgomery, Mary. *Home Is Where the Heart Is: Ideas to Help Families Grow in Love and Faith*. Minneapolis, Minn.: Winston, 1985.

A relaxed book of delightful suggestions to assist the committed Christian parent in making family wholesome and holy without artificiality.

Nelson, James. *Between Two Gardens: Reflections on Sexuality and Religious Experience*. New York: Pilgrim, 1983.

Probing and insightful explorations.

Packard, Vance. *Our Endangered Children: Growing Up in a Changing World*. Boston: Little, Brown, 1983.

Assesses the multitiude of factors militating against the development of responsibility, curiosity, and drive among children in our society.

Peck, Jane Cary. *Self and Family*. Philadelphia: Westminster, 1984.

Part of the excellent series Choices: Guides for Today's Woman.

Redden, Kenneth R. *Federal Regulation of Family Law*. Charlottesville, Va.: Michie Law Publishers, 1982.

Treats, mostly for lawyers, the complex area of federal (judicial, legislative, and administrative) regulation of family law: marriage, divorce, adoption, child support, child custody, tax, abortion, pensions, etc.

Silberman, Eileen Zieget. *The Savage Sacrament: A Theology of Marriage after American Feminism*. West Mystic, Conn.: Twenty-third Publications, 1983.

An important approach that complements the standard texts in the area.

Skolnik, Arlene S. *The Intimate Environment: Exploring Marriage and the Family*. 4th ed. Boston: Little, Brown, 1987.

Covers the usual text material, presenting a balanced coverage of current debates, giving "the politics of" various topics, and highlighting a social constructionist approach to family public policy issues.

Thomas, David M. *Christian Marriage, A Journey Together*. Wilmington, Del.: Michael Glazier, 1983.

Part of the eight-volume Message of the Sacraments series; places marriage in theology and deals with love in marriage, sex, the marriage ritual, children, change, spirituality, and the sacramentality of marriage.

———. *Family Life and the Church*. New York: Paulist, 1979.

A short (120 pages) manual for leaders and participants in family ministry.

Tufte, Virginia, and Barbara Myerhoff. *Changing Images of the Family*. New Haven, Conn.: Yale University Press, 1979.

This collection of essays looks at the early American family and asks how it can help us understand the family in these last decades of the twentieth century.

Westerhoff, John. *Living the Faith Community; The Church that Makes a Difference*. New York: Seabury, 1985.

A statement of the way faith life is communicated; takes a strong stand in favor of church community with genuine familial relationships.

Church

Bouyer, Louis. *The Church of God*. Chicago, Ill,: Franciscan Herald, 1982.

In most ways a traditional Catholic ecclesiology; builds on Vatican II as well.

Dolan, Jay P. *The American Catholic Experience: A History from Colonial Times to the Present*. New York: Doubleday, 1985.

"Conduct is the key to nature," and this brief popular history of the Catholic Church in the United States gives a key to what the Catholic Church is.

Doohan, Leonard. *The Lay-Centered Church*. Minneapolis, Minn.: Winston, 1984.

A well-researched book on the place of the laity in the Church, supportive to their role.

Dulles, Avery. *Models of the Church*. Garden City, N.Y.: Doubleday, 1978.

A study of ecclesiology with special emphasis on the teachings of the Second Vatican Council.

Flannery, Austin P., ed. *Vatican Council II: The Conciliar and Post Conciliar Documents*. 2 vols. Northport, N.Y.: Costello, 1982.

English translations of the documents of Vatican II and subsequent documents pertaining to each through 1982.

Granfield, Patrick, and Avery Dulles. *The Church: A Bibliography*. Wilmington, Del.: Michael Glazier, 1985.

Much has been written on the Catholic Church, and this guide is a help to potential readers of all tastes.

John Paul II, Pope. "The Gospel Is the Soul of the Catholic School." *L'Osservatore Romano*, vol. XVII no. 29 (July 16, 1984), pp. 6–7.

Address to cardinals and collaborators of the Roman curia, with particular concern for education.

————. "To Ban Catholic Teaching Is an Offence against Human Rights." *L'Osservatore Romano*, vol. XVI no. 20 (May 16, 1983), p. 8.

Address to the Council of the World Union of Catholic Teachers in which John Paul II discussed the need for Catholic education in a pluralistic society and the values Catholic education offers.

————. "What Is the Value of Catholic Education?" *Origins*, vol. XIII no. 23 (November 17, 1983), pp. 389–95.

Address to a group of American bishops in which John Paul II stressed the importance of Catholic schools and the roles of teachers.

Kloppenburg, Bonaventure. *Ecclesiology of Vatican II*. Trans. Matthew J. O'Connell. Chicago: Franciscan Herald, 1974.

The author, a *peritus* at Vatican II, presents an exposition of the Council documents organized around some basic themes: mystery, sacrament, brotherhood, mission, and service.

National Conference of Catholic Bishops. *To Teach as Jesus Did*. Washington, D.C.: National Conference of Catholic Bishops, 1972.

Pastoral message of the U.S. bishops concerning education, reflecting on such issues as adult education, ministry to youth, and Catholic schools.

O'Brien, David J., and Thomas A. **Shannon**, eds. *Renewing the Earth*. Garden City, N.Y.: Doubleday, 1977.

A collection of papal and U.S. Bishops' statements on social justice. Of special importance to education is *Mater et Magistra* and *Christianity and Social Progress*.

Rahner, Karl. *Theological Investigations*. 20 volumes to date. Baltimore, Md.: Helicon, 1961–1974; New York: Seabury, 1974–1980; New York: Crossroad, 1980–1981.

Has much material on conciliar and postconciliar ecclesiology. Volume 14 is especially pertinent.

Schillebeeckx, Edward. *Christ the Sacrament of the Encounter with God*. New York: Sheed and Ward, 1963.

A theological treatise on Christ, the Church, and the Sacraments.

Tobak, J. W., and P. A. Zirkle. "Home Instruction: An Analysis of the Statutes and Case Law," *University of Dayton Law Review*, Fall 1982, pp. 2-60.

Analyzes in detail the legal aspects of the statutory and case law of home instruction as regards fulfilling regulations for compulsory school attendance.

Chapter 7

THE OTHER PARTNER: THE STATE

Long ago, the family was considered the sole agency responsible for education. Then the Church and, even later, the State, became co-partners.[1] Today, the Western world takes State participation in schooling and education for granted, even to the extent of according the State the major, if not sometimes the only, share of the "partnership." Frequently people forget that it was once otherwise, and many people never question other possibilities.

DEFINITIONS AND DISTINCTIONS

In the civil sense as understood here, "society" is the collection of people living within the boundaries of a territory. "Government" is an instrument which, in addition to administrative agencies, normally consists of executive, legislative, and judicial branches; at its best, it carries out the wishes of the people. "State" comprises both society and government, plus sovereignty. The State is the supreme and final legal authority, beyond which there is no further legal power — for better or worse.[2]

ORIGINS OF STATE RIGHTS

The family and the Church, unable to develop to perfection in isolation, need the State, a natural institution which promotes the public welfare and which thereby also has rights and duties. We cannot help but be mindful of Jesus' generic dictum to "give to Caesar what is Caesar's, but give to God what is God's"[3] and of St. Paul's admonition that "all [true, good] authority that exists is established by God."[4] This does not, however, give us the right to expect that — in schooling, education, or anywhere else — Caesar is to be God's enforcer.

179

There are various theories about the origins of the State and its rights. The "Divine" theory, the oldest, maintains that God alone ordained and established the State. This theory remained unquestioned throughout the Middle Ages. The Protestant Reformation strengthened it, backing the claims of national monarchs that they had received their authority directly from God.

The "Force" theory holds that the State had its origins in conquest and coercion. Early writers felt that the State was based on injustice and evil, that the strong imposed their views on the weak. Later writers did not see this force as being necessarily evil. As nationalism became increasingly powerful, a school of thought arose in Germany which argued that the State is *the* power, superior to other forms of human association.

The "Natural" theory agrees with the ancient Greeks in viewing man as inseparable from the State. It continued the Aristotelian view that man is by nature a "political being," the State being not artificial but natural, a force for progress toward the good life.

The "Social Compact" theory, versions of which were advanced by Thomas Hobbes, John Locke, and Jean-Jacques Rousseau, is based on the notion that the State was originally created by people, by means of a social contract to which each individual had consented. Hobbes argued that people were sufficiently anxious for safety and peace to sacrifice all their rights to the State in exchange for permanent security. Locke believed that it was desirable to have an agency which could adjudicate the conflicting claims of individuals in pursuit of their rights. Therefore people voluntarily entered into a compact to form the State to promote and extend people's natural rights of "life, liberty, and property." Though few people today would contend that governments actually originated in a social contract, the concept of the consent of the people is basic to modern versions of democracy.

JUDEO-CHRISTIAN HISTORICAL PERSPECTIVE

To understand the beginnings of Church-State relations in schooling, it is necessary to have a historical perspective. Neither ancient Judaism nor early Christianity believed in State involvement in schools, their emphasis in education being on home and Church. For the ancient Jews the Church, the theocratic State, and the family were always mixed and there was no clear distinction among them.[5] Christianity, however, perceived the order of priority as being the family, the Church, and lastly the State.

The beginnings of State involvement and the ideas of Church-State separation and religious freedom began with the Renaissance and the Reformation. Martin Luther (1483–1546) taught that civil government is a divine institution and that schools were important to train able and skillful rulers and to maintain civil order. Whether humankind acknowledged God or not, Luther hoped to show how God exercised His sovereignty over all phases of existence.[6] John Calvin (1509–64) carried some of these ideas further in his concept of a theocratic state.

Beginning with the Puritans, Calvin's ideas had a deep influence in the United States. And from the early colonies to recent times, Americans looked to schooling as the means of solving their worst problems and achieving their most cherished goals — of developing the enlightened citizenry necessary for a democracy and, as time went on, helping in economic growth and assimilating the increasing number of immigrants. State involvement in schooling in the United States began early, especially with laws like the Massachusetts "Old Deluder Satan Act" of 1647, whereby local communities were to establish schools in order to prevent the Old Deluder, Satan, from corrupting youth.

The dominance of the State over schooling, which most moderns take for granted because they have never experienced anything different, was not always so. It began when the bitter religious controversies of the 1840s, and the controversies' later resurgence increased the downward slide of the dominance of the family and the Church. State dominance in schooling was furthered by decisions on church-affiliated schools rendered by the United States Supreme Court. Most of these decisions have been on the basis of the "establishment clause" of the First Amendment, whose meaning the Court has broadened much more than that of the same amendment's correlative "free exercise" clause.

In 1925, *Pierce v. Society of Sisters*[7] acknowledged the right of nongovernment schools to exist. Since *Pierce*, however, arguments for a "wall of separation" between Church and State, and between government and religion, have won out before the Supreme Court. Most were five-to-four votes, with all kinds of tortuous twists and turns. Bus transportation to and from school can be provided for parochial-school students, but bus transportation to and from field trips cannot. State money can pay for standardized tests in parochial schools, but not for teacher-made tests. Government aid for textbooks for church-school students is acceptable; aid for school supplies such as maps is not. The last gave rise to Senator Daniel Patrick Moynihan's facetious question, "What do you do with a map that's in a textbook?" At present a principle for an "accommodation of religion" appears in the sky like a hopeful dawn, but its light is tenuous and uncertain.[8]

TRUE CHOICE

"Choice" in schooling means the free, conscious, deliberate selection of a school, program, or set of academic courses, as opposed to involuntary assignment to the same. This means government financial provisions to make this possible.[9] True choice of schooling in the United States does not exist for all people. Yet the United States has been called a land of choices. We can choose among one hundred breakfast cereals, two hundred makes of automobiles, three hundred different church denominations. Thus, it is ironic that there is so little choice in the school system. When people speak of "choice" in schools, it is usually limited to only the options available among government schools. The alternatives to government schools are not provided free by the State.

The Roman Catholic Church favors true choice and does not agree with the current State monopoly over schools:

> The task of educating belongs fundamentally and primarily to the family. The function of the State is subsidiary: its role is to guarantee, protect, promote and supplement. Whenever the State lays claim to an educational monopoly, it oversteps its rights and offends justice. It is parents who have the right to choose the school to which they send their children and the right to set up and support educational centres in accordance with their own beliefs. The State cannot without injustice merely tolerate so-called private schools. Such schools render a public service and therefore have a right to financial assistance.[10]

The Church gives valid reasons for this in the individual's right to an education, and within that to the choice of one's own culture:

> Every human being has a right to culture, which is the specific mode of a truly human existence to which one gains access through the development of one's intellectual capacities, moral virtues, abilities to relate with other human beings, and talents for creating things which are useful and beautiful.[11]

Before the family can even begin its responsibilities to its children, it must have freedom of choice — *real* freedom, *true* choice.[12]

Though a relationship between freedom and money may be philosophically difficult to establish, it is even harder to argue that money and freedom have nothing to do with each other. In United States schooling, those who can afford it routinely exercise freedom of choice by selecting a residence in their preferred government-school attendance area, or (less frequently) by choosing nongovernment schools. So when we speak of freedom in schooling, we are really talking about giving *working-class* and *poor* people what the more affluent already have. What everyone has in other areas—such as food stamps, Medicare, and the GI Bill—the poor do not have in a choice of schools.

Nevertheless, there are, in some areas of United States schooling, quiet examples of true choice. In many rural areas and small towns in Vermont[13] and Maine, for example, where they have no government high schools and do not belong to union high school districts, the local public community pays tuition at a school, government or nongovernment, including church-affiliated, chosen by the family. Other communities throughout the country have "public-private" schools, in which religious bodies run schools that are almost completely financially supported by government agencies. These kinds of programs argue against the lack of confidence in government schools of those who contend that readily available meaningful choices will destroy the government schools.[14] Other types of educational choice (for example, for dropouts and for handicapped children), are spreading, but usually only among government schools.

Other democratic nations have a far wider range of choice. In the Netherlands, since the early part of this century the national government has financed government and nongovernment (mostly church-affiliated) primary schools on a virtually equal basis. Canada institutionalized public assistance to sectarian schools in 1867, at the time of the Confederation. Australia provides extensive aid of varying kinds to nongovernment schools—most of which are again church-affiliated. True freedom of choice has been a major theme and value of schooling in Denmark for over a century. England promotes parental choice through various types of subsidy for nongovernment schools. And so on and on.

Freedom of choice is a right due to parents in distributive justice, the justice which accords to every individual basic rights that the community as a whole and each of its agencies and members must recognize. Such justice would enable parents to choose the school which their conscience perceives to be in the best interest of their children.[15] The Church insists that parents have a right to choose a school in conformity with their religious faith, and this right should be absolutely guaranteed.[16] Again,

> From this [the importance of the role of the school in education] it
> clearly follows that, in principle, a State monopoly of education is
> not acceptable, and that only a pluralism of school systems will
> respect the fundamental right and the freedom of individuals.[17]

The United States Supreme Court has enunciated the concept that
the child is not the mere creature of the State.[18] The principle is
sound. A gardener who grows different kinds of flowers—violets,
roses, orchids—knows that all of them require the same basics: air,
water, heat, and nutrients. But giving all of them identical treatment
would result in many not reaching their full potential. It is like that
with children and the schools they attend.

True choice provides many benefits. When provided choices, students from the most academically disadvantaged to the most outstanding seem to produce significant growth and achievement in the
cognitive, social, and affective domains. Diversity enriches and need
not divide. With media penetrating the previously inaccessible moun-
tains and valleys of the country, there is less reason than in the horse-
and-buggy days to depend on schools to homogenize the citizenry.
Choice fosters greater satisfaction, involvement, and commitment.
One who chooses a school has a stake in it and wants to make it work.
Choice is in itself a learning experience: one who wants to make an
intelligent choice has to investigate the alternatives.

The beneficial results of choice are consonant with national goals.
One goal is equity—that the poor may enjoy some of the opportunities which the rich already have by virtue of their wealth. Many inner-
city children are trapped in inferior government schools, without alternatives. For a large number this means a life of functional illiteracy,
unemployment, and poverty. Schools which receive children under
compulsory education laws, and are the only ones to do so, are not
motivated to be responsive; the enlargement of competition between
schools and school systems would help.

Still another national goal is the centrality and strength of the
family. This is enhanced by opening the system to a challenge to the
majority beliefs, values, and philosophies and to the homogenized
orthodoxy of a monopolistic government-school pattern. Schools that
serve a truly functional community provide for "intergenerational
closure"—the web of relationships that binds parents and children—in
contrast with the current basis of school-residential proximity, which
no longer serves well. The welfare of the State is dependent on the
welfare of the family, and can be realized only by the State understanding, respecting, and deferring to the welfare of the family.

Though many parents do not have the time, inclination, or ability to completely take over their children's schooling, they want the dignity in their children's eyes of making the important decisions. Parental choice of schooling would have the supremely important effect of communicating to children the State's endorsement of their parents. Love is as much a need in school choice as it is in all other aspects of child rearing. Parental love is all-consuming and has credibility. The State's custodial concern, even at its best, is incomprehensible to the child.

The principle of true choice is the people's preference. In polls, people have indicated that they would like to be able to choose their schools for reasons of discipline, more individual attention, better student-teacher ratio, religion, cost, convenience, and a host of other reasons.[19] It is instructive that the ones who want educational choice the most tend to be those who enjoy it the least: parents with children in school, blacks, central-city residents, the poor with a grade-school education, and those who judge their local schools least satisfactory. Those who oppose freedom of choice include the more affluent, people most satisfied with their local government school, older people, rural and suburban populations, and medium-sized-city residents.[20]

TWO WAYS OF STATE IMPLEMENTATION OF EDUCATIONAL FREEDOM

The State's responsibility to implement and make meaningful the parents' right to freedom of choice in schooling can be done in a variety of ways. The most prominent today in the United States are tuition tax credits, tax deductions, and vouchers. Tuition tax credit is a procedure whereby income-tax-paying parents receive a credit from their income tax for an agreed-upon amount for each of their children's tuition, no matter what school their children attend, and non-income-tax-paying poor parents receive an enabling fee for the same purpose.

This is not to be confused with a tax deduction, a subtraction from income in items like medical bills. It was a tax deduction that was adjudicated in the 1983 case of *Mueller v. Allen*.[21] In that 1983 case, the United States Supreme Court ruled that a Minnesota law providing for state tax deductions for school expenses did not violate the establishment clause of the United States Constitution when taxpayers took deductions for expenses incurred at religious schools. The Court gave as its reason the fact that the deductions were available across the board to parents with children in government and nongovernment schools alike. Furthermore, the Court ruled that even though the deductions eventually benefited religious schools they did so only as a result of the free choice of parents. As this is being written, *Mueller*-type bills are pending in several state legislatures.

Vouchers as we speak of them here are certificates given to parents to pay for tuition or other specific school costs at any eligible government or nongovernment school, religious or secular, within or outside the student's school district. Vouchers eliminate the assignment of children to schools by districts, zones, or any other currently mandated designation; students would attend schools of their own choice. A good example of vouchers already existing is the federal government's food stamp program. Recipients of the stamps use them as vouchers to buy groceries — not at government food stores, but at stores of the choice of the food-stamp recipients.

Vouchers embody a mainstream American principle: citizen sovereignty. In schooling, this translates into the principle of parental choice. Currently, most American parents have no say in where their children attend school unless they can afford to choose where to live. Unfortunately, many families cannot afford to move to the areas where good schools are located. If they cannot afford tuition at a nongovernment school they have to take what they get. As a result, control of schooling has become more and more remote from parents. Over the past twenty-five years, educational decision making has been shifting from local areas to state governments, the U.S. Department of Education, and the federal courts. Contemporary research provides an empirical base for what many people have known all along: schools will not be effective without the personal commitment of parents, which can best be secured by parental choice of schooling.

Moreover, because the voucher goes directly to parents and only indirectly to the schools, each school is in direct competition with all other schools for students. Good schools would attract many students, redeem many vouchers, and prosper, while bad schools, avoided by parents, would either have to improve or close down. In addition, the administrative setup of schooling is an anomaly among government programs. Most government programs — student loans, welfare, Social Security, Medicaid, Medicare — subsidize the individual recipients rather than the institutions that supply the services.[22] Unfortunately, the history of educational vouchers reflects the "establishment's" displeasure with the idea. Nevertheless, responses to 1983 and 1985 Gallup polls indicated that close to half of the public favored a voucher plan.

Critics of vouchers give many counterarguments. First, a voucher system would undermine government schools. Nongovernment schools, they say, could accept the most promising students, leaving the government schools to educate those with low aptitude, emotional problems, or physical disabilities. Proponents of vouchers counter that current attendance figures do not bear this out. They also claim that government schools warrant a higher level of confidence than the opponents imply.

Second, critics contend that vouchers either offer false hope to poor people or the initial amounts mentioned in voucher proposals represent a camel's nose under the tent, unavoidably to be followed by the whole camel of equal financial treatment for nongovernment schools. Choice proponents counter that this is too speculative and hypothetical to deal with at the present time.

Third, voucher critics suggest that parents could not make informed, intelligent choices. Choice proponents counter that this position is elitist and paternalistic. If parents are eligible to vote, they should be able to choose their children's school. Fourth, critics argue that, under the United States Supreme Court's 1985 *Aguilar v. Felton* decision, it would not be constitutional to use federal funds to pay for instruction in parochial schools because it would lead to "excessive entanglement of church and state."[23] Choice proponents counter that the principle that Church and State "work together" and have "frequent contacts"—words which in the *Felton* decision seemed to be dirty words—is to be praised, not condemned. They also argue that, in any case, vouchers issued directly to parents avoid such entanglement.

Fifth, critics say that vouchers' primary effect would be to advance religion, which the Supreme Court has struck down in state programs providing tuition grants for the parents of parochial-school students. Voucher proponents counter that it is high time the country stopped perceiving the spread of religion as analogous to the spread of a contagious disease. Finally, argue the critics, voucher money could be used in schools that discriminate along racial, ethnic, political, ideological, or religious lines. Proponents counter that this can easily be avoided by carefully crafted legislation.

ADVANTAGES AND DISADVANTAGES
OF GOVERNMENT HELP

One of the advantages of equal government aid to church-affiliated and government schools is the avoidance of elitism:

> In some countries Catholic schools have been obliged to restrict their educational activities to wealthier social classes, thus giving an impression of social and economic discrimination in education. But this occurs only where the State has not weighed the advantages of an alternative presence in their pluralistic society.[24]

Another advantage is that it helps church-affiliated schools in their desire to open themselves to cooperate with other schools and to share their anxieties and their hopes.[25] And it is to the advantage of society that the Catholic school be not only particularly sensitive to the call for a more just society, but that it be able to try to make its own contribution towards that worthy end.[26] And certainly the other public services provided by Catholic schools are a help to the nation.[27]

Among the disadvantages of government aid to church-affiliated schools is that "he who pays the piper calls the tune." If the church-affiliated school is interested in maintaining its identity, it must prudently ask the question, "How much government interference is tolerable in our schools in curriculum, textbooks, student deportment, educational philosophy, teacher hiring and firing, and so on?"

There are examples of disadvantages of government aid. The French "contract schools" have entered into contract with the State, which pays their teachers and gives schools on the secondary level a set fee per pupil. There are in return some legitimate government regulations about security, corridor space, and the like. The schools cannot charge the fees they might require, but must act within the limits given by the government. Then, where the French schools are traditionally off on Wednesdays in order that State primary-school children may attend religious instruction at their parish, the government is currently arguing for school on Wednesdays; the government is also raising arguments over who makes teacher appointments.[28] Canada provides another example. There, volunteerism, commitment, and loyalty decreased after government aid.[29]

In the United States, another danger involves the issue of a candidate's religion in the hiring of faculty. College-level Church-related schools which receive government money are coming under increased fire on this score. Church officials say that faculty members' religion is essential to maintaining an institution's religious identity. A spate of legal actions across the country, however, pit the First Amendment's guarantee of the institution's religious liberty against the right of the individual to protection from unfair employment practices.

Some institutions define their preferential-hiring practices narrowly, applying them only to faculty who teach religion. Others say that, for a variety of reasons, they want all of their employees to share their religious affiliation. The latter institutions believe in the relevance of faith to everything they do, and do not believe that one who is earnest about his or her faith can compartmentalize it. Some publicize the basic mission and goals of the institution and have the candidate as well as the administrators try to ascertain whether the potential employee can support these goals.

Most are willing to make trade-offs between professional academic qualifications and religious affiliation, similar to the way they do between teaching and research. And many agree with a sermon delivered in 1972 by the Reverend James Burtchaell at Notre Dame University, in which he wanted a "critical mass" of faculty members to be "committed and articulate believers, who purposefully seek the comradeship of others to weave their faith into the full fabric of their intellectual life."[30]

U. S. GOVERNMENT OPPOSITION
TO CATHOLIC POSITIONS
Legislative Branch

In the legislative branch of government, there seems to be sufficent responsiveness to the positions of constituencies to indicate an awareness of the financial need of nongovernment schools. There is, for instance, in many parts of the country a continuance of a greater number of "public-parochial" schools than is admitted. Public-parochial schools are those which, though church-affiliated, have most of their expenses paid by government money. This is a procedure in most enlightened Western democracies, and has deep historical roots in the United States. Many legislators would like to see the eminently successful GI Bill (Servicemen's Readjustment Act) of 1944 applied to lower schools. Giving forms of aid to nongovernment as well as government schools was the National Defense Education Act, enacted in 1958, renewed in 1961, and broadened in 1964, and the Elementary and Secondary Education Act of 1965.

Even when the legislative branch tries to be agreeable, however, it often falls far short of Catholic ideals and expectations to strengthen the family. Even the new income-tax law, for example, continues to charge more against the incomes of two working people who are married over the same two incomes of single persons. Also, public policy should support the decision of mothers to stay home when their children are very young, devoting their full energies to child care (by, for instance, paid maternity leave and children's allowances, as in most other developed nations, or by a system of special tax treatment to offset the lost wages of mothers at home). Widowed and divorced mothers should be protected from later poverty, when because of their years of child care they receive lower earnings and less retirement income.

Women should also not be discriminated against in the work force. In order for the evolution of society to be fully human, women must have opportunities to "harmoniously combine" their private and public, family and occupational roles.[31] The ultimate goal of profamily policies is the good of society: the health of the whole society is heavily dependent on healthy families which can provide care for the very young and the very old.

Judicial Branch

The jurisprudence of the United States Supreme Court applying the First Amendment's "establishment clause" to governmental help for religiously affiliated schools is in a state of ambivalence, chaos, and unpredictable change. The determining philosophy behind the confusion is said to be a merging of Positivism and Utilitarianism into legal "Realism." Opponents of putting denominational schools on a par with government schools assert the unconstitutionality of government financial assistance to church-affiliated schools. The inclusion of religion, they say, makes it impossible not to violate the "wall of separation between church and state."[32]

This position is erroneous and dangerous—as Robert Frost indicated when he wrote:

> Before I built a wall I'd ask to know
> What was I walling in or walling out.[33]

The Constitution contains no absolutes in this matter, and any attempt to construct a high and impregnable wall in this area would lead to the elimination of all reference to religion in all schools and thus to an absurd set of consequences.[34]

Education can never be morally neutral, and moral interest pervades the entire educational program. This is true in government schools, where the religion is secularism, as well as others.[35] Exclusion of religion from education leads to the absurdities perceived by C. S. Lewis:

> Such is the tragic comedy of our situation—we continue to clamor for those very qualities we are rendering impossible. . . . In a sort of ghastly simplicity we remove the organ and demand the function. . . . We laugh at honor and we are shocked to find traitors in our midst. We castrate and bid the geldings be fruitful.[36]

Or, as a former president of Boston University, D. L. Marsh, said: "When we leave religion out of our educational program we practically announce that life can be explained without God, which is the same thing as saying that either God does not exist or is of no consequence."[37]

Historical and cultural considerations of religion and schooling in the United States make manifest the complexities of the issues involved and the varieties of interpretation of the foundational documents of the United States on this subject. From the earliest colonial times until well into the nineteenth century — a period of over two hundred years — Americans commonly assumed that religion was the foundation of a complete education and that education was regarded as a function of the Church. Denominational groups accepted their responsibility regardless of whether state aid was available, and state financial support for various types of denominational schools was the rule rather than the exception in the early days of the new nation.[38]

It was really *disestablishment* of churches that the Founding Fathers had in mind, which is completely different from *separation* of religion from education. Ten of the thirteen original states had official sanctions for religion; three had established churches. On the day the first Congress passed the First Amendment in September 1789, it also called for a day of national prayer and thanksgiving. Most of the Founding Fathers favored equal financial treatment for church-affiliated schools. Senator Robert Packwood said in a Senate subcommittee hearing on tuition tax credits:

> Every member of the Constitutional Convention came from a state that, prior to the adoption of the Constitution and after, levied taxes . . . , collected those taxes, and gave the taxes to churches to run primary and secondary schools for the education of those children who chose to go to school.[39]

It was not until Andrew Jackson, the seventh president of the United States (1829–1837), that we had a chief executive who had attended a government school.

The Supreme Court ignores the fact that, even on their own terms of adherence to the Constitution, to exclude religious schools from eligibility is to deny a welfare benefit to a child because of his religion. This is a religious test condemned by the Constitution. A good area for research would be the legally valid philosophies of the dissent, especially in the many five-to-four decisions.

Religious instruction in the curriculum is the principal reason churches sponsor schools, but from the viewpoint of civil society it is only *one* of the reasons to look with favor upon the benefit to society of church-affiliated schools. The government may be well advised to promote purposefully, for the general welfare, the secular aspects of church-affiliated schools. The government has done this in other areas — for example, the GI Bill of 1944, the Hospital Survey and Construction Act of 1946, the venerable tax exemption of religious organizations, and the age-old inclusion of God in the Pledge of Allegiance to the flag. Just as the national interest has been this country's tradition with respect to highways, hospitals, unemployment compensation, urban redevelopment, and other areas, so should it be in schooling.

The fact that church-affiliated schools accomplish purposes of their own is irrelevant, so long as their purposes are compatible with the national interest. The coinciding of private interest with the public welfare should be no barrier to the accomplishment of the common good. Congress cannot constitutionally give public funds to business corporations for the distribution of dividends, but Congress may, and in fact does, subsidize businesses affecting the public interest. The "no establishment" clause and the "free exercise" clause of the First Amendment should be given the unitary construction that was the intent of their authors. Both clauses together are necessary to secure true and full religious liberty.[40]

That denominational schools provide a curriculum that complies with state requirements is a fact, and a fact with legal significance. The Supreme Court's holding in *Bradfield v. Roberts* that a direct appropriation might be made for the performance of a public function to an institution conducted under the auspices of a church which exercised "perhaps controlling influence"[41] over it is significant; it should be applied not only to hospitals, which was the issue in *Bradfield*, but also to schools.

Pierce v. Society of Sisters[42] in 1925 held that Oregon's denial of accreditation of religious schools to fulfill compulsory schooling requirements was a denial of the free exercise of religion. This "Oregon School Case" has been deemed a charter for the right of the existence of nongovernment schools. This right is, however, exercised at the cost of an increasingly heavy burden, financial and otherwise, for parents who choose to send their children to nongovernment schools. A free education seems conditioned on the surrender of *Pierce* rights, a condition which the Supreme Court has condemned elsewhere: "conditions upon public benefits cannot be sustained if they so operate, whatever their purpose, as to inhibit or deter the exercise of First Amendment freedoms."[43]

The Court in *Pierce* interpreted the right of parents to choose nongovernment schooling for their children to be fundamental. But it has refused to confront the fact that many are denied the exercise of this right. Some parents can neither financially afford to send their children to church-affiliated schools nor refuse their children's attendance at government schools because of compulsory schooling laws. Yet the

Court has held unconstitutional the denial of fundamental rights due to such an economic status.[44]

Current Trends

In the United States

In some respects lately, in both legislatures and courts there seems to be an "accommodation" of religion. The Court approved payments to nongovernment schools for costs of administering and reporting state-mandated, state-approved tests as well as for other required record keeping and reporting. It condemned as unconstitutional the State's denial to religious groups of access to government-school facilities allowed for similar but nonreligious groups. It upheld the paid employment of religious chaplains by state legislatures and the recitation of prayers at the beginning of legislative sessions.

It approved state income-tax credits for educational expenses incurred by parents of nongovernment- as well as government-school children. It allowed the public display of a Christmas crèche by the city of Pawtuckett, Rhode Island, at public expense.[45] In its important 1984 accommodation decision, *Lynch v. Donnelly*, the Court came to see that the "wall" of separation between Church and State is a useful metaphor, but not an accurate description of the reality. The Constitution, the Court saw, does not require

> complete separation of church and state; it affirmatively mandates accommmmodation, not merely tolerance, of all religions, and forbids hostility toward any. . . . Anything less would require the "callous indifference" . . . [that] was never intended by the Establishment Clause.[46]

These cases said that the original intent of the establishment clause was to prevent government from favoring one or more religions as opposed to others and, by extension, from favoring traditional religions as opposed to other views of life and reality.[47] There is little danger of this kind of favoritism today.[48] An absolute separation of government and religion is impossible, and could result in an unconstitutional inhibition of religion, contrary to the First and Fourteenth Amendments.[49] The "wall of separation" metaphor cannot be taken literally, and simply means nonintrusion of Church and State into one another's special provinces and affairs.[50] Accommodation of religion by government is not only allowed, but is positively mandated by the Constitution.[51] Rejection of indirect forms of government aid to church-related schools, such as tax deductions for educational expenses, is not required by the establishment clause of the Constitution, and such an extreme result was never intended by those who adopted the Constitution.[52] Private education makes many important contributions to the public welfare.[53] Government and the public at large have an interest in the health and survival of independent education.[54]

Whether this accommodation of religion, which is a more realistic interpretation of the establishment clause and a better balance between the establishment and free exercise clauses, marks a trend remains to be seen. Church-State cases relative to schools were usually decided by the narrow majority of five-to-four, and there have been contrary decisions, some seemingly senseless, like the denial of government funding of remedial educational programs for parochial school children on the premises of the parochial school.[55]

In the United States, the three dominant current values in deciding Church-State issues in schooling are neutrality, religious accommodation, and guarantees of the separation of Church and State. Pertaining to the last, the "wall of separation" concept, though a metaphor (and rules of law are not supposed to be drawn from metaphors), has a history of use. Close examination, however, reveals the "wall" to be "blurred, indistinct, and variable."[56] The current three-pronged test (which is supposed to be a helpful signpost rather than a set formula) for the validity of government money going into programs that involve religion is that there be a secular legislative purpose, that the principal effect must neither advance nor inhibit religion, and that there be no excessive government entanglement.[57] But nothing could be more divisive than to try to channel all government aid toward the subsidization solely of secularism as a national "culture" and even "religion."

In Other Countries

In Australia, which in 1898 adopted a constitution copied from that of the U.S., decisions have been less confused and more direct than those in the U.S. The Australian Constitution's Section 116 is, almost word for word, the U.S. First Amendment:

> The Commonwealth shall not make any law for establishing any religion, or for imposing any religious observance, or for prohibiting the free exercise of any religion, and no religious test shall be required as a qualification for any office or public trust under the Commonwealth.[58]

In 1973, the Attorney-General for the state of Victoria brought suit in behalf of twenty-seven plaintiffs, including the National Council of Independent Schools (NCIS), against the Commonwealth of Australia and others, including the Council for the Defence of Government Schools (DOGS), for financial assistance to independent schools, most of which were owned by "the Roman Catholic church or its agencies."[59] The suit fought its way up to the High Court of Australia. After duly recognizing the dependence of the Australian Constitution on that of the U.S., the majority opinion declared for the plaintiffs. It forthrightly stated, among other things, that "a law which establishes a religion will inevitably do so expressly and directly and not, as it were, constructively."[60]

The decision indicated that establishing a religion involves religion's entrenchment as a feature of and identified with the body politic. Such establishment also involves the identification of the religion with the civil authority such that it involves the citizen in a duty to maintain it and the obligation of, in this case, the Commonwealth to patronize, protect, and promote it. In other words, establishing a religion involves its adoption as an institution of the Commonwealth, part of the Commonwealth "establishment."[61] The High Court noted that in the case at issue the "financial aid is expressly limited to the educational activities of such schools."[62] Expressly declaring itself independent of American case law, the court stated, "A law which in operation may indirectly enable a church to further the practice of religion is a long way away from a law to establish religion. . . . "[63]

The United States Supreme Court seems at best to encourage "civil religion," a secularist religion begun by Jean-Jacques Rousseau, which sees the United States in transcendent terms.[64] Its Supreme Being is Thomas Jefferson's rights-giving Creator, George Washington's First Author, or Abraham Lincoln's Judge. Its calendar sets aside days to honor its saints (Washington, Lincoln, Martin Luther King) and to celebrate its civic virtues: the Fourth of July (liberty), Memorial Day (sacrifice), Veteran's Day (service), Thanksgiving (recognition of providential bounty). Ironically, if we were to take this civil religion as seriously as some of our forebears did, the Supreme Court by its current principles would have to rule civil religion unconstitutional.

One result is that a bitter French-type conflict between secularists and a reactionary religious right is beginning to stir in this country. Another result is secular humanism, the man-as-God dogma that packages humanism as psychology in an attempt to avoid being attacked as a religion. But this deification of man is a *religion*, albeit not perhaps in the traditional sense. Its creed is summarized in *The Hu-*

manist Manifesto I (1933), *The Humanist Manifesto II* (1973), and *A Secular Humanist Declaration* (1980),[65] documents which are a profession of anthropological atheism. Their definition of humanism is vague: "Humanism is faith in the supreme value and self-perfectibility of human personality." When the U.S. Supreme Court cited humanism as a religion,[66] the Court was recognizing that in form — particularly in the context of what it called a "world view" — humanism qualifies as a religion, albeit not a *theistic* one.[67]

OVERLAPS, COMPLICATIONS, AND GOVERNMENT USURPATIONS

We have given some principles concerning the family, the Church, and the State as partners in education. In theory, they look fine. In theory, between the partners in schooling and education there should be cooperation, understanding, tolerance, goodwill, and mutual recognition of the definite rights of each — all for the good of students, parents, community, and nation. In practice, however, the agents do not always act in harmony. There are many overlaps of interest. In the current climate it is too easy for the government to usurp the rights of the family and the Church.

The Supreme Court, for example, recently has more and more eroded the legal basis for the family and emphasized radical individualism. Beginning in the midsixties, two parallel developments show this: the elaboration of the right of privacy and the advancement of the rights of minors. In 1965, in *Griswold v. Connecticut*,[68] the Court invalidated a law in Connecticut which forbade distribution or use of contraceptives, even by married persons. The Court said that the family is prior to the State and has rights higher and more sacred than any claim of government (thus carving out a place for the family in constitutional law), and then went on to invent a new fundamental constitutional right, the right to privacy.

In extending this right to privacy to the distribution or use of contraceptives to unmarried persons in the 1972 case *Eisenstadt v. Baird*,[69] the Court was indirectly eliminating the premise that the right of privacy is based on the sanctity of marriage — in other words, declaring the irrelevance of marriage for the sake of supporting radical individualism. William Baird is fond of claiming that this case was the stepping-stone to the Supreme Court's legalization of abortion on demand a year later.[70]

A simultaneous step in the process of the Court's denigrating the family was the furtherance of the rights of minors. In the 1967 case of *In re Gault*,[71] the Court sensibly declared that the rights of minors are protected by the Constitution. The next case in the development of the "children's liberation" movement was *Tinker v. Des Moines*[72] in 1969. Young Tinker, in protest against the Vietnam war, wore a black armband to school. The Court ruled in favor of his free-speech rights. In 1970, the Court extended to juvenile determinations the "beyond a reasonable doubt" burden of proof applied in adult criminal cases. No child could be found delinquent unless the facts underlying the delinquency determination were beyond a reasonable doubt.[73] Thus, there is now a great deal of difficulty determining delinquency. Finally, the Court extended the protections of due process into the government schools, ruling that due process required some sort of adequate, regularized procedures whereby a child could defend himself or herself against charges that would lead to school suspension.[74]

These strands came together in 1976, when the Supreme Court handed down its most antifamily decision ever, in its 1976 decision on *Planned Parenthood of Cent. Missouri v. Danforth*.[75] The Missouri legislature, after the Supreme Court's abortion decisions, had passed a law to restrict abortions. Two key provisions required that a married woman seeking an abortion would first have to obtain the consent of her husband and that an unmarried minor seeking an abortion would first have to obtain the consent of a parent or guardian. The state's intention was, in addition to saving babies, to protect the rights of families—first of all by protecting the rights of the husband in a matter having very serious consequences for the marital relationship. This was not a novel theory. The consent of both husband and wife is required before a couple may enter any such important arrangements as the adoption of a child or before disposition of jointly owned property. The Court ruled that both Missouri provisions on abortion were unconstitutional.

The Court did not say that a husband's rights are of less weight than a wife's, but simply ignored the marital relationship entirely. The Court sidestepped central family issues by shifting its focus to the power of the State. Because the State had no right to prohibit abortion, said the Court, the State could not give such a right to a husband. The implication of this reasoning was that the husband has no rights on his own, and is invested by the State with whatever rights he has.

Missouri's position on children was also nothing new. It was simply specifying a well-established principle of common law that minors may ordinarily not consent to their own medical treatment, and that parents bear the primary legal responsibility for their health and welfare. Minors having their ears pierced would be another specification implied in the common law. The Court, in rendering its decision, invoked its children's rights precedents. The Court's decision results in children needing parental consent for having their ears pierced, but not for an abortion. It should be noted that the Court's concept of increased child sophistication is not backed by psychodevelopmental research.

In 1979, in *Bellotti v. Baird*,[76] the Court decided that the only occasions in which the State may require parental notification prior to an abortion are those in which a court determines that the minor seeking the abortion is not mature *and* that the abortion would not be in her best interest. Since *Bellotti*, there is no instance in which a court has made both of these determinations. The reasoning is usually that if a minor is not mature enough to consent to the abortion, she is not mature enough to assume the responsibilities of parenthood, and so the abortion is in her best interest.[77]

Even when the government tries to do good, it often confuses principles and usurps what others can probably do better. In providing welfare benefits, for example, the proper concept of the family must be central. Too often the government phrases the issue in terms of how to get welfare mothers out of the home and into the workplace. The government frequently pays little attention to the impact of mothers' full-time employment on very young children growing up in single-parent families with few resources. Public policy offers little support of the ideal of children being cared for in their own homes by their own mothers. Welfare policy should be more sensitive.

Further inevitable conflict is caused by the *values* taught in government schools. In the first stage of U.S. history, lasting well into the nineteenth century, the government schools taught evangelical Protestant values. Next came a relatively brief period of nondenominational religious values, which never quite took hold before it was overtaken by the current era of secular values. Just as the reaction to the initial Protestant values helped bring about the inception of the Catholic-school pattern, the current phenomenon is bringing about a Protestant response. The Protestant response is twofold: forming their own schools and turning to home instruction.[78]

The formation of Protestant schools has been successful. Though they are usually small, and frequently fundamentalist, the number of their schools is so great that their student population is rapidly catching up with the Catholic. But their founders believe so strongly that the school is an extension of the Church and teachers akin to pastors, that they argue that these schools should not have to obtain approval from the State. In some of these schools, teachers who are certifiable refuse to be certified as a matter of principle. Critics are concerned about the adequacy of the physical facilities of many of these schools, worry about poorly qualified or too few teachers, and at times claim that some of these schools are teaching political views that sharply differ from the mainstream of American democratic thought. Litigation over State regulation of religious schools has increased sharply.

Home instruction is also rapidly increasing. While estimates vary, the proportion is probably less than one percent of school-age children, about half motivated by religion. The legal permissibility of home schooling varies from jurisdiction to jurisdiction.[79] With home-school advocates relying on the protection of the Ninth Amendment of the Constitution, and with no state expressly declaring home schooling illegal, most court cases weigh the balance in favor of the state's compelling interest in education. Critics in the education profession focus on four requirements for approvable home instruction: sound curriculum, determined through educational research; certified teachers; evaluation of students' academic achievement; and the same health requirements as for schools.

Although the socializing experience gained from going to school cannot easily be provided at home, home-education advocates say that school is only one of the places where children can meet other children; they contend that home-educated children more advantageously make friends with people of all ages rather than only with children who are within a year of their own birthday. The Virginia State Board of Education, in an advisory opinion for the state legislature, summed up the position of many states:

> [E]ducation is provided to a greater extent in an environment where discipline and control is more objective [than in the home environment], where a program and progress of study are verifiable, where the teacher has a singular role as teacher, where the student has a singular role as student, and where the exclusive focus and reason for meeting is the educational program.[80]

In a case concerning Catholics in home schooling, the Catholics did not fare well. In September, 1982, Margaret Snider, who lived with her husband, Richard, and their family near Richmond, Virginia, began teaching her two children at home, using the "Our Lady of Victory" home-study course. Eventually brought to "justice," Circuit Court Judge L. Paul Byrne acknowledged that Mrs. Snider was a good teacher and her children were probably getting at least as good an education as they would in government schools. But he ruled that the Sniders were guilty of truancy because their belief that sending their children to government schools would be wrong was philosophical, not religious in the sense of being based on Catholic dogma.[81]

The Sniders' views, however, had persuasive precedents. In 1972, the Supreme Court's *Wisconsin v. Yoder* had ruled in favor of an Amish family in almost exactly similar circumstances, saying:

> This case involves the fundamental interest of parents, as contrasted with that of the state, to guide the religious future and education of their children. . . . This primary role of the parents in the upbringing of their children is now established beyond debate as an enduring American tradition.[82]

And in 1981, Chief Justice Warren Burger, writing for the Court, laid down a policy that Judge Byrne ignored: "Intrafaith differences . . . are not uncommon . . . and the judicial process is singularly ill equipped to resolve such differences . . . Courts are not arbiters of scriptural interpretation." Burger at the same time ruled that "the guarantee of free exercise is not limited to beliefs which are shared by all members of a religious sect."[83]

The U.S. Supreme Court has often been the arbiter between the rights of parents and those of the State over children. It has consistently recognized the parents as having the fundamental right and duty to exercise custody, care, and control in the upbringing of their children.[84] It has adjudged that the State has the right to limit these duties only if parental conduct seriously endangers the health and safety of the child or if the limitation is necessary to avoid a significant social burden. Therefore parents cannot physically abuse their children and must educate them according to minimal government requirements. Beyond these limits, parents have near absolute power over their children. On the other hand, children are not mere possessions.

The State's heavy intrusion into the privacy of parent-child relations yields two observations. First, even in the case of families alleged by the State to be incompetent, the State does not appear to be skilled at providing the necessary training and experience. Secondly, the provision of State services may conflict with the desires of parents, and this renders the State the adversary of the parent.[85]

We should at the same time recognize that the court cases reviewed do not normally arise from harmonious familial structures; they are more the exception than the rule. Nonetheless, the legal decisions concerning weighty value conflicts regarding autonomy, liberty, and rights demand attention in evaluating the rights and roles of parents during the child's development. In fact, the Court's opinions mirror as well as form the social and moral changes of the past two decades regarding family structures and roles.

WHAT TO DO ABOUT IT

The solution to the problems of overlaps and complications among parents, Church, and State, and the aggressive incursions of the State on the other two, is multifaceted. The solution involves, at an initial minimum, instruction in the rights and duties of the family and the Church, affirmative and realistic programs of encouragement for those agencies, and familiarization with the realities of life in our republic.

Proponents of Church-affiliated schools should familiarize themselves, first of all, with the fact that the philosophies by which their government works are often inimical to their own. The two dominant philosophies in twentieth-century jurisprudence are Legal Positivism and Utilitarianism. Legal Positivism has many different forms, but in general it says that the only rights and duties that exist are those explicit in man-made positive law, that is, legislative statutes and past judicial decisions. These statutes and decisions have been rendered by people who have no necessary reference beyond themselves in the direction of individual justice, which is the heart of the matter. Beyond their decisions, in fact, for them there is no "heart of the matter." Utilitarian theorists argue that, in hard cases, judges decide on the basis of what is good for society. In the words of Jeremy Bentham, the nineteenth-century founder of Utilitarianism, the basis is the greatest good for the greatest number.

The courts seem oblivious to the societal harms brought about by positivistic interpretation of law. This philosophy defeats that inquiry into justice which ought to be one of the contributions of jurisprudence. Legal Positivism can contribute to the dangerous tendency of people, including members of the legal profession, to accept as respectable whatever has been officially recognized or proffered as such. In Germany, it was adherence to legal positivism that aided the Nazi drive for the establishment of dictatorship. In the United States, the doctrine provided a convenient principle for *Korematsu v. United States* crediting as law what had been administratively formulated as the legal basis for placing a person in a concentration camp, depriving a person of his life irrespective of any knowledgeable commission of wrong.[86]

Church members cherish belief in the dignity of the person. One of the United States' documents that manifests the same belief is the Declaration of Independence, which calls upon unalienable rights. The difference between the Founding Fathers and many modern jurisprudes is in the source and protector of those rights. The Founding Fathers wrote, "We hold these truths to be self-evident, that all

men are . . . *endowed by their Creator* with certain unalienable rights."
The Founding Fathers understood that without a fair degree of virtue
in the people and without a sense of societal morality, democracy
might not endure.

Most of the Founding Fathers believed that an important source of
that morality was religion. Alexis de Tocqueville observed in 1835 that
it was precisely religion that "has enabled Americans to use liberty
and to preserve it." There is no such thing as "a naked public square"
that is free of religion of one kind or another. If religions of the Judeo-
Christian tradition, with which our history is inextricably intertwined, are pushed out of that square, religious nihilism or other
value systems will rush in to occupy it.

From the First Congress on, government aided religion. The First
Congress, for example, established a congressional chaplaincy and
authorized the president to create a military chaplaincy. The Second
Congress created a separate chaplaincy for the navy. Congress ratified
with Indian tribes treaties which respectively provided for the building of a church on an Indian reservation at government expense and
provided a priest and a church, both at government expense, for the
religious education of the Indians.

Those who are complacent with the religious illiteracy of the modern products of our schools, on the other hand, are content with the
later U. S. Supreme Court's suppression of religion. For them, "separation of Church and State," which though a good idea is not in the
Constitution, has a preferred position over the Constitution's "free exercise" of religion clause. The American idea of the separation of Church
and State, which was intended to protect the freedom of religion, has
become a basis for the secularization of American culture.

In the area of familiarization with the realities of life in our republic for proponents of equal treatment of parochial schools with government schools, it is consoling that the courts, all the way up to the
Supreme Court, issue "opinions." A Court opinion is the embodiment
of the Court's reasons for a judgment, a "statement by a judge or court
of the decision reached in regard to a cause tried or argued before
them, expounding the law as applied to the case, and detailing the
reasons upon which the judgment is based."[87]

Opinions are not certainties, and they reflect current times, political pressures, and cultural influences. In 1856, the U. S. Supreme
Court ruled that children born of black slaves could never become
citizens and enjoy the rights and liberties of citizens, a ruling that
helped bring on the Civil War. In 1896, the Court declared that the
State had no right to limit to sixty hours a week the amount of time an
employer could demand of his employees. In the same year, the Court

said that black children could be segregated from white children, with no right to attend the quality schools set up for white children.

The sources for the Court's opinions can be pathetically wrong. In an opinion against aid to parochial schools,[88] Justice William O. Douglas, in writing for the majority, cited as a source of Catholic attitudes an anti-Catholic book comparable in spirit to the "Protocols of the Elders of Zion". Among the author's observations was: "Our American freedoms are being threatened today by two totalitarian systems, communism and Roman Catholicism. And of the two . . . Romanism . . . is the more dangerous."[89]

Justice Hugo Black indulged himself on Paul Blanshard's anti-Catholic books. His dissent against the loaning of secular textbooks to Catholic school children verged on the hysterical, accused the religious "propagandists who have succeeded in securing passage of the present law . . . [of seeking] complete domination and supremacy of their particular brand of religion," and saw as the nation's enemy the Catholic Church.[90] In a released-time case, Justice Robert Jackson expressed the view that in Church-State cases justices follow their own prejudices and prepossessions.[91]

Jackson's position was not original: in the famed *Lochner* case of 1906, Justice Oliver Wendell Holmes condemned the Supreme Court for reading into the Constitution the economic theories of Herbert Spencer, founder of the so-called Darwinist movement in sociology and economics. Justice Charles Evans Hughes is said to have advised the newly appointed Douglas, "At the constitutional level where we work, 90 percent of any decision is emotional. The rational part of us supplies the reasons for supporting our predilections." In the 1972 case of *Flood v. Kuhn* on the issue of whether professional baseball's reserve system is within the reach of the federal antitrust laws, the Court wrenched consistency and logic to decide in the negative, citing a history of previous cases that had done the same.[92] The concept that the Supreme Court justices are people who act like the rest of us should not be suprising.

These realizations are not new. Thomas Jefferson feared the unchecked power of the Supreme Court: "The Constitution is a mere thing of wax in the hands of the judiciary which they may twist and shape into any form they please."[93] Abraham Lincoln's reaction to the *Dred Scott* decision was rage. In that case the Court ruled, among other things, that blacks were not citizens and therefore had no right to sue in the federal courts. Lincoln told the American people that if they quietly acquiesce in "the next *Dred Scott* decision and all future decisions [you] familiarize yourselves with the chains of bondage." The power of judges, Lincoln continued, "is the more dangerous as they are in office for life and not responsible, as the other functionaries are, to the elective control."[94]

To those who do not agree with Court opinions, there are consolations. It should be consoling to realize, for one, that the Court has changed its mind hundreds of times in all areas of law.[95] This is not necessarily bad. Suppose, for example, the Court continued to adhere to its 1872 opinion that said: "The natural and proper timidity and delicacy which belongs to the female sex evidently unfits it for many of the occupations of civil life," and that "[t]he paramount destiny and mission of woman are to fulfil the noble and benign offices of wife and mother."[96]

Changes take place also in the area of education.[97] The Court's 1968 *Flast v. Cohen*[98] decision, for example, overturned the 1923 *Frothingham v. Mellon*[99] decision. *Frothingham* had declared that the individual taxpayer lacks standing in Court to challenge how federal funds are spent, on the ground that the taxpayer's interest is "too remote." In *Flast*, a taxpayer challenged a federal program granting benefits to parochial schools. *Flast* provided standing, with Justice William O. Douglas convinced that taxpayers "can be vigilant private attorneys general."[100] This narrow exception to taxpayer standing, which applies exclusively to parochial schools, is the only area in which the ordinary taxpayer automatically has standing solely by virtue of the fact that he is a taxpayer.

Also, Supreme Court decisions publish the opinions of the minority. The minority opinions have the respectability of having been rendered by justices who are equally qualified in constitutional law as those in the majority. And minority opinions frequently become the majority opinions.[101] The minority opinions that there should be equal support for nongovernment schools from all levels of government as is given to government schools may eventually prevail.

That is all to the good, because some majority opinions at times contain catch-22s, intrinsic contradictions, and inherent inanities. The Court decided, for example, to permit the use of pornographic materials in the privacy of one's home,[102] but at the same time eliminated the possibility of legal means of getting it there.[103] The Court decided to prohibit the provision of government-paid counsel for those indigents wanting to file bankruptcy,[104] so there are some who are too poor to go bankrupt!

States can limit judicial review of welfare termination to persons willing and able to pay a twenty-five-dollar fee.[105] The only time the government will waive filing fees for an indigent seeking a welfare claim is when it involves the exercise of a fundamental right (physical liberty, voting, interstate travel, "privacy," and First Amendment rights). So again the poor, even when they want government-granted rights to welfare, can, according to Supreme Court rulings, be too poor to pursue methods of relief. In schooling, *Aguilar v. Felton*[106] ruled that public funds for church-affiliated schools may be used for limited purposes in some circumstances, if carefully supervised to avoid excessive entanglement — *but sufficient supervision is excessively entangling!*

The bottom line for nongovernment-school proponents is action. Nongovernment-school proponents must be less politically naive, not psychologically passive, and more aware. Despite Jerome Frank's dictum that lawyers can't distinguish between stability and paralysis, lawyers and judges *are* interested in rational grounds for change. The system itself has said: "The law helps those who help themselves, generally aids the vigilant, but rarely the sleeping, and never the acquiescent."[107] And a storm of protest can change law as well as Court opinions.[108]

Of course, interested parties must create the climate necessary for government action. In the judicial branch, the U.S. Supreme Court is, despite opinions to the contrary, a political body — some say the most political of the branches of government.[109] Senator Daniel Patrick Moynihan's answer to the question, "What do you do when the Supreme Court is wrong?" is: debate, litigate, and legislate.[110]

If necessary, congressional legislation can overcome the Court in several ways, one of which is to remove the Court's jurisdiction over specific issues under Congress's powers stemming from the Constitution's Article III: "The Supreme Court shall have appellate jurisdiction, both as to law and fact, with such exceptions, and under such regulations as the Congress shall make." The breadth of Congress' powers under "such exceptions" has never been fully tested, and were it to begin, the Congress and the Court might have a hard time knowing where to stop.

A good model of what should be done is connected with the Supreme Court's 1954 *Brown*[111] desegration decision. This declared that separate facilities for blacks are inherently unequal, thus providing for Blacks *de jure* equality and overturning the 1896 *Plessy*[112] decision declaring the propriety of "separate but equal" facilities for blacks. Before that happy result could be brought about, the National Association for the Advancement of Colored People (NAACP) and other astute organizations diligently saw to it that other, carefully selected, cases had worked their way up through the courts and set proper precedents to make the *Brown* decision possible.[113]

Nongovernment-school proponents have probably not been sufficiently active in procedures for creating a climate for change. They may not have used sufficient diligence to escort carefully selected cases up through the system to overcome the present confusion. The success of Catholic-public schools could very well be one basis. These are parochial schools in educational partnership with the local community and financially supported by public taxes. They are more numerous than supposed, efficient, and satisfactory to teachers, students, parents, and communities.[114] There are other constitutional grounds, as yet underemphasized or unexplored, upon which pleas for equalization of treatment for nongovernment schools can be made.

One example is the Constitution's "general welfare" clause (Article I, Section 8).[115] The Constitution's Preamble, which is broader and also applicable here, asserts as the purpose of the document "to form a more perfect union, establish Justice, ensure domestic tranquillity, provide for the common defence, promote the general Welfare, and secure the Blessings of Liberty to ourselves and our Posterity." In connection with equal treatment for church-affiliated schools, there are historical, sociological, and psychological reasons to emphasize all those clauses, especially the one concerning the "general welfare."

Historically, the U.S. government and state governments for the first hundred or so years of the Republic were interested in nongovernment schools, and funded them. Recent historical trends to the contrary, it is not difficult to see benefits accruing to the public welfare if the control of schools were transferred back to parents from central district offices, states, the federal government, and such ancillary structures as textbook publishers, testing services, and accreditation agencies.

Sociologically, unequal treatment of government and church-affiliated schools leaves all kinds of solvable difficulties unsolved: complaints about the lack of values in government schools, protests about textbooks, fundamentalist schools defying government regulations, home instruction, inner-city contributions of parochial schools, and many more. Unequal treatment encourages not only court cases like the one from Greeneville, Tennessee, in which fundamentalist Christian children refused to read textbooks with material offensive to their religious beliefs, but its mirror suit from Jacksonville, Florida, in which parents charged that the local board of education violated their children's rights when it banned a humanities textbook because of objections raised by a Baptist minister.[116] These "catch-22" situations could be avoided, to benefit the general welfare, if parents had a true choice of schools for their children.

Psychologically, equal treatment of nongovernment schools is more satisfactory to parents, students, teachers, and the community. All are comforted when they know that there is harmony between the values which children are taught in their schools and what their parents teach them, or would like to teach them, at home.

CONCLUSION

The State, comprising both society and government plus sovereignty, has true rights in schooling and education, and not merely as God's enforcer. But the State is not, as some have come to think because of current circumstances, schooling and education's sole, or even dominant, partner. The confused, chaotic, and mutually contradictory decisions of the U. S. Supreme Court contravene the Judeo-Christian historical and philosophical perspective, denying substantive Church participation beyond the right of Church-school existence, making possible government monopoly over schools, and preventing meaningful parental choice.

The Catholic Church favors true choice, because it avoids any suggestion that the child is the mere creature of the State, avoids any debasing ideology which can turn schools into instruments of political power, is a right due to parents in distributive justice, and provides to all human beings the fundamental right to their own culture. True choice fosters satisfaction, involvement, and enrichment; is inherently instructive; through its market influences can help teachers and administrators; substitutes parental love for State custodial care; communicates to children the State's endorsement of their parents; and provides decision-making ability, already possessed by the rich, to the poor.

Aside from currently existing public-parochial schools, the two most widely proclaimed methods of achieving true choice in schooling are vouchers and tuition tax credits. Vouchers in this sense are certificates given to parents to pay for tuition or other costs at any eligible government or nongovernment school, religious or secular, within or outside the student's school district. Tuition tax credits is a procedure whereby income-tax-paying parents receive a credit from their income tax for an agreed-upon amount for each of their children's tuition, no matter what school their children attend, and non-income-tax-paying poor parents receive an enabling fee for the same purpose.

Among the arguments for government financial help to nongovernment schools are the American principle of citizen sovereignty, beneficial cooperation and competition among schools, the streamlining of bureaucracy, and the enabling of Catholic and other nongovernment schools to contribute to a more just society. Among the arguments given against it are the undermining of government-school support, the offer of false hope to poor people who would be incompetent to avoid entrepeneurial school charlatans, loss of Catholic-school identity under the principle that "he who pays the piper calls the tune," the unconstitutional advancement of religion, discrimination along racial, ethnic, or ideological lines, and the potential loss of volunteer interest.

The United States government, though comprised of many Catholics and other individuals well-disposed to Catholic schools, opposes government help to nongovernment schools, even in the current need. Government legislation often counters the important role which the Catholic Church accords to family life: in income-tax law, for example, and nonsupport of mothers who want to devote their energies to the care of their young children. The judiciary, whose philosophy of legal "Realism" is a merging of Positivism and Utilitarianism, is in these matters in a state of ambivalence. Though some recent judicial opinions on the First Amendment's establishment clause provide hope for what seems to be an "accommodation" of religion, there is no telling what direction they will take in the future.

Current values in deciding Church-State issues in schooling are neutrality, religious accommodation, and guarantees of Church-State separation and of lack of entanglement between Church and State. Inasmuch as the United States is the only country in the Western world that deliberately excludes formal religion from schooling, the situation is different in other democratic countries, even those which have copied the U.S. Constitution. U.S. citizens have fought back against Court decisions with a proliferation of Christian fundamentalist schools and with home instruction.

What to do about government usurpations of individual, family, and Church rights involves, at an initial minimum, instruction in the rights of the family and the Church, encouragement of those two partners, and familiarization with the realities of life in our republic. The last includes knowledge of the dignity of the person as found, among other places, in the founding documents of the United States, and in the nature and values of religion, whose importance to this republic was observed early on.

Another suggestion concerning what to do about the matter is contained in court dicta cited in our text (*Hannan v. Dusch*): "The law helps those who help themselves, generally aids the vigilant, but rarely the sleeping, and never the acquiescent." One good example of this is the civil rights movement. Catholic-school proponents have many unused constitutional rights open to them. For church-affiliated school proponents to fight for these rights would be like the fall of a stone into quiet water. It would have ever-widening implications.

QUESTIONS FOR DISCUSSION

From the viewpoint of the State, how might the existence of Catholic schools be justified?

If the State were to recognize Catholic schools on an equal footing with government schools in funding, what would be the rights of the State concerning administration, curriculum, and so on, in Catholic schools?

How do you account for the increasing tendency in the United States toward a greater degree of State control of education and schooling?

Evaluate arguments for and against State financial aid to church-affiliated schools.

How do you account for the basic controversy in the United States between the Church and the State concerning the support of church-affiliated schools?

As dictum, the Virginia Court of Appeals wrote, "The law helps those who help themselves, generally aids the vigilant, but rarely the sleeping, and never the acquiescent." If this is applicable to the Catholic school situation in the United States, how would you implement it?

What, if anything, may the State expect the Church to do to advance the purposes of the State?

What, if anything, may the Church expect the State to do to advance the purposes of the Church?

What is the proper relationship between law and morality, and between law and religion?

How far do the constitutional rights of children go when one must, for instance, determine whether delinquency has taken place, or see to it that children have received constitutional due process, or decide the rights of schools and parents in applying corporal punishment to misbehaving children? How far is it legitimate for the State to intrude into the privacy of parent-child relations in the home? How much can or should the State and the Church provide for children of parents adjudged to be incompetent or for parents whose goals for their children are hostile toward those of the State or the Church?

What rights should parents and the Church have when the State decides procedures for children to achieve societal benefits: for example, providing contraceptives to prevent pregnancy and disease; allowing minor children to have abortions without parental knowledge, counsel, or consent; providing medical services for venereal disease in complete privacy? Who decides at what age children are capable of making such "life or death" decisions? How autonomous should children be from parents, Church, and State?

The U.S. Supreme Court's increased recognition of the rights of minors leads to a number of interesting questions. Just how far will children's rights be extended? What role do the parents actually play in the development of the child? How autonomous are children from State as well as parental control? When are children capable of making "life or death" decisions in terms of their moral and intellectual development?

SUGGESTED BIBLIOGRAPHY

Background

Buetow, Harold A. *Of Singular Benefit: the Story of U. S. Catholic Education*. New York: Macmillan, 1970.

A history of the growth and place of Catholic schools in our democracy.

_____. *A History of United States Catholic Schooling*. Washington, D.C.: National Catholic Educational Association, 1985.

An update of the above.

Fellman, David, ed. *The Supreme Court and Education*. 3rd ed. Classics in Education Series, no. 4. New York: Teachers College, 1976.

Excerpts from Supreme Court cases, along with introductions and comments, on education and religion (pp. 3–124), racial segregation, academic freedom, the rights of students, and government-school financing.

Friendly, Fred W., and Martha J. H. Elliott. *The Constitution: That Delicate Balance*. New York: Random House, 1984.

A popularized presentation of a public-television series on the Constitution.

Kraushaar, Otto F. *American Nonpublic Schools: Patterns of Diversity*. Baltimore: Johns Hopkins University Press, 1972.

Discusses all nongovernment schools, including Catholic; treats the historical perspective, the nongovernment-school world, and nongovernment schools and the public interest.

The State and Religion

Antieau, Chester James, Arthur T. Downey, and Edward C. Roberts. *Freedom from Federal Establishment: Formation and Early History of the First Amendment Religion Clauses*. Milwaukee: Bruce, 1964.

An old but good treatment, presenting Establishment in colonial America and relating the struggle in the states for freedom from established churches; early areas of Church-State accommodation; the banning of religious test oaths; drives for religion amendments to the Constitution; the meaning of the establishment clause in the first Congress, what early citizens thought they were adding to the Constitution by the establishment clause, and the practices relating to the Establishment clause in the early times; and views of Church-State relations in early times outside the Congress.

Cord, Robert L. *Separation of Church and State: Historical Fact and Current Fiction*. New York: Lambeth, 1982.

Treats the genesis of the Constitution's establishment clause, the views of Madison and Jefferson, extensions of the clause through the Fourteenth Amendment, and later interpretations.

Ferrara, Peter J. *Religion and the Constitution: A Reinterpretation*. Washington, D.C.: Free Congress Research and Education Foundation, 1983.

An attempt to correct current historical inaccuracies with regard to First Amendment interpretations.

Gaffney, Edward McGlynn, ed. *Private Schools and the Public Good: Policy Alternatives for the Eighties*. Notre Dame, Ind.: University of Notre Dame Press, 1981.

Articles from authorities in three areas: educational freedom for minorities, legislative proposals for broadening educational opportunity, and constitutional perspectives.

Gaffney, Edward McGlynn, and Philip R. Moots. *Government and Campus: Federal Regulation of Religiously Affiliated Higher Education*. Notre Dame, Ind.: University of Notre Dame Press, 1982.

After an empirical profile of religiously affiliated colleges and universities based on a two-year study by Notre Dame's Center for Constitutional Studies, presents government regulation and the problem of governmental overreaching in religious preference in employment policies; in student admissions and student discipline; in the use of publicly funded facilities; with regard to the handicapped, alcoholism, and drug addiction; in tax matters; in labor law problems; and in the segregation of students by sex in student housing.

Kelley, Dean M., ed. *Government Intervention in Religious Affairs*. New York: Pilgrim, 1982.

Noted authors on various aspects of government interventions; reprinted from conference papers on the subject, the keynote address of which was "Government as Big Brother to Religious Bodies."

Levy, Leonard W. *The Establishment Clause: Religion and the First Amendment*. New York: Macmillan, 1986.

Treats as objectively as possible colonial and state establishments of religion, the Constitution and religion, the Supreme Court and the establishment clause, and the "wall of separation."

McBrien, Richard. *Caesar's Coin: Religion and Politics in America*. New York: Macmillan, 1987.

Addresses the interlocking network of questions involved in controversies concerning religion and the U.S. polity.

Murphy, Walter F. "Who Shall Interpret: The Quest for the Ultimate Constitutional Interpreter." *The Review of Politics*, vol. 48 no. 3 (Summer 1986), pp. 401–23.

Treats one of the fundamental problems of constitutional theory: *who* is the ultimate constitutional interpreter. Presents the three principal theories—judicial supremacy, legislative supremacy, and departmentalism—and opts for a modified version of departmentalism.

Organization of American Historians. *OAH Newsletter*. (August 1983). OAH, 112 North Bryan Street, Bloomington, Ind. 47401.

In this forty-page issue, Wilcomb E. Washburn laments the Supreme Court's ignorance of history, as evidenced by the biased texts it uses to prepare opinions.

Pfeffer, Leo, and Anson P. Stokes. *Church and State in the United States*. Westport, Conn.: Greenwood, 1964.

Takes a position against State aid to church-affiliated schools.

Sanders, Thomas C. *Protestant Concepts of Church and State*. New York: Holt, Rinehart and Winston, 1964.

A clarification of Protestant views on Church and State.

Sorauf, Frank J. *The Wall of Separation: The Constitutional Politics of Church and State*. Princeton, N.J.: Princeton University Press, 1976.

The Constitution and separation, the legal and religious context, separationists in litigation, accommodationists, the court cases, and the impact on policy.

Williams, Mary F. *Government in the Classroom*. New York: Praeger, 1979.

A compilation of essays on the impact of government in the classroom.

United States Commission on Civil Rights. *Religion in the Constitution: A Delicate Balance*. Washington, D.C.: The Commission, Clearinghouse Publication no. 80, 1983.

The history of separation, the nature of the First Amendment, religious discrimination in employment, and religious freedom in prison.

Chapter 8

WHAT CATHOLIC SCHOOLS HAVE TO DEAL WITH: THE ATMOSPHERE

Many proponents, when asked what they like about the Catholic school, point to what they call its unique atmosphere. But they often find that difficult to define. We shall try to pinpoint what constitutes the Catholic-school atmosphere and makes it singular. The atmosphere of all schooling comprises all those circumstances which may not be the essence of education, but which are integral to it, or important to it, or both. It constitutes the medium, the external and internal environments, the conditions which in some measure circumscribe and determine, at a particular time and place, the kind of schooling provided.

The *external* atmosphere is constituted by those conditions which come from society: aspects like whether the society encourages schooling by making upward mobility possible; what values the society cherishes that influence what the school will do and teach; whether the society stresses a schooling for *doing* rather than for *being*, thus determining whether a school will provide goals of spiritual and intellectual formation or skills for earning a livelihood; how society defines the educated person; and the existence of freedom of choice of schools. In the case of the Catholic school, it adds, for example, the value the Church puts upon education in general and its schools in particular, the priorities it establishes, and what it looks for in its graduates. The *internal* atmosphere is that within the school: such items as whether enough funding has been provided for adequate heat and light, sufficient space, and up-to-date materials; whether the teachers have proper training; and the numbers and quality of such support personnel as counselors, administrators, and therapists. The internal atmosphere of the Catholic school adds the most important element of the spiritual.

213

EXTERNAL ATMOSPHERE
Our complex world consists of four structures, with considerable interaction between them, all working through primary levels of social reality such as the family, and through the local, national, and international communities. The four structures are the economic, political, cultural, and social.[1] All four structures inevitably bear upon schooling and education.

Economic Structure
The *economic* structure deals with how we organize resources. Different parts of the world have different supplies of resources: oil, for example, or fertile land, or a highly skilled labor force. These factors have brought it about that the world is unjustly stratified. The stratification extends to schooling, whereby the wealthy have the best range of choice and resources and the poor the least. This pertains in some measure to Catholic schools: The economic structure in some countries, for example, encourages elitist Roman Catholic schools for girls; in the United States, it has resulted in serious attempts to include the poor. The economic structure affects the quality of staff, facilities, and programs.

Many Catholics have been on a free financial ride at the expense of a dedicated few, especially teaching religious sisters, for a long time — so long that some have come to take it for granted. Because of the American economic injustice of insufficient government financial backing, Catholic schools need financial support from both Catholics and non-Catholics to the same extent of sacrifice as has been present in U.S. history. This is true for those who do not have children in Catholic schools as well as for those who do. As long ago as 1874, in what has become known popularly as the Kalamazoo Case,[2] the Supreme Court of Michigan showed the benefits to the general public of the existence of high schools in explaining their decision that it was legal to tax the general public for their support. *A pari*, schools that are truly Catholic provide benefits not only to the children who attend them and their parents, but to the Catholic and civic communities at large, the unmarried, and the married childless as well.[3]

By their financial and spiritual support the laity make it possible for Church schools to go beyond the wealthy who can afford them to the poor, to those who are deprived of family help and affection, and to those who are far from the faith. Should financial conditions compel Catholic schools to go only to "the wealthier social classes, it could be contributing towards their privileged position, and could thereby continue to favour a society which is unjust."[4] As Martin Luther pointed out in 1530, even businessmen should support schooling: without the scholars they produce, he wrote,

> it would not be long till business men in their perplexity would be ready to dig a learned man out of the ground ten yards deep with their fingers; for the merchant will not long remain a merchant, if preaching and the administration of justice cease.[5]

This connection applies preeminently to our citizenry and to the values contributed to them by Catholic schools.

U.S. Catholics' generosity is superior to that in most other nations. But the full potential of their contributions is usually underestimated and, as a result, donations are less than they could be. Since the Great Depression in the early 1930s, Catholics as a group have been climbing the socioeconomic ladder at a pace far faster than the general population. But the rate of giving to the Church has not kept pace with that climb. Apart from parents who treasure having their children in Catholic schools, few Catholics have had the experience of giving until it hurts.

Most church support is painless, but Catholic-school teachers endure plenty of pain, and the efforts of the clergy to raise money entails pastoral pain. Ultimately, however, justice will be achieved only if the laity become convinced of the worth of Catholic schooling and are willing to make the sacrifices necessary to finance school needs. This will call for the Church to be a model of what it teaches, and for the sacrifices necessary for the Church to realign its priorities so that schools, even though financially costly, are kept open.

One financing procedure coming more and more to the fore is tithing. It may be a wave of the future. It is deeply rooted in the Bible, where it is mentioned forty-six times. It has been around since Abraham and was approved by Christ. Unlike bazaars or bingo, tithing encourages people to give totally on their own and for the right reasons.

Political Structure

The *political* structure deals with how we organize power. Who makes the key decisions, and how is power organized? Control of the power structure can be used effectively to challenge those with economic preeminence. Although laws are necessary for society to function, if the laws are made by society's formal political structures they may unjustly support the status quo. Some laws may be perceived by some as unjust, depending upon where a person is located in a stratified society. But the laws are ultimately enforced by the police, the courts, and — in some cases — the army.

Catholics should be educated to take part in the political process. This is not only because of the need for political power to get things done, but also because society has duties that must be seen to as well as rights, in schooling as well as in other important spheres of life.[6] Unfortunately, education to civic responsibility has not been a strong suit in the formation of many Catholics.

Cultural Structure

Still another structure outside the schools, but influencing them, is the *cultural*. The culture is the whole way of life of a people, including the beliefs and values upon which that way of life is based. A society must have *meaning*, and culture is its carrier. Every society has a dominant core meaning: a society may have a number of cultures within it, but at any particular time only one of these will be dominant.[7] The dominant culture supports the economic and political structures. The key question here is, "How is meaning organized?" Attitudes are a contributing factor: for example, possible smugness in the attitude of the well-off top of the social pyramid, or apathy in those poor who are trapped at the bottom of the pyramid. Mass media, the educational system, and religion are among the persuaders of people to accept the dominant culture.

The media — press, radio, and television — throughout the world are, for the most part, owned and controlled by those at the top of the economic and political structures. That they support the status quo is therefore not surprising. At least as bad is the fact that television — more and more the leading part of the media — empties both religion and education of substance. On television, the sacred becomes so deeply associated with the commercial and entertainment worlds that it is difficult to present it in a frame worthy of sacred events. Also, on television everything that makes religion an historic, profound, and sacred human activity is stripped away; there is little ritual, no dogma, scarcely any theology, and above all no sense of spiritual transcendence.

What we said of television as it pertains to religion is also true, *mutatis mutandis*, of television as it pertains to education. Education is now in the early phase of a revolution, the rapid dissolution of assumptions organized around the printed word and the equally rapid emergence of a new education based on the speed-of-light electronic image. So far the response has been to accommodate education to television, rather than vice versa. Many children's programs encourage children to love television rather than to love school. Television is hostile toward the discipline, thought, and self-restraint demanded by true education. Television "education" has no prerequisites, no perplexity beyond the imparting of information, and no encouragement to thought.[8]

But because the media are where the people are, the Church should acquire access to the mass media for the proclamation of the Good News. This access should not be only in the wee hours of Sunday morning to satisfy a network's "public service" requirements, or in the production of amateurish renditions of materials for Catholic-school classroom use, but for a presence that will compete with the best in prime time: "the mass media impart an air of reality and actuality to the facts, institutions and opinions on which they report and on the other hand they diminish the popular estimation of whatever they pass over in silence."[9]

The Church simply must become aware that "the language in which the faith is expressed [is often] too tied to ancient and obsolete formulae or too closely linked with Western culture."[10] In this updating, the Church seems at times to be lacking in sophistication. At a time when to be considered anything other than "modern" is pejorative, the Church continues to call "modernism" a heresy. And in an age when no one wants to be considered "unenlightened," the Church continues to refer to a way of thinking completely opposed to her own as "The Enlightenment."[11]

No cultural structure is value-free. *All* schools teach values. One out of many available examples of government schools teaching dominant cultural values is an advertisement by the National Education Association. Without reference to the "value-free" appearance that government schools often try to assume, the advertisement chooses as its title, "Teaching Invaluable Values." Its first sentence is, "The values we teach in our classrooms sustain and invigorate our democracy." Its succeeding statements further illustrate the government schools' purpose to socialize students to the existing society as it is:

> We continue to teach students the moral, spiritual, and cultural values that unify the union. . . . The health of our democracy demands, as our official NEA resolutions unreservedly assert, a concerted effort to teach the values that undergird this nation's social, economic, and political structure . . . And that is as it should be. That is right.[12]

Catholic schools' values are the Kingdom values of Jesus Christ: Catholics believe that the power of God is active in the world, confronting it and seeking to transform it. That does not mean, however, that Catholics look at reality through jaundiced eyes.

Religion also plays an important part in handing on culture. Unfortunately, religion has at times been used to legitimate the status quo, even when that status quo has been oppressive. Religion at times has preached that oppressive situations must be accepted as God's will, that they are only temporary, and that there will be "pie in the sky when you die." Fortunately there are also many recent examples of religion being an agent of change toward justice: for example, in the Philippines, Haiti, Chile, Poland, the U.S. bishops' pastoral letters on peace and on economic justice. In our time, the Catholic school must continue insightfully to address contemporaneous issues — as the U.S. Catholic bishops' pastoral, *To Teach as Jesus Did*, indicates.[13]

The Catholic school exists now no less than in early Christianity as an institution conditioned by and influencing the culture in which it finds itself.[14] Although "the faithful ought to work in close conjunction with their contemporaries and try to get to know their ways of thinking and feeling, as they find them expressed in current culture,"[15] there are difficulties in attempts at harmonization of the Church's culture with the world's:

> In Christian antiquity, religion was considered as it were the major unifying principle among people. Things are much different today. The phenomenon of democratization has resulted in people forming a cohesive whole, a fact which favours harmony among the different spiritual families. Pluralism is no longer regarded as an evil to be combatted, but as a fact that has to be taken into account. Each individual can make his own decisions without thereby becoming an outcast from society.[16]

Democratization and pluralism are obviously not bad. But if Catholic positions are to be made reconcilable with contemporary culture, there must be Catholic dialogue with the larger community, those without faith as well as those with it. After the Second Vatican Council's initiatives began to show themselves in the school environment, Catholic schools — like the Church — became less unyielding and absolutist, more concerned with the environments that students came from. Catholic schools have thus assumed a more central role in the lives of their students. There is now dialogue between Catholic culture and the cultures outside it — a dialogue that is without fear on the part of the Church and is beneficial to the outside world to whom the Church is servant. And "catechesis is more effective when speaking about what actually exists visibly in the community."[17]

Because many modern cultures are different from the culture of faith, we face the task of handing on the faith as almost entirely separate from the regular "transmission of culture" which goes on in other education. This demands a process which is different from ordinary "socialization," which will, as a matter of fact, sometimes be in conflict with it. Much of the dialogue, for many reasons, must take place within the Church community itself. For one thing, the witness of that community is needed for support. Another reason is frankly financial. Then, too, as the Church sees it, the local Church community has a positive obligation to see to the religious instruction of those baptized in their Church: "A Christian community which bears witness to the Gospel, lives out its fraternal charity, and actively celebrates the mysteries of Christ, is for the children that live there the best school of Christian and liturgical education."[18]

The laity should share in the salvific work of the Church according to their means and ability and the needs of the times:

> The laity . . . are given this special vocation: to make the Church present and fruitful in those places and circumstances where it is only through them that she can become the salt of the earth. Thus, every lay person, through those gifts given to him, is at once the witness and the living instrument of the mission of the Church itself "according to the measure of Christ's bestowal" (Eph. 4:7).[19]

It is vital to culture that all parents, rich and poor all over the world, have access to different kinds of schools—not only those dominated by the State—in order to be able to select one that reflects the totality of their culture. Benefits to religion in today's age of secularism are not a bad thing for our cultural structure.

Social Structure

The fourth set of structures having a bearing on the external atmosphere of education is the *social*. The key question here is, "How are *relationships* organized?" A good illustration of the different social groups in society is a pyramid divided horizontally into sections. At the bottom of this social pyramid are the unemployed and the societally marginalized. Above them are the producers (in agriculture, industry, the crafts, and so on). The third group consists of the service sector (management, security, professional, public servants, and so on). Above them is a very small group of entrepreneurs who use other peoples' resources (for example, bankers), and at the very top are those who have economic resources of their own: owners of land or capital.[20] Despite Karl Marx, class is not the only source of division.

There are others, like the divisions between men and women, young and old, and urban and rural dwellers.

Among the social conditions that will influence Catholic schools are many contradictions and paradoxes:

> In no other age has mankind enjoyed such an abundance of wealth, resources and economic well-being; and yet a huge proportion of the people of the world is plagued by hunger and extreme need while countless numbers are totally illiterate. At no time have men had such a keen sense of freedom, only to be faced by new forms of slavery in living and thinking. There is on the one hand a lively feeling of unity and of compelling solidarity, of mutual dependence, and on the other a lamentable cleavage of bitterly opposing camps. . . . There is lastly a painstaking search for a better material world, without a parallel spiritual advancement.[21]

These themes, and such added ills as drugs, aggression, and violence, demand, among other things,

> that Catholic educators develop in themselves, and cultivate in their students, a keen social awareness and a profound civic and political responsibility . . . [and a commitment] to the task of forming men and women who will make the 'civilization of love' a reality.[22]

Among the worst of the facets of the current social scene is the fact that there is no true brotherhood of humankind: "every man and every group is interested only in its own affairs, not in those of others."[23]

Much of this has been caused by the materialistic underpinnings of our time which, combined with the current social situation, present social structures detrimental to Catholic faith and to Catholic schools:

> Christians today must be formed to live in a world which largely ignores God or which . . . too often flounders in a debasing indifferentism, if it does not remain in a scornful attitude of "suspicion" in the name of the progress it has made in the field of scientific "explanations".[24]

In many ways "our scientific, technical, industrial and urban civilization . . . turns people's minds away from the divine. . . . For many, God is perceived to be less present, less necessary. . . . "[25] But God can speak to, in, and through all models, and it is the work of the Church to adapt the Word of God to all hearers.

Most societies in the past have had, at least to some extent, an "otherworldly" outlook.[26] They have looked to some reality outside human affairs — God or fate or Nirvana — for their ultimate meanings and purposes. They have lived and understood secular life in a context beyond itself. In our world of secularism, this is no longer true. Religion is looked down upon. The prevailing attitude is one of questioning and criticism, with everything relative and nothing absolute. The large measure of control that humankind has gained over the material world prompts attempts at greater and greater personal autonomy. These social conditions encourage a retreat from the supernatural and are inimical to a faith in which important elements are a denial of human self-sufficiency and a dependence on God.

In addition, Western industrial societies are more and more urban; this has led to alienation. Frequently, work is no longer a real part of a person's life: it is considered a necessary but regrettable condition of making a living.[27] And there is an enormous increase in mobility, geographical as well as social. So life becomes fragmented. All of this makes religious formation more difficult. Religious formation is made easier by stability, which makes it possible to think of formation as the handing on of a heritage.

Another factor of the social atmosphere external to schools which makes the Catholic school's mission more difficult is the current decline in public morality. Most societies in the past, and preliterate societies today, have embodied some moral ideal and reflected it in their organization. But the dominant view today is that society should only legislate about acts which are likely to harm others. The large sphere of private life is left to personal decision. It can therefore "happen that the Christian faith can become contaminated by a new form of paganism, even if a certain religious sense still remains and a certain belief in a supreme Being."[28]

The Catholic school should work closely with other bodies of activity in society which have an educational influence, thus adding a kind of "parallel school" for the purpose of further integrating faith and life. Together, all these efforts will be an active systematic force to form pupils' critical faculties to "take what is good, and integrate it into their Christian human culture."[29] In the face of economic, political, cultural, and social pluralism, the Church also advocates the principle of a plurality of school systems. She

> encourages the coexistence and, if possible, the co-operation of diverse educational institutions which will allow young people . . . to be trained to take an active part in the construction of a community through which the building of society is promoted.[30]

INTERNAL ATMOSPHERE
Importance

A Christian atmosphere and tone within the school has a profound formative influence on the development of faith. In a real sense, the tone *is* the Christian message. As a complement of the home, the school environment is, besides, a form of precatechesis, a preparation (*propaedeutic*) for the school's formal program of education in the faith. As used by Pablo Nebreda, precatechesis is that preparation which removes the obstacles to persons' encounter with the Word of God and enables catechesis to have meaning in peoples' present situation.[31] While the importance of the environment is increasingly recognized, the idea is old. Pope Pius XI referred to it in his 1929 encyclical, *The Christian Education of Youth*: "it is of the utmost importance to see . . . that the combination of circumstances which we call environment, correspond exactly to the end proposed."[32]

Of utmost gravity, the internal conditions incorporate the staff's keeping abreast of all modern pedagogical, ecclesiastical, cultural, and other developments,[33] including pedagogy as a science and the pedagogy of faith. Catholic school education should by Church law be "at least as academically distinguished as that given in the other schools of the region."[34] Sciences like biology, psychology, and sociology are providing education with valuable elements that should find their way into the atmosphere of the school. And the "techniques perfected and tested for education in general should be adapted for the service of education in the faith," with the caution that "account must always be taken of the absolute originality of faith. Pedagogy of faith is not a question of transmitting human knowledge, even of the highest kind; it is a question of communicating God's Revelation in its entirety."[35]

Physical Atmosphere of the Place Called "School"
Need of School Building

What is the importance of having an actual building called "school," which is expensive when one considers alternative premises like the home or religious instruction center? From a *realist* philosophical perspective, the school premises are necessary in order that the pupil come in contact with reality. This includes social reality: schools are "a must if disaster is to be avoided."[36] The *idealist* viewpoint agrees with the realist that people are social beings as well as individuals and that therefore students need to come together in a school building: "education is necessarily a social process and not altogether individualistic. . . . man must have a social setting in which to become a man."[37]

The *pragmatist* clearly defines education as a social function. John Dewey stated that "education is scarcely anything at all unless it is a social institution."[38] In our complex world, school is necessary as a place where experiences can be organized and learning facilitated. In Dewey's words: "School exists to provide a special environment for the formative years. A special environment is needed."[39] The *existentialist* may see school as "an institution which meddles with the lives of individuals in an unwelcome manner."[40] If, however, the place does not demand that the student conform and encourages the student's awakening to the responsibility of authentic personal choice, school could be a place of some value, because it could require participation, confronting, and experiencing with others.

Catholics as such favor the existence of the school building. Their reasons usually follow their philosophical persuasion. While agreeing that parents are the "first and foremost educators of their children," Catholics see the school as providing the assistance of society and the Church that parents and their children need. The school has an "irreplaceable function in our society. . . . The family is less and less capable of facing . . . serious problems on its own."[41]

Nature of the Building

Even the nature of the school building—its size, the seating arrangements, the placing of the walls, the positioning or elimination of the teacher's desk, and the like—is determined by one's philosophy. *Realists* emphasize a building that will facilitate the sharpening of students' perceptions and the broadening of their awareness of the world, through the arts and sciences.[42] *Idealists*, not too far from the realists, emphasize the mind, and want plenty of space to provide students with a "common experiencing of something significant,"[43] often the lives and minds of the great.

Pragmatists see less need for lecture halls. Education for them is less formal, and is in touch with society. The episodic character of learning and the emphasis on a problem-solving, group-project approach entail an ever changing physical setup, with learning centers, interest areas, and fewer traditional classrooms. *Existentialists* want to dedicate much space to creative expression. They want places for artwork and music, areas for discussion, a theatre, and nothing that promotes conformity. It is possible that their school will have no walls, no formal classrooms, no assigned seats, and no set schedules.

Catholics as a rule will opt for facilities that are suggested by their philosophy. The optimal setting in a Catholic school has areas for small group discussions, gymnasium, playground, science and math laboratories, and a library well-stocked with the works of the masters (including much on Christ and the Church) and plenty of reference material. In the perfect situation, there might be a theater, an art studio, and a music room for creative work. The optimal Catholic school also has a place to pray and to celebrate the Liturgy. Unfortunately, the dream often slams into hard fiscal reality.

Minimum Facilities Necessary for Staying Open

In view of the studies which have shown Catholic schools in the United States to have constantly achieved great results with meager resources, it is perhaps inadvisable to ask what minimum facilities are required for the schools to stay open. In the way of the physical building and classrooms, there must be resources for good maintenance and repair. In the way of finance, worry and concern cannot be so constant as to distract from academic endeavor and achievement. Class size and playgrounds must be sufficient to meet student needs.

While there must be textbooks of good quality, Catholic educators must remember that "no text can substitute for the live communication of the Christian message."[44] There should be audiovisual aids, which should be wholly accurate, carefully chosen, and clearly presented, things of beauty with emotive power which appeal to the imagination.[45] Religious as well as other schooling should also not neglect programmed instruction. In the area of visual presentations of truth for religious pedagogy, educators should have recourse to the collaboration of experts in theology, catechesis, and in the art of audiovisual education.[46] And there should be financial resources for scientific research, without which the "catechetical movement will be totally incapable of making progress."[47]

In these areas, as with the hiring of teachers, one advertises for God, hopes to avoid the devil, and compromises somewhere in between. Considering the cost of maintaining a school building, it is easy to resort to "deferred maintenance," resulting in school buildings that are under par, one hopes temporarily. We must, of course, be careful to point out that not all parts of a school's physical atmosphere are indications of the school's philosophy or worth. A decrepit school building, for example, does not necessarily mean that health, safety, and care are low priorities; it may indicate simply that despite adverse circumstances the school has been kept open because of the loving concern of the local Church community for their young.[48]

The Spiritual Atmosphere

More important than the physical atmosphere of the Catholic school is the spiritual. Outside the Catholic community, one scientific model (that of Toennies) requires as a cohesive force the qualities of commitment, pride in the school, interdependence, social cohesion, friendliness, and a consensus of values. Catholic schools must take those qualities into consideration. More important than their scientific competence, however, is that they should be known "for the witness of their ardent faith, and for the climate of respect, mutual aid, and evangelical joy permeating the entire establishment."[49] This climate of "living and acting in conformity with the Gospel" should encourage pupils' maturing in the faith given in baptism.[50]

Christian Community

The Catholic school should be forthright about providing a community of faith which is living, conscious, and active, a genuine community bent on imparting, over and above an academic education, all the help it can give to its members to adopt a Christian way of life. Both human nature and the nature of the educational process demand community: "No Catholic school can adequately fulfil its educational role on its own."[51]

This concept of Christian community is vital to the Catholic school. Only community makes possible the kind of sharing that is necessary and "is one of the most enriching developments for the contemporary school."[52] Without community, the school drifts aimlessly. The Catholic school community is more than a group, a mere conglomeration of individuals.[53] And it has a common purpose. This "common purpose both expresses community and also forms it."[54]

There are many more characteristics of the Catholic school as community: it is an agency for the transmission of Christian values; an enlivener of the Gospel spirit of charity and liberty; a provider of opportunities for cooperation, participation, and coresponsibility; a showcase of the principles of subsidiarity and collegiality; and a channel of divine grace through communal public worship. As a major agency for the transmission of Christian values for living, the Catholic school, being the center of the educative Christian community, promotes a faith relationship with Christ, in whom all values find fulfillment. This faith is principally assimilated through contact with people inside a community.[55]

An important quality of true Catholic-school community is openness. One aspect of that which perhaps may be overlooked is cooperation with government schools. Many government-school personnel, religious people themselves, are concerned for the survival of Catholic schools as an alternate value-oriented system. Government-school personnel also see the Catholic school as a check and balance on them in terms of a nontunneled form of education.[56] Beyond that, Catholic-school people should involve themselves in the total community.

There should be more interaction. This does not necessarily involve big things. But Catholic-school personnel should not just talk to each other. They have to believe in their ability to reach out and influence — and be influenced by — other people. They are in the same business — excellence — not in competition. They have ways of looking at things — for example, at values — that can be of use to others.[57]

The Gospel spirit that distinguishes and enlivens the Catholic-school community is a spirit of charity and liberty — *true* charity, *true* liberty. The school helps the student's personality development match the growth of that new creation which he or she became at baptism.[58] Concrete expressions of charity entail a sense of mutual responsibility, and of care and concern for one another.

True liberty entails freedom — to risk, to trust, to grow, to seek God — and the realization that mistakes will be accepted, because people will be accepted as persons. Many Catholic-school students consider that their schools do not allow them sufficient freedom. Deducting somewhat from this criticism because of our permissive era, where true it is tragic. It is sad especially in view of the fact that school climate is related to the development of faith: if the Catholic school is excessively *authoritarian* in structure, students will be more likely to view God as someone distant and mysterious. If the school and its teachers are *overexacting*, children will have as their image of God one who is a demanding perfectionist. If teachers are *unforgiving*, the young will find it much more difficult to think of God as a loving Father who readily forgives them.[59]

The ultimate criteria for assessment of the responsible use of freedom are not to center around immediate efficiency — important though that is — but the integration of freedom and grace, "which defies any merely temporal assessment."[60] The cooperation, participation, and coresponsibility to be found in the Catholic-school community are by their "very nature a witness not only to Christ as the cornerstone of the community, but also as the light which shines far beyond it."[61]

Overriding all responsibilities is the principle of subsidiarity, whereby decisions are made at the lowest possible level. That which affects the local community must be determined by that community. In its application to Catholic schools, subsidiarity means that "ecclesiastical authority respects the competence of the professionals in teaching and education."[62] Also involved must be the principle of collegiality, whereby the community arrives at decisions together through a dialectic of agreement and disagreement, resulting in consensus.

Assisting these endeavors, which are admittedly sometimes difficult, is the offer of divine grace. This can come to both staff and pupils through community celebrations of the Liturgy. Prayer makes the one praying aware of his or her own lack of wholeness, and of the need to unite with other human beings to bring about the needed wholeness—especially in the service of others by uniting one's own ability with that of others. Private, personal prayer becomes more powerful when lifted up in communal public worship. This is the highest act of the community, because it praises the ultimate mystery of God with all the talents and hopes of the community, and because it unifies the school's intrinsic goals and focuses the school's resources on the extrinsic goal of service to the larger community. In the Eucharistic Liturgy's moment of godliness one witnesses the marriage of secular and sacred, of contemplative and active, of the individual and the community, of the local and the wider community.[63]

School-sponsored Liturgy "should always aim at making the daily life of the children conform more and more to the Gospel."[64] Provided with care and common sense, liturgical celebrations can have great pedagogical value.[65] Some occasions, like the preparation for First Communion, are worthy of more diligence than others.[66] In all, common sense suggests such prudent care as proper timing, avoiding overfrequency, and grouping according to progress in religious formation.[67] These duties in conscience include everyone from hierarchy to laity, embracing all equally in a spirit of respect and cordiality.[68]

Most importantly, the Catholic-school community has a commitment to Christ at its center:

> Christ is the foundation of the whole educational enterprise in a Catholic school. His revelation gives new meaning to life and helps man to direct his thought, action and will according to the Gospel, making the beatitudes his norm of life. The fact that in their own individual ways all members of the school community share this Christian vision, makes the school "Catholic".[69]

Christ's centrality is not, however, as a hub to the spokes of a wheel; it is, rather, Christ at the heart of every member of the community. When that is the case, the school's Christ-centered nature will reach out to involve more and more people and events.

Those in Control in a Major Way

HIERARCHY

Canon Law unequivocally gives to the local bishop the primary responsibility for Catholic schools, including "those schools which are directed by religious, with due regard for their autonomy regarding the internal management of their schools."[70] This authority is, of course, to keep in mind the prescriptions mentioned above of community, subsidiarity, and collegiality. In particular, the specific charism of the religious institute or local sponsoring community is to be considered. If the opinions of the local community differ from those of the Church hierarchy, a dilemma is present, Canon Law giving the edge to the bishop, but not without recourse. This calls for a good deal of genuine communication and mutual respect.

ADMINISTRATORS

Administrators and others who work outside the classroom must complete the teacher's work, in an "authentic Christian dynamism."[71] It is because of their importance that so much is expected of them. We shall mention most of these expectations in chapter 9, on teachers, but we mention here those expectations in which the administrator is relevant to the school's internal atmosphere, especially to what we have said about community. One such expectation is balance. No matter what their philosophy, good administrators accept the fact that the buck stops with them. If a philosophical classicist, the good administrator has well-defined goals, substance to be imparted, and appropriate methods to be used. If an existentialist, the good administrator may be more flexible, and sees to it that school members are free to explore and confront the world with no requirement of stifling conformity. Freedom for the good administrator has with it an emphasis on *responsibility*. Another important balance is between the directives from the Church hierarchy and the local school community's focus. The administrator must walk a line (at times a delicate one) between them.

At a time when funds are hard to come by, near-divine wisdom is called for in getting the best the school's money can buy in the allocation of resources. The good administrator must make proper decisions about which educational tools to buy, how many teachers to hire, what parts of the building demand attention. A proper set of priorities will enable the administrator to convince people to use quality textbooks that "provide for a fuller exposition of the documents of Christian tradition"[72] and are well-grounded in good pedagogical theory. Even if these are the community's or others' decisions, the administrator is the one to advise, lead, and approve. For the Catholic-school administrator, financial strains make this task a great challenge. The task calls for courage, wisdom, and strength, in addition to the support of the community and the guidance of the Church.

The good administrator will be open, sharing with teachers, parents, the laity, and other interested parties all that will be of benefit. He or she "should keep the families informed about the ways in which the educational philosophy is being applied or improved on, about formation, about administration, and, in certain cases, about the management."[73] Good administrators will use their contacts with all the school's constituents in a leadership role to help develop community. A genuine community of faith

> will not take place, it will not even begin to happen, unless there is a sharing of the Christian commitment among at least a portion of each of the principal groups that make up the educational community: parents, teachers, and students.[74]

While the task of building community is sometimes difficult and may seem never ending, the valuable fruit it yields makes it eminently worthwhile. If the administrator is a principal, she or he must be careful that distance from central offices will not result in insensitivity. The good administrator will at the same time be mindful of the prescription of Canon Law "that the instruction given in them [Catholic schools] is at least as academically distinguished as that given in the other schools of the region."[75] In a word, the good Catholic-school administrator is a leader.[76]

Even so, administrative conflicts will arise. If the often quoted statement from the National Commission on Excellence in Education applies at all to Catholic schools, perhaps it could be in the area of administration. That statement is, "If an unfriendly foreign power had attempted to impose on America the mediocre educational performance that exists today, we might well have viewed it as an act of war."[77]

Part of the reason for this is that the present arrangement may contain too many bosses: a local pastor, perhaps, and a religious order, the diocesan office, the principal, and more. For greater efficiency, coordination, and cooperation, a rethinking of the system is necessary. In fact, a motto for good administrators might be adapted from an old axiom about the Church: *ecclesia semper reformanda*, "the Church must always be in the process of being reformed." For schools, the motto could be *schola semper recogitanda*: "schools must always be in the process of being rethought." We must never forget that the school is always in the process of being created. Where schools have no challenge, there is no stimulus to rethink.

Because of the importance of the principal of the parish school, the hiring decision cannot be the pastor's alone. In the past, too often his decision rested upon his perception of whether the candidate was a "good Catholic." Frequently what he meant by "good Catholic" was that, no matter what the professional qualities, the candidate went to Mass on Sunday. If the pastor was himself insecure, he settled upon a candidate who provided security in such ways as having invited him regularly to dinner.

TEACHERS

Also in control in a major way are teachers. Though most of what we have to say on teachers is contained in chapter 9, we include here observations on teachers as they appertain to the internal conditions of schools. Teachers are important enough to mention them often. The quality of learning, after all, depends very largely on the quality of teaching, and by their witness and their behavior teachers are of the first importance in imparting a distinctive character to Catholic schools. But the teachers' importance is often belied by the treatment they receive. The National Commission on Excellence in Education found that "the professional working life of teachers is on the whole unacceptable."[78] While not written about Catholic schools, the statement pertains to them as well.

It has been found that, for good morale on the part of teachers (as well as other staff), the components minimally include identification with the school and acceptance of its religious goals related to education in faith, pride in what the school community is aiming to achieve, confidence in the leadership, satisfaction of one's personal needs and aspirations through involvement in the school, a feeling of personal worth and importance in the school community, a share in the decision-making processes, reasonable job satisfaction with regard to work conditions like class sizes and duty-free lunch, good communication between the principal and staff, social integration of staff through socials and celebrations, and regular staff prayer sessions and liturgies.[79]

Unfortunately, there is a social-justice gap (whose proportions vary from time to time and place to place) between the dream and the reality. Among the problems in both government and Catholic schools (and sometimes worse in Catholic schools) are low salaries for teachers and administrators, heavy work loads, excessive extracurricular assignments, limited facilities, lack of opportunities for promotion and professional growth, and lack of adequate satisfaction in work. A good argument can be made that there is nothing seriously wrong with Catholic schools that money could not solve.

It is true that none of the Church's famous encyclicals on economic justice explicitly call upon the Church to apply to itself the moral principles explicitly applied to management, labor, and government. Neither *Gaudium et spes*, Vatican II's great document on the Church in the modern world, nor Vatican II's *Declaration on Catholic Education*, which praises Catholic-school teachers, has anything explicit to say about justice to church employees. In 1968, the U.S. bishops, in a major document, for the first time said that the Church had better practice what it preaches:

> If Catholic performance does not match Catholic promise, then truly we shall have failed. We were once warned: It is not your encyclicals which we despise; what we despise is the neglect with which you yourselves treat them.[80]

In 1971, the second synod of bishops did what Vatican II had envisioned synods would do: it added new specificity to the Council's decrees and, as it were, updated them. This synod, among other things, made a landmark declaration on justice in the Church:

> Those who serve their Church by their labor, including priests and religious, should receive a sufficient livelihood and enjoy that social security which is customary in their region. Lay people should be given fair wages and a system for promotion.[81]

In 1982, Rome's education department sent out a letter of commitment to Catholic schools and the rights of their teachers. Among other things, it said:

> If the directors of the school and the lay people who work in the school are to live according to the same ideals, two things are essential. First, lay people must receive an adequate salary, guaranteed by a well defined contract, for the work they do in the school; a salary which will permit them to live in dignity, without excessive work or a need for additional employment that will interfere with the duties of an educator. This may not be immediately possible without putting an enormous financial burden on the families, or making the school so expensive that it becomes a school for a small elite group. . . . [82]

The papal encyclicals have upheld as a basic human right the prerogative of Church employees to engage in collective bargaining with the Church through unions of the employees' choice. By far the most explicit declaration of this has been in the U.S. bishops' 1986 pastoral on the economy: "All the moral principles that govern the just operation of any economic endeavor apply to the Church and its many agencies and institutions. The Church should be exemplary."⁸³ The document also says that the "Church has a special call to be the servant of the poor" and insists on a "preferential option for the poor."⁸⁴ In keeping with this mandate, the Church should continue to conduct its inner-city schools for the education of the poor: the most important act anyone can do for the poor is to educate their children.

The reality is at times different. On the good side, many Catholic schools, especially high schools, have developed excellent contracts with teacher unions. And episcopal pronouncements have condemned all sorts of social evils like secularism, materialism, atheism, racial injustice, evils in government, and immoral weapons of war, and they have recommended solutions to all kinds of social problems based on the Gospel principles of justice and charity. On the bad side, the bishops' pronouncements have at times seemed olympian and lacking in feasibility. Part of the reason for this is that, for Catholic as well as other schools, progress comes at financial cost. Increased upward social mobility means Catholics can afford to give more to the Church, and should be educated to do so. Our non-Catholic brothers and sisters contribute more per capita than we do. If we are convinced of the value of Catholic schools and of the need of social justice for teachers, we must either pay up or surrender the Catholic schools. It's "your money or your life."

One of the biggest scandals today is the extreme poverty of religious sisters, many of whom helped build the nation's parochial-school system by working long years for subsistence wages. With a median age now over sixty, the nation's more than one hundred thousand sisters are beset by a lack of meaningful retirement programs and a sharp decline in the number of young women entering the ranks. A recent study showed a gap of almost two billion dollars between the available retirement money for the sisters and what it will take to meet their financial and medical needs. A growing number of religious communities are selling off their schools, their land, and even their mother houses, to raise enough cash to pay the mounting expenses of caring for older members. The problem promises to worsen as more religious communities run out of money.⁸⁵

This is an embarrassment to the bishops, of course, who complain, in their recent pastoral letter on economic justice, that wage discrimination against women is a "major factor" in high rates of poverty in the U.S. It should be an even greater embarrassment to the laity whom the sisters have served and whose contributions have not been adequate. But the above-cited study showed that some young laity feel that "what the sisters did, they did in charity," and do not feel obligated to do anything about it.

Those in Control in a Lesser Way: Students

Students should be able to find in the Catholic school a climate which complements that of the Catholic home. Religion is, after all, a way of living rather than the mere acquisition of knowledge, and its culture requires a medium, an atmosphere, an environment. *Morale* is an important component of that climate. Morale in a school is that inner confidence on the part of staff and students and *the mutual faith between them* which leads to identification with the school, acceptance of its vital goals, and cooperative striving toward accomplishing the goals. It implies a proper relatedness between oneself and one's environment and is a measure of human faith in the school situation.[86]

High morale among students, the opposite of alienation, points to a congruence between the reality of what is in the school situation and the utopian what ought to be. Morale tends to be high when there is a balance, or creative tension, between the two extremes of overcontrol and undercontrol. Overcontrol (overstrict molding of individuals in conformity with established patterns) leads to powerlessness, depersonalization, and meaninglessness. Undercontrol (permissiveness, lack of restraint, and disintegration of all boundaries) leads to normlessness, frustration, and isolation.

If students find themselves in continual failure at school or home, they will slowly come to believe that God is against them. If they feel that their teachers do not care for them personally or if teachers or parents are not interested in what youth have to say, youth will find it more difficult to appreciate that God loves them and listens to their prayers. If students find enjoyment and happiness at a Catholic school and feel that their parents and teachers are genuinely interested in them, they will be more likely to think of God as kind and gracious, a loving Father to whom they will want to commit themselves in faith. Clearly, the image of God that Catholic-school youth gradually develop will be influenced first of all by their home, and then by their experience of school.[87]

Innovative Situations

Among the beneficial aspects of the internal atmosphere of nongovernment schools in general and Catholic schools in particular, all of which are relatively free from political and other interference, is the ability to experiment. For whatever reasons—tight schedules, busy staff, insufficient funds, conservatism, narrow vision—Catholic schools perhaps do not engage in experimentation and innovation as often as many might wish. In addition to such practical local arrangements as interparochial schools that must be financially viable, as in the archdiocese of Baltimore, and the cost-sharing and the revitalization of the schools in the archdioceses of Chicago and Washington, D.C.,[88] two important areas in which they are involved in innovation are ecumenical schools and lay-run schools.

Ecumenical Schools

Ecumenical schools constitute a phenomenon that is still small but growing and therefore deserving of mention. They are a product of the Church's expression of concern for ecumenism in Vatican II. Among its statements, the Church sees ongoing interior conversion as an essential concomitant of ecumenism.[89] As applied to education, the Church has, as one example, this to say:

> The purpose of programs of this type [ecumenical education] is to increase among students a deeper knowledge of the faith, the spirituality and the entire life and doctrine of the Catholic Church, so that they may wisely and fruitfully take part in ecumenical dialogue each according to his capabilities, to direct their attention both to that inward renewal of the Catholic Church itself which will help so much to promote unity among Christians, and to those things in their own lives or in the life of the Church which hinder or slow down progress towards unity; a further purpose is that teachers and students should learn more about other Churches and communities, and so understand better and assess more correctly what unites Christians and what divides them; finally, since these efforts are not to be mere intellectual exercises, the aim is that those taking part in them should better realize the obligation of fostering unity between Christians and so be led to apply themselves more effectively to achieving it. They will also be led to do what is in their power to give joint Christian witness to the contemporary world.[90]

Ecumenical schools, of course, go beyond ecumenism in a curriculum: they put ecumenism into practice by having two or more Christian denominations participate in the total running of the school. In practice, some say that no ecumenical schools arise from pure devotion to ecumenism, but rather from a practical necessity. One side needs students, for example, and the other money or buildings, so they merge to form an ecumenical school.[91] Be that as it may, they have special internal atmospheres.

In England, most ecumenical schools are under the auspices of the

Church of England and the Roman Catholic Church. Christ's School, in the London Borough of Richmond upon Thames, is one such. Among its declared aims are the following:

> Christ's School aims to provide for the full ability range and to draw out the best qualities of each member of its community in a caring and stimulating Christian environment. It is concerned with the development of each individual to his or her full potential in terms of knowledge, imaginative understanding of the world in which we live and awareness of spiritual and moral values.[92]

The school badge depicts the "Chi-Rho", the first two letters of the Greek word *Christos*; the motto is "One in Christ," reflecting what is hoped to be the true nature of the school. The school hopes also that this is "evident in the ethos of the school, where a loving and caring attitude to all people is fostered."[93]

Insights into the special practical atmosphere of an ecumenical school come from St. Bede's Ecumenical School of Roman Catholics and the Church of England in Red Hill, Surrey, England.[94] St. Bede's found insufficient doctrinal difference in religious education to justify separate presentations by Roman Catholics and Anglicans. How does each denomination retain its identity? All participants are expected to know the doctrinal differences that make them Roman Catholic or Anglican. Each must be proud of their own tradition, respect the others' tradition and allow them to be proud of theirs, be open to and learn from the traditions of others, and look to what they have in common while honestly not denying what divides.

At the time of which we speak, at least once a month St. Bede's had sessions prepared and led by the chaplains on various topics that might lead to problems: infallibility, the place of Mary, and the celibacy of the clergy. Religious education teachers especially had to understand, as much as humanly possible, the beliefs of the other denomination on the principle that love comes from knowing and understanding. Every member of the staff had to understand what St. Bede's as an ecumenical school was about: the teachers of mathematics as well as the formal teachers of religion.

St. Bede's was luckier than most in getting both an Anglican and a Catholic chaplain whose first duty was to the school. The chaplaincy is a key position, and requires deep commitment. At St. Bede's, this commitment resulted in the chaplains' being well equipped with office, telephone, money, and so on. The Liturgy is important; denominational liturgy in an ecumenical school must be done even better than elsewhere. To be together in prayer is beautiful, and does not happen accidentally. On special occasions, like the death of a student's relative, there may be a joint prayer service.

The staff must be honest with themselves with regard to where their faith is. Whereas principals or teachers in a Catholic school might get by if their faith were wishy-washy, in an ecumenical school one has to believe genuinely. Other teacher qualities specially necessary in ecumenical schools are abilities at communication and public relations, because of the nature of the school; patience with frustration, because for every giant step forward there are two tiny steps backward; and understanding of the small number of parents who belittle the school because it is not sufficiently Catholic for them. There must be frequent get-togethers, luncheons, and the like, to keep lines of communication open. (St. Bede's principal had to be at every Catholic meeting, every Anglican meeting, and every ecumenical meeting, and to give more in terms of energy than many might like.)

The leaders must be tough but fair, with a lot of human compassion. They must set standards high, so that incompetent staff will leave of their own accord without being fired. The religious involved must get on well with each other. And ecumenical schools are better if they have a good governing body who are deeply committed, meet regularly, and ask questions.

If an ecumenical school is not a very good school, it could be a very dangerous one. Staff is vital, an ecumenical school needing a strong core of committed Christians. St. Bede's had all teachers take their turn in leading the assembly in prayer; unusual at first, this quickly became the norm. Extremely important also is student admissions. The school cannot exclude youngsters because they are Catholic only in name. If it puts on the application form that parents must be Church members, the parents go to church for three months prior to application in order to be on the parish records or be known to the priest or minister.

What is to prevent the students from becoming eclectic? Staff and governing body have to be secure and show it. They cannot pretend, and must be very honest. All have something to give. The ability to communicate is very important. Educated people must also learn to respect and trust other people. And they must respect self: have self-esteem and confidence in what talent each possesses. And it is most essential that they use their freedom responsibly. Relationship to the Church hierarchy is also worthy of note. One must not go beyond what one thinks the local bishop would allow. This is a delicate line, and requires balance. And the bishop must trust the school, too.

Of course, much of what we have said about ecumenical schools could also be said of good Catholic schools.

Completely Lay-Run Catholic Schools

An increase in the proportion and objective numbers of laity engaged in Catholic schools is common. Not as common, however, are Catholic schools completely run by laity. One innovation in this respect is St. Michael's Academy in the diocese of Austin, Texas. Starting in February 1982, Dr. Leonard Dolce and friends formed a lay board of trustees, negotiated with the local bishop and priests, developed a school board, defined a curriculum, acquired land, built a school, hired staff, and (in late August 1985) opened classes. The board of trustees' report recommended not only an "institution of the first class," but also that "Christian values must be stressed in all disciplines."

Whereas in some previous institutions lay boards stepped in and took over only when the last of the religious left, the newness of St. Michael's consisted in a school designed and planned from the outset by lay people who assumed responsibility for the entire operation. (Religious sisters helped on a temporary basis in setting up various aspects of the program.) The purpose of the school is to take a part in the training of lay leaders, Dolce believing that whereas heretofore some religion was by emotion, from here on it will have to be more by brain. The laity involved are serious, interested, competent, solid, and committed.[95]

CONCLUSION

Every school must deal with an atmosphere, parts of which come from outside the school, others from inside. The atmosphere is not of the essence of education, but is integral to it and gives the school its flavor, and thus is important. The external atmosphere comprises the economic, political, cultural, and social structures of the culture in which the school finds itself. At least as important to the Catholic school is its internal atmosphere, particularly the spiritual. This means especially the formation of Christian community. The hierarchy, other administrators, and teachers must do all in their power to form the school community.

The Church must make this possible by living up to her many encyclicals about personnel. This means just wages guaranteed by contract, the granting of due dignity, obviating the necessity of outside work, providing just working conditions, granting social security, putting in place a system for promotion, making collective bargaining possible, and granting without difficulty the right to join unions. Students, too, must be active participants in the Christian community that is the Catholic school, and should be able to find there a climate which complements that of the Catholic home.

In the next chapter, we shall discuss more details of teachers and students that can bring about the creation of this atmosphere.

QUESTIONS FOR DISCUSSION

What means are currently available for financing the Catholic school, and what alternatives, in your opinion, remain unused?

There are many sociocultural lampoons of Catholic schools (for example, caricatures like "Father" Guido Sarducci of "Saturday Night Live"; negative plays and movies like "Do Patent Leather Shoes Shine Up" and "Sister Mary Ignatius Explains It All For You"; myths about nuns' silly teachings about white tablecloths, dancing, male-female relationships, manners, and dress codes). Do these perceptions have any bearing on the reality of the Catholic school? Do they have any lasting detrimental influence on student perceptions of the school, community support, or societal images?

Should the janitor, sexton, or custodian mirror the existence of true community in a Catholic school? How or how not?

How can the Catholicity of Catholic schools run by the laity be assured?

Can a case be made to say that the Catholic school should be a revolutionary institution in a nonviolent way?

What are the optimal roles and functions of the Catholic community vis-a-vis the Catholic school?

How do you form a Catholic community, and how do you measure the result?

Do the Catholic schools of your experience teach and live community? If not, how would one operationalize it?

What distinguishes a school with Christian community over and against one that ignores it?

In the face of the hostile mind-set that Catholic-school graduates meet, the decline in public morality, and the like, can Catholic-school graduates realistically be expected to carry with them anything unique from the Catholic school?

How do the school building, the seating arrangements, the structure of the rooms, the positioning of the teachers' desks, and the like, demonstrate a school's philosophy of life and of education?

What are the cohesive forces that hold the Catholic school together and make it Catholic?

Why is the living of a community of faith in a Catholic school so important?

What are the characteristics of the Catholic school as a community?

Do Catholic schools allow students sufficient freedom?

Can a Catholic school truly create a climate that replicates that of the good Catholic home? If so, how?

Why are social structures important to Catholic schools?

Can God speak in, to, and through all social models in the world? How?

Is it prudent to rely upon tithing as a way to support Catholic schools?

Are Catholic-school students sufficiently educated in civic responsibility?

Aside from words, and based on the overall evidence of actions and demonstrable priorities, what value does the Church *really* put on its schools?

Does the Catholic Church put sufficient emphasis upon the intellectual life?

What are the benefits, if any, of Catholic schools to the unmarried and the married childless to merit their support?

For solid religious formation, would Catholics be better advised to place their time, money, and energy into other areas than a place called "school"?

What aspects of the spiritual atmosphere of the Catholic school do you deem the most important?

What is (are) the difference(s) between a school with Christian community and one that ignores it?

In an ecumenical school, how can students keep their identity as members of each participating denomination?

If Martin Luther's opinion on the worth of religious schools to business people is valid, how would you appeal to the business people in your neighborhood for financial support for the local Catholic school?

SUGGESTED BIBLIOGRAPHY

Aronowitz, Stanley, and Henry Giroux. *Education under Seige: The Conservative, Liberal, and Radical Debate over Schooling*. South Hadley, Mass.: Bergin and Garvey, 1985.

Synthesizes some of the best insights and thinking of radical educational analyses and offers some of the clearest analyses of neoconservative educational rhetoric and reform.

Augenstein, John J. *A Collaborative Approach to Personnel Relations*. Washington, D.C.: National Catholic Educational Association, 1980.

Describes what is promised in the title, for Catholic schools.

Behan, Sister Helen Marie. *Dynamics of Community*. New York: Corpus, 1970.

Explores various forms of community and discusses the formation of truly Christian communities.

_____. *Living Community*. Milwaukee: Bruce, 1967.

Discusses concepts related to community: man's natural need for community, its meaning, participation in a loving community, freedom and responsibility in community.

Dunphy, Joan S. *To Save Our Schools*. Fair Hills, N. J.: New Horizon, 1985.

An adaptation of a television documentary, this book provides an incisive analysis of the crisis conditions confronting U.S. schools. These conditions include alienated and apathetic students who reflect socioeconomic factors of poverty, broken homes, and cultural impoverishment; an aging, demoralized teaching corps that is poorly paid, suffers loss of community and student respect, and is subject to oppressive work conditions; and a loss of public faith in the schools.

Goodlad, John I. *A Place Called School: Prospects for the Future*. New York: McGraw-Hill, 1984.

Asserting that our educational system is nearing collapse, cites the public's dissatisfaction, the decline of family and church, segmentation in schooling, the death of the political power of educational institutions, loss of the feeling of community, and the lack of universal schooling.

Henry, Jules. *Culture against Man*. New York: Random House, 1963.

A cultural anthropologist, Henry traces the development of social problems that underlie educational conflicts through the ages.

Illich, Ivan. *Deschooling Society*. New York: Harper and Row, 1972.

An indictment of school systems that "crank out" a steady flow of robot-consumers.

Powers, Richard H. *The Dilemma of Education in a Democracy*. Washington, D.C.: Regnery Gateway, 1984.

Continues in the tradition of Maritain in its rejection of modern schools' experiential, child-centered approach. Pleads for a return to the traditional approach in which structure, prescribed curriculum, and discipline lead to an understanding of the values of the Judeo-Christian tradition and the intellectual heritage of Western civilization.

Shor, Ira. *Culture Wars: School and Society in the Conservative Restoration, 1969–1984*. New York: Routledge and Kegan Paul/Methuen, 1986.

Recent educational history from a leftist perspective; sees the 1960s as a dynamic period of promise followed by the establishment's movements to restore the status quo: career education (1971–75), back to basics (1975–82), and desire for excellence (1982–84).

Sizer, Theodore. *Horace's Compromise: The Dilemma of the American High School*. Boston: Houghton Mifflin, 1984.

The dilemma of Horace, the capable teacher who wants to teach his students how to think, is that in order to hold his job he must compromise ideals and accept mediocre learning, because the school provides conditions that are not conducive to optimal learning. Sizer proposes drastic surgery to eliminate these conditions.

Chapter 9

WHO GETS CATHOLIC SCHOOLS THERE: TEACHERS

IMPORTANCE OF TEACHERS

It is teachers (which term includes administrators, counselors, staff, and others) who represent the school's philosophy to the students and the larger public. When teachers help pupils to appreciate the cultural heritage of humankind, they are guiding those pupils toward eternal realities. To the child, what "the teacher is, as a person, may represent, for good or for evil, educated people, virtue, life beyond the barrio, or one's own future grown-up self."[1]

The Church continuously reaffirms the importance of teachers:

> The extent to which the Christian message is transmitted through education depends to a very great extent on the teachers. The integration of culture and faith is mediated by the other integration of faith and life in the person of the teacher. The nobility of the task to which teachers are called demands that, in imitation of Christ, the only teacher, they reveal the Christian message not only by word but also by every facet of their behaviour.[2]

Catholic-school teachers should "help to insert the Catholic school into pastoral activities, in union with the local Church."[3] Pope John Paul II said that teachers

> carry out one of the most important tasks of the church and of society . . . [in order] that [students] may be prepared to live their personal lives according to a new nature in justice and holiness in truth so that they may reach perfect maturity, the measure of the fullness of Christ.[4]

241

HISTORICAL PERSPECTIVES

Jesus was essentially a teacher.[5] Pope John Paul II points this out beautifully and succinctly:

> Jesus taught. It is the witness that he gives of himself: "Day after day I sat in the Temple teaching". It is the admiring observation of the evangelists, surprised to see him teaching everywhere and at all times, teaching in a manner and with an authority previously unknown: "Crowds gathered to him again; and again, as his custom was, he taught them"; "and they were astonished at his teaching, for he taught them as one who had authority." It is also what his enemies note for the purpose of drawing from it grounds for accusation and condemnation: "He stirs up the people, teaching throughout all Judaea, from Galilee even to this place". . . . One who teaches in this way has a unique title to the name of "Teacher." Throughout the New Testament, especially in the Gospels, how many times is he given this title of Teacher! . . . But above all, Jesus himself at particularly solemn and highly significant moments calls himself Teacher: "You call me Teacher and Lord; and you are right, for so I am" . . . One can understand why people of every kind, race and nation have for two thousand years in all the languages of the earth given him this title with veneration, repeating in their own ways the exclamation of Nicodemus: "We know that you are a teacher come from God."[6]

Jesus is frequently referred to as the model teacher. When he was dealing with people, he showed virtues essential to teachers, like love, patience, kindness, and gentleness. Also, he was more gentle with ordinary people and more demanding with the educated.[7] When dealing with the apostles, he was doing what we would today call teacher training. His methodology is well illustrated by his teaching of the difficult and theretofore unheard-of doctrine of the Eucharist.[8] His parables are frequently referred to as model stories which could be emulated with benefit by teachers today, the parable of the Good Shepherd being an especially fine example.[9] Good advice for teachers is present throughout the New Testament.[10]

The apostles quickly shared their ministry with others, including their ministry of teaching.[11] St. Paul, while continuing the noble Jewish tradition of respect for the rabbi, was not unaware of the difficulties and the hardships connected with teaching, and saw that teaching is connected with religion.[12] St. Augustine beautifully summed up the motivation that teachers should receive from the New Testament:

With this love [of God for humankind] set before you as a criterion
by which you should measure everything you say, go on to teach all
your lessons in such a way that the person who listens to you may
believe in consequence of listening to you and, by believing, may
hope and, by hoping, love.[13]

This mission of teaching continued in the early Church.[14] By and
large, the Fathers of the Church used even the pagan learning and
literature of the day to further the Church's mission. They used pagan
secular education as a means for the conceptual framework of the
Church's teaching, as an end toward elevating the minds of the leaders
of the day who were educated in it, and as a necessity because there
was no other learning known at the time.

This noble tradition of respect for teachers and teaching has continued through history, right up to and including the United States.
From the beginnings of this country, both laity and religious have
proved their high calibre by their success against adversity, their courage in facing the hardships of frontier life and early death, and their
anonymity, the last being dictated by their humility and zeal. Their
gifts to our country go far beyond the financial. In addition to contributing to the country as well as their church a cultural enrichment and
a fullness of life, they eradicated religious illiteracy and were role
models and saviors of many needy children. The impact of their
dedication, especially on the underprivileged, can only be inferred
from empirical studies like those of James S. Coleman. It is on their
sacrifices and dedication that the United States pattern of Catholic
schools is built. They deserve the utmost gratitude not only of Catholics but of our entire citizenry.[15]

DEFINITIONS
Overall Criteria

Our understanding of "teacher" in the present context "is not simply
a professional person whose contribution is limited to the systematic
transmission of knowledge in a school; 'teacher' is to be understood as
'educator'—one who helps to form human persons."[16] We include in
our definition

all who are involved in this formation . . . : especially those who
are responsible for the direction of schools, or are counselors,
tutors or coordinators; also those who complement and complete
the educational activities of the teacher or help in administrative
and auxiliary positions.[17]

At the same time, the activity of teaching is different from all others—like indoctrinating, conditioning, preaching, training, instructing, or demonstrating.

The characteristics that differentiate and define teaching do not necessarily imply the criteria for *good* teaching, or *successful* teaching, or *effective* teaching. Good teaching is hard to discern.[18] Successful teaching is simply teaching which brings about the desired learning. Learning a concept is like learning to play tennis or golf, not like learning to mouth the rules and principles that govern play. Effective teaching is determined objectively by the nature of the subject itself and how best to teach it.

Fundamentally, the intention of teaching activities, whatever the activities may be, is to bring about learning. But, while all educational processes are processes of learning, not all processes of learning are processes of education. Much that is learned must be excluded from teaching or true education either as inevitable, like natural physiological or maturational growth, or as undesirable, like a sexual perversion, or as trivial, like wiggling one's ears.

Definitions That Are More Remote from Catholic

Pragmatism sees the teacher as facilitator, guide, resource person, innovator, and change agent. Behind most of these characterizations is Pragmatism's emphasis on the process of learning as problem solving. The desire for creativity in finding challenging ways of presenting problems that stimulate critical thinking which pragmatists love so much are, however, as old as humankind. Many Catholic-school teachers might profit from the imaginative and innovative procedures of some pragmatists' ideas of the teacher.

But most of what is new in Pragmatism's definition of teacher is unacceptable to Catholics. Among these aspects are the preference for action rather than contemplation; belief in the changing character of knowledge as opposed to unchanging truths; and the view of the teacher as facilitator and innovator wherein student stimuli, experiences, and interactions alone are considered to constitute the learning process. Catholics do not agree, either, with the pragmatist's belief that it is the process rather than the content which is all-important. And Catholics want to give prominence to the teacher's role in the student's spiritual and moral development.

Existentialism's emphasis is on the teacher as a presenter of choices. Such teachers want to nurture the individuality of each student. Catholic-school teachers believe in human freedom, and that people define themselves by their choices. But they object to excessive permissiveness. The Catholic-school teacher also wants to present universal values, and not—as some nontheistic existentialists define the teacher's role—to mold values to suit the individual, or to hold that actions and values are relevant only to a specific person in a specific situation.

Definitions That Are Closer to the Catholic

Closer to the Catholic idea are the definitions of Realism, Idealism, and theistic Existentialism. The realist teacher, seeing knowledge as a process of the discovery of truth, sees the teacher's role as transmitting past and present knowledge and cultural values, conveying information, and disciplining students, all within a structural framework. Realist teachers, in other words, see themselves as presenters, lecturers, and causal agents—but most of all in the rather priestly role of mediators: in this case between the learner and the world of reality.

Idealism, with its belief in the supreme value of the intellect and the importance of ideas over sensory experience, stresses a kind of teaching which strives to transmit the best of humankind's traditional heritage and provides opportunities for students to challenge their intellectual capabilities, treasuring these above modern preference for personal self-acceptance over intellectual values. The Catholic-school teacher who is comfortable with this definition wants to develop in students a proper sense of God, direction, responsibility, and mission. The idealist teacher also accepts the responsibility of being a role-model.

The connotation of "teacher" in a Catholic sense is of one who has authority over others for the purpose of improving them in knowledge, skills, habits, attitudes, or ideals consonant with their true nature, ultimate end, and highest good. Authority for Catholic teachers is not authoritarianism, a tyrannical or domineering control. Authority is rather the dynamic influence and wholesome guidance of the mature person over the less mature. Personal presence is necessary—a presence which is comprised of an awareness which gives people credit for having a continuity, dialectic in terms of trust in people to make them feel free to respond and be heard, and willingness to be of help. Speaking to teachers, Pope John Paul II said:

> Through you, as through a clear window on a sunny day, students must come to see and know the richness and the joy of a life lived in accordance with his [Jesus'] teaching. . . . To teach means not only to impart what we know, but also to reveal who we are by living what we believe. It is this latter lesson which tends to last the longest.[19]

Profession or Vocation?

Professions like medicine and law have certain characteristics.[20] Some of these, like working for a fee instead of a salary and making individual contractual arrangements with one's clientele, are not as important as the claim to a specific body of knowledge unique to the profession and the mastery of which is necessary for accredited membership. Whether education has such a body of knowledge, or borrows from other sciences to the extent that it is a bastard that doesn't know its own parentage, is controverted.[21] Another requirement for a profession is that it be self-evaluating, self-governing, and self-policing; on this ground, too, the admissibility of education to professionship is controverted.

Regardless of whether or not education is a profession, teaching is, for Catholic teachers, a noble personal vocation in the Church.[22] For teachers, the profession is the vocation. This vocation calls for detachment, commitment, and generosity, and it provides for an enthusiastic fullness of life. The realization of teaching as vocation applies to Catholics teaching in all kinds of schools as well as Catholic ones. In schools with non-Catholic philosophies, "it will frequently happen that the presence of lay Catholics . . . is the only way in which the Church is present."[23] In these circumstances, Catholic teachers "should be influenced by a Christian faith vision."[24] This will be evident to all if the Catholic teacher "brings to the task professional commitment, concern for truth, justice and freedom, breadth of vision, an habitual spirit of service, personal commitment to the students, fraternal solidarity with all and total moral integrity."[25] Even in the face of apparent failure to gain perceptible results, "everyone who ventures into education [must be reminded] of the need for humility and hope and the conviction that [their] work cannot be assessed by the same rationalistic criteria which apply to other professions."[26]

One of the qualities that raises teaching from a mere profession to a vocation is commitment (from the Latin *com* + *mittere*, "to send with"; similar in origin to *commission*), a pledge by both intellectual conviction and emotional ties to involvement which embraces the future as well as the present. This kind of dedication involves loyalty, identification, and participation.[27] Commitment is passionate, with plenty of heart as well as head, and is driven by the motivation to achieve a goal.[28] It goes outside oneself, being related to what psychologist Gordon W. Allport called "self-extension," for him a characteristic of psychological maturity. With teaching, commitment reaches out to such as pupils, the faith, and good teaching, infusing both methodology and one's subject matter.

People who "hang loose" and "play it cool" see commitment as especially difficult.[29] Indeed, is it even even possible to *have* commitment? Friedrich Nietzsche answered that only some men—those in the category of *Übermensch* ("Superior Man," whom Americans, in their impatience with the use of two words when one will do, term "Superman")—are capable of commitment. Only the Superman has the autonomy that can rise above the herd morality sufficiently to make promises. Nietzsche saw all candidates for vows—baptismal, marital, religious, as well as those of public office—in this light. Jean-Paul Sartre found commitment to be as contradictory as its source, which is love. Seeing people placed in the uncomfortable position of having to choose between freedom and love, he unhesitatingly said that freedom comes before love, fidelity, and all else.

Sartre's fellow existentialist Gabriel Marcel took the opposite position. He contended that a person can only know himself—have true self-consciousness—and grow if he commits himself. He based his position on three views. First, every act is in a way a commitment of the agent, and to say that commitment is impossible is equivalent to saying that human activity is impossible. Second, the real question is not whether there is commitment or not, but rather to what a person is committed. Third, the human being is not totally process; what distinguishes the human being from things is the fact that the person is at the same time being *and* becoming, not just becoming.

Although Marcel's argument involves a certain circularity,[30] he made the very important contribution of showing that human freedom and commitment are not only not contradictory, but are necessarily correlative. So, like Nietzsche, he held that all those forces that rob a person of humanity—habit, custom, force, mechanization, and the like—deprive one of freedom and hence of the ability to commit oneself. Also like Nietzsche, but with greater sadness, Marcel maintained that not everyone is actually able to commit him/herself. But unlike Nietzsche, Marcel held that commitment remains a realistic goal for all people, simply because they are human.

Is it possible to *teach* commitment to anyone—teacher or student—who does not have it? One's answer will depend in part on which position one accepts concerning *having* commitment. Those espousing the negative position give as one reason for their negativity that (contrary to Socrates' belief) virtue cannot be taught. The negative position argues further that any attempt to teach commitment to students demands a response that today's students are usually unable to give, and that such a demand infringes drastically on students' freedom even if they could respond. Students must be taught, not importuned. Christ must be chosen, not imposed. The attempt to elicit commitment is *sermonizing*, and the teacher is to teach, not preach.

Those who take an affirmative approach decry these allegations as distortions.[31] They admit that, if we have a flight from authentic intellectual content in religion classes—downgrading challenging content matter, imposing objective testing, underlining systematic grading, and the like—teaching commitment becomes an impossibility. The answer to that, they say, is to provide a more substantive approach.

TEACHER ETHICS AND PROFESSIONAL RESPONSIBILITY

In contrast to the legal and medical professions, neither secular nor Catholic teaching has much of a code of ethics or professional responsibility to speak of.[32] Indeed, the question is often asked whether, in teacher-student relationships, a special ethics is at all required (as with doctor-patient, attorney-client), or if general ethics is sufficient. In addition to allegiance to Christian values, a properly developed Catholic-school teacher's code of professional responsibility would have to include obligations to students, parents, the community, and the profession.

To Students

The classroom should not be like a parade ground in which generation after generation of quasi-anonymous marchers pass through. It should rather be permeated by a happy atmosphere which is the result of good personal relationships between teachers and students. These personal relationships are not like the good personal "relations" which a salesman might have with his customers, but more the style of the grocer in the village store. One of the prime moral principles that holds in personal relationships is mutual respect between persons. Respect responds to another person because both sides are human beings, subject to joy, pain, hope, love, anger, and a whole gamut of other emotions and desires. It knows the difference between saying "How do you do?" as a matter of manners, and entering into a concerned discussion about the other's health.

The teacher's respect for the student should impel concern about a boy breaking his leg, irrespective of whether this hinders or helps him as a learner. But teachers should not be so overwhelmed with awe at students expressing their innermost thoughts that they would hesitate to point out that the students' thoughts were not clearly expressed, or irrelevant to a matter under discussion, or wrong. That would make one deficient as a teacher. Teacher-student relationships might be fully developed, embryonic, or somewhere in between. Most pupils would be too young for the degree of reciprocity which is required for fully developed personal relationships, and to have full reciprocal relationships with every member of a class of forty would be wearing, to say the least.

Good teachers are able to allow glimpses of themselves as human beings to slip through to their pupils and are receptive to the same from the pupils. Such embryonic personal relationships entail no obvious incompatibility with the fairness that is required of a teacher, because the relationship can be rather widely distributed. If such relationships are reasonably relaxed, spontaneous, and unselfconscious, they can act as a catalyst to teaching.

Teachers must be sufficiently self-possessed so that they do not react to, but rather respond to, children. The teacher's own psychological needs must be satisfied before the teacher can reach out to students and in turn reap the benefits of the relationship. To "love your neighbor—or your students—as yourself" must psychologically begin with a proper love and esteem of oneself. Although teaching (including Catholic-school teaching) is not immune from the entry of persons with deep-rooted psychological dysfunctions which prevent teachers from seeing the value of interpersonal relationships with students, the effectiveness of Catholic secondary schools[33] can be attributed in part to the relationships that are formed between teachers and students.

Catholic-school teachers will, then, have a lively concern for the personhood of each student, try to establish an atmosphere of trust and openness, and have a real care for the less able and underprivileged. Responsibilities to students must be given special consideration. A criterion for choosing the teacher "should be the practice of a pedagogy which gives special emphasis to direct and personal contact with the students."[34]

Teachers' contact with students is to be warm and congenial yet professional, and adapted to the individual needs of each student.[35] Teachers are to be accepting of and accessible to all students, show Christian concern for student problems and well-being, and continue to offer advice and friendship even after students have left school,[36] encouraging students to achieve their maximum potential. Not many others have the same kinds of opportunities to accomplish "the incarnation of the Christian message in the lives of men and women."[37]

To Parents

The best teachers welcome and encourage opportunities for contact with parents, respecting the parents' right to know about the education of their children and to share in decisions affecting it. Teachers supplement and intensify the education begun at home. On a regular basis, teachers should keep parents informed of current policies and of their children's progress. The philosophical basis for all this is that

the educational task of the family and that of the school complement one another in many concrete areas [and that] such contacts
will offer to many families the assistance they need in order to
educate their own children properly, and thus fulfill the "irreplaceable and inalienable" function that is theirs.[38]

Here again, modern empirical research corroborates the philosophy
which the Catholic Church has been teaching for generations.[39]

To Community

Community is of the utmost importance to Catholic belief.[40] Its
special importance in the school enterprise points up Catholic-school
teachers' moral responsibilities in its regard:

> The communitarian structure of the school brings the Catholic
> educator into contact with a wide and rich assortment of
> people; . . . The Catholic educator must be a source of spiritual
> inspiration for each of these groups, as well as for each of the
> scholastic and cultural organizations that the school comes in con-
> tact with, for the local and parish Church, for the entire human
> ambience in which he or she is inserted and should influence in
> various ways.[41]

Teachers should help prepare future civic and Church leaders by
offering instruction and practice in leadership skills, by providing
opportunities for taking responsible moral positions on current issues,
by actively involving their students in Church functions, and by
stressing the importance of a partnership between school and parish.

To Colleagues

Essential for the full accomplishment of responsibilities to students,
for meaningful cooperation with parents, and for building a sense of
community in the school is the teacher's being supportive of colleagues:

> Catholic educators are also members of the educational communi-
> ty; they influence, and are influenced by, the social ambience of
> the school. Therefore, close relationships should be established
> between colleagues; they should work together as a team.[42]

Catholic-school teachers must be active in organizations at the local,
state, and national levels in order to be aware of the current issues in
the profession. They must plan and participate in conferences and
retreats that focus on particular issues relevant to them. They should

also be sensitive to their need to undergo continuing education in order to remain on top of developments in their specialty.

TEACHER FORMATION
In General

There are long lists of desirable teacher qualities.[43] These qualities may in part be inborn, but the fine details, at least, for the most part are acquired. Teachers "should therefore be prepared for their work with special care."[44] This preparation should be a happy and harmonious blend of professional training, a faith dimension, and personal growth and development. All three are, however, not separate, but intertwined in the "Catholic attempting to make his educational work the fundamental means of his personal sanctification and of his apostolate."[45]

Professional Training

Teacher-training calls for an emphasis on the liberal arts, an immersion in one's own field, and some exposure to methodology courses. Many recent studies have made these and other good recommendations for changes in teacher education.[46] In the student teaching experience, it is imperative that a skilled, experienced, and committed teacher provide the necessary guidance, so that professional growth is nurtured to the fullest. When attending college was becoming commonplace, undergraduates viewed "education courses" as an easy way to obtain a degree. Teacher-education programs can no longer allow such a viewpoint. Catholic teacher-training should be especially exacting. For the Catholic, professionalism "includes competency in a wide range of cultural, psychological, and pedagogical areas."[47] This must always be maintained, deepened, and kept current.

What is required of the Catholic-school teacher surpasses what is required of others. For example, the Catholic-school teacher trainee should be substantially exposed to, in addition to the liberal arts, programs in religious studies. These religious programs should encourage formational activities like discussion groups, retreats, prayer groups, and communal liturgy celebrations.[48] To bring about the important integration of the theory of Catholic school teaching with practice, the program should also include opportunities for related field experiences, such as attending local parish school-board meetings and student-teaching in a Catholic school.

One area of profound significance for Catholic-school teachers is the communication of truth. For many other teachers, truth is subjective, voluntaristic, relative, and changing. For the Catholic educator, every truth is a participation in Him who is the Truth; the communication of truth, therefore, as a professional activity, is thus fundamentally transformed into a particular participation in the prophetic mission of Christ, carried on through teaching.[49]

For reasons of economy and convenience, some religious communities at times send their trainees to secular universities for professional preparation. Such institutions are often better than Catholic ones for strictly professional matters, but are sometimes dangerous for the philosophically unprepared. Among the inherent risks is that philosophically unprepared Catholic-school teachers can sometimes absorb the very positions which occasioned the establishment of Catholic schools: empiricism, for example, and relativism, form over substance and process over content, a predilection for "methods" courses, solipsism, naturalism, materialism, and positivism. They have at times unwittingly brought some of these positions into their schools. All should be made to realize "the close relationship that exists between the way a discipline (especially in the humanities) is taught, and the teacher's basic concept of the human person, of life, and of the world."[50]

Faith Dimension

Catholic Identity

Often, "lay Catholics have not had a religious formation that is equal to their general, cultural, and, most especially, professional formation" and "religious formation must be broadened and be kept up to date, on the same level as, and in harmony with, human formation as a whole."[51] Formation of the Catholic-school teacher in the faith dimension toward Catholic identity must begin with philosophical awareness. This means, first, a realization that attitudes of life are very much intertwined with school work: "a determined attitude to life (*Weltanschauung*) . . . comes into every decision that is made."[52] Philosophical awareness means, secondly, consciousness "of the ideals and specific objectives which constitute the general educational philosophy of the institution."[53] Then, the harmony of the many different dimensions of the Catholic teacher must lead to a synthesis of faith, culture, and life in the teacher, and the Catholic teacher's being a witness to faith. This will lead to a deeper level of the interior synthesis of faith, culture, and life in students.[54]

The precious ideal of the faith identity of the Catholic teacher can be lost through personal reasons like identity crises, loss of personal convictions, loss of a proper concept of authority, lack of a proper use of freedom, and serious family problems, or by reason of deficiencies in schools and society, like secularization. To combat these dangers, teachers should have opportunities for activities involving prayer, discussion, and the sharing of faith and personal experiences. One way to do this is faculty retreats.[55] These retreats could center around such themes as the ministry of teaching, discipleship, the needs and expectations of the People of God today, the history of one's particular institution, and the community of faith. Such nurturing of the faith dimension is best served by ongoing, integrated opportunities for prayer and reflection incorporated into faculty meetings and staff development activities.

Teachers and the Church

Catholic-school teachers, including the non-Catholics among them, historically have had a great respect for the Church and her teachings. They have been leaders with imagination and courage in applying Christian principles to current socioeconomic and other problems, and have to a preeminent degree possessed such important teacher virtues as charity, patience, and commitment.[56] The vast majority of Catholic-high-school teachers place a supreme value on religion, being considerably more committed to religion than other Catholics and than the public in general.[57]

What is to be done about the teacher who has no loyalty and commitment and whose personal life does not reflect moral conduct consistent with the Church's ideals? One solution comes from countries, like Ireland, which have tried teacher contracts.[58] If contracts are to be used as part of the solution, they must be specific, not broad or vague, and spell out clearly and distinctly what constitutes the Roman Catholic character of the school and what teacher conduct would be considered detrimental to that character. And teachers should have opportunities for healthy discourse in which all parties have their position heard, understood, and respected, even if disagreed with.

Personal Development

For the expected and necessary maturity,[59] personal formation must be according to the latest and best psychological and spiritual findings. Catholic teachers' maturity ought to match the high level of their generosity, so as to be a fit witness to the faith. A very important component of maturity is the development of a philosophy of life and of education. Without it, teachers can be buffeted by the winds of change, superficial, subject to fads, and, instead of judging matters by way of solid principle, inclined to judge issues on an *ad hoc* basis. With a formal and consistent philosophy of life and of education, they have solid underpinnings, vision, understanding, depth, and insight.

Beside personal maturity and philosophical awareness, conduct is also important: "Students should see in their teachers the Christian attitude and behaviour that is often so conspicuously absent from the secular atmosphere in which they live."[60] Part of the conduct deemed important is participation in the liturgical and sacramental life of the school: "Students will share in this life more readily when they are given good example."[61]

Updating

Faced with the reality of constant change, Catholic teachers are expected to update themselves continuously "in personal attitudes, in the content of the subjects that are taught, in the pedagogical methods that are used."[62] Reading periodicals and pertinent books, taking brush-up courses, participating in workshops and seminars, attending assemblies and conferences, and taking advantage of other opportunities will prevent intellectual dry rot from setting in. Continuing care to update pastoral religious knowledge and concerns will also "animate [teachers] as witnesses of Christ in the classroom."[63]

TEACHER CERTIFICATION AND EVALUATION

There are practical and philosophical difficulties in teacher evaluation.[64] Along with legitimate philosophical differences in the basic definition of "teacher," there are different emphases in criteria for evaluation. These emphases differ particularly in areas like the importance of clarity of course objectives, enthusiasm, openness to other viewpoints, use of class time, the nature of competence, contests about the "relevant" in what a teacher teaches and does, and a "scientific" verification principle in an area that is not always all that scientific. The issue of teacher-competency tests for the certification and evaluation of teachers is also controverted.

Added to this are the human differences in perceptions and emphases among principals, parents, and students. Principals' ratings of teachers may be influenced by situational factors and the extra work that establishes some teachers' leadership. Parents' ratings may be influenced by the connections teachers make with families and the quality of classroom life their children experience. Feedback from students can become a popularity contest, the difficult distinction between teacher popularity and teacher effectiveness often not being addressed.

An equally practical problem is the matter of evaluating the evaluators. It makes a difference, for example, whether the evaluator is an A student or a failing one, mature or immature, one with a personality difficulty or charisma, of a philosophical allegiance congenial with or opposed to the teacher's, truthful or inclined to lying. In addition to these ordinary certification and evaluation criteria, the Catholic school adds a host of others. For example, should Catholic-school teacher certification and evaluation differ from others in containing qualities like commitment, or loyalty to the faith, or practice of religion?

THE TEACHER OF RELIGION

Religion is not only nice to have in education, or integral to education, but is essential to it.[65] Preeminent in the Catholic school, therefore, is the one who teaches directly this *raison d'etre* of Catholic schools. This is because religion

> should be very carefully imparted. . . . In imparting this instruction the teachers must observe an order and method suited not only to the matter in hand but also to the character, the ability, the age and the life-style of their audience. This instruction should be based on holy scripture, tradition, liturgy, and on the teaching authority and life of the Church.[66]

It is mostly from the religion teacher that "religion is 'caught rather than taught,' attitudes are absorbed rather than imposed, [and] example is more powerful than precept."[67] Therefore, the religion teacher is present in the Catholic school on solid educational grounds.

The definition of the religion teacher is not easy. Because every teacher in a Catholic school is responsible for the religious formation of students,[68] whatever one says about the religion teacher would apply, *mutatis mutandis*, to other Catholic-school teachers as well. Keeping that in mind, almost everyone would agree with some elements of a descriptive definition. The religion teacher is a person (1) of faith; (2) who cultivates a deep personal prayer life and sacramental relationship with God; (3) who has compassion, forgiveness, understanding, and patience; (4) who corrects but does not judge; (5) who interprets the world in the light of Christ's revelation, sharing the purpose of life with Christian optimism; and (6) who introduces young people to Jesus so that they may get to know him as a person alive and through him to know God our Father.

The constant terms of reference for the religion teacher are: God is our Father/Mother; Creation is good; we are like God; Jesus is Lord of all creation; each one of us is unique; human beings have failed to live up to their nature; we are saved by Christ; we are destined to live forever; we must decide for or against God by loving or not loving our fellow human beings. The religion teacher should be addicted to learning. He or she should view learning as much more than simply coming to know something. Learning is a profound event, a real change in a person's way of living.

There is also a plethora of adjectives to describe how the religion teacher should act. The religion teacher should be informative, provocative, evocative, studious, practical, challenging, interesting. Teachers of religion are animators, not dictators. From the very beginning, they seek to build a bridge of trust. They foster both the intellectual and "feeling" potential of each child. They are persons of keen observation, and have an ability to listen, to provide stimuli, to be available, and to appreciate effort. They are caring. They know the children, their strengths and weaknesses, and are aware of home support or lack thereof. They encourage children to relate to other children and to adults with growing confidence. They have genuine concern for people, good sense, imagination, adaptability, sensitivity, and infectious enthusiasm for the search after meaning in life. They realize that inevitably teachers teach as much by what they are as by what they say.

One who teaches religion should ideally teach another subject also: mathematics, English, biology, or some other. From the student viewpoint, this gives a certain credibility in the classroom; the students then have greater respect in religion class because they see that an intelligent person can accept belief. From the teacher's perspective, to teach four or five religion classes every day is draining, because religion teachers have to give a great deal of themselves in personal values, commitment, and total being.

Effective religion classes are more varied in activity than many other subject areas. The student's attitude in the religion class is often more, "You can't make me believe that," than "I will accept that two plus two equals four" or "Columbus discovered America in 1492." Experience seems to indicate that those who teach only religion suffer burnout more easily than those who distribute their teaching load. On the high school level, teachers of religion should have a graduate degree, use a buddy system, visit classrooms, and the like, to learn what goes best.[69]

The selection of religion teachers must, therefore, receive the greatest of care: "Only those who are distinguished by ability, learning and spiritual life are to be chosen for so important a task."[70] Their formation should begin with the acquisition of correct doctrine. This "should always include an adequate knowledge of Catholic teaching and in the higher institutes of catechetics should reach the level of scientific theology. Sacred Scripture should be the soul of this formation. . . ."[71] The objective, summit, and center of religious formation "consists in the aptitude and the ability to communicate the gospel message."[72]

Those involved in religious formation must be aware also of the human sciences, of which our age has seen an enormous development, and which "penetrate the awareness that modern men and women have of themselves."[73] This will include "careful consideration of methods which have stood the test of experience."[74] Methodological expertise will be imparted by practical exercises as well as theoretical instruction, in-service as well as preservice. Religion teachers will, however, also realize that catechesis is not only a science, but an art. Their preparation will therefore

> fit them to interpret accurately the reactions of a group or of an individual, to discern their spiritual aptitude and to choose the method that will enable the gospel message to be heard fruitfully and effectively. . . . The art is a synthesis of apostolic aptitude and knowledge of the faith, of people and of the laws which regulate the progress of individuals and of communities.[75]

The area is not without its difficulties. Some are mentioned in our discussions of curriculum, others in the Questions for Discussion at the end of this chapter.[76] There are still others. For example, high school teachers are expected to be trained in theology, Scripture, liturgy, group dynamics, counseling, sociology, psychology, the principles of catechetics, and audio-visual procedures; to be personally appealing to students, dynamic in the classroom, acquainted with the latest developments, both secular and religious; and to be sufficiently political to fend off members of the community from the ultra left and the extreme right. It is no wonder that they fail to measure up to all that and are then criticized by parents, principals, pastors, faculty members, students—and each other.

Further, "it is an insult to teachers to expect impartiality (as distinct from neutralty) only from those without convictions."[77] The adequate religion teacher should be capable of putting the religion he or she teaches into perspective and, in a pluralistic society, to set it off against other people's search for meaning: other denominations, humanism, communism, counterculture, fascism, and whatever other "nonreligious" philosophies may be current. Such a procedure facilitates the teaching of both religion and the other philosophies.[78]

Because of the importance of religion in education, the necessary care, and the dangers involved, the Church has insisted upon religion teachers being a special responsibility of bishops.[79] The Code of Canon Law, for example, states:

> The local ordinary [bishop in charge] is to be concerned that those who are assigned as religion teachers in schools, even in non-Catholic ones, be outstanding for their correct doctrine, their witness of Christian living and their pedagogical skill.[80]

The Code is very solicitous about orthodoxy: "For his own diocese the local ordinary has the right to name or approve teachers of religion and likewise to remove or to demand that they be removed if it is required for reasons of religion or morals."[81]

THE PRINCIPAL: THE MASTER TEACHER
Importance

Studies on effective schools reveal that one of the critical variables separating good schools from poor ones is strong administrative leadership. Unfortunately, administrative leaders too often follow Al Capone's law: "We don't want no trouble." When that becomes the main rule, everything becomes *ad hoc*, nothing is philosophical or ultimate in any way, and all depends on who gets the administrator's ear. Principals might also be tempted to follow widespread modern adaptations of Machiavellian rules that appearance rather than reality is of uppermost importance and that only manipulation pays off. The principal who follows these conventions will give the outward appearance of observing the status quo.

Studies highlighting the position of the principal have identified several key role demands, which in order of importance are: instructional leader; manager of time and resources; communicator; observer and evaluator of staff; creator of school climate; and leader in goal setting and attainment, school-community relations, discipline, and teacher support. The principal's central administrative role in Catholic schools requires expertise in many diverse areas: personnel, finances, community relations, curriculum and supervision, and Catholic leadership.[82] Another interesting study describes private-school principals as having four to five more years of teaching experience than government-school principals, and as usually not viewing their jobs as steppingstones to higher administrative posts.[83]

Principals have been judged on everything but teaching—their paperwork, their skill at avoiding conflict, their popularity with parents, and their ability to get classes covered, buses loaded, and lunches served. But principals are first and foremost the master teachers. As such, principals should lead or resign. If their true possibilities as master teachers matter, the system should recognize this by upgrading their certification requirements, adding professional examinations, installing performance evaluations, encouraging risk taking, recognizing initiative, and rewarding improvements in student outcomes—all geared toward the idea of "master teacher."

Nature and Requirements of the Position

A main function of the principal is to take the talent of the staff, release it, and put it to purpose. As U.S. Secretary of Education William J. Bennett put it, the principal leads, inspires, and brings out the best from dedicated, motivated teaching staffs. That is an art. The principal is not to be someone who only takes care of details, but one who sets the tone, makes the major decisions.[84] That is in accord with the ideals of the National Association of Secondary School Principals.

The principal sets the spirit of the Catholic school, establishes its patterns of discipline, and inspires in the school community a vision of what it can become. She or he is at once the exemplar and the facilitator. In the Catholic school, the principal cannot have any doubts about the school's exact identity. It is the Christian vision that must orchestrate the whole. Principals, and other Catholic-school administrators, must never lose a clear mental vision of Christ's face, or their hearts' hearing of his word.

Principals, like all good administrators, are to be open. St. Benedict said that the role of the abbot is to listen to every monk, including the youngest, and affirm the truth wherever it is present. St. Ignatius in his rule for the discernment of spirits relates the same ideal.[85] The good Catholic principal will follow Aristotle on the concept of the common good and Christ on worth of the individual, always with concern for the *other*. In place of the self-centeredness of the image of the principal as Machiavellian prince will be that of the principal as choreographer: creative, unique, responsive to persons (on stage and off), and at the same time both pleasant and pleasing.

The National Catholic Educational Association (NCEA) has synopsized the requirements for principal into categories: spiritual, pastoral, professional, professional educational, professional managerial, and personal. Under spiritual qualities, they say the principal is committed as a believing and practicing Catholic to the Lord Jesus; is prayerful, faith-filled, and committed to spiritual growth; and is loyal to the Church and accepts its authentic teaching.

Under pastoral competencies, the association lists as uniquely Catholic that the principal is familiar with and creates an environment where the process of faith and moral development as it relates to working with youth and adults can be put into action; is familiar with and creates an environment where the content and methods of religious education are utilized; and knows and applies Church documents and other religious resources that relate to schools. Also, the principal has the capability to provide opportunities which foster the spiritual growth of faculty, students, and other members of the school community; to lead the school community in prayer; to link the school and the local community; to integrate Gospel values and Christian social principles into the curriculum and the life of the school; and to articulate the Catholic educational vision.

Not least among the pastoral duties of the principal is the school's timetable for what gives the Catholic school its special character: religion. The principal is like a trusted counselor who facilitates the marriage of God and His people, or a parent whose decisions make Christ's presence more palpable in people's lives, or even a priest who encourages sacrificial love as expressions of the community's *esprit de corps*. This, at least, is the role of the principal when he or she sees Christ.

That vision of Christ is one of the most sensitive and challenging areas. If principals are to avoid giving the impression that religion is just another subject, they must give it careful thought when planning the schedule. Because students sometimes consider religion less important than other academic areas, it is encumbent upon the principal as leader to ennoble the religion class and continually emphasize its importance to both teachers and students. Among areas that require care are the duration of periods, how the periods are used, the division of students into classes, department meetings, and prayer opportunities both within religion classes and for the school as a whole.

Principals must, of course, relate to students and make the students know they care. Even when principals are angry, the students should know they are angry because they care. The principal needs to know as many students as possible by name, as per the emphasis in the Book of Genesis on the importance of a name. When principals make requirements—for example, a dress code—it should be because of their concept of the student's personal dignity and worth. The principal should deal in a Christ-like way with the "special needs" of students who present disciplinary problems.

The NCEA lists as requisite professional qualities that the principal be committed to the philosophy of Catholic education; broadly educated; open to professional growth, familiar with professional literature, and committed to self-evaluation; able to articulate educational values; an active member of professional organizations; and have successful teaching experience (preferably in Catholic schools), the requisite formal academic preparation, and leadership capabilities.

Under "professional educational competencies," the NCEA lists no requirements as being completely unique to the Catholic-school principal. It lists as partly unique that the Catholic-school principal be capable of working collaboratively with a variety of groups, promoting staff morale and a sense of community, providing leadership in curriculum development, shaping a school philosophy which reflects the character of the school, initiating and conducting appropriate staff development activities, and providing effective instructional leadership and supervision.

The principal must also recognize, respect, and be capable of facilitating the primary role of parents as educators. Principals should welcome parents' interest, talk to them about their children, and show sincere concern. They should provide occasions that unite parents (and clergy, too) in the school's ventures in learning and celebration. Perhaps they should require parents to pick up students' report cards to establish contact, show care, and keep the lines open between principal and parent, principal and teacher, and principal and child.

The principal should relate well to teachers. Often the attitude created by how the principal welcomes and orients a new teacher on the first day lasts for years. The principal must immediately convey the importance of the ministry of teaching and foster a climate of trust in which teachers can share ideas, ideals, and their faith experience. The principal should alert teachers about children who will be absent or late. She or he should attend meetings on the evaluation of teachers. As head teacher, the principal must also be head learner, to give good example and to help make the school a true "community of learners"—on the opposite end of the scale from authoritarian schools.

Finally, the principal should relate well to aides and non-certified staff. Because of administrative duties, principals may regret having to limit their time for personal relationships—with staff as well as pupils. Their authority is nevertheless benevolent and informed. Principals work to unite all personnel for a common purpose. Relations with aides and other staff are not confined to problem-solving, but are open to occasions when praise, encouragement, and compassion are called for. The principal should let aides and noncertified staff have precise and up-to-date job descriptions, let them know they are a necessary part of the team, and be considerate in giving work orders.

Other knowledge is important to the Catholic-school principal. Preeminent is current historical and philosophical information: pertaining, for example, to how schools might be improved from within, the necessary components of innovation, how a school leader can respond creatively to public interest, and how to both initiate and sustain change. The principal should know something about education law: the U.S. Constitution, especially the First and Fourteenth Amendments; Church-State education relationships in such provisions as released time; the local school situation, government as well as Catholic; malpractice; finance and budgetary procedures; the use of school money; the transportation of students; insurance; medical and other special services; permissible uses and disposal of school property; tort and other responsibilities of employed and voluntary personnel; contract liability; the conditions of the employment, discharge, and retirement of teachers; rules of student conduct and punishments; and discrimination.

Among "professional managerial" competencies, the NCEA writes that the Catholic-school principal be sensitive to the demands of justice in making financial decisions. It states that Catholic-school principals hold as partly in common with and partly distinct from government-school principals the ability to provide leadership for long-range planning and development activities. Under personal qualities, the association asks that the principal be mature and open to growth; intelligent; organized and flexible; caring and supportive; challenging; a person of hope and trust; a critical thinker; and able to show a sense of humor, an interest in youth and their future, good judgment, verbal and writing competence (for speeches, conversations, and paperwork), courage, and a positive self-concept.[86] We might add the need for a personal charisma: an ability to lead and inspire people of all ages.

The scope of the job of principal is fatiguing even to contemplate. Its pace is frenetic. Principals' activities are usually the same time-consuming staples. They deal constantly with the late, absent, or misbehaving student. They must take walks through the building to see how things are going, and to be visible, in order to reassure and let people know they care. In accord with good psychology (which is also good Christianity), they must look for "positive" things to say. They should be actively involved in developing continuing education programs for teachers, be a public relations person to market the school and, until adequate funding is realized, help with fund raising. Sometimes, when others are low, all they need is someone to say, "You can do it!"—and that is best coming from the principal. Of course, the principal's duties are impossible without delegation and faculty-committee assistance.

The principal must look with love up the ladder as well as down, acknowledging responsibility to higher administration and using every opportunity to keep them in touch. Because we still do not have, in the Roman Catholic system, any concept of a constitution of a local Church, most diocesan manuals make the principal of the school the delegate of the pastor—despite the possibility that the pastor may not know much of schooling or education. So a new pastor can simply change everything.

One of the nicest things about the new Code of Canon Law is that the pastor has a *munus*, an "office." The educational leader's *munus* in the school, as the pastor's in the parish, is to discern and then dialogically and accountably to establish the school's leadership community, based on insight, vision, and the willingness to listen to the community in terms of discernment. In some parishes, the preference is that the principal be the rector, or pastor, of the school. That means, among other things, that all complaints about the principal or the school must go, instead of to the pastor, to the superintendent of schools.[87]

Lay Catholic-school principals face a number of additional challenges. First, because of the low pay scale for teachers, many potential administrators cannot afford the costs of graduate-school preparation, and thus do not pursue a career in Catholic-school administration. To assist, dioceses might consider establishing a fund which would provide loans or grants or both to candidates for administration. Second, as is the case with teachers, principals' pay and benefits are not commensurate with the demands or with parallel government-school positions.

Third, because of the decentralization of school financing, the movement of lay principals from one school to another is severely limited. Thus, a principal's term at a school can become too long for the well-being of either the principal or the school. A plan needs to be devised which will allow for principal movement.[88] Fourth, because of the importance of religious education and the religious preparation of lay principals, quality training programs need to be provided at least at the diocesan level. Finally, more Catholic-school administrator preparation programs need to be developed and made easily accessible to aspiring Catholic-school administrators.

Not to be forgotten throughout is the very important assistant principal, who is the principal in designated areas, with specific responsibilities. The definition of the assistant principal will depend on the intention of the principal. The principal has to be free to do his chief job. The assistant principal frees up the principal to work on such areas as require cogitation. It is from the position of assistant principal that the leadership of tomorrow will be formed.

Preparation

Some of the requirements of a Catholic-school principal can be prepared for. For the pastoral component, in addition to the obvious matter of acquiring the competencies mentioned, the NCEA lists exposure to some basic knowledge: of the philosophy and history of Catholic education and Catholic schools (especially in the United States), religious education and religious psychology, available religious resources, and how to apply this pastoral component to the religious life of the school community.[89]

For the educational component, without repeating what has been said above, the NCEA lists a basic knowledge of curriculum development, educational philosophy and research, approaches to supervision and instructional leadership, approaches to staff development, adult development theory, approaches to the evaluation of religious and educational programs, and the ways to foster personal growth, especially that growth which is uniquely Catholic. It also lists how to apply this educational component to the educational life of the school community.[90]

To prepare for the managerial component, the NCEA lists basic knowledge that pertains to Catholic schools in the areas of development activities, long-range planning, and financial management; public and community relations; what sustains an orderly school environment that promotes student self-discipline consonant with Gospel values and Christian principles; school law; group dynamics, conflict management, problem-solving, building staff morale, and other organizational development skills; approaches to providing for legitimate cultural differences; how the Catholic notion of justice and other Catholic social teachings pertain; and how to apply managerial subject matter to the daily management of the school community.[91] The NCEA also lists questions for self-evaluation of principals in the various components of competencies.[92]

CURRENT AGENDA
The Modern Teacher Situation

Today's teachers' work, no matter the school, is stressful and often thankless. Some problems, like the difficulty of innovation and experimentation in a bureaucracy, seem more applicable to government schools. Others, like the shortage of teaching religious and noncompetitive salary schedules, are specifically Catholic.

Teachers must too often contend with insolent, disrespectful, insubordinate, discourteous, disruptive, and violent children. The alliance between school, Church, and home has run amok, with parents refusing to accept responsibility and the Church being relatively powerless. The media, especially television, are perhaps responsible for student attention span being minimal and for the expectation that the teacher be an entertainer. The result is teacher frustration and dissatisfaction.

As one example, a 1985 survey of the 4,350 government-school teachers in Prince Georges County, Maryland, revealed that 48 percent wanted out of the profession.[93]

Salary levels of all teachers in objective amounts, benefits, and pay raises, are low when compared with opportunities in business. In Catholic schools, this is a poor reflection of social justice, particularly for lay teachers with families. Poor salaries, among other things, can be a factor in the important phenomenon of teacher burnout.[94] Another offshoot of the economic situation is that only about 28 percent of all Catholic high schools offer tenure. One result is high turnover, with less than half of Catholic-high-school teachers having more than five years' teaching experience.[95] This compares unfavorably with government-school teachers, whose average tenure is fifteen years or more. While an influx of new teachers can have an invigorating effect on the life of the school, this rapid a change can also disrupt the transmission of traditions and values and the establishment of community. It may mean weaker bonds between colleagues and less firm bonds with parents. Because teacher demand is high and resources scarce, in all schools there is a tendency to employ persons with substandard qualifications.

For all teachers, there is also a lack of other rewards, such as respect and prestige. The changing attitudes of students, parents, and society at large contribute to this situation. In addition, with higher education more commonplace, the teacher no longer receives respect for being more educated than others. Lastly, teachers in the United States have never had the social status that many other countries accord them and which the importance of their position deserves.[96]

Lay teachers today have come to hold almost the same majority that religious sisters, brothers, and priests held in the 1960s: On the elementary level the lay teaching staff is about 80 percent, on the secondary level about 75 percent. Overall, this has not resulted in any less Catholicity, despite the misgivings of some parents: effectiveness in that regard is measured by the nature of the goals and the extent to which they are successfully implemented.

Lay teachers are an important benefit, and their involvement has a strong theological base.[97] The lay teacher is "a sharer in 'the priestly, prophetic, and kingly functions of Christ', and their apostolate 'is a participation in the saving mission of the Church herself. . . . "[98] While this call is common to all believers, the teacher's work in a special way transforms his or her life into an admirable vocation within the Church.[99] The laity are in a position that is in some ways more advantageous than that of the religious:

The lay faithful belong fully both to the people of God and civil society. They belong to the nation into which they were born, they begin to share in its cultural riches by their education, they are linked to its life by many social ties, they contribute to its progress by personal effort in their professions, they feel its problems to be their own and they try to solve them. They belong also to Christ because by faith and baptism they have been reborn in the Church, so that by newness of life and work they might belong to Christ (cf. 1 Cor. 15:23), in order that all things might be subjected to God in Christ and that God might be all in all (cf. 1 Cor. 15:28).[100]

The roles and functions of lay faculty are many: to animate the world with the spirit of Christianity, to be witnesses to Christ in all circumstances,[101] and uniquely to bring about the all-important synthesis between faith and culture and faith and life.[102] By serving as a role model and helping students to bring about this synthesis, the lay teacher becomes an important element in the effective operation of Catholic schools.[103] The more the lay teacher conforms to a Christian ideal in attitude and behavior, the more willing the student will be to accept the ideal.[104] The lay teacher should therefore participate in the liturgical and sacramental life of the community, and be aware of opportunities to witness to faith. To do all this, the professional and religious formation of teachers must be substantial, and teachers must enjoy what they are doing, want to do it, and be reasonably good at it.

In a special category are non-Catholic teachers in Catholic schools. In some places, as much as one-third of the teaching staff is non-Catholic. The Church does not automatically keep them out: "For it is on . . . lay people, whether believers or not, that a school's success in achieving its aims depends."[105] When non-Catholics are hired they should be asked about their familiarity with Catholic teachings and their willingness to support the philosophy and goals of the school.[106] Seminars, workshops, and other means can help committed non-Catholic teachers attain a grasp of these values. Another area deserving of attention is the lack of minority teachers. While 18 percent of students in Catholic schools are members of a racial or ethnic minority, only 5 percent of teachers are.[107] Financial exigencies make it difficult for Catholic schools to compete for trained minorities, who are in great demand in other schools. In many cases, the effort of Catholic schools to supply minority teachers promotes the hiring of non-Catholics.

What to Do about It

All schools, and the communities they serve, if they want to upgrade teaching and acquire good teachers, are going to have to do something about the problems connected with current teaching.[108] There should be opportunities for advancement as good as those in business. Catholic-school teachers should be given opportunities for innovation and experimentation. There should be a career ladder for teachers in Catholic schools. This ladder might be in several steps, starting with internship, then going to regular teacher, and winding up with a mentor teacher at the top. Very importantly, the Church, as well as other institutions, must learn what keeps teachers happy and act upon it. On top of the list of what made teachers happy in one study was simply the love of teaching. Then came, in order, rapport with students and the sense of fulfillment that comes with helping students progress toward their goals, and finally all the other challenges of teaching that contribute to personal growth.[109]

And we must enhance the parents' role. The role of parents as the prime educators of their children is crucial, resulting (when successful) in a multiplier effect on the educational efforts of the school. Parents themselves must be taught to lend their support to their children by providing the children with a fixed time and place to study, helping when possible with their assignments, and taking an active interest in their academic progress and school activities.

Administrators should exchange information on such issues as administration, curriculum, and new technology. There should be funding to keep the brightest and best: capable teachers have to be lured away from other positions that are higher paying and be enabled to provide materially for their families and themselves. Proper salary levels can motivate teachers to maintain high-level performance.[110]

Church support should not end with the financial, however: moral support is equally necessary. To this end, public awareness should be enhanced: all in charge should help see to it that issues affecting school policy are visible to the public eye by bringing the issues to public forums, board meetings, church groups, the media, and the like. Most important of all, from many points of view, there should be Church support for teacher-training institutions, from which the brightest and the best should emerge to lead the system and to help the schools, which are "always in the process of being created."[111]

With their experience and capacity to conduct research, teacher-training institutions carry a high level of responsibility for ensuring that only the truly committed and professionally prepared enter the ranks of teaching.[112] An interesting trend in this direction has been teacher-training institutions offering warranties on their new graduates. If in the course of the recent graduate's beginning work, usually about a year, the new teacher has difficulty with instruction or discipline, the teacher-training institution will dispatch a professor to work with the student-teacher. If remediation is necessary, the institution will waive its cost. Not only does this help the fledgling teacher and enhance the institution's prestige, but it also helps tie higher education into the nitty-gritty of the teacher's work.

Presently, there is a promotion by the U.S. Department of Education and several state departments of education for colleges and universities to establish, for mutual benefit, stronger programs and ties with local elementary and secondary schools. Catholic colleges and universities could easily and beneficially encourage such ties with Catholic elementary and secondary schools. Such programs might include teacher and administrator in-service training, local extensions of courses for certification updating, experimentation, research, and some joint publication of exemplary programs.

CONCLUSION

The one who is in the front line (in more ways than one) of bringing about the Catholicity of the Catholic school is the teacher. There are many terms for the teacher: guide, resource person, change agent, presenter of choices, instigator, director, shepherd, role model. No matter what the term, Catholic philosophies emphasize the teacher as one who helps form human beings. Because Realism sees knowledge as a discovery—literally a dis-covery—of truth, realist teachers emphasize the transmission of knowledge and a priestly role as mediator between the learner and the world of reality. Idealist teachers, with their belief in the supreme value of the intellect, offer a style of teaching which strives to transmit the best of humankind's heritage and to provide opportunities to challenge a student's intellectual capabilities; they zealously accept the responsibility of being a role model. Existentialist teachers are careful to distinguish legitimate teacher authority from domineering authoritarianism, and emphasize the former.

Whether teaching is a profession is a hotly debated and unanswered question. Prescinding from that debate, Catholics see in teaching a noble vocation that calls for detachment, a commitment that avoids sermonizing, and generosity. It also requires concern for truth and justice, breadth of vision, an habitual spirit of service, fraternal solidarity, and total moral integrity. Because the standards are high and the demands difficult, many, including religious, are leaving the school apostolate.

Teachers are important. Catholic teachers guide youth toward eternal realities; no one can tell where the teacher's influence ends. Teachers personify the integration of culture and faith and faith and life. Christ-like, they represent their individual incarnational model. They effectuate a union of the Catholic school with the local Church. Historically, they are in the tradition of the New Testament: Jesus the teacher, the apostles' ministry, and St. Paul's inheritance of the Jews' tremendous respect for teaching. They share in the noble tradition of the early Church and in the history of Christianity in their love of learning, desire for God, and preservation of culture and civilization.

Good Catholic teachers are ethically sensitive about their obligations to students, parents, the community, and colleagues. With their students, Catholic teachers strive not only for a meeting of minds, but for a personal relationship. This entails respect, sensitivity, sympathy, concern, some degree of self-revelation, reciprocal dialogue, trust, openness, and warm and congenial relationships. Good Catholic teachers welcome and encourage opportunities for contact with parents, respect parental rights, supplement the education begun in the students' homes, meaningfully cooperate with parents, and keep parents informed. They realize their importance to the community, especially the local community of faith. To accomplish all this, they are supportive of colleagues: working together as a team, being active in professional organizations, participating in retreats, and being selflessly enthusiastic about continuing education.

To form such high-caliber teachers requires special care. Formation should be a happy blend of professional training, progress in faith, and personal growth. Professional training will take for granted proficient background in such areas as language, art, literature, mathematics, and science, and ability in thinking, reasoning, and understanding. The formation should be in a wide range of cultural, psychological, and pedagogical areas in accordance with the discoveries of modern times.

Superadded for the Catholic teacher is the faith dimension. A realization of Catholic identity begins with the awareness that philosophies of life are very much intertwined with schoolwork. The Catholic teacher must have a synthesis of faith, culture, and life, and be alert for opportunities to witness to faith. Retreats, prayer, sharing, service, follow-up kindnesses, and other exercises should inculcate habits of reflection and deepening faith.

The personal growth expected of Catholic teachers begins with psychological and spiritual maturity, which recognizes the need for a philosophy of life and of education. Conduct is also important, giving students an example of Christian behavior that includes participation in the liturgical and sacramental life of the school and of the Church. In the face of the constant change which is a fact of modern life, good Catholic teachers continuously update themselves. In the thicket of problems in teacher certification and evaluation, Catholic teachers try to develop qualities which leave no doubt of competence.

Preeminent among Catholic-school teachers is the teacher of religion, the subject area that is the *raison d'etre* of Catholic schools and the heart of their identity. The qualities that describe all Catholic-school teachers should apply in an outstanding way to religion teachers. Among these qualities is that they be persons of faith, of a deep personal prayer life and Christian virtue, who correct but do not judge, interpret the world in the light of Christ's revelation, and introduce young people to Jesus. In addition, the religion teacher is informative, provocative, evocative, studious, practical, challenging, interesting, addicted to learning, an animator rather than a dictator, caring, trusting, aware of student potential, and encouraging, and with good sense, imagination, adaptability, and infectious optimism and enthusiasm.

For adequacy, religion teachers should have appropriate graduate degrees in the human sciences, but especially in religious pedagogy. For greater credibility with students as well as for relief from the demands of teaching religion, they should probably teach another subject as well. For greater competence, they should have a buddy system to learn what works best. To alleviate tension and prevent burnout, they must develop a thick-skinned maturity that will fend off criticisms of their not measuring up to the impossible expectations and demands made of them.

The "master teacher" is the principal. Principals are to be instructional leaders, managers of time and resources, communicators, observers and evaluators of staff, creators of the school's climate, and leaders in goal setting and attainment, school-community relations, discipline, and teacher support. They must have no doubt about the Catholic school's identity, because confused ideas here make for shaky *ad hoc* decisions all around. Their qualifications—spiritual, pastoral, professional, and personal—must all be tinged with a Catholic perspective. They must strive to relate well with higher administration as well as with the entire school staff, parents, and student body.

Today's poor teaching situation makes for dissatisfaction. The Church, as well as other institutions, will do well to learn what keeps teachers happy and act upon it.

QUESTIONS FOR DISCUSSION

Should the characteristics needed by a teacher in a Catholic school be different from those in, for example, the recommendations of the National Commission for Excellence in Teacher Education? If so, how?

In teacher-student relationships, is a special ethics required (as it is with doctor-patient and attorney-client relationships), or is a general ethics sufficient?

How necessary is the personal presence of the teacher? Can the teacher who videotapes his or her course, makes it available at the library twenty-four hours a day, and then goes on vacation, said to be teaching? Will technological improvements, like computer-assisted instruction, do away with the need for the teacher? If the personal presence of the teacher is necessary, what consequences flow from that?

If teaching and learning are correlative terms, is it necessary for true teaching that learning take place?

To what extent does our pluralistic society have a right to expect a teacher to be a role model? What are the rights of a role-model teacher to free expression? Inside the school? Away from school?

In Catholic schools in a democratic country, how can one resolve the tensions between teacher loyalty and teacher freedom (especially in areas like organizational affiliations, moral life, leisure pursuits, personal appearance, and self-expression)?

What are the characteristics of commitment? In light of uncertainties about the future, is commitment in principle possible? If it is possible, ought one, even a person with the high vocation of teaching, commit oneself? If it is possible and proper, on what grounds? Can one who has commitment teach it?

By what right does one called "teacher" enter into the sacred precincts of the personhood of another called "student"?

What is the source of the teacher's authority: subject-matter mastery, superiors, delegation from parents, participation in the parenthood of God, or what?

How can a teacher develop personal relationships in classes of forty pupils? Is it sloppy sentimentality to expect a personal relationship between a teacher and a child of ten? Can the desired personal relationship between teacher and student take place without either one liking, loving, or respecting the other?

What about atheists being permitted to teach in Catholic schools? Non-Catholic Christians? Non-practicing Catholics? Ex-nuns, ex-seminarians, ex-brothers, ex-priests?

Should the criteria for the evaluation of the teacher be as mediator, as realists would say, or for the teacher as role model from the idealist viewpoint, or for the pragmatist teacher as resource person and problem-presenter, or for the existentialist teacher as choice facilitator? What does one do when the teacher espouses one philosophy and the evaluator(s) another?

For the purpose of the certification and evaluation of teachers, are criterion-referenced tests or norm-referenced tests better? (Criterion-referenced tests are those which measure the test taker's mastery of information; norm-referenced tests are those which compare individual performance to those of the whole test group.)

Do teachers of religion in Catholic elementary and high schools have a right to express in the classroom dissent from noninfallibly defined matters of faith or morals? Do teachers of other subjects?

In the order of their importance, what are the essential qualifications of the best teacher of religion?

Recognizing that not everyone can teach religion successfully, how does one choose who shall teach it?

In the process of student self-activity, which is a primary agent of education, what is your idea of the function of the teacher?

What are the differences, if any, between *good* teaching, *successful* teaching, and *effective* teaching?

For Catholic-school teachers, how can you harmonize a commendable academic freedom with the need to teach the official doctrines of the Church?

SUGGESTED BIBLIOGRAPHY

Benson, Peter L., Carolyn H. Elkin, and Michael Guerra. "What Are the Religious Beliefs of Teachers in Catholic Schools?" *Momentum*, vol. XIV no. 1 (February 1985), pp. 24–27.

A report on the religious beliefs of Catholic high-school teachers based on a survey of 1,062 teachers in 45 Catholic high schools.

Bleich, Russell. "Teachers and Teaching: What Makes Catholic Schools Different?" *Momentum*, vol. XV no. 3 (September 1985), p. 34.

A response to national concerns about teachers from the perspective of Catholic education.

Koob, Albert C. "Making Smooth the Way for Lay Leadership." *Momentum*, vol. XV no. 2 (May 1984), pp. 23–24.

Discusses the need to update the laity on the Church's interpretations of the Gospel before allowing them decision-making power.

McBride, Alfred A. *The Christian Formation of Catholic Educators*. Washington, D.C: National Catholic Educational Association, 1981.

Guidelines reflecting the Catholic Church's methods for the continuing formation of Christians and especially of Catholic educators.

National Catholic Educational Association. *The Catholic High School: A National Portrait*. Washington, D.C.: NCEA, 1985.

This major study of American Catholic secondary education includes sections on students, teachers, administration, parents, finances, five-year trends, schools serving students from low-income families, and comparison of private, diocesan, interparochial, and parochial schools.

———. *Code of Ethics for the Catholic School Teacher*. Washington, D.C.: NCEA, 1982.

A description of the attitudes and practices of the Catholic-school teacher in relation to the student, the parent, the community, and the profession.

———. *The Pre-service Formation of Teachers for Catholic Schools.* Washington, D.C.: NCEA, 1983.

Explores the Christian formation of teachers by developing program criteria and components, suggesting possible models for the ongoing pre-service formation of teachers.

Sacred Congregation for Catholic Education. *Lay Catholics in Schools: Witnesses to Faith,* in Austin Flannery, *Vatican Council II: The Conciliar and Post Conciliar Documents.* 2 vols. Northport, N. Y.: Costello, 1975. Vol. II, pp. 630–61.

The role, importance, and criteria of good lay teachers in Catholic education.

Sokolowski, Robert S. "De Magistro: The Concept of Teaching According to St. Thomas Aquinas," in John K. Ryan, ed. *Studies in Philosophy and the History of Philosophy.* 6 vols. Washington, D.C.: The Catholic University of America Press, 1961–73. Vol. I, pp. 160–193.

Outlines the three general complementary philosophical principles of teaching according to Thomistic Realism: movement toward the discovery of truth implied in knowledge we already possess, the discovery of explanatory relationships between a problematic statement and propositions already in our store of knowledge, and the communication of new insights.

Vatican Council II. *Declaration on Christian Education,* in Austin Flannery, *Vatican Council II: The Conciliar and Post Conciliar Documents.* 2 vols. Northport, N. Y.: Costello, 1975. Vol. I, pp. 725–37.

One of the Vatican II documents outlining the Church's views on Catholic Christian education.

———. *Decree on the Church's Missionary Activity,* in Austin Flannery, *Vatican Council II: The Conciliar and Post Conciliar Documents.* Vol. I, pp. 813–62.

Exploration of the Catholic Church's missionary activity, emphasizing the role of the laity.

Chapter 10

THE OBJECT AND END
OF IT ALL: STUDENTS

STUDENTS AS THE PURPOSE
OF SCHOOLING AND EDUCATION

All schooling and education exist on behalf of the individual person called the student. The student, not the teacher, parent, Church, school, State, or any other person or institution, is the principal agent of the educational process.[1] Today's students deserve special understanding: they are growing up in a world in transition in which people are groping for meaning. Youth see in society little example that religion is relevant. Many adults — often their parents — are living as though religion were peripheral and unimportant.

THE DEFINITION OF STUDENT

All educational procedures are determined in accordance with how one defines the student. The definition of the student in turn depends on one's definition of the person: mechanistic, or open to the heavens, or something in between. People have been asking about definitions of humankind from their beginnings, putting forward "views that are divergent and even contradictory. Often he [man] either sets himself up as the absolute measure of all things, or debases himself to the point of despair."[2]

The Dignity of the Student

An important aspect of any definition of person refers to the person's dignity. Our concept of the dignity of the person presents a paradox. This seems to be epitomized in Hamlet's apostrophe to man, which begins:

274

What a piece of work is man! How noble in reason! how infinite in
faculty! in form, in moving, how express and admirable! in action,
how like an angel! in apprehension how like a god! The beauty of
the world! the paragon of animals.[3]

But the apostrophe ends in disillusionment: "And yet to me, what is
this quintessence of dust? Man delights not me; no, nor woman
either . . . ." Elsewhere, Hamlet gives another view of man: "What
should such fellows as I do, crawling between heaven and earth? We
are arrant knaves, all; believe none of us."[4] Outside Christian circles
today, the concept of the individual's worth appears to be more and
more approaching the state of disillusionment.

Superdignity for Catholics

The high dignity which Catholicism accords the person begins with
the ancient Hebrews. Nothing surpasses the Hebrew Scripture's
teaching that man was created "to the image of God," and no expression of worth is more beautiful than the Psalmist's, "What is man that
thou are mindful of him . . . that thou dost care for him? Yet thou has
made him little less than God. . . ."[5] This was a new dignity for
humankind, higher than any that had gone before.

The status of personhood in the Judeo-Christian value system is
both richer and more secure than in secular ethics. The Bible indicates that each individual is created for her or his own sake. Each
person is created from nothing, and has an eternal destiny. Hence
each is unique, created from the superabundance of God's love from
which a multiplicity of persons is produced. But when each person is
produced it is, in modern terminology, as though God throws away
the mold. In the New Testament, Jesus "showed a reverence and a
solicitude for the human person which nobody had ever shown before."[6]

After the Christological controversies of the early Church, appreciation of the Christian idea of the dignity of the person reached new
heights in St. Augustine, perhaps "the first thinker who brought into
prominence and undertook an analysis of the philosophical and psychological concepts of person and personality."[7] Boethius' sixth-centu-
ry definition became a tremendous influence; he said that person is an
individual substance of a rational nature.[8] That simple definition has
subtle and intense implications. St. Thomas Aquinas, after asserting
himself in favor of Boethius' definition, added that person "signifies
what is most perfect in all nature."[9]

Defense of that attitude has continued in Catholic education. Catholic educators see the dignity of human persons as the origin of the

very right to an education: "All men of whatever race, condition or age, in virtue of their dignity as human persons, have an inalienable right to education."[10] The significance of the concept of the dignity of the student for Catholic pedagogy will show in many areas. The Church, in fact, has positive advice for Catholic educators vis-a-vis our concept of the dignity of the person of the student: the Christian concept of the person

> is a concept which includes a defence of human rights, but as something befitting the dignity of a child of God. . . . It establishes the strictest possible relationship of solidarity among all persons, through mutual love and in an ecclesial community. It calls for the fullest development of all that is human, because we have been made masters of the world by its Creator. Finally, it proposes Christ, Incarnate Son of God and perfect Man, as both model and means; to imitate Him is, for all men and women, the inexhaustible source of personal and communal perfection. Thus, Catholic educators can be certain that they make human beings more human.[11]

If the Catholic educator is doing his/her job, in the Catholic-school setting "the pupil experiences his dignity as a person before he knows its definition."[12]

For Catholics, the superdignity of the person flows from one's entire being and from every part thereof. It is the whole human being who is the subject of Christian education:

> man whole and entire, soul united to body in unity of nature, with all his faculties natural and supernatural, such as right reason and Revelation show him to be; man, therefore, fallen from his original estate, but redeemed by Christ and restored to the supernatural condition of adopted son of God. . . . [13]

Dignity of Intellect, Will, and Body

The intellect, which has as its object the pursuit of truth and of wisdom, shares preeminently in this dignity:

> Man, as sharing in the light of the divine mind, rightly affirms that by his intellect he surpasses the world of mere things. . . . For his intellect is not confined to the range of what can be observed by the senses. It can, with genuine certainty, reach to realities known only to the mind, even though, as a result of sin, its vision has been clouded and its powers weakened.[14]

Intellect refers to a person's power to pierce through appearances to the essential nature or core of inner meaning. It embraces the process of getting ideas, making judgments, and engaging in reasoning. It is the capacity to understand, among other things, nonmaterial entities such as God, soul, beauty, values, and truth. For Aristotle and those in his tradition, the intellectual virtues fall into two groups, the speculative and the practical. The speculative are known as understanding, knowledge, and wisdom. The practical are prudence and art.

If there is an area in which contemporary people are becoming increasingly conscious of the dignity of the human person, it is in the area of the will: "more and more people are demanding that men should exercise fully their own judgment and a responsible freedom in their actions and should not be subject to the pressure of coercion but be inspired by a sense of duty."[15]

For all educators, this refers especially to character education. "Character" (from the Latin word meaning a distinctive mark, in turn from a Greek word meaning to scratch or engrave) is the sum total of a person's hereditary tendencies, modified by environment, and fashioned by acquired moral habits. Character from a Catholic perspective emphasizes two things: a disciplined will and firm adherence to moral principles. It includes controlled emotions and strong feelings. Moral integrity, that highest degree of human excellence, is the outcome of a will informed by an enlightened intellect.

Character education, which is akin to moral education, is the capstone in the complete development of the child. It purports to inculcate those habits of thought and conduct, having permanent individual and social value, which are in conformity with the moral law. Its ultimate purpose is to bring the person into a more intimate relationship with his God. Good character education is integrally, if not essentially, related to religion. In religion one finds the most edifying motives; the basic virtues of moral life; ultimate sanctions of worthy living; numerous examples of true character; and the perfect model, Jesus Christ.

For the Catholic, there are additional reasons why the will enhances the person's dignity. For one thing, it is free. Humankind's dignity requires one to act out of free choice, "as moved and drawn in a personal way from within, and not by blind impulses in himself or by mere external constraint."[16] Very specially, the will enhances the person's dignity because more than any other faculty it is connected with the ability to love.

Plato's dialogues contain the image of the soul being imprisoned by the body; for him, life's vocation was the freeing of the soul from the body. While the people of the time of the early Church Fathers shared something of this view, Christians, especially since St. Thomas Aquinas, have emphasized the psychosomatic unity of human beings. Man's body and soul do not exist only on parallel lines in what is called psychophysical parallelism; the two are in substantial unity. Jesus' incarnation confirmed and restored the unity of the flesh and the spirit, of earth and of heaven: God himself actually assumed human flesh.[17] On the other hand, "[m]an is not deceived when he regards himself as superior to bodily things and as more than just a speck of nature or a nameless unit in the city of man."[18] And the Incarnation comes about "not by the conversion of the Godhead into man, but by the taking up of humanity into God" (Athanasian Creed); "God becomes man, so that man may become God" (patristic axiom).

Grace

The true and full dignity of the human being consists in the vocation to walk with God, to relate to Him in love and friendship. This is the meaning of grace. The Church gives an excellent summary definition of the totally new graced way of being:

> Justification from sin and God's indwelling in the soul are called grace. When sinners are said to be justified by God, to be enlivened by the Spirit of God, to possess the life of Christ in themselves, or to have grace, we are using expressions which say the same thing in different words—that is, that they die to sin, they become sharers in the Son's divine nature through the spirit of adoption and that they enter into an intimate shared life with the Most Holy Trinity.[19]

Christianity continues the Jewish tradition that the person is created in God's image and likeness.[20] St. Paul speaks of man being in "the image and glory of God,"[21] and requests that "just as we resemble the man from earth, so shall we bear the likeness of the man from heaven."[22] For the Christian, the highest norm is Christ.

Ancient non-Christians, and modern ones too, have a different understanding of graced existence. Apotheosis (that is, the ability of the human person to become like God) was a belief of the ancient Greeks: Plato, for example, spoke of happiness to be found "by becoming like the divine so far as we can."[23] But this Greek apotheosis is not pure gift from God offered to all human beings, as with Christianity; it is the achievement of the hero (as with Nietzsche's *Übermensch*, "Superman"). Today's secular humanists do not speak of a person being godlike and able to become more and more like God, but of man himself being God: for the nontheistic humanist, nothing that exists is higher than humankind.

Thus for many non-Christian humanists, including such a great intellectual as Plato, ethics is *autonomous*, that is, it depends solely upon the efforts of the individual. For the Christian, although the natural, acquired moral virtues may be autonomous, supernatural salvation is *theonomous*: the virtues of the "good life" are the fruits of a life permeated by God's gift of grace. Grace begins the journey and enters each step of the process. It builds on nature, and adapts itself to the inherent characteristics of nature—not only in a general sense, but concretely, respecting the individual capacities of each particular human being.

While the task of studying, formulating, describing, and understanding the workings of grace is the work of theology, the same process of personal development is examined on another level by the discipline of psychology. Every human personality has an individual history which is the product of grace and nature working together. A person's formational schooling ideally integrates these natural and supernatural orders. By the natural realm as applied to persons we mean that which is essential to our nature: powers of reason, will, imagination, sense ability, and all else that is related to our bodies and souls, plus the natural ends to which our activities are directed. The supernatural realm, on the other hand, refers to our elevation to a higher order by virtue of the gift from God called grace; it is beyond our natural potential.

The supernatural order is not superadded to the natural like cream on top of milk; the secular and the sacred are both intertwined in one reality, one organic whole. In a political campaign at the end of the last century, a charge against Catholics was the shibboleth, "Rum, Romanism, and Rebellion." If there is any truth to the charge, it may rest with Catholics' notion of the convergence of the sacred and the secular and their conception of the celebratory nature of life: grace does not contradict nature, but builds upon it. Grace can help in the process of a person's actualization, or becoming, or growing to perfection:

> grace does not supersede, but presupposes human nature and brings it to perfection; it rests on the natural ability to know and to love as well as the integration of every one of the human powers.[24]

Theologian Karl Rahner developed a contemporary theology of grace: one which safeguards God's free initiative and at the same time avoids seeing grace as a foreign element in the universe, extrinsic to the world in which we live. He envisions the human person as "spirit-in-the-world"—always oriented toward God, because this is the orientation of spirit. Grace is God's free, personal fulfillment of this inborn openness, since nothing less than the infinite God can satisfy the human heart. This grace, God's self-gift, actualizes the core of human life.

True, nature does not require that grace be given; there could be a different relationship to God that would be meaningful without grace. But the real historical order of things is a graced one. Grace is offered to all; it touches the core of human life and permeates every aspect of human history and human existence. Adapting both Scholastic vocabulary and the philosophical terminology of Martin Heidegger, Rahner coined the term "supernatural existential" to describe this transformation of the human condition: it is "supernatural" because a result of God's free self-gift, "existential" because it permeates the whole of human existence.

God's self-gift to the world is not limited to the interior life of isolated individuals; in keeping with the social and historical dimension of human existence, of spirit-in-the-world, grace seeks expression in human history. In Jesus, the definitive Savior, God's self-gift reached an unsurpassable historical climax; so, too, did the history of its human acceptance.

Catholic schools train their students in this exalted vocation of grace: All baptized Christians "should be trained to live their own lives in the new self, justified and sanctified through the truth (Eph. 4:22–24)."[25] Coming to true personhood in this way is for the benefit of society as well as for the individual: Christians

> should learn to give witness to the hope that is in them (cf. 1 Pet. 3:15) and to promote the Christian concept of the world whereby the natural values, assimilated into the full understanding of man redeemed by Christ, may contribute to the good of society as a whole.[26]

INDIVIDUAL-COMMUNITY TENSION

We do not exist alone, but co-exist with God and with others. The individual's relations with other people inevitably entail individual-community tensions. The New Testament gives us leads to develop a philosophy and a theology about this. It raises both the individual and the community to their perfect expression. All of the New Testament mentions of the individual's relations to the community refer to the "Suffering Servant" passage of Isaiah 53, which perhaps best shows the tension. There an individual takes upon himself the sins of the whole world; he is allied, yet alone. In St. John's Gospel, Christ is the Lamb who bears the sins of the world.[27] St. Paul says, speaking of Christ the Redeemer: "Through his blood, God made him the means of expiation for all who believe."[28] And the author of the Letter to the Hebrews applies to Christ as priest the passages which refer to the theology of expiation, and especially the ritual of yom kippur (atonement),[29] to which Isaiah 53 had referred.

As humans, we must be aware of our individuality and separateness from all around us, but we must at the same time be in relationship to our universe, to nature, and to other people. As Christians, we are called to form one immense body in the charity of Christ. Jesus said, "I am the vine," and Paul said of him that "he is the head"; Jesus' followers are branches of the vine and bodily members of the head. As the modern Church puts it, "For by his innermost nature man is a social being; and if he does not enter into relations with others he can neither live nor develop his gifts."[30] The best of sociological research indicates that on almost every standard of measure Catholic high schools outrank others because of the Church as a functional community behind them.[31]

So Catholic schools show the communitarian aspects of personal development in both theory and practice: "students should be guided . . . toward the development of a sense of community: toward others in the educational community, in the other communities that they may belong to, and with the entire human community."[32] But sin makes this difficult:

> [man] has broken the right order that should reign within himself as well as between himself and other men and all creatures.
>
> Man therefore is divided in himself. As a result, the whole life of men, both individual and social, shows itself to be a struggle, and a dramatic one, between good and evil, between light and darkness.[33]

CONCERN FOR ALL, ESPECIALLY THE POOR AND DISADVANTAGED
Early Christianity

Church teachings about the dignity of the person embrace especially the *anawim* — the poor, lepers, women, children, and other helpless and voiceless outcasts of society. The New Testament, beginning with St. John's prologue, ushered in a new and revolutionary concept of dignity for all people. Jesus began his Sermon on the Mount, a synopsis of his doctrine, with "Blessed are the poor in spirit [*anawim*]."[34] He carried out his teaching by his example. He incurred the displeasure of some of his contemporaries by eating and drinking with despised tax collectors and sinners.[35] Toward the end of his public ministry, Jesus taught, "As long as you did it for one of these [the hungry, thirsty, stranger, naked, sick, and imprisoned], the least of my brethren, you did it for me."[36]

Jesus' words and example pertaining to the dignity and worth of the individual were much higher than anything that had gone before. The ancient lawgiver always knew that there would be disadvantaged people in the land, as did Jesus.[37] But Jesus transfigured attitudes toward the poor. Whereas the Old Testament forbade unkindness, such as mocking the poor, Jesus taught his listeners to look upon the poor as a sacrament of his own presence.[38] Jesus' observation that the meek are blessed[39] reflects an Old Testament vocabulary, but his meaning is much more revolutionary than is commonly imagined.

It is the *anawim*, not the high and mighty, who have the Gospel preached to them.[40] The life of Jesus in poverty and the strong elements of care for the poor in the first Christian communities, especially those recorded in Luke's Gospel, inaugurated the Christian tradition of the *anawim*. Christian saints have continued the tradition: Augustine, Basil, Francis of Assisi, John of the Cross, Peter Claver, and many others.

Catholics Today

Catholic schools today are expected to be no less concerned with the *anawim* than were Jesus and his early followers. The Church continues to teach that Jesus' "goodness embraced all, the just and sinners, the poor and the rich, fellow-citizens and foreigners. If he loved any people more than the rest, it was the sick, the poor and the lowly."[41] The Church's respect for the human person continues to extend to the *anawim*: "Today there is an inescapable duty to make ourselves the neighbor of every man, no matter who he is, and if we meet him, to come to his aid in a positive way."[42] And the equal dignity of all persons demands struggle for more humane conditions for all people: "Excessive economic and social disparity between individuals and peoples of the one human race is a source of scandal."[43]

In U.S. history, Catholics and their schools have by and large been true to this tradition; elitism in schools, if and when true, has been caused by a critical need for funds (hence tuition charges), more than any other reason. A study by Andrew Greeley concluded that, contrary to the assumption that Catholic schools are more effective with the affluent, they are actually most successful with the poor. This is especially true with those whom Greeley describes as thrice disadvantaged: "of minority status, whose parents did not attend college, and who are in a general track because their prior school record did not qualify them for an academic program placement."[44] Further, valid and reliable statistics belie the stereotypes put forth by the enemies of Catholic schools.[45]

Catholic schools' ability to continue their work with the *anawim* has been complicated by many factors. Modern research indicates that complex social, economic, and political factors are creating a class of poor children in the United States who are the first society in the history of this country who are worse off than adults. Both the number and rate of births to unmarried teenagers have been increasing. The child of the unemployed mother is frequently born underweight for lack of prenatal care, becomes sicker more often, and places more financial strains on treatment facilities. Welfare payments from Aid to Families with Dependent Children have fallen.[46]

Added to this are other factors within the system: the large declines in the number of religious community members, inflation, the increase in lay teacher salaries, and so on. Also, Catholic doctrine is alien to some ethnic groups such as blacks, Indians, and Orientals whose forebears did not embrace the Catholic religion, whereas it is culturally acceptable to Hispanic peoples.

Even with these factors, the percentage of ethnic minority students in Catholic schools increased from 10.8 percent in 1970/71 to 18.4 percent in 1980/81, and to 20.4 percent in 1982/83. Catholic schools, with a long tradition of welcoming newcomers, continue to provide multicultural education to the new arrivals: the Hispanics, blacks, Vietnamese, Koreans, Haitians, and others who have replaced the Irish, Germans, Italians, and Poles of yore.[47] Catholic schools, wary of attempting a "melting pot" that might rob minority students of their identity, try instead for a sensitive course between isolationism and assimilation.

When Jesus indicated that we will always have the *anawim* with us, he did not mean that we should complacently accept social injustice. Yet, as usual for the *anawim*, society in general is largely is ignoring them, and they are its victims. Considering their available resources, Catholic schools have a record in this matter of which they can be proud.

WOMEN

In Jesus' time, the leaders of the people allowed a woman to be divorced but not to institute divorce proceedings, never allowed a woman in public to be addressed by or to speak with a man, did not bother to teach the Law to a woman, and taught that contact with a woman during her menstrual period meant liturgical uncleanness.

Jesus, on the other hand, allowed his radical conduct to become public knowledge: Mary Magdalene was his close friend, he publicly conversed with the penitent woman, instructed the Samaritan woman at Jacob's well, showed kindness to the woman who touched his cloak for a cure, and so on.

The Church continues to observe Christ's acceptance of women. For example, harking back to the Genesis account of God creating male and female, the Church asserts that this "partnership of man and woman constitutes the first form of communion between persons."[48] Restricted by historical and cultural influences and prejudices, however, the Church's statements sometimes sound to some degree vague — for example that it "is up to everyone to see to it that woman's specific and necessary participation in cultural life be acknowledged and fostered."[49]

There remain among some Catholics as among some others the remnants of a double standard. Some theologians (as well as some historians, philosophers, psychologists, and sociologists) at times continue to define women solely as the helpmates and subordinates of men. Some male scholars and teachers frequently inculcate in women the notion that their destiny is anatomy and tradition, not personal autonomy and culture, and they socialize youth into sex-stereotyped molds. Further research can come up with more and more Christian applications to these issues.[50]

NON-CATHOLIC STUDENTS

In a spirit of freedom and respect, Catholic schools, where possible without injustice to her own people, accept students of other faiths or of none. This has been in increasing numbers.[51] The percentage of non-Catholics increased from 2.7 percent in 1969/70 to 10.6 percent in 1982/83; the 1982/83 percentage in secondary schools increased to 11.2 percent. Much of this is the Church's contribution to blacks. Also, a small "new immigration," mostly to cities, has comprised such mostly Catholic minorities as Puerto Ricans and Mexicans.

For these reasons as well as because of Catholics' confidence in their faith and their perception of their duty, the acceptance of non-Catholics into their schools is no more than right:

> Faith . . . is a free response of the human person to God as he reveals himself. Therefore, while Catholic educators will teach doctrine in conformity with their own religious convictions and in accord with the identity of the school, they must at the same time have the greatest respect for those students who are not Catholics. They should be open at all times to authentic dialogue, convinced

that in these circumstances the best testimony that they can give of their own faith is a warm and sincere appreciation for anyone who is honestly seeking God according to his or her own conscience.[52]

DISCIPLINE

Young people today bring to the Catholic educator the same psychological problems they bring to other schools, the same sociological factors like the conditions of students' homes, the same secularized world:

> [i]dentity crisis, loss of trust in social structures, the resulting insecurity and loss of any personal convictions, the contagion of a progressive secularization of society, loss of the proper concept of authority and lack of a proper use of freedom.[53]

Catholic schools, therefore, like others, must deal with discipline.

Discipline means many things—teaching, for example, and learning, and hence a branch of instruction. The *Oxford English Dictionary*, which devotes over a page to the word "discipline," mentions only seventh its meaning in terms of correction and chastisement. The word comes from *discipulus*, pupil, with the same root as the word for a follower of Jesus. More important are the philosophical and theological factors involved, such as the concept of the redemption of humankind.

This means that student discipline in Catholic schools should be different from that in all other schools. For one thing, because Catholic schools view the student as a child of God, they should look upon their students with higher aspirations than do other schools. Also, what motivates discipline must be a deeper kind of love. In the age-old controversy of the use of fear or love, Machiavelli and his followers—and they are many, within and outside education—opted for fear.[54] Catholic-school educators will ineluctably choose love,[55] and their students will be made to understand why. Disciplinary procedures should be made educationally beneficial to the extent possible.

SOME PSYCHOLOGICAL THEORIES IN RAPPORT
The Connection between Psychological Theories and Catholicism

A psychiatrist wrote a long time ago to the effect that, if you were to take the sum total of all the authoritative articles ever written by the most qualified of psychologists and psychiatrists on the subject of mental hygiene; if you were to combine them, refine them, and cleave out the excess verbiage; if you were to take the whole of the meat and none of the parsley; and if you were to have these unadulterated bits of pure scientific knowledge concisely expressed by the most capable of living poets, you would have but an awkward and incomplete summation of the Sermon on the Mount.

This is not to say simplistically that Christianity is a panacea, a solution to all personality problems, or a comfort in all difficulties. It is to say that many major psychological theories of personality growth and development admit of a connection between Christianity and the personal formation that is education.[56]

Importance of Psychological Insight

Because of the awesome importance of the formation of the human person which is the purpose of education, psychological insight is necessary for the Catholic-school educator.[57] This insight must extend to all levels of development. Infancy is important because that is when religious and moral life make their first appearance.[58] Childhood is important because the pleasure derived during this period from doing things and doing them properly, collaboration with others, and the discipline arising out of these experiences assist both involvement in society and active participation in the Church's life.[59]

Because preadolescence is characterized by the arduous birth of self-awareness, the religious instruction which may have been appropriate for children should not be continued.[60] When childish religious instruction is continued during this period, this added to current societal conditions will put youth less in danger of positively opposing the Church than of being tempted to leave it.[61]

The period of adolescence is of special importance because of adolescent crises which can arise from youth's profound physical and psychological changes, their immersion in mutually opposing values, and their search for a basic orientation which will enable them to unify their lives once more.[62] In their efforts to help, adults should remember "that for adolescents commitment to the faith and their confirmation in it come not from identifying with adults but as a result of personal conviction gradually arrived at," and:

> In their search for their own autonomy, adolescents like to form associations in order to facilitate the search for their own ideas and identity and in order to protect their autonomy from adult groupings. . . . In ordinary daily life, adolescents communicate more easily with young people of the same age than with adults.[63]

This is sometimes forgotten by pastors who complain that high-school-age youth participate little, if at all, in parish life, and spend most of their time at their high school.

Developmental Theories: Piaget and Erikson

People can teach religion, but faith is a gift of God's grace. To realize that no one can teach faith may reduce frustration. Nevertheless, Catholic educators must aim not merely at presenting religious knowledge accurately, but at personal commitment to Christ and his teaching.[64] In this pursuit, a knowledge of some developmental theories may indirectly help. For one thing, the Catholic-school teacher must learn to speak the languages evolved by the other disciplines and experiences to which the student is subject. For another thing, there are preconditions of faith. As we mention elsewhere, a young person who has had so little experience of being trusted that he or she is unable to trust anyone else is thereby incapable of reaching full faith in God. People who resent the way life has turned out for them, who are so embittered that they are never prepared to say a meaningful thank-you, are not capable of celebrating the Eucharist.

Unfortunately, conclusions about how religious instruction should proceed in the light of developmental psychology are still too elemental to say anything definitive at present. James Fowler, a colleague of Lawrence Kohlberg, has begun a theory of faith development that can enlighten and enrich the Catholic school's task of religious education.[65] Somewhere between the ages of six and eleven, the child leaves what Fowler calls the "intuitive-projective" stage and arrives at the "mythic-literal" stage. The transition to the third or "synthetic-conventional" state occurs toward the end of childhood. This stage, which may last only until the late teens or may persist through middle age, is a "conformist" phase, characterized by keen awareness of the expectations and judgments of others. In this stage are many features of Kohlberg's conventionally moral person, the uncritical patriot, the unquestioning loyalist, the "true believer." It is also a strikingly accurate description of the kind of Catholic who dominated the Church before Vatican II.

It is in Fowler's fourth stage, the "independent-reflexive," that we find a description of the type of Catholic who emerged in great numbers after the Council. The transition to this stage may begin as early as the late teens, or much later, or perhaps not at all. These people are autonomous, and feel newly aware of their personal responsibility for their faith; they place a high value on authenticity and consistency. Whether they work for companies, serve in armies, or belong to churches, these stage-four people are going to be a threat to those in stage three, especially when the latter remain fixated at that stage of development long past young adulthood.

For better or for worse, the Church now has a large population of independent-reflexive members, many of whom are priests and a few of whom are bishops. The later steps on Fowler's ladder of faith maturity occur only well into adult years. The fifth or "paradoxical-consolidative" stage rarely (if ever) occurs before the age of thirty. People at this stage often become peacemakers between members of stages three and four, and the Church and the world never needed them more than it does now.[66]

The Church's theories of personality growth and development are consonant with many modern psychological theories. For effectiveness, Catholic educators should learn the general developmental principles and put them into operation. Chief among them are the cognitive development theory of Jean Piaget (1896–1984) and the psychosocial development theory of Erik Erikson (b. 1902).

For Piaget, learning depends upon the laws of development. For him, the child's *actions* show what the child is really about.[67] So teaching by telling is not totally adequate. For successful learning, the sequence of presentation should match the competencies of the pupil's stage of development. Piaget established an order in which specific competencies develop.[68] Educational success depends upon this sequence being followed. Piaget held that intellectual growth is promoted best when one places a high premium upon self-initiated and self-regulated "discovery" activities in situations that call for social interaction.[69]

Whereas Freud concentrated on psychosexual development, Erikson focuses on psychosocial development. Erikson is the first theorist to recognize that personality continues to develop in a series of stages over the entire life cycle. Throughout life, the individual is always a personality in the making, striving to incorporate the irreconcilable opposites presented by the particular phase which the individual is going through. One's solution to the particular phasal dilemma of one period generates a struggle for the dilemma of the next period.[70] Each stage of Erikson's developmental process poses a unique developmental task, in confronting individuals with a crisis or dilemma through which they must struggle. A crisis, however, is not "a threat of catastrophe but a turning point, a crucial period of increased vulnerablity and heightened potential."[71]

Erikson posits eight stages of life, all of which have psychosocial modes, crises, radii of significant relations, basic strengths, and the like, many of which have religious connections and overtones. He borrows a term from embryology—epigenesis. In embryology, epigenetic development refers to the step-by-step growth of the fetal organs. Whereas in Erikson's psychology it indicates growth and development, it "by no means signifies a mere succession."[72] One is continually building on the past for the future.

For Erikson the psychosocial origins of religious faith lay in the infant's very first crisis. This is the stage of "trust versus mistrust." Just as trust characterizes the relationship that exists between mother and child, basic trust should characterize the relationship that exists between the person and religion: "Erikson sees religion as the institution which safeguards the basic trust persons develop in their earliest years. Religions provide persons with the opportunity to express their childlike trust in life and in God."[73] Erikson writes:

> Of all institutions that of organized religion has the strongest claim to being in charge of the numinous; the believer, by appropriate gestures, confesses his dependence and his child-like faith and seeks, by appropriate offerings, to secure the privilege of being lifted up to the very bosom of the divine which, indeed, may be seen to graciously respond, with the faint smile of an inclined face.[74]

Because of this stage's connection with awesome aspects, of which religion is one, it is also known as the stage of numinous ritualization. The "numinous" for Erikson contains "the aura of a hallowed presence."[75]

In the second stage of development, "autonomy versus self-doubt," the child begins to assert his will and prove his muscular mobility and independence. In this stage children should be encouraged to acquire a sense of independence and competence, and need to be given encouragement and support so they are not overcome by shame and doubt. Erikson views the development of autonomy as essential in order to develop a mature religious faith. Because of the will of others, limitations are placed upon the child, which inhibit his or her freedom of self-expression. Erikson feels it important that this problem be resolved, since at some point in life each person must face conflict between his own faith and will and the will of others.[76]

In the third stage, "initiative versus guilt," the child must assume responsibility for himself and other elements of his world such as toys, pets, and siblings. This stage, characterized by the development of imagination and conscience, gives rise to religious imagination. This religious imagination is cultivated by great myths, legends, and games, with their interaction of free will and determined rules.[77]

A major factor in healthy ego development for both Erikson and Piaget is the role of play.[78] Both theorists agree that through play the child is able to deal with frustrations, suffering, and defeats. It is through the imaginative spirit of play that the child develops a foundation for the "religious impulse which finds its expression in stories, rituals, and the law."[79]

The fourth stage of the epigenetic process, "industry versus inferiority," takes place when the child must control his active imagination and settle down to formal education. According to Erikson, the child now becomes interested in the wider society such as the school, the church, and the neighborhood. Contributions and cooperation toward society are expressions of religious involvement. The significance of this stage is especially crucial to Catholic educators.

Erikson's fifth stage, "identity versus role confusion," is concerned with the adolescent's struggle to find his or her own identity. For the adolescent, the capacity to reach out and make contact with other people while groping with romantic involvement and vocational choices is an essential part of ego development. The adolescent needs to feel a sense of involvement in personal ideals and values. Erikson believes that while some rejection of religion is to be expected at this time, religious educators must attempt to maintain understanding and loving relationships with their students.[80]

To prevent the adolescent from suffering through what Erikson refers to as "ego diffusion" or "identity confusion," the adolescent must develop intellect, values, and self concept to the fullest. It is the strength of his or her identity that will give definition to his or her environment. The Church agrees:

> [T]he school must give constant and careful attention to cultivating in students the intellectual, creative, and aesthetic faculties of the human person; to develop in them sound judgement and the correct application of will and affectivity; to promote in them a sense of values; to encourage just attitudes and prudent behaviour; to introduce them to the cultural patrimony handed down from previous generations; to prepare them for professional life, and to encourage the friendly interchange among students who differ in character and social background that will lead to mutual understanding.[81]

Erikson's next three stages deal with young adulthood through middle adulthood to old age.

Erikson encourages educators' awareness of the value of the various types of religious personalities. One student may be of a mystical bent and interested in personal prayer and religious experience, another attracted to the ritualistic in religion, another impressed by religion's social activist thrust.[82] Erikson believes it is important for all educators, religious as well as others, to understand that every person has his own social history and identity. Thus, religious education cannot be mass-produced. It must involve real relationships between people.[83]

For Erikson, the religious dimension is inextricably bound up in the cycle of life, and religion is essential for wholeness. Wholeness is what life is all about for reasons to be found in the Judeo-Christian religion as well as in psychology. But there is the danger that religion can also be totalistic; this differs from wholeness in being exclusive of other persons and ideas, counter to efforts to integrate, and delineative of absolute boundaries between what is within and without.[84]

PERSONALITY THEORIES IN RAPPORT

In addition to these developmental theories, there are many theories about the very nature of personality in which a rapport with the Christian religion can be posited as being an essential, or at least an important, integrative, and perfective power for personality. Among them are the following.

Classical and Traditional

As early as the fourth century, St. Gregory of Nyssa mentioned the integrative and perfective power of religion on the person when he shrewdly observed, "Each of us is born by his own choice . . . and we are in some sort our own fathers because we bring ourselves to birth as we will."[85] A modern author in the Catholic tradition, Jean Mouroux, puts it another way, in speaking of the person as

> a being who is simultaneously spirit and body, closed and open, existent and yet to be achieved; or, if you prefer it, the paradox of a being in a state of tension between the two principles of his composition, between himself and his fellows, between himself and his God.[86]

The same author continues:

> [The person] bears in himself a mystery he will never exhaust: an ontological mystery, since his own being can never become transparent to himself save only by another who is God: to see himself he must see himself in God; a psychological mystery which echoes the former, since the embodied spirit can never apprehend himself save only through his body, the I only through his *me*; and this interior tension, this ceaseless pursuit that never ends in a capture, expresses the mystery of a spirit too great for its matter—the mystery of the spiritual individual.[87]

Mouroux further expresses acceptance of the view that the Christian religion can integrate and perfect personality: the person "is open on the world, on humanity, and on God; and that means that his first and fundamental impulse will be to augment, to surpass, and to fulfill his being by entering into union with all three."[88] Going further, he says that "it is in Christ that the person is called to being. The bond with God essential to the person is, in fact, a bond of grace with Christ."[89]

Psychoanalytical Theories

Psychoanalysis has moved beyond Freud and his negative theories of religious development. Some psychoanalytic theories are positive and favorable to the need of religion in education. Such would be the thesis that religious experience, like many other areas of human involvement, reflects the underlying dynamics of human personality development.

Ana-Maria Rizzuto's observations are representative. The first stage of the God representation, she says, the infants find mirrored in their surroundings. The mirroring components find their first experience in eye contact, early nursing, and maternal personal participation in the act of mirroring. Eye contact is meaningful only between humans: no grateful dog or other pet can ever take part in the kind of life-giving encounter that occurs between mother and child, and the child is simply fascinated with the configuration of the human face. And the mirroring is extremely important: in the first period of narcissistic relation to the object, the child needs the object to see himself or herself as an admirable, appealing, and wonderful being reflected in the maternal eye. This is the child's first direct experience which is used in the formation of the God representation. If the mother's face is unresponsive, then the mirror is a thing to be looked at but not to be looked into.

The need for mirroring evolves and changes in the course of life but never ceases completely. If at a stage of more mature mirroring the image is that of a bad child, there is a conflict. A child might conclude that she or he is a person whom God could not possibly love, or have fears that God is a destructive, dangerous, rejecting being with no interest in him or her, as the child knows the parent to be. When the mirroring stage evolves normally, the child begins slowly to separate his or her own representation from the maternal and moves to the next stage of separation-individuation. Soon the child separates God from other intense anal, phallic, or vaginal preoccupations, fantasies, wishes, and fears. She or he gives God a special and superior status because of multiple phenomena. Socioculturally, the child hears special people talk respectfully about God and sees special buildings, pieces of art, and celebrations having to do with the "big person" called God.

Epigenetically, at two and one half years of age the child starts to discover (in a rudimentary notion of causality) that things are made by people, but that nobody made God. So God is no ordinary being. By the age of three, if children are not stifled by adult attitudes, they will verbalize their curiosity about God's reality. Four-year-olds have a good grasp of the representation of God: they think about God in relation to their enlarged experience of parents and the world. Five-year-olds do not soar as high and have a tendency to bring God within the scope of their everyday world.

By the time children are sent to school, in a great number of families they are also asked to go through a rite of passage as they are officially introduced to religious indoctrination and told that they belong to "the people of God." They now like to hear Bible stories. They also feel the awe of participation in short ritualistic services. They are beginning to develop a feeling relationship with God, and prayers are becoming important. If the God representation is not revised to keep pace with epigenetic changes, that representation soon becomes asynchronous and is experienced as ridiculous or irrelevant or, to the contrary, threatening or dangerous. Each epigenetic phenomenon offers a new opportunity to revise the representation or leave it unchanged.

After the oedipal or electral crisis of conflict with the opposite-sex parent, there are two other important times for the God representation. One is puberty, when for the first time youth are able to grasp a concept of God beyond the limits of their experience. The second is the last part of adolescence, which confronts the growing individual with the need to integrate a more cohesive self-representation which will enable him or her to make major decisions about life, marriage, and work. That developmental crisis, with its intense self-searching and reshuffling of self-images, brings about encounters with new as well as old God representations.

It is during these years that most people who cease to believe drop their God. Many who keep Him may load Him with anachronistic and restrictive notions — an indicator of unresolved developmental issues, sometimes due to lack of proper education. In fact, each new crisis of growth during the life cycle creates similar possibilities of belief ceasing to have meaning because the God representation has remained developmentally anachronistic or, being unrevised, incompatible with development. All children in the Western world initially form a God representation — which may later be used, neglected, or actively repressed, depending in some measure on one's education.

The entire process occurs in a wider context of the family, social class, organized religion, and particular subcultures as well as education.[90]

Some psychoanalysts present a different breakdown, seeing various successive modes of religious experience. A first mode is a primitive and/or deeply regressive state which is dominated by the conditions of narcissism and of nondistinguishability of self and object. The religious experience on this level is one in which the self-representation and the God representation are diffuse and obscure. The sense of self is without cohesion.

The second mode is one of idealization and dependence on the parental *imago*. The God representation at this stage is in terms of the omnipotence and omniscience of the perfected and idealized parent. The quality of the faith experience is riddled with a sense of utter dependence and a terror at the omnipotence of the godhead. The anally determined issues of submission, the conflicts between autonomy and relative dependence, and the obsessional quality of magical necessity to placate by ritual permeate the religious experience. God is likely to be highly concretized, personalized, and given predominantly anthropomorphic features.

The third modality of religious experience is conditioned upon the achievement of an integration of a cohesive self. Narcissistic vulnerabilities are now focused in more extrinsic terms having to do with self-esteem. Matters of belief or valuative judgment are based primarily on the appeal to trusted authority, although there is an increasing capacity to use thought processes. The quality of belief systems is generally less magical. Constructs underlying distinctions between natural and supernatural have become operative. The major dimensions of religious experience are cast in terms of fear of punishment for transgressions and preoccupation with rectitude and ritual performance. In contrast to the overriding maternal quality of earlier projections in the image of the deity, these projections now exhibit more of a paternal quality, reflecting the underlying fear of the punitive and harshly judging father.

A fourth mode of religious experience is articulated around the developmental achievement of the superego. The internalization of ideals and values means the organization of conscience. Discrimination develops between the idea of the spiritual, as it relates to both the existence of God and the spiritual aspect of human beings, and the realm of the nonspiritual. Awareness of the faith orientation of others tends to be cast in prejudicial terms. Institutional authority or sacramental community, or both, tends to sustain this level of synthesis and provides a powerful motivation for institutional adherence. Probably the largest portion of adult religious behavior falls into this modality.

The final modality of religious experience contains a number of significant developmental achievements. There is, for example, an integration with relatively autonomous functional capacities of the ego. The individual reaches a higher level of wisdom, empathy, humor, and creativity. Faith becomes a lived source of sustaining support and strength. At the higher reaches of this modality, one touches a realm of the integration of the faith experience which bridges over into spiritual experience that one may describe in terms of mystical gifts and spiritual genius.

This is an inner life of lucidity, simplicity, and harmony which, though it escapes the generality of human experience, nevertheless seems somehow more fully and more profoundly human. In persons who have reached this modality, the love of God seems wholly unselfconscious, stripped of the residues of the infantile, and capable of integration into a life of activity, responsibility, and fulfillment. Such persons often seem capable of profoundly meaningful outside relations, which are characterized by a selfless love and acceptance of others.[91]

These qualities are most often found in the lives of the saints. In regressive Freudian terms, saints' states of fusion with God represent a reactivation or a re-creation of primitive states of symbiotic fusion with the all-good, all-giving, all-nurturing maternal breast. This Freudian interpretation, however, is denied by those who believe in authentic mystical experience. Within the Judeo-Christian tradition, mystical experiences share the attributes of ineffability and immersion in divine love, as well as a sense of fusion with the object of that love. The capacity to reach beyond the boundaries of self and to empty the self out in the loving embrace of the object is a transcendent capacity of the psyche to immerse itself in a loving object relationship, and need not be considered regressive.

Social Psychological Theories

At the same time that Freud and Jung were being inspired by the Positivism of the nineteenth century, others were developing theories based on dynamic-cultural forces due to the findings of the social sciences. Like Erikson, they emphasized the social nature of man. Their social psychological theories are not only consonant with the Christian religion; they see the Christian life as integrative and perfective of the human personality.

First and foremost in this group is one of Freud's disciples who eventually broke with him, Alfred Adler. Adler's belief in the inherent positive nature of humankind substantiates the nature of humankind as perceived by Catholic philosophies. That belief posits that the person is intrinsically a social being whose main goal is to work cooperatively and harmoniously with his fellow human beings. The broadening of one's sense of incompletion or imperfection in some department of life leads to compensation by one's trying to achieve completion and perfection. This in turn leads to Adler's notion of social interest.

The individual, in accord with this drive, wants to help society as well as himself to attain the goal of perfection. Another of Adler's major concepts, "style" or "plan of life," is difficult to define, but means in general that each person seeks his goal of superiority in his own way: some by developing intellect, others through muscular perfection, and so on. This part of his theory gives the theory its name: "individual psychology." To explain what determines the individual's "style of life," he postulated the creative self.

Social interest, an important concept in Adlerian psychology, is one's feeling of belonging in group situations—one's family, community, or work environment. This potential is inborn and must be carefully cultivated. Catholic educators agree with Adler that the child must develop a healthy self-concept and strong, positive community feelings: "love your neighbor as yourself" implies that you must love yourself in the right way and then go on from there. Adler feels that if children are not trained at an early age to partnerships with other people, they will be inclined to work for the wrong kind of self-fulfillment instead:

> At one time dependent on other people, at another longing to supress them, such children are soon confronted with the insurmountable problem of living in a world that demands fellowship and cooperation. Robbed of their illusions, they blame other people and always see the hostile principle of life.[92]

Consistent with these views, the Catholic Church has long believed that children need systematic direction beginning in early childhood.[93]

The classroom can be an opportunity for the child to learn a sense of cooperation with others. The child's social interest can be aroused by caring adults like parents and teachers. Catholic educators should reflect

> an understanding of religion in which the community of believers is understood to be part and parcel of the religious experience. Emphasis on a spirit of community within the school for its importance is an educational goal.[94]

Another social psychologist was Karen Horney, who considered the basic determining principle of the human personality to be the need for security. A child raised in a good home—one where there has been love, tolerance, warmth, and so on—will triumph over all socially caused conflicts. She listed ten neurotic needs, and classified these needs under three heads: (1) moving toward people—for example, the need for love; (2) moving away from people—for instance, the need for independence; and (3) moving against people—for example, the need for power.[95]

The major representative of the social psychological theorists, however, was Harry Stack Sullivan, who introduced a new viewpoint: the interpersonal theory. He defined personality as "the relatively enduring pattern of recurrent interpersonal situations which characterize a human life,"[96] and asserted that personality "is a dynamic center of various processes which occur in a series of interpersonal fields."[97]

Organismic Theories

Dissatisfied with the mind/body dualism first proposed in the seventeenth century by Rene Descartes and continued by such experimental psychologists as Wilhelm Wundt (1832–1920), some theorists wanted to put the person back together again and treat people as a unified, organized whole. This point of view began with those German psychologists who posited a system based on *Gestalt*. This word has no exact English equivalent, but approximations are "configuration," "meaningful organized whole," "structural relationship," and "theme." The "Gestalt" in this context is the meaningful organized whole of a figure (act or person) together with its background. The background, or "ground" in Gestalt psychology, is the context against which the figure stands out. The Gestaltists contend that only a consideration of this entirety gives a natural and undistorted approach to the human being's wholeness of life.

Each of the several persons who embrace this theory has his own variations. Its chief representative is Abraham Maslow, who calls his version of the organismic theory a holistic-dynamic point of view. In his theory of motivation, Maslow arranged needs in a hierarchy of priority. He found the self-actualizing people he studied to have these characteristics in common: realistic orientation; acceptance of themselves, other people, and the world; spontaneity; problem-centeredness rather than self-centeredness; detachment and need for privacy; autonomy and independence; fresh rather than stereotyped appreciation of others; most with profound spiritual experiences (not necessarily religious); identification with humankind; intimate relationships that are profound; democratic values; distinction of means from ends; a philosophical rather than hostile sense of humor; creativeness; and resistance to conformity.

Maslow's theory, as well as the other organismic theories of personality, lend themselves most readily to observations on the advantages of the Christian religion in personality development. In fact, though the proponents of these theories do not say so, Christianity has the wherewithal for deep, satisfying, and lasting solutions to the searches posited by their theories.

Self Theory

Another theory harmonious with psychological personal development through the Christian religion is what has been called the "self theory." Ever since psychology became a science about a hundred years ago, it has searched for an agency within the person that regulates behavior and explains his or her higher processes. Formerly this was the role of the soul and its faculties which had served this purpose since Plato. Psychology has substituted the ego or the self, each term having different meanings for different writers.

Perhaps the most famous theorist on the self is Carl Rogers (1902–1987), who is identified with nondirective or client-centered psychotherapy. The first ingredient of his theory is the *organism*, the total individual. This possesses several qualities: it reacts as an organized whole; it has the one basic motive of trying to actualize, maintain, and enhance itself; and it may bring its experiences within the realm of consciousness, refuse them admittance, or ignore them. Second, there is the *phenomenal field*, or totality of experience. Third, there is the *self*, a separated part of the field consisting of the pattern of conscious perceptions and values of the person.

Christianity can fulfill the "organism," can put peace and order into the "phenomenal field" and remove threat from it, can perfect the values of the "self," and can remove tension and maladjustment from interactions of all three. Rogers, in describing the process of the therapeutic "good life," says that it involves an increasing openness to experience which is the "polar opposite to defensiveness": a situation in which

> the individual is becoming more able to listen to himself, to experience what is going on within himself. He is more open to his feelings of fear and discouragement and pain. He is also more open to his feelings of courage and tenderness and awe.[98]

The careful reader may notice an affinity of Rogers's statement with St. Paul's description of Christian growth: "We know that affliction makes for endurance, and endurance for tested virtue, and tested virtue for hope. And this hope will not leave us disappointed."[99] Also reminiscent of the good Christian is the Rogerian technique of "listening." Listening, for Rogers, is an active process, not a passive waiting. It is a matter of striving to understand what the other is trying to accomplish. It is similar to good spiritual direction. It is also similar to listening in prayer, in which a relaxed alertness is called for.

Existential Psychology

Another system (at least for the theists in it) which can relate positively to the formational value of the Christian religion is Existential Psychology. Less empirical and more philosophical, it pursues the "I" rather than the "it." It is subjective, in two senses: its center is the existing thinker, and it does not mean the same for any two existentialists. Despite its subjectivism, theistic Existentialism does have some major themes which are found in most of its adherents. For example, one is alone with oneself and hence is tempted to anguish and its variants that have degrees of ascending seriousness: boredom, melancholy, and despair. The self is at the opposite pole from "the masses" or "the world"; at best, the world is the testing ground for self-realization.

One is limited by a hostile environment, by one's psychological makeup, and by the finiteness and contingency of one's existence. Theistic existentialists "take seriously the widespread withdrawal of intelligent men from God and religion during the past century and a half."[100] The theist Kierkegaard had as his major problem how to be a Christian in Christendom. And the existentialists in general see freedom as the ability to accept one's responsibility.

Here Albert Camus joins the witness of Christ, and consequently of Christianity, in the emphasis on revolt, freedom, and responsibility. Revolt at its best is a standing up to be counted, a swimming against the tide, a commitment to one's beliefs and desires even when they run counter to the status quo—all despite the isolation which such a state necessarily entails. Christ died essentially because he revolted against the priestly status quo and freely gave up his life for his principles, taking responsibility for his actions. Christianity is only truly lived by those "free" people who can take personal responsibility for trying to live by their principles, embodied in their faith, which is often seen as "revolt" against the establishment.

Pedagogically, Existentialism teaches the primacy of existence in all its variable aspects: oneness, authenticity, tragic optimism, concrete situation, involvement, freedom, and an attitude favorable to dialogue. It seems possible, however, to reduce these eight characteristics to three: *authenticity*, since that is inseparable from the realization of a unique existence with its manifold possibilities; *involvement*, which leads to the discovery of one's concrete situation, together with its difficulties, conflicts, and tragic aspects; and *aptitude for dialogue*, based on respect for one's own freedom and that of others. These three characteristics of the human person can be considered to be the foundation of the pedagogical categories which should be introduced into an existential Christian education.[101]

Allport's Psychology of the Individual

Gordon W. Allport, in discussing the development of personality, mentions that it is "a system within a matrix of sociocultural systems."[102] He defines personality as "the dynamic organization within the individual of those psychophysical systems that determine his characteristic behavior and thought."[103] But more important than searching the past is the simple question of intention. Allport prefers to look to the intended future, which is, he says, the key to the present. "Motivation," he says, "is the 'go' of personality, and is, therefore, our most central problem."[104]

Allport, distinct from other psychologists, most of whom dwell upon aspects of the negative personality, goes into some descriptions of the mature personality of the normal individual. Of maturity, he states:

> One terse definition says that a healthy personality actively *masters his environment*, shows a certain *unity of personality*, and is *able to perceive the world and himself correctly*. Such a personality stands on his own two feet without making excessive demands on others.[105]

The mature personality, according to him, must be first of all an extension of the self—that is, not tied narrowly to one's own immediate needs and duties. An important part of this aspect of one's "self" is involvement in projecting into the future—planning, hoping, and the like.

The mature individual will, further, be able to relate warmly to others and to possess a fundamental emotional security and self-acceptance. She or he will have self-objectification—that is, be realistically oriented with respect to herself or himself—and will be realistically oriented toward outer reality as well. Two main components of this self-objectification are humor and insight. A sense of humor implies in this context the ability to maintain positive relations with oneself and loved objects, while at the same time being able to see incongruities and absurdities connected with them. Insight here means the individual's capacity to understand himself or herself. Finally, to Allport maturity implies that the individual possesses a unifying philosophy of life.

He calls the process of growth "integration," of which he says: "Integration means the forging of approximate mental unity out of discordant impulses and aspirations."[106] Allport's "integration" means much the same as the "single-hearted" whom Jesus called blessed and those of whom St. Paul spoke when he advised Christ's followers to "turn from youthful passions and pursue integrity, faith, love, and peace, along with those who call on the Lord in purity of heart."[107]

This integration and maturity provide an underlying thread of seriousness that give purpose and meaning to all else. The Christian religion represents one of the most important sources, though not the only source, of unifying philosophies. Allport considered as immature those "many personalities who deal zealously and effectively with all phases of becoming except the final task of relating themselves meaningfully to creation."[108] Specifically of the religious fulfillment of personality, he wrote:

> While religion certainly fortifies the individual against the inroads of anxiety, doubt, and despair, it also provides the forward intention that enables him at each stage of his becoming to relate himself meaningfully to the totality of Being.[109]

CONCLUSION

The end, purpose, and center of the Catholic-school enterprise is the student. Since the time of Jesus, who showed a reverence and a solicitude for the human person which nobody has ever shown before or since, Catholics see the person, and hence the student, as having a dignity greater than all the rest of God's vast creation. In a good Catholic-school setting, the student experiences his dignity as a person before he knows the definition of personhood.

For Catholics, though the superdignity of personhood flows from one's entire being, it is perceived especially in intellect, will, and body. The intellect shares preeminently in this superdignity because it has as its object the achievement of truth and of wisdom. The will shares in it because it invests one with the power of responsibility, freedom, and love. The body shares because it is in substantial unity with the soul, is created by God, and has a worth that is confirmed by Jesus' incarnation.

What raises the person to his or her highest dignity is grace, the call to share in God's own nature. This apotheosis, the person becoming like God, does not depend upon the individual's efforts alone, but is theonomous: dependent upon God. But grace acts through nature, and does not contradict it. Grace's being of the supernatural order does not make it something added to the top of nature like cream on milk, but the sacred and the natural permeating each other, intertwined as one organic whole. Grace brings human nature to perfection. The life of grace is therefore an aspect of the education which Catholic schools provide their students.

Because the individual does not live alone, but coexists with others, there are inevitable individual-community tensions. Isaiah's Suffering Servant passage and its New Testament referents remind the Catholic that how to live this phenomenon is exemplified in Jesus: an individual who takes upon himself the sins of the world, one who is allied yet alone. Students, too, must come to realize their individuality and separateness from all around them, but at the same time their relationship to the universe, to nature, and to other people — the last especially as a member of one immense body in the charity of Christ.

All people by virtue of the simple fact that they are persons have a right to be educated in such a way as to help in the working of divine grace toward full and complete personal formation. This embraces the underprivileged of all faiths and of none. With roots in the Hebrew Scriptures, this embrace finds a new and higher expression in Jesus' words and example, and continues today. It includes women, with whom Jesus allowed his radical conduct to become public knowledge. It includes non-Catholic students, before whom the Church allows her teaching to speak for itself.

An area in which we have a right to look for great things in Catholic schools is discipline. The word is from *discipulus*, which has the same root as the word for a follower of Jesus. More important are the philosophical and theological factors behind discipline, such as the concept of redemption. This means that Catholic schools should look upon their students with higher aspirations than do other schools. In the age-old controversy of the use of fear or love, Machiavelli and his followers — and they are many, within and outside education — opt for fear. Catholic-school teachers inevitably try to choose love, and attempt to help their students understand why.

Psychological insight into the stages of individual growth and development — infancy, childhood, pre-adolescence, adolescence, and all the stages of adulthood — is important because religious growth takes place commensurate with the readiness of each period. Many major psychological theories admit of a connection between Christianity and the personal formation that is education. The cognitive theory of Jean Piaget and the psychosocial theory of Erik Erikson are in the forefront of such theories.

Many personality theories admit of the Christian religion being an important integrative and perfective power for personality. Classical and traditional theories show individual personalities as being born by their own choice, in some way being their own fathers. Psychoanalytical theories which have moved beyond Sigmund Freud favor the need of religion in education and the thesis that religious experience, like many other areas of human involvement, reflects an underlying dynamic of human personality development. Social theorists like Alfred Adler, Karen Horney, and Harry Stack Sullivan, who emphasize the social nature of humankind, could also admit of the Christian religion as being integrative and perfective of the human personality. So, too, with the self theory of people like Carl Rogers, the personality theories of Existentialism, and Gordon W. Allport's psychology of the individual.

QUESTIONS FOR DISCUSSION

From all possible perspectives—philosophical, theological, psychological—who or what is a person?

What are the educational consequences of the doctrine of original sin?

What is the importance, if any, of philosophical principles in formulating norms along with psychological findings about the periods of child growth and development?

Given that many families are constantly "on the move," thus making changes of school necessary, how can Catholic schools impart formation that will be consistently, deeply, and truly Catholic?

In view of the true and complete nature of children as perceived by Catholics, what fundamental items should be stressed throughout children's schooling and education?

The U.S. Declaration of Independence states, "We hold these truths to be self-evident, that all men are created equal. . . . " Does this statement agree with reality?

To what extent should a child be encouraged to acquire self-direction over and against being dependent upon authority?

How does the concept of "the whole person" differ from the secular psychologist to the Catholic theologian? What meaning does this have for Catholic schooling?

Do the psychological theories pertaining to the growth and development of the person address the idea of spirituality?

If the Catholic school is to be involved in developing wholeness in its students, what does this entail?

In spiritual formation, do many Catholic schools in your experience pay attention to the stages of youth developmental milestones? Why or why not?

Are the students who enter Catholic schools "typical" youth, or are they different from the start? Do they differ from other school graduates when they leave?

How can a Catholic school at the same time respect the freedom of the student and enforce discipline and responsibility?

Can a school teach self-discipline? What is the purpose of discipline in a Catholic school?

Catholic-school proponents often proudly point to scientific studies' evidence of the academic superiority of their students, especially minorities in inner cities. Do these claims to fame negate the formation of the whole person, including character and spiritual growth, that Catholic schools are supposed to be about?

Do you think that Catholic-school discipline may breed passivity (passive acceptance) in later years, which stunts the overall growth of the person?

Is the admission of non-Catholic students into Catholic schools a legitimate mission of the Church? Is there a point at which the number of non-Catholic students affects the Catholic identity of the school? If so, when is the point reached (for example, 60 percent, 75 percent, 90 percent)? What principles, if any, should rule in admitting non-Catholic students?

SUGGESTED BIBLIOGRAPHY

Adler, Alfred. *What Life Should Mean to You*. New York: Capricorn, 1958.
    An interesting and somewhat popular psychological discussion on a wide range of topics, including dreams, social influences, occupations, and love. Emphasizes the place and importance of meaning.
Allport, Gordon W. *Becoming*. New Haven, Conn.: Yale University Press, 1955.
    Seeks to lay the groundwork for a psychological discussion on personal development. It remains conceptually open-ended, with a brief but insightful section on the nature of personality.
_____. *The Individual and His Religion*. New York: Macmillan, 1950.
    Discusses the psychological aspects of religion in personal life.
_____. *Pattern and Growth in Personality*. New York: Holt, Rinehart and Winston, 1961.
    Comprehensive discussion of the nature, structure, and development of personality.
Arbuckle, Gerald. "Inculturation, Not Adaptation," *Worship*, vol. 60 no. 6 (November 1986), pp. 511–20.
    Defines inculturation as incarnating the Christian mystery in a particular culture, and sees it as a positive need.

Conn, Walter E., ed. *Conversion*. New York: Alba House, 1978.

Designed to work as a teacher's aid; encompasses the main elements in conversion and thereby facilitates raising pertinent questions.

Eliade, Mircea. *The Sacred and the Profane*. New York: Harcourt Brace, 1959.

Draws on the wealth of religious and social history, psychology, anthropology, and sociology to demonstrate primitive humankind's search for the sacred in all of life.

Elias, John L. *Psychology and Religious Education*. Bethlehem, Pa.: Booksellers of Bethlehem, 1975.

Explains for the religious educator contributions of six influential psychologists: Rogers, Kohlberg, Allport, Goldman, Skinner, and Erikson. Presents various ways in which psychology can be of interest to religious educators.

Erikson, Erik H. *Childhood and Society*. New York: Norton, 1963.

A unique and profound integration of psychoanalysis and history in a study of emergent leadership.

_____. *Identity, Youth and Crisis*. New York: Norton, 1968.

In this collection of revised essays, Erikson considers the nature of psychosocial identity and the importance of personal growth through conflict or crisis.

_____. *The Life Cycle Completed*. New York: Norton, 1984.

Erikson's own summation of his work. Also published as an article, "Elements of a Psychoanalytic Theory of Psychosocial Development," in *The Course of Life: Psychoanalytic Contributions Toward Understanding Personality Development*, Stanley I. Greenspan and George H. Pollock, eds. Washington, D.C.: U.S. Department of Health and Human Services, 1980, pp. 11–61.

Fowler, James. *Becoming Adult, Becoming Christian: Adult Development and Christian Faith*. San Francisco: Harper & Row, 1984.

In this follow-up to *Stages of Faith*, Fowler applies to Christianity his research on the development of faith. Presents insights from the four dominant adult development theories today, highlighting their images of wholeness, maturity, and human potential: Erik Erikson's existential psychology (see Erikson's *Childhood and Society* [2nd ed. New York: Norton, 1963], Daniel Levinson's *Seasons of a Man's Life* [New York: Knopf, 1978], Carol Gilligan's feminist reinterpretations in *In a Different Voice: Psychological Theory and Women's Development* [Cambridge: Harvard University Press, 1982]), and Fowler's own work on faith development theory.

_____. *Stages of Faith: The Psychology of Human Development and the Quest for Meaning*. San Francisco: Harper & Row, 1981.

Building on such key thinkers as Piaget, Erikson, and Kohlberg, and a wide range of literature and firsthand research, presents six stages that emerge in working out the meaning of our lives—through the imitative faith of childhood to the self-transcending faith of full maturity.

Furth, Hans. *Piaget and Knowledge: Theoretical Foundations*. University of Chicago Press, 1981.

Explains Piaget's theories in easily understood prose; see also Furth's *Piaget for Teachers* (New York: Prentice-Hall, 1970).

Gilligan, Carol. *In a Different Voice: Psychological Theory and Women's Development*. Cambridge, Mass.: Harvard University Press, 1982.

Records different modes of thinking about relationships and the association of these modes with male and female voices in psychological and literary texts.

Goble, Frank. *The Third Force: The Psychology of Abraham Maslow*. New York: Grossman, 1970. Especially chap. 16, "Education and Personal Potential," pp. 150–169.

A condensation and explanation of Maslow's works with an added section on related findings of psychiatrists, managers, and consultants.

Grant, W. Harold, Magdala Thompson, and Thomas E. Clarke. *From Image to Likeness: A Jungian Path in the Gospel Journey.* New York: Paulist, 1983.

Combines a biblical and historical understanding of the Christian pilgrimage with the insights provided by the type theory suggested by Jung and worked out by Isabel Briggs Myers.

Gregson, Vernon. *Lonergan, Spirituality and the Meeting of Religions.* Lanham, Md.: University Press of America, 1985.

From the viewpoint of subjectivity and interiority, offers a concise, nuanced, and lucid introduction to all of Lonergan.

Hall, Calvin S., and Gardner Lindsey. *Theories of Personality.* 3rd ed. New York: Wiley, 1978.

Presents an organized summary of the major contemporary theories of personality. Discusses relevant research and provides a general evaluation of each theory.

Hall, Calvin S., Gardner Lindsey, and Martin Manosevitz, eds. *Theories of Personality: Primary Sources and Research.* 3rd ed. New York: Wiley, 1973.

A collection of essays by both the great psychologists of the twentieth century and current researchers in the field.

Homans, Peter, ed. "The Significance of Erikson's Psychology for Modern Understandings of Religion," in *Childhood and Selfhood: Essays on Tradition, Religion, and Modernity in the Psychology of Erik H. Erikson.* London: Associated University Presses, 1978, pp. 231–263.

Describes and assesses Erikson's contribution to the nonclinical and more humanistic disciplines in psychology from the perspective of the disciplines of psychoanalysis and the humanities.

Jung, Carl Gustav. *Psychology and Religion.* New Haven, Conn.: Yale University Press, 1938.

Considers religion in both its Eastern and Western forms from a psychological perspective.

Kraft, William. *The Search for the Holy.* Philadelphia: Westminster, 1973.

From a phenomenological-existential perspective, examines questions about the meaning of God. Identifies the emergence of a yearning for God in the psychotherapeutic context. Attempts to answer questions of where and how to find meaning in life.

Küng, Hans. *Freud and the Problem of God.* Trans. Edward Quinn. New Haven, Conn.: Yale University Press, 1979.

Brief (126 pages). Traces the nature of religious longings. Shows the importance of religion for Freud and traces Freud's views of religion. Compares Freud with Jung and Adler. Concludes with questions about what psychoanalysis might be able to teach the Catholic Church.

Leeuw, Gerardus van der. *Religion in Essence and Manifestation.* New York: Harper and Row, 1963.

An analysis of the phenomenology of religion, incorporating varied viewpoints and extensive documentation.

Luke, Helen. *Woman, Earth and Spirit: The Feminine in Symbol and Myth.* New York: Crossroad, 1985.

Like some other works on this list, examines another area of interest to Catholic schools: women's studies.

Maier, Henry W. *Three Theories of Child Development.* New York: Harper and Row, 1978.

Presents and parallels the work of Piaget, Erikson, and Sears.

Maslow, Abraham Harold. *Religion, Values, and Peak Expereiences.* New York: Penguin, 1964. Especially chap. 7, "Value-Free Education?"

A brief but thorough psychological review of religious experiences following in the path of William James, John Dewey, and Erich Fromm.

Meissner, W. W. "Psychoanalytic Aspects of Religious Experience," *Annual of Psychoanalysis*, vol. 6 (1978), pp. 103–141.

This Jesuit psychiatrist reassesses the psychoanalytic understanding of religious phenomena, using as a frame of reference the Judeo-Christian religious tradition.

————. "The Psychology of Religious Experience," *Communio*, vol. 4 (1977), pp. 36–59.

Meissner here contends that whatever of religious experience can be focused and understood through the methodology of psychology must be seen inherently and specifically as a human experience.

Moore, Thomas Verner. *The Life of Man with God*. Garden City, N.Y.: Doubleday, 1962.

Examines spiritual formation and the highest reaches of the self, an area that Catholic schools should be concerned about.

Murphy, Gardner, and Lois Murphy, eds. *Western Psychology*. New York: Basic Books, 1969.

A comprehensive review of Western thought on humankind's search for understanding of ourselves from the Greeks to William James. Consists predominantly of primary-source selections, with some interpretive material.

Nordby, Vernon J., and Calvin S. Hall. *A Guide to Psychologists and their Concepts*. San Francisco: Freeman, 1974.

A compilation of short biographical and conceptual synopses of over forty leading psychologists and related thinkers of the twentieth century. Concise and accessible to the popular reader.

Nuttin, Joseph. *Psychoanalysis and Personality*. Trans. George Lamb. New York: Mentor, 1962.

The result of years of study of the Freudian system which Nuttin has explored as philosopher, experimentalist, and consulting psychologist.

Oates, Wayne Edward. *The Religious Dimensions of Personality*. New York: Association Press, 1957.

Explores the relationship of religion and personality; defines religion and personality; examines the religious dimension of man's heredity, birth, and innate desires. Also describes some spiritual laws of personality and the spiritual goals of man's becoming.

Oraison, Marc. *Love or Constraint? Some Psychological Aspects of Religious Education*. New York: Paulist, 1959.

A study of the elementary psychology that is required for developing an authentic spiritual life if one is to arrive at a morality that embodies the teaching of God and the nature of the person.

Otto, Rudolf. *The Idea of the Holy*. 2nd ed. New York: Oxford University Press, 1950.

This landmark piece is both a philosophical and a poetic discussion of the nonrational factor in the idea of the divine and its relation to the individual.

Piaget, Jean, and Barbel Inhelder. *The Psychology of the Child*. New York: Basic Books, 1969.

A comprehensive synthesis of Piaget's child psychology, tracing the stages of cognitive development over the period of childhood.

Pruyser, Paul W. *The Play of the Imagination: Toward a Psychoanalysis of Culture*. New York:

International Universities Press, 1983. Especially chap. 8, "Illusion Processing in Religion," pp. 152–178.

Answers questions about the manner in which children are trained to use their imagination so as to become adept at dealing with cultural symbol systems.

_____. "Sigmund Freud and His Legacy: Psychoanalytic Psychology of Religion," in *Beyond the Classics? Essays in the Scientific Study of Religion*, ed. by Charles Y. Glock and Phillip E. Hammond. New York: Harper and Row, 1973, pp. 243–290.

The eight essays attempt to summarize the central ideas of modern "classical" writers on religion, to report on subsequent work inspired by those ideas, to evaluate their present status, and to point out a direction for future research.

Reimer, Joseph, Diana Paolitto, and Richard Hersh. *Promoting Moral Growth*. 2nd ed. New York: Longman's, 1983.

Explains Kohlberg's theory, and its practical implications for the teacher, curriculum, and school.

Rizzuto, Ana-Maria. *The Birth of the Living God: A Psychoanalytic Study*. University of Chicago Press, 1979. Especially pp. 13–39, on Freud.

Deals from a psychoanalytic viewpoint with the questions of the origin of an individual's belief in God, how the God representation is created in childhood, and how that representation is altered in the course of a lifetime. Shows that belief or nonbelief in God is the result of a complex adaptive process.

Rogers, Carl R. *On Becoming a Person: A Therapist's View of Psychotherapy*. Boston: Houghton Mifflin, 1961.

From the viewpoint of Rogers's nondirective client-centered therapy technique, addresses such fundamental questions as the meaning of personal growth, the conditions under which growth is possible, how one person can help another, and the meaning of creativity and how it can be fostered.

Rychlak, Joseph F. *Introduction to Personality and Psychotherapy. A Theory-Construction Approach*. 2nd ed. Boston: Houghton Mifflin, 1981.

An excellent textbook overview giving a framework for the study of personality and the theories of such as Locke, Freud, Adler, Jung, Harry Stack Sullivan, Dollard and Miller, Skinner, and others.

Sanford, John A. *Evil, the Shadow Side of Reality*. New York: Crossroad, 1984.

For the specialist. After discussions of the problem of evil in mythology, and in the Old and New Testaments, treats how to deal with evil as the "shadow" side of life.

_____. *The Kingdom Within*. Ramsey, N.J.: Paulist, 1970.

An excellent treatment of the inner meaning of Jesus' sayings, combining both spirituality and psychology.

Schneiders, Sandra. *Women and the Word: the Gender of God in the New Testament and the Spirituality of Women*. New York: Paulist, 1986.

Suggestions for resolving the problem of an exclusively male God-image that are both faithful to tradition and liberating for women.

Schüssler Fiorenza, Elizabeth. *In Memory of Her: A Feminist Theological Reconstruction of Christian Origins*. New York: Crossroad, 1983.

Explores the hermeneutical presuppositions, methodological difficulties, and theological problems raised by a feminist reassessment of early Christianity.

Spender, Dale. *Women of Ideas and What Men Have Done to Them*. Boston: Ark Paperbacks, 1983.

In a survey of English and North American women, seeks to correct several misconceptions about feminism.

Thorn, Ivan, and William Kirk Kilpatrick. "The Drift of Modern Psychology: A Critical Appraisal," *The Freeman*, August 1984, pp. 478–487.

Discusses the controversy of the infiltration of psychology into religion.

Tyrrell, Bernard J. *Christotherapy: Healing through Enlightenment.* New York: Seabury, 1981.

Discusses the theories of therapy in the field; the meaning of healing through Christ; the mysterious law of death and resurrection for each of us; transcendence, indwelling, and service; and healing in the Church.

————. *Christotherapy II: The Fasting and Feasting Heart.* Ramsey, N.J.; Paulist, 1982.

Begins with the development and deformations of the human subject. Proceeds to the new wisdom of principles and methods of a spiritual-psychological synthesis, spiritual directing and counseling of the Christotherapist. Concludes with the process of the healing of sin, neurosis and addiction, and the process of healing and education of feelings.

Van Kaam, Adrian. *Religion and Personality.* Englewood Cliffs, N.J.: Prentice-Hall, 1964.

Examines the structure of the religious personality, especially self-integration and religious motivation; also the perfection of the religious personality and its process of development. Also presents brief explanations of deviation in religious personality.

Vergote, A. *The Religious Man.* Dublin: Gill-Macmillan, 1969. (Originally published as *Psychologie Religieuse.*)

An attempt to synthesize much of the psychological writing on religious phenomena. Considers the religious experience and the mind during both childhood and adolescence.

Welch, John. *Spiritual Pilgrims: Carl Jung and Teresa of Avila.* New York: Paulist, 1982.

Explores the remarkably similar understanding of symbols in Carl Jung and Teresa of Avila. Jung's depth psychology is a reflection upon contemporary experience, while Teresa's *Interior Castle* is a classic on the life of prayer.

Wright, J. Eugene, Jr. *Erikson: Identity and Religion.* New York: Seabury, 1982.

After a section on the identity, method, and theory of Erik Erikson, treats ethics and religion, patterns of personal and social responsibility, and the question of whether Erikson is religious.

Zilboorg, Gregory. *Freud and Religion.* Westminster, Md.: Newman, 1961.

A short analysis of religion in the life of Freud.

Chapter 11

SOME CONCLUSIONS
AND APPLICATIONS

CONTEXT

The two major problems in Catholic schooling are identity and viability. They are closely related. Both require "clear and positive thinking, courage, perseverance and cooperation."[1] The problem of identity cuts to the heart of the matter: "Today, as in the past, some scholastic institutions which bear the name Catholic do not appear to correspond fully to the principles of education which should be their distinguishing feature."[2]

Catholic-school viability has always required "great cost and sacrifice [from] our forebears," and "the Catholic school is conscious of its responsibility to continue this service."[3] To help in the past were extremely dedicated clergy, religious, and laity. It was through their love, labors, and sacrifices—and their exquisite, subtle, keen sense of identity—that the Catholic school pattern in the United States, the greatest Catholic-school phenomenon in the world, was built. Today the Spirit seems to be calling some religious, all over the world, to apostolates other than teaching. About this, one Superior General wrote an honest and forthright appraisal:

> At a time when we are so relatively few in number, by comparison with the past, it seems to be important that each one would carry out those functions in the ministry that allow her to make maximum use of her giftedness in response to the greatest needs of her society; that, as far as possible, each one would be a "multiplier" rather than a "purveyor" of service. . . . We may discover that this response will no longer be ordinarily in the classroom or in the hospital ward. . . . I believe one strong call to us today is to re-

310

spond to the needs of adult development and personal growth, for communications, relational and leadership skills, for education in healthcare and preventitive [*sic*] medicine, and for the skills of pedagogy. For I believe also, that the school, the health centre of the future will be places where adults come, more often than their children, to discuss with the professional educator and health-care worker their own difficulties in educating their children at home and how to overcome these difficulties.[4]

Among the new apostolates are adult Christian formation, ecumenism, family life, ministry to the lonely and suffering, many kinds of options for the poor, and service to the unemployed, those under stress, and the elderly. With specific reference to education, some see new and different apostolic opportunities for Catholics — priests, brothers, sisters, lay people — teaching in the government schools in fields in which they are properly certified, engaging in education for social justice, or administering catechetical centers in a parish building.[5]

This shift in ministerial preference, together with other serious problems like funding, leaves the future viability of Catholic schools in question. The evidence from history shows that Catholic schools have contributed greatly to God and country; the evidence from the sciences of sociology and anthropology underline the worth of religion in education; the evidence from psychology praises the benefits of religion in personal formation. In view of this evidence, it is difficult to think of the loss of Catholic-school viability as God's will. It would seem better to cooperate with the Holy Spirit in seeking Catholic-school identity to maintain Catholic schools' viability.

A Catholic school will not remain Catholic for long without attention to its identity. A Catholic school without an identity does not become neutral: it comes under the influence of the current community ideology, or nationalism, or secularism, or faddism. Its mind and its heart then become those of a different community. Today more than ever before, unless a particular Catholic school is considering the principles that give it its Catholic identity and is trying to live by them, it does not deserve to stay in existence.

Catholic schools which adhere to their identity cannot, however, be perceived as being the sole answer to the furtherance of Catholicism and its ideals. Nevertheless, one of the ways that Catholic schools could be made truly Catholic and more effective, their worth discovered, and their future made more secure, is if they receive insights from their identity. In that connection, the material between these covers is not intended just to be put neatly into book form and forgotten about. It is to be reflected upon, discussed, and lived.

CATHOLIC EDUCATIONAL LEADERS' ASSOCIATION (CELA)

One of the conclusions that emerges from these pages is that Catholic schooling and education need true and good leadership. To know the meanings of philosophy, education, schooling, and the Catholic identity of each, requires leadership. To differentiate between the opponents' and proponents' mind-sets takes leadership. To set proper goals and get people to adhere to them and implement them demands leadership. To see to it that religion and values are meaningfully placed in the curriculum calls for leadership. To harmonize the partnership of family, Church, and State wants leadership. To create the proper atmosphere for the Catholic school, both internal and external to it, solicits leadership. To motivate teachers and involve students asks for leadership. This need applies to the highest member of the hierarchy as well as to the lowest teacher in the most remote school.

Leadership in the Catholic enterprise must be a bit different from most secular leadership. Secular leadership can, without any inherent contradiction with its principles, assert power and control, flowing from top to bottom, by using a hierarchical structure. Catholic leaders, on the other hand, must always be mindful that they are the servants, not the masters, of the People of God. Authority flows from the bottom to the top. Even when the People of God express opinions that seem opposed to opinions at the top, the people are to be viewed not as "the competition" to be defeated, but as potential collaborators working toward a common goal through negotation and compromise.

To paraphrase Sirach (5:1–10), good leaders are to eradicate the vices to which the powerful might easily fall heir: pride, independence, presumption, false security, and impenitence. The New Testament advises the good administrator to be always open to conversion and to be "trustworthy" (1 Cor. 4:2). Another word for this foundation of leadership might be "credibility." This means such qualities as honesty, competence, being forward-looking, and the ability to inspire. Trustworthiness is earned minute by minute. If not carefully tended, it can quickly be lost. Once lost, it is difficult to win back.

Ecclesiastical Indices

One new and encouraging idea for leadership formation is suggested by a post-Vatican II document that calls for the creation of "new groups, always searching for the type of association that will best respond to the needs of the times and the differing situations."[6] The 1983 Code of Canon Law speaks of

> associations distinct from the institutes of consecrated life and societies of apostolic life, in which the Christian faithful, either clergy or laity, or clergy and laity together, strive by common effort to . . . animate the temporal order with the Christian spirit.[7]

All such associations

> are to have their own statutes which define the end of the association . . . , its headquarters, its government, the conditions of membership and by whom its policies are to be determined, according to the need or utility of time and place.[8]

And they are "to choose a title or name . . . adapted to the usage of their time and place, selected especially in view of their intended purpose."[9]

What this suggests to promote Catholic-school identity is specifically the formation of an association, to be called something like the Catholic Educational Leaders' Association (CELA). The association would aim at providing ongoing formation of necessary leaders. It would purport to assure concerned Catholics that its member-educators would, without further ado, be trustworthy in any Catholic educational capacity. Everyone interested in the retention of the Catholic identity of Catholic schools could feel secure that members of the association would retain the schools' spiritual purposes, "especially those which propose to animate the temporal order with the Christian spirit and in this way greatly foster an intimate union between faith and life."[10]

Membership would be open to competent and knowledgeable men and women, religious and lay, married and single, living on their own as well as in religious houses and institutes. It would embrace laborers already in the vineyard as well as those being newly called. For membership eligibility, common-sense judgments would have to be made concerning the results of training, and examinations in subject matter—subject matter somewhat as contained in these pages. The association would admit to membership only those with the best qualities for academic achievement and active leadership.[11] Its members would be entitled to wear an aesthetically designed, dignified, distinctive badge or pin which would engender pride and respect.

Though open to teachers outside Catholic schools, this association

would be closely connected with the Church, in accordance with ecclesiastical definitions and characteristics. It would by its nature be
public rather than private.[12] For simplicity of organization and facility
of working out details, we propose that it begin on a diocesan level
with an interested and sympathetic bishop and, when flaws have been
eliminated and the association proven successful, that it grow region-
ally, and eventually nationally or even internationally.

CELA would not compete with existing associations, like the National Catholic Educational Association (NCEA) or any of its specialized departments like the Chief Administrators of Catholic Education
(CACE) or the Supervision, Curriculum and Personnel (SPC) group,
or any other. CELA is not administrative, has entirely different purposes, and fills a need that is not now met. Should a superintendent
want a teacher, CELA certification tells him something. Should a
bishop, pastor, religious superior, or other head of a Catholic school
have to abandon a Catholic school and want it to retain its identity,
members of CELA could be available to help. These examples could
be multiplied.

Membership Requirements

Ecclesiastical

An important requirement is that one "who has publicly rejected
the Catholic faith or abandoned ecclesiastical communion or been
punished with an imposed or declared excommunication cannot be
validly received into public associations."[13] All others are admissible,
provided they also have an understanding of and a sympathy with the
Church's creed and her positions in education as outlined in courses
under appropriate ecclesiastical jurisdiction or in approved texts. Ju-
dicious examination and compassionate discussion should ascertain
fulfillment.

Ecclesiastical training must be "many-sided and complete" and
must supplement "the education common to all Christians, . . . specific and individual . . . by reason of the diversity of persons and
circumstances."[14] It must be "an integral human education" that brings
it about that the member

> learn to accomplish the mission of Christ and the Church, living
> by faith . . . , moved by the Holy Spirit. . . . Besides spiritual
> formation, solid grounding in doctrine is required: in theology,
> ethics and philosophy, at least, proportioned to the age, condition,
> and abilities of each one.[15]

Members must be trained to see all things in the light of faith and to improve and perfect themselves by working with others. Training for this apostolate cannot consist in theoretical teaching alone. Members' education "should be steadily perfected; it requires an ever more thorough knowledge and a continual adaptation of action."[16]

Professional

One of the reasons for current criticisms of educators and one of the reasons why educators do not proceed apace from mere schoolkeeping to true professionalism is the lack of professional qualities among some members (at times the most vocal), in both aptitude and academic achievement. CELA must at all times deal only with aspirants who are capable. Capability in this instance means, to begin with, being academically above average: a cumulative grade-point score above 3.0 on a 4.0 scale at the college level, or a minimum combined score (verbal and quantitative) of 1200 on the Graduate Record Examination, or a minimum of 60 on the Miller's Analogies Examination. Intellectually outstanding people should be identified as early as possible and encouraged. Those who aspire to membership in the association must be well-qualified by local secular standards as well as by the association's standards.

Because the secular and the Catholic levels of qualification entail many intertwined facets, professionalism entails all the disciplines from which education derives benefit: philosophy, theology, sociology, psychology, history, and anthropology, to name a few. Courses in the philosophy of education would inform candidates of such areas as the consequences of specific modes of thinking, where the modern mind is, and how the Catholic mind differs and why. Philosophy would present theory, which would deal with, among other things, epistemology and theories of truth as they relate to the curriculum.

Through study of the history of education, the student would learn the relation between religion and education in the past, including theological influences on and from the still-very-influential John Dewey, the basic thought of educational reformers, and the theological as well as other factors at work in educational progress. Also important is patristic thought; the basic concepts of scholastic theology, especially Thomas Aquinas; the thought of the Protestant reformers, especially Luther and Calvin, and the Catholic response, especially of the Jesuits. An absolute "must" is a familiarization with the Catholic experience in the country in which the Catholic educator will work. This area would also include comparative education, for all of the learning experiences which this field offers.

The study of the psychology of education would impart a knowledge of child development, including the spiritual and moral, to indicate what to expect realistically and how to educate at specific chronological ages; the psychology of religion and religious experience; counseling principles and techniques; evaluative skills; and group dynamics. Allied areas would teach what the curriculum of the Western world looked upon as essential for about two thousand years: communication theories and skills, and developing creative potential (imaginative and aesthetic abilities).

The sociology of education would expose the candidate to many important questions. In the area of secularization, for example, there are the questions of the nature of the Christian presence within a secular system and the nature of Church-State relations. Under social revolution and the school, the curriculum would treat such concepts as deschooling, progressive education, roles and responsibilities through change, and political theology. This area would also present an understanding of culture and the social context of learning. In the area of politics, the student would be introduced to choices between the principles of such as Aristotle, the New Testament, and Machiavelli.

The very rich area of contemporary theology would, of course, be paramount. Students would gain the insights derived from systematic theology. They would become familiar with the implications of the idea of God for schooling and education. They would face questions like the relationship between divine revelation and human education. Students would be familiarized with the revelatory nature of all creation. Theological questions about humankind's destiny and nature, sin, punishment, and so on, are perhaps the most crucial of all. The relevance of people like Karl Barth, Martin Buber, Søren Kierkegaard, Bernard Lonergan, Karl Rahner, Friedrich Schleiermacher, Paul Tillich, and others would also have to be presented.

In the tremendously important area of Christology, there is the meaning of the lordship of Jesus for the Christian in education, to what extent the image of humankind underlying education should be molded by the image of Christ, and the meanings and implications of incarnation and atonement. In ecclesiology, there is the nature of the Church, upon which so much in schooling and education depends (as these pages have tried to show), the nature of the Church's mission in education, the educational value of the liturgy and the sacraments, and Christian community. In eschatology, the student would learn the consequences of a theology of hope for education.

Biblical theology is also important and relevant, teaching the thinking on education in the Old and New Testaments. An ecumenical presentation of confessional theology would also be included: Judaism and its rich contributions to schooling and education, Catholicism (including Jacques Maritain, the Vatican II documents, and the like), and Protestantism (especially those who have been involved in schooling, like the Lutherans, Quakers, and evangelicals). The subject of theology would also include spirituality and prayer experience—penance as a formational sacrament, the practical dimension of human relationships and of personal human development, and the work of the Spirit in the teacher and pupil.

Though the nature of the situation prevents curricula from being rigid, the association's standards would not be expected to change quite as much as secular standards from time to time or place to place. At the end of their formal schooling, members would undergo a one-year apprenticeship period, with a reduced class load and support from a mentor. Candidates would undergo "certification" and "licensing" based upon their individual performance as well as courses taken.

There would be updating through meetings and other methods. Members would keep themselves familiar with current research, qualitative as well as quantative, regarding theory as well as practical methodology. This familiarity means being acquainted with the thought processes of educators as well as of students, and the whole gamut of methods of discourse, the use of the media, and creative techniques. It goes from the social and institutional context of teaching, through adaptive techniques, to differences among learners, to specific subjects and grade levels.

Candidates would pass subject-matter tests upon entry and three quinquennial updating subject-matter tests thereafter. They would have annual evaluations, constructed for purposes of improvement in professional performance and personal growth. In all of this there should be peer assistance as well as peer review, keeping in mind charity on all sides, so that there would be neither overbearingness on the part of reviewers nor immature dependence on the part of reviewees.

There is to be no toleration of stopgap measures, like having a teacher who is certified for English teaching mathematics. There would be time allocations for work with parents, politicians, and local communities, both civil and ecclesiastical, in matters which have to do with schooling and education. Members would involve themselves in policy formation and decision making, in which all would have not only a voice but a vote. To support notices, newsletters, consultations, residences, research, and other reasonable expenses, there would be dues to the association, grants, contributions, and whatever other resources could be encouraged. Benefits from financial support would accrue to members in such terms as work toward elevated standards for all members, public representation of which would make all proud and from which all would benefit.

Personal

On a personal level, members would demonstrate self-discipline, manifested in such ways as deportment, clothing, and speech. They would manifest a mature ability to live with ambiguities and uncertainties. They would have qualities of optimism, joy in life and work, an inclination to curiosity, adventure, human understanding, and the service of others. They would have a high respect for the integrity of their vocation. They would have an outgoingness that makes easier the art of living and working on friendly terms with other people and entering into dialogue with them. They would develop that very important requirement for education, patience.

All these and other qualities would be cloaked with charity—true and profound Christian love. For spiritual sustenance, members would at least frequent the Sacraments regularly and perhaps belong to a spiritual association that would give direction and opportunities for spiritual growth such as an annual retreat.

SUMMARY OF THE BELIEFS OF CELA MEMBERS AND OTHER CATHOLIC EDUCATORS

From their personal propensities, aptitude, and training, members of the association—and, indeed, all who are interested in Catholic education—will lean toward most, if not all, of the properties of Catholic education. We summarize them here in the order in which they are discussed in this book.

Opponents' and Proponents' Mind-Sets

To be effective, all Catholic educators, and especially leaders, must be familiar with the mind-sets of both their opponents and their supporters (see chapters 2 and 3). The minds of many who are opposed to Catholic schools have been influenced, without blame, by some of the less inspiring aspects of United States history, by philosophical backgrounds opposed to what Catholicism stands for, and by some theories of personal formation. These influences are pervasive in our society.

Although Catholicism does not align itself inextricably with any one culture, ideology, or philosophy, and tries to be acceptable to all people of all times, it must nevertheless have a language in which to be heard. The New Testament adopted acceptable philosophies in its time, and we do the same. Today, moderate Realism, classical Idealism, and theistic Existentialism provide substantial roots for Catholic philosophies of education and schooling. But the thinking is not static.

While, for example, the 1929 encyclical *The Christian Education of Youth* reflected Realism, Vatican II's 1965 *Declaration on Christian Education* and subsequent documents have been more open to other philosophies.

The philosophical emphases of the Catholic mind-set nevertheless continue to focus on such elements as the objective nature of truth, the primacy of the spiritual over the material, the ultimate triumph of good over evil, Christian ideals and values, the realization of the self in the context of a relationship with the Ultimate Being, aliveness to all the anguish and care of existence, passionate concern, full commitment to life, true responsibility, the use of the humanities as a vehicle to present the problems of humankind, emphasis on personal conversion, and belief in the greatness as well as the uniqueness of the person.

Goals

We speak in these pages of goals rather than of aims and objectives, because of the connotations of goals in athletics: specific, taken seriously, prepared for, worked at, sacrificed for, and sweated over. Granting local cultural specifics, Catholic educators participate in the formulation of goals that are detailed, close, meaningful, and more than "motherhood" statements. They answer ultimate questions like "why?" and they look for "shoulds." Catholic schools, an expression of the mission of Christianity, receive their goals from such sources as the New Testament (for example, *metamorphosis* and *metanoia*) and the tradition of humanism. The shared process as well as the result of formulating goals can have many beneficial results, not the least of which is to establish a sense of community and to provide a vision that will be lived and will unite.

Catholic-school goal clusters are consonant with the best of the humanist heritage and of the United States' foundations; they establish a relationship of trust with the institutional Church, can vary from time to time and place to place and school level to school level, and aim at total student wellness. They center around the person's union with God, include a social dimension, and embrace the spiritual, intellectual, affective, moral, and physical dimensions of the self. Throughout, Catholic-school goals have Jesus as their model.

The *general* goals of Catholic education (see chapter 4) are threefold, but inseparably one: the message revealed by God (*didache*); fellowship in the life of the Holy Spirit (*koinonia*); and service to the Christian community (*diakonia*). Subsets include teaching pupils "to discern in the sound of the universe the creator whom it reveals,"[17] and are consequently entwined with worship. The Catholic educator wants to teach that knowledge "is not to be considered as a means of material prosperity and success, but as a call to serve and to be responsible for others."[18]

The Catholic educator also aspires to foster "the development of man from within, freeing him from that conditioning which would prevent him from becoming a fully integrated human being."[19] The Catholic educator, consonant with the level of the school, trains students to give "joint Christian witness to the contemporary world" with other Christians.[20] Further, Catholic schools aspire to develop students "in wisdom, which gently draws the human mind to look for and to love what is true and good."[21] A stupendous goal, when one considers its potential, is to teach "that the fundamental law of human perfection, and consequently of the transformation of the world, is the new commandment of love."[22]

Allied with that is the overriding goal to introduce students to Christ, who "is not merely the greatest of the prophets . . . [He is] the last event, focus of all the events of the history of salvation, the completion and the manifestation of God's final plans."[23] And the Catholic educator wants to form "in the Christian those particular virtues which will enable him to live a new life in Christ and help him to play faithfully his part in building up the kingdom of God"[24]—in brief, "the complete Christian formation of pupils."[25]

In that connection, the Catholic educator wants to "facilitate and stimulate interior activity [of] . . . the act of faith [which] necessarily involves a person's conversion."[26] And that requires "a synthesis of culture and faith, and a synthesis of faith and life."[27] In short, Catholic education aims at nothing less than holiness: the *metanoia*, or change of heart, of which the New Testament speaks.

Taking into account time, place, and level of schooling, the formulation of specific goals should consider such factors as the definition of an "educated" person, the meaning of Christian character, the pertinence of the Christian faith to all forms of human inquiry, and the relevancy of ultimate goals to the good of the communities and societies of which students are members and in whose responsibilities they share. Once goals have been formulated, all who will be touched by the enterprise should support them with "unity of purpose and conviction."[28]

Looking outward in openness to the situation of humankind on the various levels of communal and societal reality, Catholic educators will want to serve the contemporary needs of the Church and society. Their school will be "a place of integral formation by means of a systematic and critical assimilation of culture."[29] Catholic educational leaders will play their part in the daily purification and renewal of the

Church.[30] The schooling they support, far from having a narrow vision, will provide an interest in improving the circumstances of the world: they will prepare pupils "to contribute effectively to the welfare of the world of men and to work for the extension of the Kingdom of God."[31]

Toward this end they will prepare students, by the example of their lives and the witness of the Word, to bring the presence of the Church to those groups who have never, or barely, heard the Gospel message.[32] They will intend "not only to bring men the message and grace of Christ but also to permeate and improve the whole range of the temporal."[33] They will therefore train students "to interest themselves, and collaborate with others, in the right ordering of social and economic affairs."[34]

Curriculum

Catholic educators are interested in a curriculum (chapter 5) that will implement these goals. The two major qualities that differentiate the Catholic-school curriculum from others are the importance it openly accords to religion and its unique presentation of values. Education is essentially religious in many ways. It is by nature moral, for example, because it has to do with defining the good—the good person, the good life, the good society. Also, both religion and education deal with the underlying nature of reality. Lastly, Catholicism is an historically proven counterbalance to self-centered pride, self-serving ideologies, materialism, relativism, and excessive rationalism.

The Catholic school not only teaches *about* religion, but imparts commitment and provides Christian *witness*. This kind of inclusion of the Roman Catholic religion is a contribution not only to its students, but also to the community and the nation. The ways in which religion should best be present in the curriculum, however, are not as simple as some might think.

Personal formation in the values taught in the Catholic school is especially important, again to both community and nation, in our time of crisis in the absence of values. Like religion, their inclusion in the curriculum is not as uncomplicated as it may at first seem. Nevertheless, the Catholic school assists students to choose, prize, cherish, and act upon Judeo-Christian values. It integrates those values into contemporary life and work.

Agents and Co-Partners

The primary agents of education are God and the self-activity of the student. The secondary agents, co-principals, or partners are the family, the Church, and the State. Catholic educators should be aware of all the principles, discussions, and history involved in Catholic positions on the relationships among all of them (chapters 6 and 7).

The nuclear family — married parents and their progeny — comes first not only chronologically, but also in the order of priority. This God-ordained institution, this "domestic church," this basic unit of society, this first school forms the earliest, deepest, and most persistent influence on a person's subsequent behavior, value judgments, and life decisions. The family's role and responsibilities have to do with their begetting life — not only physical, but also spiritual. Except for cases of neglect, abuse, a rejecting circumstance, or any combination thereof, parental rights can neither be usurped nor surrendered. The basic element in parents' educational duty is love, which engenders self-esteem and proper self-love on the part of their children, from which can arise fulfillment of the basic Christian law of love of God and neighbor. The Catholic family forms a loving community of persons, serves life, participates in the development of society, and shares in the life and mission of the Church.

Because people follow witnesses more readily than formal teachers and because children need beacon personalities, Christian parenthood is a serious obligation. Parents should be given training in parenting, in home-school cooperation, and, while preserving child autonomy, in ways to bring their children up with religion in a secularist society. The Christian family is at the heart of the Church's mission to exemplify God's love for His children.

Catholic educators' realization that the priority of rights lies with the family should result, first, in sympathy for parents of children in Catholic schools for the mammoth financial sacrifice they have undertaken in behalf of their children before a quasi-hostile State and a largely indifferent culture. It should result, second, in a sincere desire to work closely with parents, to the extent of even compulsory meetings with them on a regular basis. The purpose of such meetings would be to familiarize the parents with their rights, obligations, and best ways to cooperate, and to acquaint the educators with family backgrounds. From this will come a multiplier effect for the best education of youth.

The Church is important to any consideration of Catholic schooling and education. The New Testament refers to this important sacrament of Christ among us in such terms as the mystical body of Christ, Christ's spotless bride, and the pillar and bulwark of truth. To describe the Church, the New Testament also uses the images of sheepfold, flock, cultivated field, edifice, and mother. Our day also uses "models" of the Church, none complete of itself: saving institution, mystical communion, sacrament, herald, servant.

The Church is hierarchical, entailing authority and obedience but not superiority and subjection for their own sake. Proclaiming the Gospel of Christ is one of the principal duties of bishops. Priests derive their authority from the bishop. Because baptism unites the faithful with their heavenly king, the laity's share in the common priesthood is rightly called a "royal priesthood." The laity help constitute the Church as community, as people of God, and as celebrants of the Good News.

In the particular Catholic school, the local Church—parish, religious community, or whatever—is the sponsoring organization. The local Church is the reason why the school came into existence, why the school is rooted in Catholic Christianity, and why it remains a Catholic Christian school. The local Church continuously gives the Catholic school the richness of the Christian tradition, exerts its ongoing good influence without interfering with its autonomy, is the speculative model of the Christian community and the practical model of the living faith community, interfaces with the school in a way in which the strengths of each minister to the others' weaknesses, and is a wise and compassionate mediator between the school and the Church at large.

The Church has both rights and duties in schooling and education. The Church has rights because people have a spiritual nature as well as a physical one, because of social justice, because of the need for the complete betterment of human life, and because of education's being essentially a moral enterprise dealing with the "good person," the "good life," and the "good society." Intertwined with it all is the Church's perception of herself as a loving mother. That the Church takes seriously her duties to schooling is reflected in Church legislation.

Catholic schools offer advantages to the State, individuals, society, human activity, and peace. Ideally, they offer an educational alternative for youth; provide wholesome cooperation competition with government schools; facilitate high-quality education; can be a source of commitment, direction, and vigor to the community of humankind; and offer to human activity a proper and beneficial mean between otherworldly faith and immersion in earthly endeavors, and between the faith which many profess and the practice of their daily lives. For individuals, they offer meaning to life, teachings that elevate the dignity of human nature, proclamations of the rights of humankind, and a presentation of truths of the moral order. The Catholic school, under the auspices and complements of the Church, and with no desire for power, wants to educate children toward the most elevated concrete ideal possible: Jesus Christ and his evangelical message.

The State, comprising both society and government plus sovereignty, also has rights and duties in schooling and education. But the State should not be, as current trends seem to indicate, the sole, or even the dominant, agent of schooling and education. The confused, chaotic, and mutually contradictory decisions of the U.S. Supreme Court contravene Judeo-Christian historical and philosophical perspectives, deny substantive Church rights beyond Church-school existence, make possible government monopoly over schools, and prevent meaningful parental choice.

The Catholic Church favors true parental choice of schooling, because it avoids any suggestion that the child is the mere creature of the State, avoids any debasing ideology which can turn schools into instruments of political power, is a right due to parents in distributive justice, and provides to all human beings the fundamental right to their own culture. True choice fosters greater satisfaction, involvement, and enrichment for families; is inherently instructive; through its market influences can help teachers and administrators; substitutes parental love for State custodial care; communicates to children the State's endorsement of their parents; and provides decision-making ability, already possessed by the rich, to the poor.

Aside from currently existing public-parochial schools, the two most widely proclaimed methods of achieving true choice in schooling are vouchers and tuition tax credits. Vouchers in this sense are certificates given to parents to pay for tuition or other costs at any eligible government or non-government school, religious or secular, within or outside the student's school district. Tuition tax credit is a procedure whereby income-tax-paying parents receive a credit from their income tax for an agreed-upon amount for each of their children's tuition, no matter what school their children attend, with non-income-tax-paying poor parents receiving an enabling fee for the same purpose.

Among the arguments for government financial help to nongovernment schools are the American principle of citizen sovereignty, beneficial competition among schools, the streamlining of bureaucracy, and the enabling of Catholic and other nongovernment schools to contribute to a more just society. Among the greatest dangers of government aid is the idea that "he who pays the piper calls the tune," a principle which if exercised wrongly could destroy Catholic schools' identity.

Government legislatures often stand against the important role which the Catholic Church accords to family life: in income-tax law, for example, and nonsupport of mothers who want to devote their energies to the care of their young children. Though some recent judicial opinions on the First Amendment's establishment clause provide hope for what seems to be an "accommodation" of religion, there is no telling what direction they will take in the future. Current values in deciding Church-State issues in schooling are neutrality, religious accommodation, and guarantees of Church-State separation and of lack of entanglement between Church and State. The United States is the only country in the Western world that deliberately excludes organized religion from its schooling. The situation is different in other democratic countries, even those which have copied the U.S. Constitution.

What to do about government usurpations of individual, family, and Church rights involves, at an initial minimum, instruction in the rights of the family and the Church, encouragement of these two partners, and familiarization with the realities of life in our republic. The last includes knowledge of the dignity of the person as noted in, among other places, the founding documents of the United States, and in the nature and values of religion, whose importance to this Republic was observed early on. It also includes firm belief in and action upon the court dictum cited in our text (*Hannan v. Dusch*): "The law helps those who help themselves, generally aids the vigilant, but rarely the sleeping, and never the acquiescent."

Catholics should create a climate for the U.S. Supreme Court to act. The Court *does* listen to the election returns. In addition to theories that have already brought favorable results, like "child benefit," good lawyers should constantly bring forth creative theories. Blacks gave a good model for Catholics in their careful and astute legal preparations for the Supreme Court's 1954 *Brown* decision, which declared that separate facilities for blacks are inherently unequal, thus overturning the 1896 *Plessy* decision which declared the constitutionality of "separate but equal" facilities.

There are many bases on which to build a proper climate, especially in the courts, for the equal financial treatment of Catholic schools with government schools. The benefits of Catholic schools to the general welfare are civic contributions. "Public-parochial" schools, for example, comprise plans which provide that public taxes pay for the major part of parochial school funding, especially teacher salaries and building maintenance, while Catholics run the schools. Historically, these plans have existed for generations, to the happiness of local communities, parents, students, teachers, and others. They still exist in many places.

Perhaps Catholics have not put their best foot forward. For one thing, Catholics should be aware of the gospel justification for Christian indignation: Christianity does not mean a doormat humility, as Christ showed in putting his whip to the money changers in the temple. For another thing, the Catholic laity cannot rely upon the hierarchy to do this work for them; the historical situation in which that took place can no longer exist, for a variety of reasons, and should not.

An interested laity will support Catholic-school needs, not the least of which is for more research. Research might address such areas as the extent to which current Catholic-school goals reflect the Church's mission, the question of curricular design meeting stated goals, areas of curriculum development in which Catholic schools can and should lead all other schools, the degrees of freedom permissible by the Church, the extent to which Catholic schools can be flexible or must remain firm, optimal hierarchies of goals for stated times and places, the implications of specifically Catholic educational leadership, modes of funding and finance, and constitutional and other legal issues relevant to Catholic schools.

Other possibilities for research are Catholic-school potential in an alien or even hostile culture, cultural determinants and opportunities, prudent directions for effective governmental action on behalf of justice for Catholic schools, degrees of cooperation between Catholic schools and government and other schools, procedures to help family life, the ways in which Catholic university departments and schools of education can help the Catholic-school enterprise, the ways in which Catholic-school graduates compare with those of other schools, Catholic-school teacher values, religion's role in education, innovative procedures — and many, many more.

The challenge and cooperation of government schools, church-affiliated schools, and others, are necessary for the good of "a nation at risk," whose "once unchallenged preeminence in commerce, industry, science, and technological innovation is being overtaken by competitors throughout the world."[35] Comprehending the proper definitions and roles of the family, Church, and State as partners in education should enable every good-willed person to see in the Catholic school "an irreplaceable source of service, not only to the pupils and its other members, but also to society."[36] The Catholic school by its Christian presence serves the academic world by presenting the enriching power of faith to humankind's enormous problems. It serves the faith by benefiting the human family. For church-affiliated schools to fight for their unused constitutional rights would be like the fall of a stone into still water: it has ever-widening implications.

The Atmosphere

Christians are bound by their dignity as Christians to help elevate the atmosphere or conditions of schooling and education (chapter 8). The external atmosphere comprises the economic, political, cultural, and social structures in which the school finds itself. With these, insofar as they affect the schools, Christians should do all in their power to bring about virtue, with an emphasis on justice in the economic structure, peace in the political structure, morality in the cultural structure, and love in the social structure.

Catholic educators are especially interested in the conditions internal to the schools (sometimes called the school's culture). Both the physical and the spiritual atmosphere are the field of concern, but especially the spiritual, because the medium is often the message. This spiritual atmosphere will be a marriage of the secular and the sacred, of the contemplative and the active, of the individual and the community. It will provide a form of precatechesis, a preparation for the school's formal program of education in the faith.

The spiritual atmosphere of the Catholic school will result from the professional, theological and personal competency of all staff; a climate of respect, mutual aid, and evangelical joy; an enlivened Gospel spirit of charity and liberty; the principles of subsidiarity and collegiality; and the practice of cooperation, participation, and coresponsibility. There will be communal public worship, which will be a channel of grace, and the integration of grace with freedom. Overall there will be a spirit of community, which alone makes possible the kind of sharing that is necessary for a school to be truly Catholic. With all these qualities, there is a commitment to Christ as the center.

Those in control in a major way—hierarchy, administrators, teachers, and staff—ideally will try to lead Catholic schools in these directions. The institutional Church must live up to her many encyclicals about personnel. This means just wages guaranteed by contract, the granting of due dignity, obviating the necessity of outside work, providing just working conditions, granting social security, putting in place a system for promotion, making collective bargaining possible, and granting without difficulty the right to join unions.

The hierarchy will be mindful of community, subsidiarity, and collegiality, and will encourage genuine communication and mutual respect. Administrators, especially principals, will try to complete the teachers' work, always demonstrating balance, a sense of responsibility, wisdom in all things including the spending of money, proper priorities, openness to rethinking and re-creating, and awareness of the need to develop community. Teachers, recognizing that the quality of learning will depend on the quality of teaching, will develop themselves professionally, personally, and religiously to the fullest.

Those in control in a lesser way—including the students—must be encouraged to be active participants in the Christian community that is the Catholic school, and should be able to find there a climate which complements the Catholic home. An important part of that environment is morale, which is an inner confidence held by staff and students in each other and a mutual faith between them which leads to identification with the school. It is built by a cooperative striving by students and staff toward shared vital goals.

The good Catholic school will not be afraid to take advantage of its freedom from political and other interference to go into new areas. Two important areas of such experimentation today are ecumenical schools and completely lay-run Catholic schools. Each has its own dangers to avoid—the retention of faith identity in the ecumenical schools, and overindependence in lay schools so that "trusteeism" is not revisited.

Teachers

Teachers (chapter 9) are important. Catholic teachers guide youth toward eternal realities, and no one can tell where the teacher's influence ends. Teachers personify the integration of culture and faith and faith and life which they impart. Christ-like, they represent their individual incarnational model. They effectuate a union of the Catholic school with the local Church. Historically, they are in the tradition of the New Testament: Jesus the teacher, the apostles' ministry, and St. Paul's inheritance of the Jews' tremendous respect for teaching. They share with the noble tradition of the early Church and with the history of Christianity their love of learning, their desire for God, and their preservation of culture and civilization.

Many dispute whether teaching is a profession. For a profession to exist, specific criteria apply. A true profession engages, for example, a way of work based upon a mastery of a body of specialized knowledge. The mastery of knowledge—any knowledge—is difficult, and (to the extent that teaching entails a special body of knowledge) will also make successful entry into teaching difficult. To approach proper professionalism, changes in the curricula of schools of education and the strengthening of certification requirements will not of themselves be enough. Teachers must themselves *aspire* to learn, and this aspiration must be a lifetime commitment.

At the center of any profession is a paradigm of usefulness, usually to a weaker party, with whom the professional has a fiduciary relationship in return for necessary access to intimate dimensions of the other's existence. In this connection, professionals autonomously and collectively establish the standards for their work. They take an oath to abide by these standards and can be disciplined by fellow professionals for failing to do so. And they are paid for service rather than by salary, so that they are easily able to fulfill their obligation to advise their clients about what is best for them to do, as distinguished from what the clients may themselves wish to do. In some of those senses, teaching may never become a profession.

Prescinding from that debate, Catholics see in teaching a noble vocation that calls for detachment, a commitment that avoids sermonizing, generosity, concern for truth and justice, breadth of vision, a habitual spirit of service, fraternal solidarity, and total moral integrity. Because the standards are high and the demands difficult, many, including religious, are leaving the school apostolate.

Good Catholic teachers are sensitive about their obligations to students, to parents, to the community, and to colleagues. With their students, Catholic teachers strive not only for a meeting of minds, but for a personal relationship. This entails mutual respect, sensitivity, sympathy, concern, some degree of self-revelation, dialogue, trust, openness, and warm and congenial contact. Good Catholic teachers welcome and encourage opportunities for contact with parents, respect parental rights, meaningfully cooperate with parents, and keep parents informed. Catholic teachers must realize their responsibility to the community, especially the local community of faith. It is also essential that Catholic teachers be supportive of colleagues: working together as a team, being active in professional organizations, participating in retreats, and sensitive to the need for continuing education.

To form such high-caliber teachers requires special care. Formation should be a happy blend of professional training, progress in the faith, and personal growth. Professional training will take for granted proficiency in such areas as language, art, literature, mathematics, and science, and ability in thinking, reasoning, and understanding. The formation should be in a wide range of cultural, psychological, and pedagogical areas in accordance with the discoveries of modern times.

The Catholic teacher's faith dimension begins with the awareness that philosophies of life are very much intertwined with schoolwork and contributory to Catholic identity. The Catholic teacher must have a synthesis of faith, culture, and life, and be alert for opportunities for witness to faith. Retreats, prayer, sharing, service, follow-up services, and other exercises should inculcate habits of reflection, deepening faith, and commitment to the Church.

The personal growth expected of Catholic teachers begins with psychological and spiritual maturity, which is an added aspect that recognizes the need for a philosophy of life and of education. Conduct is important, too, giving students an example of Christian behavior that includes participation in the liturgical and sacramental life of the school and of the Church. In the face of the constant change which is a fact of modern life, good Catholic teachers will continuously update themselves. In the thicket of problems in teacher certification and evaluation, Catholic teachers try to develop qualities which will leave no doubt of competence.

Preeminent among Catholic-school teachers is the teacher of religion, the subject area that is the *raison d'etre* of Catholic schools. Religion teachers must share to a supreme degree the qualities that describe all good teachers: that they be informed, practical, challenging, interesting, addicted to learning, animators rather than dictators, caring, trusting, aware of student potential, encouraging, imaginative, adaptable, and infectiously optimistic and enthusiastic. They are to be persons of faith, with a deep personal prayer life and unquestioned Christian virtue. They are to correct but not to judge, to interpret the world in the light of Christ's revelation, and to introduce young people to Jesus.

It goes without saying that religion teachers should have appropriate graduate degrees in the human sciences, but especially in religious pedagogy. For greater credibility with students as well as for balance in the demands of teaching religion, they should probably teach another subject as well as religion. For greater competence, they should collaborate with a mentor or colleague to optimize instruction. To alleviate stress, they must be mature enough to fend off criticisms of their not measuring up to the impossible expectations and unreasonable demands made of them.

The "master teacher" is the principal. The role expectations of principals are as demanding as those of religion teachers. Among them are that they be instructional leaders; good managers of time and resources; communicators; observers and evaluators of staff; creators of the school's climate; and leaders in the setting and achievement of goals, school-community relations, discipline, and teacher support. Principals must have a clear vision of the Catholic school's identity, because confused ideas in that matter provide poor leadership, shaky ad hoc decisions, confusion, and stress. Their qualifications will be spiritual, pastoral, professional, and personal—all tinged with a Catholic perspective. They must relate well with higher administration as well as with teachers, staff, parents, and students.

Students

In many ways intertwined in the entire Catholic-school enterprise is its end, purpose, and center: the student (chapter 10). Since the time of Jesus, who showed a reverence and a solicitude for the human person which nobody has ever shown before or since, Catholics see the person, and hence the student, as having a dignity greater than all the rest of God's vast creation. In a good Catholic-school setting, the student experiences his dignity as a person before he knows the definition of the concept.

In Catholic thought, though the superdignity of personhood flows from one's entire being, it is perceived especially in intellect, will, and body. Catholic schools are to help students "to develop harmoniously their physical, moral and intellectual qualities."[37] The intellect shares preeminently in this superdignity because it has as its object the achievement of truth and of wisdom; the will because it invests one with the responsibilities of freedom and love; and the body because it is in substantial unity with the soul, is created by God, and has a worth that is confirmed by Jesus' incarnation. Catholic youth should be encouraged to develop their unique new dignity as persons

> which they put on in baptism, and to reveal the power of the Holy Spirit by whom they were strengthened at confirmation, so that others, seeing their good works, might glorify the Father and more perfectly perceive the true meaning of human life and the universal solidarity of mankind.[38]

Faith tells the Catholic that what raises one to the highest dignity of personhood is grace, the call to share in God's own nature. Grace acts through nature, and does not contradict it. Grace's being of the supernatural order does not make it something added to the top of nature like cream on milk, but of the sacred order that permeates the natural, each intertwined with the other as one organic whole. Grace brings human nature to perfection. The life of grace is therefore an aspect of Catholic-school education.

Catholic schools want their graduates to "hold on to and perfect in their lives" their privilege of being children of God, working toward the fullness of Christian life, and striving for the perfection of love.[39] They are to follow Christ in being "poor, humble and cross-bearing, that they may deserve to be partakers of his glory."[40] Catholic schools are to stimulate youth "to make sound moral judgments based on a well-formed conscience and to put them into practice with a sense of personal commitment."[41]

Catholic schools are to "draw out the ethical dimension for the precise purpose of arousing the individual's inner spiritual dynamism and to aid his achieving that moral freedom which complements the psychological."[42] They should be developing people for a desparate need of our age: "men and women not only of high culture but of great personality as well."[43] They are to "develop persons who are responsible and innerdirected, capable of choosing freely in conformity with their conscience"—that is, to teach youth "to open themselves up to life as it is, and to create in themselves a definite attitude of life as it should be."[44]

Because of the Catholic-school view of the dignity of each student, an area in which we have a right to look for great things in Catholic schools is discipline. The word is from *discipulus*, which has the same root as the word for a follower of Jesus. The theological factors behind discipline involve such concepts as redemption and formation. This means that Catholic schools should look upon their students with higher aspirations than discipline as mere punishment. In the age-old controversy of the use of fear or love, Machiavelli and his followers opt for fear. Catholic-school teachers ineluctably choose love, and make their students understand why.

Psychological theories show the stages of individual growth and development—infancy, childhood, preadolescence, adolescence, and all the stages of adulthood—insight into which is important because religious growth can take place only commensurate with the readiness of each period. And many personality theories admit of the Christian religion being an important integrative and perfective power for personality. Gordon W. Allport said of religion that it provides the forward intention that enables people at each stage of their becoming to relate themselves meaningfully to the totality of Being.

Because the individual does not live alone, but coexists with others, there are inevitable individual-community tensions. The New Testament's attribution of Isaiah's Suffering Servant passages[45] to Jesus reminds the Catholic that how to live in the world community is exemplified in Jesus: an individual who takes upon himself the sins of the world, one who is allied yet alone. Students must be made to realize their individuality and separateness from all that is around them, but at the same time to realize their relationship to the universe, to nature, and to other people—the last especially as a member of one immense body in the charity of Christ.

A Christian view means an awareness of "mutual respect for the full spiritual dignity of men as persons."[46] It means making students aware of the "obligation on the part of the sons of God to treat each other as brothers."[47] It implies each man's duty to safeguard the notion of the human person as a totality in which predominate values of intellect, will, conscience, and brotherhood, since these values were established by the creator and wondrously restored and elevated by Christ.[48]

The Christian view of the person therefore acknowledges the duty to impart a "firm determination to respect the dignity of other men and other peoples along with the deliberate practice of fraternal love [which] are absolutely necessary for the achievement of peace."[49]

Catholic schools embrace underprivileged students of all faiths and of none — the *anawim* about whom the Scriptures speak. With roots in the Hebrew Scriptures, this dignity finds a new and higher expression in Jesus' words and example, and continues today. It includes women, for whose equality Jesus defied the customs of his time and with whom his public conduct was considered radical. It includes non-Catholic students, before whom the Church allows her teaching to speak for itself. It includes the handicapped of all kinds, among whom Jesus gave an example of special care, for whom the early Church was so solicitous, and with whom the Catholic school must do all that its resources will allow.

In brief, with respect to the student, Catholic schools' intention is nothing less than the student's Christian *metamorphosis*, in contrast with the lesser *morphosis* that is the vision of many other schools. This is, in effect, nothing less than a call to holiness.[50]

THE LAST WORD

It is a pity that the U.S. public does not have a better understanding of the the component parts of Catholic-school identity: the mind-sets of all its citizens, the mighty contributions of Catholic-school goals and outcomes to the commonwealth, religion and values in schooling and education, the roles of family and Church in schooling, the spiritual atmosphere of Catholic schools, the great work of teachers, and the Catholic-school view of the superdignity of its students. Catholics, educated to the long view, are mindful of Pope John Paul II's beautiful words about God's help overcoming all:

> The Spirit is . . . promised to the Church and to each Christian as a Teacher within, who, in the secret of the conscience and the heart, makes one understand what one has heard but was not capable of grasping: "Even now the Holy Spirit teaches the faithful," said Saint Augustine in this regard, "in accordance with each one's spiritual capacity. And he sets their hearts aflame with greater desire according as each one progresses in the charity that

makes him love what he already knows and desire what he has yet to know."[51]

In the United States of America, the identity of the Catholic school is singularly consonant with and helpful to the ideals that characterized colonial America, inspired the Declaration of Independence, sustained the early Republic, and remains a choice way to maintain the best of this great nation. Catholic-school identity, if properly reflected upon, understood, and implemented by Catholic educators, should result in Catholic schools being welcomed everywhere.

QUESTIONS FOR DISCUSSION

Specifically what steps must be taken to maintain the identity and viability of the Catholic school?

Some dedicated persons in religious communities have taken to new apostolates outside Catholic schools. Are they as important as teaching? Why or why not?

Is there any incontrovertible evidence that the Catholic school has contributed greatly to God and country? If yes, has this mode of contribution been better than other modes which would be less expensive in financial and human resources?

Is a Catholic Educational Leaders' Association (CELA) a good idea? Would you aspire to membership?

What qualities would you personally believe essential for good Catholic educational leadership? For excellence in education and schooling?

What would you insist upon as minimums for inclusion in a curriculum to form Catholic educational leaders?

In the area of belief on the part of Catholic educators, what would you posit as minimum?

SUGGESTED BIBLIOGRAPHY

Cohen, Michael D., and James G. March. *Leadership and Ambiguity.* New York: McGraw-Hill, 1974.

An analysis of the presidency of four-year colleges and universities with a focus on organization theory, decision making, governance, and leadership.

Geneen, Harold S., and Alvin Moscow. *Managing.* New York: Doubleday, 1984.

The wizard behind International Telephone and Telegraph offers some retrospective advice on management and management theory.

Hardy, Thomas. *The Mayor of Casterbridge.* New York: AMS, 1984.

Hardy examines leadership in this tale of one man's deeds and character.

Harvanek, Robert F. "The Expectations of Leadership," *The Way*, vol. 15 no. 1 (January 1975), pp. 20–33.

One of five very good articles in an issue of *The Way* dedicated to the topic of leadership. (*The Way* is a quarterly on contemporary Christian spirituality published at 39 Fitzjohn's Avenue, London NW3 5JT, England.)

Machiavelli, Niccolò. *The Prince.* Irving, Tex.: University of Dallas Press, 1980.

In this classic, the author lays out the theories of leadership practices that have come to be associated with his name.

Palmer, Parker J. *To Know as We Are Known: A Spirituality of Education.* San Francisco: Harper and Row, 1983.

From a non-Catholic Christian spiritual perspective, analyzes education and its leadership.

Peters, Thomas J., and Robert H. Waterman. *In Search of Excellence: Lessons from America's Best-Run Companies.* New York: Harper and Row, 1982.

This popularly written best seller offers a "back to basics" approach to successful leadership that emphasizes practical action, individual contact, and personal initiative.

Peters, Thomas J., and Nancy Austin. *A Passion for Excellence.* New York: Random House, 1985.

This sequel to *In Search of Excellence* attempts to clarify and extend the common-sense approach of its predecessor.

Plato. *The Republic.* (Many editions.)

This seminal classic considers myriad issues relating to the nature of leadership, education, and so on.

Rosenbach, William E., and Robert L. Taylor. *Contemporary Issues in Leadership.* London: Westview, 1984.

A collection of essays that attempt to describe the phenomenon of leadership and to identify the qualities of an effective leader.

NOTES

CHAPTER 1: INTRODUCTION

1. Mary Perkins Ryan, *Are Catholic Schools the Answer?* (New York: Holt, Rinehart and Winston, 1964).

2. Among previous works on this subject are Franz DeHovre, *Catholicism in Education*, trans. Edward B. Jordan (New York: Benziger, 1934); idem, *Philosophy and Education* (New York: Benziger, 1931); P. Marique, *The Philosophy of Christian Education* (New York: Prentice-Hall, 1939); W. McGucken, *The Catholic Way in Education* (Milwaukee: Bruce, 1934); John D. Redden and Francis A. Ryan, *A Catholic Philosophy of Education* (Milwaukee: Bruce, 1942); idem, *Freedom Through Education* (Milwaukee: Bruce, 1944); Thomas E. Shields, *Philosophy of Education* (Washington, D.C.: Catholic Education Press, 1921); John Lancaster Spalding, *Means and Ends of Education* (Chicago: A. C. McClurg, 1909); idem, *Education and the Higher Life* (Chicago: A. C. McClurg, 1922).

3. Definitions are basically either descriptive or essential. Descriptive definitions do just what they say: describe. They may deal in the etymology of a word, or present the appearance of a thing, or tell what a thing does in order to come to a knowledge of what it is, or present the appearance of a thing. Essential definitions go to the heart of the matter by telling what a thing is rather than what it does. Essential definitions can deal with the denotation of a word, which is the meaning that might be found in a dictionary, or with the connotation of a word, which consists in those overlays which have accrued with time and are particular to a person, place, time, or culture. Though essential definitions are usually more profound than descriptive definitions, they are not always possible. One of the many reasons for this is that sometimes a definition will depend on what philosophy one espouses.

4. Eros's *joie de vivre* is commemorated in Picadilly Circus, the hub of London's entertainment world, by a statue of a winged archer. The sculptor, Sir Alfred Gilbert, in readying it for an unveiling that took place in 1893, intended it as the Angel of Christian Charity. Christians have usually associated charity with *agape* raised to a higher level.

5. See Gilbert C. Meilaender, *Friendship: A Study in Theological Ethics* (Notre Dame, Ind.: University of Notre Dame Press, 1985).

6. Some of the material on secular and Christian wisdom is loosely synthesized

from David J. Hassel, S.J., *City of Wisdom: A Christian Vision of the American University* (Chicago: Loyola University Press, 1983), pp. 430–36.

7. See, e.g., Ps. 36 [37]:30; Eccles. 2:13; Prov. 3:18; 3:13–25; Wis. of Sol. 1–19.

8. Luke 2:52; Matt. 10:16; 1 Cor. 1:24.

9. See, e.g., Aeschylus, *Agamemnon*, line 177; Sophocles, *Antigone*, line 1050 (Ode 3) and line 1347 (closing lines); Euripides, *The Bacchae*, line 480. For further beneficial insights from the ancient Greeks on education, see Werner Jaeger, *Paideia: The Ideals of Greek Culture*, 3 vols., trans. Gilbert Highet, 2nd ed. (New York: Oxford University Press, 1945).

10. T. S. Eliot, *The Rock* (Toronto: Ryerson Press, 1934), 1. See also Plautus, *Trinummus*, act 2, scene 2, line 88; Horace, *Epistles*, book 1, epistle 2, lines 40, 41; Shakespeare, *Henry IV*, part 2, act 2, scene 2, line 155; Anne Bradstreet, *Thirty-Three Meditations*, line 12; Alfred Lord Tennyson, *Locksley Hall*, line 141; James Stephens, *The Crock of Gold* (New York: Macmillan, 1912).

11. Peter Stoler, "A Conversation with Jonas Salk," *Psychology Today*, vol. 17 no. 3 (March 1983), p. 55.

12. *Pastoral Constitution on the Church in the Modern World* (*Gaudium et spes*) # 15, in Austin Flannery, ed., *Vatican Council II: The Conciliar and Post Conciliar Documents*, 2 vols. (Northport, N.Y.: Costello, 1982), vol. 1, p. 916. (Hereafter cited as Flannery.)

13. The following is a summary of some of these benefits of philosophy.

Critical Thinking

Critical thinking is reflective questioning by one who has some experience in a field of knowledge, a familiarity with the field, and a disposition to think carefully about it. Along with moral discernment and aesthetic discrimination, critical thinking constitutes the mark of an educated person and leader. People need to think, now perhaps more than ever. Business offices are divided into thinkers of "high abstraction" and "low abstraction," whose pay scale is commensurate with their degree of abstraction. Among the high abstractors are scientists, engineers, and managers, much of whose time is taken up with meetings, conferences, drafting memos, and in other ways formulating policy. Among the low abstractors are the industrial and office work forces. Even with the latter, however, the increasing use of "smart" typewriters and other new technology calls for higher levels of abstraction. Everybody competent enough to know the "how" of their job will always have a person who knows the "why" as their boss.

But thinking is often difficult. Oliver Wendell Holmes said that there are one-story intellects, two-story intellects, and three-story intellects with skylights. All fact collectors, who have no aim beyond their facts, are one-story people. Two-story people compare, reason, and generalize, using the labors of the fact collectors as well as their own. Three-story people idealize, imagine, and predict; their best illumination, said Holmes, comes from above, through the skylight.

Educated Person

In a former time, society considered the formation of an educated person to be in great measure the work of one or another facet of philosophy. Philosophy confronts the most basic conceptions used in arguing about underlying causes of phenomena and the nature of reality, analyzing contending positions on questions of life and worth, evaluating the basic principles and criteria we employ when making claims, and synthesizing and collating theories. Philosophy is not merely an expression or development of personal opinions; it uses technical principles for analyzing and evaluating meanings, premises, reasoning, and arguments.

We have a remnant of all this in the fact that we still call most of the highest earned academic degrees "Doctor of Philosophy." The degree retains this name even though the work is done in other fields, because people once assumed that the integration of every discipline took place through philosophy. The approach which teaches whatever students want to learn (usually for a salable skill rather than a philosophy of life), with no integration, is an abrogation of this. Few would hold that schools should eliminate giving students salable skills, but many would like them to restore the integrating contribution of a philosophy of life.

Essentially what philosophy intends to do is to make one a free person. It helps accomplish this in many ways. For example, it analyzes all the concepts, propositions, and arguments that come before it. It synthesizes, putting things together where possible and trying to make sense of them. It speculates and theorizes, mulling over meanings, finding transcendence where appropriate, and coming up with universals when warranted. It establishes norms or prescriptions as necessary. Always, the perspective is one of being critical in the best sense—a realization that not even a sacred cow is free of flies.

Everything involves a philosophy. The way students' chairs are arranged will show one's overall philosophy of education: the "liberal" secondary school in Paris that un-bolted its desks from the floor, but didn't move them, showed a philosophy whose rigidity the leaders couldn't escape despite good will; the teacher's high platform in the same classroom demonstrated a philosophy about the teacher. But not everything is philosophy: There are other influential factors as well, like psychology and sociology.

Competencies for Greater Comprehension of Self and Others

The pursuit of philosophy will result in a greater comprehension of oneself and of others on the cognitive level. With regard to oneself, it will, for one thing, result in the development of desirable discernment. In reading, for example, it can improve the ability to comprehend and summarize the ideas in a written work, to interpret inferentially, to separate one's own assumptions from a writer's, and to adjust one's reading to the type of material.

In writing, philosophy helps with the ability to conceive ideas, to organize and develop them, to form correct sentences and paragraphs, to vary writing style with different materials and audiences, and to gather and arrange information. With speaking and listening competencies, philosophical principles assist in the ability to engage critically and constructively in the exchange of ideas, to engage in coherent and concise questioning, to identify the main and subordinate ideas in lectures and discussions, and to develop ideas for the purpose of addressing a group.

Philosophy greatly helps in reasoning, too: it assists with the ability to identify problems and to evaluate ways to solve them, to use inductive and deductive reasoning correctly, to recognize fallacies in reasoning, to draw reasonable conclusions and defend one's own conclusions, to formulate valid generalizations, and to distinguish between fact and opinion.

A well-begun formal development of a coherent and consistent personal philosophy will include deeper insights, easier facility with decision making, and greater capacity at policy formulation. It will assist in the development of a necessary creative and critical attitude toward life and one's position in it, and a reflective examination and appraisal of the entire range of one's situation.

With regard to relationships with *others*, the overall outcome of exposure to philosophy will be a better understanding, an ability to perceive backgrounds and patterns in ways of thinking, and a deeper sympathy—though not necessarily agreement—with where other people stand. More specifically it will help all those — teachers, administrators, parents, counselors, superiors, and all who aspire to any of these positions — who try to lead others to maturity in thinking, understanding, and knowing. Philosophy relates to the whole of human living, especially human needs, values, and ideals.

Finally, but by no means least, philosophy helps with needed dialogue. Ours is a time of growing solipsism (*solus*, "alone," + *ipse*, "self"). Solipsism is the belief that the whole world is me. Though its extreme version does not exist outside mental institutions, its moderate philosophical version, plural solipsism — the belief that the whole world is *like* me — does. The world it yields is, at base, a radical denial of the otherness of others. One of its central axioms is that if one burrows deep enough beneath the Mao jacket, the *chador*, or the *shapka*, one discovers that people everywhere are the same. But to say that people have commonalities like the same hopes and fears, being born and loving and suffering and dying alike, is to say very little. Ideologies, philosophies, values, cultures, and interests do clash — and a book like this one is necessary in the field of schooling.

14. Relatively early on, such as Clement of Alexandria and Origen used philosophy to explain Christianity. The first ecumenical council, at Nicaea in A.D. 325, used philosophical thought to tackle the subtleties of Arianism, which maintained that Jesus was not "the same" (*homoousios*) as God, but "like" (*homoiousios*) God — only a man, though perfect enough to be our model. The Fathers and Doctors of the Church all used existing philosophical principles to put forth solid doctrine. In its development, Christian philosophy was influenced by persecutions, migrations, invasions, wars, and other human phenomena.

St. Augustine and other Fathers had been influenced by the philosophy of Plato, among others. In the twelfth century, a new movement, Scholasticism, began under the leadership of St. Anselm of Canterbury. The Scholastics, or Schoolmen, who were heirs to the monastic and cathedral schools which had preserved learning and culture through the barbarian invasions, developed a refined technique of systematic study. In the thirteenth century, an unprecedented synthesis between faith and philosophy was achieved by St. Thomas Aquinas. For the philosophical basis of his synthesis, Thomas shifted from the Platonism of Augustine of eight centuries before to the Realism of Aristotle and others who were then being reintroduced, at the great universities. Thomas has been a leading influence in the seven centuries since his death.

In the sixteenth century, to introduce his theology Martin Luther also used philosophical principles: in explaining the total corruption of man, for example, and the subjection of reason to faith. In the early seventeenth century, René Descartes attempted a philosophy of pure reason without faith: "only reason" in contrast to Luther's "only faith." In the nineteenth century, the Catholic Church condemned faith without reason as the heresy of fideism; in the same century the Church also condemned rationalism, which was the rejection of everything outside of human reason. Modern heresies have been occasioned by those who have attempted to separate faith and reason.

The process continues today. For example, *Theological Studies* carried an interesting series of articles in philosophical theology, the central theme of which was the development of an inculturated theology for the U. S. through the retrieval, in a theological context, of classical North American philosophy. The articles deal successively with conversion, religious affectivity, discernment, the community called to conversion, and divine reverence. They develop insights from Bernard Meland and H. Richard Niebuhr, from Jonathan Edwards and Josiah Royce, from Alfred North Whitehead and William Ernest Hocking. See Donald L. Gelpi, S.J., "Conversion: The Challenge of Contemporary Charismatic Piety," *Theological Studies*, vol. 43 no. 4 (December 1982), pp. 606–28; William C. Spohn, S.J., "The Reasoning Heart: An American Approach to Christian Discernment," ibid., vol. 44 no. 1 (March 1983), pp. 30–52; John R. Stacer, S.J., "Divine Reverence for Us: God's Being Present, Cherishing, and Persuading," ibid., vol. 44 no. 3 (September 1983), pp. 438–55; Frank M. Oppenheim, S.J., "Graced Communities: A Problem in Loving," ibid., vol. 44 no. 4 (December 1983), pp. 604–24; J. J. Mueller, S.J., "Appreciative Awareness: The Feeling-Dimension in Religious Experience," ibid., vol. 45 no. 1 (March 1984), pp. 57–79.

On the "Christian philosophy" issue, see also Mark D. Jordan, "The Debate over 'Christian Philosophy,'" *Communio*, vol. 12 (Fall 1985), pp. 293–311, and John T. Wippel, "Thomas Aquinas and the Problem of Christian Philosophy," *Metaphysical Themes in Thomas Aquinas* (Washington, D.C.: The Catholic University of America Press, 1984), pp. 1–33.

15. John M. Hull, *Studies in Religion and Education* (London: Falmer, 1984), pp. 255–57.

16. Adapted from Kevin Nichols, *Cornerstone* (Middlegreen, Slough, England: St. Paul, 1978), pp. 58–69.

17. Hull, op. cit., pp. 257f.

18. Ibid., pp. 260f.

19. Adapted from Hull, op. cit., pp. 261–63. For reviews of theologies and philosophies which have influenced the place of individuality in education, see Brian V. Hill, *Education and the Endangered Individual* (New York: Teachers College Press, 1973); H. Parsons, "God and Man's Achievement of Identity: Religion in the Thought of Alfred North Whitehead," *Educational Theory*, vol. 11 (1962), pp. 228–54; Irenee Noye, "Enfance de Jesus," *Dictionnaire de spiritualité ascétique et mystique* (Paris: Beauchesne, 1969), vol. 4, cols. 652–82.

20. John Dewey, "My Pedagogic Creed," in *Dewey on Education*, compiled by Martin S. Dworking (Classics in Education series, no. 3; New York: Teachers College Press, 1971), p. 19.

21. Lawrence Cremin, *Traditions of American Education* (New York: Basic Books, 1977), p. 134.

22. Pope Pius XI, *The Christian Education of Youth* (New York: America Press, 1930), p. 4.

23. John D. Redden and Francis A. Ryan, *A Catholic Philosophy of Education* (Milwaukee: Bruce, 1942), p. 23.

24. This is a perception of, e.g., Bernard Lonergan. See his *Insight: A Study of Human Understanding* (New York: Philosophical Library, 1957); also, "Subjectivity," *New Catholic Encyclopedia* (New York: McGraw-Hill, 1966), vol. 13, pp. 758–60; Robert O. Johann, "Subjectivity," *Review of Metaphysics*, vol. 12 (1958–59), pp. 200–234.

25. Sacred Congregation for Catholic Education, *Lay Catholics in Schools: Witnesses to Faith (Les laïcs Catholiques)* # 13, in Flannery, vol. 2, p. 634.

26. E.g., *State v. Peterman*, Indiana Supreme Court (1904).

27. *Turnverein Lincoln v. Board of Appeals*, 358 Ill. 135, 192 N.E. 780 (1934).

28. *National Schools v. City of Los Angeles*, 135 Cal.App.2d 311, 287 P.2d 151 (1955), *cert. denied*, 850 U.S. 968, 76 S.Ct. 439, 100 L.Ed. 841 (1956).

29. In some cases, parents have sought legally to classify home instruction programs as schools (see chapter 6 of this book). The High Court in Oregon found that parents must meet the stricter requirements for a "parent or private teacher" teaching the child at home (*State v. Bowman*, 60 Or.App. 184, 653 P.2d 254 [1982]). Courts in Colorado and Virginia have reached the same conclusion: *Gunnison Watershed School Dist. v. Funk*, No. 81-JVB-3, Colo. Dist. Ct., Gunnison County, Dec. 30, 1981; *Grigg*

v. Virginia, 224 Va. 356, 297 S.E. 2d 799 1982. Other courts have applied a broader definition of "school." A court in South Dakota, for example, held that a parent giving instruction at home was not guilty of violating the compulsory education law because schooling was in fact occurring.

30. Unfortunately, there is a paucity of sociological research as to whether Catholic-school policy makers have given much thought to the identity of their schools, as to whether the accomplishments of the schools are consonant with their *raison d'etre*, to substantiate philosophical principles, or to suggest new areas for philosophical as well as other research. The lack of such research suggests the possibility of short-sighted allocation of resources.

In the United States, the in-depth areas of the Notre Dame study of Catholic elementary and secondary schools were done so long ago (1966) that they have lost some of their applicability. (Reginald A. Neuwien, ed., *Catholic Schools in Action* [Notre Dame, Ind.: University of Notre Dame Press, 1966].) Another massive study, by Andrew Greeley and Peter Rossi, *The Education of Catholic Americans*, published the same year, emphasized that "rather than causing the comparatively high level of minimal allegiance to be found in American Catholics, the schools may be the result of it," and "while American Catholicism would probably have survived in reasonable health without its schools, the schools have nevertheless produced a rather fervent religious elite." (Andrew M. Greeley and Peter H. Rossi, *The Education of Catholic Americans* [Chicago: Aldine Publishing, 1966] pp. 111–13.) Greeley's second study, *Catholic Schools in a Declining Church* (1976), found that Catholic schools had a 90 percent favored rating among Catholics and produce such desired results as reduction of racism, increase of client loyalty to the Church, spurs to upward mobility, etc. Less massive studies with equally positive results have taken place under the auspices of the National Catholic Educational Association and in various dioceses. (See, for example, the National Catholic Educational Association's major study of Catholic high schools, *The Catholic High School: A National Portrait*. As reported in *Momentum*, vol. XVI no. 2 [May 1985], pp. 8–25, this study is in two parts. Part I gives a composite view of the resources, programs, facilities, personnel, and policies of high schools. Part II assesses how Catholic high schools influence students in academics, life skills, values, and faith. While empirical studies like these are extremely valuable to discover what *is*, one must remember that they are not philosophical studies, which try to determine what is equally valuable and necessary: what *should be*.)

In England, sociological studies have been equally scarce. Michael Hornsby-Smith performed a valuable study on youth between the conclusion of World War II and 1978. Smith's findings were consistent with those of Greeley in the United States and M. Flynn in Australia. (Michael P. Hornsby-Smith, *Catholic Education: The Unobtrusive Partner; Sociological Studies of the Catholic School System of England and Wales* [London: Sheed and Ward, 1978]. See also Greely and Rossi, op. cit.; M. Flynn, *Some Catholic Schools in Action: A Sociological Study of Sixth Form Students in Twenty-One Catholic Boys' High Schools* [Sydney, Australia: Catholic Education Office, 1975]; B. Martin and R. Pluck, *Young People's Beliefs: An Exploratory Study Commissioned by the General Synod Board of Education of the Views and Behavioral Patterns of Young People Related to Their Beliefs* [London: General Synod, 1977], cited as being applicable to Catholics by Hornsby-Smith, p. 137.) In 1985, Michael Winter remarked upon Hornsby-Smith's conclusions that adolescents were struggling for autonomy, were antagonistic to the "official" religion of the institutional Church, rejected God and religion as "childish," and drifted lazily into their positions rather than making conscious choices. Winter then asked "the question, important but not investigated, of causation: Do Catholics send their children to Roman Catholic schools because they are good Catholics, or do people become good

Catholics because they go to Catholic schools? In other words, are Catholic schools superfluous?" (Michael Winter, *What Ever Happened to Vatican II?* [London: Sheed and Ward, 1985], p. 93.)

31. *Atlantic Monthly*, November 1948, as cited by John W. Donohue, "Voices for Parent Power," *America*, vol. 139 no. 6 (September 9, 1978), p. 125.

32. *The Oxford English Dictionary* (Glasgow: Oxford University Press, 1971), p. 1558.

33. See J. C. Esty, "The Public Purpose of Nonpublic Education," *Momentum*, vol. XV no. 3 (September 1984), pp. 48–50.

34. Pope Paul VI, "The *Credo* of the People of God" (*Solemni hac liturgia*), in Flannery, vol. 2, pp. 389–94.

35. Sacred Congregation for the Clergy, *General Catechetical Directory* (*Ad normam decreti*), in Flannery, vol. 2, pp. 553f.

36. Hull, op. cit., p. 236.

37. Paul Hirst, *Moral Education in a Secular Society* (University of London Press, 1974), p. 81, as cited in Hull, op. cit., p. 241.

38. Canon 803, in Canon Law Society of America, *Code of Canon Law, Latin-English Edition*, trans. under the auspices of the Canon Law Society of America (Washington, D.C.: Canon Law Society of America, 1983).

39. *Declaration on Christian Education* (*Gravissimum educationis*) # 5, in Flannery, vol. 1, pp. 730f.

40. National Council of Catholic Bishops, *To Teach as Jesus Did* ## 8, 14; "Teach Them," *Origins*, vol. 6 no. 1 (May 27, 1976), pp. 1–7, Part II, esp. pp. 3–5.

41. Bishop David Konstant, ed., *Signposts and Homecomings* (London: Bishops' Conference, 1981), p. 143, as cited in Winter, op. cit., p. 101.

42. Pope John Paul II, "The Catholic School" (Address to Catholic Educators December 28, 1985), *The Pope Speaks*, vol. 31 (1986), p. 79.

43. Interview with Peter Hackett, S.J., Master, Campion Hall, Oxford, on February 24, 1986.

44. Interview with Michel Bureau, S.J., Aumonier (campus minister), in Paris, March 23, 1986.

45. Sacred Congregation for Catholic Education, *Catholic Schools* (*Malgre les declarations*) # 73, in Flannery, vol. 2, p. 623.

46. Ibid., # 2, p. 606.

47. *Lay Catholics in Schools* # 39, in Flannery, vol. 2, p. 645.

48. Ian T. Ramsey, ed., *The Fourth R: The Durham Report on Religious Education* (London: National Society and S.P.C.K., 1970), p. 186.

49. See Patricia Bauch, "On the Importance of Catholic Schools," *Today's Catholic Teacher*, vol. 17 (April 1986), pp. 70–76, which explores the ways in which Catholic schools differ from government schools and cites major studies.

50. *Catholic Schools* # 14, in Flannery, vol. 2, p. 609.

51. Francis J. Stafford, "Reflections on Catholic Education," *Origins*, vol. 13 no. 3 (June 2, 1983), p. 63.

52. See Pope John Paul II, "Address to Parents, Teachers and Students of the Federation of Institutes of Education Activities on the Role of the Catholic School in Modern Society," *The Pope Speaks*, vol. 30 (Winter 1985), pp. 355–59.

53. *Catholic Schools* # 15, in Flannery, vol. 2, p. 609.

54. For the treatment of church-affiliated schools in England, Scotland, Australia, West Germany, France, Belgium, Holland, and the United States, see Sr. Raymond McLaughlin, *The Liberty of Choice: Freedom and Justice in Education* (Collegeville, Minn.: Liturgical Press, 1979).

CHAPTER 2: OPPONENTS' MIND-SET

1. For the history of Catholic schooling in the United States, see my *Of Singular Benefit: the Story of U.S. Catholic Education* (New York: Macmillan, 1970), and my summary and update, *The History of United States Catholic Schooling* (Washington, D.C.: National Catholic Educational Association, 1985).

2. In the United States, Protestantism and Enlightenment ideas were often intertwined. See Henry F. May, *The Enlightenment in America* (London: Oxford University Press, 1976); Perry Miller, *Jonathan Edwards* (Amhurst, Mass.: University of Massachusetts Press, 1981).

3. For an overall history of anti-Catholic bigotry in the United States, see Ray Allen Billington, *The Protestant Crusade 1800–1860* (New York: Macmillan, 1938); John Higham, *Strangers in the Land: Patterns of American Nativism 1860–1925* (New Brunswick, N.J.: Rutgers University Press, 1955); Donald L. Kinzer, *An Episode in Anti-Catholicism: The American Protective Association* (Seattle: University of Washington Press, 1964).

4. In a speech to the Army of the Tennessee, at Des Moines, Iowa, on September 29, 1875, Grant said: "[R]esolve that not one dollar appropriated for their support shall be appropriated to the support of any sectarian schools." ("The President's Speech at Des Moines," *The Catholic World*, vol. XXII, pp. 434–35.) On December 7 of the same year, in his annual message to Congress, Grant asked that "a constitutional amendment be submitted . . . prohibiting the granting of any school funds . . . for the benefit or in aid . . . of any religious sect or denomination. . . . " (*The Congressional Record*, IV, Part 1, p. 175.) Larger excerpts in John Tracy Ellis, *Documents of American Catholic History* (Milwaukee: Bruce, 1969), pp. 392f.

5. Sidney E. Ahlstrom, *A Religious History of the American People* (New Haven, Conn.: Yale University Press, 1972), p. 1087.

6. The historical backgrounds and cultural foundations of Catholic schooling are different in other countries. In France, when the socialist Mitterand government tried to decrease government financial aid to church-affiliated (principally Catholic) schools, one million people in Paris successfully demonstrated against it. When the socialist government of Spain tried to do the same, about three-quarters of a million marchers braved wintery showers to forcefully demonstrate their protest. (*The Washington Post*, November 19, 1984, p. A16.) They succeeded.

Many countries that have borrowed the exact wording of the U.S. Constitution have interpreted the no establishment and free-exercise of religion clauses in favor of equal treatment of church-affiliated schools. In Australia, for example, whose 1898 Constitution copied that of the United States almost verbatim, the High Court in a critical 1981 decision had no difficulty in forthrightly deciding that government financial support for church-affiliated schools is constitutional. It noted that "establishing a religion involves the entrenchment of a religion as a feature of and identified with the body politic," and common-sensically observed that "a law which establishes a religion will inevitably do so expressly and directly and not, as it were, constructively." (*State of Victoria v. Commonwealth of Australia*, February 10, 1981, slip opinion.)

7. See Daniel S. Parkinson, "Paideia, Humanitas and Modern Humanism: Some Pertinent Questions," *Educational Studies*, vol. 8 no. 1 (Spring 1977), pp. 29–35.

8. Charles S. Peirce, "Illustrations of the Logic of Science," *Popular Science Monthly*, vol. 13 (May 1878), p. 203.

9. This was in William James's famous essay "The Will to Believe." See William James, *The Will to Believe and Other Essays in Popular Philosophy* (New York: Longmans, Green, 1897), pp. 1–31; reprinted in John K. Roth, ed., *The Moral Philosophy of William James* (New York: Crowell, 1969), pp. 192–213.

10. William James, *Pragmatism: A New Look for Some Old Ways of Thinking* (New York: Longmans, Green, 1907), pp. 43–81.

11. Ibid., pp. 54–55.

12. Because Voltaire's philosophy was very much influenced by and intertwined with his life, one must know his life, at least in outline, to appreciate his philosophy. See Theodore Besterman, *Voltaire* (University of Chicago Press, 1969), a thorough biography by the man who for many years directed the Voltaire Foundation for studies of Voltaire; Ira O. Wade, *The Intellectual Development of Voltaire* (Ann Arbor, Mich: Books on Demand, Division of University Microfilms International, 1969), a scholarly biography by a man who devoted his life to the study of Voltaire; Mary Margaret Barr, *A Century of Voltaire Study: A Bibliography of Writings on Voltaire, 1825–1925* (New York: Institute of French Studies, Columbia University Press, 1929), a work whose extensiveness shows Voltaire's popularity.

13. Edward Gibbon, *The Decline and Fall of the Roman Empire* (New York: Modern Library, 1932).

14. Condorcet, *Sketch for a Historical Picture of the Progress of the Human Mind* (Westport, Conn.: Hyperion Press, 1979).

15. Robert Bryan, "History, Pseudo-History, Anti-History: How Public-School Texbooks Treat Religion" (Washington, D. C.: Learn, Inc., 1984), as cited in *Education Week*, May 2, 1984, p. 1. Bryan holds a Ph.D. in ecclesiastical history from the University of London.

16. Ibid.

17. Paul C. Vitz et al. *Religion and Traditional Values in Public School Textbooks: An Empirical Study* (Washington, D.C.: National Institute of Education, 1985, NIE Grant No. G84-0012; Project No. 2-0099). Vitz also charged that elementary- and secondary-school textbooks fail to promote "family values," criticizing elementary-school social-studies texts' complete omission of such words as "husband," "wife," "marriage," and "wedding," and noting that one book's definition of a family is "a group of people." A defender of the textbooks said that they "represent the consensus that we have in this society, whether you like it or not." As reported in *Education Week*, vol. 5 no. 5 (October 2, 1985), p. 10. For other attacks on the Vitz report, see *Education Week*, vol. 6 no. 8 (October 29, 1986), p. 6.

A study by Charles C. Haynes of thirty of the best-selling history, social studies, and civics textbooks, as well as films and supplementary materials on the Constitution, also found little or no discussion of religion. Haynes sees government schools as having gone "from assuming that every student is a Protestant to portraying America as a land of no religion." (See *Education Week*, vol. 5 no. 32 [April 30, 1986], p. 6.)

In 1985, a court case was brought by some six hundred fundamentalist Christian parents against the school board in Mobile, Ala., for secularism in their textbooks. Basing their case on their First Amendment rights, the parent-plaintiffs wanted to prove three points: that thirty-nine social studies textbooks exclude facts about traditional faiths like Christianity; that seven home economics textbooks promote "humanism"; and that humanism is a religion. University of Virginia sociologist James D. Hunter testified that humanism is the "functional equivalent" of a religion, pointing to the ordination of humanist ministers who can conduct weddings and the listing of humanist organizations under "churches" in the telephone book. William Coulson, psychologist and professor from the U.S. International University, San Diego, testified that children taught to make their own decisions about moral issues in accord with the relative values of the textbooks in question are vulnerable to dealers of drugs, sex, and pornography. Other cases involve other Bible Belt states, especially Louisiana, Mississippi, Tennessee, and Texas.

Anthony T. Podesta, president of People for the American Way, disputed the conclusions of Vitz and the parents: religion is being left out of textbooks, he said, not because of a humanist bias, but because publishers are afraid of controversy; he admitted that some of the books were poor, but "lousy books don't violate the Constitution." Paul Kurtz, philosophy professor at the State University of New York at Buffalo, and a secular humanist, testified as an expert witness that secular humanism, at least as an organized movement, is not being taught in the government schools. Others said that if the parents win there will be recurring incidents of textbook censorship. The parents countered that they were not seeking a ban of the books, but alternate readings for their children. Sincere believers in religion, they contended that their case was similar to the fact that no government school would force a Jewish child to eat pork, a Jehovah's Witnesses child to participate in Halloween activities, or Black Muslim children to read material praising the superiority of the white race.

The parents won their case on the local trial level and in the U.S. District Court. On the interesting question of whether Secular Humanism is a religion, U.S. District Court Judge W. Brevard Hand ruled in the affirmative, writing:

> All of the experts, and the [plaintiffs], agreed that [humanism] is a religion which:
>
>> makes a statement about supernatural existence a central pillar of its logic; defines the nature of man; sets forth a goal or purpose for individual and collective human existence; and defines the nature of the universe, and thereby delimits its purpose.
>>
>> It purports to establish a closed definition of reality. . . .
>
> The most important belief of his religion is its denial of the transcendent and/or supernatural: there is no God, no creator, no divinity. . . . Man is the product of evolutionary, physical forces. He is purely biological and has no supernatural or transcendent spiritual component or quality. Man's individual purpose is to seek and obtain personal fulfillment by freely developing every talent and ability, especially his rational intellect, to the highest level. Man's collective purpose is to seek the good life by the increase of every person's freedom and potential for personal development.
>
> In addition, humanism, as a belief system, erects a moral code and identifies the source of morality. . . .
>
> Secular humanism . . . has organizational characteristics. Some groups are more structured and hierarichal, others less so. . . . The entire body of thought rests as a platform: *Humanist Manifesto I*, *Humanist Manifesto II*, and the *Secular Humanist Declaration*.
>
> These factors . . . demonstrate the *institutional* character of secular humanism. They are evidence that this belief system is similar to groups traditionally afforded protection by the First Amendment religion clauses. (*Smith v. Board of School Commissioners of Mobile County*, Civ. A. No. 82-0544-BH, F. Supp., as in Westlaw, pp. 100–102.)

See also *Education Week*, vol. 6 no. 24 (March 11, 1987), pp. 1, 18f.)

As a result of the controversies, Laidlaw Educational Publishers, based in River Forest, Illinois, the textbook division of Doubleday, has promised to make "significant changes" in future publications. These changes, said the publisher, will maintain the separation of Church and State in not inculcating religious doctrine in its texts, but will include more references to religious influences in the United States. (*The Washington Post*, February 28, 1987, p. G14.)

18. An amendment to the Economic Security Act of 1984 prohibits the use of federal funds for the teaching of secular humanism, but does not define the term. In fact, People for the American Way (a lobby founded by television producer Norman

Lear) denounced the amendment and said that "trying to define 'secular humanism' is like trying to nail Jell-O to a tree." (*The New York Times*, February 28, 1986, p. A19.)

19. See Karl Rahner, *Concern for the Church: Theological Investigations XX* (New York Crossroad, 1981); idem, *Foundations of Christian Faith* (New York: Crossroad, 1978); idem with Herbert Vorgrimler, *Dictionary of Theology*, 2nd ed. (New York: Crossroad, 1981).

20. Inasmuch as Rousseau's life, like that of Voltaire, plays a large part in his thinking, and his thinking reflects the kind of person he was, the reader may wish to consult such works as Jean-Jacques Rousseau, *Confessions of J. J. Rousseau: With the Reveries of the Solitary Walker*, 2 vols. (New York: Everyman Library, 1960), an autobiography; Jean Guehenno, *Jean-Jacques Rousseau*, 2 vols. (New York: Columbia University Press, 1966), an accurate biography; F. C. Green, *Jean-Jacques Rousseau: A Critical Study of His Life and Writings* (London: Cambridge University Press, 1955), a good study of the relationship between Rousseau's life and his writings; Jacques Maritain, *Three Reformers: Luther, Descartes, Rousseau* (Westport, Conn.: Greenwood Press, 1950), a brief but good study by this eminent Catholic realist philosopher.

21. Jean Jacques Rousseau, *The Social Contract and Discourses* (New York: Dutton, 1950); idem, *Emile* (New York: Basic Books, 1979).

22. John Dewey, *A Common Faith* (New Haven, Conn.: Yale University Press, 1934).

23. Ludwig A. Feuerbach, *The Essence of Christianity* (London: J. Chapman, 1854).

24. Jean-Paul Sartre, *Existentialism and Human Emotions* (New York: Philosophical Library, 1957), p. 15.

25. For instance, the novels of Franz Kafka—e.g., *The Trial* (New York: Knopf, 1937); *The Castle* (New York: Knopf, 1930)—have his characters inhabit a nightmare landscape in which man is an alien, burdened by nameless guilt, trying to make sense out of absurdity, in a quest for a stable, secure, and radiant reality which is continually elusive. The absurd is a pervasive category. In Sartre's novel *Nausea* (Norfolk, Conn.: New Directions, 1949), the absurd takes the form of the sheer "gooey" contingency of existence. With Camus, it arises in the incommensurability between man's need for meaning and the silence of reality. Camus' novels repeat that theme in various ways: see *Caligula and Three Other Plays* (New York: Knopf, 1958); *The Plague* (New York: Knopf, 1948); *The Stranger* (New York: Knopf, 1946).

The attempt to live an authentic and free life inevitably raises the question of our relation to other persons. Sartre concentrates upon the threat presented by other people to one's own autonomy. A character in his play *No Exit* says, "Hell is just— other people" (*No Exit and Three Other Plays* [New York: Vintage Books, 1959], p. 47). Camus, on the other hand, in his novel *The Rebel* (New York: Knopf, 1953), comes to regard the solidarity of man in the common revolt against absurdity as his sole deliverance. Simone de Beauvoir, in novels remarkable for their meticulous psychological scrutiny, is preoccupied with the vitiation of interpersonal relations by various forms of bad faith: see *She Came to Stay* (Cleveland: World, 1954); *The Mandarins* (Cleveland: World, 1956); *The Blood of Others* (New York: Knopf, 1948).

26. Sigmund Freud, *Totem and Taboo* (New York: Norton, 1952).

27. Sigmund Freud, *The Future of an Illusion* (London: Hogarth Press and the Institute of Psychoanalysis, 1928).

28. "The Future of an Illusion" in *The Standard Edition of the Complete Psychological Works of Sigmund Freud* (London: Hogarth Press, 1953–1974), vol. 21, p. 49.

29. Ibid., pp. 47–48.

30. Ibid., p. 49.

31. Karl Stern, *The Third Revolution* (Garden City, N.Y.: Doubleday, 1961), pp. 80–81.

32. Gregory Zilboorg, *Freud and Religion* (Westminster, Md.: Newman Press, 1961), p. 49.

33. See Rudolf Allers, *The Successful Error* (New York: Sheed and Ward, 1940); idem, *The New Psychology* (New York: Sheed and Ward, 1938).

34. It is important to note also that terms like *id, ego,* and *superego* are inaccurate renditions by translators of Freud's simple German words. See Bruno Bettleheim, *Freud and Man's Soul* (New York: Knopf, 1983).

35. The above paragraphs are adapted from W. W. Meissner, "Psychoanalytic Aspects of Religious Experience," *Annual of Psychoanalysis*, vol. 6 (1978), pp. 108–14.

36. Carl Gustav Jung, *Psychology and Religion* (New Haven, Conn.: Yale University Press, 1938), pp. 4–5.

37. Ibid., pp. 113–14. Nevertheless, based upon Jungian typology is the Myers-Briggs Type Indicator, an instrument that is used with benefit by many who seek religious growth and many other applications. The Myers-Briggs Type Indicator is a psychological inventory that tests for four pairs of contrasting preferences said to be found in varying degrees in all people: extroversion versus introversion, sensing versus intuition, thinking versus feeling, and judging versus perceptive. This gives rise to sixteen possible combinations or personality types. These designations, however, are relative rather than absolute.

CHAPTER 3: PROPONENTS' MIND-SET

1. St. Paul, perhaps the New Testament author most acquainted with secular learning, used language replete with scholarly terms. He quoted the *Minos* of Epimenides, calling the Cretans "always liars, evil beasts, lazy gluttons" (Titus 1:12). On the Areopagus, the awesome place of discussion and judgment in front of the Acropolis of Athens, St. Luke has Paul quote the *Phenomena* of the Greek poet Aratus (Acts 17:28). To the Corinthians, he quoted Menander's *Thais* to the effect that "evil companionships corrupt good morals" (1 Cor. 15:33). The New Testament uses the pregnant Greek word *paideia* several times — advising fathers, for example, to "not provoke your children to anger, but rearing them in the *discipline* and admonition of the Lord," and asserting that "all Scripture is inspired by God and useful for teaching, for reproving, for correcting, for *instructing* in justice" (Eph. 6:4 and 2 Tim. 3:16). Other uses of *paideia* may be found: e.g., Luke 23:16, 22; Acts 7:22; 22:3; Heb. 12:6–11; Rom. 2:20; 1 Cor. 11:32; 2 Cor. 6:9; 1 Tim. 1:20; 2 Tim. 2:25; Titus 2:12.

See Edwin Hatch, *The Influence of Greek Ideas on Christianity* (New York: Harper Torchbooks, 1957). See also Werner Jaeger, *Early Christianity and Greek Paideia* (Cambridge, Mass.: Harvard University Press, 1961); Frederick C. Grant, *Roman Hellenism and the New Testament* (New York: Scribner's, 1962).

2. Rom. 12:2.

3. See John Burnet, trans. and ed., *Aristotle on Education: Extracts from the Ethics and Politics* (Cambridge: Cambridge University Press, 1967).

4. For one edition of Thomas Aquinas's masterwork, see *St. Thomas Aquinas: Summa Theologica*, 3 vols., trans. by Fathers of the English Dominican Province (New York: Benziger, 1947sqq.). For secondary sources on Thomas Aquinas on education, see, e.g., James Collins, intro. and ed., *Thomas Aquinas: The Teacher — The Mind; Truth, Questions X, XI* (Chicago: Henry Regnery, 1953); John W. Donohue, *St. Thomas Aquinas and Education* (New York: Random House, 1968). See also the many theses and dissertations on Thomas Aquinas in Catholic universities.

5. See, for example, Pope Leo XIII's 1879 "Encyclical Letter on the Restoration of Christian Philosophy according to the Mind of St. Thomas Aquinas, the Angelic

Doctor," in *St. Thomas Aquinas: Summa Theologica*, vol. I (New York: Benziger, 1947), pp. xii, xiii. See also the 1918 Code of Canon Law (e.g., canons 589 and 1366 §2).

6. W. P. Montague, Ralph Barton Perry, et al., *The New Realism* (New York: Macmillan, 1912).

7. Some nonbelievers erroneously understand by "original sin" a doctrine that connotes an innate evil in children. This sin is inherited at conception as a result of the original wrong choice of the first man, Adam. The precise nature of Adam's sin (in Gen. 3) is not known. Original sin designates a number of things. One is a condition of weakness found in human beings prior to their own free option for good or evil — a state of being rather than a human act or its consequence — for which God the Father sent His son as savior. Although this weakness causes people to set up obstacles to a state of friendship with God, it does not mean that human beings are so corrupted that they have no capacity for good. Human beings' lack of holiness is a *privation*, not a mere *absence*. Another meaning has to do with the origin of that state: its cause or source. How can the link between Adam and the rest of humankind be so close as to bring about humankind's inheritance of the consequence of original sin? This is a difficult mystery. But our age, which recognizes the influences of heredity and environment on people, should not find it difficuilt to understand that human beings, even aside from a religious point of view, can be affected both adversely by human evil for which they were not responsible and favorably by good which they did not perform.

8. *Webster's Third New International Dictionary* (Springfield, Mass.: Merriam, 1961), definition under "Idealism," p. 1122.

9. Plato, *Republic*, VII, 514ff., in Edith Hamilton and Huntington Cairns, eds., *Plato: The Collected Dialogues* (New York: Pantheon Books, 1961), p. 747.

10. Personalism as a philosophical theory is not to be confused with psychological theories of personality. The latter are usually less profound than the former: "personality," for example, has to do more with superficial traits than "personhood," a philosophical term which has to do with what makes a person himself or herself and separate from all others. Foreshadowed in Bronson Alcott (1799–1888) and Walt Whitman (1819–1892), the theory which holds that ultimate reality consists of a plurality of spiritual beings or independent persons was developed in America principally by Borden P. Bowne (1847–1910) and George H. Howison (1834–1916), and includes also people like the French Emmanuel Mounier (1905–1950).

See Borden P. Bowne, *The Essence of Religion* (Boston: Houghton Mifflin, 1910; idem, *The Immanence of God* (Boston: Houghton Mifflin, 1905); idem, *Personalism* (Boston: Houghton Mifflin, 1908); George H. Howison, *The Conception of God* (New York: Macmillan, 1897); idem, *The Limits of Evolution, and Other Essays Illustrating the Metaphysical Theory of Personal Idealism* (New York: Macmillan, 1905); Emmanuel Mounier, *Personalism* (Notre Dame, Ind.: University of Notre Dame Press, 1970); idem, *Be Not Afraid: A Denunciation of Despair* (New York: Sheed and Ward, 1962); *The Character of Man* (New York: Harper and Row, 1956); idem, *Existential Philosophies* (London: Rockliff, 1948). For a synthesis of Personalism and Moderate Realism, see Joseph W. Browne, *Personal Dignity* (New York: Philosophical Library, 1983).

11. Plato, *Laws*, bk. X, in Edith Hamilton and Huntington Cairns, eds., *Plato: The Collected Dialogues* (New York: Pantheon Books, 1961), pp. 1440–65.

12. Immanuel Kant, *Critique of Pure Reason*, trans. Norman Kemp Smith (New York: Humanities Press, 1950).

13. Immanuel Kant, *Critique of Practical Reason and Other Writings in Moral Philosophy*, trans. and ed. with intro. by Lewis White Beck (University of Chicago Press, 1949).

14. See Arthur Schopenhauer, *Essays of Arthur Schopenhauer* (New York: A. L. Bur,

1892). In England, Thomas Hill Green (1836–1882) was the first important modern idealist. In France, Idealism developed in reaction against the founder of Positivism, Auguste Comte (1798–1857): see Auguste Comte, *A General View of Positivism* (London: Trubner, 1865); see also Charles B. Renouvier, *Essais de critique generale* (Paris: Bureau de la Critique Philosophique, 1875); Antoine-Auguste Cournot, *Ouvres completes*, ed. Andre Robinet (Paris: Librarie philosophique J. Urin, 1973). Italian Idealism derived from the German Hegel, who described the dialectical advance of the human spirit in history, art, religion, and philosophy: see Georg F. W. Hegel, *Phenomenology of Mind* (Winchester, Mass.: Allen and Unwin, 1966); see also Benedetto Croce, *Il Carattero della filosophia moderna* (Rome: Laterza, 1945), and Giovanni Gentile, *Opere complete* (Firenze: Sansoni, n.d.).

15. See, for example, Perry Miller, ed., *The Works of Jonathan Edwards* (New Haven, Conn.: Yale University Press, 1957); and *The Yale Edition of the Works of Samuel Johnson* (New Haven, Conn.: Yale University Press, 1958). See also William Torrey Harris, *General Government and Public Education Throughout the Country* (Syracuse, N.Y.: Bardeen Press, 1890); *The Journal of Speculative Philosophy*, vols. 1–22 (St. Louis: Knapp, 1867–1880; New York: D. Appleton, 1880–1893); George Holmes Howison, *The Conception of God* (New York: Macmillan, 1897); idem, *The Limits of Evolution, and Other Essays Illustrating the Metaphysical Theory of Personal Idealism* (New York: Macmillan, 1905); Borden Parker Bowne, *Personalism* (Boston: Houghton Mifflin, 1908); and E. S. Brightman, *The Finding of God* (New York: Abingdon, 1931); idem, *Moral Laws* (New York: Abingdon, 1933). See also the quarterly *The Personalist*, vol. 1 (April 1920) through vol. 60 (October 1969) (Los Angeles: School of Philosophy, University of Southern California; continued by *Pacific Philosophical Quarterly*).

Probably the most outstanding of U.S. idealists is the Hegelian Josiah Royce (1855–1916). He argued that the entire universe is essentially one living thing, a mind, one great spirit: see Josiah Royce, *The World and the Individual*, 2 vols. (New York: Macmillan, 1900–1901). Because the universe is one great all-inclusive mind, the best way to acquire an understanding of it is by examining one's own conscious experience. And just as the human mind is the total of fleeting conscious experience, so also the Absolute is composed of all the conscious selves into which the Absolute is differentiated.

16. George E. Moore, "The Refutation of Idealism," *Mind*, vol. XII (1903), pp. 433–53; Bertrand Russell, "The Nature of Sense-Data," *Mind*, vol. XXII (1913), pp. 76–81; idem, *Journal of Philosophy*, vol. 12 (1915), pp. 391f.

17. See E. I. Watkin, *A Philosophy of Form* (London: Sheed and Ward, 1951) for the fullest statement of the author's "dialectical ideal-realism," an articulation of the "ideal-realism founded by Plato . . . modified by Aristotle for better and for worse and continued through Plotinus, Augustine, Boethius, 'Dionysius', Scotus-Eriugena, Anselm, Bonaventura, Albert, and Thomas Aquinas to Wust, Lossky among contemporary philosophers" (p. vii). An earlier and shorter statement of Watkin's thought may be found in his *The Bow in the Clouds: An Essay Towards the Integration of Experience* (London: Sheed and Ward, 1931). A formulation of a "dialectical theory of religion" by a Catholic philosopher may be found in Louis Dupré, *The Other Dimension: A Search for the Meaning of Religious Attitudes* (Garden City, N.Y.: Doubleday, 1972).

18. One can see these themes in *Three Plays: A Man of God, Ariadne, The Votive Candle*, rev. ed. (New York: Hill and Wang, 1965); and *La Soif* (Paris: Desclee de Brouwre, 1938); also published as *Les Colours Avides* (Paris: La Table Ronde, 1952).

On Marcel, see also Kenneth T. Gallagher, *The Philosophy of Gabriel Marcel* (New

York: Fordham University Press, 1975); Vincent P. Miceli, *Ascent to Being: Gabriel Marcel's Philosophy of Communion* (Paris: Desclee, 1965); Seymour Cain, *Gabriel Marcel* (New York: Hillary House, 1963).

19. Carl Rogers, "Can Learning Encompass both Ideas and Feelings?" in Don Hamachek, ed., *Human Dynamics in Psychology and Education* (Boston: Allyn and Bacon, 1977), p. 24, as cited in Brendan Carmody, "A Context for the Catholic Philosophy of Education," *Lumen Vitae*, vol. 36 no. 1 (1981), p. 46.

20. On Buber, see Robert E. Wood, *Martin Buber's Ontology: An Analysis of I and Thou* (Evanston, Ill.: Northwestern University Press, 1969).

21. Janusz Tarnowski, "An Existential Christian Pedagogy, The Current Problem," *Lumen Vitae*, vol. 28 no. 2 (June 1973), pp. 328f.

22. By the year 2000, it is reliably estimated that 83 percent of all youth between ages fifteen and twenty-four will be living in Asia, Africa, and Latin America. (*Maryknoll*, vol. 81 no. 3, March 1987.)

23. See Bernard Lonergan, *Insight: A Study of Human Understanding* (New York: Philosophical Library, 1957); idem, *Method in Theology* (London: Darton, Longman and Todd, 1973), especially pp. 217, 318, 338.

24. Carmody, art. cit., pp. 56f. See also Bernard J. Tyrrell, *Christotherapy: Healing through Enlightenment* (New York: Seabury, 1981), and idem, *Christotherapy II: The Fasting and Feasting Heart* (Ramsey, N.J.: Paulist, 1982), especially the latter.

25. Tarnowski, art. cit., p. 332.

26. M. Navratil, *Dialogue, vocabulaire de psychopedagogie et de psychiatrie de l'enfant* (Paris, 1963), p. 174, as in Tarnowski, art. cit., p. 333.

27. Martin Buber, *Schriften zur Philosophie* (Munich-Heidelberg, 1962), vol. 1, p. 88, as in Janusz Tarnowski, "An Existential Christian Pedagogy, The Current Problem," *Lumen Vitae*, vol. 28 no. 2 (June 1973), p. 333.

28. *Pastoral Constitution on the Church in the Modern World* (*Gaudium et spes*) # 48, in Flannery, vol. 1, p. 951.

29. Carmody, art. cit., p. 54.

CHAPTER 4: GOALS

1. Adapted from Kevin Nichols, *Cornerstone* (Middlegreen, Slough, England: St. Paul, 1978), p. 43.

2. John Goodlad, *A Place Called School: Prospects for the Future* (New York: McGraw-Hill, 1984), p. 48.

3. For example, a 1985 study found that more than 65 percent of the country's Catholic school systems lack written long-range development plans. The study, by William J. Amoriell and Joseph Procaccini of Loyola College, Baltimore, surveyed 197 Catholic-school superintendents (95 of whom responded), and interviewed over 50 school superintendents, principals, and development officers. (*Education Week*, September 11, 1985, p. 5.)

4. Michael Winter, *What Ever Happened to Vatican II?* (London: Sheed and Ward, 1985), pp. 99f., citing W. T. Glynn's pamphlet *Aims and Objectives in Catholic Education* (Stoke-on-Trent: Catholic Teachers Federation, 1980), p. 3.

5. Werner Jaeger, *Paideia: The Ideals of Greek Culture*, 3 vols., trans. Gilbert Highet, 2nd ed. (New York: Oxford University Press, 1945), vol. I.

6. Rom. 12:2. See also 2 Cor. 3:18; 1 Cor. 1:24.

7. Sacred Congregation for Catholic Education, *Catholic Schools* (*Malgre les declarations*) # 9, in Austin Flannery, ed., *Vatican Council II: The Conciliar and Post Conciliar Documents*, 2 vols. (Northport, N. Y.: Costello, 1975), vol. 2, p. 608.

8. National Conference of Catholic Bishops, *Sharing the Light of Faith: National Cate-*

chetical Directory for Catholics of the United States (Washington, D.C.: United States Catholic Conference, 1979), # 224, p. 138.

9. Ralph W. Tyler, *Basic Principles of Curriculum and Instruction* (Chicago: University of Chicago Press, 1949).

10. Mary Ann Eckoff, "Speaking of Standards and Expectations," *Momentum*, vol. XV no. 4 (December 1984), pp. 14–15, gives a brief comparative discussion of goals in government and Catholic schools and of what Catholic-school expectations should be.

11. B. S. Bloom et al., *Taxonomy of Educational Objectives* (New York: McKay, 1956).

12. Paul H. Hirst and R. S. Peters, *The Logic of Education* (London: Routledge and Kegan Paul, 1970), chap. 4, "The Curriculum," pp. 60–73.

13. Paul H. Hirst, *Knowledge and the Curriculum: A Collection of Philosophical Papers* (London and Boston: Routledge and Kegan Paul, 1974), p. 27.

14. Goodlad, op. cit. p. 50.

15. Ibid., p. 59.

16. As cited in John Whitney Evans, "Americanism: Acculturation and Aggiornamento," *The Critic*, vol. 41 no. 2 (Winter 1986), p. 24.

17. H. I. Marrou, *A History of Education in Antiquity*, trans. George Lamb (New York: Sheed and Ward, 1956), pp. 217–26

18. *Catholic Schools* # 49, in Flannery, vol. 2, p. 617.

19. *The Church in the Modern World* (*Gaudium et spes*) # 59, in Flannery, vol. 1, p. 963.

20. Winter, op. cit., p. 104, from the Conference of Catholic Chaplains to Universities and Polytechnics.

21. *Catechetical Directory* # 104, in Flannery, vol. 2, p. 588.

22. *Catholic Schools* # 37, in Flannery, vol. 2, p. 614.

23. From mimeographed 1986 Self-Study, p. 1.

24. The Loreto Sisters of Dublin, *The Loreto Tradition* (Dublin: Loreto Sisters, 1984), pp. 3–12.

25. *Catholic Schools* # 35, in Flannery, vol. 2, p. 614.

26. Adolf Exeler, "Faith and Education," in Kevin Nichols, ed., *Voice of the Hidden Waterfall: Essays on Religious Education* (Middlegreen, Slough, England: St. Paul, 1980), pp. 51–52.

27. *Decree on the Church's Missionary Activity* (*Ad gentes divinitus*) # 11, in Flannery, vol. 1, p. 825.

28. Janusz Tarnowski, "An Existential Christian Pedagogy, The Current Problem," *Lumen Vitae*, vol. 28 no. 2 (June 1973), p. 335.

29. Ibid., p. 337.

30. Col. 1:15; *Catechetical Directory* # 42, in Flannery, vol. 2, p. 553.

31. *The Church in the Modern World* (*Gaudium et spes*) # 30, in Flannery, vol. 1, p. 930.

32. *Decree on the Apostolate of Lay People* (*Apostolicam actuositatem*) # 5, in Flannery, vol. 1, p. 772.

33. *Gaudium et spes* # 25, in Flannery, vol. 1, p. 926.

34. *Lay Catholics in Schools: Witnesses to Faith* (*Les laïcs Catholiques*) # 34, in Flannery, vol. 2, p. 643.

35. *Gaudium et spes* # 23, in Flannery, vol. 1, p. 924.

36. U. S. Catholic bishops, *To Teach as Jesus Did* (Washington, D.C.: United States Catholic Conference, 1973), ## 22, 23, p. 7. See also ## 24–26, p. 8.

37. *Gaudium et spes* # 78, in Flannery, vol. 1, p. 986f.

38. *Catholic Schools* # 56, in Flannery, vol. 2, p. 618.

39. U. S. Catholic bishops, *To Teach as Jesus Did*, # 29, p. 9.

40. *Decree on the Church's Missionary Activity (Ad gentes divinitus)* # 12, in Flannery, vol. 1, p. 826.

41. Adapted from the Loreto Sisters of Dublin, op. cit., pp. 3–12.

42. Apoc. 22:13, and *Gravissimum educationis* # 45, in Flannery, vol. 1, p. 947.

43. See *Gaudium et spes* # 78, in Flannery, vol. 1, p. 987; # 32, in Flannery, vol. 1, p. 932; and *Catechetical Directory* # 52, in Flannery, vol. 2, p. 558.

44. Adapted from the Loreto Sisters of Dublin, op. cit., pp. 3–12.

45. *Gaudium et spes* # 31, in Flannery, vol. 1, p. 931.

46. *Pastoral Constitution on the Church in the Modern World (Gaudium et spes)* # 59, in Flannery, vol. 1, p. 963.

47. *Catholic Schools* # 31, in Flannery, vol. 2, p. 613.

48. *Declaration on Christian Education (Gravissimum educationis)* # 1, in Flannery, vol. 1, p. 727. The harmonious development of physical, moral, and intellectual qualities was also in Pius XI's 1929 encyclical, *The Christian Education of Youth*.

49. *Catholic Schools* # 26, in Flannery, vol. 2, p. 612.

50. Ibid., # 45, in Flannery, vol. 2, p. 616; *Gaudium et spes* # 61, in Flannery, vol. 1, p. 965.

51. Canon 795, from Canon Law Society of America, *Code of Canon Law, Latin-English Edition*, trans. under the auspices of the Canon Law Society of America (Washington, D.C.: Canon Law Society of America, 1983).

52. See, for example, Richard Hofstadter, *Anti-intellectualism in American Life* (New York: Knopf, 1963).

53. The 1981 study *Public and Private Schools*, by James S. Coleman et al., concluded:

> A) On average, Catholic schools are more effective than public schools; B) Catholic schools are especially beneficial to students from less advantaged backgrounds; C) There are strong indications that higher levels of discipline and academic demands account in large part for the differences between the sectors' levels of achievement. (Sally Kilgore, Thomas Hoffer, and Bruno Manno, "An Update on the Coleman Study," *Momentum* 13 [October 1982], p. 7.)

Compared to government schools, Catholic-school students scored about two grade levels higher in mathematics, reading, and vocabulary scores. No differences were found in sciences. The study found that factors which accounted for this were more effective school discipline, fewer student absences, higher enrollments in academic coursework, and about 50 percent more homework.

54. *Catechetical Directory* # 94, in Flannery, vol. 2, p. 583.

55. *Catholic Schools* # 46, in Flannery, vol. 2, p. 616.

56. Ibid., # 30, in Flannery, vol. 2, p. 613.

57. *Catechetical Directory* # 40, in Flannery, vol. 2, p. 551f.

58. *Gaudium et spes* # 22, in Flannery, vol. 1, p. 923f.

59. See Martin Kaplan, *What Is an Educated Person?: The Decades Ahead* (New York: Praeger, 1980), p. 9.

60. John M. Hull, *Studies in Religion and Education* (London: Falmer, 1984), pp. 198–205.

61. Adapted from Adolf Exeler, "Faith and Education," in Nichols, op. cit., pp. 51–60.

62. *Catholic Schools* # 29, in Flannery, vol. 2, p. 612f.

63. In the sixteenth century, some missioners like Bartolome de las Casas, witnessing the suffering of Indians, discovered that their mission was to call for liberation. But a theology of liberation as we know it today started in the 1960s, when pastoral agents, including theologians, religious sisters, brothers, and priests, not only lived among the poor but also began to listen to them. After World War II, the gap between the rich and the poor in the third world was ever widening. Then came the Second

Vatican Council, whose documents, along with great social encyclicals like *Mater et magistra*, *Pacem in terris*, and *Populorum progressio*, prepared the groundwork further.

Liberation theology's birth, however, came with the second Latin American Bishops' Conference in Medellin, Colombia, in 1968, when the bishops applied the Church's social teaching to conditions of the vast majority of people in Latin America. Despite some popular opinions to the contrary, liberation theology is not a call to violent revolution.

Paolo Freire, a liberation theologian, distinguishes between education as domestication and education as liberation: see Paolo Freire, *Education for Critical Consciousness* (London: Sheed and Ward/New York: Continuum, 1974), as cited in Michael P. Hornsby-Smith, *Catholic Education: The Unobtrusive Partner; Sociological Studies of the Catholic School System of England and Wales* (London: Sheed and Ward, 1978), p. 147. See also Phillip Berryman, *Liberation Theology: Essential Facts About the Revolutionary Religious Movements in Latin America and Beyond* (Philadelphia: Temple University Press, 1987); Denis E. Collins, *Paolo Freire* (New York: Paulist Press, 1977). Though a critic of formal schooling, Freire is likely to be of most value to Catholic educators with a post-Vatican-II orientation which is sensitive to the existence of worldwide social injustice and has a concern to school its young in freedom to be witnesses to the Gospel imperatives of love. (See Paul VI, *Populorum progressio*, 1967, and *Octogesima adveniens*, 1971.) For Freire, the task of the educator is to enter into dialogue with the pupil about concrete experienced situations—a dialogue "nourished by love, humility, hope, faith and trust"—and in the process culture is created and re-created and the world transformed.

A key concept for Freire is *conscientization*, which involves the process in which people achieve a deepening awareness of both their sociocultural reality and their ability to reform that reality, and "refers to learning to perceive social, political, and economic contradictions, and to take action against the oppressive elements of reality" (Paolo Freire, *Pedagogy of the Oppressed* [Hammondsworth, England: Penguin, 1972], translator's note, p. 15, n. 1). In the dialogic process of action which Freire advocates, *witness* is one of the principal expressions of the educational character of the transformation of society. Given the proclaimed goals of the Roman Catholic Church to act on behalf of the underprivileged of the world (see Paul VI, op. cit.; *Gaudium et spes*, in Flannery, vol. 1, pp. 903–1001; John XXIII, *Mater et magistra*, 1961, and *Pacem in terris*, 1963; *Justice in the World*, Third International Synod of Bishops, 1972; and the U.S. bishops' pastoral letters), it is important to examine the extent to which Catholic schools are promoting the sorts of witness to "this-worldly" concerns of social justice.

Freire criticizes traditional education as a "banking" concept, whereby educators try to deposit material into pupils against future withdrawals of their investment. For him this is too conservative, an instrument of oppression used by the establishment to mold the young into the establishment's own worldview. For Freire, liberation must be extended to the oppressed many. It is not to be too cerebral or abstract; it is to form the heart as well as the mind. It is to be, in Martin Buber's words, "speech from certainty to certainty, though from one open-hearted person to another" (Martin Buber, *Between Man and Man*, trans. Ronald Gregor Smith [Boston: Beacon, 1955]).

Freire's view of educational liberation has similarities to the Western liberal tradition. Both are concerned with enabling persons to stand on their own feet, with being conscious of the world critically, and with taking their destiny in their own hands. Freire's writings, however, from the cognitive point of view are more confused and diffuse than the traditional view. And for Freire thought is of little significance unless it results in action.

64. See Gustavo Gutierrez, *A Theology of Liberation* (New York: Orbis Books, 1973).

65. Congregation for the Doctrine of the Faith, *Instruction on Christian Freedom and Liberation* (Vatican City: Vatican Polyglot Press, 1986), # 25, p. 15.

66. Ibid., # 26, p. 16.

67. Ibid., # 18, p. 11.

68. Gen. 3:5.

69. *Instruction on Christian Freedom and Liberation* # 61, p. 35.

70. Ibid., # 20, p. 13.

71. Ibid., # 20, p. 13.

72. Ibid., # 23, p. 14.

73. Ibid., # 75 p. 45.

74. Bernard Lonergan, *Insight* (New York: Philosophical Library, 1957), chap. XX.

75. Freire, *Pedagogy*, p. 62.

76. *Instruction on Christian Freedom and Liberation* # 99, p. 58.

77. It can also mean happiness, redemption. In German, *die Heilsgeschichte* means "salvation history"; *im Jahre des Heils* means "in the year of grace," or "in the year of our Lord." As an acclamation *Heil* means "Hail! Good Luck!" Unfortunately, the National Socialists adapted it for such greetings as *Heil Hitler!* and *Sieg Heil!* ("To Victory!").

78. In the Bible, the words "save," "salvation," and "savior" passed through many stages of meaning. The first sense, never lost, is that to be "saved" is to be rescued from disaster — defeat, captivity, or death, or all three. In later parts of the Old Testament, salvation sometimes refers specifically to deliverance from sin, and to the joy that results from this. More often, however, the concept is generalized beyond the nation and related to God's entrance into the historical process as the ruler of humankind, where the purpose of His entrance is the freedom of His people and the inauguration of peace, righteousness, and love throughout creation. The New Testament speaks more forcefully of salvation being deliverance from sin. Jesus saves us from sin at a personal level and therefore from sin's impact on the social order.

When Jesus comes on the scene as Savior, his saving work, though necessarily limited during his earthly career to individuals, families, and small groups, is all-inclusive. He comes as healer as well as teacher. He asserts his program in the synagogue at Nazareth: "to announce good news to the poor, to proclaim release for prisoners and recovery of sight for the blind; to let the broken victims go free . . . " (Luke 4:18f.). And he fulfills his program: he delivers people in physical need, forgives sins, sets free the captive, and founds a Church to continue the salvation that he started and which is meant for all people and covers the whole of human life.

79. *Lumen Gentium* # 40, in Flannery, vol. 1, p. 397.

80. *Catechetical Directory* # 56, in Flannery, vol. 2, p. 566.

81. *Lumen Gentium* # 39, in Flannery, vol. 1, p. 396.

82. Ibid., # 41, in Flannery, vol. 1, p. 398.

CHAPTER 5: CURRICULUM

1. Paul H. Hirst and R. S. Peters, *The Logic of Education* (London: Routledge and Kegan Paul, 1970), chap. 4, "The Curriculum," p. 60.

2. Fenwick W. English, ed., *Fundamental Curriculum Decisions* (Alexandria, Va.: Association for Supervision and Curriculum Development, 1983), is a yearbook of articles addressing the major issues in curriculum development.

3. Interview with Peter Hackett, S. J., Master, Campion Hall, Oxford, on February 24, 1986.

4. Paul H. Hirst and R. S. Peters mention seven (among them formal logic and mathematics, physical sciences, historical truths, and religious claims), all of which are different in kind but have a network of relations. See Hirst and Peters, op. cit., pp. 62–67. Philip Phenix maintains that there are "six fundamental patterns of meaning [which] emerge from the analysis of the possible distinctive modes of human understanding." The six realms (symbolics, empirics, aesthetics, synnoetics, ethics, and synoptics) are seen as providing "the foundations for all the meanings that enter into human experience. They are the foundations . . . in the sense that they cover the pure and archetypal kinds of meaning that determine the quality of every humanly significant experience." Philip Phenix, *Realms of Meaning* (New York: McGraw-Hill, 1964), pp. 6, 8, cited in Paul H. Hirst, *Knowledge and the Curriculum: A Collection of Philosophical Papers* (London: Routledge and Kegan Paul, 1974), p. 54.

5. Phenix, p. 21, in Hirst, op. cit., p. 55.

6. Hirst and Peters, op. cit., pp. 62–67.

7. John Dewey, *Democracy and Education* (New York: Macmillan, 1923), p. 226.

8. *Constitution on the Church in the Modern World (Gaudium et spes)* # 15, in Austin Flannery, ed., *Vatican Council II: The Conciliar and Post Conciliar Documents*, 2 vols. (Northport, N.Y.: Costello, 1975), vol. 1, p. 916.

9. Hirst and Peters, op. cit., chap. 4, "The Curriculum," pp. 60–73, especially p. 71. See also Hirst, op. cit., chapter 9, "Curriculum Integration," pp. 132–51.

10. Hirst, op. cit., p. 32.

11. Ibid., p. 31.

12. Ibid., p. 47.

13. *Credo of the People of God*, in Flannery, vol. 2, p. 388.

14. *Gaudium et spes* # 57, in Flannery, vol. 1, p. 961.

15. Ibid., # 57, in Flannery, vol. 1, p. 962.

16. Ibid., in Flannery, vol. 1, p. 961.

17. Pope John Paul II at audience with the International Association of Catholic Educators, November 5, 1985, on occasion of twentieth anniversary of Vatican II's "Declaration on Christian Education," as reported in *NC News Service*, November 5, 1985, p. 12.

18. *Declaration on the Relation of the Church to Non-Christian Religions (Nostra aetate)* # 1, in Flannery, vol. 1, p. 738.

19. *Constitution on the Church in the Modern World (Gaudium et spes)* # 43, in Flannery, vol. 1, p. 943.

20. See, e.g., H. I. Marrou, *A History of Education in Antiquity* (New York: Sheed and Ward, 1956), pp. 314–29; Anders Nygren, *Agape and Eros* (New York: Harper and Row, 1969), p. 340.

21. After the conversion of Constantine, profound changes took place in the formation of Christians. For one thing, mass baptisms made it necessary that individual instruction give way to group instruction. For another, there as a gradual shift from adult instruction to that of children. And the Church had to interweave her instructions into the processes of formal education. The Christian faith was now more able to stand up for itself in the world's intellectual marketplace.

By the early Middle Ages, the Church's involvement in secular education developed from wholehearted commitment to dominance and control. During the Dark Ages the Church, through her monasteries, saved classical education and transmitted its light to the future despite the surrounding darkness of barbarism. Eventually, the Church achieved a new synthesis between classical learning and the teachings of the faith. This synthesis was the foundation of the liberal arts curriculum which in turn was the basis of the West's higher education for over a thousand years.

In this synthesis, theology became the "queen" of the other fields of knowledge. But there was also conflict between theology and the liberal arts. Liberal education by definition has as its purpose to free the person. A freed person can explore, compare, accept—and reject. This became evident with certain facets of the Renaissance. The increased religious pluralism after the Protestant revolt, the growth of secular states, the lack of Church awareness, and the general secularization of Europe contributed to the perception of a lessened importance for religious instruction on an adult level. More recent industrialization, technologization, and media pervasion have hastened the process.

22. See Josef Neuner and J. Dupuis, *The Christian Faith in the Doctrinal Documents of the Catholic Church* (New York: Alba House, 1966). (Gives corresponding references to Denzinger.)

23. *Catholic Schools* # 19, in Flannery, vol. 2, p. 610.

24. Pope John Paul II, *Catechesis in our Time (Catechesi tradendae)* # 69, in Flannery, vol. 2, p. 805.

25. Pope John Paul II on November 5, 1985, as reported in *NC News Service*, November 5, 1985, p. 12.

26. *Catechetical Directory* # 43, in Flannery, vol. 2, pp. 553f. For a fuller exposition of the Creed, see also *Credo of the People of God*, in Flannery, vol. 2, pp. 388–94.

27. *Catechetical Directory* # 44, in Flannery, vol. 2, p. 554.

28. Ibid., # 63, in Flannery, vol. 2, p. 565.

29. Marisa Crawford and Graham Rossitor, *Teaching Religion in Catholic Schools: Theory and Practice* (Sydney: Province Resource Group, 1986), p. 23; concludes that there is little evidence in recent years that religion courses are too academic or too intellectual.

30. Among the difficulties we do not treat are classroom constraints—compulsory attendance, discipline, timetable, examinations, and the like—which make the school seem the least likely setting in which to build up a "community of faith."

31. *The National Catholic Reporter*, vol. 22 no. 15 (February 7, 1986), p. 3, reporting on A. James Reichley et al., *Religion in American Public Life* (Washington, D. C.: Brookings Institute, 1986).

32. Interview with Peter Hackett, S. J., Master, Campion Hall, Oxford, on February 24, 1986.

33. Anselmo Balocco, "The Religious Sense and Religious Education," in Kevin Nichols, ed., *Voice of the Hidden Waterfall: Essays on Religious Education* (Middlegreen, Slough, England: St. Paul, 1980), p. 104.

34. *Catholic Schools* # 50, in Flannery, vol. 2, p. 617.

35. *Catechical Directory* # 2, in Flannery, vol. 2, p. 532.

36. One proponent, Michael O'Neill, divides schooling into three layers: content, methodology, and intentionality. (Michael O'Neill, "Toward a Modern Concept of 'Permeation,'" *Momentum*, May 1979, pp. 48–50.) Content he sees as the curriculum, objectives, books and other materials, assignments, tests, and the like. He sees content as open to legitimate ways to elicit Catholic contributions when they in fact exist. In methodology he includes teaching methods, disciplinary procedures, administrative styles, and school decision making processes. This important part of the school reality actually constitutes a metacurriculum which in some ways is more powerful than the school's stated curriculum. Although not all humane methodology is "Catholic," permeation in methodology is meaningful to overall purposes.

By intentionality, O'Neill means the intentions and interpersonal relationships with which people act, creating a powerful reality in the social setting of the school (or anyplace else). A man and a woman who as strangers eat at the same table in a crowded cafeteria are immensely different from a man and a woman who love each other preparing and eating a meal together. Here is where permeation is the most important. Although intentionality may not be always immediately evident, it is most powerful. When the people in a school share a definite intentionality, they set up a definite pattern of values, understandings, sentiments, hopes, and dreams. This conditions everything else: math class, athletic activities, dances, teachers' coffee breaks. This whole is greater than the sum of its parts. It is also the notion of the "hidden curriculum," sometimes called the "unstudied curriculum."

37. *Catholic Schools* # 39, in Flannery, vol. 2, p. 615.

38. *Catechetical Directory* # 25, in Flannery, vol. 2, p. 545.

39. *Directory on Children's Masses* ## 23, 47, 50, 51, in Flannery, vol. 1, pp. 262, 268f.

40. *Instruction on the Worship of the Eucharistic Mystery* (*Eucharisticum mysterium*) # 6, in Flannery, vol. 1, p. 107.

41. *Directory on Children's Masses* # 9, in Flannery, vol. 1, p. 257.

42. *Constitution on the Sacred Liturgy* (*Sacrosanctum concilium*) ## 11, 14, 19, 48, in Flannery, vol. 1, pp. 6, 7, 8, 9, 16.

43. Ibid., ## 12f., in Flannery, vol. 1, p. 7.

44. Hirst, op. cit., p. 174.

45. Rom. 2:14f.

46. Lawrence Kohlberg, "The Child as a Moral Philosopher," *Psychology Today*, September 1968, as cited in John W. Donohue, "Farther Than the Moon," *America*, vol. 135 (September 11, 1976), pp. 110–13.

47. Among them, Sidney Simon, Leland Howe, and Howard Kirschenbaum, *Values Clarification: A Handbook of Practical Strategies for Teachers and Students* (New York: Hart, 1972), and Michael Silver, ed., *Values Education* (Washington, D.C.: National Education Association, 1976).

48. *Declaration on Certain Problems of Sexual Ethics* (*Personae humanae*) ## 3, 4, in Flannery, vol. 2, pp. 487f.

49. Clyde Kluckhohn et al., "Values and Value-Orientations in the Theory of Action: An Exploration in Definition and Classification," in Talcott Parsons et al., eds., *Toward a General Theory of Action* (Cambridge, Mass.: Harvard University Press, 1951), p. 395.

50. *The Washington Post*, April 4, 1987, p. A8. Among the normally opposing camps taking this position are Bill Honig, California superintendent of schools; District of Columbia superintendent Floretta D. McKenzie; liberal television producer and founder of People for the American Way Norman Lear; former U.S. Secretary of Education Terrel H. Bell; current U.S. Secretary of Education William J. Bennett; and White House domestic policy adviser Gary L. Bauer. What prompted the attention are current social trends like teenage pregnancy, drug problems, high school dropouts, racial violence, and single-parent families. Honig observed that there should be no disagreement about teaching most civic and personal values—honesty, responsibility, self-discipline, and compassion, for example—because there is wide social consensus on most of these values. This group of about 250 educators, religious leaders, textbook publishers, and policy makers also agreed that schools cannot teach values adequately by simply adding a course on the subject, but must weave lessons in virtue and morality throughout the curriculum. Granting the pluralistic nature of our society, however, it would seem that the only way to accomplish this is to provide better conditions for the equal existence of nongovernment schools.

51. Ernest L. Boyer, "Communicating Values: The Social and Moral Imperatives of Education," *Momentum*, vol. XVII no. 3 (September 1986), pp. 6–8, presents excellent material on the importance of values, especially the sacred, in education.

Patricia Feistritzer, "Transmitting Values through Education: A Conversation with William J. Bennett," *Momentum*, vol. XVI no. 4 (December 1985), pp. 8–10, gives the U. S. Secretary of Education the opportunity to make his case for values in education. He uses the Greeks, Shakespeare, and the Federalist Papers as means to transmit values.

52. Carl R. Rogers and Barry Stephens, *Person to Person* (Lafayette, Ind.: Real People Press, 1968), p. 47.

53. Søren Kierkegaard, "Either/Or," *A Kierkegaard Anthology*, ed. Robert Bretall (Princeton, N.J.; Princeton University Press, 1967), p. 106.

54. Ibid.

55. See Simon, Howe, and Kirschenbaum, op. cit., # 24, p. 123.

56. See Robert N. Bellah et al., *Habits of the Heart: Individualism and Commitment in American Life* (Berkeley: University of California Press, 1985).

57. See, for example, Aristotle, *Nicomachean Ethics* (Indianapolis, Ind.: Bobbs-Merrill, 1981); also in Loeb Classical Library and many other editions.

58. John Dewey, *Theory of the Moral Life* (New York: Holt, Rinehart and Winston, 1960), and his *Theory of Valuation* (University of Chicago Press, 1939); also, John Dewey and James H. Tufts, *Ethics* (New York: Holt, Rinehart and Winston, 1932), and James Gouinlock, *John Dewey's Philosophy of Value* (New York: Humanities, 1972).

59. See Jean Piaget, *The Moral Judgment of the Child* (Glencoe, Ill.: Free Press, 1948).

60. See Lawrence Kohlberg, "Stages of Moral Development as a Basis for Moral education," in C. M. Beck et al., eds., *Moral Education: Interdisciplinary Approaches* (University of Toronto Press, 1971), pp. 23–92.

61. Lawrence Kohlberg, *Essays on Moral Development, Vol. I: The Philosophy of Moral Development* (New York: Harper and row, 1981), especially chap. 9, "Moral Development, Religious Thinking and the Question of a Seventh Stage," pp. 311–72.

62. Kohlberg himself saw it necessary to address his philosophical underpinnings in his *The Philosophy of Moral Development: Moral Stages and the Idea of Justice* (San Francisco: Harper and Row, 1981). This is the first part of a projected monumental three-volume magnum opus. Although this was probably not finished before Kohlberg's death in 1987, it was expected to be followed by *The Psychology of Moral Development: Moral Stages and the Life Cycle*, to put forth the psychological evidence supporting his hypothesized stages (most of it based on structured interviews which elicit reactions to "moral dilemmas"), and by *Education and Moral Development: Moral Stages and Practice*, to develop the implications of his theory for moral education (a work already largely begun). Throughout, Kohlberg sets himself the gigantic task of establishing morality as a science and rendering the good efficacious. He posited moral development as the aim of all education.

63. Leopold and Loeb, for example, were geniuses, but did not possess much in the way of proper affections and will. They therefore conspired to commit the "perfect crime" of killing a child, immortalized in the motion picture *Compulsion* and in literature written and read by those who are fascinated by this dichotomy.

64. By what right, for example, can anyone claim that fear of punishment is a lower form of moral reasoning and thus a less worthy form of ethical behavior than that which is instrumental in satisfying needs?

65. Sacred Congregation for Catholic Education, *Lay Catholics in Schools: Witnesses to Faith (Les laïcs Catholiques)* # 30, in Flannery, vol. 2, p. 641.

66. Carleen Reck, *Vision and Values in the Catholic School: Participant's Guide* (Washington, D.C.: National Catholic Educational Association, 1986); presents a different approach than the one here, but attempts a reflective guide to help in developing a

Catholic value-oriented curriculum and in translating some key gospel values into concrete terms.

67. Matt. 23:12; Mark 10:43.

68. E.g., Mark 7:21-23; 1 Tim. 6:3-12; Titus 2:1-8; Gal. 5:22.

69. See, e.g., Matt. 22:34-40; John 13:34f.; 14:15; 14:23; 15:9,13; Rom. 12:9; 13:8-10; Gal. 5:14; James 2:8; 1 Cor. 8:3; 2:9; 1 Thess. 4:9; 1 John 2:15; 3:11, 18, 23; 4:7, 11f., 19-21; Jude 21.

70. Matt. 18:3; 19:13.

71. Deut. 6:4f.; Mark 12:29-31.

72. For an interesting analysis of youth and faith in the Jewish and Christian traditions, see Rabbi Gordon Tucher, "Youth: Faith and the Quest for Life's Meaning," *Origins*, vol. 14 no. 5 (June 14, 1984), pp. 75-80.

73. See Matt. 26:42, 44; Mark 1:35, 39; Luke 5:16; 9:29; 22:32, 41, 43; Acts 4:31; 9:40; 14:22; 20:26; 21:5.

74. See Matt. 12:21; 1 Tim. 1:1; 4:10; 1 Thess. 4:12; 5:8; Col. 1:23, 27; Acts 24:15; 26:6f.; 27:20; 26:7; Rom. 4:18; 5:2,5; 8:20, 24f.; 12:12; 15:12f.; 1 Cor. 9:10; 10:15.

75. Enunciated by Jesus in Matt. 25:31-46, and shown by his example in Matt. 4:24; 8:16; 9:2; 14:14.

76. Matt., chaps. 5, 7, and 18.

77. James 3:1-12.

78. Matt. 12:10; Mark 3:1,3; Luke 6:8; Matt. 21:12; John 2:14.

79. John 4.

80. Matt. 5.

81. U.S. Catholic bishops, *To Teach as Jesus Did* (Washington, D.C.: National Catholic Educational Association, 1973), ## 28, 29, p. 9.

82. Matt. 10:39.

83. Service is not, of course, to be equated with adolescent employment, which can be harmful. See Ellen Greenberger and Lawrence Steinberg, *When Teenagers Work: The Psychological and Social Costs of Adolescent Employment* (New York: Basic Books, 1986), and *Education Week*, December 10, 1986, pp. 24, 17.

84. Ford Foundation and St. Mary's Catholic Foundation, *The Catholic High School: A National Portrait* (Washington, D.C.: National Catholic Educational Association, 1985), p. 37.

85. Among current injustices are ideologies that favor structural injustice, violations of human rights, the arms race, repression, marginalization, the deprivation of religious liberty, unequal distribution of wealth, consumerism, unemployment, the disadvantaged situation of the developing countries, migration, racism, violence, public and private corruption, discrimination against women, and innumerable abandoned children and youth who find no meaning in life.

For resource material for Catholic schools on violence, see Loretta Carey, "Teaching Alternatives on Violence in the Resolution of Conflict," *Momentum*, vol. XIV no. 4 (December 1983), pp. 16-18.

86. The breaking of God's Covenant was for the Hebrews a failure of justice. Though this failure deserves and receives punishment, one must exercise caution in describing the God of the Old Testament as vindictive. There is no Old Testament text which equates God's justice with vengeance against the sinner. God's justice is a *saving* justice, and punishment is an integral part of restoration. The prophets — those who were forthtellers and not necessarily foretellers — spoke in behalf of Yahweh and the voiceless (see, e.g., Jer. 22:1-16; Isa. 58:6-10; Ezek. 16:48-51).

In the Old Testament, the Psalms (which were the liturgical prayer of the Israelites and thus of Jesus) saw justice as a constitutive dimension of living the Covenant relationship. The prophets, who saw themselves as speaking for God and as being sent by God, read the signs of the times, spoke for the poor and the marginalized as well as for God directly, and challenged their hearers to respond (See, for example, the Books of Amos, Hosea, Isaiah, Jeremiah, Ezekiel, and Job). John the Baptist, Joseph, and Mary in the New Testament felt called in the same way: for John the Baptist, see especially Matt., chaps. 3, 11, 14; Mark, chaps. 1, 6; Luke, chaps. 1, 3, 7; John, chap. 1; for Joseph, see especially Luke, chap. 2; Matt., chaps. 1, 2 (especially 1:19, which describes Joseph as a just man). For Mary, see particularly her *Magnificat* and especially Matt., chaps. 1, 2, 27; Mark, chap. 15; Luke, chaps. 1, 2, 23, 24; John, chaps. 2, 19; and Acts, chap. 1.

From the Exile to the time of Jesus, the understanding of justice underwent three major transformations. One was an emphasis on the justice of the individual. While in exile, the Jews had to learn how to worship Yahweh in a place where other gods seemed to be in control, and the Hebrew community was very dispersed. One response was that the Pharisees originated the concept of the pious or separated ones, the *hasidim*. Pharisaic spirituality fostered the individualization of justice. Another transformation was the establishing of justice as a characteristic of the end time: the full accomplishment of God's justice will come only at the end of time. And third, there was a shift in language whereby justice (*sedaqah*) came to be equated with almsgiving or care for the poor: concern for neighbor is conceived as not simply an overflowing of love, but justice.

A message of the New Testament is that "God is justice." A few themes will illustrate this. The message of Jesus centers upon the Kingdom of God: For example, the first act of Jesus' public ministry, related in all three synoptic Gospels, was his preaching that "the Kingdom of God is at hand" (Mark 1:15). For Jesus, the Kingdom is the power of God active in the world, transforming it and confronting the powers of the world. Another theme is the fact that Jesus' disciples are called to serve, to be committed to the kind and quality of life that he led, dedicated to a mission of compassion to the outcast, and prophetic in their confrontations with the powers of evil (Mt. 5:17). After leaving his desert retreat that prepared him for his public ministry, Jesus' first public appearance according to St. Luke was in the synagogue in Nazareth where, asked to do the reading according to custom, he read: "The spirit of the Lord has been given to me . . . He has sent me to bring good news to the poor, to proclaim liberty to captives, sight to the blind . . . " (Luke 4:18f., from Isa. 61:1-2).

87. See Luke 1:51-53.

88. Matt. 25:31-46.

89. Acts 2:45; 4:34. The Epistle of James makes very clear that among the people of God all are equal and none should go in need, and speaks against discrimination and the exploitation of the poor (James 2:1-4; 5:1-6). Paul dwells on the mystery of Christ's option for the poor (see, e.g., 1 Cor. 1:17-31; 11: 17ff.; 2 Cor. 5:1-10; 8).

90. Matt. 5:1-7, 29.

91. The new economic order is well documented in Acts 2:42-47; 4:34.

92. Matt. 16:13, 20; 18:21-22; Mark 8:27-30; 9:2-8; 14:32-42; Luke 9:18ff.; 22:54ff.; John 13:38; 21:15-18.

93. For these instances, see respectively Luke 7:18-23; Matt. 19:16-22; Mark 10:17ff.; Luke 18:18ff.; John 12:24ff.; John 4:1-42; John 3:1-21; Matt. 15:21-28.

94. For these instances see respectively Matt. 19:23-30; Matt. 20:1-16; Matt. 8:1-4; Mark 9:33-37; Luke 9:46ff.; 22:24-27; Matt. 28:16ff.; Mark 6:9-13; Luke 9:1-6; 10:1-20; Mark 10:42.

95. John 12:1-11.

96. Matt. 5:1–7:29; Luke 6:20ff.; Matt. 19:1–12; Matt. 6:24–34; Luke 12:13ff.,32; Luke 12:33; Luke 14:12ff.

97. Mark 6:1–6; Luke 4:16–30; Matt. 23:37–39; Luke 19:41–44; John 8:32–44.

98. Matt. 9:10–13; Mark 2:15–17; Luke 5:29ff.; 11:37ff.; Luke 19:1–10; Luke 16:19–31.

99. Luke 7:38–50; John 8:1–11; John 7:14–24; 8:1–11; Matt. 21:12–17; Mark 11:15–19; Luke 19:45ff.; John 2:13ff.; Luke 22:66ff.; John 18:12–27; Mark 11:27–33; Luke 20:1–8; Matt. 4:1–11.

100. Matt. 27:11ff.; Luke 23:2ff.; John 18:28ff.; Luke 23:8–12; John 7:45ff.; John 18:1ff; Mark 15:39; Luke 7:1–10; 23:47ff.

101. For the historical dimension as well as others, see Joe Holland and Peter Henriot, S.J., *Social Analysis: Linking Faith and Justice* (Washington, D.C.: Center of Concern, 1984).

102. This begins with Pope Leo XIII's response to the Industrial Revolution, the 1891 encyclical *Rerum novarum*, which was the first of the Social Encyclicals and dealt with the condition of labor. As one good example of the encyclicals' teachings on justice, Pope John XXIII's *Pacem in terris* listed twenty-one rights of human beings, including "the right to life, to bodily integrity, and to the means which are suitable for the proper development of life; these are primarily food, clothing, shelter, rest, medical care, and finally the necessary social services." (Pope John XXIII, *Pacem in terris*, 1963, ## 11, 18.) Vatican II continued the trend.

In 1968, at Medellin, Colombia, the Latin American bishops discussed means of implementing Vatican II and *Populorum progressio* in the specific situation of Latin America. They produced sixteen documents, the two main themes of which were justice and peace. In 1971, on the eightieth anniversary of *Rerum novarum* and the tenth of *Mater et magistra*, Pope Paul VI issued *Octogesima adveniens*, an open letter to Cardinal Roy of Quebec, which was a call to action to all Catholics to begin more seriously to incorporate the new sense of Christian responsibility in the world. In the same year, the Synod of Bishops issued, among other things, a document on *Justice in the World*. The most quoted statement from the document is: "Action on behalf of justice and participation in the transformation of the world fully appear to us as a constitutive dimension of the preaching of the Gospel." In other words, if we are not actively concerned for justice, we are not Christian.

Pope John Paul II's first encyclical, issued in 1979, was *Redemptor hominis*. Dealing with, among other things, redeemed man and his situation in the modern world, it talks about "each man, an unrepeatable reality" (¶14), and raises the question, "Is man, as man, developing and progressing, or is he regressing and being degraded in his humanity?" (¶15), ending the discussion with a large section on human rights.

In 1979, the Latin American bishops met in Mexico and issued the "Puebla Document," which, in a pastoral overview, presented divergent views on the mission of the Church and the challenge to evangelization of unjust structures. Part II, "God's Saving Plan for Latin America," is a more positive view. It shows that the mission of the Church is enormous and is the task of us all. There have also been other works on justice by national conferences of bishops, such as the Irish bishops in 1977, and the United States bishops on *War and Peace* in 1983 and the 1986 pastoral letter on *Economic Justice for All*.

On the ninetieth anniversary of *Rerum novarum* in 1981, Pope John Paul II issued his encyclical *Laborem exercens* ("Human Work"), which greatly enriched and developed the social teaching of the Church. From an understanding of Genesis 1:28, he defined man as laborer: *Homo laborans*. Calling both capitalism and communism erroneous, he talked about the priority of labor over capital, indicating that capital must serve labor (¶15). He included the right to work as being among human rights (¶16) and spoke of elements for a spirituality of work.

103. For a stimulating discussion of some of the foregoing material, the author wishes to thank Fr. Sean Healy, S.M.A., and Sr. Brigid Reynolds, S.M., in an interview on March 18, 1986, at the justice office, Conference of Major Religious Superiors, Dublin, Ireland. See also Sean J. Healy, S.M.A., and Brigid Reynolds, S.M., *Social Analysis in the Light of the Gospel* (Dublin: Folens, 1983). And see the criticisms of current capitalism which Pope John Paul II made on a 1984 visit to Canada, particularly at Flatrock. The Flatrock remarks were an endorsement of the 1983 statement, "Ethical Reflections on the Economic Crisis," by the Social Affairs Commission of the Canadian Conference of Catholic Bishops. These and other statements so criticize current practices of capitalism that some have called them Marxist. One strong demonstration of continued interest in the U.S. is the bishops' 1986 pastoral letter on the economy, initial drafts of which left some people aghast: see the National Conference of Catholic Bishops, *Economic Justice for All* (Washington, D.C.: United States Catholic Conference, 1986). For books, papers, cassettes, slides, tapes, and other resources containing more information on justice in the teachings of the Church, contact the Center of Concern, 3700 13th Street N.E., Washington, D.C. 20017; telephone: (202) 635-2757.

Even those who take a position that "peace and justice" groups seem too action-oriented and propagandistic admit that Catholic schools should promote at least *cognitive* approaches to foster genuine insight into the causes of social problems.

104. *Gaudium et spes* # 76, in Flannery, vol. 1, p. 985.

105. Ibid., # 82, in Flannery, vol. 1, p. 992.

106. Dorene Wagner, "Is Peace a Religious Education Activity?" *Momentum*, vol. XIII (December 1983), p. 38.

107.

Gen. 4:10	From all eternity God loved His creation. By sin evil entered the world and injustice was born in the human heart. All through the history of humankind, however, God manifested His
Mic. 6: 6	will to liberate His people.
Ex. 3:23	Yahweh heard the cry of the poor and called His people to
Amos 5:21-24	justice. Through His prophets He never ceased to remind us
Is. 58	that sacrifice without action for justice is of no value in
Ez. 34	His eyes.
Jn. 3:16f.	In His great love, God sent His Son to redeem the world from
Rom. 8:15	the slavery of sin, and reveal that we are all children of the same Father.
1 Jn. 3:16	Jesus has given us an example of love, to the extent of laying down one's life. He shows how to love one another and how to
Mt. 4:43-48	forgive even our enemies. The love of God cannot be separated
Lk. 10:25-37	from the love of one's neighbor.
Mt. 5:2-10	Christ calls us to establish with Him a Kingdom of truth, love
Lk. 1:46-55	and justice, a Kingdom where the "little ones" have the first place.

108. Contact Fordham/NCEA Center for Justice and Peace Education, Room 1024B, 113 W. 60th Street, New York, N.Y., 10023; telephone: (212) 757-7516. See also David M. Johnson, ed., *Justice and Peace Education: Models for College and University Faculty* (New York: Orbis Books, 1986); this book is adaptable to lower levels of schooling and to learners outside academe, and contains good bibliographies. And see George Weigel, *Tranquillitas Ordinis* (New York: Oxford University Press, 1987), for

a comprehensive treatment of the full spectrum of American Catholic theological writings on peace.

109. *Decree on Ecumenism* # 9, in Flannery, vol. 1, p. 461.

110. Ibid., # 12, in Flannery, vol. 1, pp. 462f.

111. Rose Thering, O.P., Ph.D., *Jews, Judaism, and Catholic Education* (South Orange, N.J.: Anti-Defamation League of B'nai B'rith and the American Jewish Committee, Seton Hall University, 1986), p. 70. This study is a documentary report of Catholic institutions' implementation of the 1965 conciliar statement on the Jews (*Nostra aetate*), the 1974 Roman Catholic guidelines/suggestions, and the 1975 U.S. bishops' statement on the Jews. The study contains good source material.

112. Ibid., pp. 70f.

113. Ibid., p. 74.

114. Ibid., p. 77.

115. Secretariat for the Promotion of the Unity of Christians, *Directory Concerning Ecumenical Matters* (*Spiritus domini*) # 70, in Flannery, vol. 1, p. 520. (Written of higher education, but *mutatis mutandis* applicable to lower.)

116. Ibid., # 68, in Flannery, vol. 1, p. 517.

117. *Decree on Ecumenism* # 7, in Flannery, vol. 1, p. 460.

118. Jean Bouvy, "Education in Values for the Societies of the Year 2000, Echoes of a Recent Congress," *Lumen Vitae*, vol. 37 no. 3 (1982), pp. 249–75.

119. *Declaration on Certain Problems of Sexual Ethics* # 1, in Flannery, vol. 2, p. 486.

120. On sex education in the context of moral right and wrong and character formation, see *America*, vol. 156 no. 6 (February 14, 1987), which is devoted to "Teen-Age Sexuality"; in the issue, see especially William J. Bennett, "Sex and the Education of Our Children," pp. 120–25; James J. DiGiacomo, "All You Need Is Love," pp. 126–29.

121. See Bishop Lawrence Walsh, "Education for Human Sexuality," *Origins*, vol. 13 no. 5 (June 16, 1983), pp. 81–84.

122. For a popular summary of pros and cons on sex education in schools, see *Time*, vol. 128 no. 21 (November 24, 1986), pp. 54–63. For current complexities in both government and Catholic schools, see Karen Sue Smith, "Sex Education: A Matter of Body and Soul," *Commonweal*, vol. CXIV no. 7 (April 10, 1987), pp. 206–10.

123. Vatican Congregation for Catholic Education, "Educational Guidance in Human Love," *Origins*, vol. 13 no. 27 (December 15, 1983), pp. 449–61, addressed specifically to educators, gives excellent guidelines for sex education for educators and parents, and provides further source material.

124. *Declaration on Certain Problems of Sexual Ethics* # 12, in Flannery, vol. 2, p. 496.

125. *Constitution on the Sacred Liturgy* (*Sacrosanctum concilium*) # 122, in Flannery, vol. 1, p. 34.

126. *Mediator dei* (translated as "On the Sacred Liturgy"; New York: America, 1965). See also Jacques Maritain, *Art and Scholasticism*, trans. Joseph W. Evans (New York: Scribner's, 1962); Francis Kovach, *Philosophy of Beauty* (Norman, Okla.: University of Oklahoma Press, 1974).

127. *Gaudium et spes* # 62, in Flannery, vol. 1, p. 967.

128. *Constitution on the Sacred Liturgy* (*Sacrosanctum concilium*) # 122, in Flannery, vol. 1, p. 34. See also Titus Burckhardt, *Sacred Art in East and West: Its Principles and Methods*, trans. Lord Northbourne (Middlesex, England: Perennial, 1967).

129. *Pastoral Instruction on the Means of Social Communication* (*Inter mirifica*) # 67, in Flannery, vol. 1, p. 316.

130. Ibid., # 142, in Flannery, vol. 1, p. 339. See also Harold A. Buetow, *An Evaluation of the Effectiveness of the 1961 Film "King of Kings" in Reflecting its Message on Jesus*

Christ and His Times, unpublished master's thesis (Washington, D.C.: The Catholic University of America, 1963).

131. *Pastoral on Social Communication* # 144, in Flannery, vol. 1, p. 339.

132. Ibid., # 142, in Flannery, vol. 1, p. 339.

133. Ibid., # 16, in Flannery, vol. 1, p. 290.

134. Ibid., # 108, in Flannery, vol. 1, p. 328.

135. Ibid., # 109, in Flannery, vol. 1, p. 328.

136. Ibid., # 110, in Flannery, vol. 1, p. 328.

CHAPTER 6: FAMILY AND CHURCH

1. Pope Pius XI, *Education of the Redeemed Man* (*Divini illius Magistri*), December 31, 1929, in Benedictine Monks of Solesmes, eds., *Education: Papal Teachings* (Boston: St. Paul Editions, 1979), p. 47.

2. Thomas C. McGinnis and Dana G. Finnegan, *Open Family and Marriage: A Guide to Personal Growth* (St. Louis: Mosby, 1976), pp. 54–61.

3. David Cooper, *The Death of the Family* (New York: Pantheon, 1970), especially pp. 135–41. Cooper is not alone: see also Herbert Otto, ed., *A Family in Search of a Future* (New York: Appleton-Century-Crofts, 1970), pp. 1–9. Many scholars understand the fragmentation of the family in terms of the great change in society over the past century. For aeons, the family was society's unit of *production*: e.g., family farms, craft apprenticeships. As such, the family was needed as a strong, integrated entity. Now, however, *individuals* are the units of production (along, of course, with corporations), and are even more importantly units of *consumption*. As society is presently structured, families are less necessary for production or consumption: *individuals* are more necessary. Since societies think of themselves as needing families less, we have the cult of the individual, and the family and the Church can no longer depend on society's support; they have to protect families against society's newly developed indifference.

4. Pope John Paul II, "What Is the Value of Catholic Education?" (address to a group of U.S. bishops on October 28, 1983, during their *ad limina* visit to the Vatican), *Origins*, vol. 13 no. 23 (November 17, 1983), p. 390.

5. Nathan Ackerman, *The Psychodynamics of Family Life* (New York: Basic Books, 1958), p. 15; notes of the family:

> None of us lives his life alone. Those who try are foredoomed; they disintegrate as human beings. Life is a shared and sharing experience. In the early years this sharing occurs almost exclusively with members of our family. The family is the basic unit of growth and experience, fulfillment or failure. It is also the basic unit of illness or health.

6. See Gen. 1; Eph. 5; Col. 3; 1 Pet. 3.

7. *The Christian Family in the Modern World* (*Familiaris consortio*) ## 47–50, in Austin Flannery, ed., *Vatican Council II: The Conciliar and Post Conciliar Documents*, 2 vols. (Northport, N. Y.: Costello, 1975), vol. 2, pp. 854–57. See also the edition published by Daughters of St. Paul (Boston: 1982), pp. 31ff.

8. Vatican II, *Dogmatic Constitution on the Church* (*Lumen gentium*) # 11, in Flannery, vol. 1, p. 362.

9. "Charter of the Rights of the Family," *Origins*, vol. 13 no. 27 (December 15, 1983), pp. 461ff.

10. Article 6.

11. *Declaration on Christian Education* # 3, in Flannery, vol. 1, p. 728. For a closely argued and detailed work on educational freedom, see John E. Coons and Stephen D. Sugarman, *Education by Choice: The Case for Family Control* (Berkeley: University of

California Press, 1978). Interestingly, Coons and Sugarman do not award the primacy of rights to parents, but emphasize instead the child's right to the best schooling possible. See also John W. Donohue, "Voices for Parent Power," *America*, vol. 139 no. 6 (September 9, 1978), pp. 123-27; M. B. McKinney, "Parental Leadership in a Vatican II Church," *Momentum*, vol. XV (September 1984), pp. 18-20.

12. Pope Pius XI, *Quadragesimo anno*, in *Acta apostolicae sedis*, vol. XXIII (Vatican City: Vatican City Press, 1931), p. 203.

13. *Declaration on Christian Education (Gravissimum educationis)* # 3, in Flannery, vol. 1, p. 729.

14. Ibid., in Flannery, vol. 1, pp. 728f.

15. Carle Clark Zimmerman, *Family and Civilization* (New York: Harper Bros., 1947), pp. 784-810.

16. *The Christian Family in the Modern World* # 18, in Flannery, vol. 2, p. 828.

17. *Pierce v. Society of Sisters*, 268 U.S. 510 (1925).

18. Department of State Publication no. 3381 (Washington, D.C., 1948).

19. *The Christian Family in the Modern World* # 15, in Flannery, vol. 2, p. 826.

20. *Commonweal*, vol. CXIV no. 3 (February 13, 1987), p. 68.

21. Jean Piaget, *Six Psychological Studies* (New York: Random House, 1967), p. 36.

22. Pope Paul VI, *On Evangelization in the Modern World* (apostolic exhortation *Evangelii nuntiandi*; Washington, D.C.: United States Catholic Conference, 1976).

23. British Council of Churches, *Understanding Christian Nurture* (London: British Council of Churches, 1981), especially pp. 51-80, "Christian Parenthood."

24. Ibid., p. 145.

25. Ibid., p. 148.

26. Theodore Lidz, " The Family, Language, and Ego Functions," in *The Family and Human Adaptation: Three Lectures* (New York: International Universities Press, 1963), pp. 3-38; Selma Fraiberg, *Every Child's Birthright* (New York: Basic Books, 1977), p. 27.

27. Catholic Education Council, *Evidence to the Central Advisory Council on Primary Education* (London: Catholic Education Council, 1965), p. 5.

28. See, e.g., William Stanmeyer, *Clear and Present Danger* (Ann Arbor, Mich.: Servant Books, 1983).

29. T. H. McLaughlin, "Parental Rights and the Religious Upbringing of Children," *Journal of Philosophy of Education*, vol. 18 no. 1 (1984), p. 81. Many of the ideas in the present section of my work are from this article (pp. 75-83) as well as Eamonn Callan, "McLaughlin on Parental Rights," ibid., vol. 19 no. 1, (1985), pp. 111-18, and T. H. McLaughlin, "Religion, Upbringing and Liberal Values: A Rejoinder to Eamonn Callan," ibid., pp. 119-27.

30. Morris Zelditch, Jr., "Role Differentiation in the Nuclear Family: A Comparative Study," in T. Parsons and R. Bales, *Family, Socialization and Interaction Processes* (Glencoe, Ill: Free Press, 1955), pp. 307-52; Theodore Lidz, *The Person* (New York: Basic Books, 1983), pp. 71-73.

31. Lidz, *The Person*, pp. 54-61.

There is a growing body of literature on women. Following is part of a list compiled by the staff of the Regis College Graduate Program in Adult Christian Development (Dr. David M. Thomas, Director), Denver, Colo. In the area of Scripture, see Elizabeth Schüssler Fiorenza, *In Memory of Her: A Feminist Theological Reconstruction of Christian Origins* (New York: Crossroad, 1983): a milestone in New Testament studies and a good place to begin; idem, *Bread Not Stone: The Challenge of Feminist Biblical Interpretation* (Boston: Beacon Press, 1984): explores the Bible as "an empowering resource" for women and men; John H. Otwell, *And Sarah Laughed: The Status of Women in the Old Testament* (Philadelphia: Westminster, 1977): argues that while men were clearly dominant, women were not as subservient or passive as some interpretations have suggested; Letty M. Russell, ed., *The Liberating Word: A Guide to Nonsexist Interpretations of the Bible* (Philadelphia: Westminster, 1976): articles for lay study groups on biblical authority and interpretation, images of women, and language; idem, *Feminist Interpretation of the Bible* (Philadelphia: Westminster, 1985): essays by historians, theologians, and biblical specialists on a range of topics; Phyllis Trible, *God and the Rhetoric of Sexuality* and *Texts of Terror: Literary Feminist Readings of Biblical Narratives* (Philadelphia: Fortress, 1978 and 1984, respectively): feminist interpretations of various parts of the Old Testament; Leonard Swidler, *Biblical Affirmations of Woman* (Philadelphia: Westminster, 1979), a comprehensive survey of biblical texts dealing with women.

In feminist theology and spirituality, see Walter Burghardt, ed., *Woman: New Dimensions* (New York: Paulist, 1977): treats feminist theology and ethics with attention to such issues as home and work, ministry, and anthropology; Betsy Caprio, *The Woman Sealed in the Tower: A Psychological Approach to Feminine Spirituality* (New York: Paulist, 1982): combines the psychology of Carl Jung with the Christian tradition; Joann Wolski, ed., *Women's Spirituality: Resources for Christian Development* (New York: Paulist, 1986): demonstrates the compatibility of feminist values and traditional sources in Christian spirituality; Carol Christ and Judith Plaskow, eds., *Womanspirit Rising: A Feminist Reader in Religion* (San Francisco: Harper and Row, 1979): essays on woman's place in traditional and postpatriarchal religion; Nancy Auer Falk and Rita M. Gross, eds., *Unspoken Worlds: Women's Religious Lives in Non-Western Cultures* (San Francisco: Harper and Row, 1980): a valuable anthology, focusing on case studies and beginning to explore women's religious experience in comparative cross-cultural perspective; Janet Kalven and Mary I. Buckley, eds., *Women's Spirit Bonding* (New York: Pilgrim, 1984), brief essays on "survival issues" (e.g., poverty, racism, war, peace) and "resources," including rituals; Carol Ochs, *Women and Spirituality* (Totowa, N.J.: Rowan and Allanhead, 1983): based on the premise that women can bring a unique perspective to spiritual questions.

In the area of feminist theology and ethics, there are Barbara Hilkert Andolsen, Christine E. Gudorf, and Mary D. Pellauer, eds., *Women's Consciousness, Women's Conscience: A Reader in Feminist Ethics* (Minneapolis: Winston, 1985): introductory essays covering a wide range of topics; Margaret A. Farley, *Personal Commitments: Making, Keeping, Breaking* (Minneapolis: Winston, 1985): an excellent work; Maria Riley, "Women: Carriers of a New Vision" (a paper given in 1983, available from Center of Concern, 3700 13th Street N.E., Washington, D.C. 20017, and also as an audio cassette with study guide from Leadership Conference of Women Religious); Rosemary Radford Ruether, ed., *Womanguides: Readings Toward a Feminist Theology* (Boston: Beacon, 1985): an assemblage of texts for theological reflection, from various cultures and historical periods; Joan Timmerman, *The Mardi Gras Syndrome: Rethinking Christian Sexuality* (New York: Crossroad, 1984): an historical-theological study which proposes that sexuality should be rethought in a feminist social-justice context; Patricia Wilson-Kastner, *Faith, Feminism and the Christ* (Philadelphia: Fortress, 1979): an affirmation of both feminism and Christianity.

For women and psychology, the following titles are self-explanatory: Luis Eichenbaum and Susie Orbach, *What Do Women Want? Exploding the Myth of Dependency* (Berkeley, Calif.: Berkeley Publications, 1984); Carol Gilligan, *In a Differing Voice: Psychological Theory and Women's Development* (Cambridge: Harvard University Press, 1982); Madonna Kolbenschlag, *Kiss Sleeping Beauty Good-bye: Breaking the Spell of Feminine Myths and Models* (New York: Bantam, 1979); Jean Baker Miller, *Toward a New Psychology of Women* (Boston: Beacon, 1976); Georgia Witkin-Lanoil, *The Female Stress Syndrome: How to Recognize and Live with It* (New York: New Market Press, 1984); Marion Woodman,

The Owl and the Baker's Daughter (Toronto: Inner City Books, 1980): about the price the body pays for being cut off from feminine energies.

In the area of worship and language, see Linda Clark, Marian Ronan, and Elinor Walker, *Image-breaking/Image-building: A Handbook for Creative Worship with Women of Christian Traditions* (New York: Pilgrim, 1981); Sharon Neufer Emswiler and Tomas Neufer Emswiler, *Women and Worship: A Guide to Non-Sexist Hymns, Prayers and Liturgies*, rev. ed. (New York: Harper and Row, 1984); Lutheran Church of America, *Guidelines for Inclusive Language* (L.C.A. Office for Communication, 231 Madison Avenue, New York, N.Y. 10016; Casey Miller and Kate Swift, *Words and Women: New Language in New Times* (Garden City, N.Y.: Doubleday, 1977).

32. Erik H. Erikson, *Identity, Youth and Crisis* (New York: Norton, 1968), pp. 91–141; A. Rossi, "Family Development in a Changing World," *American Journal of Psychiatry*, vol. 128 no. 9 (March 1972), pp. 1057–66.

33. See Erik Erikson, *Childhood and Society* (New York: Norton, 1950).

34. M. D. S. Ainsworth, "Infant-Mother Attachment," *American Psychologist*, vol. 34 no. 10 (October 1979), pp. 932–37.

35. M. E. Lamb, "Effects of Stress and Cohort on Mother-and Father-Infant Interaction," *Developmental Psychology*, vol. 12 no. 5 (September 1976), pp. 435–43; idem, "Father-Infant and Mother-Infant Interaction in the First Year of Life," *Child Development*, vol. 48 no. 1 (March 1977), pp. 167–81; M. E. Lamb, M. Frodi, C. P. Hwang, and A. M. Frodi, "Effects of Paternal Involvement on Infant Preference for Mothers and Fathers," *Child Development*, vol. 54 no. 2 (April 1983), pp. 450–58.

36. See recent issues of *The Journal of Marriage and the Family*.

37. K. A. Clarke-Stewart "Popular Primers for Parents," *American Psychologist*, vol. 33 no. 4 (April 1978), pp. 359–69.

38. H. H. Bohen and A. Viveros-Long, *Balancing Jobs and Family Life* (Philadelphia: Temple University Press, 1981).

39. W. Emmerich, "Family Role Concepts of Children Ages 6–10," *Child Development*, vol. 32, 1961, pp. 609–24; J. Kagan and J. Lemkin, "The Child's Differential Perception of Parental Attributes," *Journal of Abnormal and Social Psychology*, vol. 61 (1960), pp. 440–47.

40. K. W. Fischer and A. Lazerson, *Human Development: From Conception Through Adolescence* (New York: Freeman, 1984), pp. 525–29.

41. Theodore Lidz, *The Family and Human Adaptation*, pp. 11–38.

42. Pope John Paul II, "The Role of the Family in the Modern World" (*Familiaris consortio*; Boston, Mass.: Daughters of St. Paul, 1982), # 17, pp. 31f.

43. *Familiaris consortio* ## 6, 7.

44. For resources see, e.g., Mala Powers, *Follow the Year: A Family Celebration of Christian Holidays* (New York: Harper and Row, 1985); Evelyn Birge Vitz, *A Continual Feast: A Cookbook to Celebrate the Joys of Family and Faith Throughout the Christian Year* (New York: Harper and Row, 1985); Diana Carey and Judy Large, *Festivals, Family and Food* (Gloucestershire, England: Hawthorn, 1982). Or subscribe to *The Family's Home Gazette*, a bimonthly newsletter (Box 5870, The Vicarage, Takoma Park, Md. 20912; telephone: [301] 270-0598); *Festivals*, a bimonthly magazine that explores creative rituals for family life (160 E. Virginia Street, Suite 290, San Jose, Calif. 95112; telephone: [408] 286-8505).

It is equally interesting and valuable to look into the history of the institution of the family — see some of the entries in the bibliography at the end of the chapter.

45. *The Washington Post*, March 3, 1987, p. D5.

46. This longitudinal research on the social and academic development of elementary-school children began in 1982 on a $450,000 grant from the National Science

Foundation, under Karl Alexander and Doris Entwisle, researchers at the Johns Hopkins University. The research, which will follow the original group of children through the sixth grade, is intended to be completed in 1988 (but will probably be later). *Education Week*, vol. V no. 15 (December 11, 1985), p. 8.

47. Lidz, *The Person*, pp. 54–56.

48. Robert O. Blood, Jr., *Marriage*, 2nd ed. (New York: Free Press, 1969), pp. 446–62; see also Ackerman, op. cit., p. 21.

49. Ackerman, op. cit., pp. 23–25. See also Craig Dykstra and Sharon Parks, eds., *Faith Development and Fowler* (Birmingham, Ala.: Religious Education Press, 1986).

50. Lidz, *The Person*, pp. 59–63.

51. E. Pavenstedt, "Review of Findings and Recommendations," in E. Pavenstedt, ed., *The Drifters: Children of Disorganized Lower-Class Families* (Boston: Little, Brown, 1967), pp. 323–35.

52. See, e.g., Lawrence Kohlberg, *Essays on Moral Development* (New York: Harper and Row, 1981).

53. R. P. Selman and C. Rubenstein, "Childhood Attachment Experience and Adult Loneliness," *Review of Personality and Social Psychology*, vol. 1 (September 1980), pp. 42–73.

54. Justin Aronfreed, "The Concept of Internalization," in Justin Aronfreed, ed., *Conduct and Conscience: The Socialization of Internalized Control over Behavior* (New York: Academic, 1968), pp. 18–42.

55. Ibid.

56. S. Coopersmith, *The Antecedents of Self-Esteem* (San Francisco: Freeman, 1967).

57. Ibid.; Diana Baumrind and A. E. Black, "Socialization Practices Associated with Dimensions of Competence in Pre-School Boys and Girls," *Child Development*, vol. 38 no. 2 (June 1967), pp. 291–327; Diana Baumrind, "Harmonious Parents and Their Pre-School Children", *Developmental Psychology*, vol. 4 no. 1 (January 1971), pp. 99–102; idem, "Current Patterns of Parental Authority", *Developmental Psychology*, vol. 4 no. 1 pt. 2 (January 1971), pp. 1–103.

58. See K. W. Fischer and A. Lazerson, *Human Development: From Conception through Adolescence* (New York: Freeman, 1984), pp. 525–29.

59. See 1 Cor. 13.

60. See David Heller, *The Children's God* (University of Chicago Press, 1986); part of the thesis is that the cozy, familiar quality of Catholic children's God often reflects the children's experiences with their parents.

61. See *De La Salle Institute v. United States*, 195 F.Supp. 891, 897–901 (N.D.Cal. 1961).

62. *Young Life Campaign v. Patino*, 122 Cal.App.3d 556, 570 (1981).

63. See *Words and Phrases* (St. Paul, Minn.: West, 1952), vol. 7, pp. 194–203. See also *American Jurisprudence*, 2nd ed. (Rochester, N. Y.: Lawyers Cooperative; San Francisco: Bancroft-Whitney, 1973), vol. 66, pp. 756–58.

64. *Young Life Campaign v. Patino*, 122 Cal.App.3d 556, 570 (1981).

65. Ibid., 574, 575.

66. Sacred Congregation for the Doctrine of the Faith, *Declaration in Defence of the Catholic Doctrine on the Church Against Some Present-Day Errors (Mysterium ecclesiae)*, in Flannery, vol. 2, p. 429.

67. See 1 Tim. 3:15; Eph. 5:27; Matt. 28:20; and John 14:17.

68. *Mystici corporis* ## 13, 17.

69. See, for example, *Dogmatic Constitution on the Church* ## 2, 4, 7, in Flannery, vol. 2, pp. 351f., 355.

70. Pope Paul VI, *Ecclesiam suam*, encyclical of Pope Paul VI on the Church, August

6, 1964, in Claudia Carlen, ed., *The Papal Encyclicals 1958–1981* (Wilmington, N.C.: McGrath, 1981).

71. *Dogmatic Constitution on the Church* # 6, in Flannery, vol. 1, pp. 353f.

72. Matt. 28:18–20. Avery Dulles, *Models of the Church* (Garden City, N.Y.: Doubleday, 1978), p. 39.

73. Sacred Congregation for the Clergy, *General Catechetical Directory (Ad normam decreti)* # 67, in Flannery, vol. 2, p. 568.

74. Ibid., # 65, in Flannery, vol. 2, pp. 566f; see also Dulles, op. cit., p. 53.

75. Dulles, op. cit., pp. 47f.

76. Ibid., pp. 48–50.

77. *Dogmatic Constitution on the Church* # 7, in Flannery, vol. 1, p. 355.

78. 1 Cor. 12:12–14.

79. Dulles, op. cit., pp. 62f.

80. *General Catechetical Directory* # 55, in Flannery, vol. 2, p. 560.

81. *Dogmatic Constitution on the Church* # 9, in Flannery, vol. 1, p. 360.

82. Edward Schilebeeckx, *Christ the Sacrament of the Encounter with God* (New York: Sheed and Ward, 1963), p. 14.

83. Dulles, op. cit., p. 77.

84. Ibid., pp. 78f.

85. *Dogmatic Constitution on the Church* # 13, in Flannery, vol. 1, p. 363.

86. Dulles, op. cit., pp. 92f.

87. *Dogmatic Constitution on the Church* # 8, in Flannery, vol. 1, p. 358.

88. *General Catechetical Directory* # 67, in Flannery, vol. 2, p. 569.

89. *Dogmatic Constitution on the Church* # 18, in Flannery, vol. 1, p. 369.

90. Sacred Congregation for the Doctrine of the Faith, *Declaration in Defence of the Catholic Doctrine on the Church Against some Present-Day Errors (Mysterium ecclesiae)*, in Flannery, vol. 2, pp. 430f.

91. *The Dogmatic Constitution on the Church* # 22, in Flannery, vol. 1, p. 375.

92. Ibid., # 25, in Flannery, vol. 1, p. 380.

93. *Decree on the Pastoral Office of Bishops in the Church (Christus Dominus)* ## 12, 15, in Flannery, vol. 1, pp. 569, 571.

94. *The Dogmatic Constitution on the Church* # 23, in Flannery, vol. 1, pp. 376f.

95. Apostolic exhortation *Quinque iam anni, AAS* 63 (1971), p. 100, as cited in *Declaration in Defence of the Catholic Doctrine on the Church Against Some Present-Day Errors*, in Flannery, vol. 2, p. 431.

96. *The Dogmatic Constitution on the Church* # 26, in Flannery, vol. 1, p. 381; *Decree on the Pastoral Office of Bishops in the Church* # 28, in Flannery, vol. 1, p. 580.

97. *Decree on the Pastoral Office of Bishops in the Church* # 30 (2), in Flannery, vol. 1, pp. 581f.

98. John Paul II, *Catechesis in Our Time* # 64, in Flannery, vol. 2, p. 802.

99. *Declaration on Christian Education* # 2, in Flannery, vol. 1, p. 728.

100. *Declaration in Defence of the Catholic Doctrine on the Church Against Some Present-Day Errors*, in Flannery, vol. 2, p. 435.

101. *The Dogmatic Constitution on the Church* # 35, in Flannery, vol. 1, p. 392.

102. *Decree on the Pastoral Office of Bishops in the Church* # 30 (1), in Flannery, vol. 1, pp. 581f.

103. *Dogmatic Constitution on the Church* # 10, in Flannery, vol. 1, p. 361.

104. *General Catechetical Directory* # 66, in Flannery, vol. 2, pp. 567f.

105. Adapted from David J. Hassel, S.J., *City of Wisdom: A Christian Vision of the American University* (Chicago: Loyola University Press, 1983), p. 439.

106. In one large parish (St. Joseph's, Ronkonkoma, N.Y.) in which the continued

existence of the school was fiscally precarious, the statement that "the school is part of the parish as I want it to be" was supported by a surprising number of nonparents and older people among the parishioners. The school was seen as being run as a catalytic agent for the creation of the Church as it ought to be. Everything that was poured into the school was done to make it a child- and parent-oriented nucleus for formation. Even the religious education program was primarily piloted and enabled by the parochial school. The school is something around which much else in a parish can center; most other things in a parish are occasional. The school is an ecclesial phenomenon to which people can point and say, "This is what the Church ought to be like." A support group even solicited financial help from the non-practicing Catholics, so the school would be there when they came home. (Interview, January 3, 1987, with the Reverend Charles Kohli, Pastor, St. Joseph's Church, Ronkonkoma.)

107. Matt. 28:19f.

108. See Eph. 4:1–6.

109. Acts 2:42.

110. Pope John XXIII, *Christianity and Social Progress (Mater et magistra)* # 1, in David J. O'Brien and Thomas A. Shannon, eds., *Renewing the Earth* (Garden City, N. Y.: Doubleday, 1977), p. 51. See also Jean Leclercq, *The Love of Learning and the Desire for God* (New York: New American Library, 1961).

111. *Declaration on Christian Education* # 5, in Flannery, vol. 1, pp. 730–31.

112. For an overview of the Church's right to educate, see Marvyn Davies, "The Church's Role in Education," *The Tablet*, 237 (October 8, 1983), 975–81.

113. Interview with Fr. Sean Healy, S.M.A., and Sr. Brigid Reynolds, S.M., March 18, 1986, at the Justice Office, Conference of Major Religious Superiors, Dublin, Ireland.

114. Pope John XXIII, *Christianity and Social Progress* # 1, in O'Brien and Shannon, op. cit., p. 50.

115. *Gravissimum educationis* # 3, in Flannery, vol., pp. 729f.

116. *Pastoral Constitution on the Church in the Modern World* # 40, in Flannery, vol. 1, p. 940.

117. Ibid., # 3, in Flannery, vol. 1, p. 905.

118. See Kevin Nichols, *Cornerstone* (Middlegreen, Slough, England: St. Paul, 1978), pp. 58–69.

119. *Catechesis in Our Time* # 14, in Flannery, vol. 2, p. 770.

120. Canon Law Society of America, *Code of Canon Law, Latin-English Edition*, trans. under the auspices of the Canon Law Society of America (Washington, D.C.: Canon Law Society of America, 1983), canon 794 §§1 and 2.

121. Ibid., canon 800 §§1 and 2.

122. *Declaration on Christian Education* # 8, in Flannery, vol. 1, p. 734.

123. *Code of canon Law*, canon 802 §1.

124. Ibid., canons 804, 806§1. See also *Decree on the Pastoral Office of Bishops in the Church* # 35 (4), in Flannery, vol. 1, p. 585.

125. *Declaration on Christian Education* # 2, in Flannery, vol. 1, p. 728.

126. Pope John Paul II, "The Gospel Is the Soul of the Catholic School," *L'Osservatore Romano*, vol. XVII no. 29 (July 16, 1984), p. 7.

127. Harold A. Buetow, *Of Singular Benefit: the Story of U.S. Catholic Education* (New York: Macmillan, 1970).

128. See, for example, Pope Pius IX, *Cum nuper*, January 20, 1858, in Benedictine Monks of Solesmes, eds., *Education: Papal Teachings* (Boston: St. Paul Editions, 1979), p. 47.

129. In *Wolman v. Walter*, 433 U.S. 229, 262 (1977) (Powell, J., concurring in part).

130. *Pastoral Constitution on the Church in the Modern World* # 42, in Flannery, vol. 1, p. 942.

131. Ibid., # 43, in Flannery, vol. 1, p. 943.

132. Ibid., # 76, in Flannery, vol. 1, p. 985.

133. Ibid., # 41, in Flannery, vol. 1, p. 940.

134. Sacred Congregation for the Doctrine of the Faith, *Declaration on Certain Problems of Sexual Ethics* (*Personae humanae*) # 4, in Flannery, vol. 2, p. 488.

135. James S. Coleman and Thomas Hoffer, *Public and Private High Schools: The Impact of Communities* (New York: Basic Books, 1987), p. 214.

136. Ibid., p. 216.

137. Ibid., p. 215.

138. Pope John Paul II, "To Ban Catholic Teaching Is an Offense Against Human Rights," *L'Osservatore Romano*, vol. XVI no. 20 (May 16, 1983), p. 8.

CHAPTER 7: THE STATE

1. Catholics have not been as fast as others to recognize the State's rights in schooling and education. As recently as the end of the last century, when a Catholic theologian published a booklet that recognized the rights of the State, it started a controversy among Catholics. The booklet was Thomas Bouquillon, *Education: To Whom Does It Belong?*, 2nd ed. (Baltimore: John Murphy, 1892). For a brief history of the controversy, see Harold A. Buetow, *Of Singular Benefit: the Story of U.S. Catholic Education* (New York: Macmillan, 1970), pp. 170–75.

2. Totten J. Anderson, Carl Q. Christol, and Carlton C. Rondee, *Introduction to Political Science* (New York: McGraw-Hill, 1967), p. 39.

3. Matt. 22:21; see also Mark 12:17; Luke 20:25. See also Richard P. McBrien, *Caesar's Coin: Religion and Politics in America* (New York: Macmillan, 1987).

4. Rom. 13: 1 and 7. See also Jacques Ellul, *The Theological Foundation of Law* (New York: Doubleday, 1960).

5. According to the Jewish Scriptures (Deut. 6:7, 11, 19, and elsewhere) and the Talmud, the duty to educate children rested on the parents, the father first of all (Prov. 1:8; 6:20). The sages spoke of the great reward prepared for parents who discharge the function of educator adequately. In the patriarchal age, when there were no schools and the Jews, like the bedouins today, lived as nomads, the nation gradually came to see itself as one family (Amos 3:1–2; Jer. 31:1). The sages said also that when a father neglects his duties to educate his children, he forfeits the right to fatherhood—because the one who teaches the child, and not the mere progenitor, is the real father. The literature also emphasized the obligation of the community to provide for schooling. The Talmud said, "a city where there is no school for children deserves to be destroyed." And among the means of national training mentioned in the Old Testament are monuments of stone, sacred feasts (see, for example, Joshua 4:5–7, Exodus 12:25–39, and Deut. 6:20–25), and the teaching of the law by the official representatives of the nation and the Church, the priests and the Levites.

6. Thomas G. Sanders, *Protestant Concepts of Church and State* (New York: Holt, Rinehart and Winston, 1964), p. 25.

7. *Pierce v. Society of Sisters*, 268 U.S. 510, 535 (1925).

8. Yet the connection between religion and law is definite. Among the voluminous writings on the subject are: "Religion and the Law," *The Hastings Law Journal*, vol. 29 no. 6 (July 1978); "Symposium: The Secularization of the Law," *Mercer Law Review*, vol. 31 no. 2 (Winter 1980); "Symposium: Religion and the Law," *Capital University Law Review*, vol. 8 no. 3 (Fall 1979); Harold J. Berman, *The Interaction of Law and*

Religion (Nashville: Abingdon, 1974); Note, "Toward a Constitutional Definition of Religion," *Harvard Law Review*, vol. 91 no. 5 (March 1978), pp. 1056–89; Richard John Neuhaus, "Law and the Rightness of Things," *Valparaiso Law Review*, vol. 14 no. 1 (Fall 1979), pp. 1–13; *The NICM Journal*, vol. 2 no. 3 (Summer 1977): Harold J. Berman, "The Prophetic, Pastoral, and Priestly Vocation of the Lawyer," pp. 5–9, and James F. Bresnahan, S.J., "Theology and Law: Responsibilities of Vocation," with responses, pp. 10–51; Council on Religion and Law (CORAL) *Newsletter*, P.O. Box 30, Cambridge, Mass., 02140; "Symposium on Education," *Notre Dame Journal of Law, Ethics and Public Policy*, vol. 1 no. 4 (Spring 1985).

Some of these works have Judaism as their reference point: e.g., "The Exodus as the Desacralization of Politics," in Harvey Cox, *The Secular City* (New York: Macmillan, 1965), pp. 25–36; Milton R. Konvitz, *Judaism and Human Rights* (New York: Norton, 1972), pp. 16–19; Stanley A. Cook, *The Laws of Moses and the Code of Hammurabi* (London: Adam and Charles Black, 1903); Edward Nielsen, *The Ten Commandments in New Perspective* (London: SCM Press, 1968), especially pp. 132–44; Roland De Vaux, *Ancient Israel: Its Life and Institutions* (London: Darton, Longman and Todd, 1961), especially pp. 98–99, 143–63; Abraham J. Heschel, *The Prophets* (New York: Harper and Row, 1962), pp. 198–220; Will Herberg, *Judaism and Modern Man: An Interpretation of Jewish Religion* (New York: Harper and Row, 1965), especially pp. 145–65; Moshe Greenberg, "The Biblical Grounding of Human Values," *Samuel Friedland Lectures, 1960–1966* (New York: Jewish Theological Seminary of America, 1966), pp. 39–52.

Other writings on religion and law have Christianity as their origin: e.g., Richard J. Cassidy, *Jesus, Politics and Society: A Study of Luke's Gospel* (Maryknoll, N.Y.: Orbis Books, 1978), especially chap. II, "The Social Stance of Jesus," pp. 101–4, and chap. VI, "Was Jesus Dangerous to the Roman Empire?" pp. 108–13; Dietrich Bonhoeffer, *The Cost of Discipleship* (London: SCM Press, 1959), especially pp. 109–14, 162–68; Rudolf Bultmann, "The Sermon on the Mount and the Justice of the State" (1936), reprinted in *Existence and Faith* (London: Collins, 1960), pp. 240–43; idem, *Theology of the New Testament* (London; SCM Press, 1952), especially vol. I, pp. 11–19 ("Jesus' Interpretation of the Demand of God"), 259–69 ("The Law"), and 340–45 ("Freedom from the Law and the Christian's Attitude toward Men"); Johannes Baptist Metz, *Theology of the World* (New York: Herder and Herder, 1971), especially chap. II, "The Future of Faith in a Hominized World," pp. 64–70, and chap. V, "The Church and the World in the Light of a 'Political Theology,'" pp. 107–20; Karl Barth, *Community, State and Church: Three Essays* (Garden City, N.Y.: Doubleday & Co., 1960), especially pp. 114–48 ("The Essence of the State," "The Significance of the State for the Church," "The Service Which the Church Owes to the State"; Oscar Cullmann, *The State in the New Testament* (New York: Scribner's, 1956), pp. 34–37, 50–55, 90–92; John Howard Yoder, *The Politics of Jesus* (Grand Rapids: Eerdmans, 1972), pp. 193–214 ("Let Every Soul Be Subject: Romans 13 and the Authority of the State"); William Stringfellow, *Conscience and Obedience: The Politics of Romans 13 and Revelation 13 in Light of the Second Coming* (Waco, Texas: Word Books, 1977), especially chap. II, "The Problem of Political Legitimacy," pp. 35–51, and chap. III, "Anarchy, Apocalyptic Reality, and the Antichrist," pp. 55–71.

The literature involves Christian theorists and insights from many quarters: e.g., Ernst Troeltsch, *The Social Teaching of the Christian Churches*, vol. I (New York: Macmillan, 1931), pp. 143, 150–55; idem, "Natural Law and Humanity," *Natural Law and the Theory of Society, 1500–1800* (Cambridge University Press, 1950), pp. 205–9; Gerd Tellenback, *Church, State and Christian Society* (New York: Harper and Row, 1970), pp. 10–25; Charles Norris Cochrane, *Christianity and Classical Culture* (London: Oxford

University Press, 1940), esp. pp. 177–80, 213–16, 221–23, 254–56, 259, 294–99, 318, 321–27, 328–37; T. M. Parker, *Christianity and the State in the Light of History* (London: Adam and Charles Black, 1955), pp. 53, 56–59, 63f.; *Augustine: City of God*, ed. with intro. David Knowles, trans. Henry Bettenson (Baltimore: Penguin Books, 1972); Henry Paolucci, ed., *The Political Writings of St. Augustine* (Chicago: Henry Regnery, 1962), pp. 163–83; John Neville Figgis, *The Political Aspects of St. Augustine's "City of God"* (London: Longmans, Green, 1921), pp. 51–67; Herbert A. Deane, *The Political and Social Ideas of St. Augustine* (New York: Columbia University Press, 1963), pp. 220–43; Christopher Dawson, *Religion and the Rise of Western Culture* (New York: Sheed and Ward, 1950), pp. 224–28; Thomas Aquinas, "Commentary on the Ethics," Lessons 15 and 16, reprinted in Ralph Lerner and Mushin Mahdi, eds., *Medieval Political Philosophy: A Source Book* (New York: Free Press, 1963), pp. 290–96; Thomas Aquinas, *Summa Theologica* (New York: Benziger, 1947), I–IIae, QQ. 90, 91, 94, and 96, arts. 2–5; II–IIae, QQ. 40 and 42, art. 2 (pp. 993–1000, 1008–13, 1018–20, 1359–63, 1365f: "Of the Essence of Law," "Of the Various Kinds of Law," "Of the Natural Law," "Human Law," "Of War," "Of Sedition"); Thomas Gilby, *The Political Thought of Thomas Aquinas* (University of Chicago Press, 1958), pp. 125–42, 172–78, 288f.

Many theories originate in Protestantism. See, for example, James Atkinson, *The Christian in Society* (Philadelphia: Fortress, 1966), especially pp. xiv–xv, on Luther's works; Martin Luther, "Two Kinds of Righteousness," (Sermon, 1519), reprinted in John Dillenberger, ed., *Martin Luther: Selections From His Writings* (Garden City, N.Y.: Doubleday, 1961), pp. 93–96; Martin Luther, "Secular Society; To What Extent It Should Be Obeyed," *Works of Martin Luther*, vol. III (Philadelphia: Muhlenberg, 1930), pp. 231, 233f., 236, 239–241, 247–49, 264–66, 268, 270f.; Heinrich Bornkamm, "An Exposition of Luther's Doctrine of the Two Kingdoms," *Luther's Doctrine of the Two Kingdoms in the Context of His Theology*, trans. Karl H. Hertz (Philadelphia: Fortress, 1966), pp. 5–11, 16–18, 34–36; R. H. Murray, "Political Consequences of Luther's Doctrine of Religious Freedom," *The Political Consequences of the Reformation; Studies in Sixteenth-Century Political Thought* (New York: Russell and Russell, 1960), pp. 55, 57–64, 74–77; Ernst Troeltsch, "The Social Ethic of Lutheranism," *The Social Teachings of the Christian Churches*, vol. II, trans. Olive Wyon (London: Allen and Unwin, 1950), pp. 515f., 519–25, 529–32, 540–42, 548f., 555–57, 561–67, 569–73; J. W. Allen, "Martin Luther," in Fossey John Cobb Hearnshaw, ed., *The Social and Political Ideas of Some Great Thinkers of the Renaissance and the Reformation* (New York: Brentano, 1925), pp. 171–91; John Calvin, *Institutes of the Christian Religion* (New York: J. Clarke, 1949); Peter Barth, "John Calvin," in Jaroslav Pelikan, ed., *Twentieth Century Theology in the Making*, vol. 3 (London: Collins, 1969), pp. 238–49; John T. McNeill, "John Calvin on Civil Government," in George L. Hunt, ed., *Calvinism and the Political Order* (Philadelphia: Westminster, 1965), pp. 23–45; Ernst Troeltsch, *The Social Teaching of the Christian Churches*, trans. Olive Wyon, intro. Charles Gore, 2 vols. (New York: Macmillan, 1931), vol. 2, pp. 691–714); Franklin H. Littell, *From State Church to Pluralism: A Protestant Interpretation of Religion in American History*, 2nd ed. (New York: Macmillan, 1971), pp. 4–9, 14–20, 26–31; James Hastings Nichols, *Democracy and the Churches* (Philadelphia: Westminster, 1952), pp. 29–41; Robert T. Handy, *A History of the Churches in the United States and Canada* (New York: Oxford University Press, 1977).

Religion enters most problems and facets of living. See, for example, Michael J. Malbin, *Religion and Politics: The Intentions of the Authors of the First Amendment* (Washington, D.C.: American Enterprise Institute, 1978); Arthur Sutherland, "Historians,

Lawyers, and Establishment of Religion," in Donald A. Giannella, ed., *Religion and the Public Order*, vol. 5 (Ithaca: Cornell University Press, 1969), pp. 28–46; Chester James Antieau, Arthur T. Downey, and Edward C. Roberts, *Freedom from Federal Establishment: Formation and Early History of the First Amendment Religion Clauses* (Milwaukee: Bruce, 1964); Elizur Wright, "The Sin of Slavery and Its Remedy: Containing Some Reflections on the Moral Influence of American Colonization" (New York: n.p., 1833), in Louis Ruchames, ed., *The Abolitionists: A Collection of Their Writings* (New York: Capricorn, 1964), pp. 58–60; Robert N. Bellah, "Civil Religion in America," *Daedalus*, vol. 96 (1966), pp. 1–21; Roger Shinn, "Population and the Dignity of Man," in Preston N. Williams, ed., *Ethical Issues in Biology and Medicine* (Cambridge, Mass.: Schenkman, 1973), pp. 78–91; John Courtney Murray, "War and Conscience," and Paul Ramsey, "Selective Conscientious Objection, Warrants and Reservations," in James Finn, ed., *A Conflict of Loyalties: The Case for Selective Conscientious Objection* (New York: Pegasus, 1968), pp. 19–22, 25–30; Martin Luther King, Jr., "Letter from Birmingham Jail," in *Why We Can't Wait* (New York: Signet, 1963), pp. 76–95; idem, "Declaration of Independence from the War in Vietnam," in Michael P. Hamilton, ed., *The Vietnam War: Christian Perspectives* (Grand Rapids: Eerdmans, 1967), pp. 115–30; Andrew Carnegie, "The Gospel of Wealth" (1889) in Edward C. Kirkland, ed., *The Gospel of Wealth and Other Timely Essays* (Cambridge, Mass.: Harvard University Press, 1962), pp. 14–29, 47–49; Walter Rauschenbusch, *Christianizing the Social Order* (New York: Macmillan, 1914), especially chap. VII, "The Case of Christianity against Capitalism," pp. 311–23; U.S. Catholic bishops, *Pastoral Letter on the Economic System*, 1986; Pope John XXIII, *Mater et magistra*, encyclical on christianity and social progress (May 15, 1961); United States Catholic Conference, *The Reform of Correctional Institutions in the 1970s* (Washington, D.C.: United States Catholic Conference, 1973); Gerald Austin McHugh, *Christian Faith and Criminal Justice: Toward a Christian Response to Crime and Punishment* (Ramsey, N.J.: Paulist, 1978); Roger C. Cramton, "The Ordinary Religion of the Law School Classroom," and Edward M. Gaffney, Jr., "The Role of Biblical Religion in the Law School Classroom—A Reply to Dean Cramton," *NICM Journal*, vol. 2 no. 3 (Summer 1977), pp. 72–91, 98–107.

9. Federal assistance to government schools amounts to about 7 percent of the total government-school budget. Some state and local governments have sponsored programs that permit and fund some education choices in non-government schools, such as loans or grants of textbooks and of other materials, transportation, testing services, counseling services, tax benefits (including property-tax exemptions and other tax advantages which are granted to all nonprofit organizations), compensatory-education programs, services for handicapped children, dual or part-time enrollment in government schools, health services, meals, some therapeutic services, remedial instruction, hearing and vision screening, physical medical examinations at parent option, and aid for street-crossing guards. (See *Education Week*, vol. VI no. 30 [April 22, 1987], pp. 18–19.) These programs provide for only a minimal portion of the total nongovernment-school budget.

10. Congregation for the Doctrine of the Faith, *Instruction on Christian Freedom and Liberation* (Vatican City: Vatican Polyglot Press, 1986), # 94, pp. 54f. See also Holy See, *Charter of Rights of the Family*, art. 5, in *L'Osservatore Romano*, November 25, 1983. Robert B. Everhart, ed., *The Public School Monopoly: A Critical Analysis of Education and the State in American Society* (Cambridge, Mass.: Ballinger, 1982), gives a comprehensive examination of education in the United States from historical, political, cultural, and moral perspectives, and discusses the private-versus government-school controversy.

11. Congregation for the Doctrine of the Faith, *Instruction on Christian Freedom and*

Liberation (Vatican City: Vatican Polyglot Press, 1986), # 92, p. 54. See also John Paul II, *Discourse to UNESCO*, June 2, 1980, 8: *AAS* 72 (1980), pp. 739–40.

12. *Freedom* comes in so many tones that there should be many words for it; for example, the Eskimo has one hundred words for snow—such are the subtleties he detects in its color and tone and depth and temperature. The opposite of freedom may be slavery, but the range of unfreedoms is as wide and subtle as the range of freedoms.

13. See John McClaughry, *Educational Choice in Vermont* (Concord, Vt.: Institute for Liberty and Community, 1987).

14. For a good summary, see Joe Nathan, "The Rhetoric and the Reality of Expanding Educational Choices," *Phi Delta Kappan*, March 1985, pp. 476–81.

15. *Declaration on Christian Education* (*Gravissimum educationis*) # 6, in Austin J. Flannery, ed., *Vatican Council II: The Conciliar and Post Conciliar ocuments*, 2 vols. (Northport, N.Y.: Costello, 1982), vol. 1, p. 731.

16. Pope John Paul II, *The Role of the Christian Family in the Modern World* (Boston: Sisters of St. Paul, 1981), # 40.

17. Sacred Congregation for Catholic Education, *Lay Catholics in Schools: Witnesses to Faith* (*Les laics Catholiques*) # 14, in Flannery, vol. 2, p. 634.

18. *Pierce v. Society of Sisters*, 268 U.S. 510, 535 (1925). See also *Meyer v. Nebraska*, 262 U.S. 390, 401–402 (1923).

19. See various Gallup polls (especially 1970, 1971, 1979, 1981–1985); *Public Policy and Private Choice: The Case of Minnesota*, a study by the Rand Corporation of the Minnesota tuition tax deduction plan, 1984; *Parental Views on Student Financial Aid*, a survey of parents on federal aid to college students, National Center for Education Statistics, U.S. Deaprtment of Education, 1982; *Survey of Montgomery County Parents Who Transferred Their Children between Public and Private Schools in 1980–81*, Department of Educational Accountability, Montgomery County Public Schools, Montgomery County, Maryland, 1982; *Survey of Parents Regarding Parent Involvement in Schools*, survey done as part of a larger study that also surveyed teachers and principals, Southwest Educational Development Laboratory, Austin, Texas, 1982; *Study of Attitudes Among Parents of Elementary School Children in Boston*, Martila and Kiley, Inc., for the Boston City-Wide Education Coalition, 1985; *Parents and School Choice: A Household Survey*, School Finance Project, U.S. Department of Education, 1983; Robert Bezdek and Ray Cross, "Tax Breaks for Parents of Private School Students: Who Favors Them and Who Would Take Advantage of Them?," *Integrated Education*, December–January 1983, pp. 202f.; *USA Today* poll of 807 adults, *USA Today*, May 1985, p. 1.

20. For this and other material here, see testimony of Chester E. Finn, Jr., Assistant Secretary, Office of Educational Research and Improvement, U.S. Department of Education, on "Education Choice: Theory, Practice, and Research," before the Senate Subcommittee on Intergovernmental Relations, Committee on Governmental Affairs, October 22, 1985.

21. *Mueller v. Allen*, 463 U.S. 388 (1983).

22. For further information, contact the Clearinghouse on Educational Choice, 1611 North Kent Street, Suite 805, Arlington, Va. 22209; telephone: (703) 524-1556. This nonpartisan, nonprofit, tax-exempt organization is dedicated to the issue of parental choice in schooling, including the issues of vouchers, tuition tax credits, magnet schools, alternative schools, and the role of parents in their children's academic achievement. Also excellent for information on choice in schooling is Citizens for Educational Freedom, at the same address (telephone: [703] 524-1991). See also *Educational Freedom*, a publication of the Educational Freedom Foundation, 20 Parkland, Glendale, St. Louis, Mo., 63122.

23. *Aguilar v. Felton*, 105 S. Ct. 3232, 3239 (1985).

24. Sacred Congregation for Catholic Education, *Catholic Schools* (*Malgre les declarations*) # 21, in Flannery, vol. 2, pp. 610f.

25. Ibid., # 57, in Flannery, vol. 2, p. 619.

26. Ibid., # 58, in Flannery, vol. 2, p. 619.

27. Ibid., # 82, in Flannery, vol. 2, p. 626.

28. This information was provided in interviews with Sr. Mary Fitzpatrick, Faithful Companions of Jesus, at Notre Dame de France School, Paris, on March 21, 1986, and with Sr. Philomena O'Higgins, S.S.L., on March 9, 1986, at Newmarket, England.

29. Donald A. Erikson, "Disturbing Evidence about the 'One Best System,'" in Robert B. Everhart, *The Public School Monopoly* (Cambridge, Mass.: Ballinger, 1982), pp. 393–422.

30. *The Chronicle of Higher Education*, vol. XXXI no. 13 (November 27, 1985), pp. 1, 23.

31. *Familiaris consortio* # 23, p. 40.

32. *Reynolds v. United States*, 98 U.S. (8 Otto) 145, 164 (1878).

33. Robert Frost, "Mending Wall," *The Poetry of Robert Frost*, ed. Edward Latham (New York: Holt, Rinehart and Winston, 1974), p. 33.

34. For early state constitutions and statutes encouraging support for religion in schools by grants of money and land to denominational schools, see Richard J. Gabel, Jr., *Public Funds for Church and Private Schools* (Washington, D.C.: The Catholic University of America, 1937).

35. See Daniel D. McGarry's excellently thorough analysis in his "Public Schools Teach Religion Without God and Should Not Have a Monopoly: Secularism in American Public Education and the Unconstitutionality of Its Exclusive Governmental Support," distributed by the Thomas J. White Educational Foundation, 940 West Port Plaza, Suite 264, St. Louis, Mo. 63146.

36. As cited in E. E. Ellis, "If Only a Secularist Religion Is Taught," *Educational Freedom*, Spring–Summer 1984, p. 36.

37. As cited in P. A. Kienel, *The Philosophy of Christian Education* (Whittier, Calif.: ACSI, 1978), p. 130.

38. Otto F. Kraushaar, *American Nonpublic Schools: Patterns of Diversity* (Baltimore: Johns Hopkins University, 1972), p. 20.

39. Senate Committee on Finance, Subcommittee on Tuition Tax Credits, 1978.

40. See Nancy H. Fink, "The Establishment Clause According to the Supreme Court: The Mysterious Eclipse of Free Exercise Values," *Catholic University Law Review*, vol. 27 no. 2 (Winter 1978), pp. 207–62.

41. *Bradfield v. Roberts*, 175 U.S. 291, 298 (1899).

42. *Pierce v. Society of Sisters*, 268 U.S. 510 (1925).

43. *Sherbert v. Verner*, 374 U.S. 398, 405 (1963), citing to *Speiser v. Randall*, 357 U.S. 513, 526 (1958).

44. *Griffin v. Illinois*, 351 U.S. 12, 19 (1956): "There can be no equal justice where the kind of trial a man gets depends on the amount of money he has"; *Harper v. Virginia State Board of Elections*, 383 U.S. 663, 666 (1966): "We conclude that a State violates the Equal Protection Clause of the Fourteenth Amendment whenever it makes the affluence of the voter or payment of any fee an electoral standard"; *Murdock v. Pennsylvania*, 319 U.S. 105, 111 (1943): "Freedom of speech, freedom of the press, freedom of religion are available to all, not merely to those who can pay their own way." In *Everson v. Board of Education*, 330 U.S. 1, 16 (1947), Justice Hugo Black wrote that, under a "child benefit" theory, to deny transportation to children attending religious schools

would make the State an adversary of religion. See also Stephen Arons, "The Separation of School and State: Pierce Reconsidered," *Harvard Educational Review*, vol. 46 no. 1 (February, 1976), pp. 76–104.

But confusion is not limited to the area of church-affiliated schools. It exists also in, for example, workman's compensation cases. Article III of the U.S. Constitution provides that the judicial power of the United States should be exercised through Article III courts. The Founding Fathers felt that it was significant for judicial power to be exercised before courts headed by judges with life tenure and thus placed beyond dependency on the executive branch of government. Workman's compensation cases, however, have been decided by the U.S. Supreme Court as being constitutionally placed before an administrative agency which does not have the protections that the Founding Fathers found to be significant enough to write into Article III and thus is a denial of those protections. Similarly, all such cases are supposed, under the Seventh Amendment, to be guaranteed the right to a jury trial. Placing these cases before an administrative agency constitutes a negation of such a right.

A contradiction seems to exist also in the area of remittitur and additur. Though remittitur is firmly established in federal practice, additur has been found by the Court to be in violation of the Seventh Amendment and therefore not allowed in federal trials. *Dimick v. Schiedt*, 293 U.S. 474 (1935). The first argument was on historical grounds: It said that the "according to the rules of common law" clause of the Seventh Amendment was violated because at the time that the Amendment was enacted in 1791, the practice of additur was not allowed at common law. But if this strict an adherence to history is controlling in this instance, why not with nongovernment schools and the monopoly of government schools, today's practice in this regard being the reverse of what it was in 1791?

45. *Committee for Public Education & Religious Liberty v. Regan*, 44 U.S. 646 (1980); *Widmar v. Vincent*, 454 U.S. 263 (1981); *Marsh v. Chambers*, 463 U.S. 783 (1983); *Mueller v. Allen*, 463 U.S. 388 (1983); *Lynch v. Donnelly*, 465 U.S. 668 (1984).

46. *Lynch v. Donnelly*, 465 U.S. 668, 673 (1984) (cites omitted). See also Neal Devins, "The Supreme Court and Private Schools: An Update," *This World* 8 (Spring–Summer 1984), pp. 13–26.

47. *Lynch*, 465 U.S. at 678–79; see *Mueller*, 463 U.S. at 399–400.

48. *Wolman v. Walter*, 433 U.S. 229, 263 (1977); *Mueller*, 463 U.S. at 400 (cite omitted); *Lynch*, 465 U.S. at 686 (cite omitted).

49. *Lynch*, 465 U.S. at 672–73; see also *Meek v. Pittenger*, 421 U.S. 349, 386–87 (1975) (Burger, C.J., dissenting).

50. *Lynch*, 465 U.S. at 673–74.

51. *Ibid.*, at 673 (cites omitted).

52. *Mueller*, 463 U.S. at 395, 400.

53. *Wolman*, 433 U.S. at 262 (Powell, J., concurring and dissenting; *Mueller*, 463 U.S. at 394–95, 401–402.

54. *Wolman*, 433 U.S. at 262; *Mueller*, 463 U.S. at 395.

55. *Aguilar v. Felton*, 105 S.Ct. 3232 (including related cases Nos. 84–238, 239).

56. *Lemon v. Kurtzman*, 403 U.S. 602, 614 (1971).

57. Ibid., at 612–613.

58. Geoffrey Sawyer, *The Australian Constitution* (Canberra: Australian Government Publishing Service, 1975), p. 61.

59. *Her Majesty's Attorney-General for the State of Victoria v. Commonwealth of Australia*, Slip Opinion, February 10, 1981, p. 1.

60. Ibid., p. 5.

61. Ibid., p. 7.

62. Ibid.

63. Ibid., p. 8. When the U.S. Constitution was adopted, in 1787, nothing like it had been seen before. Hardly any of the Constitution's ideas, however, were the brainchildren of Americans: They came from French *philosophes* and English political thinkers. The American innovation was to give life to their ideas by weaving them into a single document, and to give them teeth. By declaring the Constitution "the supreme law of the land," the framers paved the way for effective judicial review to make even the government comply with the Constitution's high directives.

Today, all but seven of the world's more than 170 nations are committed to a single written charter. Some constitutions pay no more than lip service to the notion of individual freedom. But every one of them owes something to the American model. India and Japan established supreme courts modeled on the American version. So have some African states. Italy, West Germany, and France set up special tribunals with the authority to resolve constitutional questions.

American constitutionalism has traveled abroad along many paths. Sometimes it took the express route: in the Philippines, for example, as part of the 1934 arrangement for independence from the U.S.; in West Germany, by way of the victorious Allies after World War II; and in postwar Japan, whose language lacked even a word for rights until the mid-nineteenth century, by way of General Douglas MacArthur's command. More commonly, the U.S. model traveled indirectly. Some governments have even sought help in drafting their constitutions along U.S. lines: the Marshall Islands, for example, and Bangladesh, Liberia, and Zimbabwe.

All of the countries that have adopted the U.S. Constitution (including military dictatorships like Liberia) have in their case law interpreted the constitutionality of government aid to church-affiliated schools more favorably than the U.S. Supreme Court. A comparison of these countries with the United States would make a valuable study.

Aside from the influence of the U.S. Constitution, a review of the U.S. position on freedom to children in church-affiliated schools is enlightening. Countries with whom the United States is allied in denying true freedom (freedom meaning no serious financial penalty) are Albania, Bulgaria, China, Ceylon, Cuba, East Germany, Hungary, South Africa, Russia, Turkey, and Yugoslavia. Among the countries that provide true freedom (that is, without serious financial penalty, and out of consideration for the public welfare), are the following: in North America, Canada; in Latin America, Argentina, Bolivia, Brazil, Chile, Columbia, Costa Rica, Dominican Republic, Ecuador, Guatemala, Haiti, Honduras, Jamaica, Mexico, Panama, Peru, El Salvador, Venezuela; in the Near East, Iran, Iraq, Israel, Jordan, Lebanon, Syria; in Europe, Austria, Belgium, Denmark, England, France, Finland, Holland, Ireland, Norway, Portugal, Scotland, Spain, Switzerland, Wales, West Germany; in Asia and Oceania, Australia, India, Indonesia, Japan, Laos, New Zealand, Pakistan, Thailand, Taiwan.

64. Robert Bellah et al., *Habits of the Heart: Individualism and Commitment in American Life* (Berkeley: University of California Press, 1985).

65. The "Humanist Manifesto I" (*The New Humanist*, vol. VI no. 3 (May–June, 1933), promulgated by a group including John Dewey, included the following dogmas: the universe is self-existing and not created; humankind is a part of nature and has emerged as the result of a continuous process; the traditional dualism of mind and body must be rejected; humankind's culture and civilization are the product of a gradual development due to its interaction with its natural environment and social heritage; the nature of the universe makes unacceptable any supernatural or cosmic guarantees of human value; religion must formulate its hopes and plans in the light of

the scientific spirit and method; the time is past for theism, deism, modernism, and the several varieties of "new thought"; the complete realization of human personality is the end of man's life, and its development and fulfillment is to be sought in the here and now; religious institutions, their ritualistic forms, ecclesiastical methods, and religion's communal activities must be reconstructed as rapidly as experience will allow.

For the "Humanist Manifesto II," see *The Humanist*, vol. 33 no. 5 (September–October 1973), pp. 4–9. See also Paul Kurtz, ed. *Humanist Manifestos I and II* (Buffalo, N. Y.: Prometheus, 1973). For a good criticism, see Charles H. Hagan, *The Humanifestos: The Creed of Secular Humanism* (Rome: Pontificia Universitas Gregoriana, 1975), pp. 15–26 presents the full text of the 1973 "Humanist Manifesto II," which is essentially the same as "Humanist Manifesto I." See also Paul Kurtz, *A Secular Humanist Declaration* (Buffalo, N.Y.: Prometheus, n.d.), reprinted from *Free Inquiry*, vol. 1 no. 1 (Winter 1980). For Secular Humanist literature, contact Prometheus Books, 700 East Amherst Street, Buffalo, N.Y. 14215; telephone: (800) 421-0351, in New York State (716) 837-2475.

66. *Torcaso v. Watkins*, 367 U.S. 488, 495 n. 11 (1961).

67. For further information on Secularism as a religion, see chapter II under "Secularism: Voltaire," including notes.

68. 381 U.S. 479 (1965).

69. *Eisenstadt v. Baird*, 405 U.S. 438 (1972).

70. *Roe v. Wade*, 410 U.S. 113 (1973).

71. 387 U.S. 1 (1967).

72. 393 U.S. 503 (1969).

73. *In re Winship*, 397 U.S. 358 (1970).

74. *Goss v. Lopez*, 419 U.S. 565 (1975). Nonetheless, juveniles are still distinct from adults in the eyes of the law. For example, in *Ginsberg v. New York*, 390 U.S. 629 (1968), the Supreme Court upheld a state statute that prohibited the sale of obscene material to children—material which would not be considered off-limits to adults. The Court held that it was permissible to restrict the rights of minors more than adults, and claimed that the statute did not invade constitutionally protected rights of minors. A second major decision distinguishing the minor from the adult was in *McKeiver v. Pennsylvania*, 403 U.S. 52 (1971), wherein the Court held that delinquents were not constitutionally entitled to a trial by jury in determining delinquency. Finally, in *Ingraham v. Wright*, 430 U.S. 651 (1977), the Court upheld the rights of schools to apply corporal punishment to misbehaving students. The Supreme Court ruled that the Eighth Amendment ban on cruel and unusual punishment did not apply to the disciplinary "spanking" of children. But it held the right of school children to be free from corporal punishment as a constitutional liberty. Thus, the question became one of what procedural protections were due to children before punishment.

75. 428 U.S. 52 (1976).

76. *Bellotti v. Baird*, 443 U.S. 622 (1979); see also its precessors, *Carey v. Population Services International*, 431 U.S. 678 (1977), which originated in New York; *Doe v. Irwin*, 449 U.S. 829 (1980), originating in Michigan; and *Parham v. J. R.*, 442 U.S. 584 (1979), a case challenging on due process grounds the constitutionality of a Georgia statute authorizing parents to commit their minor children to a mental institution without an adversary hearing. In *Doe*, Federal District Court Judge Noel P. Fox's lengthy and scholarly opinion of November 23, 1977, is forthrightly profamily against State intrusion and makes for beneficial reading. He concluded that, even if minors do have a fundamental right to obtain contraceptives, "that right need not

exist to the total exclusion of any rights of the child's parents" (*Doe v. Irwin*, 428 F.Supp. 1198 (W.D. Mich. 1977). Fox was overturned by the U.S. Court of Appeals for the Sixth Circuit on February 26, 1980, and the Supreme Court declined to hear an appeal from that decision. In *Parham*, the Court, after giving a ringing endorsement of parental rights, denied to parents the right even to know about medical procedures carried out on their children without the parents' consent.

77. Both the "mature minor" doctrine and the "best interest" test contradict established principles of law. Juvenile courts have traditionally been empowered to inquire into the "best interest" of minors, but it is a well-established principle of law that this inquiry cannot be undertaken without a prior finding of parental unfitness. The principle is: "It is a serious matter for the long arm of the state to reach into a home and snatch a child from its mother." *Rinker Appeal*, 180 Pa. Super. 143, 148, 117 A.2d 780, 783 (Pa. Super. Ct. 1955). The "mature minor" doctrine is excessively vague: there are no agreed-upon criteria for maturity, apart from age, which is admittedly an arbitrary criterion. The doctrine enshrines a rule of men instead of the rule of law. It violates the due process rights of parents: it suspends or curtails their custodial rights without any showing of parental unfitness, without any adversary proceeding, and without giving parents the knowledge that their rights and responsibilities are no longer in force. The doctrine violates the concept of equal protection of the law: one minor may be declared "mature" by one judge, while another minor of the same age may be regarded "immature" by another judge. And the doctrine invites chaos. Is a minor who is declared sufficiently "mature" for an abortion without parental knowledge also "mature" enough to have her ears pierced without parental consent? Is she legally competent to take out a bank loan to pay the abortionist? Do her parents remain legally responsibile for her medical bills if she has to be treated for complications arising from the abortion?

78. See Patricia M. Lines, "The New Private Schools and Their Historic Purpose," *Phi Delta Kappan*, vol. 67 no. 5 (January 1986), pp. 373–79.

79. In the writer's immediate jurisdictions, the District of Columbia requires parents who want to school their children between ages seven and sixteen at home to file an application and meet the criteria of approvable curriculum and certifiable instructor. Virginia requires one of four criteria, to be approved by local school superintendents: the instructor's having a B.A. degree from any accredited college, or a teaching certificate, or enrolling the child in an approved correspondence course, or submission of a statement of curriculum and qualifications. At the end of each year, the child must be evaluated by standardized tests and must score at least in the fortieth percentile in mathematics and language arts. Maryland regulations deal with instruction programs, materials, teacher qualifications, and monitoring, evaluation, and approval; county superintendents make all decisions, which can range from strict interpretation to waiving all requirements.

80. Perry A. Zirkel, "Defense of Home Instruction 'Not Warranted,'" *Education Week*, October 30, 1985, p. 19. On home education, see also John W. Whitehead and Wendell R. Bird, *Home Education and Constitutional Liberties* (Westchester, Ill.: Crossway, 1984).

For further information, contact Growing Without Schooling, Holt Associates, 729 Boylston Street, Boston, Mass., 02116; telephone (617) 437-1550; Hewitt Research Foundation, Box 9, Washougal, Wash., 98671; telephone (206) 835-8708.

81. Jack Anderson and Dale Van Atta, "School at Home," *The Washington Post*, July 14, 1985, p. B7.

82. *Wisconsin v. Yoder*, 406 U.S. 205, 232 (1972).

83. *Thomas v. Review Bd.*, 450 U.S. 707, 715–16 (1981).

84. *Meyer v. Nebraska*, 262 U.S. 390 (1923); *Pierce v. Society of Sisters*, 268 U.S. 510 (1925); *Wisconsin v. Yoder*, 406 U.S. 205 (1972).

85. John T. Noonan, Jr., in 1973 presented the interesting thesis that the Supreme Court's treatment of marriage may be divided into three phases: phase one, beginning in the last quarter of the nineteenth century, in which the Court was the defender of Christian marriage; phase two, beginning during World War II and perduring through its aftermath, in which the Court was the creator of partial marriage; and phase three, the modern, in which the Court became the upholder of no marriage.

Until the late eighteenth century in America, and until still later in England, marriage was created, ruled, and ended in accordance with ecclesiastical law. When secular courts took over, the adjustments were often awkward and inconsistent. Nevertheless, the institution survived, and the consensus was broad. Even eighteenth-century rationalism and nineteenth-century agnosticism did not attack it.

Lately, however, the consensus weakened and then finally disappeared. Among the propositions Noonan infers from the modern phase is that the unique legal privileges of heterosexual monogamy are constitutionally obsolete. Whereas in a 1965 case Justice William O. Douglas, writing for the Court, could say that "Marriage is a coming together for better or for worse, hopefully enduring, and intimate to the degree of being sacred," (*Griswold v. Connecticut*, 381 U.S. 479, 486 [1965]), the marriage contract in a state like California today is less than any other contract: terminable, without penalty, at the option of either party. And unfortunately the law, while far from omnipotent, has a pedagogic role in the shaping of society; in our secular age, when ecclesiastical authority has diminished, the specific importance of the Supreme Court as the expositor of moral doctrine increases.

See John T. Noonan, Jr., "The Family and the Supreme Court," *Catholic University Law Review*, vol. 23 no. 2 (Winter 1973), 255–74. For further thoughts, see also William J. Byron, "Needed: A New Educational Partnership between Government and Families," *America*, vol. 156 no. 22 (June 6, 1987), pp. 460–62, 469.

86. *Korematsu v. United States*, 323 U.S. 214 (1944); *In re Yamashita*, 327 U.S. 1 (1946).

87. *Black's Law Dictionary*, rev. 5th ed. (St. Paul, Minn.: West. 1979), p. 985.

88. *Lemon v. Kurtzman*, 403 U.S. 602 (1971).

89. Loraine Boettner, *Roman Catholicism* (Philadelphia: Presbyterian and Reformed, n.d.), p. 62.

90. *Board of Education of Central School District no. 1 v. Allen*, 392 U.S. 236, 251 (1968).

91. *McCollum v. Board of Education*, 333 U.S. 203 (1948).

92. 407 U.S. 258 (1972).

93. Thomas Jefferson, "Letter to Judge Spencer Roane, Poplar Forest, September 6, 1819," *The Portable Thomas Jefferson*, ed. Merrill Peterson (New York: Penguin, 1975), p. 563.

94. Paul Angle, *Created Equal? The Complete Lincoln-Douglas Debate of 1858* (University of Chicago Press, 1972), p. 78.

95. For a review of the history of Supreme Court decisions overruled by subsequent decisions, see Albert R. Blaustein and Andrew H. Field, "Overruling Opinions in the Supreme Court," *Michigan Law Review*, vol. 57 (December 1958), pp. 151–94. Some examples of Supreme Court changes of opinion follow.

On the exclusionary rule, *Mapp v. Ohio*, 367 U.S. 643 (1961) overruled *Wolf v. Colorado*, 338 U.S. 25 (1949), and continues to be fought about. The doctrine on the right to counsel has evolved from *Powell v. Alabama*, 287 U.S. 45 (1932), through *Betts v. Brady*, 316 U.S. 455 (1942), to *Gideon v. Wainwright*, 372 U.S. 335 (1963): for a fascinating narration of *Gideon*, see Anthony Lewis, *Gideon's Trumpet* (New York: Vintage, 1966). Most of the opinions concerning the "cruel and unusual punishment" prohibition of the Eighth Amendment rely on the statement in *Trop v. Dulles*, 356 U.S. 86 (1958), that the Eighth Amendment standard is one of "evolving standards of decency" — a common phrase in Court elaborations of procedural due process as well.

Changes have taken place in the interpretation of the Constitutions's Article I, Section 8, Par. 3 (the "Commerce Clause"), which empowers Congress to "regulate commerce with foreign nations and among the several states, and with the Indian tribes." For a while, the Court required the government to show that a disputed act was regulating an activity which had a "direct effect" on commerce; it was this interpretation which led to the refusal of important New Deal legislation. This direct effect has now been eliminated. Beginning with *NLRB v. Jones and Laughlin Steel Corp.*, 301 U.S. 1 (1937), the Court has sustained congressional power to regulate any activity, local or interstate, which either in itself or in combination with other activities has a "substantial economic effect upon" or "effect on movemement in" interstate commerce. *United States v. E. C. Knight Co.*, 156 U.S. 1 (1895), ruled that the connection between "local" and "interstate" activities had to be a *logical* nexus; *Houston E. & W. Texas Ry. Co. v. United States* (*The Shreveport Rate Case*), 234 U.S. 342 (1914), ruled that the connection between "local" and "interstate" activities for involving the Commerce Clause had to be rather a *practical, empiric* one of *economic impact*.

Important applications of "Commerce Clause" changes in interpretation exist in the areas of Congressional control of an individual farmer's production of wheat for home consumption (*Wickard v. Filburn*, 317 U.S. 111 [1942]), federal regulation of local loan-sharking (*Perez v. United States*, 402 U.S. 146 [1971]), and key sections of the Public Accommodations title of the Civil Rights Act of 1964 (*Katzenbach v. McClung*, 379 U.S. 249 [1964]; *Heart of Atlanta Motel v. United States*, 379 U.S. 241 [1964]).

In the matter of privileges vs. rights, the Supreme Court has changed from a concept of privileges to one of entitlements (see the watershed case of *Goldberg v. Kelly*, 397 U.S. 254 [1970]). There has been a great change in the view of the beneficiary of life insurance. *Central Bank of Washington v. Hume*, 128 U.S. 195, 206 (1888), decided that the "policy, and the money to become due under it, belong, the moment it is issued, to the person or persons named in it as the beneficiary or beneficiaries, and . . . there is no power in the person procuring the insurance by any act of his, by deed or by will, to transfer to any other person the interest of the person named"; *Gordon v. Portland Trust Bank*, 201 Or. 648, 271 P.2d 653, 655 (1954), decided that "there is considerable authority for the view that the beneficiary gets a vested right only as his expectancy or contingent interest matures on the death of the insured."

Frank v. Maryland, 359 U.S. 360 (1959), authorized warrantless inspections by health inspectors during daytime hours of residential private premises. *Camara v. Municipal Court*, 387 U.S. 523 (1967), overruled *Frank* and said that in accord with the Fourth Amendment warrants are necessary, as "no Warrants shall issue, but upon probable cause." In anti-child-labor regulation, *United States v. Darby*, 312 U.S. 100, (1941) explicitly overruled *Hammer v. Dagenhart*, 247 U.S. 251 (1918).

Products liability is an area of change for the better, the landmark case of *MacPherson v. Buick Motor Co.*, 217 N.Y. 382 382, 111 N.E. 1050 (1916), overruling *Winterbottom v. Wright*, 10 M. & W. 109, 152 Eng. Rep. 402 (Ex. 1842), an English case.

Many of the Court's overturnings are indirect. Some are express and direct: e.g., *Boys Markets, Inc. v. Retail Clerks Union*, 398 U.S. 235, (1970), expressly overturned *Sinclair Refining Co. v. Atkinson*, 370 U.S. 195 (1962). *Swift v. Tyson*, 41 U.S. 1 (16 Pet.) (1842), was expressly overturned by the very important *Erie v. Tompkins*, 304 U.S. 64 (1938); important on the speculative as well as the practical level, *Swift* was based on a natural law philosophy, *Erie* on a realist philosophy.

Even items of long standing are sometimes overturned. The "Hawkins Rule" emanated from a 1958 decision that gave a spouse on trial the right to veto the intention of the other spouse to offer incriminating evidence in court. In *Trammel v. United States*, 445 U.S. 40, 52 (1980), Chief Justice Warren Burger in rendering the opinion of the Court explained that the old notions about married women having no separate legal identity had broken down "chip by chip," and that marriage was not what it used to be; so a spouse, instead of being an accomplice for every imaginable crime, when willing can testify against a spouse, except for conversations that were intended to be private (like "pillow talk").

96. *Bradwell v. State*, 83 U.S. (16 Wall) 130, 141 (1872) (Bradley, J., concurring).

97. One quick about-face (in three years) was the government-school flag-salute cases: *Minersville School Dist. v. Gobitis*, 310 U.S. 586 (1940); *West Virginia State Bd. of Education v. Barnett*, 319 U.S. 624 (1943). Graphically illustrating perhaps the quickest "flip-flop-flip" ever accomplished by the Supreme Court on a major issue, however, were the 1968–71 cases on legitimacy and illegitimacy: See *Levy v. Louisiana*, 391 U.S. 68 (1968); *Glona v. American Guarantee & Liability Ins. Co.*, 391 U.S. 73 (1968); *Labine v. Vincent*, 401 U.S. 532 (1971); *Weber v. Aetna Casualty & Surety Co.*, 406 U.S. 164 (1972).

98. *Flast v. Cohen*, 392 U.S. 83 (1968).

99. *Frothingham v. Mellon*, 262 U.S. 447 (1923).

100. *Flast v. Cohen*, 392 U.S. 83, 109 (1983) (Douglas, J., concurring).

101. The minority opinions in, for example, the *Slaughter-House Cases*, 83 U.S. (16 Wall.) 36, (1873), became the majority opinions.

102. See *Stanley v. Georgia*, 394 U.S. 557 (1969).

103. *Paris Adult Theatre I v. Slaton*, 418 U.S. 939 (1974), which negates the right to sell, purchase, receive, or transport obscene material.

104. The Federal government can condition a bankruptcy discharge on the payment of fifty dollars: *United States v. Kras*, 409 U.S. 434 (1973).

105. *Ortwein v. Schwab*, 410 U.S. 656 (1973).

106. 105 S.Ct. 3232 (1985).

107. *Hannan v. Dusch*, Supreme Court of Appeals of Virginia, 154 Va. 356, 379, 153 S.E. 824, 831 (1930).

108. In *Pirie v. Chicago Title & Trust Co.*, 182 U.S. 438 (1901), the Supreme Court barred the claims of a creditor who had received a preference without notice of insolvency. There was a storm of protest, so that in 1903 the word "voidable" was inserted in Section 57b of the Bankruptcy Act.

109. As one example out of many, the decision in *South Carolina State Highway Dept. v. Barnwell Bros., Inc.*, 303 U.S. 177 (1938) was affected by the fact that it came right after the Franklin D. Roosevelt court-packing controversy.

110. Daniel Patrick Moynihan, "What Do You Do When the Supreme Court Is Wrong," *Public Interest*, no. 57 (Fall 1979), pp. 3–24.

111. *Brown v. Board of Education*, 347 U.S. 483 (1954).

112. *Plessy v. Ferguson*, 163 U.S. 537 (1896).

113. The efforts of the NAACP and Thurgood Marshall in setting up the necessary case law precedent to justify the overturning of the "separate but equal" doctrine is chronicled in Richard Kluger's *Simple Justice: The History of Brown v. Board of Education and Black America's Struggle for Equality* (New York: Vintage, 1977). See also J. Harvie Wilkinson III, *From Brown to Bakke: The Supreme Court and School Integration: 1954–1978* (New York: Oxford University Press, 1979); Kenneth F. Ripple, "Thurgood Marshall and the Forgotten Legacy of *Brown v. Board of Education*," *Notre Dame Lawyer*, vol. 55 no. 4 (April 1980), pp. 471–75.

114. As early as 1942, Redden and Ryan reported on these schools, dealing with

the schools and pupils, property arrangements, public and Catholic supervision, the teaching staff, religious instruction and practices, special aids to pupils, and opinions. See John D. Redden and Francis A. Ryan, *A Catholic Philosophy of Education* (Milwaukee: Bruce, 1942), pp. 131–34, See also Harold A. Buetow, *Of Singular Benefit: the Story of U.S. Catholic Education* (New York: Macmillan, 1970), p. 481, n. 258.

115. See Robert F. Drinan, "The Constitutionality of Public Aid to Schools," in Dallin H. Oaks, ed., *The Wall Between Church and State* (University of Chicago Press, 1963), pp. 55–61.

116. See *Education Week*, vol. VI no. 14 (December 10, 1986), pp. 1, 15. Nuissance cases could also be avoided, such as the case (no. LR-C-86-653 in Federal District Court, Little Rock, Ark.) brought to prevent the celebration of Halloween in government schools because some satanic churches believe that Satan is reborn on that day; Ibid., p. 3.

CHAPTER 8: ATMOSPHERE

1. Adapted from Sean J. Healy, S.M.A., and Brigid Reynolds, S.M., *Social Analysis in the Light of the Gospel* (Dublin: Folens, 1983).

2. *Stuart v. School Dist. no. 1 of Village of Kalamazoo*, 30 Mich. 69 (1874).

3. The Roman Catholic Church is no longer an immigrant church consisting of little islands of Italy, Ireland, Poland, or Germany. By the mid-1980s, studies found that the average level of education of adult non-Hispanic Roman Catholics was slightly below that of Jews, Episcopalians, and Presbyterians, and above that of the large Protestant bodies such as Methodists, Lutherans, and Baptists. While Catholics are a little over 22 percent of the population, they account for 40 percent of the enrollment in universities and colleges. Unlike their Protestant counterparts, the higher the education level of young Catholics the more likely they are to attend Mass fairly regularly.

Studies conducted by the Institute for Pastoral and Social Ministry at Notre Dame University revealed findings on the upward mobility of Catholics that confirmed those of the National Opinion Research Center at the University of Chicago. See Andrew M. Greeley, "Making It in America: Ethnic Groups and Social Status," *Social Policy*, September–October 1973, pp. 21–29; Marjorie Hyer, "Parish Activity Flourishing Among Catholics After Vatican II," *The Washington Post*, December 5, 1985, pp. A33–A34.

For conclusions that Catholic contributions have not kept pace and are affected by Catholics' objections to the Church's official teaching on matters like birth control, and by a nonresponsive hierarchical leadership, see Andrew Greeley and William McManus, *Catholic Contributions: Sociology and Policy* (Chicago: Thomas More Press, 1987). (Retired Bishop McManus, the co-author, disagrees with some of Greeley's conclusions.) Sociologist Greeley says that Catholics are putting $6 billion less in the collection plate than they should. Except for parents of Catholic-school pupils, who contribute much more than average, Catholics give only half as much proportionately as they did 25 years ago (1.1% of their income today against 2.2% formerly), and give only half as much proportionately as do U.S. Protestants (as compared with roughly the same percentage 25 years ago). Catholics' contributions to their Church rank last in quantity among the major denominations. All these figures are national averages, which may not pertain to a particular locality. The authors urge new strategies to involve Catholics in the budget process and suggest alternatives to the traditional Sunday collection basket.

4. Sacred Congregation for Catholic Education, *Catholic Schools (Malgre les declara-*

tions) # 58, in Austin Flannery, ed., *Vatican Council II: The Conciliar and Post Conciliar Documents*, 2 vols. (Northport, N.Y.: Costello, 1984), vol. 2, p. 619.

· 5. Martin Luther, "Sermon on the Duty of Sending Children to School," from F. V. N. Painter's "Luther on Education," in Robert Ulich, *Three Thousand Years of Educational Wisdom* (Cambridge, Mass.: Harvard University Press, 1963), p. 247.

6. *Declaration on Christian Education (Gravissimum educationis)* # 3, in Flannery, vol. 1, p. 729.

7. See Sean J. Healy, S.M.S., and Brigid Reynolds, S.M., "Irish Society and the Future of Education," in *Urbanisation — Ireland in the Year 2000* (Dublin: St. Martin's House, 1985), p. 1.

8. Neil Postman, *Amusing Ourselves to Death* (New York: Viking, 1985).

9. Sacred Congregation for the Clergy, *General Catechetical Directory (Ad normam decreti)* # 123, in Flannery, vol. 2, p. 595.

10. Ibid., # 8, in Flannery, vol. 2, p. 535.

11. How can Catholics, to whose religion the symbol of light means so much, allow themselves to go along with terming a mind-set whose whole spirit is so against their own, the "Enlightenment"? For the Judeo-Christian symbolism of light, see Gen. 1:3–5; Ps. 103:2; Sir. 46:18; Wis. 7:26; Isa. 9:2; 1 John 1:5; 1 Tim. 6:16; Col. 1:12; 1 Pet. 2:9; John 3:19; 1 John 2:8; Eph. 5:9; Heb. 1:3; Luke 1:79; Luke 2:32; John 1:4f., 9; John 3:19–21; 8:12; 9:5; 12:35; Eph. 5:8; 1 Thess. 5:5; John 12:36; John 5:35; Matt. 5:14–16.

12. *The Washington Post*, April 20, 1986, p. C5; and *Education Week*, vol. V no. 32 (April 30, 1986), p. 10.

13. *To Teach as Jesus Did*, pp. 29, 31.

14. Sacred Congregation for Catholic Education, *Lay Catholics in Schools: Witnesses to Faith (Les laïcs Catholiques)* # 20, in Flannery, vol. 2, p. 636.

15. *Pastoral Constitution on the Church in the Modern World (Gaudium et Spes)* # 62, in Flannery, vol. 1, p. 967.

16. *General Catechetical Directory* # 3, in Flannery, vol. 2, p. 532.

17. Ibid., # 35, in Flannery, vol. 2, p. 549.

18. Sacred Congregation for Divine Worship, *Directory on Children's Masses (Pueros baptizatos)* # 11, in Flannery, vol. 1, pp. 256f.

19. *Dogmatic Constitution on the Church (Lumen Gentium)* # 33, in Flannery, I, pp. 390–391.

20. One wag said that some people wrest a living from nature; this is called *work*. Some people wrest a living from those who wrest a living from nature; this is called *trade*. And some people wrest a living from those who wrest a living from those who wrest a living from nature; this is called *finance*.

21. *The Church in the Modern World* # 4, in Flannery, vol. 1, p. 906.

22. *Lay Catholics in Schools* # 19, in Flannery, vol. 2, 636.

23. *The Church in the Modern World* # 37, in Flannery, vol. 1, p. 936.

24. Pope John Paul II, *Catechesis in our Time (Catechesi tradendae)* # 57, in Flannery, vol. 2, p. 797. See also *Catholic Schools* # 12, in Flannery, vol. 2, pp. 608f.

25. *General Catechetical Directory* # 5, in Flannery, vol. 2, p. 533.

26. See Baron Walter Ernest Christopher Northbourne, *Religion and the Modern World* (London: Dent, 1963).

27. See Eric Gill, *A Holy Tradition of Working* (West Stockbridge, Mass.: Lindisfarne, 1983).

28. *General Catechetical Directory* # 7, in Flannery, vol. 2, p. 535.

29. *Catholic Schools* # 48, in Flannery, vol. 2, p. 617.

30. Ibid., # 13, in Flannery, vol. 2, p. 609.

31. Adapted from Brother Marcellin Flynn, *The Milieu Is the Message: Building the Environment and Climate of a Catholic School* (Drummoyne, Ireland: Marist Brothers' Provincial House, n.p., n.d.).

32. Pius XI, "The Christian Education of Youth," in *Seven Great Encyclicals* (Glen Rock, N.J.: Paulist, 1963), p. 57.

33. *Catholic Schools* # 52, in Flannery, vol. 2, p. 617f.

34. Canon 806 §2, in Canon Law Society of America, *Code of Canon Law, Latin-English Edition*, trans. under the auspices of the Canon Law Society of America (Washington, D.C.: Canon Law Society of America, 1983).

35. *Catechesis in our Time* # 58, in Flannery, vol. 2, pp. 797f.

36. John Wild, "Education and Human Society: A Realistic View," *Modern Philosophy and Education*, ed. Nelson B. Henry (University of Chicago Press, 1955), p. 38.

37. Herman Harrell Horne, "An Idealist Philosophy of Education," *Philosphies of Education* (Bloomington, Ill.: Public School Publishing, 1942), p. 89.

38. John Dewey, *Democracy and Education* (New York: Macmillan, 1916), p. 23.

39. Ibid.

40. Donald J. Butler, *Four Philosophies and Their Practice in Education and Religion* (New York: Harper and Row, 1968), p. 426.

41. *Lay Catholics in Schools* # 13, in Flannery, vol. 2, p. 634.

42. Harry S. Broudy, *Building a Philosophy of Education*, 2nd ed. (Englewood Cliffs, N.J.: Prentice-Hall, 1964), p. 312.

43. B. B. Bogoslovsky, *The Ideal School* (New York: Macmillan, 1936), p. 136.

44. *General Catechetical Directory* # 120, in Flannery, vol. 2, p. 594; see also ## 119, 121, pp. 593f.

45. Ibid., # 122, in Flannery, vol. 2, pp. 594f.

46. Ibid., # 124, in Flannery, vol. 2, p. 595.

47. Ibid., # 131, p. 598.

48. There are two facets of the school's physical atmosphere that should at least be mentioned. One is something that many ignore for understandable reasons of saving time and red tape: the importance of record keeping (memos, letters, etc.). Records are important for such purposes as self-examination and history. The other concerns the display of religious ornaments: crucifixes, images of saints, and the like. Considering what we know of how education takes place, these, too, are important.

49. Pope John Paul II on November 5, 1985, to an audience with the International Association of Catholic Educators on the occasion of the twentieth anniversary of Vatican II's "Declaration on Christian Education", as reported in *NC News Service*, November 5, 1985, p. 12.

50. *Catholic Schools* # 47, in Flannery, vol. 2, p. 616.

51. Ibid., # 54, in Flannery, vol. 2, p. 618.

52. *Lay Catholics in Schools* # 22, in Flannery, vol. 2, p. 637; see also # 39, p. 645.

53. This is not to say that the Church does not recognize the importance of groups, especially in connection with the psychological and sociological phenomena of the adolescent years:

> To catechize children in groups helps to educate them for life in society . . . Adolescents and young adults discover themselves, are supported and stimulated in groups. . . . In a group comprising adolescents or adults, catechesis takes on the character of a quest in common. (*General Catechetical Directory* # 76, in Flannery, vol. 2, pp. 573f.)

54. Sr. Helen Marie Behan, *The Dynamics of Community* (New York: Corpus, 1970), p. 84.

55. *Catholic Schools* # 53, in Flannery, vol. 2, p. 618.

56. Interview January 3, 1987, with the Reverend Charles Kohli, Pastor, St. Joseph's Church, Ronkonkoma, N.Y.

57. Interview January 3, 1987, at with Michael Daly, Principal, St. Joseph's School, Ronkonkoma, N.Y.

58. *Declaration on Christian Education* (*Gravissimum educationis*) # 8 (in Flannery, vol. 1, p. 730), as cited in *Lay Catholics in Schools* # 38, in Flannery, vol. 2, p. 645.

59. Adapted from Brother Marcellin Flynn, op. cit.

60. *Catholic Schools* # 84, in Flannery, vol. 2, p. 627.

61. Ibid., # 61, in Flannery, vol. 2, p. 620.

62. Ibid., # 70, in Flannery, vol. 2, p. 622.

63. Adapted from David J. Hassel, S.J. *City of Wisdom: A Christian Vision of the American University* (Chicago: Loyola University Press, 1983), pp. 282f., 436.

64. *Directory on Children's Masses* # 15, in Flannery, vol. 1, p. 259.

65. Ibid., pp. 258f.

66. Ibid., p. 258.

67. Ibid., ## 27, 28, in Flannery, vol. 1, p. 263.

68. *Catholic Schools* ## 70, 71, in Flannery, vol. 2, pp. 622f.; *Lay Catholics in Schools* # 77, in Flannery, vol. 2, p. 657.

69. *Catholic Schools* # 34, in Flannery, vol. 2, p. 614; see also ## 54, 55, p. 618.

70. Canon 806 §1, from Canon Law Society of America, *Code of Canon Law, Latin-English Edition*.

71. Pope John Paul II, address to U.S. bishops Oct. 28, 1983, in *Origins*, vol. 13 no. 23 (Washington, D.C.: United States Catholic Conference, 1984), pp. 389–91.

72. *General Catechectical Directory* # 120, in Flannery, vol. 2, p. 594

73. *Lay Catholics in Schools* # 80, in Flannery, vol. 2, p. 659.

74. Ibid., # 41, in Flannery, vol. 2, p. 646.

75. Canon 806 §2, from *Code of Canon Law*, op. cit.

76. For more specific leadership qualities, see chapter 9, on teachers, and chapter 11.

77. The National Commission on Excellence in Education, *A Nation at Risk: The Imperative for Educational Reform* (Washington, D.C.: U.S. Department of Education, 1983).

78. Ibid., p. 22.

79. Adapted from Brother Marcellin Flynn, op. cit.

80. U.S. Catholic bishops, *The Church in Our Day* (Washington, D.C.: United States Catholic Conference, 1968), p. 24.

81. Synod of Bishops, *Justice in the World* (*Conveniens ex universo*), in Flannery, vol. 2, p. 703.

82. *Lay Catholics in Schools* # 78, in Flannery, vol. 2, pp. 657f.

83. U.S. Catholic bishops, *Economic Justice for All* (Washington, D.C.: National Conference of Catholic Bishops, 1986), § 337, p. 93.

84. Ibid., §§ 86–90, pp. 25–26.

85. *The Wall Street Journal*, vol. CCVII no. 97 (May 19, 1986), pp. 1, 17. The study was done by the accounting firm of Arthur Andersen and Co. and sponsored by the National Council of Catholic Bishops. One New York community, whose members continued uncomplainingly to teach in a poor inner-city neighborhood, was in debt to its undertaker because it was unable to pay for the funerals of its members. Practices like clipping grocery coupons from newspapers, meatless meals to help make ends meet, and stopping summer-school tuitions have only a minuscule impact on the sisters' money problems. Increasingly, small orders of sisters, especially those who serve poorer communities, are applying for public welfare as a last resort.

86. Adapted from Brother Marcellin Flynn, op. cit.

87. Ibid.

88. For details on the Washington situation, see "A Report from the Archbishop to the People of the Archidocese of Washington" (The Archdiocese, March 1987), and *The Washington Post*, March 12, 1987, pp. A1, A35.

89. *Decree on Ecumenism (Unitas redintegratio)* # 7, in Flannery, vol. 1, p. 460.

90. Secretariat for the Promotion of the Unity of Christians, *Directory Concerning Ecumenical Matters: Part Two: Ecumenism in Higher Education (Spiritus Domini)* # 68, in Flannery, vol. 1, p. 517.

91. Interview with Peter Hackett, S.J., Master, Campion Hall, Oxford University, on February 24, 1986.

92. *Christ's School Prospectus 1985–1986* (Christ's School, Queen's Road, Richmond, Surrey, TW10 6HW), p. 2. Christ's School is a six form entry, all ability, ecumenical, voluntary-aided school for boys and girls aged eleven to sixteen.

93. Ibid., p. 16.

94. This information is from a lengthy interview generously given on March 2, 1986, by Dr. Philomena Dineen-Reardon, at Woldingham School, Surrey, England, where she is now headmistress. For seven years Dr. Dineen-Reardon was in charge of St. Bede's.

95. Robert J. Bueter, "Lay Catholics Build a School," *America*, vol. 154 no. 13 (April 5, 1986), pp. 273–76.

CHAPTER 9: TEACHERS

1. Frances F. Fuller and Oliver H. Brown, "Becoming a Teacher," in Kevin Ryan, ed., *Teacher Education: 74th Yearbook of the National Society for the Study of Education* (University of Chicago Press, 1975), p. 26, as cited in Mildred Haipt, "Preparing Teachers for a Changing Culture," *Momentum*, vol. XVII no. 4 (December 1986), p. 12.

2. Sacred Congregation for Catholic Education, *Catholic Schools (Malgre les declarations)* # 43, in Austin Flannery, ed., *Vatican Council II: The Conciliar and Post Conciliar Documents*, 2 vols. (Northport, N.Y.: Costello, 1975), vol. 2, p. 615. See also ibid., # 41; *Declaration on Christian Education (Gravissimum educationis)*, # 5, in Flannery, vol. 1, p. 731.

3. Sacred Congregation for Catholic Education, *Lay Catholics in Schools: Witnesses to Faith (Les laïcs Catholiques)* # 44, in Flannery, vol. 2, p. 647.

4. *NC News Service*, September 14, 1984. Conversely, by virtue of the power inherent in what the teacher does, the teacher could be the most dangerous person in the world. The pleasant, charismatic teacher who is attractive to students could, if not prepared or aware, or if careless about truth or deliberately indoctrinative of a false philosophy, lead tender, impressionable, and immature students in the wrong direction.

Lest the teacher's authority degenerate into authoritarianism, teachers should reflect upon the source of their authority. Before anyone is entitled to tinker with a student's self-esteem, she or he must first demonstrate her or his respect for the student as a person. When motives have been clarified and a relationship of confidence carefully constructed, the authority figure will then, and only then, have earned the right to discuss an intimate topic.

Teachers should be among the most influential members of society. That they are no longer so is evident. This is due partly to the mentality of a materialist society which does not seem to value sufficiently the formation of persons—especially the mind, the imagination, and the will—in ways that do not increase profits or productivity.

5. Matt. 11:1; Acts 1:1.

6. Pope John Paul II, *Catechesis in Our Time* (*Catechesi tradendae*) ## 7, 8, in Flannery, vol. 2, pp. 765–66.

7. Matt., chaps. 22 and 23.

8. John 6.

9. John 10:11–18.

10. See, e.g., Rom. 12:7f., 1 Tim. 5:17f., 2 Tim. 2:2, and Rom. 11:33. See also Gilbert Highet, *The Immortal Profession* (New York: Weybright and Talley, 1976).

11. *Catechesis in Our Time* # 11, in Flannery, vol. 2, p. 768.

12. Rom. 12:6ff.

13. St. Augustine, *De Catechizandis Rudibus*, quoted in George Howie, ed. and trans., *St. Augustine on Education* (South Bend, Ind.: Gateway, 1969), p. 367.

14. See Joseph A. Grassi, *The Teacher in the Primitive Church* (Santa Clara, Calif.: University of Santa Clara Press, 1973).

15. See Harold A. Buetow, *Of Singular Benefit: the Story of U.S. Catholic Education* (New York: Macmillan, 1970); idem, "Historical Perspectives on Catholic Teachers in the United States," *Notre Dame Journal of Education*, vol. 3 no. 2 (Summer 1972), pp. 171–82.

16. *Lay Catholics in Schools* # 16, in Flannery, vol. 2, p. 635.

17. Ibid., # 15, in Flannery, vol. 2, p. 635. Some of the following material is also adapted from Paul H. Hirst, *Knowledge and the Curriculum: A Collection of Philosophical Papers* (London: Routledge and Kegan Paul, 1974), pp. 103–26, and Paul H. Hirst and R. S. Peters, *The Logic of Education* (London: Routledge and Kegan Paul, 1970), chap. 5, "Teaching," pp. 74–87, and chap. 6, "Teaching and Personal Relationships," pp. 88–105.

18. See Phillip Schlechty, *Teaching and Social Behavior: Toward an Organizational Theory of Instruction* (Boston: Allyn and Bacon, 1976); N. L. Gage, *The Scientific Basis of the Art of Teaching* (New York: Teachers College Press, 1978).

19. *Origins*, vol. 14 no. 15 (September 27, 1984), p. 227. Also, the entire issue of *Momentum*, vol. XVII no. 4 (December 1986), entitled, "Teaching in a Changing World," is devoted to teaching, and treats some of the issues discussed in these pages.

20. This has been written about often. See, e.g., Paul Woodring, "Schoolteaching Cannot Be Considered a Profession as Long as Its Entrance Standards Remain So Low," *The Chronicle of Higher Education*, vol. 32 no. 11 (November 12, 1986), p. 48.

21. Dan Lortie, "The Balance of Control and Autonomy in Elementary School Teaching," in Amitai Etzioni, *The Semi-Professions and Their Organization* (New York: Free Press, 1969), p. 24.

22. *Lay Catholics in Schools* # 37, in Flannery, vol. 2, p. 644; see also ibid., # 61, in Flannery, vol. 2, p. 652.

23. Ibid., # 48, in Flannery, vol. 2, pp. 648–49.

24. Ibid., ## 49, 51, in Flannery, vol. 2, p. 649.

25. Ibid., # 52, in Flannery, vol. 2, p. 649.

26. Ibid.

27. See Maria Ciriello, *Teachers in Catholic Schools: A Study of Commitment*, unpublished Ph.D. dissertation (Washington, D.C.: The Catholic University of America, 1987).

28. For the concept of "driven" commitment, see Abraham Maslow, *The Farther Reaches of Human Nature* (New York: Viking, 1972).

29. See Richard J. Westley, "On Permanent Commitment," *America*, vol. 120 (May 24, 1969), pp. 612–17. See also Marisa Crawford and Graham Rossiter, *Teaching Religion in Catholic Schools* (Sydney: Province Resource Group, Christian Brothers,

1985), chap. V, "The Place of Commitment in Classroom Religious Education," pp. 53–62.

30. Marcel contends that a person can only know himself if he commits himself, but he also holds that a person cannot commit himself unless he knows himself.

31. See Frank McQuilkin, "Can We Teach Commitment?" *Commonweal*, March 31, 1967, pp. 48–50; Gabriel Moran, "A Failure of Structure," ibid., pp. 50–54.

32. For example, National Catholic Educational Association, *Code of Ethics for the Catholic School Teacher* (Washington, D.C.: National Catholic Educational Association, 1982), consists of three pages. The last time I saw it, the National Education Association's Code of Ethics consisted of one sheet. See also Kenneth A. Strike and Jonas F. Soltis, *The Ethics of Teaching* (New York: Teachers College Press, 1985).

33. Thomas Hoffer, Andrew M. Greeley, and James S. Coleman, "Achievement Growth in Public and Catholic Schools," *Sociology of Education*, vol. 58 no. 2 (April 1985), pp. 74–97.

34. *Lay Catholics in Schools* # 21, in Flannery, vol. 2, p. 637.

35. Ibid., # 33, in Flannery, vol. 2, p. 642.

36. *Declaration on Christian Education* (*Gravissimum educationis*) # 8, in Flannery, vol. 1, p. 734.

37. *Lay Catholics in Schools* # 31, in Flannery, vol. 2, p. 641.

38. Ibid., # 34, in Flannery, vol. 2, p. 643. See also chapter 6 of this book, part of which is on the family as a partner in schooling and education.

39. See, for example, Kevin Marjoribanks, *Families and Their Learning Environment: An Empirical Study* (London: Routledge and Kegan Paul, 1979); Anne Henderson, ed., *Parent Participation, Student Achievement: The Evidence Grows* (Columbia, Md.: National Committee for Citizens in Education, 1981); James S. Coleman, with Thomas Hoffer, *Public and Private High Schools: The Impact of Communities* (New York: Basic Books, 1987).

40. We treat the school as an ecclesial community writ small under the definition of the Catholic school in chapter 1 and under the Church as one of the partners, in chapter 6.

41. *Lay Catholics in Schools* # 23, in Flannery, vol. 2, p. 638.

42. Ibid., # 34, in Flannery, vol. 2, p. 643.

43. The effective teacher encourages perseverance and cultivates optimism; is polite, punctual, and diligent, and expects these qualities from pupils; cooperates in general school activities, willingly accepting any inconvenience that this may involve; gives long-term planning and preparation to classwork; keeps abreast of current trends by ongoing study; is an active member of professional organizations; gives careful attention to work assignments of pupils; cooperates in the giving of tests and the making of reports to parents in accord with school policy; shows delicacy, respect, and tolerance when encountering family problems; listens sympathetically to properly made representations from the pupils concerning pace of work or other aspects of classwork; and adheres to professional standards of dress and behavior, encourages refinement and courtesy at all times, and accepts responsibility for correcting roughness or unacceptable behavior. See *Declaration on Christian Education* ## 5, 8, in Flannery, vol. 1, pp. 731, 733f.; *Decree on the Apostolate of Lay People* (*Apostolicam actuositatem*) # 30, in Flannery, vol. 1, p. 795; *General Catechetical Directory* (*Ad normam decreti*) # 114, in Flannery, vol. 2, p. 592.

Inasmuch as Catholic teaching "leads the pupil on to a personal integration of faith and life" (Sacred Congregation for Catholic Education, *Catholic Schools* # 44, in Flannery, vol. 2, p. 616), this same integration of faith and life must be present in the teacher: one cannot give what one does not have. Because this work is ongoing and difficult, it requires support from the community, from the teacher's inner resources of faith in the Word, and from sacramental life. Filling in the details of faith, hope, and charity are many subcategories that have been outlined by others, like the National Catholic Educational Association. This association's *Guidelines for Selected Personnel Practices in Catholic Schools* (Washington, D.C.: National Catholic Educational Association, 1975), pp. 6–7, contains the following:

> The teacher . . . understands and accepts the fact that the schools are operated in accordance with the philosophy of Catholic education; accepts and supports the on-going building and living of a faith community, not simply as a concept to be taught but as a reality to be lived . . . ; has an overall knowledge of the goals of the entire school program and can relate his/her specific expertise to these goals; reflects . . . a commitment to Gospel values and the Christian tradition; acknowledges that faith commitment is a free gift of God . . . ; accepts the responsibility for providing an atmosphere for fostering the development of a faith commitment by the students; accepts accountability . . . ; accepts professional evaluation . . . ; demonstrates good classroom management and record-keeping techniques; provides for continuous professional growth . . . ; recognizes and appreciates the contributions of the other members of the professional staff, and shares with them his/her ideas, abilities and materials; understands the limits of his/her professional competencies and makes appropriate referals for the benefit of the student; recognizes and respects the primary role of the parents . . . ; relates to the student in an adult Christian manner and contributes to the student's sense of self worth as a Christian person; shows an understanding of the principles of human growth and development; is creative and resourceful in choosing instructional materials and in using appropriate . . . resources to facilitate optimum learning for all students; fosters the apostolic consciousness of students by encouraging them to join in experiential learning activities that give witness to Christian justice and love; motivates and guides the students in acquiring skills, virtues and habits of heart and mind required to address with Christian insight the multiple problems of injustice . . . ; demonstrates the use of skillful questions that lead students to analyze, synthesize, and think critically; provides learning experiences which enable students to transfer principles and generalizations developed in school to situations outside of the school; provides for on-going evaluation of students and the learning program in order to modify the learning process in accord with each student's needs, interests and learning patterns.

44. *Declaration on Christian Education* # 8, in Flannery, vol. 1, p. 733.

45. *Lay Catholics in Schools* # 61, in Flannery, vol. 2, p. 652.

46. See Task Force on Teaching as a Profession, Carnegie Forum on Education and the Economy, *A Nation Prepared: Teachers for the Twenty-First Century* (available from Carnegie Forum on Education and the Economy, P.O. Box 157, Hyattsville, Md. 20781). For suggestions, see also *The Chronicle of Higher Education*, vol. XXX no. 1 (March 6, 1985), pp. 1, 13–21; see also the text of the report in *Education Week*, vol. V no. 35 (May 21, 1986), pp. 11–18, commentary on pp. 1, 8; text of Carnegie Report also in *The Chronicle of Higher Education*, vol. XXXII no. 12 (May 21, 1986), pp. 43–54, commentary in ibid., pp. 1, 42; interesting commentary on the Carnegie Report by Linda Darling-Hammond in ibid., vol. XXXII no. 20 (July 16, 1986), p. 76.

See also the report of the Holmes Group of education deans from several dozen research universities, *Tomorrow's Teachers: A Report of the Holmes Group* (East Lansing, Mich. 48824-1034 [501 Erickson Hall]: Holmes Group, 1986); text of the main sections in *The Chronicle of Higher Education*, vol. XXXII no. 6 (April 9, 1986), pp. 27–37; commentary in ibid., pp. 1, 27; further commentary in *Education Week*, vol. V no. 29 (April 9, 1986), pp. 1, 12. See also Mary Anne Raywid et al. *Pride and Promise; Schools of Excellence for All the People* (Westbury, N.Y.: American Educational Studies

Association, 1984), especially "Educating Teachers for Excellence," pp. 29–38, and *Teacher Development in Schools: A Report to the Ford Foundation* (New York: Academy for Educational Development, 1985).

47. *Lay Catholics in Schools* # 27, in Flannery, vol. 2, p. 640.

48. National Catholic Educational Association, *The Pre-Service Formation of Teachers for Catholic Schools* (Washington, D.C.: NCEA, 1983), p. 8.

49. *Lay Catholics in Schools* # 16, in Flannery, vol. 2, p. 635.

50. Ibid., # 64, in Flannery, vol. 2, p. 653.

51. Ibid., ## 60, 62, in Flannery, vol. 2, p. 652.

52. *Catholic Schools* # 29, in Flannery, vol. 2, p. 612.

53. *Lay Catholics in Schools* # 38, in Flannery, vol. 2, p. 645.

54. Ibid., # 29, in Flannery, vol. 2, p. 641.

55. See Robert R. Newton, S.J., "A Systematic Approach to Faculty Religious Development," *The Living Light*, vol. 16 no. 3 (Fall 1979), pp. 328–41.

56. The National Catholic Educational Association, *The Catholic High School: A National Portrait* (Washington, D.C.: NCEA, 1985).

57. Peter Benson, Carolyn Eklin, and Michael Guerra, "What Are the Religious Beliefs of Teachers in Catholic High Schools?" *Momentum*, vol. XIV no. 1 (February 1985), p. 26.

58. Interview with Paddy Crowe, S.J., in Dublin, Ireland, March 14, 1986.

59. *Lay Catholics in Schools* # 60, in Flannery, vol. 2, p. 652.

60. Ibid., ## 32, 33, in Flannery, vol. 2, p. 642.

61. Ibid., # 40, in Flannery, vol. 2, pp. 645–46.

62. Ibid., ## 67, 68, 69, 70, in Flannery, vol. 2, pp. 654, 655.

63. *Catholic Schools* # 78, in Flannery, vol. 2, p. 625.

64. See Marjorie Powell and Joseph W. Beard, *Teacher Effectiveness: An Annotated Bibliography and Guide* (New York: Garland, 1984), a 745-page annotated listing of publications in the title field from 1965 to 1980. See also Thomas L. McGreal, *Successful Teacher Evaluation* (Alexandria, Va.: Association for Supervision and Curriculum Development, 1983), which offers not only a theory of evaluation, but also a system to evaluate teachers, including sample forms. Also, Joyce L. Epstein, "A Question of Merit: Principals' and Parents' Evaluations of Teachers," *Educational Researcher*, vol. 14 no. 7 (August–September 1985), pp. 3–10.

65. *Lay Catholics in Schools* # 56, in Flannery, vol. 2, p. 651.

66. *Decree on the Pastoral Office of Bishops in the Church* (*Christus Dominus*) # 14, in Flannery, vol. 1, p. 571.

67. Catholic Education Council, *Evidence to the Central Advisory Council on Primary Education* (London: Catholic Education Council, 1965), p. 2.

68. See Peter L. Benson, *Catholic High Schools: Their Impact on Low-Income Students* (Washington, D.C.: National Catholic Educational Association, 1986); Peter L. Benson and Michael J. Guerra, *Sharing the Faith: The Beliefs and Values of Catholic High School Teachers* (Washington, D.C.: National Catholic Educational Association, 1985).

69. Interview with Sr. Elizabeth Anne di Pippo, Sisters of St. Ursule de Tours, at Foyer Center School, Paris, on March 21, 1986.

70. Sacred Congregation for the Clergy, *General Catechetical Directory* (*Ad normam decreti*) # 115, in Flannery, vol. 2, p. 592. See also *Gravissimum educationis* # 5.

71. *General Catechetical Directory* # 112a, in Flannery, vol. 2, p. 591.

72. Ibid., # 111, in Flannery, vol. 2, p. 590.

73. Ibid., # 112b, in Flannery, vol. 2, p. 591.

74. Ibid., # 112c, in Flannery, vol. 2, p. 591.

75. Ibid., # 113, in Flannery, vol. 2, pp. 591–92.

76. An area receiving current attention is academic freedom. On the lower levels of schooling, is there a need to harmonize academic freedom with the need to teach the official doctrines of the Church? Presumably the same criteria will not apply here, where religion teachers are not considered theologians, as in higher education. In 1980, the U.S. Catholic Bishops issued their first pastoral letter on Catholic higher education: "Catholic Higher Education and the Pastoral Mission of the Church" (Washington, D.C.: United States Catholic Conference, 1980). The letter maintained: "Academic freedom and institutional independence in pursuit of the mission of the institution are essential components of educational quality and integrity." It also advised, "We should all need to recall and to work for that 'delicate balance . . . between the autonomy of a Catholic university and the responsibilities of the hierarchy.' There need be no conflict between the two."

77. Howard W. Marratt, "The Legitimacy of Religious Education," in M. C. Federhof, ed., *Religious Education in a Pluralistic Society* (London: Hodder and Stoughton, 1985), p. 83.

78. John M. Hull, *Studies in Religion and Education* (London: Falmer, 1984), p. 53.

79. Vatican II, *Decree on the Pastoral Office of Bishops in the Church* (*Christus Dominus*) # 14, in Flannery, vol. 1, p. 571.

80. Canon 804 §2. Canon Law Society of America, *Code of Canon Law, Latin-English Edition*, trans. under the auspices of the Canon Law Society of America (Washington, D.C.: Canon Law Society of America, 1983).

81. Canon 805, ibid.

82. Anthony A. Bryk, Peter B. Holland, Valerie E. Lee, and Ruben A. Carriedo, *Effective Catholic Schools: An Exploration* (Washington, D.C.: National Catholic Educational Association, 1984). See also Bruno V. Manno, "The Post-Vatican II Principalship," *Today's Catholic Teacher*, vol. 19 (September 1985), pp. 32–36.

83. This study, whose principal director was John E. Chubb, is available from the Brookings Institution, 1775 Massachusetts Avenue N.W., Washington, D.C. 20036.

84. Interview January 3, 1987, at Ronkonkoma, N. Y., with Michael Daly, Principal, St. Joseph's School.

85. Interview January 3, 1987, at Ronkonkoma, N.Y., with the Reverend Charles Kohli, Pastor, St. Joseph's Church.

86. Bruno V. Manno, ed., *Those Who Would Be Catholic School Principals: Their Recruitment, Preparation, and Evaluation* (Washington, D.C.: National Catholic Educational Association, 1985), pp. 11f. Robert L. Smith, "Quality Private and Public Schools Compared," *Momentum*, vol. XVI no. 2 (May 1985), pp. 32–39, describes the characteristics of the good principal in the National Catholic Educational Association report, *The Catholic High School: A National Portrait*. Among the characteristics are that good principals are dynamic but not domineering, strong but not autocratic, low-key but effective, make their presence felt in the halls, their door and their mind are open, biggest cheerleaders for the school, team leaders, get an enormous amount of work out of the staff, and let people know they love them.

87. Interview January 3, 1987, at Ronkonkoma, N.Y., with the Reverend Charles Kohli, Pastor, St. Joseph's Church.

88. It must accommodate those situations in which Parish A does not want principal Mary Smith because her salary is higher than principal John Jones's, whereas Parish B would be delighted to have Jones because of the lower salary.

89. Manno, op. cit., pp. 19f.

90. Ibid., pp. 20f.

91. Ibid., pp. 20f.

92. For a knowledge of spiritual qualities, the principal is to ask, How have I

deepened my commitment to the Lord Jesus as a believing and practicing Catholic; provided for my own spiritual growth; provided services in my parish community? For pastoral competencies, the questions are, In what major way(s) have I come to better know and understand: the Church's authentic teaching on [one or several topics and their] implications; the philosophy and history of Catholic education; religious education and religious psychology as they relate to youth; the religious resources available; and how to apply aspects of pastoral subject matter to a school situation.

For professional qualities, the evaluative questions are, In what major way(s) have I undertaken specific actions that demonstrate my commitment to professional growth; demonstrated leadership capabilities; become more experienced with various parish or diocesan (or both) governance groups? For professional educational competencies, the questions for the purpose of evaluation are, In what major ways have I come to better know and understand an aspect of theory and leadership in curriculum development; an aspect of educational philosophy or research; an aspect of adult development theory as this relates to facilitating and supporting the primary role of parents as educators of their children; the value of service programs as an aspect of the school's religious program, and how to establish, implement, and evaluate these; and how to apply aspects of the professional-educational-component subject matter to a school situation.

For the evaluation of professional managerial competencies, the questions are, In what major way(s) have I come to better know and understand the various components that comprise development activities as these relate to Catholic schools and the notion of Christian stewardship; those agencies and publics unique to Catholic education; what sustains an orderly school environment that promotes student self-discipline consistent with Gospel values and Christian principles; general notions and specific aspects of school law as it applies to the Catholic school; and how to apply aspects of the professional-managerial-component subject matter to a school situation. (Manno, op. cit., pp. 28f.)

93. Among them, 70 percent said they had suffered from verbal abuse during the previous year, 21 percent reported incidents of physical abuse by students, 38 percent said discipline problems affected their teaching to a "great extent," 22 percent had received professional counseling or medical attention because of job-related stress during the previous year, and 60 percent said they spent eight hours or more each week doing classroom work at home. (*The Washington Post*, June 11, 1985, pp. A1 and A9.)

94. Barry Farber and James Miller, "Teacher Burnout: A Psychoeducational Perspective," *Teachers College Record*, vol. 83 (1984), pp. 235–43. For other details of social injustice to Catholic-school teachers, see chapter 8.

95. NCEA, *National Portrait*, p. 42.

96. Mortimer J. Adler, *The Paideia Proposal: An Educational Manifesto* (New York: Macmillan, 1982), pp. 57–58.

97. *Lay Catholics in Schools* # 2, in Flannery, vol. 2, p. 630.

98. Ibid., # 6, in Flannery, vol. 2, p. 632.

99. Ibid., ## 7, 11, in Flannery, vol. 2, p. 632.

100. Vatican II, *Decree on the Church's Missionary Activity (Ad gentes divinitus)* # 21, in Flannery, vol. 1, p. 838.

101. *Pastoral Constitution on the Church in the Modern World (Gaudium et spes)* # 43, in Flannery, vol. 1, p. 944. See also *Decree on the Church's Missionary Activity* # 21, in Flannery, vol. 1, p. 838.

102. *Lay Catholics in Schools* # 20, in Flannery, vol. 2, p. 637.

103. See V. T. Cook, "Viewpoints of Lay Educators," *Momentum*, vol. XV no. 3

(September 1984), pp. 44–45; James Kearney, "The Ministry of the Teacher," *Today's Catholic Teacher*, vol. 17 (January 1984), pp. 48–49; Barbara Mahany, "The Rugged Devotion of Teachers in Catholic Schools," *U.S. Catholic*, vol. 49 (September 1984), pp. 30–35.

104. *Lay Catholics in Schools* # 34, in Flannery, vol. 2, p. 643.

105. Ibid., # 1, in Flannery, vol. 2, p. 630.

106. See Stephen O'Brien and Margaret McBrien, eds., *Personnel Issues and the Catholic School Administrator* (Washington, D.C.: National Catholic Educational Association, 1986).

107. NCEA, *National Portrait*, p. 44.

108. Jean Bettis Graham, "Serious about Keeping Good Teachers? Help Them Reclaim Lost Teaching Time," *The American School Board Journal*, vol. 172 no. 1 (January 1985), p. 36.

109. *American Teacher*, vol. 70 no. 3 (November 1985), p. 2.

110. *Lay Catholics in Schools* # 78, in Flannery, vol. 2, p. 658. See also *Code of Canon Law*, canon 1286; United States Conference of Catholic Bishops, *Economic Justice for All* # 103. Among the documents justifying teachers (as well as other employees in Catholic institutions) in forming assocations for the achievement of justice is Pope Leo XIII, *Rerum novarum* # 76; Pope Pius XI, *Quadragesimo anno* # 87; Pope John XXIII, *Mater et magistra* # 22; Pope John Paul II, *Laborem exercens* ## 94–95; Vatican Council II, *Gaudium et spes* # 68; *Code of Canon Law*, canon 215.

111. *Lay Catholics in Schools* # 78, in Flannery, vol. 2, p. 658.

112. See National Catholic Educational Association, *The Pre-Service Formation of Teachers for Catholic Schools: In Search of Patterns for the Future* (Washington, D.C.: NCEA, 1982).

CHAPTER 10: STUDENTS

1. See Thomas Aquinas, *Summa Theologica*, I, q. 117, a. 1; *II Contra gentiles*, chap. 75; *De veritate*, q. 11, a. 1.

2. *Pastoral Constitution on the Church in the Modern World (Gaudium et spes)* # 12, in Austin Flannery, ed., *Vatican Council II: The Conciliar and Post Conciliar Documents*, 2 vols. (Northport, N. Y.: Costello, 1975), vol. 1, p. 913.

3. *Hamlet*, act 2, scene ii, line 316, in William Shakespeare, *The Tragedy of Hamlet, Prince of Denmark*, ed. Tucker Burke and Jack Randall Crawford (New Haven, Conn.: Yale University Press, 1947). On the grandeur and misery of humankind, see also Pascal, *Pensées*.

4. *Hamlet*, act III, scene i, line 128.

5. Ps. 8:5–8.

6. *General Catechetical Directory (Ad normam decreti)* # 53, in Flannery, vol. 2, p. 559.

7. Paul Henry, *Saint Augustine on Personality* (New York: Macmillan 1960), p. 1.

8. Boethius, *De Duabus Naturis*, cap. 3 (P.L. 64, 1343).

9. St. Thomas Aquinas, *Summa Theologica*, i. 29. 3c.

10. *Declaration on Christian Education (Gravissimum educationis)* # 1, in Flannery, vol. 1, p. 726.

11. *Lay Catholics in Schools: Witnesses to Faith (Les laïcs Catholiques)* # 18, in Flannery, vol. 2, pp. 635f.

12. *Catholic Schools (Malgre les declarations)* # 55, in Flannery, vol. 2, p. 618.

13. Pope Pius XI, "The Christian Education of Youth," in *Five Great Encyclicals* (New York: Paulist, 1939), p. 54.

14. *Pastoral Constitution on the Church in the Modern World (Gaudium et spes)* # 15, in Flannery, vol. 1, pp. 915f.

15. *Declaration on Religious Liberty* (*Dignitatis humanae*) # 1, in Flannery, vol. 1, p. 799.

16. *The Church in the Modern World* # 17, in Flannery, vol. 1, p. 917.

17. See ibid., # 14, in Flannery, vol. 1, pp. 914f.

18. Ibid., # 14, in Flannery, vol. 1, p. 915.

19. *General Catechetical Directory* # 60, in Flannery, vol. 2, p. 563.

20. Gen. 1:26; Wisdom 2:23.

21. 1 Cor. 11:7.

22. 1 Cor. 15:49; see also 2 Cor. 4:4; 2 Cor. 3:18; Eph. 4:13; John 1:12; 2 Pet. 1:4.

23. *Theaetetus* 176b, in Edith Hamilton and Huntington Cairns, eds., *Plato: The Collected Dialogues* (New York: Pantheon, 1961), p. 881.

24. Beatrice Avalos, *New Men for New Times* (New York: Sheed and Ward, 1962), p. 90.

25. *Declaration on Christian Education* # 2, in Flannery, vol. 1, p. 728.

26. Ibid.

27. John 1:29.

28. Rom. 3:25.

29. Leviticus 16.

30. *The Church in the Modern World* # 12, in Flannery, vol. 1, pp. 913f.

31. James S. Coleman and Thomas Hoffer, *Public and Private High Schools: The Impact of Communities* (New York: Basic Books, 1987), pp. 211–43.

32. *Lay Catholics in Schools* # 34, in Flannery, vol. 2, p. 643.

33. *The Church in the Modern World* # 13, in Flannery, vol. 1, pp. 914.

34. Matt. 5:3.

35. Luke 5:27.

36. Matt. 25:34–46.

37. Deut. 15:11; Mark 14:7; Matt. 26:11.

38. Prov. 17:5; Matt. 25:34–40.

39. Matt. 5:4.

40. Matt. 11:5; Luke 4:18.

41. *General Catechetical Directory* # 53, in Flannery, vol. 2, p. 559.

42. *The Church in the Modern World* # 27, in Flannery, vol. 1, p. 928.

43. Ibid., # 29, in Flannery, vol. 1, pp. 929f.

44. *Catholic High Schools and Minority Students* (1982), as cited in Anthony S. Bryk and Peter B. Holland, "The Implications of Greeley's Latest Research," *Momentum* 13 (October 1982), p. 4.

45. Among the statistics cited by Bruno V. Manno, "Stereotypes, Statistics, and Catholic Schools," *Education Week*, vol. V no. 11 (November 13, 1985), p. 22, are the following.

During the preceding twenty years, Catholic schools had deepened their involvement in urban centers, especially the inner city. Once filled with students from poor, ethnic families, mostly of Eastern and Western European descent, those poor have been replaced by the new urban poor—primarily blacks, Hispanics, and Asians. Increasingly, Catholic and non-Catholic minorities are viewing Catholic schools as prized alternatives to public education.

In 1969–70, non-Catholic students constituted 2.7 percent of total enrollment in Catholic schools. In 1983–84, that figure was 11.6 percent.

As a percentage of total enrollment, Hispanics and Asians have a larger percentage of students in Catholic schools than in government schools.

A substantial number of the minority students enrolled in Catholic schools are non-Catholic. For example, 63.5 percent of those schools' black students are not

Catholic. There are also significant numbers of Asian and American Indian non-Catholics. . . .

Finally, there is the stereotype that Catholic schools accept and retain only the students who are academically most able and least likely to cause disciplinary problems.

In fact, in 1983, close to 20 percent of Catholic high schools admitted students expelled or dropped from public schools for disciplinary reasons. Almost 18 percent took students expelled or dropped for academic reasons. On the average, Catholic high schools annually expel only 1 percent of their students.

Furthermore, a look at admissions practices shows that one-third of Catholic high schools have open admissions policies (meaning they take anyone who applies), one-third accept almost any student, and one-third are highly selective. Overall, Catholic high schools reject fewer than 12 percent of the students who apply.

Catholic schools are not havens for whites fleeing public education or for an elite avoiding social responsibility. For the benefits of Catholic school attendance for the disadvantaged (the poor and minorities), see also James S. Coleman and Thomas Hoffer, *Public and Private High Schools: The Impact of Communities* (New York: Basic Books, 1987), chap. 5, "Achievement and Dropout in Disadvantaged and Deficient Families," pp. 118–48.

46. *The New York Times*, October 20, 1985, pp. 1, 56.

47. For global intercultural education, see Sohan Modgil et al., eds., *Multicultural Education: the Interminable Debate* (New York: Taylor and Francis, 1986). For a Catholic perspective, see the entire issue of *Momentum*, vol. XIV no. 1 (February 1983), and Catherine Rudolph, "Books and the Multicultural Classroom," *Today's Catholic Teacher*, vol. 16 (February 1983), pp. 46f., which lists comprehensively not only books classified by level and culture, but also other informational series, posters, and records.

48. *The Church in the Modern World* # 12, in Flannery, vol. 1, p. 913.

49. Ibid., # 60, in Flannery, vol. 1, p. 965.

50. Much is being published today under the heading of "women's studies." Included are publications concerning women and the Church: e.g., Helen M. Luke, *Woman, Earth and Spirit: The Feminine in Symbol and Myth* (New York: Crossroad, 1985); Sandra M. Schneiders, *Women and the Word: The Gender of God in the New Testament and the Spirituality of Women* (New York: Paulist, 1986); Elizabeth Schüssler Fiorenza, *In Memory of Her: A Feminist Theological Reconstruction of Christian Origins* (New York: Crossroad, 1983). Current and future Catholic educators need to be knowledgeable in this area.

51. See, for example, *The Washington Post*, February 20, 1987, pp. A1, A16. In the Catholic elementary schools of the Archdiocese of Washington, D.C., the non-Catholic school population in 1986 was 47 percent, with three schools having more than 70 percent. Many of these are inner-city schools which are subsidized by the archdiocese.

52. *Lay Catholics in Schools* # 42, in Flannery, vol. 2, p. 646. See also *Decree on Ecumenism (Unitatis redintegratio)* # 3, in Flannery, vol. 1, p. 455; *Catholic Schools* # 85, in Flannery, vol. 2, p. 627. ,

53. *Lay Catholics in Schools* # 26, in Flannery, vol. 2, p. 639.

54. See Niccolo Machiavelli, *The Prince* (New York: New American Library, 1952), or any other edition, chap. 17, "Of Cruelty and Clemency, and Whether It Is Better to Be Loved or Feared": "one ought to be both feared and loved, but as it is difficult for the two to go together, it is much safer to be feared than loved." Modern writers on leadership have been returning more and more to Machiavellian ideas. Elbert Hubbard's *A Message to Garcia* (New York: Daniels, 1899) was a bracing sermon about an army lieutenant who overcame all obstacles on a secret mission during the Spanish-

American War. Later, in Dale Carnegie's *How to Win Friends and Influence People* (New York: Simon and Schuster, 1936), and in Carnegie's and other self-help books of the 1950s, getting ahead meant getting along with others. Gradually the ideal of hard work receded, as in Shepherd Mead's 1952 *How to Succeed in Business without Really Trying* (New York: Simon and Schuster, 1952), which was made into a musical and a movie. With Robert J. Ringer's *Winning through Intimidation* (Los Angeles: Los Angeles Book Co., 1974) and Michael Korda's *Power! How to Get It, How to Use It* (New York: Random House, 1975), in the 1970s came another mutation in the tradition: the system is chaotically unjust, and only intimidation pays off.

55. See Michael R. Carey, "School Discipline: Better to be Loved or Feared?" *Momentum*, vol. XVII no. 2 (May 1986), pp. 20–21, which contrasts St. Benedict's philosophy of love with Machiavelli's principle of fear. Donald R. Grossnickle and Frank P. Sesko, *Promoting Effective Discipline in School and Classroom* (Reston, Va.: National Association of Secondary School Principals, 1985), provides guides to school discipline that involve respect, dignity, parental involvement, and positive praise instead of the use of fear.

56. See Ronald T. Zaffran, "Developmental Guidance in Catholic Elementary Schools: A Realistic Promise for Emotional Growth," *Journal of Humanistic Education and Development*, vol. 22 no. 4 (June 1984), pp. 170–74; idem, "Developmental Guidance in Catholic Secondary Schools: A Call for Change," ibid., vol. 23 no. 3 (March 1985), pp. 134–44.

57. *Lay Catholics in Schools* # 17, in Flannery, vol. 2, p. 635.

58. Ibid., # 78, in Flannery, vol. 2, p. 575.

59. Ibid., # 79, in Flannery, vol. 2, p. 576.

60. Ibid., # 83, in Flannery, vol. 2, p. 578.

61. Ibid., # 82, in Flannery, vol. 2, p. 578.

62. Ibid., # 84, in Flannery, vol. 2, p. 579.

63. Ibid., ## 86, 87, in Flannery, vol. 2, pp. 579f.

64. Catholic Education Council, *Evidence to the Central Advisory Council on Primary Education* (London: Catholic Education Council, 1965), p. 2.

65. See James Fowler, *Stages of Faith: The Psychology of Human Development and the Quest for Meaning* (San Francisco: Harper and Row, 1981); idem, *Becoming Adult, Becoming Christian: Adult Development and Christian Faith* (San Francisco: Harper and Row, 1984).

66. Adapted from James J. DiGiacomo, "Why Johnny Can't Pray," *America*, vol. 137 (December 10, 1977), pp. 416–18.

67. Jean Piaget and Barbel Inhelder, *The Psychology of the Child* (New York: Basic Books, 1969), p. 157.

68. Milton Schwebel and Jane Ralph, *Piaget in the Classroom* (New York: Basic Books, 1973), p. 10.

69. David Elkind, *Child Development and Education: A Piagetian Perspective* (New York: Oxford University Press, 1976), pp. 1–24.

70. Henry W. Maier, *Three Theories of Child Development* (New York: Harper and Row, 1978), p. 16.

71. Erik Erikson, "Life Cycles," in *International Encyclopedia of Sciences*, ed. D. L. Sills (New York: Macmillan, 1927), pp. 22f.

72. Erik H. Erikson, "Elements of Psychoanalytic Theory of Psychosocial Development," *The Course of Life: Psychoanalytic Contributions Toward Understanding Personality Development, Vol. I: Infancy and Early Childhood*. Stanley I. Greenspan and George H. Pollock, eds. (Washington, D.C.: U.S. Government Printing Office, 1980), pp. 18f.

73. John L. Elias, *Psychology and Religious Education* (Bethlehem, Pa.: Booksellers of Bethlehem, 1975), p. 37.

74. Erik H. Erikson, *Toys and Reasons: Stages in the Ritualization of Experience* (New York: Norton, 1977), pp. 89f.

75. Elias, op. cit., p. 29.

76. Ibid., p. 22.

77. Ibid., pp. 1–16.

78. Maier, op. cit., pp. 71–132.

79. Elias, op. cit., p. 39.

80. Ibid., pp. 28–45.

81. *Lay Catholics in Schools* # 12, in Flannery, vol. 2, pp. 633f.

82. Elias, op. cit., p. 40.

83. Ibid., pp. 1–16.

84. Donald Capps sees a relationship between the basic strengths and themes that Erikson poses for each of his eight stages of life and comparable theological themes developed by Paul W. Pruyser. See Donald Capps, *Pastoral Care: A Thematic Approach* (Philadelphia: Westminster, 1979), p. 114, and Paul W. Pruyser, *The Minister as Diagnostician* (Philadelphia: Westminster, 1976).

85. St. Gregory of Nyssa, *Vita Moysis* (New Haven, Conn.: Yale Divinity School, 1975) (P.G. xliv, 327b).

86. Jean Mouroux, *The Meaning of Man* (Garden City, N.Y.: Doubleday & Co., 1961), p. 113.

87. Ibid., pp. 115–16.

88. Ibid., pp. 124–26.

89. Ibid., p. 129.

90. Ana-Maria Rizzuto, *The Birth of the Living God: A Psychoanalytic Study* (University of Chicago Press, 1979), especially pp. 179–209.

91. The material on psychoanalytic theories is adapted from W. W. Meissner, "Psychoanalytic Aspects of Religious Experience," *Annual of Psychoanalysis*, vol. 6 (1978), pp. 130–36.

92. H. L. and Rowena Ansbacher, eds., *Superiority and Social Interest* (New York: Basic Books, 1964), p. 67.

93. Pope Pius XI, *The Christian Education of Youth* (New York: America Press, 1936), p. 20.

94. Ford Foundation and St. Mary's Catholic Foundation, *The Catholic High School: A National Portrait* (1985), p. 217.

95. Calvin S. Hall and Gardner Lindsey, *Theories of Personality*, 2nd ed. (New York: Wiley, 1970), p. 136. See also Karen Horney, *Our Inner Conflicts* (New York: Norton & Co., 1945).

96. Hall and Lindsey, op. cit., p. 137.

97. Ibid., p. 140.

98. Carl Rogers, *On Becoming a Person* (London: Constable, 1967), p. 188.

99. Rom. 5:1–5.

100. James Collins, *The Existentialists* (Chicago: Henry Regnery, 1952), p. 227.

101. Janusz Tarnowski, "An Existential Christian Pedagogy, The Current Problem," *Lumen Vitae*, vol. 28 no. 2 (June 1973), pp. 331f.

102. Gordon W. Allport, *Pattern and Growth in Personality* (New York: Holt, Rinehart and Winston, 1961), p. 194.

103. Ibid., p. 28.

104. Ibid., p. 218.

105. Ibid., p. 277.

106. Gordon W. Allport, *The Individual and His Religion* (New York: Macmillan, 1960), p. 92.

107. Matt. 5:8; 2 Tim. 2:22.

108. Gordon W. Allport, *Becoming* (New Haven, Conn.: Yale University Press, 1955), p. 97.

109. Ibid., p. 96.

CHAPTER 11: CONCLUSIONS

1. Sacred Congregation for Catholic Education, *Catholic Schools (Malgre les declarations)* # 64, in Austin Flannery, ed., *Vatican Council II: The Conciliar and Postconciliar Documents*, 2 vols. (Northport, N.Y.: Costello, 1982), vol. 2, p. 620.

2. Ibid., # 65, in Flannery, vol. 2, p. 621.

3. Ibid.

4. Sr. Dorothy McCloskey, S.S.L., "Superior General's Report," unpublished paper (Dublin, Ireland: General Chapter of Society of St. Louis, July 24, 1985), pp. 44f.

5. Interview with Sr. Elizabeth Anne di Pippo, Sisters of Ursule de Tours, at Foyer Center School, Paris, onarch 21, 1986.

6. Sacred Congregation for Catholic Education, *Lay Catholics in Schools: Witnesses to Faith (Les laïcs Catholiques)* # 75, in Flannery, vol. 2, p. 657.

7. Canon 298 §1.

8. Canon 304 §1.

9. Ibid., §2.

10. Canon 327.

11. There are many recent books on leadership contrary to the principles of Niccolo Machiavelli and some of the many "how-to" books based on him mentioned in chapter 9 of our book. See, for example, James MacGregor Burns, *Leadership* (New York: Harper and Row, 1978): this theory of transformational leadership apparently influenced the others; Warren Bennis and Burt Nanus, *Leaders* (New York: Harper and Row, 1985): the theme is that leaders are people who do the right thing; Harold J. Leavitt, *Corporate Pathfinders* (Homewood, Ill.: Dow Jones-Irwin, 1986): focuses on how leaders think and suggests that leaders should be philosopher-kings; Thomas Peters and Robert Waterman, *In Search of Excellence* (New York: Harper and Row, 1982); Samuel A. Culbert and John J. McDonough, *Radical Management* (New York: Free Press, 1985): suggests that leaders should be metaphysicians who create reality.

12. Canon 301 §3.

13. Canon 316.

14. *Decree on the Apostolate of Lay People (Apostolicam actuositatem)* # 28, in Flannery, vol. 1, p. 793.

15. Ibid., # 29, in Flannery, vol. 1, p. 793.

16. Ibid., in Flannery, vol. 1, p. 794.

17. *Catholic Schools* # 46, in Flannery, vol. 2, p. 616.

18. Ibid., # 56, in Flannery, vol. 2, p. 618.

19. Ibid., # 29, in Flannery, vol. 2, p. 613.

20. *Directory Concerning Ecumenical Matters: Part Two: Ecumenism in Higher Education (Spiritus Domini)* # 68, in Flannery, vol. 1, p. 517.

21. *Pastoral Constitution on the Church in the Modern World (Gaudium et spes)* # 15, in Flannery, vol. 1, p. 916. See also *General Catechetical Directory (Ad normam decreti)* # 94, in Flannery, vol. 2, p. 583.

22. *The Church in the Modern World* # 38, in Flannery, vol. 1, p. 937.

23. *General Catechetical Directory (Ad normam decreti)* # 12 in Flannery, vol. 2, p. 538.

24. *Catholic Schools* # 36, in Flannery, vol. 2, p. 614.

25. Ibid., # 45, in Flannery, vol. 2, p. 616.

26. *General Catechetical Directory* # 75, in Flannery, vol. 2, p.573.

27. *Catholic Schools* # 37, in Flannery, vol. 2, p. 614.

28. Ibid., # 59, in Flannery, vol. 2, p. 619.

29. Ibid., # 26, in Flannery, vol. 2, p. 612.

30. *Decree on Ecumenism (Unitatis redintegratio)* # 4 in Flannery, vol. 1 p. 458.

31. *Declaration on Christian Education (Gravissimum educationis)* # 8, in Flannery, vol. 1, p. 733.

32. *Decree on the Church's Missionary Activity (Ad gentes divinitus)* # 11, in Flannery, vol. 1, p. 825.

33. *Decree on the Apostolate of Lay People* # 5, in Flannery, vol. 1, p. 772.

34. *The Church's Missionary Activity* # 12, in Flannery, vol. 1, p. 826.

35. The National Commission on Excellence in Education, *A Nation at Risk: The Imperative for Educational Reform* (Washington, D. C.: U.S. Department of Education, 1983), p. 1.

36. *Catholic Schools* # 62, in Flannery, vol. 2, p. 620.

37. *Declaration on Christian Education* # 1, in Flannery, vol. 1, p. 727.

38. *Decree on the Church's Missionary Activity* # 11, in Flannery, vol. 1, p. 825.

39. *Dogmatic Constitution on the Church (Lumen gentium)* # 40, in Flannery, vol. 1, p. 397.

40. Ibid., # 41, in Flannery, vol. 1, p. 398.

41. *Declaration on Christian Education* # 1, in Flannery, vol. 1, p. 727.

42. *Catholic Schools* # 30, in Flannery, vol. 2, p. 613.

43. *The Church in the Modern World* # 31, in Flannery, vol. 1, p. 931.

44. *Catholic Schools* # 31, in Flannery, vol. 2, p. 613.

45. Especially Isa. 52:13–53:12.

46. *The Church in the Modern World* # 23, in Flannery, vol. 1, p. 924.

47. Ibid., # 32, in Flannery, vol. 1, p. 932.

48. Ibid., # 61, in Flannery, vol. 1, p. 965.

49. Ibid., # 78, in Flannery, vol. 1, p. 987.

50. *Dogmatic Constitution on the Church* # 39, in Flannery, vol. 1, p. 396.

51. Pope John Paul II, *Catechesis in Our Time (Catechesi tradendae)* # 72, in Flannery, vol. 2, pp. 807f.

INDEX